The Greenwood Encyclopedia of Science Fiction and Fantasy

Advisory Board

The Greenwood Encyclopedia of Science Fiction and Fantasy

Themes, Works, and Wonders

EDITED BY GARY WESTFAHL

FOREWORD BY NEIL GAIMAN

GREENWOOD PRESS
Westport, Connecticut • London

Library of Congress Cataloging-in-Publication Data

The Greenwood encyclopedia of science fiction and fantasy : themes, works, and wonders / edited by
Gary Westfahl ; foreword by Neil Gaiman.
    p. cm.
    Includes bibliographical references.
    ISBN 0–313–32950–8 (set : alk. paper)—ISBN–0–313–32951–6 (v. 1 : alk. paper)—
ISBN 0–313–32952–4 (v. 2 : alk. paper)—ISBN 0–313–32953–2 (v. 3 : alk. paper)
    1.Science fiction, American—Encyclopedias. 2. Fantasy fiction, American—
Encyclopedias. 3. Science fiction, English—Encyclopedias. 4. Fantasy fiction,
English—Encyclopedias. I. Westfahl, Gary.
PS374.S35.G74   2005
813′.0876203—dc22   2005013677

British Library Cataloguing in Publication Data is available.

Library of Congress Catalog Card Number: 2005013677
ISBN: 0–313–32950–8 (set)
      0–313–32951–6 (vol. 1)
      0–313–32952–4 (vol. 2)
      0–313–32953–2 (vol. 3)

First published in 2005

Greenwood Press, 88 Post Road West, Westport, CT 06881
An imprint of Greenwood Publishing Group, Inc.
www.greenwood.com

Printed in the United States of America

The paper used in this book complies with the
Permanent Paper Standard issued by the National
Information Standards Organization (Z39.48–1984).

10 9 8 7 6 5 4 3 2 1

Contents

Alphabetical List of Themes

VOLUME 2

Alphabetical List of Classic Works

A.I.: Artificial Intelligence (2001)

Alice's Adventures in Wonderland by Lewis Carroll (1865)

Alien (1979)

Alphaville (1965)

Animal Farm: A Fairy Story by George Orwell (1945)

Babylon 5 (1993–1998)

Back to the Future (1985)

Batman (1989)

Beauty and the Beast (1946)

Blade Runner (1982)

Blakes 7 (1978–1981)

Blood Music by Greg Bear (1985)

The Book of the New Sun by Gene Wolfe (1980–1983)

Brave New World by Aldous Huxley (1932)

Brazil (1986)

Bring the Jubilee by Ward Moore (1953)

The Brother from Another Planet (1984)

Buffy the Vampire Slayer (1996–2003)

A Canticle for Leibowitz by Walter M. Miller, Jr. (1959)

Cat's Cradle by Kurt Vonnegut, Jr. (1963)

Childhood's End by Arthur C. Clarke (1953)

A Christmas Carol by Charles Dickens (1843)

City by Clifford D. Simak (1952)

The Clan of the Cave Bear by Jean Auel (1980)

A Clockwork Orange (1971)

A Clockwork Orange by Anthony Burgess (1962)

Close Encounters of the Third Kind (1977)

The Colour of Magic by Terry Pratchett (1983)

Conan the Conqueror by Robert E. Howard (1950)

A Connecticut Yankee in King Arthur's Court by Mark Twain (1889)

Consider Phlebas by Iain M. Banks (1987)

Dawn by Octavia E. Butler (1987)

The Day of the Triffids by John Wyndham (1951)

The Day the Earth Stood Still (1951)

Deathbird Stories: A Pantheon of Modern Gods by Harlan Ellison (1975)

The Demolished Man by Alfred Bester (1953)

The Difference Engine by William Gibson and Bruce Sterling (1990)

The Dispossessed: An Ambiguous Utopia by Ursula K. Le Guin (1974)

Do Androids Dream of Electric Sheep? by Philip K. Dick (1968)

Dr. Jekyll and Mr. Hyde (1931)

Doctor No (1962)

Dr. Strangelove, or How I Stopped Worrying and Learned to Love the Bomb (1964)

Doctor Who (1963–1989)

Dracula (1931)

Dracula by Bram Stoker (1897)

Dragonflight by Anne McCaffrey (1968)

Guide to Related Topics

THEMES ENTRIES BY CATEGORY (400)

Abstract Concepts and Qualities

Absurdity
Androgyny
Anxiety
Beauty
Chivalry
Colors
Courage
Darkness
Decadence
Destiny
Eternity
Evil
Force
Freedom
Friendship
Gender
Guilt and Responsibility
Hubris
Identity
Illusion
Individualism and Conformity
Intelligence
Invisibility
Knowledge
Light
Love
Madness
Magic
Memory
Mystery
Names
Nature

Nudity
Old Age
Optimism and Pessimism
Pain
Paranoia
Personification
Progress
Secret Identities
Sense of Wonder
Sexism
Sexuality
Social Darwinism
Sublime
Taboos
Talents
Time
Virginity
Vision and Blindness
Wisdom
Xenophobia
Yin and Yang

Animals

Animals and Zoos
Apes
Birds
Cats
Dinosaurs
Dogs
Dragons
Fish and Sea Creatures
Horses
Insects

Illustration and Graphics
Journalism
Language and Linguistics
Mathematics
Medicine
Music
Philosophy
Physics
Poetry
Politics
Psychology
Religion
Technology
Theatre
Writing and Authors

Events and Actions

Apocalypse
Betrayal
Birth
Carnival
Christmas
Communication
Crime and Punishment
Curses
Cycles
Death
Disaster
Disguise
Divination
Dreams
Enlargement
Escape
Estrangement
Evolution
Exile
First Contact
Flood
Flying
Halloween
Invasion
Marriage
Metamorphosis
Miniaturization
Mutation
Nuclear War

Pantropy
Perception
Plagues and Diseases
Possession
Promise
Reading
Rebellion
Rebirth
Reincarnation
Revenge
Rituals
Role Reversals
Sacrifice
Sin
Sleep
Suicide
Survival
Teleportation
Terraforming
Theft
Time Travel
Timeslips
Torture
Touch
Trade
Transportation
Uplift
Violence
Work and Leisure

Games and Leisure Activities

Art
Carnival
Chess
Christmas
Clowns and Fools
Disguise
Dreams
Drugs
Escape
Fashion
Food and Drink
Games
Gifts
Halloween
Home

Humor
Labyrinth
Music
Pastoral
Poetry
Puzzles
Riddles
Sleep
Sports
Stories
Taverns and Inns
Theatre
Toys
Virtual Reality
Work and Leisure

Horror

Aliens on Earth
Blood
Borderlands
Curses
Dark Fantasy
Darkness
Death
Decadence
Demons
Divination
Doppelganger
Dreams
Elder Races
Estrangement
Evil
Frankenstein Monsters
Ghosts and Hauntings
Goblins
Golem
Guilt and Responsibility
Halloween
Hell
Horror
Hypnotism
Illusion
Invasion
Invisibility
Labyrinth
Mad Scientists
Madness

Monsters
Mutation
Omens and Signs
Pain
Paranoia
Parasites
Possession
Prisons
Psychic Powers
Puzzles
Reincarnation
Rituals
Sacrifice
Satan
Sin
Skeletons
Sublime
Supernatural Creatures
Torture
Vampires
Violence
Voodoo
Werewolves
Witches
Zombies

Literary Concepts

Absurdity
Allegory
Alternate History
Arcadia
Bildungsroman
Books
Carnival
Chivalry
Clichés
Comedy
Cyberpunk
Cycles
Dark Fantasy
Decadence
Deus ex Machina
Doppelganger
Dystopia
Escape
Fables
Fairy Tales

Feminism
Fin de Siecle
Future War
Globalization
Gothic
Hard Science Fiction
Heroic Fantasy
Horror
Hubris
Humor
Illustration and Graphics
Landscape
Language and Linguistics
Libraries
Magic Realism
Maps
Metafiction and Recursiveness
Microcosm
Mystery
Mythology
Pastoral
Personification
Poetry
Postcolonialism
Postmodernism
Prehistoric Fiction
Promise
Reading
Romance
Ruritanian Romance
Satire
Shakespeare
Sense of Wonder
Shared Worlds
Space Opera
Steampunk
Stories
Sublime
Surrealism
Sword and Sorcery
Taboos
Technothrillers
Theatre
Threshold
Tragedy
Trickster
Urban Fantasy
Utopia

Westerns
Writing and Authors

Love and Sexuality

Amazons
Androgyny
Decadence
Feminism
Gender
Homosexuality
Love
Marriage
Nudity
Romance
Sexism
Sexuality
Sin
Taboos
Temptress
Virginity

Magical Beings

Angels
Demons
Dragons
Dwarfs
Elder Races
Elves
Fairies
Ghosts and Hauntings
Giants
Goblins
Gods and Goddesses
Golem
Mermaids
Monsters
Satan
Shapeshifters
Superheroes
Supernatural Creatures
Talking Animals
Trickster
Unicorns
Vampires
Werewolves
Witches

Wizards
Zombies

Magical Places

Arcadia
Atlantis
Borderlands
Carnival
Dimensions
Heaven
Hell
Hollow Earth
Imaginary Worlds
Labyrinth
Lost Worlds
Parallel Worlds
Rings
Shared Worlds
Threshold
Virtual Reality
Wilderness

Objects and Substances

Antimatter
Automobiles
Blood
Books
Clocks and Timepieces
Computers
Dolls and Puppets
Drugs
Elements
Fire
Flowers
Food and Drink
Gifts
Gold and Silver
Inventions
Machines and Mechanization
Magical Objects
Maps
Mirrors
Money
Omens and Signs
Plants
Rings

Rockets
Skeletons
Statues
Swords
Television and Radio
Toys
Treasure
UFOs
Water
Weaponry

Religions and Religious Concepts

Adam and Eve
Apocalypse
Christianity
Christmas
Demons
Divination
Eschatology
Evil
Golem
Halloween
Heaven
Hell
Islam
Judaism
Messiahs
Mythology
Omens and Signs
Reincarnation
Religion
Rituals
Sacrifice
Satan
Sin
Voodoo
Witches
Yin and Yang

Social and Political Concepts

America
Anthropology
Australia
Business
Carnival

China
Chivalry
Cities
Civilization
Class System
Community
Crime and Punishment
Cultures
Decadence
Dystopia
Economics
Education
Ethics
Exile
Family
Freedom
Friendship
Future War
Galactic Empire
Globalization
Governance Systems
Guilt and Responsibility
Habitats
History
Humanity
Individualism and Conformity
Japan
Kings
Nuclear War
Overpopulation
Planetary Colonies
Politics
Postcolonialism
Post-Holocaust Societies
Prisons
Progress
Race Relations
Rebellion
Rituals
Russia
Secret History
Slavery
Social Darwinism
Space War
Taboos
Taverns and Inns
Trade
Urban Fantasy

Utopia
Violence
War
Work and Leisure
Xenophobia

Sciences and Scientific Concepts

Air Travel
Alien Worlds
Aliens in Space
Aliens on Earth
Alternate History
Androids
Antimatter
Astronauts
Biology
Black Holes
Clones
Comets and Asteroids
Computers
Cosmology
Cyberspace
Cyborgs
Dimensions
Earth
Ecology
Elements
Eschatology
Evolution
Far Future
First Contact
Force
Future War
Galactic Empire
Generation Starships
Gravity
Immortality and Longevity
Inventions
Machines and Mechanization
Mad Scientists
Mars
Mathematics
Medicine
Mercury
The Moon
Mutation
Near Future

Nuclear Power
Nuclear War
Pantropy
Parasites
Physics
Plagues and Diseases
Planetary Colonies
Predictions
Psychic Powers
Psychology
Robots
Rockets
Scientists
Sea Travel
Social Darwinism
Space Habitats
Space Opera
Space Stations
Space Travel
Space War
The Sun
Superman
Suspended Animation and Cryonics
Symbiosis
Technology
Technothrillers
Teleportation
Television and Radio
Terraforming
Time Travel
UFOs
Uplift
Venus
Virtual Reality
Vision and Blindness
Weaponry
Weather

Settings

Africa
Alien Worlds
America
Arcadia
Asia
Atlantis
Australia

Black Holes
Borderlands
Castles
Caverns
Cemeteries
China
Cities
Comets and Asteroids
Community
Cultures
Cyberspace
Desert
Dimensions
Earth
Egypt
Europe
Farms
Forests
Frontier
Galactic Empire
Gardens
Generation Starships
Habitats
Heaven
Hell
Hollow Earth
Home
Hyperspace
Imaginary Worlds
Islands
Japan
Jungles
Jupiter and the Outer Planets
Labyrinth
Landscape
Latin America
Libraries
Lost Worlds
Mars
Mercury
Microcosm
The Moon
Mountains
Parallel Worlds
Planetary Colonies
Polar Regions
Prisons

Rivers
Russia
Shared Worlds
South Pacific
Space Habitats
Space Stations
Stars
The Sun
Taverns and Inns
Threshold
Venus
Virtual Reality
Wilderness

Space

Alien Worlds
Aliens in Space
Aliens on Earth
Astronauts
Black Holes
Comets and Asteroids
Cosmology
Dimensions
Earth
First Contact
Force
Galactic Empire
Generation Starships
Gravity
Hyperspace
Invasion
Jupiter and the Outer Planets
Mars
Mercury
The Moon
Pantropy
Parallel Worlds
Planetary Colonies
Rockets
Sense of Wonder
Space Habitats
Space Opera
Space Stations
Space Travel
Space War
Stars

The Sun
Terraforming
Venus

Subgenres and Narrative Patterns

Air Travel
Allegory
Alternate History
Bildungsroman
Comedy
Cyberpunk
Dark Fantasy
Deus ex Machina
Dystopia
Exploration
Fables
Fairy Tales
Fin de Siècle
Future War
Gothic
Hard Science Fiction
Heroic Fantasy
Horror
Magic Realism
Metafiction and Recursiveness
Mythology
Pastoral
Postmodernism
Prehistoric Fiction
Quests
Romance
Ruritanian Romance
Satire
Sea Travel
Secret History
Space Opera
Space Travel
Space War
Steampunk
Surrealism
Sword and Sorcery
Technothrillers
Tragedy
Underground Adventure
Underwater Adventure
Urban Fantasy

Utopia
War
Westerns

Time

Alternate History
Clocks and Timepieces
Cycles
Cosmology
Dimensions
Divination
Eschatology
Eternity
Evolution
Far Future
Fin de Siècle
Future War
Generation Starships

History
Hyperspace
Immortality and Longevity
Medievalism and the Middle Ages
Memory
Near Future
Omens and Signs
Parallel Worlds
Post-Holocaust Societies
Predictions
Prehistoric Fiction
Progress
Seasons
Social Darwinism
Speed
Suspended Animation and Cryonics
Time
Time Travel
Timeslips

CLASSIC WORKS BY CATEGORIES

Books

Alice's Adventures in Wonderland by
  Lewis Carroll (1865)
Animal Farm: A Fairy Story by George
  Orwell (1945)
Blood Music by Greg Bear (1985)
The Book of the New Sun by Gene
  Wolfe (1980–1983)
Brave New World by Aldous Huxley
  (1932)
Bring the Jubilee by Ward Moore
  (1953)
A Canticle for Leibowitz by Walter M.
  Miller, Jr. (1959)
Cat's Cradle by Kurt Vonnegut, Jr.
  (1963)
Childhood's End by Arthur C. Clarke
  (1953)
A Christmas Carol by Charles Dickens
  (1843)
City by Clifford D. Simak (1952)
The Clan of the Cave Bear by Jean
  Auel (1980)

A Clockwork Orange by Anthony
  Burgess (1962)
The Colour of Magic by Terry Pratchett
  (1983)
Conan the Conqueror by Robert E.
  Howard (1950)
*A Connecticut Yankee in King Arthur's
  Court* by Mark Twain (1889)
Consider Phlebas by Iain M. Banks
  (1987)
Dawn by Octavia E. Butler (1987)
The Day of the Triffids by John
  Wyndham (1951)
*Deathbird Stories: A Pantheon of
  Modern Gods* by Harlan Ellison (1975)
The Demolished Man by Alfred Bester
  (1953)
The Difference Engine by William
  Gibson and Bruce Sterling (1990)
*The Dispossessed: An Ambiguous
  Utopia* by Ursula K. Le Guin (1974)
Do Androids Dream of Electric Sheep?
  by Philip K. Dick (1968)

Dracula by Bram Stoker (1897)

Dragonflight by Anne McCaffrey (1968)

The Drowned World by J.G. Ballard (1962)

Dune by Frank Herbert (1965)

Earth Abides by George R. Stewart (1949)

Ender's Game by Orson Scott Card (1985)

The Eye of the World by Robert Jordan (1990)

Fahrenheit 451 by Ray Bradbury (1953)

The Female Man by Joanna Russ (1974)

*Flatland: A Romance of Many Dimiensions*i by Edwin A. Abbott (1884)

Flowers for Algernon by Daniel Keyes (1966)

The Forever War by Joe Haldeman (1975)

Foundation by Isaac Asimov (1951)

Frankenstein, or The Modern Prometheus by Mary Shelley (1818)

From the Earth to the Moon by Jules Verne (1865)

Galapagos by Kurt Vonnegut, Jr. (1985)

The Gate to Women's Country by Sheri S. Tepper (1988)

Gateway by Frederik Pohl (1977)

Gulliver's Travels by Jonathan Swift (1726)

The Handmaid's Tale by Margaret Atwood (1986)

Harry Potter and the Sorcerer's Stone by J. K. Rowling (1997)

Helliconia Spring by Brian W. Aldiss (1982)

Herland by Charlotte Perkins Gilman (1915)

The Hitchhiker's Guide to the Galaxy by Douglas Adams (1979)

The Hobbit by J.R.R. Tolkien (1937)

Hospital Station by James White (1962)

Hyperion by Dan Simmons (1989)

I, Robot by Isaac Asimov (1950)

Interview with the Vampire by Anne Rice (1976)

The Island of Doctor Moreau by H. G. Wells (1896)

Islandia by Austin Tappan Wright (1942)

Jurassic Park by Michael Crichton (1990)

Jurgen: A Comedy of Justice by James Branch Cabell (1919)

Kindred by Octavia E. Butler (1979)

The King of Elfland's Daughter by Lord Dunsany (1924)

Last and First Men by Olaf Stapledon (1930)

The Last Man by Mary Shelley (1826)

The Last Unicorn by Peter S. Beagle (1968)

The Left Hand of Darkness by Ursula K. Le Guin (1969)

Lilith by George MacDonald (1895)

The Lion, the Witch, and the Wardrobe by C.S. Lewis (1950)

Little, Big by John Crowley (1981)

Looking Backward, 2000–1887 by Edward Bellamy (1887)

Lord Foul's Bane by Stephen R. Donaldson (1977)

Lord of Light by Roger Zelazny (1967)

Lord of the Flies by William Golding (1954)

The Lord of the Rings by J.R.R. Tolkien (1954–1955)

Lost Horizon by James Hilton (1933)

The Lost World by Arthur Conan Doyle (1912)

The Man in the High Castle by Philip K. Dick (1962)

The Martian Chronicles by Ray Bradbury (1950)

Mary Poppins by P.L. Travers (1934)

The Mists of Avalon by Marion Zimmer Bradley (1982)

More Than Human by Theodore Sturgeon (1953)

The Narrative of Arthur Gordon Pym by Edgar Allan Poe (1839)

Films

Brazil (1986)
The Brother from Another Planet (1984)
A Clockwork Orange (1971)
Close Encounters of the Third Kind (1977)
The Day the Earth Stood Still (1951)
Dr. Jekyll and Mr. Hyde (1931)
Doctor No (1962)
Dr. Strangelove, or How I Stopped Worrying and Learned to Love the Bomb (1964)
Dracula (1931)
E.T.: The Extra-Terrestrial (1982)
Field of Dreams (1989)
Forbidden Planet (1956)
Frankenstein (1931)
Godzilla, King of the Monsters (1954)
Heaven Can Wait (1978)
The Incredible Shrinking Man (1957)
Invaders from Mars (1953)
Invasion of the Body Snatchers (1956)
The Invisible Man (1933)
Island of Lost Souls (1933)
It's a Wonderful Life (1946)
Jason and the Argonauts (1962)
La Jetée (1962)
King Kong (1933)
The Lord of the Rings: The Fellowship of the Ring (2001)
Mad Max (1979)
The Man Who Fell to Earth (1976)
The Matrix (1999)
Metropolis (1926)
Planet of the Apes (1968)
Snow White and the Seven Dwarfs (1937)
Solaris (1972)
Star Trek: Generations (1994)
Star Trek: The Motion Picture (1979)

Star Wars (1977)
Stargate (1994)
Superman (1978)
The Terminator (1984)
The Thing (from Another World) (1951)
Things to Come (1936)
Topper (1937)
Total Recall (1990)
A Trip to the Moon (1902)
2001: A Space Odyssey (1968)
The Wizard of Oz (1939)

Television Series

Babylon 5 (1993–1998)
Blakes 7 (1978–1981)
Buffy the Vampire Slayer (1996–2003)
Doctor Who (1963–1989)
Farscape (1999–2003)
Futurama (1999–2003)
Hercules: The Legendary Journeys (1994–2000)
The Outer Limits (1963–1965)
The Prisoner (1967–1968)
The Quatermass Experiment (1953)
Red Dwarf (1988–1998)
The Simpsons (1989–)
Star Trek (1966–1969)
Star Trek: Deep Space Nine (1993–1999)
Star Trek: Enterprise (2001–2005)
Star Trek: The Next Generation (1987–1994)
Star Trek: Voyager (1994–2001)
The Twilight Zone (1959–1964)
Wonder Woman (1976–1979)
The X-Files (1993–2002)
Xena: Warrior Princess (1995–2001)

Volume 2, Themes L–Z

L

LABYRINTH

Overview

Most people use the terms "labyrinth" and "maze" interchangeably, although they can be differentiated by designating a maze as a **puzzle** with choices of path while a labyrinth has only a single path to the center. The most famous labyrinth was constructed for King Minos of Crete to hold the Minotaur in Greek **mythology**; actual examples of labyrinth design are found in simple stone carvings in numerous places across the world, from Syria to Ireland, dating back 3000 years. The labyrinth symbol has appeared in petroglyphs, pavement, turf, and basketry throughout the world, from Java to the Americas, **Australia**, India and Nepal. Mazes have been built with rocks, walls, hedges, and crops such as maize.

Survey

If one thinks of labyrinths in popular culture, Jim Henson's film *Labyrinth* (1986) will most likely come to mind. When the audience is first introduced to sixteen-year-old Sarah, she is play-acting in a princess-style dress, trying to memorize a scene from one of her favorite **books**, *Labyrinth*. Sarah is soon whisked into the world of **fairy tales** when her baby brother is kidnapped by the Goblin King (see **Goblins**), forcing Sarah to navigate a constantly changing fantasy labyrinth to ensure her brother's **freedom**. Another story where the labyrinth takes center stage is Mervyn Peake's ***Titus Groan***, wherein the labyrinthine Gormenghast **castle** is a living, breathing, continuously growing organism. Centuries upon centuries of ancestral rulers building new additions onto it have turned the castle into a sprawling, gigantic maze that no one has ever seen in its entirety.

Even larger than Gormenghast is the galactic-scale maze in Avram Davidson's *Masters of the Maze* (1965). This Maze is a pathway between worlds and times, and **insect**-like aliens try to find their way past the Guardians to get to **Earth** so that they can build a new hive with humans as their food supply. The **hero**, Nate Gordon, must traverse through **alien worlds** to get to the center of the Maze and alert the legendary Maze Masters. In Algis Budrys's *Rogue Moon* (1960), a man sends duplicates of himself—which keep dying along the way—to investigate an enigmatic alien labyrinth on the **Moon**. Another horrifying maze can be found in the movie *Cube* (1997), which portrays a group of strangers that wake up inside a bizarre labyrinth and discover that they must navigate through a series of identical chambers with lethal traps in order to **escape**.

Many science fiction stories describe futuristic totalitarian **cities** that have labyrinthine constructions. In *Alphaville*, intergalactic secret agent Lemmy Caution enters the maze of Alphaville to destroy the crazed **computer** Alpha 60 that runs the emotionless city. The underground city (see **Underground Adventures**) in *Metropolis* is comprised of suspended streets and zig-zagged buildings. In the future of H.G. Wells's *The Time Machine*, a portion of **humanity** has devolved (see **Evolution**) into the Morlocks, a race with lidless eyes and pale complexions that live beneath the earth in a maze of tunnels that the Time Traveller must enter in search of his missing time machine. Gene Wolfe takes a **far future** city with a maze-like environment and mixes in fantasy elements in *The Book of the New Sun*. The young **apprentice** torturer Severian finds his way through the subterranean labyrinth of the sorcerers, while in Ursula K. Le Guin's *The Tombs of Atuan* (1971), the **wizard** Ged must also penetrate a mysterious underground labyrinth (see *A Wizard of Earthsea*).

Futuristic labyrinthine cities are not limited to Earth. In *Forbidden Planet*, Morbius is stranded on a barren planet, where he explores the underground maze-like ruins of the ultra-developed **civilization** of the Krell. In Robert Silverberg's thought-provoking novel *The Man in the Maze* (1969), Dick Muller, a man who was hideously transformed in a way that has left him repulsive to all **humanity**, takes refuge on an alien world within a city that defends itself with scientific traps and **illusion**. The city of Lemnos is famed for its labyrinthine horrors, and the men that seek Muller's aid must first face the murderous maze. The reptilian aliens in H.P. Lovecraft and Kenneth Sterling's "Within the Walls of Eryx" (1939) deliberately build a labyrinthine prison to trap the humans who had inadvertently stolen (see **Theft**) their crystals. Likewise, in the movie *Dark City* (1998), humans are unknowingly stuck in an alien race's experiment (see **Mad Scientists**) like rats in a maze, and their world changes every night while they **sleep**.

There are also psychological labyrinths (see **Psychology**), as in *The Matrix*, a film which asks us to ask ourselves if we are really sure what we see and feel is real (see **Philosophy**). The Matrix is a mind-maze, ultimately leading to the Truth; the more experienced one is in the Matrix, the more **knowledge** one gains toward understanding the Truth about what the Matrix is. Labyrinths are also an important image in the works of Jorge Luis Borges, particularly his story "The Garden of Forking Paths" (1941).

Discussion

In science fiction and fantasy stories, characters often need to escape from enemies, or gain freedom from tyranny, so it is natural that storytellers will challenge heroes with the ultimate trap of the labyrinth. Even when the environment is not purposely created as a labyrinth, it may have that feel, as did the Mines of Moria and the Forest of Fangorn in J.R.R. Tolkien's *The Lord of the Rings* to suspenseful effect.

Bibliography

Hilary Crew. "From Labyrinth to Celestial City." *Journal of Youth Services in Libraries*, 2 (Fall, 1988), 84–89.
Tanya J. Gardiner-Scott. "Through the Maze." *Extrapolation*, 30 (Spring, 1989), 70–83.

John T. Irwin. "A Clew to the Clue." Shawn Rosenheim and Stephen Rachman, ed., *The American Face of Edgar Allan Poe*. Baltimore: Johns Hopkins University Press, 1995, 139–154.

Allen Malmquist. *"Labyrinth." Cinefantastique*, 17 (January, 1987), 42, 59.

Robert M. Philmus. "Wells and Borges and the Labyrinths of Time." *Science-Fiction Studies*, 1 (Fall, 1974), 237–248.

E.H. Redekop. "Labyrinths in Time and Space." *Mosaic*, 13 (Spring/Summer, 1980), 95–113.

Roger B. Salomon. *Mazes of the Serpent*. Ithaca, NY: Cornell University Press, 2002.

Stephen Scobie. "Different Mazes." *Riverside Quarterly*, 5 (July, 1971), 12–18.

David Seed. *The Fictional Labyrinths of Thomas Pynchon*. Iowa City: University of Iowa Press, 1988.

—Nick Aires

LANDSCAPE

Overview

"Landscape" entered the English language in the late sixteenth century from the technical vocabulary of **art**—denoting scenic paintings of **mountains, rivers,** prairies, or **forests**—but quickly was extended as a metaphor for an array of human affairs, including **psychology, anthropology,** and **history**. We now use terms such as cityscape, mindscape, dreamscape, soundscape, and even mediascape to describe any topic's conceptual horizon.

Survey

Some works of science fiction and fantasy are set against formidable backgrounds of polar ice (see Ursula K. Le Guin's *The Left Hand of Darkness*), open ocean (see Le Guin's *A Wizard of Earthsea* and J.G. Ballard's *The Drowned World*), arid **desert** (see Frank Herbert's *Dune*), or alien regolith (see Kim Stanley Robinson's *Red Mars*); others track how **seasons** and variations of **weather** can shape **culture** (see Brian W. Aldiss's *Helliconia Spring*). Such titles majestically foreground our **sublime** subjugation to or daring domestication of **nature**, a grandeur obvious in epic **quests,** where **heroes** traverse rugged terrain, surmount topographic **thresholds,** or journey beyond dangerous **frontiers** for **exploration** or in search of new **habitats**. Capturing vast vistas with sweeping shots, Peter Jackson's adaptation of J.R.R. Tolkien's *The Lord of the Rings: The Fellowship of the Ring* and its sequels offer an arresting example; not only do the films brilliantly realize Middle-earth, but they suggest the ways geography proves to be Frodo's antagonist as much as does Sauron—the ruthless plain of Gorgoroth is far from the idyllic **pastoral** of the Shire. Landscape can establish reality's cold equations and yet still be a source of wonder; Jules Verne's extraordinary voyages, such as *Journey to the Center of the Earth* (1863) and *Twenty Thousand Leagues under the Sea*, present geological surveys or travelogues, as does most of the last third of Greg Egan's *Schild's Ladder* (2002), where characters tour an astonishing landscape of meta-life on the scale of the Planck length, orders of magnitude smaller than atoms or electrons (see **Sense of Wonder**).

But more than just affording a strange, difficult, or distant locale, landscape indexes a *human geography*, catalogs reciprocal tensions of physical and social environments. Landscape is not simply place, setting, or site: it codes how humans encounter or conceptualize, preserve or destroy the **Earth**. This is most obvious in allegorical, archetypal, mythic, or personified landscapes (see **Allegory, Mythology, Personification**)—the **garden** of **Adam and Eve**, the sick land of the **Arthur** stories, the **utopia** of **Arcadia**, religious conceptions of **Heaven** and **Hell** (see **Religion**), and **ritual** artifacts such as Stonehenge. Ian Watson's *The Gardens of Delight* (1980) animates landscape in the eschatological tradition of David Lindsay's *A Voyage to Arcturus* (see **Eschatology**). Less obvious but equally telling is the rural ideal's cardinal opposite, the metropolitan morass of our daily lives. While the bucolic countryside can proffer a redemptive antidote to the **decadence** of moldering **cities** (as in *Blade Runner*), the cityscape constitutes a powerful representation of human culture and value. Think, for instance, of the symbolic difference between the New York skyline on September 10, 2001 and September 11, 2001: here is an unequivocal palimpsest of **memory** and **time**, not merely power and **tragedy**.

Think too of the **romance** of the open American prairie—only the poetic imagination could transform the monotony of an unvariegated landscape into a lyrical encomium, a rhetoric of national **destiny** and individual triumph (see **America**). The pattern appears in literatures of **Asia**, Canada, **Australia**, **Africa**, **Russia**, and elsewhere. Steppe or veldt, dense **jungle** or desert **island**, the landscape without feature offers an occasion for the most imperialistic imagination. Similarly, land provides a prominent trope of colonization and conquest; Daniel Defoe's seminal *Robinson Crusoe* (1719) is the emblematic parable of how geography cannot be separated from global **politics** (see **Postcolonialism**).

Science fiction is especially interested in such notional transformations, seen principally in geomorphic architecture such as the city-planet erasing natural topography through **terraforming** and **overpopulation**; examples include Trantor, Isaac Asimov's empire's capital in *Foundation*, Coruscant, the galactic hub in the *Star Wars* series, and one also thinks of the film *Metropolis*, and of the unrestrained arcologies in William Gibson's *Neuromancer*, a novel that appraises the wasteland of a lost generation gone to space. Much of that latter novel's landscape is virtual, the "matrix" of **cyberspace**. Perhaps an even more revealing urban **ecology** is the imbricated **borderland** where city meets country, mapped by "franchuates" (see Neal Stephenson's *Snow Crash*) that make one suburb indistinguishable from any other, the indiscriminate sprawl that elides **wilderness** and tames nature (as in "landscaping," the colloquialism for domesticating **plants** around buildings).

The most radical vision of human geography appears in J.G. Ballard's stark *Crash* (1973), *Concrete Island* (1974), and *High-Rise* (1975). These display the ethical and psychological consequences of a dynamic technological landscape designed to fulfill desire, but which defamiliarize (see **Estrangement**) landscape codes, producing for **readers** uncanny epiphanies impossible in most mundane fiction.

Discussion

Landscape remains one of the most significant features of fictive world-building. While some imaginary landscapes are intentionally pallid (see Edwin A. Abbott's *Flatland*), it is usually the richly developed detail, the intensely nuanced image, the exact metaphor that both realizes the world's otherness and renders it accessibly familiar. This can be vividly illustrated by comparing landscapes in crude 1960s television (the sound stages littered with enormous *papier mâché* boulders backed by clumsy matte paintings) with more visually sophisticated films. In Terry Gilliam's *Brazil, The Adventures of Baron Munchausen* (1989), or *12 Monkeys* (1995) (see *La Jetée*), texture is as important as plot or character; here visual depth, in the form of perversely particular details, provides both the concreteness and consistency to complete a *lived-in* world full of sinuous surface contours and indirect vectors.

Perhaps landscape can be even more important than characters. In an appendix to *Triton*, Samuel R. Delany comments that science fiction is science fiction only when the text's speculation operates fully within an interlocking matrix of social and scientific ideas. **Knowledge**, he says, "was *always* the secondary hero of the s-f novel—in exactly the same way that the landscape was always the primary one."

Bibliography

Samuel R. Delany. "Appendix A." Delany, *Triton*. New York: Bantam Books, 1976, 331–343.

Jean-François Lyotard. "Scapeland." Trans. David Macey. Andrew Benjamin, ed., *The Lyotard Reader*. Cambridge: Basil Blackwell, 1989, 212–219.

Rachel May. "Narrating Landscape, Landscaping Narrative." *Russian Studies in Literature*, 39 (Summer, 2003), 65–87.

Richard Muir. *Approaches to Landscape*. New York: Barnes and Noble, 1999.

Patrick Parrinder. "Landscapes of British Science Fiction." George Slusser and Eric S. Rabkin, eds., *Styles of Creation*. Athens: University of Georgia Press, 1992. 193–204.

Simon Schama. *Landscape and Memory*. New York: Alfred A. Knopf, 1995.

Anne Whiston Spirn. *The Language of Landscape*. New Haven: Yale University Press, 2000.

Raymond Williams. *The Country and the City*. London: Oxford University Press, 1973.

—Neil Easterbrook

LANGUAGE AND LINGUISTICS

"When I use a word," Humpty Dumpty said in rather a scornful tone, "it means just what I choose it to mean—neither more nor less."

—Lewis Carroll
Through the Looking Glass (1871)

Overview

Although **communication** of all kinds is broadly an issue in science fiction and fantasy, many stories focus more specifically on aspects of linguistic science, such as studying languages on **alien worlds** or in the **far future**. Authors may also foreground exotic invented languages or sprinkle their stories with neologisms.

Survey

Some stories explore a specific linguistic theory. Edgar Rice Burroughs's *Tarzan of the Apes* deals with various forms of language acquisition: raised by **apes**, Tarzan grows up learning to speak the language of **jungle** beasts (see **Animals and Zoos**), picks up English by reading his father's books, and is taught to speak French by a friend. Jack Vance's *The Languages of Pao* (1958) extrapolates the Sapir-Whorf hypothesis into caste **cultures** whose different languages prevent people from thinking the thoughts of another caste—until someone begins blending the languages. Matthew Farrell's *Thunder Rift* (2001) takes the same hypothesis, but gives the characters (see **Aliens in Space**) several choices like Language-of-Intimacy or Language-of-Command. In Charles Sheffield's "At the Eschaton" (1995), a man awakens in the far future to learn that all disciplines, like medicine and chemistry, now have their own distinct languages. And Samuel R. Delany's *Babel-17* (1966) involves an invented language that enhances the human ability to formulate and solve complex problems but is also tainted by political bias (see **Politics**).

Authors may write part or all of their story in an exotic dialect from the characters' **civilization**. In George Orwell's *Nineteen Eighty-Four* the Party (see **Governance Systems**) uses Newspeak to control the populace, and snippets from this language contribute to the novel's oppressive tone. The **youth** culture of Anthony Burgess's *A Clockwork Orange* uses the Russian-based slang dialect Nadsat to bond within their **community** while excluding others. In Jane M. Lindskold's *Brother to Dragons, Companion to Owls* (1994) the main character can speak only in repeated phrases, such as quotations from **books** like the Bible—just as the character Loyal to the Group of Seventeen in Gene Wolfe's *The Book of the New Sun* tells a story entirely in political slogans. Esther M. Friesner uses invented words and odd phrases to suggest the far future in *The Psalms of Herod* (1995).

Beyond dialect lies the realm of constructed languages. J.R.R. Tolkien said that he wrote *The Hobbit* and *The Lord of the Rings* primarily as vehicles for the languages he invented. He recorded extensive vocabulary for **elves** and other races in Middle-earth. Jacqueline Lichtenberg's *Unto Zeor, Forever* (1978) features a handful of specialized terms to express how two newly evolved human races interact (see **Mutation**); without these terms, the story would make no sense, as English has no equivalents. Linguist and author Suzette Haden Elgin designed Láadan to express the worldview and **perception** of women, as described in her novel *Native Tongue* (1984). Complete with grammar, vocabulary, lessons, and sample readings, Láadan is taught in some college classes (see **Education**) on linguistics and science fiction. The Yilanè (see **Dinosaurs**) of Harry Harrison's *Winter in Eden* (1986) use not only words but also postures and changing **colors** to communicate; the author explores much of their odd grammar and vocabulary, and his human protagonist must learn the language to survive. Marc Okrand composed the Klingon language for *Star Trek* and a passing reference in one movie led to Lawrence Schoen's *The Klingon Hamlet*

(2000), a translation of William **Shakespeare**'s play. Klingon enjoys a comprehensive grammar as well as vocabulary, with many speakers and a journal, *HolQeD*, published by the Klingon Language Institute.

Alien languages frequently appear as **puzzles** complicating the plot, especially in **first contact** stories. In *Close Encounters of the Third Kind* the **aliens on Earth** use **music** for communication with **humanity**. Humans reply with the aid of **computers**. A linguist in Janet Kagan's *Hellspark* (1988) realizes that the alien **birds** communicate by ruffling their feathers; this proves their **intelligence** and protects their **home**. In A.C. Crispin and Kathleen O'Malley's *Silent Dances* (1990), the crane-like aliens have a sophisticated sign language. The *Star Trek: The Next Generation* episode "Darmok" (1991) introduces a race of beings who talk entirely in metaphors—highly specific historical and legendary allusions that convey nothing to outsiders. In *Stargate*, a linguist must decipher the instructions for operating alien **technology**. The arboreal frogs in Amy Thomson's *The Color of Distance* (1995) speak through patterns and **colors** on their chameleon-like skins. In Janine Ellen Young's *The Bridge* (2000), **exploration** leads to **disaster** because the alien Kasarans communicate by exchanging special viruses (see **Plagues and Diseases**). Their greeting almost wipes out humanity, but implants the **knowledge** of **space travel** in the survivors. The television series *Star Trek: Enterprise* features a xenolinguist among its crew, who proves invaluable because the universal translator so essential to other *Star Trek* series is a new **invention** and only marginally reliable.

Discussion

Like other soft sciences, linguistics has often gotten shortchanged by writers who do not understand it. The result is sometimes good fiction, but usually poor science. Yet language remains the thing that most separates humanity from beasts. It shapes us as **children** and teaches us through both listening and **reading**. Even foreign languages seem tremendously alien to us; alien languages open a whole new **frontier**.

In science fiction, languages can demonstrate the effects of **alternate history**, **time travel**, or space travel. In fantasy, we find **elder races** and **magical objects** that pose linguistic puzzles. We can seek to manipulate the language process through **genetic engineering**, **globalization**, and technology. Yet it remains a **mystery** at heart, which excites our **sense of wonder**. Writers have much room left to explore languages, especially using new discoveries and solid linguistic science for inspiration.

Bibliography

Him Allan. *An Introduction to Elvish*. Hayes: Bran's Head Books, 1978.

Myra Edwards Barnes. *Linguistics and Languages in Science Fiction-Fantasy*. New York: Arno Press, 1975.

Suzette Haden Elgin. *Linguistics and Science Fiction Sampler*. Huntsville, AL: OCLS Press, 1994.

Verlyn Flieger. *Splintered Light*. Revised. Kent, OH: Kent State University Press, 2002.

M.J. Hardman. "Linguistics and Science Fiction." *Women and Language*, 22 (Spring, 1999), 47–48.

Walter E. Meyers. *Aliens and Linguists*. Athens: University of Georgia Press, 1980.

Ruth S. Noel. *The Languages of Tolkien's Middle-Earth*. Boston: Houghton-Mifflin Co., 1980.

Marc Okrand. *The Klingon Dictionary*. New York: Pocket Books, 1985.

Gary Westfahl. "Words of Wishdom." George Slusser and Eric S. Rabkin, ed., *Styles of Creation*. Athens: University of Georgia Press, 1992, 221–244.

—*Elizabeth Barrette*

LAST MAN

Overview

The last man, one of the earliest science fiction themes, rarely if ever figures in fantasy, which generally posits an overarching religious framework with an afterlife that would preclude the entire elimination of **humanity** (see **Religion**). The term is also appropriate because the **gender** of the sole survivor is invariably male— although the first English-language speculation of novel length was written by a woman. The theme dates back to the Romantic era, when poets considered **time**, mortality, and social and personal **apocalypse**. Thomas Hood's 1826 poem "The Last Man" is a whimsical version of other meditations, such as Byron's "Darkness" (1816) or Thomas Campbell's "The Last Man" (1823). The narrator of H.G. Wells's *The War of the Worlds* is discovered in a devastated London singing Hood's poem in hysterical relief at the Martians' demise.

Survey

Although the Frenchman Jean-Baptiste de Grainville published an earlier version of the idea in 1805, Mary Shelley's *The Last Man* is nearer to modern science fiction. Her future, although technologically little different from her own time, is extrapolated from it. Shelley's "Last Man" is the sole survivor of a plague (see **Plagues and Diseases**), as is the survivor of M.P. Shiel's *The Purple Cloud*, whose rampage of destruction marks the growing **paranoia** that comes to replace romantic narcissism. While Wells used references to the theme, not the theme itself, the final image in Wells's *The Time Machine* with the Time Traveller alone under a red sun is one of science fiction's classic images. The "Last Man" theme is hinted at in both **disaster** stories where people die one by one and in those that begin with the protagonist believing he is the only survivor; yet its narrative progress to the final sense of aloneness is different and is marked by the solipsism that stems from its Romantic roots. Richard Matheson's *I Am Legend* (1954), fusing science fiction, plague, and **vampire**-horror, comes close to this early sensibility.

Many later versions show the final survivor as victim of **nuclear war** or alien **invasion**. Mordecai Roshwald's *Level 7* (1959) and Richard C. O'Brien's *Z for Zachariah* (1975) both show "last people"—O'Brien's protagonist is actually a teenage girl—in the aftermath of nuclear holocaust. Alfred Bester's "They Don't Make Life Like They Used To" (1963) shows a psychotic last *couple* after an unexplained alien invasion. The story is a disturbing examination of denial. In Ray Bradbury's "The Silent Towers" (1949), incoporated into *The Martian Chronicles*, the last man on an evacuated **Mars** tracks down the last woman, only to flee in panic at her unattractiveness. Bradbury's story recalls the a common wish-fulfillment fantasy—that the Last *Man* has a world full of available women—and suggests the sexual **anxiety** beneath it; the same fantasy is presented, and exploded, in Bester's "5,271,009" (1954). A sense of unease also arose in Wallace G. West's "The Last Man" (1929): the last male in a world of sexless women is discovered by an atavistic "real" woman. Many of these stories are in fact versions of **Adam and Eve**, giving us new couples in a position to revive (or not) the human race.

A comic book series that began in 2003, Brian K. Vaughan's *Y: The Last Man*, has the modern world devastated by a plague that kills all males except for one young American. It engages **feminism** and feminist arguments for a separatist women's world, and treats with some irony the "Last Man" theme's easy incorporation in male sexual fantasy. *A.I.: Artificial Intelligence* develops another irony: the survivor is in fact a humanoid **robot**. This sense of the **absurd** is also present in the beginning of Fredric Brown's "Knock" (1948) with the famous lines about the last man alive sitting alone in a room and suddenly hearing a knock at the door. Brown gives us a science fiction story about the last man—and woman—alive after aliens have exterminated all life on **Earth** except for representative couples of each species. But the underlying joke is that such a scenario can be **horror** (what knocks is a ghost or **vampire**), science fiction (what knocks is an alien), a feminist story (what knocks is a woman), and no doubt many others.

Discussion

The "Last Man" may be a new Adam. He is also Robinson Crusoe, alone on his **island**, surviving on the remnants of the old **civilization**; or Henry David Thoreau living a romantically **pastoral** life in the woods. John Wyndham's *The Day of the Triffids*, like George R. Stewart's *Earth Abides*, begins with someone in a position to exploit the riches of society precisely because there is no one with whom to share it. By being apparently the last man, by seeing in a world of blindness (or, as in *The Invisible Man*, by being literally out of sight), the subject can indulge in the power-fantasy of taking what he wants when he wants it. This, and a subtle meditation on teenage loneliness, underlines John Christopher's *Empty World* (1977), in which yet another plague sweeps the globe. Another sort of loneliness, elegiac and ironic, marks the conclusion of Olaf Stapledon's *Last and First Men*, where after millions of years of evolutionary struggle humanity is faced with extinction. Almost the last words of the book are those of the youngest of the "Last Men": "It is very good to have been man."

Bibliography

Michael Bradshaw. "Mary Shelley's *The Last Man*." Derek Littlewood and Peter Stockwell, eds., *Impossibility Fiction*. Amsterdam: Rodopi, 1996, 163–176.

I.F. Clarke. "Introduction." Jean-Baptiste Françoise Xavier Cousin de Grainville, *The Last Man*, trans. I.F. and M. Clarke. Middleton, CT: Wesleyan University Press, 2002, xix–xli.

Ryszard Dubonski. "The Last Man Theme in Modern Fantasy and SF." *Foundation*, No. 16 (May, 1979), 26–31.

Michael Eberle-Sinatra, ed. *Mary Shelley's Fictions*. London: Macmillan, 2000.

Malcolm, Pittock. "*The Last Man* and *Nineteen Eighty-Four*." *English Language Notes*, 35 (March, 1998), 67–73.

Robert Plank. "The Lone Survivor." Eric Rabkin, Martin H. Greenberg, and Joseph Olander, eds., *The End of the World*. Carbondale: Southern Illinois University Press, 1983, 20–52.

Edward Shanks. "*The Purple Cloud* and Its Author." A. Reynolds Morse, ed., *Shiel in Diverse Hands*. Cleveland, OH: Reynolds Morse Foundation, 1983, 23–29.

W. Warren Wagar. *Terminal Visions*. Bloomington: Indiana University Press, 1982.

—*Andy Sawyer*

LATIN AMERICA

Overview

Latin America comprises the countries of Mexico, Central America, South America, and the Spanish-speaking Caribbean. The fifteenth-century European **invasion** of the Americas resulted in genocide and **slavery**; **alternate histories** dealing with Christopher Columbus and other conquistadors are concomitantly vivid and powerful. Latin Americans generally write sociological rather than **hard science fiction**, because they live amid the **anxieties** caused by unstable **governance systems**, unfair **class systems**, rocky **race relations**, and poverty. American science fiction and fantasy authors use Latin American settings to work through themes of imperialist **politics** and **guilt and responsibility**.

Survey

Latin American fantastic fiction is often conflated with **magic realism** because of the international prominence of such authors as Colombian Nobel Prize winner Gabriel García Márquez (whose *One Hundred Years of Solitude* [1967] is a primary example) and Alejo Carpentier. Jorge Luis Borges's collection *Ficciones* (1944) showcases classic instances of **metafiction and recursiveness**, employing metaphors of **labyrinths, libraries, dreams,** and **mirrors**. Adolfo Bioy Casares's *The Invention of Morel* (1940), inspired by H.G. Wells's *The Island of Doctor Moreau*, features **illusions** caused by holograms; it was adapted into film and inspired the movies *Last Year at Marienbad* (1961) and *Man Facing Southeast* (1985). Angélica Gorodischer's *Kalpa Imperial* (translated by Ursula K. Le Guin in 2003) is a fantasy of **imaginary worlds**. Cuban-American Daína Chaviano has won many awards for her best-selling novels and collections.

Pre-Columbian gods retain their violent panache; Alexander Irvine's virtuoso fantasy *A Scattering of Jades* (2002) parallels Aztec pantheonistic warfare with nineteenth-century social ills including poverty and slavery. An Aztec **trickster** god wreaks havoc in *Smoking Mirror Blues* (2002), Ernest Hogan's unique and imaginative work.

The cruelties of the conquistadors are graphic in John Kessel's "Invaders" (1990). He satirizes imperialism as mentally deranged while juxtaposing conquistador Francisco Pizarro's defeat of Inca emperor Atahualpa with an invasion by **aliens on Earth** who seek cocaine and "kicks" (see **Satire**). Orson Scott Card's *Pastwatch: The Redemption of Christopher Columbus* (1996), meanwhile, shows **far future** Africans adjusting **history** to put the Indians on a technological par with Columbus's **Europe**.

Latin America as host to **lost worlds** was popularized by Wells's Ecuadorian valley, "The Country of the Blind" (1904) (see **Vision and Blindness**). Emphasizing the savage perils of Brazil, Wells also pioneered the giant **insect** story in "Empire of the Ants" (1905); it inspired Carl Stephenson's similar "Leiningen versus the Ants" (1938) and Murray Leinster's "Doomsday Deferred" (1949). **Dinosaurs** are found on a remote plateau in Arthur Conan Doyle's *The Lost World*. His Brazil is full of wonders, but his Amazonian indigenes are treacherous slavers inferior to Europeans. Postulating that Doyle's novel was factual, Greg Bear's *Dinosaur Summer* (1998) shows American ingenuity outwitting both corrupt Latinos and subjugated Indians. Michael Crichton's *Jurassic Park* and its sequels are further descendents of Doyle's novel. Greedy American John Hammond establishes his dinosaur theme park on an **island** off Costa Rica precisely because, there, he can avoid governmental regulations.

North Americans regularly view Latin America as politically corrupt. In Ira Levin's *The Boys from Brazil* (1976), Brazil is merely a hideaway for exiled Nazis, particularly Josef Mengele, who perpetrated cruel experiments on Jewish prisoners during World War II (see **Judaism**) and is still alive and experimenting in this novel.

Harry Harrison's *The Stainless Steel Rat for President* (1982) treats Latino politics comically, using his recurring character to confront dictator General Zapilote, who has "won" elections forty-one times. Jim campaigns against Zapilote in this satire of corruption that is ultimately more hilarious than Woody Allen's 1971 film *Bananas*, but with a similar subplot.

Lucius Shepard is memorably lyrical in his fantasy *Life During Wartime* (1987), a devastating condemnation of **war** and oppressors who create misery and poverty. The war is a feudalistic **microcosm** of life for Central Americans, who are manipulated by two opposed **families** of vampiric telepaths, and thus are trapped between **magic** and **madness**. Shepard's collection *The Jaguar Hunter* (1987) returns to magic and **monsters** rendered realistic due to keen observations during his travels.

Orson Scott Card's *Speaker For The Dead* (1986) is a **first contact** novel set on a Brazilian **planetary colony**. The Brazilians are intelligent and mostly Catholic, excepting the secular humanist protagonists. Card lived in Brazil for two years and dramatizes the themes of guilt, **sin**, and atonement with profound care (see *Ender's Game*). Similarly, Mary Doria Russell's *The Sparrow* (1996) features a Puerto Rican Jesuit who uses his Catholic network (see **Religion**) to arrange a first contact; though severely traumatized, his strengths are his skills in **language and linguistics** and his "hybrid vigor, the strength of two continents."

Discussion

North-South foreign relations are rarely depicted. White men's racism and **sexism** are famously punished in James Tiptree, Jr.'s "The Women Men Don't See" (1973) when a plane carrying three Americans and a Maya crashes on the Yucatán coast. The narrator is surprised by the self-sufficiency of the women and native; his presumed superiority has blinded him to human heterogeneity. Americans are culpable again in Gregory Frost's trenchant "Madonna of the Maquiladora" (2002): a journalist investigating sightings of the Virgin Mary in a factory of "motion controller systems" discovers that the impoverished Mexicans are being controlled by Yankee corporate hegemony. Latin America remains a **frontier** for North American writers, yet it has a thriving community of autochthonous authors.

Bibliography

Andrea Bell and Yolanda Molina-Gavilán, eds. *Cosmos Latinos*. Middletown, CT: Wesleyan University Press, 2003.
Gene Bell-Villada. *Borges and His Fiction*. Austin: University of Texas Press, 1999.
Damien Broderick. "Some Informal Remarks Toward a Calculus of God." *New York Review of Science Fiction*, No. 114 (February, 1998) 1, 4–6.
Stephen Minta. *García Marquez*. New York: Harper, 1987.
Mike Resnick and Gardner Dozois, eds. *Future Earths: Under South American Skies*. New York: DAW, 1993.
Donald Leslie Shaw. *Companion to Modern Spanish American Fiction*. Rochester, NY: Tamesis, 2002.
Ilan Stavans. "Private Eyes and Time Travelers." *Literary Review*, 38 (1994), 5–20.
Tim Sullivan. *Tropical Chills*. New York: Avon, 1988.

—Fiona Kelleghan

LEISURE

See Work and Leisure

LIBRARIES

Overview

"Science," literally translated, is "knowledge." While the theme of cryptic **books** in fantasy and occasional science fiction suggest the hidden, sometimes mystic **knowledge** to be found in grimoires and magical handbooks (see **Magical Objects**), libraries stand for the classification of this knowledge, building it into a scheme of related facts and analysis. In many circumstances they also suggest a regaining of knowledge or technological exploitation of this knowledge.

Survey

When societies are brought to their knees by **disaster** (see George Stewart's *Earth Abides* and John Wyndham's *The Day of the Triffids*) the scattered survivors are too few to regain the full range of skills necessary for resurrecting civilization. What is necessary is the stored, external record of knowledge and skills, in the library. Masen and his companions, in Wyndham's novel, develop their knowledge of farming, engineering, and other skills through retrieving books from libraries. It is the irony of *Earth Abides* that Ish cannot persuade his children to exploit the systematic knowledge to be found in books. Other futures are saved by their ability to develop libraries: the work of the monks in Walter M. Miller, Jr.'s *A Canticle for Leibowitz*, recording and copying the works of the "Blessed Leibowitz" after a **nuclear war**, recapitulates the actual work of Dark Ages monasteries. Australian novelist Sean McMullen's Greatwinter series, beginning with *Voices in the Light* (1994), describes a **post-holocaust society** where the duel-fighting "Highliber" leads a caste of librarians devoted to the development of a huge calculating **computer**. In contrast, the library of Philip K. Dick's *Counter-Clock World* (1967) is devoted to *erasing* books in a world where **time** has reversed.

Science fictional futures have echoed the development of "real" libraries through records and digitalization. In Arthur C. Clarke's *Imperial Earth* (1975), Duncan Makenzie travels from Titan to **Earth** on a ship whose library contains virtually the entire cultural record of books, **music**, and film. The library in Gene Wolfe's *The Book of the New Sun*, in the keeping of a blind librarian, contains a thumb-sized cube that itself contains more books than the library itself. The sentient knowledge-banks in *A. I.: Artificial Intelligence* and the 2002 *The Time Machine* (see H.G. Wells's *The Time Machine*) update the **robot** librarians in stories like Harry Harrison's "The Robot Who Wanted to Know" (1958). Such knowledge-banks are themselves present in more sophisticated form in post-**cyberpunk** novels like Neal Stephenson's *Snow Crash*, in which a "meta-librarian" daemon or software agent organizes and retrieves information for the **hero**.

Storing information is part of the process of being a sentient species. The Great Race in H.P. Lovecraft's "The Shadow Out of Time" (1936) archives the **history** of the various species that have inhabited the Earth by kidnapping the minds of representative individuals such as the protagonist, Peaslee. Despite Peaslee's **horror** at his ordeal, we are able to recognize these **monsters** as scholars, engaged in the pursuit of knowledge.

The "world of knowledge" as envisioned by the library is also cognate with the world itself. In Jorge Luis Borges's "The Library of Babel" (1941), the Universe itself is an infinite library with all possible books, including those with blank pages and a book that is the "formula and perfect compendium" of all others. Neil Gaiman's Morpheus, in the Sandman series of comic books, possesses a library of *unwritten* books by classic authors—a knowing echo of the library in James Branch Cabell's *Beyond Life* (1919) (see *Jurgen*). Terry Pratchett's Discworld (see *The Colour of Magic*) features not only the great library of Unseen University but the audacious theory that all libraries, everywhere, are connected through the hidden corridors of "L-Space."

The magic in books of spells can escape into the reader. Cyberspace, in William Gibson's *Neuromancer*, is perhaps the model for this; a realm of networked information through which expert "console jockeys" like the hero Case have to find their way, avoiding traps and discovering routes to what is really necessary. Although Gibson's source for the novel is the video arcade game, the network of information that is the modern library is at the story's heart, partly because libraries have leaped so enthusiastically upon matrix- and web-like models for the structure of knowledge, and have eagerly adopted the benefits of information **technology**.

Discussion

Thus the traditional image of the librarian, within science fiction, is much more positive than without it. Although partly reflecting the timid stereotype, Homir Munn in Isaac Asimov's *Second Foundation* (1953) (see **Foundation**) takes an active part in the plot. Terry Pratchett's orangutan librarian (see **Apes**) is three hundred pounds of fang and muscle who frequently saves the day: in *Jingo* (1997), for instance, the plot turns on the fact that he supplies the right book at the right time, and there is a series of running jokes to the effect that he is more competent than human colleagues. Above all, there is Rupert Giles in **Buffy the Vampire Slayer**, Buffy's "Watcher" and mentor, who is inextricably part of the team. However, perhaps the most unusual library in science fiction is the *human* library to be found at the end of Ray Bradbury's **Fahrenheit 451**. In a **dystopia** where books are banned, great works of literature are committed to **memory** by individuals, and Bradbury perhaps has something to say about the library as a storehouse of **culture** rather than information.

Bibliography

Agnes M. Griffen. "Images of Libraries in Science Fiction." *Library Journal*, 112 (September 1, 1987), 137–142.

James Gunn. "Dreams Written Out." *Wilson Library Bulletin*, 69 (February, 1995), 26–29.

Kevin J. Hayes. "The Book in American Utopia Literature, 1883–1917." *Visible Language*, 31 (1997), 64–84.

Robert Molyneux. "Devil's Advocate." *Against the Grain*, 13 (November, 2001), 78–79.

Marcia J. Myers and Deborah L. Core. "Librarianship in Science Fiction." *Kentucky Libraries*, 62 (Spring, 1998), 10–12.

Andy Sawyer. "The Librarian and His Domain." Andrew M. Butler, Edward James and Farah Mendlesohn, eds., *Terry Pratchett*. Reading: Science Fiction Foundation, 2000, 66–82.

Robert Silverberg. "Reflections: Fantastic Libraries." *Asimov's Science Fiction*, 27 (March, 2003), 5–8.

Susan Spencer. "The Post-Apocalyptic Library." *Extrapolation*, 32 (Winter, 1991), 331–342.

Gillian Wiseman. "Visions of the Future: The Library in Science Fiction." *Journal of Youth Services in Libraries*, 7 (Winter, 1994), 191–198.

—Andy Sawyer

LIGHT

∎

There is no place bereft of the light, the comfort and radiance of the creator spirit. There is no place that is outcast, outlawed, forsaken. There is no place left dark.

—Ursula K. Le Guin
"The Stars Below" (1974)

Overview

Within the realms of fantasy and science fiction, light serves as a beacon of goodness and hope against those that would do **evil**, such as **vampires**. It also stands as an emblem of power for larger-than-life characters such as **superheroes**, most notably *Superman*. In futuristic stories light has more than a symbolic role, as it becomes a source of communication, propulsion for **UFOs**, and a powerful form of **weaponry**.

Survey

Whereas some fantasies fall into shades of gray, most deal with the concepts of good and evil in clear-cut terms of black and white. Fantasy literature often compares and contrasts the dual sides of nature by representing them as the forces of light and **darkness**. This is never more obvious than in J.R.R. Tolkien's *The Lord of the Rings*. Within the text we see the battle between Sauron's unrelenting evil, a force of darkness sweeping across the lands of Middle-earth, and the goodness of the **wizard** Gandalf the Grey, whose **rebirth** as Gandalf the White changes him into a beacon of light marshalling the armies of righteousness against Sauron. In a less abstract way, Frodo Baggins and Sam Gamgee use the Phial of Galadriel and light of Eärendil within to fight the forces of darkness opposing them, from the One Ring to the horrific spider Shelob (see **Insects**).

Fighting forces of darkness with light is part and parcel of fantasy literature containing **wizards**. The young wizards of Hogwarts School of Witchcraft and Wizardry in J.K. Rowling's *Harry Potter and the Sorcerer's Stone* know this all too well. Harry and his friends learn a variety of **magic** to aid them as wizards, but steer clear of the Dark Arts lest they stray down the path of evil wizards like Voldemort. Rowling fills the entire Harry Potter series with references to light being a force for good, ranging from Headmaster Dumbledore's phoenix to Harry's use of the Patronus spell to protect him from the Dementors.

This idea of bringing evil into the light to expose its true nature and utterly destroy it is the backbone of **vampire** lore. From Bram Stoker's *Dracula* to Anne Rice's *Interview with the Vampire* and even *Buffy the Vampire Slayer*, there is the constant theme of vampires being mortally averse to the light of the **Sun**. While other methods exist to destroy these undead horrors, none is so effective or permanent as exposing them to the purifying light of day; hence, we get the idea that evil must operate under the cover of darkness lest it be found out and destroyed.

Imagery of light opposing darkness permeates fantasy and science fiction: for example, Olaf Stapledon drew upon this tradition in entitling his vision of two futures, one dystopian and the other utopian, *Darkness and the Light* (1942) (see **Dystopia and Utopia**). Ursula K. Le Guin, however, reflects an awareness of Buddhism in arguing that there are similarities between apparent opposites in her line of poetry, "Light is the left hand of darkness," included in *The Left Hand of Darkness* to explain its title.

Another aspect of light in fantasy literature is touched upon in *Harry Potter and the Sorcerer's Stone*: the use of light (or more precisely, the bending of light around an object) to become invisible, which Harry Potter does with a magic cloak to achieve **invisibility**. While the power of invisibility drives *The Invisible Man* to **madness**, *Forbidden Planet* reverses the idea: a **mad scientist** actually spawns an evil invisible entity. It takes wreathing the creature in light to show its true form and discover its nature.

As seen in *Forbidden Planet* and other science fiction stories, light is far more than just a metaphor for good and evil. Just as a wizard strikes with magic lightning by a wave of his wand, so does an interstellar explorer strike with a shot from his energy pistol. Light becomes a power source for UFOs, weaponry, **teleportation** devices, and even the Man of Steel himself, Superman. Superman is empowered by the light of Earth's yellow Sun, which grants him abilities far beyond ordinary humans and what he would have on his home world. Another DC superhero, Green Lantern, uses a power ring to emit beams of light that have amazing effects.

Finally, the best-known science fiction universes, *Star Trek* and *Star Wars*, arguably revolve around the manipulation of light: the starships of *Star Trek* rely on their destructive phasers and photon torpedoes, and along with similar rays that harken back to the **space operas** of the 1930s, *Star Wars* features battles between characters wielding **swords** made out of light.

Discussion

Like a moth to a flame, light and its bearing on the battle between good and evil are what draw many readers to science fiction and fantasy literature. Light and darkness, good and evil, are integral parts to human nature. It is the exploration of this human nature in larger-than-life stories that allows readers to invest some of themselves into characters and **escape** from their ordinary lives.

Light also serves as a reminder and ward against the primal fear of the unknown in all **humanity**. As people read about the forces of light beating back the darkness, it instills hope that they, too, can beat back the darkness.

Bibliography

Bronislaw Braczko. *Utopian Lights*. New York: Paragon House, 1989.
Peter Brigg. "Night Dream and the Glimmer of Light." *Foundation*, No. 36 (Summer, 1986), 31–34.
Bryan Dietrich. "Prince of Darkness, Prince of Light." *Journal of Popular Film and Television*, 19 (1991), 91–96.

Highfield, Roger. *The Science of Harry Potter*. New York: Viking Press, 2002.

Linda W. Hobson. "The 'Darkness That Is Part of Light.'" Jan N. Gretlund, ed., *Walker Percy*. Jackson: University Press of Mississippi, 1991, 119–130.

Catherine Madsen. "Light From an Invisible Lamp." *Mythlore*, 14 (Spring, 1988), 43–47.

Anthony S. Mercatante. *Good and Evil in Myth and Legend*. New York: Barnes & Noble, 1996.

Lane Roth. "*Metropolis*, the Lights Fantastic." *Literature/Film Quarterly*, 6 (Fall, 1978), 342–346.

Roger C. Schlobin. "Dark Shadows and Bright Lights." Martha Bartter, ed., *The Utopian Fantastic*. Westport, CT: Praeger, 2004, 11–16.

—Frederick A. Jandt

LINGUISTICS

■

See Language and Linguistics

LIONS AND TIGERS

■

Lions, and tigers, and bears! Oh, my!

—Noel Langley, Florence Ryerson,
and Edgar Allan Woolf
The Wizard of Oz (1939)

Overview

Fantasy and science fiction abound in lions and tigers. This essay excludes other large felines, cat-like aliens, and household **cats**; blended creatures like the sphinx and griffin are discussed under **Supernatural Creatures**.

Survey

In the nineteenth and early twentieth centuries, tigers and lions had not been relegated to zoos; they were ferocious natural forces, over which human beings demonstrated their superiority. In Helen Bannerman's *Story of Little Black Sambo* (1898), a child dissuades a series of tigers from eating him by giving each an article of clothing. The vain tigers quarrel, racing around a tree until they melt into butter. Sambo and his parents turn the tables on the man-eating tigers, gorging themselves on pancakes covered with tiger butter. In Rudyard Kipling's *The Jungle Book* (1894), a tiger is Mowgli's most relentless enemy. Shere Khan attacks the toddler, who **escapes** and is adopted by wolves. Because Shere Khan continues to menace him, Mowgli lures him to a narrow ravine, where stampeding buffalo trample him to **death**. Thus, through human **intelligence**, Sambo and Mowgli triumph over more powerful, animal enemies.

Influenced by Mowgli, Edgar Rice Burroughs's Tarzan kills a series of lionesses (Sabor) and lions (Numa). Simpler in motivation than Shere Khan, the lions in *Tarzan of the Apes* and its successors threaten Tarzan and his friends with "a cruel death beneath tearing claws and rending fangs" because they are hungry, but Tarzan demonstrates his enormous strength by slaying them.

Late twentieth-century and early twenty-first-century fantasy, in contrast, depicts lions and tigers sympathetically. Set in a world that is completely mapped, Russell Hoban's *The Lion of Boaz-Jachin and Jachin-Boaz* (1973) begins mournfully: "There were no lions any more." In John Crowley's *Beasts* (1976) the leos, human-lion hybrids, are persecuted by their creators. At the end, a devastated natural world begins to flourish, but only because civil **war** has fragmented **America**. In Ziziou Corder's *Lion Boy* (2003), Charlie helps drugged, depressed circus lions escape from an intolerable existence.

In *The Bloody Chamber* (1979), Angela Carter's retelling of classic fairy tales, are two versions of "Beauty and the Beast." Feminist critics rightly regard "The Courtship of Mr. Lyon" and "The Tiger's Bride" as critiques of a male-dominated society that preys upon and commodifies women (see **Feminism**). The Beast character in both stories, however, exists unhappily on the margins of human society. Each "Beauty" character realizes that "wild things" are right in fearing people.

Fantasy lions and tigers are often emblematic of principles, both kingly and savage, within human beings. In *Songs of Experience* (1794), William Blake juxtaposes "The Tiger" with poems about adults who cruelly exploit children. Tanith Lee's "Bright Burning Tiger" (1986) and Stephen King's *The Dead Zone* (1979) feature characters whose tigerish energy overcomes their humanity. In Lee's story, Pettersun, a tiger hunter, is torn to pieces in his bed. Encountering the hunter transformed into a burning tiger, the narrator concludes that the beast within Pettersun "had to tear him to pieces to get out." In King's novel, a redneck buffoon, Greg Stillson, rises to political power through systematic intimidation (see **Politics**). Ngo, a refugee, says that Stillson plays the Vietnamese game, the Laughing Tiger: wearing a tiger skin, a child clowns and bites. Johnny Smith, who can foresee possible futures, has a vision in which he looks through tiger stripes to see Stillson becoming president and starting a **nuclear war**.

Ray Bradbury's "The Veldt" (1950) and Hoban's *The Lion of Boaz-Jachin and Jachin-Boaz* feature imaginary lions that come to life, fueled by human rage. In Bradbury's story, a **family's** "Happylife Home" has a nursery that projects images of the **children's** fantasies. Because the spoiled children are angry at being denied luxuries, the nursery becomes an African veldt with lions that devour the parents. Though lions are extinct, a **father** and son in Hoban's novel are haunted by a lion that, while invisible to others, inflicts real wounds (see **Invisibility**). The lion represents the **pain**, rage, and fear that each man has repressed.

Lions have a long association with kingship. *The Lion King* (1994) and *The Wizard of Oz* depict lions who become kings by demonstrating **courage** in the service of others. In L. Frank Baum's **The Wonderful Wizard of Oz**, the Lion overcomes his cowardice by protecting Dorothy. At the end, he becomes king of forest animals. Brilliantly depicted by Bert Lahr, the Cowardly Lion in *The Wizard of Oz* covers his fearfulness with bullying. Like the lion in Baum's book, the Lahr character reclaims his masculinity through altruism.

Two Christian fantasies feature especially influential lions. In Charles Williams's *The Place of the Lion* (1931), a small English village is invaded by the Platonic archetype of the lion, embodying the principles of strength and majesty, which has pushed through the barrier that separates appearance from reality. The lion, as well as an archetypal serpent, eagle, and butterfly, begins to dismantle mundane life. In the Christian **allegory** that informs C.S. Lewis's seven Narnia books, the lion Aslan represents Christ. Aslan lovingly shapes the moral character of the children who visit Narnia. He enacts the Passion of Christ when, in **The Lion, the Witch and the Wardrobe**, he dies in place of the erring Edmund.

Discussion

An increasingly fragile **ecology** has changed fictional lions and tigers from savage threats to vulnerable beings in need of protection. From earliest times, however, people have internalized large cats, making them metaphors for such principles as kingship, rage, courage, or libido.

Bibliography

Kelli Brew. "Metanoia." *Lamp Post*, 21 (Spring, 1997), 11–17.

Elaine Casella. "A Lion Is Still a Lion." *The Burroughs Bulletin*, No. 23 (July, 1995), 24–30.

Reid Davis. "What WOZ." *Film Quarterly*, 55 (2001), 2–13.

Aidan Day. "*The Bloody Chamber and Other Stories*." Day, *Angela Carter*. Manchester: Manchester University Press, 1998, 132–166.

Sarah Gamble. "*The Bloody Chamber*." 1979. Gamble, *Angela Carter*. Edinburgh: Edinburgh University Press, 1997, 130–141.

Thomas Howard. "*The Place of the Lion*." Howard, *The Novels of Charles Williams*. New York: Oxford University Press, 1983, 96–121.

Kathryn Ann Lindskoog. *The Lion of Judah in Never-Never Land*. Grand Rapids, MI: Eerdmans, 1973.

Peter J. Schakel. *Imagination and the Arts in C.S. Lewis*. Columbia: University of Missouri Press, 2002.

—*Wendy Bousfield*

LONGEVITY

See Immortality and Longevity

LOST WORLDS

■

Overview

Lost worlds are to be distinguished from **imaginary worlds,** in that they purport to be hidden corners of the real world, unlike Gormenghast (see Mervyn Peake's *Titus Groan*) or Middle-earth (see J.R.R. Tolkien's *The Lord of the Rings*), which are totally disconnected from **history** and geography. The lost world story differs from the **Ruritanian romance,** which takes place in imaginary lands that are supposedly part of contemporary **Europe,** but in no way lost or hidden. A typical lost world exists in a remote, inaccessible place. It usually contains a long-isolated population of cave-men, ancient Atlanteans (see **Atlantis**), and, not infrequently, **dinosaurs.** The archetypal example is Arthur Conan Doyle's *The Lost World.*

Survey

The whole charm of the lost world motif is the inaccessibility of the setting. Such stories have earlier antecedents, such as Robert Patlock's *The Life and Adventures of Peter Wilkins* (1751), which is about a winged race discovered in Antarctica (see **Polar Regions**), but the great bulk of lost world stories are a product of the period from 1880 to 1930, at the high tide of European imperialism, when white men really were penetrating the world's last unexplored regions (see **Quests**). The discovery of real lost cities, such as Great Zimbabwe, could only excite the public imagination. The next step was to describe such a place still inhabited and containing fabulous **mysteries.**

H. Rider Haggard perfected the form in *She,* which has absolutely everything the next fifty years would reduce to **cliché:** the gloomy **city** in the lost valley of Kor, complete with degenerate natives, supernatural mystery (the Flame of Immortality) and the white goddess (see **Gods and Goddesses**) who has been waiting all this time for a suitable mate, namely the **hero.**

Doyle added the dinosaurs, when his Professor Challenger and companions scaled a plateau in South America, after which the stock elements of the lost world story were complete, to be rehashed endlessly in the pulp magazines, as in Rex Stout's *Under the Andes* (1914). William L. Chester's *Hawk of the Wilderness* (1936) and its sequels combined the lost world and Tarzan motifs: a boy is raised by bears on a balmy lost island in the Arctic. Edmond Hamilton, the noted master of **space opera,** wrote numerous lost world adventures, of which *The Valley of Creation* (1948) is a culmination. A. Merritt played up the sexual elements (see **Sexuality**). His lost worlds usually come with a **temptress** modelled after Haggard's Ayesha.

It has been remarked that Edgar Rice Burroughs's **Africa** in the Tarzan series contains so many lost regions that all of them together would not merely fill the continent, but a good deal of the Indian Ocean as well. Tarzan found yet another lost city in the posthumously published *Tarzan and the Madman* (1964). But Burroughs's most impressive creation of this sort is the **island** of Caprona in *The Land That Time Forgot* (1924), with its inevitable dinosaurs, an unscalable **mountain** wall (the heroes get in by submarine, through an underwater tunnel), and a very odd view of **evolution** in which the inhabitants begin as very primitive creatures, but develop beyond humanity in a single lifetime. A similar lost world, minus the evolutionary aspect, is found in the film *King Kong*.

Since the standard plot of a pulp lost world adventure could be as formularized as an English country-house mystery, soon the only interest lay in where the lost world was placed. All the world's **jungles** were soon used up. Lost valleys in the Arctic or Antarctic had to be conveniently heated by volcanoes. John Wyndham's *The Secret People* (1935) placed its lost world in a **cavern** under the Sahara. H.P. Lovecraft (see **Horror**), ghost-writing for Zealia Bishop, developed a suitably ghastly realm beneath the American Southwest in "The Mound" (1940). There was no princess in this one, just a Spanish conquistador who meets a hideous fate when he tries to carry forbidden secrets to the outside world.

As available places to tuck a lost world began to diminish, Burroughs showed superior foresight by moving the entire routine, complete with princess, to **Mars** in *A Princess of Mars*, creating a whole new species of interplanetary **romance**. He also cleverly exploited the **hollow Earth** in his Pelludicar series, beginning with *At the Earth's Core* (1922).

Another sort of lost world story is that in which the hidden **civilization** guards, not merely a beautiful princess and assorted monsters, but ineffable wisdom (see **Philosophy**). The best-known example is James Hilton's *Lost Horizon*, modeled, like many such, on hearsay about the mysteries of Tibet (see **Utopia**).

Discussion

Although the lost world story might have its origins with Patlock, or even Voltaire (see *Candide* [1759]) or Jonathan Swift (see *Gulliver's Travels*), who used it for satirical purposes (see **Satire**), the appeal has mostly been one of sheer wish-fulfillment. It is a product of the age of **exploration**, and ultimately becomes a day-dream, in which the brave and stalwart bring the rationality of civilization into remote places, showing their superiority while getting the best of both worlds, in the form of **immortality and longevity**, enlightenment, or the princess. We all wonder what is over the horizon. For a time it was possible to imagine lost worlds, still flourishing. But now the globe is too well-known for that. Alas, lost worlds transported to other planets have not fared much better, and there is no incomparable princess on Mars.

Bibliography

Alan Barnard. "Tarzan and the Lost Races." Eduardo P. Archetti, ed., *Exploring the Written.* Stockholm: Scandinavian University Press, 1994, 231–257.

Allienne R. Becker. *The Lost Worlds Romance.* Westport, CT: Greenwood Press, 1992.

Lin Carter. *Imaginary Worlds.* New York: Ballantine Books, 1973.

L. Sprague de Camp. *Lost Continents.* New York: Dover Publications, 1970.

L. Sprague de Camp and Willy Ley. *Lands Beyond.* New York: Rinehart & Co., 1952.

Nadia Khouri. "Lost Worlds and the Revenge of Realism." *Science-Fiction Studies*, 10 (July, 1983), 170–190.

Mark R. Leeper. "Six Lost Worlds." *Argentus*, No. 3 (Summer, 2003), 22–29.

Stuart Teitler. "In Search of Zion." Kenneth M. Roemer, ed., *America As Utopia.* New York: Franklin, 1981, 186–191.

Samuel H. Vasbinder. "Aspects of Fantasy in Literary Myths About Lost Civilizations." Roger C. Schlobin, ed., *The Aesthetics of Fantasy Literature and Art*. Notre Dame, IN: University of Notre Dame Press, 1982, 192–210.

—*Darrell Schweitzer*

LOVE

Overview

Love is a potent force in science fiction and fantasy, defining what it means to be human, inspiring characters to fight against **evil** and oppression, and enabling them to transcend boundaries. Love that turns into long-term relationships is covered under **Romance**, while non-romantic love is discussed in **Friendship, Children, Family, Fathers,** and **Mothers.**

Survey

The ability to love is seen as a defining characteristic of **humanity**, yet fictional **robots** often show emotion. The artificial child's love for its mother is supposed to be only a matter of programming in *A.I.: Artificial Intelligence*, but the robots in the Flesh Fair are more compassionate than the humans. Until he receives an emotion chip in *Star Trek: Generations*, the **android** Data cannot feel love, as stated in an episode of *Star Trek: The Next Generation*, "In Theory" (1991), yet often demonstrates affection for those he regards as family members and friends. In Tanith Lee's *The Silver Metal Lover* (1981), it is the robot who explains the nature of love to his human lover.

The word "love" means many things, and some authors create new words to distinguish between love and sexual attraction, as in Austin Tappan Wright's *Islandia* (see **Languages and Linguistics**). However, it is romantic love that generates **quests** and ends **fairy tales**, both happily and not. The protagonist of *Heaven Can Wait* falls in love at first sight, the tragic love triangle of Arthurian legend is retold in Marion Zimmer Bradley's *The Mists of Avalon* and Guy Gavriel Kay's Fionavar Tapestry series, beginning with *The Silver Tree* (1984) (see **Arthur**), and *Buffy the Vampire Slayer* **sacrifices** her true love to save the world in the episode "Becoming II" (1998). Unrequited love, which leads to a tragic ending for the **mermaid** in Hans Christian Andersen's "The Little Mermaid" (1836), is also featured in E.R. Eddison's *The Worm Ouroboros* and to a lesser extent J.R.R. Tolkien's *The Lord of the Rings*, where the beloved is little more than the **heroes'** reward. While the message conveyed by *Beauty and the Beast*—that love sees past physical appearance—is positive, it is sometimes more troubling, in tales such as *Snow White and the Seven Dwarfs*, that for the heroine, love must end in **marriage.**

The belief that love conquers all enables lovers to transcend social and other boundaries. The **class system** is no barrier to love at first sight in *Metropolis*, while issues of **race relations** are often symbolically addressed in science fiction by demonstrating loving relationships between humans and aliens, as in Octavia E. Butler's *Dawn*, or humans and animals, as in Olaf Stapledon's *Sirius* (1944) and the film *King Kong*, although the beast's love for **beauty** remains unrequited. Love also crosses **gender** lines, complicating the question of **sexuality**. In the world of Pern, the telepathic bond between **dragons** and their mostly male riders does not fade during mating in Anne McCaffrey's *Dragonflight*, although the resulting physical relationships are seldom explicitly dealt with in the narrative. **Space travel** requires dealing with aliens whose **biology** and sexual **taboos** are different, as in Ursula K. Le Guin's *The Left Hand of Darkness*. While television is more conservative about **homosexuality**, occasional episodes of *Xena: Warrior Princess* show Xena and Gabrielle as soulmates, suggesting a more physical relationship, as in "The Quest" (1997) and "Déjà Vu All Over Again" (1999). Even **time** and **death** are no obstacles to love; H. Rider Haggard's *She* is willing to wait through **eternity** for the **reincarnation** of her lover, while **time travel** stories such as *La Jetée* often center on star-crossed lovers reunited.

In **dystopias**, love between individuals is presented as a potential force of **freedom** from oppression that more often than not fails, demonstrated intriguingly in the alternate endings of *Brazil*, one happy and one not. Falling in love incites the protagonist of Yevgeny Zamiatin's *We* to futile **rebellion** against the State, and Winston's love for Julia, which both see as a political act, ends in **betrayal** in George Orwell's *Nineteen Eighty-Four* (see **Politics**). Some **utopias** are predicated on the belief that love might be a positive force if it were not limited to exclusive and conventional pairings, **weaponry** in the battle of the sexes. Joanna Russ's *The Female Man* and Marge Piercy's *Woman on the Edge of Time* depict societies in which love is not confined by monogamy or gender. In other works, love is re-imagined as a force for building a stronger **community**. Robert A. Heinlein's *Stranger in a Strange Land* celebrates polygamy and unfettered sexual intercourse leading to fuller understanding, while Theodore Sturgeon's *More Than Human* posits a new kind of love through mental union (see **Hive Minds**) as an essential step in the **evolution** of humanity, perhaps leading to a sort of immortality (see **Immortality and Longevity**).

Discussion

Love in all its forms and permutations is a driving force in science fiction and fantasy in part because it is so central to the human condition but also because it is an essential element of the **fairy tales**, legends, and **mythology** from which such narratives derive much of their form and content. Because love is a powerful component in the construction of both **identity** and community, a key concern of writers in the field seems to be the definition, or rather redefinition, of a simple word whose full meaning cannot be contained or easily explained.

Bibliography

P.J. Day. "Love and the Technocracy." Richard D. Erlich and Thomas Dunn, eds., *Clockwork Worlds*. Westport, CT: Greenwood Press, 1983, 195–211.

Joel N. Feimer. "Alchemy of Love in *A Fine and Private Place*." *Journal of the Fantastic in the Arts*, 1 (1988), 69–78.

Matthew A. Fike. "Hero's Education in Sacrificial Love." *Mythlore*, 14 (Summer, 1988), 34–38.

John Huntington. "Impossible Love in Science Fiction." *Raritan*, 4 (Fall, 1984), 85–99.

Paul N. Hyde. "Emotion With Dignity." *Mythlore*, 17 (Autumn, 1990), 14–19.

Farah Mendlesohn. "Surpassing the Love of Vampires." Rhonda V. Wilcox and David Lavery, eds., *Fighting the Forces*. Lanham: Rowman & Littlefield, 2002, 45–60.

Charles W. Nelson. "But Who Is Rose Cotton?" *Journal of the Fantastic in the Arts*, 3 (1994), 6–20.

Marge Piercy. "Love and Sex in the Year 3000." Marleen Barr, ed., *Envisioning the Future*. Middletown, CT: Wesleyan University Press, 2003, 131–145.

Anca Vlasopolos. "Technology as Eros's Dart." *Foundation*, No. 73 (Summer, 1998), 59–66.

—Christine Mains

MACHINES AND MECHANIZATION

Why should you sweat yourselves to
death to benefit the Lord of Metropolis?
Who keeps the machines going?
Who are the slaves of the machines?
Let the machines stop.
Destroy the machines.

—Fritz Lang and Thea von Harbou
Metropolis (1926), translator unknown (1926)

Overview

Extrapolating from contemporary **technology, hard science fiction** lauds technological **progress** and its liberating power primarily in the form of advances in **transportation, communication** and **weaponry**. Increasingly, the social impact of technology and machines as a collective force, and of transforming humans into automatons or creating intelligent human–machine interfaces (see **Computers; Cyborgs; Robots**) has been critically examined in science fiction. Fantasy rarely if ever addresses such issues, although some see dark intimations of industrialization in, for example, the activities of Saruman in J.R.R. Tolkien's *The Lord of the Rings*.

Survey

Spurned by an enthusiastic belief in industrialization, the exploding advances in technology and science, and the rapid rise of the **city** in Western societies, early science fiction stories created all kinds of **inventions** and presented the **scientist**/inventor as the cultural hero of the new technological age. At the **fin de siècle,** despite his rather pessimistic view of human **evolution,** H.G. Wells nevertheless invents one of the most influential devices in *The Time Machine* that quickly replaces the then-standard trope of utopian **time travel**: the **dream.**

Generally, **utopias** of the late nineteenth century reverently view machines as symbols for individual **freedom** and as the unlimited means for the betterment of society at large, solving all problems of **humanity**. Advocating technological perfection for the good of humankind in *Looking Backward 2000–1887*, Edward Bellamy envisions an industrial army in a planned economy, and H.G. Wells's *A Modern Utopia* (1905) combines social progress with the advantages of technological progress. Before the 1930s critical views such as Samuel Butler's antitechnological stance in *Erewhon* (1872) and its sequel *Erewhon Revisited* (1901), where citizens ban machines for fear of being supplanted by them, are exceptions.

A few stories of the early nineteenth century, such as E.T.A. Hoffmann's "The Sandman" (1816) and "Automata" (1817) or Hermann Melville's "The Bell-Tower" (1855), problematize the indistinguishable and diabolical similarity between human and machine. In the 1920s, this motif of duplication and ambiguity is taken up by the almost **Gothic** film *Metropolis* in which the robot Maria tricks workers into **rebellion**. Since the 1990s the increasing valorization of human/machine hybridization is effectively captured with the figure of the cyborg, which is the merging of biological and mechanical systems: to become a machine is the highest aspiration of a technologized humanity. This blurring of boundaries between humans and machines is also an ambiguous issue in Philip K. Dick's *Do Androids Dream of Electric Sheep?*, adapted as the film *Blade Runner* in the 1980s.

In contrast, **dystopia** criticizes the ever more sophisticated techniques for social control that go hand-in-hand with the advance of machines. As rising totalitarianism in Europe seemingly depended upon the mechanization of society and the perfected machinery of a bureaucratic apparatus, machinery was seen as dehumanizing and destructive. For dystopia, technology is therefore not a misused neutral tool but the totalitarian logic of the future. Criticizing the uncontrolled prevalence of scientism, Aldous Huxley's *Brave New World* imagines the willful abuse of technology to allow the artificial mass production of humans according to selective genetic criteria (see **Clones; Genetic Engineering**) that follow the principles of Fordism, a parody of the philosophy of industrialization. Humans are hatched from assembly-line incubators for their pre-classified social destinies as mere appendages to machines in a conformist society. Anthony Burgess's *A Clockwork Orange* and Kurt Vonnegut, Jr.'s *Player Piano* (1952), for instance, equate the state organism with a mechanism, while others prophesy the domination of machines and the mechanization of human life or the transformation of humans into machines. In "The Machine Stops" (1909), E.M. Forster describes a mechanistic society, controlled by a machine, in which technology replaces individual contact. The totality of human dependence on machines is elucidated when the machine malfunctions and the society collapses. D.F. Jones's *Colossus* (1966), filmed as *Colossus: The Forbin Project* (1969), depicts how the computer Colossus gains consciousness and usurps the world: machines are getting out of human control.

This theme of the machine striking back is further elaborated in films from the 1980s onwards that depict a **war** between machines and humans, as in *The Terminator* and its sequels, where humans fight inexorable machines and computers to avoid being wiped off the face of the **Earth**. In *The Matrix* and its sequels this war has already been won, for machines have become more powerful than humans. The power system has been reversed and humans are adapted to the machines' needs: humans are mechanically bred for the machines' energy supply. Even one of the human protagonist–saviors, Trinity, must symbolically transform herself into a machine, acting as precisely and inevitably as a machine or a computer program, to survive.

Discussion

From the beginning, science fiction has been fascinated by the seemingly endless possibilities that technological inventions, machines, and mechanization offer. Increasingly, the transfer of the parameters of machines to humans and human society has been problematic and leads to the pressing question of whether the equation of humans, the human body, and human activities with the logic of machines dehumanizes us. With the integration of machine parts, prosthetics, and nanotechnology into our bodies and the all-prevalent dominance of computer technology and the Internet, the human dependence on machines, and the fusion of humans and machines, are increasingy becoming our reality.

Bibliography

Brian W. Aldiss. "All Those Big Machines." *Journal of the Fantastic in the Arts*, 7 (1996), 83–91.

Beatrice Battaglia. "Losing the Sense of Space." Alan Sandison and Robert Dingley, eds., *Histories of the Future*. Basingstoke: Palgrave, 2000, 51–71.

Jane Donawerth. "Woman as Machine in Science Fiction by Women." *Extrapolation*, 36 (Fall, 1995), 210–221.

Thomas P. Dunn and Richard D. Erlich. "List of Works Useful for the Study of Machines in Science Fiction." Dunn and Erlich, eds., *The Mechanical God*. Westport, CT: Greenwood Press, 1982, 225–273.

Lauric Guillaud. "From Bachelor Machines to 'Cybernetic Fiction.'" *New York Review of Science Fiction*, No. 75 (November, 1994), 12–17.

Daniel W. Ingersoll Jr. "Machines Are Good to Think." Richard D. Erlich and Thomas P. Dunn,. eds., *Clockwork Worlds*. Westport CT: Greenwood Press, 1983, 235–262.

Ray Kurzweil. "The Human Machine Merger." Glenn Yeffeth, ed., *Taking the Red Pill*. Dallas: Benbella, 2003, 185–197.

Janez Strehovec. "Machines for Ultimate Questions." *Popular Culture Review*, 12 (February, 2001), 135–144.

—Dunja M. Mohr

MAD SCIENTISTS

Overview

Throughout western **culture**, the master narrative involving **scientists** is of a dangerous male figure with varying degrees of mania (see **Madness**). Mad scientists vary from conscious **villains** seeking power or revenge, to harmless **clowns and fools**, focused on research and oblivious of conventions. In between are obsessive characters, not malevolent yet socially irresponsible.

Survey

Although Mary Shelley's character *Frankenstein* was irresponsible rather than malevolent, he is stereotyped as the **evil** mad scientist because of the **disasters** resulting from his secret research. *Frankenstein* has inspired at least twenty-three films and become shorthand in **journalism** for any potentially dangerous science—termed "frankenscience" in Greg Egan's *Distress* (1995). Two of the earliest silent films, *Dr. Jekyll and Mr Hyde* (1908) and *Frankenstein* (1910), established the cinematic image of the mad scientist. In America the charisma of the **heroes** of **inventions** was such that initially evil scientists were rarely drawn from **physics** (associated with Thomas Edison and Nicolas Tesla) but, rather, from **biology**. Mad biologists attempt to modify life by destroying, shrinking, enlarging, transmuting, perpetuating, or cloning it (see **Clones; Miniaturization; Enlargement**). From the early films featuring a "radium ray" to *Jurassic Park*, such tampering is condemned and punished. *The Monster* (1925), *Frankenstein* ("the most famous horror movie of all time"), *Dr. X* (1932), *Island of Lost Souls* (based on H.G. Wells's *The Island of Doctor Moreau*), and *Dr. Cyclops* (1940) involve the spawning of monstrous progeny either by deliberate design or by accident, and the scientists responsible are universally condemned. David Cronenberg's 1986 remake of the 1958 film *The Fly* and the 1996 version of *The Island of Dr. Moreau* attest to continuing ethical discussion about the dangers of controlling life (see **Ethics**).

Evil, mad physicists achieved notoriety in comics, such as *Superman*, where mastermind inventor Lex Luthor, forever plotting to gain wealth and power, is Superman's entrenched enemy. Early fears concerning radioactivity and **nuclear power** were boosted by the development of nuclear weapons. Pre–World War II treatments cast scientists working on atomic bombs as megalomaniacs or as driven by **revenge**, but the actual development of the bomb suggested that physicists were culpable through denial of responsibility—a new category of evil. In *Cat's Cradle* Kurt Vonnegut, Jr. explored the kind of insane irresponsibility represented by nuclear physicist Hoenikker. The most influential antinuclear war film was Stanley Kubrick's *Dr. Strangelove*. Comprising elements of physicists Otto Hahn and Edward Teller, Strangelove introduced a different mad scientist archetype. A macabre combination of mad scientist, former Nazi, and civil servant, Strangelove shocked audiences by suggesting that a scientific–military–industrial alliance was self-interestedly driving the arms race. Like medieval **witches**, the evil scientist was frequently identified by a physical deformity. Rotwang with his withered hand in *Metropolis*, one-armed Dr. Wells of *Dr. X*, and crippled Dr. Strangelove with a withered right hand hidden in a black glove are almost parodic examples of the evil scientist who, having no respect for **nature**, has lost his natural attributes.

A more sophisticated treatment of the mad physicist was Dr. Bluthgeld in Philip K. Dick's *Dr. Bloodmoney* (1965), a response to *Dr. Strangelove*. The paranoiac Bluthgeld believes that, as the instrument of God, he has **psychic powers** to summon nuclear thunderbolts and in one sense he is right for, having invented the atomic bomb, he is responsible for radioactive fallout (see **Paranoia**). In the rigidly moral world of Hollywood, nemesis invariably counters the **hubris** of mad scientists, usually via their own inventions. These simplistic endings pandered to desires by audiences to see science-generated dangers controlled and perpetrators appropriately punished, frequently by insanity, as in *Seven Days to Noon* (1950), *The Terror Beneath the Sea* (1966), *The Spy Who Loved Me* (1977), and *Never Say Never Again* (1983) (see *Doctor No*).

The absent-minded, comic version of the mad scientist derived from the foolish virtuoso of the Restoration stage, who was preoccupied with his collections and out of touch with the real world. Variations survive in *Doctor Who*, with his unruly hair and long scarf, and in the Einstein figure of *Back to the Future* and its sequels. The persona adopted by Albert Einstein conformed readily to this already entrenched image and provided symbols for its perpetuation: the shock of hair and inattention to dress.

Between the insane, evil scientist and the absent-minded comic stands the obsessive scientist, fixated on research and lacking balance and responsibility. This figure often exhibits characteristics of the mad scientist. Wells's Doctor Moreau works in isolation on secret research that is morally repugnant to society, whereas Hoenikker of *Cat's Cradle* is both sinister like the evil scientist and comic in his childish helplessness.

Discussion

In our highly technologized culture it may seem anomalous that mad scientists feature so widely in film, fiction, and fantasy, but there are numerous reasons for this. Scientists are the only individuals with sufficient power to pose a threat to powerful societies. As malevolent, insane, and powerful figures they provide a narrative of power and fear of that power that allows us to examine nebulous fears embodied in a particular form. The simplified mad, evil, and dangerous scientist underlies our contemporary mythology of **knowledge**, justifying latent fears of depersonalized rationalism and legitimizing Romantic longings in a materialist culture.

Bibliography

Mick Broderick. *Nuclear Movies*. Northcote, Australia: Post-Modem Publishing, 1988.

Carlos Clarens. *An Illustrated History of the Horror Film*. New York: Capricorn, 1967.

Roslynn D. Haynes. *From Faust to Strangelove*. Baltimore: Johns Hopkins University Press, 1994.

———. "Celluloid Scientists." Alan Sandison and Robert Dingley, ed., *Histories of the Future*. Basingstoke, Hampshire and New York: Palgrave, 2000, 34–50.

———. "From Alchemy to Artificial Intelligence." *Public Understanding of Science*, 12 (July, 2003), 243–254.

Daniele Jörg. "The Good, the Bad, and the Ugly." *Public Understanding of Science*, 12 (July, 2003), 297–306.

George Levine and U.C. Knoepflmacher, eds. *The Endurance of Frankenstein*. Berkeley and Los Angeles: University of California Press, 1979.

Milton Millhauser. "Dr. Newton and Mr. Hyde." *Nineteenth Century Fiction*, 28 (1973), 287–304.

Andrew Tudor. *Monsters and Mad Scientists*. Oxford: Blackwell, 1989.

—*Roslynn Haynes*

MADNESS

Overview

The inspiration and genius necessary to scientific **progress** have sometimes been considered close to madness—hence the numerous stories about **mad scientists** who, while well-intentioned at first, drifted into insanity in the course of their research.

However, other forms of dementia have also figured in science fiction and fantasy. Separate entries address the general discipline of **psychology** and the specific problem of **paranoia**.

Survey

One thing that can drive people mad is a restrictive, confining environment. One pioneering parable of **feminism**, Charlotte Perkins Gilman's "The Yellow Wall Paper" (1892), describes the plight of an unnamed woman who is denied any preoccupation—such as people, writing, or **books**—that could provide solace or meaning to her life. Changes in the wallpaper, providing her only contact with the rest of the world, ultimately drive her to a mental breakdown. The story can be read metaphorically as an indictment of how society generally limited, and hence maddened, the women of its day. One of fantasy's most beloved madmen is the prisoner in L. Sprague de Camp and Fletcher Platt's "The Roaring Trumpet" (1940) who, utterly insane after years of confinement in a dungeon, does nothing but scream "Yngvi is a louse!" again and again and again. In Stephen King's *The Shining*, a protagonist is driven over the edge by the oppressive atmosphere of the deserted Overlook Hotel where he is living, which turns out to be a site for **ghosts and hauntings**.

Science fiction stories set in the future express concern about **astronauts** going mad in the cramped conditions of **space travel**; as Lester del Rey memorably observed in *Siege Perilous* (1966), "space gnawed at men's minds." So, in James Gunn's *Station in Space* (1958), travelers to **Mars** go insane before they arrive, and in Charles L. Harness's *The Paradox Men* (1953), workers in a **space station** near the **Sun** develop what seems to be a beneficial form of madness to help them work in that environment. It is not surprising, then, that an effort to establish an asylum to cure mental illness in a space station, depicted in Frank Belknap Long's *This Strange Tomorrow* (1966), is a complete failure.

People can also go insane due to traumatic circumstances in their life. Alfred Bester's *The Demolished Man* offers a poetic vision of madness. Reich is terrorized in his dreams by The Man With No Face and becomes unhinged when he believes that his rival D'Courtney has refused a merger offer. In response, he murders his rival and bribes a high-ranking telepath with **psychic powers** to help him cover his tracks. Isaac Asimov's "Nightfall" (1941) describes a **civilization** that goes mad every two thousand years when the sky becomes dark. In the film *Psycho* (1960), Norman Bates is driven mad by his domineering **mother** and, after she dies, begins to dress and act like her, and in that guise kills the woman who had come to stay at his motel. In King's *Misery* (1987), filmed in 1990, a devoted fan becomes so disturbed when a writer decides to kill off a favorite character that she kidnaps him and forces him to write a new story featuring the character.

Madness can more prosaically be a result of adverse stimuli or **drugs**, often leading to homicidal impulses. In S.P. Meek's "The Madness Ray" (1930), a Russian agent uses a strange ray to drive the President of the United States insane. Bester's "Fondly Fahrenheit" (1954) describes an intelligent **android** who becomes a killer whenever the temperature around him reaches a certain level. In the film *The Crazies* (1975), a virus from a military experiment pollutes the local water supply and makes residents insanely homicidal, while in *Blue Sunshine* (1976), a bad batch of LSD belatedly turns indulgers into bald murderers. The lurking influence of **aliens on Earth** maddens crowds of people in the film *Five Million Years to Earth* (1968) (see **Quatermass and the Pit**) and in Adrian Cole's *Madness Emerging* (1976).

Madness, however, is not always a debilitating or dangerous condition. In Lewis Carroll's **Alice's Adventures in Wonderland**, Alice encounters quite a number of people who seem to be insane, including a man called the Mad Hatter, but they all seem able to carry on with their everyday routines in the strange context of Wonderland. Philip K. Dick—a writer who repeatedly returned to the theme of madness as he himself drifted toward insanity—pictured in *Clans of the Alphane Moon* (1964) a functioning society on a distant moon consisting entirely of people suffering from various mental illnesses; originally confined there for treatment, these people were later left to their own devices and managed to develop **governance systems** and cooperative arrangements that resist an attempt by officials from **Earth** to reassert their control. And in Mary Chase's play *Harvey* (1944), filmed in 1950, a carefree man who devotes his life to heavy drinking—in the company of an imaginary rabbit that only he can see—is ultimately vindicated and allowed to continue living harmlessly in the way that he pleases, despite efforts to commit him to an asylum.

Discussion

Finally, a favorite category of science fiction and fantasy stories involve people who are *believed* to be mad by those around them because they alone can observe or detect strange phenomena. A classic example is "Nightmare at 20,000 Feet" (1963), an episode of **The Twilight Zone**, in which everybody on an airplane believes a passenger is insane because he keeps saying that there is a gremlin sabotaging the airplane wing—and there actually is. The **hero** of *Invasion of the Body Snatchers* is also regarded as crazy when he reports an alien **invasion**, though a modified ending produces evidence that eventually convinces the authorities. Such works remind us that an individual's madness or sanity is ultimately determined only by the predominant beliefs of those around that person—beliefs that could very well be wrong.

Bibliography

Charles Ardai, ed. *Great Tales of Madness and the Macabre*. New York: Galahad, 1990.

Nancy Topping Bazin. "Madness, Mysticism, and Fantasy." *Extrapolation*, 33 (Spring, 1992), 73–87.

Joan C. Kessler, ed. *Demons of the Night*. Chicago: University of Chicago Press, 1995.

Kenneth Krabbenhoft. "The Uses of Madness in Cervantes and Philip K. Dick." *Science Fiction Studies*, 27 (July, 2000), 216–233.

Kaley Kramer. "Madmen in the Middle." Karen Sayer and Rosemary Mitchell, eds., *Victorian Gothic*. Trinity and All Saints, UK: Leeds Centre for Victorian Studies, 2003, 69–80.

Tony Magistrale. "Art Versus Madness in Stephen King's *Misery*." Donald E. Morse, ed., *The Celebration of the Fantastic*. Westport, CT: Greenwood Press, 1992, 271–278.

John McCarty. *Movie Psychos and Madmen*. Secaucus, NJ: Carol, 1993.

Steven J. Schneider. "Barbara, Julia, Carol, Myra, and Nell." Steve Chibnall and Julian Petley, eds., *British Horror Cinema*. London: Routledge, 2002, 117–130.

—Joyce Scrivner

MAGIC

∎

He thought no more of performing the lesser arts of magic than a bird thinks of flying. Yet a greater, unlearned skill he possessed, which was the art of kindness.

—Ursula K. Le Guin
A Wizard of Earthsea (1968)

Overview

Most fantasy stories involve magic. Even in some science fiction magic takes the form of extremely advanced **technology**. Magic often seems an intrinsic part of the **landscape** but can also be an acquired **force**. Related entries discuss **talents, magical objects**, and magical persons like **witches** and **wizards**.

Survey

The presence of magic is a defining characteristic of fantasy, reflecting its origins in **fairy tales** and **mythology**, although magic can sometimes be a matter of **illusion**, as practiced by L. Frank Baum's *The Wonderful Wizard of Oz*. Magic can be part of the landscape, as in Piers Anthony's *A Spell for Chameleon*, or invested in **names**, as in Ursula K. Le Guin's *A Wizard of Earthsea*, or in magical objects such as **rings, swords**, and other **weaponry**. Magic users cast spells, often of healing (see **Medicine**), as in Katherine Kurtz's *Deryni Rising* (1970), and of **metamorphosis**, as when the witch in *Snow White and the Seven Dwarfs* transforms herself, or in Peter S. Beagle's *The Last Unicorn*, when the **unicorn** becomes a woman. Magic can be invoked in **rituals**, such as the black mass depicted in James Branch Cabell's *Jurgen* (see **Sexuality**).

Magic is sometimes divided into two types: high magic, a product of **knowledge** contained in **books** and practiced by wizards, and wild magic inherent in **nature** and related to the **elements**. The tension between the two is a source of conflict in Alan Garner's *The Moon of Gomrath* (1963) and Guy Gavriel Kay's the Fionavar Tapestry, beginning with *The Silver Tree* (1984). The **mathematics** of magic underlies Fletcher Pratt and L. Sprague de Camp's *The Compleat Enchanter* (1975). Magic as a creative force is associated with **music**, as in Patricia McKillip's *Song for the Basilisk* (1998) and Emma Bull's **urban fantasy** *War for the Oaks* (1987), and with **art**, as in Charles de Lint's *Memory and Dream* (1991).

Though magic is often a matter of talent or **birth**, as in David Eddings's *Pawn of Prophecy*, it can be taught to **apprentices**, as in T.H. White's *The Once and Future King* (1958) and Marion Zimmer Bradley's *The Mists of Avalon*, or in schools (see **Education**) such as Hogwarts in J.K. Rowling's *Harry Potter and the Sorcerer's Stone* or Unseen University in Terry Pratchett's *The Colour of Magic*. Magical power is sometimes the **destiny** of the seemingly ordinary man; Rand in Robert Jordan's *The Eye of the World* is able to work magic only practiced by women.

Magic is a neutral force that can be used for both good and evil purposes, as the children learn in Alan Garner's *The Owl Service*. Black magic gives villains power over others and over death; the task of the hero in tales of sword and sorcery, like Robert E. Howard's *Conan the Conqueror*, and heroic fantasy, like J.R.R. Tolkien's *The Lord of the Rings*, E.R. Eddison's *The Worm Ouroboros*, and Terry Brooks's *The Sword of Shannara*, is to defeat attempts to misuse magic. In C.S. Lewis's *The Lion, the Witch and the Wardrobe*, magic is explicitly connected to faith (see **Christianity**).

Magic can be depicted in environmental terms as a resource that must be kept in balance, as Ged's **mentor** observes when he refuses to control the **weather** in Ursula K. Le Guin's *A Wizard of Earthsea*, or risk depletion, as in Larry Niven's *The Magic Goes Away* (1978), especially when its source lies in human **blood** or energy, as demonstrated in Kay's Fionavar Tapestry series and, repeatedly, in *Buffy the Vampire Slayer*. The absence of magic in the present world is explained by the departure of **gods and goddesses** in mythology-based stories such as *Xena: Warrior Princess, Hercules: The Legendary Journeys*, and *Jason and the Argonauts*, or the departure of **elves** and **fairies** in fantasy set in an idealized past (see **Medievalism and the Middle Ages**), like Lord Dunsany's *The King of Elfland's Daughter*, Tolkien's *The Lord of the Rings*, and Lloyd Alexander's *The High King* (1968).

In science fiction, advanced or unexplained technology can seem like magic, and the **scientists** who use it, like wizards. While more common in tales of the **far future**, like Gene Wolfe's *The Book of the New Sun*, Roger Zelazny's *Lord of Light* and Joan D. Vinge's *The Summer Queen* (1991), it is also true of those who **time** travel into the past, like Mark Twain's *A Connecticut Yankee in King Arthur's Court*, or inhabitants of an **alternate** history such as Randall Garrett's **detective** Lord Darcy, observed in *Too Many Magicians* (1967), who solves **mysteries** with deductive skills and his assistant's forensic magic.

Discussion

Magic is what makes the impossible possible, what allows the reader inhabiting the ordinary world of consensus reality to enter the **imaginary world** of the story. It lies at the heart of all subgenres of fantasy, animates the **supernatural creatures** that inhabit **horror** and **dark fantasy**, and even, in the guise of technology, evokes the **sense of wonder** that marks a work of science fiction. As the once-rigid distinction between realism and fantasy dissolves (see **Postmodernism**), narrative elements characteristic of magic appear more often even in mainstream literature (see **Magic Realism**). Without our shared belief in the magic of storytelling, in the powers of **writing and authors**, not even realistic mainstream fiction would exist, let alone the genres of speculative fiction.

Bibliography

John Algeo. "Magic Names." *Names*, 30 (June, 1982), 59–67.
Dainis Bisenieks. "Children, Magic and Choices." *Mythlore*, 6 (Winter, 1979), 13–16.
Bernadette Bosky. "Grace and Goetia." *Mythlore*, 12 (Spring, 1986), 19–23.
Gilbert K. Chesterton. "Magic and Fantasy in Fiction." *The Bookman*, 71 (March, 1930), 27–30.

John Crowley. "A Modern Instance." *Journal of the Fantastic in the Arts*, 12 (2001), 147–156.

Patricia Dooley. "Magic and Art in Ursula K. Le Guin's Earthsea Trilogy." *Children's Literature*, 8 (1979), 103–110.

Sarah Gilead. "Magic Abjured." *PMLA*, 106 (March, 1991), 277–293.

William M. Schuyler, Jr. "Ethical Status of Magic." Jan Hokenson, ed., *Forms of the Fantastic*. Westport, CT: Greenwood Press, 1986, 25–29.

Will Shetterly and Emma Bull. "The Relevance of Magic." *Utne Reader*, 21 (May/June, 1987), 136–140.

—*Christine Mains*

MAGIC REALISM

Climb up on the Moon? Of course we did. All you had to do was row out to it in a boat and, when you were underneath, prop a ladder against her and scramble up.

—Italo Calvino
Cosmicomics (1965)
trans. William Weaver (1968)

Overview

Popularized by the "boom" in Latin American literature of the late 1950s through 1970s (see **Latin America**), magic realism quickly became an internationally prominent style, admired by critics and general audiences alike. Essentially a liminal or "slipstream" genre, it imperceptibly blends a fundamentally realistic framework with powerful elements of **magic** or the mystical.

Survey

"Magic Realism" was coined by Franz Roh in 1925 to describe certain tendencies of German literature and painting. Roh's term tried to characterize the co-mingling of quotidian life with **dream**-fantasy refracted through the kaleidoscopic patterns of the Munich surrealists (see **Surrealism**); it was later appropriated to describe painting and photography at the New York Museum of Modern Art in 1943 ("American Realists and Magic Realists"). In 1949, the Cuban writer Alejo Carpentier discussed a kind of writing structured around the "marvelous real," and by the late 1950s the phrase had metamorphosed into magic (sometimes *magical*) realism. By the late 1970s, it would describe a diverse, eclectic group of writers who came to include Carpentier, the Argentinean Jorge Luis Borges, the Mexican Juan Rulfo, the Columbian Gabriel García Márquez, the Portuguese José Saramago, the German Günter Grass, the American Toni Morrison, the Czech Milan Kundera, the Indian

Salman Rushdie, the Nigerian Ben Okri, and many others. Ironically, as magic realism became more important internationally, it became less important in Latin America—where writers such as Roberto Bolaño and Alberto Fuguet have created and explored many new styles, something only beginning to be understood in the Anglophone world.

While clearly of the fantastic, there is no more consensus on magic realism's precise definition than on definitions of fantasy or science fiction. Virtually every important writer involved with the genre denies being so: even García Márquez, whose magnificent *One Hundred Years of Solitude* (1967) is magic realism's very paradigm, calls himself a "social realist." As he told the *New York Times*, "What gives literary value is mystery, the magic in commonplace events," or as he has it in his novel, the genre presents "an intricate stew of truths and mirages." This stew has four distinctive traits: the seamless weaving of the quotidian real and the most extraordinary fantasy; the use of various magical emblems (see **Magical Objects**) or emblematic events; a tone or style of dreamy, hazy lyricism (which could range from spare poetic reverie to hallucinatory psychorealism); and, consequently, an anamorphic sense of spacetime.

It is hard to identify works of fantasy or science fiction to which the term is unequivocally germane. In fantasy, the appellation has some loose use with novels like Charles Dickens's **A Christmas Carol**, Oscar Wilde's **The Picture of Dorian Gray**, or Octavia E. Butler's **Kindred**, where the magical events (incidents of **ghosts and hauntings** or **time travel**) simply happen without explanation. Films such as *Field of Dreams* or *Big Fish* (2003) seem a closer match, though still the later case questions the line between real events and characters' imaginations. A mélange of fantasy, science fiction, and political **allegory**, China Miéville's **Perdido Street Station** has been called magic realism, though Miéville prefers "new weird." Better examples appear in the fiction of the Jamaican-born Canadian Nalo Hopkinson, who blends Afro-Caribbean folklore, magical **metamorphosis**, and science fiction together with mainstream appeal in *Brown Girl in the Ring* (1998), *Midnight Robber* (2000), *Skin Folk* (2001) and *The Salt Roads* (2003). Harlan Ellison actually embraces the category, and a good deal of his work—from television scripts for *Star Trek* ("The City on the Edge of Forever" [1967]) and *The Outer Limits* ("Demon with a Glass Hand" [1963]) to stories collected in *Slippage* (1997)—shows generic connections. The term also helps describe some science fantasy such as Italo Calvino's remarkable *Cosmicomics* (1965) and *T Zero* (1967), complex hybrids of **hard science fiction**, animism, and heart-wrenching wistfulness. Calvino's earlier *The Cloven Viscount* (1952) and *The Nonexistent Knight* (1959), built on absurd premises, resemble surrealism more than magic realism (see **Absurdity**).

Discussion

The term "magic realism" has only limited application to fantasy and science fiction, except as a transgressive comparison with wonder. Like fantasy, it uses magic, although like science fiction its emphasis on "realism" makes it more mainstream literature than *identifiable* fantasy. In fantasy, the magic is literally true, but the fantasy world is discontinuous with ours; magic realism's worlds remain both continuous and contiguous (its diaphanous **thresholds** don't merely leak; they are completely fluid). In magic realism, the magical events are *always* literal; while it may include even aggressively political themes (see **Politics**), the magical event *is* simply a fact, not allegorical of some higher or greater purpose. Unlike science fiction, the magical events are not given a rational or material explanation; unlike fantasy, they are not woven into a fabric of the supernatural or supranatural; perhaps their very *lack of explanation* identifies their separate generic status.

Whereas profitable comparisons could also invoke the ghost story or the **Gothic, fable** or **fairy tale**, its closest parallels concern **postmodernism**—typically displaying boundary ambiguity, bifurcated or imbricated narratives, subtle irony, playful metafictional elements (see **Metafiction and Recursiveness**), and lack of hermeneutic closure—but unlike postmodernism it remains rooted in the common world rather than intellectual abstraction. In certain respects, magic realism simply rediscovers or heightens some traditional traits of literature that, for reasons too numerous and too well-known to invoke here, fell out of fashion in the nineteenth-century novel. In this sense, magic realism restores a traditional genre founded by Cervantes in *Don Quixote* (1605, 1615).

Bibliography

Maggie Ann Bowers. *Magic(al) Realism*. New York: Routledge, 2004.

Amaryll Chanady. *Magical Realism and the Fantastic*. New York: Garland, 1985.

Wendy B. Farris. *Ordinary Enchantments*. Nashville: Vanderbilt University Press, 2004.

Francisco Goldman. "In the Shadow of the Patriarch." *The New York Times Magazine*, 2 (November, 2003), 38–43.

Carl Malmgren. "Towards a Definition of Science Fantasy." *Science-Fiction Studies*, 15 (November, 1988), 259–281.

Greer Watson. "Assumptions of Reality." *Journal of the Fantastic in the Arts* 11 (2000), 164–172.

Kenneth Wishnia. "Science Fiction and Magic Realism." *Foundation*, No. 59 (Autumn, 1993), 29–41.

Lois Parkinson Zamora and Wendy B. Farris, eds. *Magical Realism*. Durham, NC: Duke University Press, 1995.

—Neil Easterbrook

MAGICAL OBJECTS

Overview

Sometimes a magical object is simply the goal of a **quest**: a **ring** has to be obtained (or destroyed). Sometimes it engages with the plot, like the **sword** "Stormbringer" in Michael Moorcock's Elric series, or the "palantir" through which Sauron in J.R.R. Tolkien's *The Lord of the Rings* can observe what happens elsewhere. Indeed, the palantir, though magical in the context of Tolkien's epic, reminds us of Arthur C. Clarke's Third Law: "any sufficiently advanced technology is indistinguishable from magic" (see **Magic**). Magic carpets or seven-league boots in a **fairy tale**, or time machines and faster-than-light spaceships in a science fiction story, each allow characters to travel in a way that breaks the laws of science as we know them.

Survey

Many magical objects are either **weaponry** or the focus of power, like traditional magic wands, or the **wizard's** staff wielded in *The Lord of the Rings*. Terry Pratchett's Discworld series (see *The Colour of Magic*) satirizes such props: the wizard's staff is the subject of one of Nanny Ogg's bawdy songs (see **Satire**). Power is present in everyday objects or garments. Dorothy's shoes in L. Frank Baum's *The Wonderful Wizard of Oz* give her the power to return from Oz to Kansas. The Sorting Hat in J.K. Rowling's *Harry Potter and the Sorcerer's Stone* allocates **children** to the Houses in Hogwarts School that best fit their characters. Harry Potter himself possesses numerous magical objects: naturally a wand, but also a cloak which, like the "tarnhelm" in Richard Wagner's Ring cycle, gives **invisibility**. Lloyd Alexander's *Book of Three* (1964) and its sequels borrow magical objects from Celtic folklore: a broach that brings foreknowledge, hazelnuts that confer understanding of animal speech, and the "Black Cauldron" from which living–dead warriors spring.

"Lucky" objects may also act as intermediaries between owners and more powerful beings. Aladdin's lamp, when rubbed, summons a genie who grants wishes. Such objects are not necessarily beneficent. The whistle in M.R. James's "Oh, Whistle and I'll Come to You, My Lad" (1904) summons a disturbing ghost (see **Ghosts and Hauntings**). W.W. Jacobs's "The Monkey's Paw" (1902) grants three wishes, but of the horrifically ironic sort in which the wisher gets *exactly* what they wish for.

Magical objects can be "plot coupons," objects that confer power, or objects that suggest the ironic and double-edged nature of such power. In the first instance, a series of objects have to be "collected" before the plot can progress, or, as in episodes of *Buffy the Vampire Slayer* and other popular fantasy series, the **villain** can be defeated. They can be helmets, shields, or even a collection of objects which, like the "Key to Time" in the series of *Doctor Who* episodes under that umbrella title beginning with "The Ribos Operation" (1978), make up a greater whole. In the second instance, the garment, talisman, or amulet gives the owner invisibility, say, or invulnerability. This leads almost inexorably to a third instance: the apparent blessing is discovered to be either ambiguous or a downright curse. In Moorcock's series, Elric's sword Stormbringer heals his albinism-induced weakness by infusing into him the souls of those it kills, but is as likely to turn upon his friends as his enemies. Bilbo's ring in Tolkien's *The Hobbit* is a simple object of power, but in Tolkien's sequel it possesses larger implications. Especially where these objects are weapons, we might infer an **anxiety** about the threatening possibilities of **technology**.

In science fiction, the "magical object" is usually *explained* in some way as a technological artifact. Often this explanation is cursory. There is very little difference between the wizards' duels in the film *The Lord of the Rings: The Fellowship of the Rings,* using staffs, and those in *Star Wars* using **light** sabers. In E.E. "Doc" Smith's "Lensman" series (see *Triplanetary*) the power-inducing "lens" acts and looks like a magic jewel. Some science fiction employs a "magical object" in a more knowing, sophisticated fashion. Cordwainer Smith's "Think Blue, Count Two" (1963) nods to the idea of the incantation/spell and Dorothy's "red shoes" when a protector for Veesey on her journey through space is constructed by three technicians. Gene Wolfe's *The Book of the New Sun* oscillates between science fiction and fantasy in its employment of "magical" objects such as the "Sword of the Lictor" or the apparent jewel known as the "Claw of the Conciliator." We return, perhaps, to Clarke's Third Law in science fiction like Arkady Strugatsky and Boris

Strugatsky's *Roadside Picnic* (1972), filmed as *Stalker* (1979), and Frederik Pohl's *Gateway* (1977), where human scavengers seek half-understood alien technology.

Everyday objects can be brought to life by magic: the wooden sawhorse, glass cat, and rug in Baum's Oz series owe their "lives" to magic, as does the Luggage in Terry Pratchett's "Discworld" series (see *The Colour of Magic*). Conversely, in Alan Garner's *Elidor* (1965) the symbolic objects the children bring to our reality manifest as drab, everyday things: a broken cup, an iron rail.

Discussion

The object as numinous symbol is found especially in the swords, spears, and cauldrons derived from Celtic/Christian mythology featuring the Holy Grail. In epics involving the "matter of Britain" such as T.H. White's *The Once and Future King* (1958), **Arthur** sends his knights to find the Grail as a symbol of the healing necessary to bring the wounded land to peace. Arawn's "Black Cauldron" is a sinister version of this, while in James Branch Cabell's sardonic *Jurgen* we see a parody of the theme in accordance with Freudian sexual **psychology**. Finally, an object's true power may not be known to the owner until part-way through the story. Susan's "Tear" in Garner's *The Weirdstone of Brisingamen* (1960) is the key to the safety of the Sleepers in Fundindelve, lost by the wizard to whom it was entrusted. "Magic" here, and more so in the later *Elidor*, may be spiritual and emotional resources invested in the object by its possessor rather than any supernatural power.

Bibliography

Michael Andre-Driussi. *Lexicon Urthus*. San Francisco: Sirius Books, 1994.
Brian Attebery. "Oz." Attebery, *The Fantasy Tradition in American Literature*. Bloomington: Indiana University Press, 1980, 83–108.
Diana Wynne Jones. *The Tough Guide to Fantasyland*. London: Gollancz, 1996.
Roger Sherman Loomis. *The Grail*. Cardiff: University of Wales Press, 1963.
John Moore. "Roadside Stalker." *Foundation*, No. 71 (Autumn, 1997), 63–76.
Neil Philip. *A Fine Anger*. London: Collins, 1981.
Joe Sanders, *E.E. "Doc" Smith*. Mercer Island, WA: Starmont House, 1986.
Elizabeth D. Schaffer. *Exploring Harry Potter*. London: Ebury, 2000.
Donna R. White. "Lloyd Alexander's Chronicles of Prydain." White, *A Century of Welsh Myth in Children's Literature*. Westport, CT: Greenwood Press, 1998, 97–120.

—*Andy Sawyer*

MAPS

Overview

Maps accompany most fantasy and many science stories, where they can function as an integral part of the text. In stories, maps can be consulted and used to find something of value, perhaps **treasure** or **lost worlds**.

Survey

The use of maps in the literature of the fantastic has a long tradition. Dante's Divine Comedy (c. 1306–1321) presents its moral **landscapes** in a geographical way, additionally establishing the parallels between topographies of the underworld and those of the human body. Jonathan Swift's *Gulliver's Travels* is specific about fitting its imaginary locations into the accepted geographies of the eighteenth-century world—the practice that at once enhances the verisimilitude of Gulliver's adventures and satirizes the belief in contemporary **knowledge**. Many late nineteenth-century and early twentieth-century adventure stories by such authors as Robert Louis Stevenson or H. Rider Haggard were accompanied by maps and plans, which in some cases authenticated the narration and in others provided additional help for the reader in imagining the realities of the text; the same was true of L. Frank Baum's fantasy *The Wonderful Wizard of Oz*. Cartographic materials were also of key importance in the turn-of-the-century **lost worlds** narratives, which tried to fit the fantastic lands or **cities** into real-world geographies.

The fundamental problem of the relationship between the map and the represented space, real or imagined, is probably best conveyed in Jorge Luis Borges's fable titled "On Exactitude in Science" (1972). The story describes a society obsessed with cartography, which, to be precise, draws the map of the Empire, whose size is exactly the same as the size of the land itself and each point on the map overlaps precisely its physical equivalent. Borges borrowed the idea from Lewis Carroll's *Sylvie and Bruno Concluded* (1893), in which it is concluded, "So now we use the country itself, as its own map, and I assure you it does nearly as well."

In the twentieth century, maps became a integral part of fantasy texts. Among the many to add them to narratives were Robert E. Howard and J.R.R. Tolkien, who used them respectively in *Conan the Conqueror* and its sequels, and *The Hobbit* and *The Lord of the Rings*. While some maps, for example those in *The Hobbit*, are schematic and unsophisticated, and others, like the maps compiled in the Middle-earth atlases, are extremely detailed and extensive, their function is the same as that of numerous volumes of appendices, glossaries, and encyclopedic data—to enhance the experience of reading and help visualize **imaginary worlds** with no connection to mundane reality.

With the explosive development of the genre, maps have become a fixture in fantasy, and it is probably easier to find fantasy texts without them than to enumerate those with them. Still, in many cases they appear to function more as a decorative element and a validation of the imaginative integrity of the work's setting than as a true aid in following the course of the narrative. Maps can also accompany science fiction texts but, because of science fiction's reliance on mundane geographies, their presence is far less crucial for the plot. Star maps or schematic maps of constellations, such as those in Sean Williams and Shane Dix's *Echoes of Earth* (2002) and its sequels, are a variation, as are maps of newly colonized worlds (see **Exploration**), such as one of the titular planet found in C.J. Cherryh's *Cyteen* (1988).

Within stories, maps are consulted probably as often or as rarely as in the real world as part of **quests** or **escapes**, but the act itself hardly ever acquires any broader significance. In many late twentieth-century science fiction texts and movies traditional maps are replaced with electronic screens displaying grids or plans of installations—this is the case in *Aliens* (1986) (see **Alien**) and *The Matrix Revolutions* (2003) (see **The Matrix**)—or automated voice systems informing their users about their current position. In **cyberpunk**, the cartographic focus is shifted to charting the geographies of **virtual realities** rather than physical spaces—the topography of Metaverse in Neal Stephenson's **Snow Crash** is as important in the novel as the real-world locations.

Discussion

While maps played a major role in the narratives of the late nineteenth and early twentieth centuries, the period in which certain parts of the globe had not yet been fully charted, their importance rapidly decreased in the twentieth century with the fast disappearing stretches of unexplored territories. At the end of the century maps had become a relatively minor element in science fiction. Simultaneously, their popularity in fantasy appears to be well-secured, as stories of fully imagined secondary worlds always benefit from cartographic addenda.

Bibliography

Tobias Doring. "Scales and Ladders." Elmar Schenkel and Stefan Welz, eds., *Lost Worlds and Mad Elephants*. Glienicke: Galda & Wilch Verlag, 1999, 243–258.

Rob Kitchin and James Kneale, ed. *Lost in Space*. London: Continuum. 2002.

Ursula K. Le Guin, "Mapping Imaginary Countries." David Wingrove, ed., *The Science Fiction Source Book*. New York: Van Nostrand, 1984, 77–79.

Naomi Mitchison. "Maps of Middle Earth." *Books and Bookmen*, 23 (October 1977), 28–30.

J.B. Post. *An Atlas of Fantasy*. New York: Ballantine, 1979.

———. "Toward an Atlas of Fantasy." *Bulletin of the Geography and Map Division, Special Libraries Association*, 75 (March, 1969), 11–13.

Brian Sibley and John Howe. *The Maps of Middle-earth*. Boston: Houghton Mifflin, 2003.

Brian Stableford. *The Dictionary of Science Fiction Places*. New York: Wonderland Press, 1999.

R.E. Walker. "Cartography of Fantasy." *Mythlore*, 7 (Winter, 1981), 37–38.

—Pawel Frelik

MARRIAGE

Overview

Science fiction and fantasy frequently depict unusual forms of social and **family** organization, in societies remote from those of the immediate audience. Thus they are well placed to undertake a cognitive examination of institutions such as marriage. What is, perhaps, surprising is how little published science fiction and fantasy takes advantage of that opportunity.

Survey

Traditional forms of **comedy** and **romance** are festive at heart: they celebrate **youth** (especially young **love**), fertility, and the triumph of good. Here, the marital union of at least one pair of lovers represents in **microcosm** the defeat of whatever forces threatened them, their love for each other, or their ascendant society. After a period of confusion, desolation, or misrule, the natural and social orders are restored. Mainstream love stories typically conclude in this way, and many **fairy tales**, fantasies, and science fiction adventures follow the same pattern. Modern examples include the interplanetary and **jungle** adventures of Edgar Rice Burroughs's muscular **heroes** (see *A Princess of Mars; Tarzan of the Apes*), Walt Disney's version of *Snow White and the Seven Dwarfs*, J.R.R. Tolkien's *The Lord of the Rings*, the monumental saga of the *Star Wars* movies, and many others.

A more pessimistic variation is the story in which love fails, and the natural or social order is left unredeemed. An extreme case is George Orwell's terrifying **dystopia**, *Nineteen Eighty-Four*, in which the all-powerful totalitarian regime breaks the will of the lovers. In the *Mad Max* movies, the postnuclear wasteland (see **Nuclear War**) is only partly redeemed, and Max is left with no significant human relationships to replace those with his wife and child (both killed in the first movie). He becomes a destructive figure who can do no more than clear the way for his symbolic **children** (the Feral Kid and Savannah Nix) to build new societies.

Fictional narratives can also examine the institution of marriage with a knowing eye, alert for foibles and problems. The effect achieved may be humorous, satirical, melodramatic, or tragic (see **Humor; Satire; Tragedy**). Science fiction and fantasy elements sometimes heighten the **absurdity** of family relationships, as in many television situation comedies (including the more bizarre episodes of *The Simpsons* and similar programs, which are not essentially works of science fiction or fantasy).

Since antiquity, however, utopian thinkers have taken a far more radical approach to criticism of marriage and the **family**. Thomas More's *Utopia* strongly reaffirms the need for patriarchal institutions, with only minimal reforms, such as allowing prospective brides and grooms to view each other naked (see **Nudity**); however, more recent utopian works have advocated major changes. Some **utopias** favor the eugenic control of marriage and procreation by the state. The future society of Edward Bellamy's *Looking Backward, 2000–1887* emphasizes free selection of marital partners, but still for eugenic reasons. Such dystopian novels as Aldous Huxley's *Brave New World* and Margaret Atwood's *The Handmaid's Tale* describe societies in which social control of **sexuality** and reproduction has been taken to repugnant extremes.

Because science fiction examines social changes that arise from the advance of science and **technology**, it provides an ongoing literary forum for such issues as whether monogamy should be retained. It sometimes critiques monogamy from an alien viewpoint, as in Robert A. Heinlein's *Stranger in a Strange Land*, or describes alternatives, such as the line marriages of Heinlein's *The Moon is a Harsh Mistress* (1966). In Arthur C. Clarke's *Imperial Earth* (1975), exclusive marriage and sexual possessiveness are said to be things of the past, and Clarke shows us successful polygynous and polyandrous marriages in **Rendezvous with Rama**.

Feminist utopias typically reject traditional relationships between the sexes, including marriage (see **Feminism**). Some feminist novels, such as Charlotte Perkins Gilman's **Herland** and Joanna Russ's **The Female Man**, describe societies without men. Marge Piercy's **Woman on the Edge of Time** depicts a utopia in which women have achieved freedom from male domination, and sexuality is free of guilt (though not of all interpersonal conflict). Ectogenesis is used to separate reproduction from recreational "coupling," and there is no marriage bond. Individuals may have unlimited numbers of "sweet friends," while three social mothers (who may be of either sex) are provided for each child. Ursula K. Le Guin's **The Dispossessed** depicts a similarly utopian, though stagnating, society. Once again, many forms of sexual involvement are acceptable, but the focus of interest and sympathy is on monogamous, heterosexual relationships.

Some science fiction works describe unusual familial/sexual arrangements for their alien characters, as in Isaac Asimov's **The Gods Themselves** (1972), without considering anything very radical for future humans. However, Anne McCaffrey (see **Dragonflight**), Samuel R. Delany (especially in *Stars in My Pocket Like Grains of Sand* [1984]), and others have imagined more extraordinary sexual arrangements involving the interactions of humans and nonhumanoid aliens, or even (in *Stars in My Pocket*) direct human–alien sex.

Discussion

Despite their potential to re-imagine love, courtship, and marriage, science fiction and fantasy are usually quite conservative. Most authors assume that the marital customs of their own times will last into the distant future—or would apply in magical, ontologically remote worlds. Ample scope remains for science fiction and fantasy writers to explore alternatives and show their effects on the characters involved.

Bibliography

Anne Cranny-Francis. "Feminist Fantasy" and "Feminist Utopias." Francis, *Feminist Fiction*. New York: St. Martin's, 1990, 75–142.

Val Clear, Martin H. Greenberg, Joseph D. Olander, and Patricia S. Warrick, eds. *Marriage and the Family through Science Fiction*. New York: St. Martin's Press. 1976.

Chris Ferns. *Narrating Utopia*. Liverpool: Liverpool University Press, 1999.

Peter Fitting. "So We All Became Mothers." *Science-Fiction Studies*, 12 (1985), 156–183.

Peter C. Hall and Richard Erlich. "Beyond Topeka and Thunderdome." *Science-Fiction Studies*, 14 (November, 1987), 316–325.

Betty King. *Women of the Future*. Metuchen, NJ: Scarecrow Press, 1984.

Tarya Malkki. "The Marriage Metaphor in the Works of Ursula K. Le Guin." Robert A. Latham and Robert A. Collins. eds., *Modes of the Fantastic*. Westport, CT: Greenwood Press, 1995, 100–109.

Fred D. Miller, Jr. and Nicholas D. Smith. "Introduction: The Philosophical Appeal of Science Fiction." Smith, ed., *Philosophers Look at Science Fiction*. Chicago: Nelson-Hall, 1982, 1–19.

Patricia Monk. "The Future of Imperfect Conjugation." *Mosaic*, 17 (1984), 207–222.

—Russell Blackford

MARS

∎

I opened my eyes upon a strange and weird landscape. I knew that I was on Mars; not once did I question either my sanity or my wakefulness.

—Edgar Rice Burroughs
A Princess of Mars (1917)

Overview

Mars, fourth planet from the Sun, once commanded attention as a likely home of intelligent life. Today, though scientists aware of its harsh climate can only hope for evidence of microbes or fossils, Mars remains an object of interest as a world humans may colonize or transform into a habitable environment by **terraforming**.

Survey

In the late nineteenth century, Percival Lowell proposed that an ancient Martian **civilization** had constructed canals to bring water to drought-stricken **cities**. Lowell suspected these Martians were almost extinct, and a few stories, like George O. Smith's "Lost Art" (1943) and H. Beam Piper's "Omnilingual" (1957), involve vanished Martian **cultures** represented only by puzzling ruins. But generally, writers preferred to envision living Martians.

If Martians were older and wiser than humans, their civilization might be a **utopia**, as in Hugo Gernsback's *Baron Munchausen's Scientific Adventures* (1915–1917) and Alexei Tolstoy's *Aelita* (1922). This notion influenced novels like C.S. Lewis's *Out of the Silent Planet*, which depicts Mars as a world without original **sin** (see **Christianity**). Such Martians might visit Earth to enlighten humanity, as in Richard Gathony's play *A Message from Mars* (1899); other examples include Klaatu in *The Day the Earth Stood Still*, whose journey of 250 million miles suggests a Martian origin, and Valentine Michael Smith of Robert A. Heinlein's *Stranger in a Strange Land*, who brings Martian **religion** and **psychic powers** to Earth.

However, an imperiled Mars might invade Earth to seize its resources, as occurs in H.G. Wells's *The War of the Worlds*. Martian **invasions** of Earth became a staple of science fiction, even figuring in Olaf Stapledon's *Last and First Men* as well as films ranging from *Invaders from Mars* to *Mars Attacks!* (1996). As a subtler variation on the theme, *Five Million Years to Earth* (1968) (see *The Quatermass Experiment*) posits that ancient Martian invaders endowed humans with **intelligence** while embedding images of **demons** in their **memories**.

Along with utopian Mars and sinister Mars, there is decadent Mars—a once-great civilization now requiring assistance from vigorous young Earthlings (see **Decadence**). Edgar Rice Burroughs portrayed such an environment in *A Princess of Mars* and its sequels, where John Carter mystically teleports to Mars to battle for princess Dejah Thoris (see **Teleportation**). Breaking Burroughs's pattern of humanoid Martians, Stanley G. Weinbaum crafted more enigmatic creatures to inhabit the declining Mars of "A Martian Odyssey" (1934), but others followed in Burroughs's footsteps, including Leigh Brackett, whose exotic Martian adventures began with "Queen of the Martian Catacombs" (1949). While Burroughs and Brackett produced upbeat, exciting sagas (see **Sword and Sorcery**), Ray Bradbury more soberly portrayed a dying Mars in *The Martian Chronicles*.

Bradbury's elegiac tone reflected new data in the 1940s indicating that Mars was barren, lacking canals or breathable air. Arthur C. Clarke's *Sands of Mars* (1951) was an early work featuring this inhospitable world. Surrendering to scientific realities, stories about Mars became grim sagas of **survival** amidst desperate conditions, as in Rex Gordon's *No Man Friday* (1956), the unacknowledged basis of the film *Robinson Crusoe on Mars* (1964). D.G. Compton's *Farewell, Earth's Bliss* (1966) even depicts Mars as a penal colony (see **Prisons**). To inhabit Mars, one possibility was **pantropy**, biologically transforming humans into creatures that could survive on the Martian surface, but except for the surgical modifications in Frederik Pohl's *Man Plus* (1976), this process was rarely considered.

Instead, stories emphasized the more attractive prospect of terraforming Mars. The idea was not entirely new, since scientists in *Sands of Mars* create a miniature sun to orbit Mars and raise its temperature, and a new atmosphere for Mars is generated in *Total Recall*. The most noteworthy saga of Martian terraforming is Kim Stanley Robinson's *Red Mars* and its sequels, describing how Mars is gradually made habitable through centuries of effort, though preservationists insist that some areas remain untouched (see **Ecology**). Another strategy for improving Mars's climate is conveyed by the title of Greg Bear's *Moving Mars* (1993).

Other works pondered the question of how humans, in light of political and budgetary restraints, might colonize Mars in the **near future**, including Terry Bisson's satirical *Voyage to the Red Planet* (1990; see **Satire**) and Ben Bova's practical-minded *Mars* (1992). Discovering signs of life on Mars, even simple lifeforms or ruins, also figured in works like Gregory Benford's *The Martian Race* (1999) and the films *Mission to Mars* (2000) and *Red Planet* (2000).

Discussion

Because Mars was regarded as older than Earth, its civilizations were often idealized redactions of older human societies. Martians appear in togas or armor recalling ancient Greece or Rome, and Bradbury's Mars seems a version of **America's frontier**, with displaced, exterminated Martians representing **Native Americans**. Martians invading Earth may reflect concerns about despised contemporary cultures, like **Asia's** "Yellow Peril" or the Communist Soviet Union (see **Russia**). However, while such recycled imagery reverberates through Martian stories, the planet also figures as an icon of **humanity's** glorious future, a world humans can remake into a new and better Earth. As in the final story of *The Martian Chronicles*, "The Million-Year Picnic" (1946), humans who cannot meet Martians may instead become Martians, the prospect most appealingly developed in Robinson's novels.

Bibliography

Stephen Baxter. "Martian Chronicles." *Foundation*, No. 68 (Autumn, 1996), 5–16.

Martin Caidin and Jay Barbree, with Susan Wright. *Destination Mars*. New York: Viking, 1997.

T.E. Dikty, ed. *Great Science Fiction Stories about Mars*. New York: Frederick Fell, 1966.

Christine Hawkins. "Voyages to Mars." *Sirius*, No. 3 (November, 1993), 16-21, and No. 4 (February, 1994), 12–22.

Jane Hipolito and Willis E. McNelly, eds. *Mars, We Love You*. Garden City: Doubleday, 1971.

Edward James. "Building Utopias on Mars, from Crusoe to Robinson." *Foundation*, No. 68 (Autumn, 1996), 64–75.

Thomas J. Morrissey. "Ready or Not, Here We Come." *Journal of the Fantastic in the Arts*, 10 (2000), 372–394.

Oliver Morton. *Mapping Mars*. London: Fourth Estate, 2002.

Gary Westfahl. "Reading Mars." *New York Review of Science Fiction*, 13 (December, 2000), 1, 8–13.

—*Gary Westfahl*

MATHEMATICS

Overview

For many people today, mathematical formulas are as incomprehensible and numinous as **magic** spells. It is a natural, even inevitable step to assume that the symbolic techniques that so effectively model **nature** may themselves form a **technology** capable of manipulating the universe.

Survey

Since **knowledge** equals power, mathematical understanding of reality brings **psychic powers** in James Blish's *Jack of Eagles* (1952), Mark Clifton's *Eight Keys to Eden* (1960), and Henry Kuttner and C.L. Moore's "The Fairy Chessmen" (1946) (see **Chess**). Charles L. Harness's "The Rose" (1953) dramatizes the "two **cultures**" clash with seventeen universal equations whose interpretation as **physics** yields potent new technology as **art** or exquisite **music**. **Space travel** in David Zindell's *Neverness* (1988) is an exhilarating mathematical dance in which pilots negotiate interstellar flux by solving its ever-changing equations.

Mathematical predictions are a recurring science fiction theme (see **Divination**). Extrapolating **cycles** in Robert A. Heinlein's "The Year of the Jackpot" (1952) foretells **apocalypse**. One subplot of E.E. "Doc" Smith's *The Vortex Blaster* (1960) (see *Triplanetary*) involves a human/**computer** race to make short-term, split-second predictions. Isaac Asimov's *Foundation* employs "psychohistory," a mixture of statistics and **psychology**, for detailed forecasting of sociology and **politics**. A peak of predictive **absurdity** is Colin Kapp's *The Patterns of Chaos* (1972), with key human figures accurately targeted by **weaponry** aimed and launched 700,000,000 years previously.

"Random" numbers themselves become predictable through advanced math in Terry Pratchett's *The Dark Side of the Sun* (1976) and Barrington J. Bayley's *The Grand Wheel* (1977). Infinity is frequently invoked in science fiction, though often confused with the merely very big. The **library** of Jorge Luis Borges's "The Library of Babel" (1941), containing all possible book-length permutations of typographic symbols, is strictly finite although too large to be contained in our universe.

Genuine infinities feature in Greg Bear's *Eon* (1985), with a tubular corridor that extends forever; in Christopher Priest's *The Inverted World* (1974), whose distorted, hyperboloid **Earth** extends to infinity at poles and equator (perhaps only an artifact of **perception**); and in mathematician Rudy Rucker's tour-de-force *White Light* (1980), presenting the dizzying heights of transfinite set theory through an **allegory** of endless mountain climbing. The protagonist of Greg Egan's "The Infinite Assassin" (1991), who can strike simultaneously in an infinity of **parallel worlds,** is ingeniously neutralized by mapping him to a mathematical set of points ("Cantor dust"), which is infinite yet so sparse as to have no effective presence.

Ordinary geometry offers less excitement, though providing background in Kim Stanley Robinson's "The Blind Geometer" (1987). Poul Anderson's "The Three-Cornered Wheel" (1963) uses triangular curves of constant width for rollers when **religion** forbids perfect circles (see **Taboo**). Edwin A. Abbott's *Flatland* imagines a two-dimensional world as a springboard to understanding four-dimensional space, a concept that has inspired many science fiction stories (see **Dimensions**). Norman Kagan's "The Mathenauts" (1964) portrays physical **exploration** of mathematical spaces, and Lewis Carroll's wonderlands (see *Alice's Adventures in Wonderland*) include warped mathematical logic.

Many science fiction implausibities are explained away by mathematical handwaving not far from sympathetic **magic**. In Heinlein's "—And He Built a Crooked House" (1940), a house built as a three-dimensional "unwrapping" of a 4-D hypercube or tesseract collapses inexplicably into an actual tesseract. Topology, in terms of a **transportation** system's connectivity, excuses anomalies and **time travel** in A.J. Deutsch's "A Subway Named Mobius" (1950). David Duncan's *Occam's Razor* (1957) uses minimal-path theory, interestingly represented by soap films, to access parallel worlds. Contemplation of symbolic logic transfers characters into fantasy settings in L. Sprague de Camp and Fletcher Pratt's *The Incomplete Enchanter* (1941).

Recreational mathematics (see **Games**) can provide narrative **puzzles:** Piers Anthony's *With a Tangled Skein* (1985) recycles an old problem about detecting false coins by weighing, laboriously transposed into fantasy. Anthony's *OX* (1976) draws on John Horton Conway's cellular-automata game "Life," which Egan's *Permutation City* (1994) audaciously develops into a **virtual reality** mechanism requiring no **computer.**

Mathematical weaponry builds on the idea that human minds can be overloaded with information, as in Fred Hoyle's *The Black Cloud* (1957), or that they function like computer programs, which certain inputs can halt or crash, causing brain **death**. Examples include the Destroyer logic-sequence of Anthony's *Macroscope* (1969) and David Langford's lethal imagery in stories like "Different Kinds of Darkness" (2000). Less explicable pure-math weapons are deployed against tumors afflicting **cosmology** in Paul J. McAuley's *Eternal Light* (1991).

Discussion

The remorseless effectiveness of mathematics can provoke resentment, exemplified by generations of amateurs who attempted proven impossibilities like squaring the circle using only a straight edge and compass. Stories tapping this vein include William F. Orr's "Euclid Alone" (1975) and Ted Chiang's "Division By Zero" (1991), where math proves fundamentally flawed. Colin Kapp's "Getaway from

Getawehi" (1969) features construction difficulties in conditions where, when adding *physical* lengths, one plus one equals not two but 1.5708. In Egan's "Luminous" (1995), computer analysis locates the **borderland** of an alternative mathematics corresponding to a different **physics** from our own. Carl Sagan's *Contact* (1985) proposes that the endless digital expansion of *pi* contains a message from our universe's creators. Asimov's "The Feeling of Power" (1958), in which omnipresent computers have made mathematics a lost art, and the rediscovery of mental arithmetic is co-opted for weaponry, seems a more prophetic **satire** today than when first published.

Bibliography

Elwyn R. Berlekamp, John H. Conway, and Richard K. Guy. *Winning Ways, Volume 2.* London and New York: Academic Press, 1982.

E.A. Boyno. "Mathematics in Science Fiction." Donald M. Hassler, ed., *Patterns of the Fantastic II.* Mercer Island, WA: Starmont, 1985, 39–44.

Clifton Fadiman, ed. *Fantasia Mathematica.* New York: Simon & Schuster, 1958.

———. *The Mathematical Magpie.* New York: Simon & Schuster, 1962.

Martin Gardner. *Wheels, Life, and Other Mathematical Amusements.* New York: W.H. Freeman, 1983.

Lila M. Harper. "Mathematical Themes in Science Fiction." *Extrapolation,* 27 (Fall 1986), 245–269.

Douglas Hofstadter. *Gödel, Escher, Bach.* New York: Basic Books, 1979.

Rudy Rucker. *Infinity and the Mind.* Boston; Basel; Stuttgart: Birkhäuser, 1982.

Rudy Rucker, ed. *Mathenauts.* New York: Arbor House, 1987.

—*David Langford*

MECHANIZATION

∎

See Machines and Mechanization

MEDICINE

∎

Earth had become Hospital Earth, physician to a Galaxy, surgeon to a thousand worlds, midwife to those susceptible to midwifery and psychiatrist to those whose inner lives zigged when their outer lives zagged.

—Alan E. Nourse
"Contamination Crew" (1958)

Overview

The profession of medicine, while increasingly important in a contemporary society much concerned with maintaining good health, is only occasionally the focus of science fiction and fantasy. Topics related to medicine include **Biology, Frankenstein Monsters, Immortality and Longevity, Plagues and Diseases, Suspended Animation and Cryonics,** and **Uplift.**

Survey

Fantasy stories may feature figures with a magical **talent** for healing (see **Magic**), like Alvin Maker in Orson Scott Card's *Seventh Son* (1987) and its sequels, Paksenarrion of Elizabeth Moon's *Sheepfarmer's Daughter* (1988) and its sequels, and Sulis of Tanya Huffs's *Healing Magick* (2004). There are also those who heal using more conventional means, like Croaker of Glen Cook's *The Black Company* (1984) and its sequels, who treats the wounds of his fellow soldiers. Altruistic physicians may appear in stories set in contemporary times like the film *Field of Dreams*, where doctor and former baseball player Moonlight Graham, after magically reverting to **youth** on a special baseball diamond, gives up playing the **game** and returns to being an elderly doctor to save a child who is choking to death.

Considering science fiction, one might first think of the blasphemous activities in Mary Shelley's *Frankenstein, or, The Modern Prometheus* and H.G. Wells's *The Island of Doctor Moreau*, though Frankenstein was not actually a physician. These novels provided a model for the strange transplants performed by the sinister Ras Thavas in Edgar Rice Burroughs's *The Master Mind of Mars* (1928) and *Synthetic Men of Mars* (1939) (see *A Princess of Mars*) while also inspiring so many twentieth-century **horror** films about doctors performing ill-fated experiments that the phrase "mad doctor" became synonymous with "**mad scientist**"; examples include the doctor switching minds from one body to another in *The Man Who Lived Again* (1936), the doctor endeavoring to raise the dead in *The Man They Could Not Hang* (1939), *The Awful Dr. Orloff* (1961) attempting bloody face transplants, and the homicidal doctor afflicting the *Horror Hospital* (1973). The film *Dr. Cook's Garden* (1971) is the creepy tale of a physician who secretly decides which of his patients shall live and which shall die. But a medical doctor is the **hero** in the film *Invasion of the Body Snatchers*, alerting the authorities about an insidious alien **invasion**.

Also set in the present are the "medical thrillers" by former physician Robin Cook, Ken McClure, and others. These variants of **technothrillers** involve **near-future** medical advances with potentially catastrophic results; Cook's first and best-known novel *Coma* (1977), filmed in 1978, involves a surreptitious scheme to kill patients to sell their organs. The medically trained Michael Crichton also has dabbled in the form with works like *The Terminal Man* (1972), filmed in 1974, about a patient turned into a crazed murderer by a **computer** implant.

Moving into future worlds of **space travel**, some writers focus on issues of medical care. Works like Lee Correy's *Space Doctor* (1981) and Moon's "ABCs in Zero-G" (1986) examine the problems of medical treatment in an Earth-orbiting **space station**. More extravagantly imaginative are the series of stories about physicians traveling through interstellar space and addressing the ailments of **aliens in space**;

three examples can be observed in L. Ron Hubbard's *Ole Doc Methuselah* (1970); Murray Leinster's *Med Service* (1959) and its sequels; and S.L. Viehl's *StarDoc* (2001) and its sequels. An author who was also a working physician, Alan E. Nourse, wrote novels in this vein like *Star Surgeon* (1959) and *The Mercy Men* (1968). Unique sorts of medical series include the stories collected in Piers Anthony's *Prostho Plus* (1971), chronicling the travails of a spacefaring dentist; the stories in Sharon Webb's *The Adventures of Terra Tarkington* (1985), the memoirs of a space nurse; and the British television series *Spacevets* (1992–1994), a comedy about future veterinarians treating sick alien animals.

However, the preeminent author in this subgenre was James White, who produced many stories and novels, beginning with **Hospital Station**, about the dedicated physicians working at the Sector Twelve General Hospital, a huge **space habitat** where a wide variety of bizarre aliens receive treatment for often inexplicable ailments. The short-lived television series *Mercy Point* (1998–1999) featured some less memorable doctors working in a space station hospital. Instead of functioning as protagonists, though, future physicians are more often supporting characters, as most prominently observed in *Star Trek*, its successor series, and *Babylon 5*, which all include a ship's doctor in a secondary role; *Star Trek*'s Dr. Leonard "Bones" McCoy is the most beloved of these figures, while *Star Trek: Voyager*'s sentient hologram, known only as the Doctor, is the most unusual (see **Virtual Reality**).

One story about the future's advanced medical care takes place in the present—C.M. Kornbluth's "The Little Black Bag" (1950), in which a washed-up, drunken physician obtains a satchel of advanced medical equipment from the future (see **Time Travel**) and becomes capable of seemingly miraculous cures. There are also future **dystopias** wherein citizens are smothered by excessive medical care, imposed by a government run by doctors in Ward Moore and Robert Bradford's *Caduceus Wild* (1978) and by overzealous computers in John Sladek's "The Happy Breed" (1966).

Discussion

In an essay in Gary Westfahl and George Slusser's anthology *No Cure for the Future*, "The Missionary Physician, from Asclepius to Kevorkian," Frank McConnell argues that science fiction is characteristically obsessed with *transcending* the human body—whether by means of being transformed into beings of pure energy, forming a **hive mind**, or being downloaded into a computer—and hence is not particularly interested in *treating* and *preserving* the human body with advanced scientific medicine. This might explain why physicians—increasingly the most important figures in people's real lives—remain somewhat marginalized figures in science fiction.

Bibliography

John Baxter. "The Doctor Will See You Now." Baxter, *Science Fiction in the Cinema*. New York: Paperback Library, 1970, 39–52.
Arthur C. Clarke. "Life Meets Death and Twists Its Tale." Clarke, *July 20, 2019*. New York: Macmillan, 1986, 229–247.
James J. Hughes and John Lantos. "Medical Ethics Through the *Star Trek* Lens." *Literature and Medicine*, 20 (Spring, 2001), 26–38.

Nina Lykee and Rosa Braidotti, eds. *Between Monsters, Goddesses and Cyborgs*. London: Zed, 1996.

Nickianne Moody. "Medicine, Morality and Faith." Edward James and Farah Mendlesohn, eds., *Parliament of Dreams*. Reading: Science Fiction Foundation, 1998, 145–152.

Lorena Laura Stookey. *Robin Cook*. Westport, CT: Greenwood Press, 1996.

Gary Westfahl. "Sector General: The Next Generation?" *Interzone*, No. 179 (May, 2002), 52–54.

Gary Westfahl and George Slusser, eds. *No Cure for the Future*. Westport, CT: Greenwood Press, 2002.

D.E. White. "Medical Morals and Narrative Necessity." R.E. Myers, ed., *The Intersection of Science Fiction and Philosophy*. Westport, CT: Greenwood Press, 1983, 185–194.

—*Gary Westfahl*

MEDIEVALISM AND THE MIDDLE AGES

Overview

The Middle Ages is often considered the last period in history when a majority of humans believed in **magic** rather than science; therefore, it is a key setting for fantasy. Medieval codes and practices, like **chivalry**, give moral weight and purpose to both fantasies set in the period and some science fiction that reflects medieval modes.

Survey

Many European folk and **fairy tales,** in their familiar form, originated in the Middle Ages (see **Europe**); these stories provided the poor with a temporary **escape** from oppression, suggesting the possibility of social mobility through magic or quick thinking. The Middle Ages also produced epic **romances** like *The Song of Roland* (c. 1050), in which brave **heroes** fought for their native lands and people. Both these traditions provide a basis for the modern use of medievalism in science fiction and fantasy.

It should be noted, however, that depictions of the Middle Ages in modern fantasy and science fiction are rarely historically accurate. Rather, it is generally portrayed as an antitechnological, morally superior paradise, providing counterpoint to a technological and corrupt modern world. This depiction derives partly from the simplified moral universe found in fairy tales and epics, but also from the influence of William Morris and the pre-Raphaelites. They described an unrealistically beautiful and magical version of the medieval world in their paintings, **poetry,** and novels. The literary fairy tales of George MacDonald (whose books were illustrated by pre-Raphaelite Arthur Hughes) and the Victorian revival of interest in the legends of Robin Hood and King **Arthur** during this period, underline the pre-Raphaelite influence.

Even in a work like Mark Twain's *A Connecticut Yankee in King Arthur's Court,* the **satire** of the cult of medievalism is balanced by an equally, if not more, unfavorable portrayal of modern science and **technology**. While Twain exposes medieval society as superstitious and backwards, he stops short of arguing that modern society is superior. Twain also suggests that magic is just science by another name, and that "signs and wonders" depicted in medieval literature could easily be explained away by scientific means.

Many twentieth-century works, however, blend medievalism with elements of science fiction. Thus, E.R. Eddison's *The Worm Ouroboros* is set on the planet **Mercury**, but is reminiscent of a medieval epic with its heightened language and battles between heroes and royal kingdoms. Although the setting of *The Worm Ouroboros* is merely a device to start the story, this trend of blending science fiction elements with medievalism would continue throughout the century, even though the attitude toward the Middle Ages might change. Eddison is decidedly enamored of chivalric codes, but later works were not so clear; John Christopher's Tripods series, beginning with *The White Mountain* (1967), an alien **invasion** series, suggests the Middle Ages were a dark time of conformity and oppression. Anne McCaffrey's Pern sequence (see *Dragonflight*) details a human colonization of another planet. The colonizers, though capable of **genetic engineering** to turn lizards into planet-saving **dragons**, live in a replica of a medieval society with bards (harpers) and kitchen maids who are disguised **queens**. The heroes of the story must combat anti-technological and superstitious attitudes to succeed.

Many fantasies that use medievalism as a mode also contain consistent, recognizable tropes, most notably the **castle** and the **forest**. The castle is the home of magic, often dark magic, although sometimes the hero or heroine can redeem it. This is the case in several twentieth-century fantasy films, including **Dracula, Snow White and the Seven Dwarfs**, and Jean Cocteau's **Beauty and the Beast**. Although *Dracula* is based on the **Gothic** tradition, and the other two films are derived from European fairy tales, all three use the remote castle as a dark place where magic has a grip over the protagonist. The forest, on the other hand, allows the protagonist to escape from danger while drawing him or her closer to the magic; it acts as a place of both safety and the unknown.

Because of its connection with the chivalric age, medievalism almost always has a political message (see **Politics**). Many authors use it conservatively, to promote a wished-for return to a mythical past of peace. This is the case in C.S. Lewis's *The Lion, the Witch and the Wardrobe*, where the symbol of the redemption of Narnia is the castle of Cair Paravel once again inhabited by a High King. Lewis's friend, J.R.R. Tolkien, in *The Hobbit* and *The Lord of the Rings*, insisted that **evil** is real and must be combated by even the most lowly. *Star Wars* argues that a return to chivalric codes by those destined to be Jedi Knights is the only way to save the universe. Marion Zimmer Bradley presents a feminist revisionist version of the medieval period in *The Mists of Avalon* to suggest that pre-Christian societies, like that of the Welsh druids, were more open to and accepting of women (see **Feminism**).

Discussion

Use of the Middle Ages and medieval codes and practices gives many fantasies their guiding principle. Medievalism allows for easy acceptance of magical events and creatures, the principles of chivalry, and a simplified moral universe through common tropes and themes. It can, therefore, often serve to underline a conservative, patriarchal society. However, many authors and creators of science fiction and fantasy have deliberately reversed hierarchies found in traditional medievalism, to offer a more inclusive vision.

Bibliography

Stephanie Barczewski. *Myth and National Identity in Nineteenth Century Britain*. Oxford: Oxford University Press, 2000.

Norman F. Cantor. *Inventing the Middle Ages*. New York: Morrow, 1991.

Alice Chandler. *A Dream of Order*. Lincoln: University of Nebraska Press, 1970.

Kathryn Hume. "Medieval Romance and Science Fiction." *Journal of Popular Culture*, 16 (Summer, 1982), 15–26.

Kim Ileen Moreland. *The Medievalist Impulse in American Literature*. Charlottesville: University Press of Virginia, 1996.

Donald Scragg and Carole Weinberg, eds. *Literary Appropriations of the Anglo-Saxons from the Thirteenth to the Twentieth Century*. Cambridge: Cambridge University Press, 2000.

Clare Simmons, ed. *Medievalism and the Quest for the "Real" Middle Ages*. London: Cass, 2001.

Charlotte Spivack. *Merlin's Daughters*. Westport, CT: Greenwood Press, 1987.

—*Karen Sands-O'Connor*

MEMORY

———————————————■———————————————

It's a poor sort of memory that only works backwards.

—Lewis Carroll
Through the Looking Glass (1871)

Overview

Memory, whether individual and cultural, is a psychological, genetic, or technological recording of the past. Works of science fiction and fantasy involve not only the process of remembering but also the problem of forgetting or amnesia, while characters struggle with separating true memories from implanted false memories. Sometimes memories are recovered with the aid of **drugs**, during **dreams**, or through **hypnotism**.

Survey

Human memory is elusive and inaccurate, but the **magic** of fantasy and the **technology** of science fiction offer other methods for archiving the past. The Renaissance palace of memory takes form in Edgewood, the five-sided house in John Crowley's **Little, Big**, while the protagonist of James White's *The Dream Millennium* (1974) dreams Jung's racial memory during a thousand-year cryosleep. The parasitical Goa'ulds use a different form of genetic memory in *Stargate SG:1* (1997–) (see **Stargate**; **Parasites**). In Gene Wolfe's *The Book of the New Sun*, Severian, who claims to have an eidetic memory, is able to access Thecla's memory after consuming her flesh in a **ritual**. **Computers** as a means to store, access, and enhance memory are a defining characteristic of **cyberpunk**, as in William Gibson's *Neuromancer* and the film *Johnny Mnemonic* (1996).

A familiar figure is the amnesiac **hero** in **exile**, on a **quest** to recover **identity**, such as Gilbert Gosseyn in A.E. van Vogt's *The World of Null-A* (1948), Valentine in Robert Silverberg's *Lord Valentine's Castle* (1979), Red in Roger Zelazny's *Roadmarks* (1979), and Corwin in Zelazny's *Nine Princes in Amber* (1970). The narrator of the film *Lost Horizon* (1937) (see James Hilton's **Lost Horizon**), self-exiled from Shangri-La, recounts his tale as he regains his memories, and *Star Trek III: The Search for Spock* (1984) (see *Star Trek: The Motion Picture*) ends with Spock beginning to remember his crewmates after his **rebirth**. Recovering one's **name** and **family** is essential for rejoining the **community**, as Tenar learns when she regains the name symbolically eaten by the **gods and goddesses** she serves in Ursula K. Le Guin's *The Tombs of Atuan* (1971), the sequel to *A Wizard of Earthsea*.

The trauma of losing memory is evident in the experience of Sol Weintraub's daughter, regressing towards infancy in Dan Simmons's **Hyperion**, and of Charley Gordon, as his **intelligence** regresses in Daniel Keyes's *Flowers for Algernon*. Although Charley learns that the recovery of childhood memory can prove equally painful, generally memory recovery is considered a positive experience. Attempts by aliens at **communication** through memories of **love** lead to healing for the **robot** David in a single perfect day with the **clone** of his **mother** in *A.I.: Artificial Intelligence*, and for Kelvin who is able to deal with the **guilt and responsibility** he feels about the **death** of his wife in the 2002 remake of the film *Solaris*. In a fragmented consumer society (see **Postmodernism**), the power of nostalgia for a lost world leads to recovering cultural memories, illustrated by the film *Field of Dreams* in its depiction of an idealized **America**.

Because memory is a temporal process, it can be affected by **time travel**, which sometimes results in **alternate histories** or in **parallel worlds**. In Isaac Asimov's *The End of Eternity* (1955), adjustments to the timeline affect everyone except time travelers; the same is true in Ward Moore's **Bring the Jubilee**. The protagonist of *La Jetée* is haunted by the memory of a childhood event to the point that he is able to return there from his future. The introduction of a sister for *Buffy the Vampire Slayer* necessitates the alteration by magic of the memories of everyone around her.

Memory tampering includes both the implanting of false memories, as in the film *Total Recall*, and the repressing of true ones, as a machine-controlled system represses the inhabitants' true memories of the world and implants the false **illusion** of *The Matrix*. To teach him a lesson about **home** and **friendship**, George Bailey's guardian **angel** leaves him with a memory of his world while transporting him to a world where he never existed in *It's a Wonderful Life*, while Joe's love for Betty survives another angel's interference after his **reincarnation** in *Heaven Can Wait*.

Sometimes memories are altered with the deliberate intent to control, particularly in **dystopias**. The society of Alfred Bester's *The Demolished Man* erases the memories of criminals as a form of rehabilitation (see **Crime and Punishment**), whereas the State uses **technology** to wipe the memory of rebellious citizens in

Yevgeny Zamiatin's *We*. In an attempt to control **knowledge** of **history**, the Party in George Orwell's *Nineteen Eighty-Four* alters documents, while in Ray Bradbury's *Fahrenheit 451*, people memorize works of literature to counteract their society's burning of **books**. Memories of past **freedom** are considered dangerous to future social stability.

Discussion

Writing, of both fiction and fact, is a form of memory, capturing thoughts, feelings, and events for history; it is humanity's attempt to achieve **immortality and longevity**. Fantasy in particular seems concerned with the possibility of redemption, of dealing with the terrible memories of **war** by imparting some sense of meaning or significance. The ability to record and access memories is of particular interest in the fiction of the information age, as computer technology offers the possibility of remembering events completely and accurately at the same time that the postmodern fragmenting of the self calls such memories into question.

Bibliography

Erik Davis. "Techgnosis." *South Atlantic Quarterly*, 92 (Fall, 1993), 585–616.

Tanya Gardiner-Scott. "Memory Emancipated." *Mythlore*, 14 (Winter, 1987), 26–29.

Vincent Geoghegan. "The Utopian Past." *Utopian Studies*, 3 (1992), 75–90.

Brooks Landon. "Not What It Used to Be." George Slusser and Tom Shippey, eds., *Fiction 2000*. Athens: University of Georgia Press, 1992, 153–167.

Alison Landsberg. "Prosthetic Memory." Mike Featherstone and Roger Burrows, eds., *Cyberspace / Cyberbodies / Cyberpunk*. London: Sage Publications, 1995, 175–190.

Peter Malekin. "Remembering the Future." Donald E. Morse, ed., *The Fantastic in World Literature and the Arts*. Westport, CT: Greenwood Press, 1987, 47–57.

Jennifer Stevenson. "Memory and the World of John Crowley." *New York Review of Science Fiction*, No. 119 (July, 1998), 1, 8–11.

Ellen R. Weil. "The Door to Lilith's Cave." *Journal of the Fantastic in the Arts*, 5 (1993), 90–104.

Scott A. Winkler. "Is This Heaven? No, It's Iowa." *Journal of Popular Culture*, 37 (May, 2004), 704–718.

—Christine Mains

MENTORS

Overview

Mentors are usually, but not always, older adults who guide younger **heroes**, occasionally acting as surrogate **fathers** or **mothers**. In addition to imparting philosophical or spiritual advice, mentors also teach particular skills or occupations to **apprentices**, sharing the **wisdom** or **knowledge** developed through long experience.

Survey

The mentor acts as a guide to the hero on a **quest** for knowledge or **identity**, much as the **wizard** Merlin does for **Arthur** and Gandalf for both Bilbo in J.R.R. Tolkien's *The Hobbit* and Frodo in *The Lord of the Rings*. Dumbledore in J.K. Rowling's *Harry Potter and the Sorcerer's Stone* and Master Ogion in Ursula K. Le Guin's *A Wizard of Earthsea* teach younger wizards to control their **talents** (see **Education**), while Halloran guides the development of Danny's **psychic powers** in Stephen King's *The Shining*. The mentor's teachings are not always reserved for a single individual; in Roger Zelazny's *Lord of Light*, Sam seeks to share with everyone the **technology** that allows his peers to impersonate **gods and goddesses**.

The mentor is often like a father, as **mad scientist** Doc Brown is to Marty McFly in *Back to the Future* and Alfred is to *Batman*, although the relationship can also be one of **friendship**, as between *Doctor Who* and his many companions. Mentors are not only male, however. The female heroes of Jean Auel's *The Clan of the Cave Bear*, Marion Zimmer Bradley's *The Mists of Avalon*, L. Frank Baum's *The Wonderful Wizard of Oz*, and *Xena: Warrior Princess* learn from female mentors, and in Philip Pullman's *The Amber Spyglass* (2000), Mary, a **scientist** and former nun, guides the two **children** who become the new **Adam and Eve**. Nor are mentors necessarily human. In *A.I.: Artificial Intelligence*, David is guided by the **robots** Gigolo Joe and Teddy Bear; the Caterpillar and the Cheshire Cat advise Alice in Lewis Carroll's *Alice's Adventures in Wonderland*; and the multilingual Polynesia the Parrot teaches Doctor Dolittle to talk to the animals in Hugh Lofting's *The Story of Doctor Dolittle*. Faber, afraid to take action himself, becomes a helpful voice in Guy's ear in Ray Bradbury's *Fahrenheit 451*, and the software **reincarnation** of Dixie Flatline guides Case through **cyberspace** in William Gibson's *Neuromancer*.

The mentor's role can be partly to ease the passage into a new **community** by teaching the protégé about appropriate customs and behaviors. Lestat introduces Louis to the ways of **vampires** in Anne Rice's *Interview with the Vampire*. Edgar Rice Burroughs's primitive *Tarzan of the Apes* learns about **civilization** from his friend Paul d'Arnot, and Mike, raised on the **alien world** of Mars in Robert A. Heinlein's *Stranger in a Strange Land*, learns about **America** from Jubal Harshaw. The mentor may be more concerned with spiritual guidance, as is Aslan in C.S. Lewis's *The Lion, the Witch and the Wardrobe* and its sequels, and the **angels** in *Heaven Can Wait* and *It's a Wonderful Life*. To prepare their charges for **war**, mentors such as Morpheus in *The Matrix* and Mazer Rackham in Orson Scott Card's *Ender's Game* share their **philosophy** about good and **evil** in addition to conveying necessary physical skills. The **destiny** of Paul Atreides is shaped by the teachings of many different mentors, including his mother, in Frank Herbert's *Dune*, much as Giles and the Watcher's Council attempt to control the destiny of *Buffy the Vampire Slayer* until her **rebellion** against them.

Often, the pupil becomes the teacher to others in an ongoing process of sharing knowledge, as depicted in the Jedi training in the universe of *Star Wars* and in the practices of the Immortals in the world of *Highlander* (1986). Mentorship as a continuing process of **evolution** underlies the concept of **uplift** in David Brin's *Startide Rising*; similarly, the Overlords of Arthur C. Clarke's *Childhood's End* oversee the **rebirth** of **humanity** as it joins the Overmind.

Unfortunately, the mentor relationship does not always function as it should. Mentors do not always act in the best interests of their pupils, as Shevek's mentor demonstrates when he takes credit for Shevek's work in Le Guin's *The Dispossessed*, and in science fiction of the **near future,** the failings of the academic mentoring system can even impede scientific **progress,** as in Gregory Benford's *Timescape*, where a younger scientist is hindered in efforts to properly interpret a message from the future by a senior colleague. The advice of the older generation is not always heeded by **youth**; the new generation in the **post-holocaust society** of George R. Stewart's *Earth Abides* no longer finds knowledge of **history** or reading **books** useful, and the protagonists of Alan Garner's *The Owl Service* only break the cycle of **guilt and responsibility** by ignoring the advice of their elders.

Discussion

Because so many works of science fiction and fantasy focus on the journey towards knowledge and the growth of understanding, characters who provide guidance and wisdom to make that journey easier are important figures. Recognizing that narrative knowledge is as useful as other forms of knowledge, and in a much more interesting form, readers turn to stories to discover more about the physical world around them and the emotional or spiritual world within. Readers of science fiction and fantasy often describe the impact that reading particular books has had upon their lives; in a real sense, authors act as mentors to their readers, sharing knowledge and a way of looking at the world that shapes the kind of people that readers become.

Bibliography

Sarah Beach. "Breaking the Pattern." *Mythlore*, 20 (Winter, 1994), 10–14.

Gwyneth Evans. "Three Modern Views of Merlin." *Mythlore*, 16 (Summer, 1990), 17–22.

David Gooderham. "Fantasizing It as It Is." *Children's Literature*, 31 (2003), 155–175.

Thomas D. Hanks, Jr. "T.H. White's Merlin." Jeanie Watson and Maureen Fries, eds., *The Figure of Merlin in the Nineteenth and Twentieth Centuries*. Lewiston, NY: E. Mellen Press, 1989, 100–120.

John Huntington. "The Unity of *Childhood's End.*" *Science-Fiction Studies*, 1 (Spring, 1974), 154–164.

Sue Misheff. "Beneath the Web and Over the Stream." *Children's Literature in Education*, 29 (September, 1998), 131–142.

Elaine Ostry. "Magical Growth and Moral Lessons." *The Lion and the Unicorn*, 27 (January, 2003), 27–56.

Thelma J. Shinn. "The Wise Witches." Marjorie Pryse and Hortense Spillers, eds., *Conjuring*. Bloomington: Indiana University Press, 1985, 203–215.

Charlotte Spivack, ed. *Merlin versus Faust*. Lewiston: E. Mellen Press, 1992.

—Christine Mains

MERCURY

■

Overview

Mercury, the closest planet to the **Sun**, is difficult to observe from the **Earth** because of its position. Aside from its size and mass, therefore, essentially nothing was known about the planet until the 1960s, and the one "fact" that astronomers were certain of furthermore proved to be wrong. Mercury had been thought to keep the same face toward the Sun as the **Moon** does to the Earth. Even sober textbooks routinely described the hellish Dayside, with its bloated Sun hanging over a landscape hot enough to melt lead, and the frozen Nightside, the coldest place in the solar system. Moreover, due to the high eccentricity of Mercury's orbit, there would be an intermediate region—the "twilight zone"—where the Sun would bob up and down over the horizon during the Mercurian year.

In fact, however, Mercury rotates three times for every two orbits, so all parts of the planet experience sunrise and sunset except possibly for small, permanently shadowed areas near the poles. Although this 3:2 ratio also leads to some bizarre effects, few science fiction stories have taken advantage of the "new" Mercury.

Survey

Early stories about Mercury, when not completely fanciful, inevitably focused on the contrast between the Dayside and the Nightside, with action typically set around the Twilight Zone. Reasonably serious stories included technical **survival** tales such as Isaac Asimov's "Runaround" (1944), in which two astronauts must figure out how to persuade a malfunctioning **robot** to fetch critical material from the Dayside. Asimov's juvenile adventure *Lucky Starr and the Big Sun of Mercury* (1956) is similar. Such stories have been set even on the "new" Mercury: in Grant Callin's "The Tortoise and O'Hare" (1982), for example, an **astronaut** stranded on foot must stay ahead of the advancing dawn to survive.

Asimov's mystery "The Dying Night" (1956) exploited the once-standard picture of Mercury: the culprit was unmasked when, used to the permanent **darkness** around his observatory on the Nightside, he hid unexposed film outside on Earth. Indeed, a Mercury settlement was often a scientific base, as in Arthur C. Clarke's "Out of the Sun" (1958).

Alan E. Nourse's "Brightside Crossing" (1956) describes what might be termed an "endurance stunt": as with mountaineering, an expedition is to cross the Brightside at perihelion for no deeper reason than "because it's there." Such stories seem to have become even more common by the late twentieth century (one example being G. David Nordley's "Crossing Chao Meng Fu" [1997]), perhaps because they provide a convenient justification for why *humans* are attempting such feats. Presumably purely scientific or commercial purposes would be carried out as much as possible with robots or telepresence. The growing popularity of extreme **sports** in wealthy societies may also help rationalize such plots.

Even apart from the fanciful descriptions in early pulp tales, such as Leslie F. Stone's "Hell Planet" (1932) and "The Fall of Mercury" (1935), the desire to find life remains strong. Robert Silverberg's "Sunrise on Mercury" (1957) described a telepathic molten pool, and Poul Anderson's "Life Cycle" (1957) showed aliens that metamorphosed from female to male (see **Metamorphosis**) upon migrating to the Dayside. Larry Niven's "The Coldest Place" (1965) featured a creature based on helium-II on the Nightside. (This is probably the last serious "traditional" Mercury story, too, as between its sale and its publication Mercury had been discovered to rotate after all.) A wish to rationalize life persists, however, as in Stephen Baxter's "Cilia-of-Gold" (1994), which features a geothermally driven ecosystem lying below the ice trapped in a permanently shadowed area near the Mercurian pole.

A number of stories on "modern" Mercury echo a version of the **frontier**, with the protagonists struggling against venal bureaucrats, greedy governments, or clueless corporations (see **Freedom**). In Eric Vinicoff and Marcia Martin's "Render unto Caesar" (1976), a Mercury colony must thwart a United Nations takeover, whereas in Lee Goodloe's "MercuryMine" (1990), the protagonists must solve a problem before the unimaginative home office shuts their project down. Frank Herbert's satirical "Transcript: Mercury Program" (1985) has as its background a heavily exploited Mercury that also supports a largely robotic solar observatory.

In John Varley's "Retrograde Summer" (1974), Mercury mostly serves as the background, although the tale does feature an improbable "quicksilver pool" that seems straight out of the pulp era. The story did describe matter-of-factly the extraordinarily advanced **technology** that would be needed for humans to prosper in such an environment.

In the nineteenth century, slight changes in the orientation of Mercury's orbit were attributed to gravitational perturbations from a hypothetical planet, "Vulcan," inside of Mercury's orbit, which figured in a few stories like Leslie F. Stone's "The Hell Planet" (1932), Ross Rocklynne's "At the Center of Gravity" (1936), and Leigh Brackett's "Child of the Sun" (1941). Despite reported sightings, however, Vulcan now seems certain not to exist, since Einstein's General Theory of Relativity satisfactorily explains the orbital discrepancies.

Discussion

The searing Dayside, the frigid Nightside, and the barely temperate "Twilight Zone" (a phrase that has passed into popular culture) have joined **Venus's jungles** and **Mars's** canals as the mental furniture of a solar system that never existed. Perhaps this is a salutary reminder that reality pays no attention to consensus. In fact, the sheer abundance of tales set in the "consensus solar system" probably helped obscure the extremely tenuous chain of inferences on which it had been based.

Another issue meriting further study is the degree to which even serious tales have attempted to rationalize life in such an improbable setting as Mercury. Perhaps a "dead" universe is simply too unsettling. Alternatively, perhaps living things merely provide an easy way to generate the conflicts needed to drive storytelling.

Bibliography

John W. Campbell, Jr. "Mercury." *Astounding Stories*, 17 (August, 1936), 91–95.
Clark R. Chapman. "Mercury, the Sun's Closest Companion." Byron Preiss, ed., *The Planets*. New York: Bantam, 1985, 248–258.

Andrew Darlington. "I Remember Hell Planet." *The Zone*, No. 2 (1995), 30–33.

Andrew Fraknoi. "Science Fiction Stories with Reasonable Astronomy." *Mercury*, 19 (January/February, 1990), 26–30.

Stephen L. Gillett. "Mercury." *Amazing Stories*, 69 (Winter, 1995), 110–116.

Joe Haldeman. "The Surprising World Called Mercury." Ben Bova with Trudy E. Bell, eds., *Closeup: New Worlds*. New York: St. Martin's Press, 1977, 107–136.

Brian Stableford. "Mercury." Stableford, *The Dictionary of Science Fiction Places*. New York: Wonderland Press, 1999, 198.

Batya Weinbaum. "Space and the Frontier in Leslie F. Stone's 'The Fall of Mercury.'" Gary Westfahl, ed., *Space and Beyond*. Westport, CT: Greenwood Press, 2000, 109–114.

—*Stephen L. Gillett*

MERMAIDS

From the coral grottoes is to be heard a sound, at once the most musical and the most melancholy in the Never Land, the MERMAIDS calling to the moon to rise.

—J.M. Barrie
Peter Pan (1904)

Overview

Mermaids figure in a range of gendered myths that position women as both alluring and fatal. During Europe's Age of Exploration, sailors crossing the world's oceans insisted that they sighted mermaids—beautiful, dangerous, attractive women combing their long hair, sitting on rocks in the sea. Today, scientists prosaically argue that they actually saw sea creatures like dolphins or manatees (see **Fish and Sea Creatures**), but mermaids nevertheless have become fixtures of popular culture, icons of male desire and the fear of woman as alluring but deadly—a kind of foreign, other femme fatale. They appear in hosts of stories, poems, and films.

Survey

Legends of mermaids date back to the Nereids of Greek **mythology**, said to be half-woman and half-fish, so they appeared in a television series based on Greek myths, *Hercules: The Legendary Journeys*. Mermaids are also related to the Greek sirens, who charmed sailors with their songs and lured them to their doom; in Homer's *Odyssey* (c. 750 BCE), Odysseus gets past them by plugging his sailors' ears and listening to their call himself while strapped to the mast. Odysseus encounters another relative of the mermaid, Scylla, a woman turned into a **monster** with six heads and twelve feet. This abomination of dangerous allure appears in various literary texts, including John Milton's *Paradise Lost* (1667). Also relevant are Scottish legends of selkies, seals who turn into women and live with human males until a broken **taboo** forces them back to sea.

Since mermaids are in a sense **shapeshifters**, they have been viewed as exciting, wonderful women, to be rescued into everyday life. Thus, while the mermaid in Hans Christian Andersen's "The Little Mermaid" (1836) was ultimately saddened by life on land, the story was rewritten to provide her with joyful **marriage** and a sense of fulfillment as a legged mortal in the animated adaptation *The Little Mermaid* (1989). Another version of the story with a happy ending is the film *Splash* (1984), which comically explores the difficulties of having a tail instead of legs. Other stories about mermaids brought into human society include H.G. Wells's *The Sea Lady* (1902) and Guy Jones and Constance Jones's *Peabody's Mermaid* (1946), filmed in 1948 as *Mr. Peabody and the Mermaid*.

Two Victorian and Edwardian tales featuring mermaids are J.M. Barrie's *Peter and Wendy* and Charles Kingsley's *The Water Babies*; these **children**'s stories provide social commentary, figuring mermaids as delightful, childlike sea creatures offering alternative modes of living and **freedom** for children oppressed by authoritarian upbringings in middle-class homes (Barrie) or oppressive working conditions in Victorian London (Kingsley).

Other fantastic tales involving mermaids are more abrasive. The vagina dentata myth of the female castratrix informs images of voracious mermaids and sirens, recalling Scylla. Sigmund Freud identifies the terror women cause with their seemingly castrated bodies, more obviously when a scaly fish tail is involved. Terror of castration is transferred to the body of the woman/mermaid/siren herself, demonizing women in image and myth. However, this demonization is explored, revelled in, and exploited by some women writers. Valerie Martin's "Sea Lovers" (1991) delights in body **horror** and dramatization of the terrors of the femme fatale. The tale recognizes that a mermaid would be part fish, part woman, and thus aggressive other, predatory, Scylla's daughter. Beaching herself like a killer whale seeking to lure dolphins and penguins, she awaits the desires of a passing male. When he appears and resolves to accept this gift of a seemingly somnolent, fascinating, sexy woman, she attacks, like a crocodile or shark, grasping and rolling him under the waves. This reinforces male fears of castrating femme fatales, while turning the tables on male fantasies of attracting beautiful women of the sea.

Single- and double-tailed mermaids inspire similar tales, although the little mermaid with her single fishtail seems more virginal than the siren who exhibits herself, holding up two tails. Andersen's mermaid bleeds when her tail is divided into legs and she becomes human. The siren survives in **fairy tales** and legends about female initiation in **love**, sexual activity, and sexual power. Marina Warner's *No Go The Bogeyman* (2000) notes that the double tail suggests the onset of menarche and sexual maturity, with the accompanying threats of Greek myths like Scylla; in pictorial representations of Scylla she has a double tail linking her mythic associations to issues of female **sexuality** and appetite. Warner also recognizes images of Scylla— her multiple limbs, rearing and snatching snakey heads—in popular cultural graphics referencing energy, power, and aspiring **Satanism**, such as heavy metal album covers, bikers' tattoos, pinball, and video games.

Rarely, fantasies also feature mermen, one interesting example being Fredric Brown's "Fish Story" (1961), in which a man accepts transformation into a merman in order to enjoy the ecstacies of mermaid love but sadly learns that his only role is to swim over to the egg and fertilize it. Here, Brown's **knowledge** of the true sexual habits of fish transforms the traditional **sexuality** of mermaids into a subject for wry **humor**.

Discussion

Creatures of myth and men's desires and fears, mermaids have been portrayed as beautiful, alluring, and dangerous femmes fatales. They also represent ways to investigate similarities and interrelations between beasts, mythic creatures, and humans.

Bibliography

Ruth Berman. "Mermaids." Malcolm South, ed., *Mythical and Fabulous Creatures.* Westport, CT: Greenwood Press, 1987, 133–145.

Barbara Creed. *The Monstrous Feminine.* London: Routledge, 1993.

Jack Dann and Gardner R. Dozois, eds. *Mermaids!* New York: Ace Books, 1986.

Bram Dijkstra. *The Idols of Perversity.* York: Oxford University Press, 1986.

Helen King. "Half-Human Creatures." John Cherry, ed., *Mythical Beasts.* London: British Museum Press/Pomegranite Artbooks, 1995, 138–167.

Mike Mayo. "How to Make a Mermaid." *Cinefantastique*, 14 (September, 1984), 92–99.

Marina Warner. *No Go the Bogeyman.* New York: Farrar, Straus, and Giroux, 1999.

Michael J. Wolff. "Mermaid Tales." *Starlog*, No. 149 (December, 1989), 17–20, 36.

—Gina Wisker

MESSIAHS

■

> *Yesterday's monomaniac is tomorrow's messiah.*
>
> —Philip Jose Farmer
> "Riders of the Purple Wage" (1967)

Overview

Messiahs figure in fantasy and science fiction as agents of **apocalyptic** transformation. **Heroic fantasy** often features religious **allegories** in which messianic **heroes** pursue epic **quests** to redeem worlds fallen into **sin** and **decadence** (see **Religion**). Science fiction secularizes this myth, depicting superhuman saviors whose **destinies** are linked to epochal rejuvenation of their societies, planets, or galaxies.

Survey

In the apocalyptic **eschatologies** of **Judaism** and **Christianity**, the messiah is a divine agent whose earthly arrival, presaged by **omens and signs**, brings about the cleansing and renewal of **humanity**. A number of early fantasy authors, such as George

MacDonald and Marie Corelli, adapted this myth into quirky, sentimental **fables** of **reincarnation** and **metamorphosis**: George MacDonald's *Lilith*, for example, reworks the Victorian **Bildungsroman** into an allegory of spiritual regeneration. Many of Oscar Wilde's **fairy tales**, such as "The Happy Prince" (1888), offer more ironic treatments of divine mediators whose blessings are rejected by a cold, unfeeling society.

In the twentieth century, the Cambridge-based Inklings—C.S. Lewis, Charles Williams, and J.R.R. Tolkien—pioneered a strain of Christian fantasy in which messianic deliverance forms the central narrative action. In Lewis's Chronicles of Narnia, begun with *The Lion, the Witch and the Wardrobe*, the Christlike figure Aslan undergoes a heroic **sacrifice** and **rebirth** that revitalizes a moral **community**. Tolkien's *The Lord of the Rings* melds a Christian worldview with Arthurian legend (see **Arthur**), depicting a militant elite of the faithful led by a regal savior, the "true **king**" of Gondor, as they struggle to purge Middle-earth of the corruptions engendered by **demonic** forces though admittedly, the true protagonist Frodo does not appear messianic. The popularity of Tolkien's brand of heroic fantasy has spawned hosts of imitations like Robert Jordan's series the Wheel of Time (see *The Eye of the World*) in which Rand al'Thor, the "Dragon Reborn," struggles to fulfill his prophesied destiny through volume after volume. The most imaginative of Tolkien's successors is Gene Wolfe, whose luxuriant science fantasy *The Book of the New Sun* follows the exploits of Severian, a torturer and reluctant messiah whose complex quest transforms a dying Urth.

Despite its seeming lack of theological commitments, science fiction persistently deploys messiah figures, often depicting them as brave champions battling corrupt societies. This basic plot animates texts as diverse as Victor Rousseau's *The Messiah of the Cylinder* (1917), in which the protagonist leads a revolt against a decadent **utopia**, and *The Terminator* films, which feature a charismatic leader seeking to overthrow a regime of merciless machines. In Robert A. Heinlein's *Sixth Column* (1949), a **rebellion** against tyranny is led by a scientific elite whose liberationist **politics** make cynical use of the ideology of messianic deliverance. The travesty of evangelical faith in this novel presages more ironic treatments of the theme in science fiction texts of the 1950s and 1960s. For instance, Gore Vidal's *Messiah* (1954) offers a stark **satire** of a delusive spiritual leader, a cunning **trickster** whose gospel is **death**, while J.G. Ballard's *The Drowned World* features a half-mad protagonist who champions apocalyptic dissolution (see **Madness**). In Michael Moorcock's "Behold the Man" (1966), Christ Himself is revealed to a modern time traveller as a cretinous imbecile, requiring the visitor to take his place as the historical messiah and martyr, and Harlan Ellison's *Deathbird Stories* is filled with derisive portraits of hubristic saviors (see **Hubris**) and hollow **gods and goddesses**.

Another trend in science fiction involves cloaking messiahs in futuristic guise as superhuman entities. Characters transformed by **mutation** into superior beings capable of ethical leadership figure prominently in Theodore Sturgeon's *More Than Human* and Frank Herbert's *Dune* (see **Ethics**). Heinlein's human raised by Martians in *Stranger in a Strange Land* (see **Mars**) and the **alien on Earth** of the film *The Man Who Fell to Earth* are figures whose Christlike innocence contrasts sharply with the casual corruption of secular humanity. However, Philip K. Dick's delirious *Valis* (1981) and its sequels portray an ambiguous extraterrestrial salvation. **Heroes** with **psychic powers** or **secret identities** who stand apart from and seek to guide humanity became common in science fiction from the 1940s onward, a classic example being A.E. Van Vogt's *Slan* (1946). American popular culture, beginning with *Superman* comic books, has picked up this theme, and it appears in numerous mass-media texts featuring **superheroes**, including the film *The Matrix* and the series *Buffy the Vampire Slayer*.

Discussion

Messiah figures in fantasy and science fiction are significant because they fuse the destinies of individual characters with the fates of **civilizations**. The ability to deploy heroes as symbolic representatives of wide-scale political change is particularly important for genres that are marked by a sharp contrast between good and **evil** and that deal with broad social transformations, whether futuristic or fantastic in form. In fantasy, the tendency is for the hero to serve as a moral savior whose mission is essentially restorative—to recover a lost purity metaphorically corrupted by sin. Tolkien's 1947 essay "On Fairy-Stories" defines fantasy as essentially a redemptive mode, its transfiguring happy endings, where good triumphs over **evil**, conveying an apocalyptic joy. Science fiction treats the theme more flexibly, and often more ironically: while many science fiction messiahs are unproblematic emblems of the cleansing force of moral apocalypse, ushering in worlds redeemed from **slavery** or corruption, a sizeable number of texts display ambivalence, if not outright contempt, toward such ethical exemplars, viewing them as misguided and even dangerous.

Bibliography

Thomas Andrae. "From Menace to Messiah." *Discourse*, 2 (Summer, 1980), 84–111.

Robert Galbreath. "Salvation Knowledge." Gary K. Wolfe, ed., *Science Fiction Dialogues*. Chicago: Academy Chicago, 1982, 115–132.

Colin Gunton. "A Far-Off Gleam of the Bible." Joseph Pearce, ed., *Tolkien: A Celebration*. London: Fount, 1999, 124–140.

Donna Larson. "Machine as Messiah." *Cinema Journal*, 36 (Summer, 1997), 57–75.

R.D. Mullen. "H. G. Wells and Victor Rousseau Emanuel." *Extrapolation*, 8 (May, 1967), 31–63.

Hugh Ruppersburg. "Alien Messiahs in Recent Science Fiction Films." *Journal of Popular Film and Television*, 14 (Winter, 1987), 158–166.

Jay Ruud. "Aslan's Sacrifice and the Doctrine of Atonement in *The Lion, the Witch and the Wardrobe*." *Mythlore*, 27 (Spring, 2001), 15–23.

Susan Stratton. "The Messiah and the Greens." *Extrapolation*, 42 (Winter, 2001), 303–316.

—Rob Latham

METAFICTION AND RECURSIVENESS

Overview

Metafiction and recursiveness refer broadly to fiction about fiction. The terms have been used loosely and often synonymously, varying in application from scholar to scholar and from work to work. "Metafiction" will refer here to fiction that somehow interpenetrates with other fictional worlds. "Recursiveness" will refer to fiction about *writing* fiction. Science fiction and fantasy are prime literary territory for both types of stories, though certain mainstream works also qualify as metafiction or recursive fiction. A related entry is **Writing and Authors.**

Survey

Fantasy fiction began to exhibit metafictional tendencies early in its history. Mark Twain's *A Connecticut Yankee in King Arthur's Court,* based on the literary world of **Arthur,** became a model for similar but inferior stories. Sixty years later, L. Sprague de Camp and Fletcher Pratt's Harold Shea series (first collected as *The Incomplete Enchanter* [1949]) featured a modern hero who finds himself in various fantasy worlds. A school of writers dedicated to H.P. Lovecraft pastiches and homages brought characters from outside Lovecraft's fiction into the Cthulhu mythos (as in Jim Turner's anthology *Cthulhu 2000* [1995]). Among mass media metafictions (such as *Van Helsing* [2004]), some of the most entertaining are the annual "Treehouse of Horror" telecasts, which insert *The Simpsons* into a variety of familiar **horror** and science fiction scenarios. Similarly but more elaborately, *Who Framed Roger Rabbit?* (1988) brought together animated film characters from multiple sources, along with a "real" hardboiled **detective** from another Hollywood tradition.

Science fiction came later to metafiction but embraced the approach enthusiastically. The existence of multiple universes or of revivifying **technologies** (such as **computer** reconstructions of long-extinguished personalities) can be posited to bring together characters from numerous literary sources and legends as well as historical figures. Prominent examples are Philip Jose Farmer's Riverworld series, beginning with *To Your Scattered Bodies Go* (1971), and Robert A. Heinlein's *The Number of the Beast* (1980). **Shared world** novels or anthologies, where writers locate new stories in settings already created and described in a book, film, or television series, like **Star Trek, Star Wars,** and **Doctor Who** novels, may serve as crutches for lazy readers and writers. But shared worlds can be exploited in ingenious ways, complementary to the original author's work, as in K.W. Jeter's *Blade Runner 2: The Edge of Human* (1995), which extends and interweaves elements of the **Blade Runner** film with others from the film's source, Philip K. Dick's **Do Androids Dream of Electric Sheep?** The animated series **Futurama** may be said to have used the entire corpus of popular twentieth-century science fiction as a shared world throughout its four-year run.

Recursive fantasy fiction—that is, a fantasy about writing fantasy—is scarce. Luigi Pirandello's play *Six Characters in Search of an Author* (1921) offered a non-genre model. An early genre example, perhaps inspired by Pirandello, was L. Ron Hubbard's "Typewriter in the Sky" (1940). A more complex extra-genre model was Flann O'Brien's *At Swim-Two-Birds* (1939), in which a young writer struggles to create the Great Irish Epic while his efforts are insistently disrupted by his own characters and creatures from Irish **mythology.** Using a different recursive strategy, Geoff Ryman's *Was* (1992) depicts an **alternate history** in which L. Frank Baum is inspired by a "real" and sexually abused Dorothy to create a compensatory *The Wonderful Wizard of Oz.*

In the first prominent example of recursive science fiction, Fredric Brown's *What Mad Universe* (1946), a science fiction magazine editor gets trapped in a pulp universe based on the imagination of one of his magazine's most devoted fans. Another example also involves a magazine editor and a writer: Paul Di Filippo's "Campbell's World" (1993) imagines how *Astounding Science Fiction* would have changed the world had it been edited by the Jungian mythicist Joseph Campbell, not the scientifically-trained John W. Campbell, Jr. Other works incorporate prominent science fiction writers into stories large and small. Mary Shelley becomes a part of her own ***Frankenstein*** story, both in the film *Bride of Frankenstein* (1935) and Brian W. Aldiss's novel *Frankenstein Unbound* (1973). Philip K. Dick is a central character in Michael Bishop's *The Secret Ascension* (1987). Cordwainer Smith, under another pseudonym, plays a role in unraveling a vast historical conspiracy in Howard V. Hendrix's *The Labyrinth Key* (2004). Anticipating Saddam Hussein's literary efforts, an alternate-world Adolf Hitler pursues a career as a passionate but untalented pulp science fiction writer in Norman Spinrad's *The Iron Dream* (1972).

Recursive science fiction has become popular enough to have an anthology devoted to it, Mike Resnick's *Inside the Funhouse* (1992); two single-author collections by the most prolific science fiction recursivists, Barry N. Malzberg's *The Passage of the Light* (1994) and Paul Di Filippo's *Lost Pages* (1998); and a lengthy bibliography of the field, Anthony R. Lewis's *An Annotated Bibliography of Recursive Science Fiction* (1990).

Discussion

Science fiction and fantasy writers often employ metafiction and recursive fiction as a playful tribute to favorite works or writers. But recursive science fiction may also be a means of dealing with marginalized writers' self-esteem issues, either by asserting the unacknowledged importance of science fiction writers to the continued existence of the world, **humanity**, or the universe, or by distancing writers from silly fans, the silly ghettoization of science fiction, or the silly human race. Alternatively, recursiveness may represent a simple case of "Write what you know."

Bibliography

Marleen S. Barr. "Feminist Fabulation." *Women's Studies*, 14 (1987), 187–192.

Bernd Engler and Kurt Muller, eds. *Historiographic Metafiction in Modern American and Canadian Literature*. Paderborn, Germany: Ferdinand Schöningh, 1994.

N.B. Hayles. "Metaphysics and Metafiction in *The Man in the High Castle*." Martin H. Greenberg, ed., *Philip K. Dick*. New York: Taplinger, 1982, 53–71.

Anthony R. Lewis, *An Annotated Bibliography of Recursive Science Fiction*. Boston: NESFA Press, 1990.

Stephen Prickett. "Fictions and Metafictions." William Raeper, ed., *The Gold Thread*. Edinburgh: Edinburgh University Press, 1990, 109–125.

Mike Resnick, ed., *Inside the Funhouse*. New York: Avon, 1992.

Robert Scholes. *Fabulation and Metafiction*. Urbana: University of Illinois Press, 1979.

Takayuki Tatsumi. "Comparative Metafiction." *Critique*, 39 (Fall, 1997), 2–17.

Peter Wright. "Grasping the God-Games." *Foundation*, No. 66 (Spring, 1996), 39–58.

—Alan C. Elms

METAMORPHOSIS

■

Overview

Derived from the Greek, the word "metamorphosis" means a changing of shape or substance. The most common metamorphoses are physical, human-to-animal changes; however, any physical, mental or emotional transformation can be included. Regardless of physical manifestations, the metamorphosis usually represents the individual's inner or "true" nature. Beings who regularly engage in metamorphosis—shapeshifters, vampires, and werewolves—have separate entries.

Survey

Metamorphoses have been prominent in literature since 800 BCE in Greek and Roman **mythology**. Transformations occurred when Greek or Roman **gods and goddesses** became impassioned and acted either angrily, vengefully, lovingly, or whimsically (see **Love; Revenge**). Sometimes a means of punishment, sometimes a reward, transformations include humans turning into animals, **plants**, or inanimate objects, and vice versa. Two early texts describing metamorphoses are Ovid's *Metamorphoses* (8 CE), relating mythological tales of transformation, and Apuleius's *The Golden Ass* (c. 158 CE), describing a man changed into a donkey.

Common in folk and **fairy tales**, metamorphoses are firmly rooted in **magic**. To "become animal" is a **curse** or punishment; restoration to human form must be warranted and awarded. Although some characters are cursed at **birth**, as in the Brothers Grimm's "Hans My Hedgehog" (1812) and Giovan Francesco Straparola's "The Pig Prince" (1553), others are cursed later in life, like the title characters in Jeanne-Marie Leprince de Beaumont's "Beauty and the Beast" (1756) (see **Beauty and the Beast**) and the Grimms's "The Frog King, or Iron Henry" (1812) and "The Six Swans" (1812).

The Victorian era heralded new uses for metamorphoses. **Children**'s literature like Charles Kingsley's *The Water Babies* and Lewis Carroll's *Alice's Adventures in Wonderland* employ physical transformations to comment on characters' mental states of being as well as the authors' ideologies. Kingsley's Tom undergoes "cleansing" transformations that teach him how to behave and think as would befit a "proper" Victorian gentleman. On Kingsley's **island** of "Readymade," men are transformed into **ape**-like creatures because of stupidity and laziness; on "the island of the Golden Asses," referencing Apuleius's tale, men have been turned into donkeys for meddling in the affairs of others. Kingsley creates human-to-animal metamorphoses to punish unacceptable human behavior (see **Animals and Zoos**).

Carroll's metamorphoses, on the other hand, enable a mockery and outright defiance of Victorian practices, while simultaneously privileging animal over human. Carroll's Alice experiences a series of alterations in size (see **Enlargement; Miniaturization**) as her behavior becomes more "adult" than the adults she should respect as her elders. Other Carroll characters, like the Duchess's **baby** and Uggug in Carroll's *Sylvie and Bruno Concluded* (1893), experience a permanent metamorphosis into a pig and porcupine, respectively, both transformations representing the inner nature of human male children (of whom Carroll was not fond).

Classic works such as Robert Louis Stevenson's *Strange Case of Dr. Jekyll and Mr. Hyde*, H.G. Wells's *The Island of Doctor Moreau*, and Franz Kafka's *The Metamorphosis* (1915) also reflect the inseparability of mind and body; outer, physical, transformations reflect characters' "true" self. Stevenson's Henry Jekyll and Kafka's Gregor Samsa experience the eclipse of their **humanity** by their bestial nature and in Samsa's case, the treatment he has received at the hands of an impersonal, uncaring society. Moreau's attempts to surgically transform animals into humans fail when animals rebel and revert to their original natures (see **Uplift**).

The film *Werewolf of London* (1935) began the trend of were-animal films that peaked in the 1980s with *An American Werewolf in London* (1981) and the 1982 remake of *Cat People* (1942). For were-animals, the metamorphosis may be voluntary, as with shapeshifters, or involuntary, as with transformations caused by lunar **cycles**; changes can be inherent or caused by an interaction (often a bite) by another were-animal. A science fiction series, K.A. Applegate's Animorphs series, beginning with *The Invasion* (1996), involves a group of young teens given the ability to "morph" into animal form to save the human race from a great **evil**, "The Controllers."

Although the term metamorphosis is commonly applied to human-to-animal alterations, especially in fantasy, technological innovations of the late twentieth and early twenty-first centuries necessitate consideration of human-to-machine or animal-to-machine metamorphoses that appear in science fiction. The altering of a human into a technological hybrid, or **cyborg**, has been part of American pop culture since the television series *The Six Million Dollar Man* (1974–1978) in which Steve Austin, a crippled test pilot, is rebuilt with bionic parts. Although the show ran for four years, **cyborgs** gained fame when *Star Trek: The Next Generation* aired the episode "Q, Who?" (1989) featuring the Borg—half-human, half-machine beings working as a **hive mind**.

Discussion

In a society in which human supremacy is an accepted norm, metamorphosis is important because it subverts and questions people's "humanity." Whether a person is replaced by the "other" or the transformation entails liberation of an inherent but repressed inner self, metamorphosis enables humans to cross taxonomic boundaries and interrogate issues of human nature, evolutionary hierarchy, and technological possibility.

Bibliography

Caroline Walker Bynum. *Metamorphosis and Identity*. New York: Zone Books, 2001.
Gilles Deleuze and Felix Guattari. "1730: Becoming-Intense, Becoming-Animal, Becoming Imperceptible . . . ." Deleuze and Guattari, *A Thousand Plateaus*, trans. Brian Massumi. Minneapolis: University of Minnesota Press, 1987, 232–309.
Nancy Gray Diaz. *The Radical Self*. Columbia: University of Missouri Press, 1988.
Donna Haraway. "A Cyborg Manifesto." 1985. Haraway, *Simians, Cyborgs, and Women*. New York: Routledge, 1991, 149–181.
W.R. Irwin. "Metamorphosis." Irwin, *The Game of the Impossible*. Urbana: University of Illinois Press, 1976.
Rosemary Jackson. *Fantasy*. London: Routledge, 1981.

Irving Massey. *The Gaping Pig*. Berkeley: University of California Press, 1976.

Harold Skulsky. *Metamorphosis*. Cambridge: Harvard University Press, 1981.

Marina Warner. *Fantastic Metamorphoses, Other Worlds.* Oxford: Oxford University Press, 2002.

—*Cat Yampell*

MICE

See Rats and Mice

MICROCOSM

We were privileged to witness the birth of a universe, now we must, perforce, witness its death.

—Donald A. Wollheim
Edge of Time (1958)

Overview

The term "microcosm" applies to science fiction and fantasy in two ways. First, as in other forms of literature, writers can present groups of people in isolated places as allegorical representations of the societies of their origin (see **Allegory**); typical settings include **islands** or boats (see **Sea Travel**), as in Sebastian Brant's *Ship of Fools* (1494), the work that set the pattern for later stories. Second, writers can envision, employing a magical or scientific rationale, literally miniaturized worlds, or even miniaturized universes, existing within our world (see **Magic; Miniaturization**).

Survey

Many stories about small and isolated communities might be regarded as microcosms. Robinsonades about people stranded on remote islands, like J.M. Barrie's *The Admirable Crichton* (1902) and William Golding's *Lord of the Flies,* function as commentaries on contemporary society. **Utopias** in remote or hidden places—the island of Thomas More's *Utopia*, the Himalayan **mountain** valley of James Hilton's *Lost Horizon*, the unknown South American region of Charlotte Perkins Gilman's *Herland*—provide small working models of superior **governance systems** applicable to larger **civilizations**. Some **fables** are explicitly miniature versions of larger realms, as George Orwell's ***Animal Farm*** provides a capsule **history** of the Soviet Union. **Lost worlds** in unexplored areas—like those encountered in **Africa** by H. Rider

Haggard's **heroes** (see *She*) and Edgar Rice Burroughs's Tarzan (see *Tarzan of the Apes*)—are typically remnants of once-mighty empires, which embody and represent both ancient **wisdom** and **decadence**.

There are many fantastic variations on such settings. In fantasy, examples include the **flying** city of Laputa in *Gulliver's Travels*, filled with eccentric **scientists** who convey Jonathan Swift's acerbic commentary on the scientific community; the legendary **city** of Brigadoon, a nostalgic image of the simpler lifestyle in eighteenth-century Scotland, which appears only once every hundred years, seen in the 1947 Broadway musical and 1954 film of that name; and the fair in a sidewalk chalk drawing magically visited by Mary Poppins and the Banks children in *Mary Poppins* (1964) (see P.L. Travers's *Mary Poppins*). In science fiction, Fredric Brown's "Arena" (1944) reduces a **space war** to single combat between a human and alien on an **alien world**. Brown's hero kills his opponent, but when the story was adapted as the *Star Trek* episode "Arena" (1967), Kirk refuses to kill the alien, making the story a statement about the need for different races and **cultures** to live in harmony. The point is also made in another story about a human and alien stranded on an uninhabited planet, Barry B. Longyear's "Enemy Mine" (1979), filmed in 1985. **Space stations** may serve as microcosms of larger space communities of humans and various alien races, as in the television series *Star Trek: Deep Space Nine* and *Babylon 5*, and a **generation starship** includes representatives of various **Earth cultures** in the series *The Starlost* (1973). Remnants of vanished Earth civilizations may be surprisingly found on **alien worlds**, like the **Native American** tribe Kirk joins in the *Star Trek* episode "The Paradise Syndrome" (1968) and the ancient Egyptian society visited by **teleportation** in *Stargate* (see **Egypt**).

As for literally miniature worlds, one early instance is Lilliput, the remote realm of tiny people in *Gulliver's Travels*, but fantasy more typically locates such societies in unexplored corners of everyday existence: examples include Mary Norton's *The Borrowers* (1952) and its sequels, envisioning tiny humans secretly living in the nooks and crannies of people's houses; Margery Sharp's *The Rescuers* (1959) and its sequels, depicting a society of intelligent mice covertly operating underneath human civilization; and Terry Pratchett's *The Carpet People* (1971), describing a tiny society within a carpet. Straddling the border between science fiction and fantasy are Burroughs's Minuni, an African realm of inhabitants only eighteen inches tall in *Tarzan and the Ant Men* (1924), and his Martian moon Phobos, where all visitors shrink to interact with a world of miniature beings, in *Swords of Mars* (1936) (see *A Princess of Mars;* **Mars**).

In science fiction, visions of miniature human civilizations date back to at least 1858, when Fitz-James O'Brien's "The Diamond Lens" described the tragic plight of a scientist who falls in love with a tiny woman he sees through a microscope. In the early twentieth century, Ernest Rutherford's early atomic model briefly sanctioned the notion that atoms might be miniature solar systems, leading to many stories like Ray Cummings's *The Girl in the Golden Atom* (1921) involving **heroes** who shrink to adventure on microscopic worlds. There are intimations at the conclusion of *The Incredible Shrinking Man* that its ever-diminishing hero might someday encounter other microscopic beings. There were also stories about scientists creating their own tiny worlds, like Jack Williamson's "Pygmy Planet" (1932) and Theodore Sturgeon's "Microcosmic God" (1941); later, entire micro-universes were created in Donald A. Wollheim's *Edge of Time* (1958) and Gregory Benford's *Cosm* (1998).

Discussion

Figuratively miniature worlds appeal to writers who can employ them to make a point without the bothersome complexities of describing vast civilizations. Literally miniature worlds appeal to **children,** who understandably relate to stories about little people carrying on without being noticed or bothered by big people, though writers like Swift and Sturgeon demonstrate that this is not exclusively a theme for children. Finally, since the very process of writing a story or making a film represents an effort to reduce a huge world to a manageable size, stories about creating tiny worlds might be regarded as metaphors for acts of artistic creation, which is one of many ideas explored in John Crowley's *Little, Big.*

Bibliography

Max P. Belin. "Infinity in Your Back Pocket." George Slusser and Eric S. Rabkin, eds., *Mindscapes*. Carbondale: Southern Illinois University Press, 1989, 234–241.

Gregory Benford, ed. *Microcosms*. New York: DAW Books, 2004.

James Blish. "Theodore Sturgeon's Macrocosm." *Magazine of Fantasy and Science Fiction*, 23 (September, 1962), 42–45.

Clark A. Brady. "Minuni" and "Thuria." Brady, *The Burroughs Cyclopedia*. Jefferson, NC: McFarland, 1996, 219, 336.

Thomas A. Bredehoft. "Cosms and Lacks." *New York Review of Science Fiction*, No. 121 (September, 1998), 9–10.

L.L. Dickson. *The Modern Allegories of William Golding*. Tampa: University of South Florida Press, 1990.

Robert Solomon. "Ant Farm." Robert Mulvihill, ed., *Reflections on America, 1984*. Athens: University of Georgia Press, 1986.

Gary Westfahl. "Small Worlds and Strange Tomorrows." *Foundation*, No. 51 (Spring, 1991), 38–63.

—Gary Westfahl

MIDDLE AGES

See Medievalism and the Middle Ages

MINIATURIZATION

Overview

Miniaturization is the shrinking of a human, animal, or object with the aid of **magic** or advanced **technology.** Such shrinking sometimes occurs as the consequences of **curses** or other misfortune, but it is often intentionally done so that characters can go on **quests** in smaller worlds (see **Microcosm**).

Survey

Miniaturization in speculative fiction has its roots in **mythology** and **fairy tales**, which often involve shrinking characters so they may live in fairy-sized worlds. Many myths involve humans encountering **giants** and enormous **monsters**. The natural extension of this idea is a situation in which people and objects in the ordinary world become huge and fantastic.

Thus, miniaturization became a common theme early in the evolution of speculative fiction. The Lilliputians of Jonathan Swift's *Gulliver's Travels* have inspired later versions of miniaturized characters. In Lewis Carroll's *Alice's Adventures in Wonderland*, protagonist Alice shrinks to less than a foot in height after drinking a bottle labeled "Drink Me." Edgar Rice Burroughs's Tarzan series (see *Tarzan of the Apes*) features instances of miniaturization: in *Tarzan and the Ant Men* (1923), Tarzan enounters a race of miniaturized people and later is himself shrunk by a **scientist** named Zoanthrohago.

Science fiction has also been fascinated by the idea of worlds with extremely tiny people. Writers shrink **heroes** to visit miniature civilizations in works like Ray Cummings's *The Girl in the Golden Atom* (1920) and R.F. Starzl's "Out of the Sub-Universe" (1928). In Francis Rufus Bellamy's *Atta* (1953), a man shrunk by lightning befriends an ant. Miniaturization also has caught the fancy of science fiction filmmakers throughout the twentieth century. The **evil** Doctor Thorkel shrinks unwilling victims in the 1940 **horror** movie *Dr. Cyclops*, a scenario repeated in the film *Attack of the Puppet People* (1957). The film **The Incredible Shrinking Man** centers on a protagonist who begins shrinking—and must struggle to survive in an increasingly hostile, gigantic world—after being exposed to a strange mist. It was so popular that it spawned other films involving tiny people interacting with giant people and objects, including *Tom Thumb* (1958), based on the classic fairy tale, and the television series *World of Giants* (1960) and *Land of the Giants* (1968–1970).

During this same period, comic book writers took up the theme of heroes who could shrink, including DC Comics' second version of the Atom, who appeared in 1961, and Marvel Comics' Ant-Man. The progenitor of these heroes, though, was Quality Comics' Doll Man and Doll Girl, who premiered in the 1940s.

The 1966 movie *Fantastic Voyage* involves a team of five scientists and a submarine being shrunk to microscopic size and injected into a professor's bloodstream so they can destroy a **blood** clot threatening his life. Though its story had been anticipated by Joseph W. Skidmore's "A World Unseen" (1936), *Fantastic Voyage* inspired more tales of adventurers being shrunk and placed in the human body, including Isaac Asimov's reworking of his 1966 film novelization, *Fantastic Voyage II: Destination Brain* (1987), the film *InnerSpace* (1987), and various episodes of the series *Futurama*. The "shrinking ray" has become a well-established bit of science fictional paraphernalia and has been employed to miniaturize characters in films like *Honey, I Shrunk the Kids* (1989) and its sequels and the series *Dexter's Laboratory* (1996–2005).

In the latter part of the twentieth century, when science-fictional presentations of miniaturization were regressing into laughable gimmicks in movies and television, the theme took on new life as writers began to explore nanotechnology, the process of making molecule-sized machines. No longer were people shrunk and injected into bloodstreams; tiny **robots** (called nanites or nanobots) were used instead and quickly became a staple of science fiction. Nanotechnology, treated seriously as plausible future technology, has been especially influenced by Japanese culture, which particularly loves miniaturized objects and technology due to the space constraints of the **island** nation (see **Japan**).

Discussion

Miniaturized characters appeal to writers and readers on a variety of levels. An ant is beneath the notice of normal-sized humans, but to miniaturized characters it becomes a monster. The ordinary becomes exotic. Shrinking literally represents a character's loss of power, control, and status, and a fear of the world's hugeness; in many works, it also can become a metaphor for how ordinary people feel overwhelmed by their fast-changing world. In science fiction, miniaturization has been used to explore worlds and environments previously only imagined through a microscope lens. The intersection of artificial **intelligence** with nanotechnology means that different kinds of miniaturized characters will remain on the scene in science fiction.

Bibliography

Leroy W. Dubeck. *Fantastic Voyages*. New York: American Institute of Physics, 1994.
Steven B. Harris. "*A. I.* and the Return of the Krell Machine." *Skeptic*, 9 (2002), 68–79.
Cyndy Hendershot. "Darwin and the Atom." *Science Fiction Studies*, 25 (July, 1998), 319–335.
Ron Magid. "*Innerspace*: A Microscopic Adventure." *American Cinematographer*, 68 (August, 1987), 54–63.
Wil McCarthy. "Nanotechnology." *SFWA Bulletin*, 35 (Fall, 2001), 20–23.
Colin Milburn. "Nanotechnology in the Age of Posthuman Engineering." *Configurations*, 10 (2002), 261–295.
W.M.S. Russell. "They Who Shrank." *Foundation*, No. 82 (Summer, 2001), 74–83.
David Zinman. "*The Incredible Shrinking Man*." Zinman, *50 From the 50s*. New Rochelle, NY: Arlington House, 1979, 133–140.

—Lucy A. Snyder

MIRRORS

∎

> *There comes a time when you look into the mirror and realize that what you see is all that you will ever be. Then you accept it, or you kill yourself. Or you stop looking into mirrors.*

> —J. Michael Straczynski
> "Chrysalis," episode of *Babylon 5* (1994)

Overview

Mirrors and other reflecting surfaces, literary symbols of truth and insight, are transformed by science fiction and fantasy into objects that facilitate observation across distances, serve as a means of **communication** through space and **time**, and open portals into other worlds similar to but often different from our own.

Survey

In **fairy tales** and folklore, mirrors are **magical objects** associated with many super-stitions. As the **Moon** reflects the **light** of the **Sun, magic** mirrors reflect not only the surface appearance but also the inner soul of the person looking into them. For that reason, **vampires** cannot cast a reflection, a tradition followed in Bram Stoker's *Dracula* and in *Buffy the Vampire Slayer*, but discarded in Anne Rice's *Interview with the Vampire*. Mirrors reveal not only a character's **identity** but also their desires, as the Mirror of Erised shows Harry his dead parents in J.K. Rowling's *Harry Potter and the Sorcerer's Stone*. Harry's **mentor** Dumbledore warns him that such reflections can be **illusions**. Reflections can be distorted, as in **carnival** or fun-house mirrors; in Hans Christian Andersen's "The Snow Queen" (1845), a magi-cian's distorting mirror shatters, corrupting human souls. When two mirrors face each other, their reflections seem to continue into infinity, an image used to great effect in Father Inire's specula and mirror-leaved **book** in Gene Wolfe's *The Book of the New Sun*.

Witches and **wizards** use magic mirrors to observe others from a distance, as does the Queen to spy on Snow White in *Snow White and the Seven Dwarfs*. Mirrors play similar roles in several Patricia McKillip novels. *The Tower at Stony Wood* (2000) re-imagines Alfred Lord Tennyson's "Lady of Shalott" (1842), who is **cursed** to watch the reflection of the world rather than participate in it (see **Free-dom**), while the **villains** in *Ombria in Shadow* (2002) and *In the Forests of Serre* (2003) use mirrors to exert power over their domains. In science fiction, mirrors can be technological rather than magical means of communication, as in Andre Norton's *Merlin's Mirror* (1975), where the mirror is an alien device used in Merlin's **education**.

Images in the mirror communicate possible futures, often influencing **heroes** on **quests**. In J.R.R. Tolkien's *The Lord of the Rings*, Frodo and Sam look into the Mirror of Galadriel, a basin filled with **water**, but are cautioned against using its images as a guide. When characters base their actions on **divination**, they often find they cannot avoid **destiny**. In Delia Sherman's *Through a Brazen Mirror* (1989), a sorceress makes a futile attempt to avoid the image of her own **death**.

Mirrors also serve as portals to other worlds. A closeted mirror leads to a world in which outward appearance reflects inner personality in George MacDonald's **allegory** *Lilith*, while in Lewis Carroll's *Through the Looking Glass* (1871), the sequel to *Alice's Adventures in Wonderland*, Alice steps through a mirror and crosses a **threshold** into a **dream** world where natural laws seem reversed. In MacDonald's *Phantastes* (1858), the mirror reflects Cosmo's room but not Cosmo; instead, he sees a woman trapped in the reflected room until he breaks the mirror and with it the spell. Crossing between worlds is one use of mirror magic in Stephen R. Donaldson's *The Mirror of Her Dreams* (1986).

In science fiction, a **parallel world** sometimes lies on the other side of the mir-ror, accessed in *Stargate: SG1* (1997–) (see *Stargate*) by touching a quantum mirror that reflects the room of the destination reality rather than of the origin. In "There But for the Grace of God" (1998), Daniel Jackson finds himself in a version of Stargate Command about to be destroyed, but is able to return with the **knowledge** to avoid that fate; "Point of View" (1999) sees an alternate version of Samantha Carter come through the mirror from an already overrun **Earth**. Sometimes an actual mirror is not necessary to access the parallel world; superior **technology** can serve a similar function. In an episode of *Star Trek*, "Mirror, Mirror" (1967), an ion storm occurring in both realities interferes with a simultaneous transport process. Just as writing is reversed in a mirror, the mirror universe of *Star Trek* reveals reversed values and personalities (see **Role Reversals**); the Federation is an **evil** empire bent on domination through terror, and Kirk's **doppelganger** rises in rank through assassination. *Star Trek: Deep Space Nine* not only maintained this reversal of values in several episodes dealing with the mirror universe, but also used the mirror conceit to explore issues of death and **rebirth** by resurrecting Sisko's dead wife. A common theme in stories about mirror worlds is the need to maintain balance and harmony, perhaps influenced by theories about matter and **antimatter**.

Discussion

Mirrors appear in different forms—magical, technological and metaphorical—because they concretize the metaphor that **art** holds a mirror up to reality. The imagined worlds of science fiction and fantasy are reflections of readers' real worlds, both imitating and distorting their surfaces while revealing what is concealed outside the frame and within the human psyche.

Bibliography

A.S. Byatt. "Ice, Snow, Glass." Kate Bernheimer, ed., *Mirror, Mirror on the Wall.* New York: Anchor, 1998, 64–84.

Beverly Clark. *Reflections of Fantasy.* New York: Lang, 1986.

Cath Filmer-Davies. *The Fiction of C.S. Lewis.* New York: St. Martin's, 1992.

Laurel L. Hendrix. "A World of Glass." Joe Sanders, ed., *Functions of the Fantastic.* Westport, CT: Greenwood Press, 1995, 91–100.

John Pennington. "From Elfland to Hogwarts, or the Aesthetic Trouble with Harry Potter." *The Lion and the Unicorn*, 26 (January, 2002), 78–97.

George Slusser. "Death and the Mirror." George Slusser, Eric S. Rabkin, and Robert Scholes, eds., *Coordinates.* Carbondale: Southern Illinois University Press, 1983, 150–176.

John Allen Stevenson. "A Vampire in the Mirror." *PMLA*, 103 (1988), 139–149.

Carl B. Yoke. "Magic and Mirrors." *Journal of the Fantastic in the Arts*, 9 (1998), 34.

Jane Yolen. "Magic Mirrors." *Children's Literature Association Quarterly*, 11 (Summer, 1986), 88–89.

—Christine Mains

MONEY

Things *were not money, any more than water shared was growing-closer. Money was an* idea, *as abstract as an Old One's thoughts—money was a great*

*structured symbol for balancing and
healing and growing closer.*
      *Mike was dazzled with the magnifi-
cent beauty of money.*

—Robert A. Heinlein
Stranger in a Strange Land (1961)

Overview

Ever since coins were introduced to obviate barter and facilitate **trade**, money and acquisition of wealth, through **theft, treasure** hunts (see **Gold and Silver**), trade, and **business**, have been central human concerns. In fantasy and science fiction, new and old monetary systems are examined, their weaknesses laid bare, and alternatives suggested.

Survey

One major challenge to currencies is the threat of forgery. Hence matter-replicating **technology**, which creates exact copies of objects and materials, is a potential problem. Although such technology could decrease the need for trade, it requires some non-replicable material to be used as a medium of exchange, like the gold-pressed latinum used by the Ferengi in *Star Trek: Deep Space Nine*. George O. Smith suggests a similar solution in "Pandora's Millions" (1945), introducing a substance that explodes when scanned for replication. This can be used for currency and also thwarts forgery of legal documents. Even barring full replication, advanced technology facilitates forgery. In Jack Vance's *The Killing Machine* (1964), the currency's integrity is maintained by checking money for a secret property. After discovering this property, the protagonist gains access to unlimited funds simply by making the money himself.

In fantasy, **magic** may copy or create money and is thus subjected to restrictions ranging from the plausible to the absurd. Only a feeling of civic responsibility seems to stop **wizards** from conjuring up as much money as they want. In some stories, the cost is disproportionately high, as in Ursula K. Le Guin's Earthsea (see *A Wizard of Earthsea*), where changing the essence of something (or creating something from nothing) disturbs the Equilibrium of the world. In others, money created by magic only lasts a limited time. J.K. Rowling's *Harry Potter and the Goblet of Fire* (2000) (see *Harry Potter and the Sorcerer's Stone*) foregrounds the moral implications of using such money inadvisably; and in Edith Nesbit's *Five Children and It* (1902), the morals are that unearned riches result in suspicion and accusations, and one cannot eat money.

Although occasional fantasy **heroes** are well off (like Frodo Baggins and Harry Potter), fantasy tends to feature poor protagonists, and affluence and greed come with severe drawbacks. In Megan Lindholm's *Wizard of the Pigeons* (1986), a homeless wizard is prohibited by his magic from carrying more than one dollar's worth of change, allowing him to display both ingenuity and vulnerability. The traditional motif of a cursed object that fulfills the owner's wishes but promises damnation unless it is sold for less than its purchase price figures in Robert Louis Stevenson's "The Bottle Imp" (1896).

Science fiction writers also warn that wealth, along with power, corrupts. Deprived of his privileged life, the advertising executive in Frederik Pohl and C.M. Kornbluth's *The Space Merchants* finally sees the errors of his, and society's, ways and abandons his corrupt lifestyle. When **aliens on Earth** with vast amounts of cash arrive in Clifford D. Simak's *They Walked Like Men* (1962), they realize that everything is for sale if the price is right and thus begin to buy the **Earth**. Like fairy money, their cash disappears, leaving banks with a cash deficit and the economy in confusion (see **Economics**). Pohl turns poverty and affluence around in "The Midas Plague" (1954), where wealth is tantamount to **freedom** from consumption.

Whereas many writers envision a future of electronically managed credits, others describe alternative monetary systems and standards. In Iain M. Banks's *Consider Phlebas*, a banker species offers the only universally acceptable currency. Each coin can be converted into any stable element, area of land, or **computer**, so the currency offers guaranteed conversion into something with intrinsic value. Steel rather than precious metals is the currency in the fantasy game world Krynn and other intrinsically valuable substances are used in place of currency in Frank Herbert's *Dune* books and Piers Anthony's Apprentice Adept series beginning with *Split Infinity* (1980).

In *The Hitchhiker's Guide to the Galaxy*, Douglas Adams pokes fun at the idea of currencies on a galactic scale, also observing that a penny deposited in a bank account and left there until the end of the universe will grow enormously owing to compound interest. This is a common theme in science fiction: awakening after centuries of **sleep**, the protagonist of H.G. Wells's *When the Sleeper Wakes* (1899) finds himself owner of the world. Conversely, Pohl's *The Age of the Pussyfoot* (1968) introduces the problem with inflation: his sleeping protagonist wakes up to find the value of his fortune reduced to almost nothing.

Discussion

Money might not be the root of all **evil**, but fantasy and science fiction often portray it as such. Also, despite some interesting treatments of money, the genres generally pay little attention to how monetary systems work. In *Star Trek*, the Federation no longer uses money, but no amount of replication explains how payment for labor and allocation of resources are carried out. In J.R.R. Tolkien's *The Lord of the Rings*, no government guarantees the hobbits' silver pennies, and Bilbo's spending part of Smaug's hoard (see *The Hobbit*) in the Shire apparently fails to cause inflation. In general, monetary systems are taken for granted, and though money is something to be short of, steal, and pay with, little attention is given to what makes it work.

Bibliography

Anna Kornbluh. "For the Love of Money." *Historical Materialism: Research in Critical Marxist Theory*, 10 (2002), 155–172.

Kevin McLaughlin. "The Financial Imp." *Novel*, 29 (Winter, 1996), 165–183.

Leonard Mustazza. "Divine Folly and the Miracle of Money in *God Bless You, Mr. Rosewater*." Harold Bloom, ed.. *Kurt Vonnegut*. Philadelphia: Chelsea House, 2000. 49–62.

Diane Purkiss. "Desire of Gold and the Good Neighbours." Purkiss, *At the Bottom of the Garden.* New York: New York University Press, 2000, 117–157.

Robert A. Smart. "Blood and Money in Bram Stoker's *Dracula*." John Louis DiGaetani, ed., *Money.* Westport, CT: Greenwood Press, 1994, 253–260.

David Trotter. "Gold Standards: Money in Edwardian Fiction." *Critical Quarterly*, 30 (Spring, 1988), 22–35.

Warren Salomon. "The Economics of Interstellar Commerce." *Analog*, 109 (May, 1989), 76–90.

———. "The Wealth of Galaxies." *Analog*, 109 (December, 1989), 4–13.

Gary Westfahl. "In Search of Dismal Science Fiction." *Interzone*, No. 189 (May/June, 2003), 55–56.

—Stefan Ekman

MONSTERS

Overview

Since **humanity**'s earliest days, people have imagined and feared varieties of menacing creatures. Several frightening beings that might be deemed monstrous are discussed elsewhere: **Demons, Dinosaurs, Dragons, Frankenstein Monsters,** ghosts (see **Ghosts and Hauntings**), **Giants, Goblins,** the **Golem, Robots, Skeletons, Vampires, Werewolves,** and **Zombies;** there is also an entry on **Supernatural Creatures.**

Survey

One type of monster frequently envisioned in ancient times was a bizarre amalgam of human and animal characteristics. Some of these, like **mermaids,** centaurs (see **Horses**), or satyrs (half-human and half-goat), were usually benign. Some that were more monstrous include the Minotaur, the half-man, half-bull who terrorizes the **youth** of Athens in his **labyrinth;** the Sphinx, a woman's head with a lion's body and eagle's wings, who challenges Oedipus with her famous **riddle;** the griffin, a mixture of lion and eagle; and the chimera, mentioned in Homer's *Iliad* (c. 750 BCE), a combination of lion, goat, and serpent (see **Lions and Tigers; Snakes and Worms**). These creatures from **mythology** sometimes appear in later fantasies like Lewis Carroll's ***Alice's Adventures in Wonderland,*** where Alice and the Queen encounter a "Gryphon"; Thomas Burnett Swann's *Day of the Minotaur* (1966), a story about the Minotaur set in ancient Greece; and Esther M. Friesner's *Sphynxes Wild* (1989), which brings the Sphinx to modern-day Atlantic City in the guise of a businesswoman. The Greeks also described menacing giants like the one-eyed Cyclops and metallic Talus, as well as a sea monster that threatened Andromeda before she was rescued by Perseus (see **Fish and Sea Creatures**).

Modern-day monsters come in several forms. Monsters with magical origins (see **Magic**) are often the basis of longstanding film franchises, including the implacably homicidal Jason of *Friday the Thirteenth* (1980) and its sequels, master of **dreams** Freddy Krueger of *Nightmare on Elm Street* (1984) and its sequels, and the possessed doll Chucky of *Child's Play* (1988) and its sequels (see **Dolls and Puppets**). A favorite film monster is the reanimated Egyptian mummy stalking human prey, first featured in the film *The Mummy* (1932) (see **Egypt**).

There are also accounts of monstrous offshoots of humanity living in remote areas of the world. The tall, furry humanoid known as the Yeti, or Abominable Snowman, is observed in the film *The Abominable Snowman of the Himalayas* (1958). His American cousin, Bigfoot, appeared in two episodes of *The Six Million Dollar Man*—"The Secret of Bigfoot" (1975) and "The Return of Bigfoot" (1976)—and was humorously domesticated in the 1987 film *Harry and the Hendersons*. In *The Creature from the Black Lagoon* (1954) and its sequels, an aquatic humanoid called the Gill Man is discovered deep in the **jungles** of Brazil.

Ill-advised science might also create a *Man Made Monster* (1941), as in the film of that name involving a man transformed by electricity into an emotionless murderer. Robert Louis Stevenson's **Strange Case of Dr. Jekyll and Mr. Hyde** was a pioneering story about a man who drank a potion and became bestial, inspiring film adaptations and other films about **mad scientists** who made themselves monsters like *The Neanderthal Man* (1953) and *Monster on the Campus* (1958). One horribly transformed victim of his own experiments, however, became a **hero**—*Swamp Thing*, featured in the 1982 film of that name as well as a sequel and television series.

Aliens—whether **aliens in space** or **aliens on Earth**—can also be monsters. H.G. Wells's **The War of the Worlds** memorably described the loathsome physiology of his invaders from **Mars**, and A.E. van Vogt wrote a number of stories about alien monsters, including the shapeshifting alien (see **Shapeshifters**) of "Vault of the Beast" (1940) and the ferocious killer menacing a spaceship in "Black Destroyer" (1939). Memorable alien monsters appeared in films like *It Conquered the World* (1956), *I Married a Monster from Outer Space* (1958), *Alien*, and *Predator* (1987), while the series **The Outer Limits** specialized in presenting grotesque alien monsters in episodes like "Nightmare" (1963), "The Zanti Misfits" (1963), "The Mice" (1964), and "Second Chance" (1964).

All these menaces are of roughly human dimensions, but the success of *Godzilla, King of the Monsters* and similar films inspired an increasing tendency to associate the term "monster" with gigantic creatures resembling dinosaurs or other enlarged animals (see **Enlargement**). Indeed, in later Godzilla films like *Destroy All Monsters* (1968) and *Godzilla on Monster Island* (1971), all of **Earth**'s immense menaces have been gathered together in the future to live peacefully on "Monster Island."

Discussion

When monsters first appear, they are frightening and repulsive, but monsters that linger in popular consciousness may come to be regarded more sympathetically, evolve into heroic figures (like Swamp Thing and Godzilla), or even become objects to be laughed at or ridiculed. Still, gifted storytellers can always recapture a monster's original aura of **mystery** and power or create a new monster to be perceived by readers and audiences with fresh eyes. Clearly, monsters fulfill some elemental human need, so one can safely predict that they will always be around to thrill and entertain us.

Bibliography

Stuart Galbraith. *Monsters Are Attacking Tokyo!* Venice, CA: Feral House, 1998.
Leslie Halliwell. *Dead That Walk*. New York: Continuum, 1988.

E. Michael Jones. *Monsters from the Id*. Dallas, TX: Spence, 2000.

Georgess McHargue. *Beasts of Never*. Revised. New York: Delacorte, 1988.

Jeff Rovin. *The Encyclopedia of Monsters*. New York: Facts on File, 1989.

Joanna Russ. "Alien Monsters." Damon Knight, ed., *Turning Points*. New York: Harper, 1977, 132–143.

Per Schelde. *Androids, Humanoids, and Other Science Fiction Monsters*. New York: New York University Press, 1993.

Jan Stacy and Ryder Syvertsen. *The Great Book of Movie Monsters*. Chicago: Contemporary Books, 1983.

Andrew Tudor. *Monsters and Mad Scientists*. Oxford: Blackwell, 1989.

—*Gary Westfahl*

THE MOON

Overview

In ancient times all sorts of **magic** was attributed to the influence of the Moon. **Werewolves** transformed from human to beast under its **light**. **Witches** could harness its power for fearsome spells. Ancient priests watched the phases of the Moon to predict good fortune or calamities. Some dreamed of journeying to that distant place and wrote adventurous tales. In 1969, science fiction became science fact when **astronaut** Neil Armstrong stood on the Moon's surface.

Survey

Although humans first traveled to the Moon in Lucian's satirical *True History* (c. 160 CE), serious moon exploration began in 1634, when astronomer Johannes Kepler's *Somnium* was published. During a lunar eclipse the earth's shadow provided the tunnel of **darkness** required to protect the vulnerable Moon voyager. Other early speculative fiction includes Francis Godwin's *The Man in the Moone* (1638), where the protagonist is flown to the Moon by geese; Cyrano de Bergerac's *The Comical History of the States and Empires of the Moon and Sun* (1687), in which Cyrano travels to the Moon in something resembling a **rocket**; and Edgar Allan Poe's "The Unparalleled Adventure of One Hans Pfaall" (1835), with Hans reaching the Moon in a balloon. The works of Jules Verne (***From the Earth to the Moon***) and H.G. Wells (*The First Men in the Moon* [1901]) captured the imagination of popular audiences. A pioneering film, ***A Trip to the Moon***, was made by Georges Meliès, loosely based on Verne's and Wells's novels.

For many writers the Moon has not been a dead world. Kepler populated the moon with nomadic creatures of monstrous proportions. Godwin inhabited his lunar world with **giants** who live long lives with gorgeous women as wives. Edgar Rice Burroughs's space adventure *The Moon Maid* (1926) showed **Earth**'s satellite teeming with life and fraught with dangers. Murray Leinster's "Keyhole" (1951) described the unexpected discovery of life on the Moon.

As a close neighbor the Moon offers a starting place for extraterrestrial **exploration**. In Robert A. Heinlein's works, the Moon plays a prominent role. The young heroes of *Rocket Ship Galileo* (1947) build a rocket to take them to the Moon; *Destination Moon* (1950), the film version of that story, attempts to provide a realistic look at what **space travel** would be like. "The Man Who Sold the Moon" (1950) and "Requiem" (1940) feature entrepreneur D.D. Harriman who first cajoles a reluctant **humanity** to journey to the Moon and eventually realizes his dream of going there himself. In later stories in Heinlein's "Future History" (see *The Past Through Tomorrow*), the Moon recedes into the background as a place where travelers to **alien worlds** begin their journeys.

In some cases, the Moon becomes humanity's new **home** when Earth must be abandoned. In Stephen Baxter's *Moonseed* (1998) a powerfully destructive microscopic entity reaches Earth through a Moon rock brought back by an Apollo mission; then, ironically, the Moon offers a haven to humanity. In Jack Williamson's *Terraforming Earth* (2001), after Earth's disastrous collision with an asteroid, the cloned children of the few survivors plan to make Earth habitable once more (see **Clones**). In Arthur C. Clarke's "If I Forget Thee, Oh Earth" (1951), a **father** takes his young son to the Moon's nearside to see Earth for the first time. The **beauty** of this sight is marred by the glow resulting from a **nuclear war**. John Varley's *Steel Beach* (1992) uses the setting of a lunar colony that has become the primary residence for humans after an alien attack devastates Earth.

In most stories, humans colonize the Moon by choice, not by necessity. Once permanent bases are established, lunar residents face all the inherent problems and perils of establishing a new **planetary colony**. Murray Leinster wrote a trilogy—*Space Platform* (1953), *Space Tug* (1953) and *City on the Moon* (1957)—in which he described a landing on the Moon and subsequent establishment of a lunar station. Once people feel settled, bits from Terran homes become part of life. Nancy Holder demonstrates this in her novels about Moonbase Vegas—*The Six Families* (1998), *Legacies and Lies* (1999), and *Invasions* (2000)—where six Mafia families vie for control of the casinos. The teenage adventurers in David Gerrold's *Bouncing Off the Moon* (2001) and *Leaping to the Stars* (2002) get more than they bargained for when they arrive on the Moon with its technological marvels and deadly natural environment.

Our Moon may be important not only for humans but also visiting **aliens in space**. **Scientist** Edward Hawks in Algis Budrys's *Rogue Moon* (1960) has developed a matter transmitter that is used to explore an ancient and dangerous alien artifact on the Moon. In Clarke's novel and the film *2001: A Space Odyssey*, scientists discover a monolith buried on the Moon three million years ago. In James P. Hogan's *Inherit the Stars* (1977), the discovery of an ancient **skeleton** on the Moon leads to revelations about humanity's extraterrestrial origins. And in David Weber's Dahaks series (*Mutineer's Moon* [1991], *The Armageddon Inheritance* [1993], and *Heirs of Empire* [1996]), the Moon itself turns out to be a giant, self-aware, alien starship.

Discussion

The Moon's proximity can make it seem a mere extension of Earth, our next logical **frontier**. Many stories have been written with our lunar neighbor as a home for lunar inhabitants, steppingstone to the **stars**, haven from terrestrial calamities, place to colonize, and site for alien encounters.

Bibliography

Brian W. Aldiss. "Some Early Men in the Moon." Aldiss, *The Detached Retina*. Syracuse, NY: Syracuse University Press, 1995, 150–158.

Stephen Baxter. "Moon Believers." *Foundation*, No. 74 (Autumn, 1998), 26–37.

Paul A. Carter. "Rockets to the Moon 1919–1944." *American Studies*, 15 (Spring, 1974), 31–46.

Dona A. Jalufka and Christian Koeberl. "Moonstruck." *Earth, Moon and Planets*, Nos. 85/86 (2001), 179–200.

Rob Latham. "The Men Who Walked on the Moon." Joe Sanders, ed., *Functions of the Fantastic*. Westport, CT: Greenwood Press, 1995, 195–204.

Marjorie Hope Nicolson. *Voyages to the Moon*. New York: Macmillan, 1948.

David Sandner. "Shooting for the Moon." *Extrapolation*, 39 (Spring, 1998), 5–25.

L.G. Wells. *Fictional Accounts of Trips to the Moon*. Syracuse, NY: Syracuse University Library, 1962.

Donald A. Wollheim, ed. *Men on the Moon*. New York: Ace Books, 1958.

—*Patricia Altner*

MOTHERS

A boy's best friend is his mother.

—Joseph Stefano
Psycho (1960)

Overview

Mothers in science fiction and fantasy have been depicted in a variety of ways, both literally and figuratively. The latter expressions include concepts like Mother **Earth** or Mother Ship, symbolizing a secure **home** or place of sanctuary. The literal mother, however, is approached more ambivalently as someone who may offer both security and repression; for feminists, motherhood is equally ambivalent, representing both limitation and empowerment. Related entries include **Babies, Birth, Children, Family, Fathers, Feminism,** and **Marriage.**

Survey

Motherhood is usually celebrated in fantasy; in J.M. Barrie's ***Peter and Wendy***, for example, Mrs. Darling strives to mitigate the harshness of her husband, and Peter and the Lost Boys enjoy having Wendy as their surrogate mother. The **evil** maternal figure in fantasy is normally the stepmother, as observed in two **fairy tales** adapted as animated films, ***Snow White and the Seven Dwarfs*** and *Cinderella* (1950).

Mothers in science fiction may be associated with **horror.** The covert theme of Mary Shelley's ***Frankenstein*** is motherhood, as the novel can be interpreted as a cautionary tale of a man's attempted maternity. Also noteworthy is Frankenstein's response to the female creature, whom he destroys for fear that she will engender a race of **monsters**. As in Michael Crichton's ***Jurassic Park***, the female is threatening because of her fecundity; her potential motherhood makes her powerful and thus alarming. Philip Jose Farmer's "Mother" (1953) employs a blatantly Freudian perspective: a determinedly immature young man chooses to dwell in the outsized womb of an alien mother rather than face the demands of adult life. On this **alien world**, the female has been reduced to the basic function of reproduction; only males have **freedom** of movement, but after they perform their sexual role the mother devours them.

The threatening aspect of the mother is explored in ***Alien*** and its sequels. In the first film the Mother Alien is unseen, but there is a profusion of maternal imagery, including a catastrophic male "birth." The ship's **computer** is ironically named "Mother." In subsequent films the theme of motherhood is foregrounded, with the Mother Alien portrayed as an insectoid hive queen, a model found in other stories like C.J. Cherryh's *Serpent's Reach* (1980) and Orson Scott Card's ***Ender's Game*** and its sequels. This plays upon both the authoritative nature of the matriarch and her ominous alien aspect.

Aldous Huxley's ***Brave New World*** offers a different view of motherhood: children are produced entirely by artificial means and the concept of biological mothers seems disgusting. The one real mother, Linda, is an abject creature filled with self-loathing and reviled by society. Linda is one of many science fiction mothers who are effectively Madonnas *manquées*. Other examples are Rosemary Woodhouse, the mother of the anti-Christ in Ira Levin's *Rosemary's Baby* (1967); Sarah Connor of ***The Terminator***, whose son will someday liberate **humanity** from machines; and Jessica of Frank Herbert's ***Dune***, another mother of a future **messiah**.

The emphasis on woman as mother concerns female writers who acknowledge the importance of the role but wish to **escape** its limitations. Charlotte Perkins Gilman described the horrors of postnatal depression in patriarchal society in "The Yellow Wall Paper" (1892) and explored an alternative model in her separatist **utopia, *Herland***. There women reproduce by parthenogenesis and because motherhood is greatly valued, child-rearing is entrusted only to women trained for the task, freeing women to be something more than mothers. A similar model had been imagined in Mary E. Bradley Lane's *Mizora* (1890), but such ideas did not come to the forefront until the 1970s and the advent of feminism. Some writers, like Marge Piercy in ***Woman on the Edge of Time***, created egalitarian worlds where men and women, aided by **technology**, shared parenting on equal terms. Others, like Joanna Russ in ***The Female Man***, envisioned separatist societies where motherhood is an integral part of life.

Suzy McKee Charnas produced an elaborate separatist society in her Motherlines series: *Walk to the End of the World* (1974) describes a patriarchal **dystopia** in which women are kept in abject **slavery**, primarily for breeding purposes, but their parenthood is unacknowledged. Its sequel, *Motherlines* (1978), depicts a utopian alternative in which an all-female community develops a form of parthenogenesis using the sperm of their stallions as a catalyst. This results in clone-like "Motherlines" in which each succeeding generation has identical traits. Along with birth mothers, each child has several "sharemothers" who support the birth mother and share child-rearing responsibilities.

A different feminist perspective occurs in Margaret Atwood's ***The Handmaid's Tale***, where motherhood is crucial: fertile women, as "handmaids," are again reduced purely to the role of child-bearers, becoming in effect "two-legged wombs for infertile couples." Any child is handed over to the legal wife who is "mother" in all respects except giving birth. Here, the dichotomy between limitation and empowerment inherent in motherhood becomes a literal division.

Discussion

The concept of the mother incorporates many paradoxes: she is comforting but threatening, nurturing but voracious, limiting but empowering, a sexual being but a Madonna. There is also a gendered division in perceptions: to male children the mother represents the Other, the Alien, as well as the home to which he is drawn; to daughters she is the potential Self, with all the hopes and fears which that implies. In science fiction and fantasy, Freudian anxieties may be worked out and monstrous mothers subdued, perhaps with the comforting image of Mother Earth in the background.

Bibliography

Lynda K. Bundtzen. "Monstrous Mothers." Gill Kirkup, Linda Janes, Kathryn Woodward, and Fiona Hovenden, eds., *The Gendered Cyborg*. London: Routledge, 2000, 101–109.

Nancy Chodorow. *The Reproduction of Mothering*. Berkeley: University of California Press, 1978.

Dorian Cirrone. "Millenial Mothers." *Femspec*, 3 (2001), 4–11.

Catherine Constable. "Becoming the Monster's Mother." Annette Kuhn, ed., *Alien Zone II*. London: Verso, 1999, 172–202.

Jane Donawerth. "Mothers Are Animals." *Graven Images*, No. 2 (Fall, 1995), 237–247.

Bernie Heidkamp. "Responses to the Alien Mother in Post-Maternal Cultures." *Science Fiction Studies*, 23 (November, 1996), 339–354.

Robin Roberts. "Adoptive versus Biological Mothering in *Aliens*." *Extrapolation*, 30 (Winter, 1989), 353–363.

Marc A. Rubenstein. "My Accursed Origin." *Studies in Romanticism*, 12 (1976), 65–94.

Stephen Scobie. "What's the Story, Mother?" *Science-Fiction Studies*, 20 (March, 1993), 80–93.

—Liz Fielden

MOUNTAINS

Perhaps "because it is there" is not sufficient reason for climbing a mountain.

—David Loughery
Star Trek V: The Final Frontier (1989)

Overview

Mountains have long fascinated people as remote and mysterious realms where **gods and goddesses** might dwell, or **monsters** may lurk. Reaching the top of a mountain might also represent fulfillment of a **quest**.

Survey

As places close to the sky, mountains have special significance in many **religions**. In Greek **mythology**, Mount Olympus was the home of Zeus, Hera, and other major gods; it is visualized in the film *Jason and the Argonauts* and the series

Hercules: The Legendary Journeys. As punishment for giving **fire** to **humanity**, the god Prometheus was chained to a mountain in the Caucasus where an eagle constantly devoured his liver. Significant mountains in the Bible include Mount Ararat, where Noah's Ark came to rest after the **flood**, and Mount Sinai, where Moses met with God and received the Ten Commandments. Dante's *Purgatory* (c. 1306–1321) describes Purgatory, the virtuous souls' pathway to **Heaven**, as a mountain with seven levels, where the seven deadly **sins** are purged as souls ascend.

The ancients were also much impressed with volcanoes. The Hawaiians were one ancient **culture** that personified and worshipped great volcanoes (see **Personification**), as depicted in Dan Simmons's *Fires of Eden* (1994). The erupting Mount Vesuvius, which buried the Roman city of Pompeii, figures in the **horror** film *The Curse of the Faceless Man* (1958), wherein an ash-covered man from Pompeii is revived to stalk present-day Italy in search of his lover. Volcanoes menace contemporary people in three 1997 **disaster** films: in *Dante's Peak* and *Volcano: Fire on the Mountain*, a remote town is menaced, but in *Volcano*, a volcano improbably springs up right in the middle of downtown Los Angeles.

One of fantasy's most famous mountains is also a volcano: Mount Doom in J.R.R. Tolkien's *The Lord of the Rings*, where Frodo Baggins must travel to destroy his powerful **ring** in its fires. Previously, his uncle Bilbo Baggins had also traveled to a mountain to assist some **dwarfs** seeking to reclaim **gold and silver** hoarded by a **dragon**. H. Rider Haggard's African explorers may climb mountains to discover hidden **treasures** or **lost worlds**, as in *King Solomon's Mines* (1886) and *She* (see **Africa**). In Esther M. Friesner's *The Silver Mountain* (1986), a sinister sorceress lives in a mountain fortress.

Monsters and aliens are often found atop mountains. A high mesa in South America is home to **dinosaurs** in Arthur Conan Doyle's *The Lost World*. The Himalayan Mountains of **Asia** are the traditional abode of the Yeti, or Abominable Snowman, as observed in the films *The Abominable Snowman of the Himalayas* (1957) and *My Friend, the Yeti* (2001). A tentacled alien with **psychic powers** hides atop a mountain in the Alps in the film *The Crawling Eye* (1958), while the **hero** of *Close Encounters of the Third Kind* must climb up Wyoming's Devil's Tower to participate in humanity's **first contact** with **aliens on Earth**. Frightening intimations of a sinister **elder race** are found at mountains in the Antarctic in H.P. Lovecraft's "At the Mountains of Madness" (1936) (see **Polar Regions**).

Mountains may also be where even grander quests may begin. In Jules Verne's *Journey to the Center of the Earth* (1864), explorers climb up an extinct volcano to find a passage into the earth's interior (see **Underground Adventure**). In contrast, a mountain becomes a conduit to outer space in Arthur C. Clarke's *The Fountains of Paradise* (1979), where fulfillment of an ancient prophecy causes monks to abandon a mountain of religious significance in a nation resembling Sri Lanka and allows a future engineer to construct a space elevator stretching from the mountain to an orbital **space station**. The adventures of television's *Captain Video* (1949–1955) usually began and ended at his mountain headquarters. A mountain may even be a starting point for **time travel**, as in Edgar Allan Poe's "A Tale of the Ragged Mountains" (1844), wherein a man strolling through the Virginia mountains is mysteriously transported back in time to a battle in India.

Mountain climbing today is primarily a **sport**, which many find challenging and exhilarating, and at least one story—the film *Star Trek V: The Final Frontier* (1989)—predicts that it will remain popular in the future, albeit with advanced safety features (see *Star Trek: The Motion Picture*). Mountain climbers in the Alps discover the mysterious remains of prehistoric humans in Greg Bear's *Darwin's Radio* (1999). Mountain climbing can also occur on **alien worlds** like **Mars,** in Kim Stanley Robinson's **Red Mars** and its sequels, and **Mercury,** in Alan E. Nourse's "Brightside Crossing" (1955). The techniques of mountain climbing become useful when people are miniaturized, so they must use ropes and hooks to climb up tables or flights of stairs that seem like mountains to them—as observed in films like *The Incredible Shrinking Man* and *Attack of the Puppet People* (1958) (see **Miniaturization**).

Discussion

Mountain climbing was humanity's first form of **space travel,** a way to almost touch the sky and magisterially look down on Earth's faraway surface; hence, it is appropriate that Clarke used a mountain as his steppingstone to the stars, and Captain Kirk enjoys mountain climbing as a hobby. Now, with orbital flight becoming an everyday experience, the excitement of climbing a mountain should be diminishing, although mountains may always retain a certain aura of majesty and **mystery.**

Bibliography

Robert Carmichael. "*Star Trek V: The Final Frontier.*" *American Cinematographer*, 70 (July, 1989), 38–48.

Joe Christopher. "Mount Purgatory Arises Near Narnia." *Mythlore*, 23 (Spring, 2001), 65–90.

Gary W. Ciuba. "Walker Percy's Enchanted Mountain." Jan Nordby Gretlund and Karl-Heinz Westarp, eds., *Walker Percy*. Jackson: University Press of Mississippi, 1991, 13–23.

Jason C. Eckhardt. "Behind the Mountains of Madness." *Lovecraft Studies*, 6 (Spring, 1987), 31–38.

F. Colin Kingston. "*Volcano.*" *Cinefantastique*, 28 (June, 1997), 30–31.

Jennifer L. McMahon and B. Steve Csaki. "Talking Trees and Walking Mountains." Gregory Bassham and Eric Bronson, eds., *The Lord of the Rings and Philosophy*. Chicago: Open Court, 2003, 179–191.

J.C. Nitzsche. "The King Under the Mountain." *North Dakota Quarterly*, 47 (Winter, 1979), 5–18.

Diana Waggoner. *The Hills of Faraway*. New York: Atheneum, 1978.

—*Gary Westfahl*

MUSIC

Overview

Many fantastic stories feature the playing or singing of music, as well as characters who are musicians. Songs also play an integral role in fantastic musicals, and music may become a medium of **communication** alternative to language.

Survey

In fantasy, the central form of music is the songs sung by characters; J.R.R. Tolkien's *The Hobbit* and *The Lord of the Rings* most famously illustrate the use of songs in fantasy narrative, but readers have been equally impressed by the songs of John Myers's *Silverlock* (1949). Musical instruments are sometimes **magical objects**, like the flute that lures both rats (see **Rats and Mice**) and **children** to their doom in the classic **fairy tale** of the Pied Piper. Many fantasy texts also feature characters who are bards or minstrels; sometimes they simply entertain, but they may also mediate between various levels of creations with music that literally has **magic** powers, as in Greg Bear's *The Infinity Concerto* (1984) and *The Serpent Mage* (1986).

Early examples of music in science fiction include the "Sound Houses" in Francis Bacon's **utopia** *The New Atlantis* (1627) and H.P. Lovecraft's "The Music of Erich Zann" (1921). However, it was only after the 1960s that science fiction and music, frequently rock music, entered into a dialogue as two channels for the **rebellion** of **youth**. One early rocker-protagonist was Michael Moorcock's Jerry Cornelius, who first appeared in *The Final Programme* (1968). As a rebellious icon of ambiguous **sexuality**, Cornelius was styled after contemporary rock musicians. The same applies to Rick Rickenharp, the protagonist of John Shirley's trilogy of *Eclipse* (1985), *Eclipse Penumbra* (1988) and *Eclipse Corona* (1990), a disgruntled musician, who over time becomes leader of the underground movement seeking to overthrow the totalitarian regime. The name of Shirley's actual band, Panther Moderns, made it into the text of William Gibson's *Neuromancer*, but that novel relies on other types of music—in crucial scenes dubbed reggae music epitomizes the visceral, biological rhythm of life antithetical to the mechanical logic of artificial intelligences and **cyberspace**. Gibson also explores music stardom and fandom in *Idoru* (1996), as does Bruce Sterling in *Zeitgeist* (2000). Orson Scott Card's "Unaccompanied Sonata" (1979) is the haunting story of a talented musician denied the ability to express himself by a repressive society.

While most **cyberpunk** narratives do not directly refer to music, they still generate the sense of anarchic techno-noise underlying high-tech panoramas of **near future** societies. Among the fictions extending the common portrayals of music are Paul Di Filippo's *Ciphers* (1997), whose text contains—if it is not literally constructed from—hundreds of allusions and references to songs listed at the end of the novel; Jack Womack's *Elvissey* (1993), which plays with the Elvis Presley myth; and Richard Kadrey's *Kamikaze d'Amour* (1995), in which artistic synaesthesia centered around music drives the story. Other music genres are also relevant; jazz and blues are central metaphors of Kathleen Ann Goonan's tetralogy *Queen City Jazz* (1994), *Mississippi Blues* (1997), *Crescent City Rhapsody* (2000), and *Light Music* (2002), not only infusing their plots but also constituting a structural metaphor for the novels themselves. The latter is true of Geoff Ryman's *The Child Garden* (1988), which revolves around musical adaptations of Dante's works.

Music, or musical sounds, may serve as a medium of communication: a five-note musical phrase famously initiates contact with aliens in *Close Encounters of the Third Kind*. Future musicians are featured in Jack Vance's *Space Opera* (1965), which describes a spacefaring opera ensemble acting out a sort of ambassadorial function, and early episodes of *Star Trek* showed Spock playing his Vulcan harp to accompany Uhura's singing. Music is uniquely central to Ursula K. Le Guin's *Always Coming Home* (1985), which was published accompanied by a cassette recording of the music and lyrics of the reprimitized inhabitants of her **post-holocaust society**. One might regard this emphasis on music as a feminist's attempt to break up the linear and medium-specific hegemony of a type of story traditionally associated with masculinity (see **Feminism**).

Discussion

Though not central to a focus on literature and film, the crossover from narrative to music is worth mentioning. Many enthusiasts have provided music for lyrics from literature, as prominently occurred when Donald Swann put some of Tolkien's lyrics to music and published the results as *The Road Goes Ever On* (1967). There is also the tradition of so-called "filk music"—the folk music of the science fiction and fantasy community, heavily although not exclusively drawing on the subject matter of fantastic literature. Finally, virtually all genres of popular music, from rock to jazz to electronic music, occasionally reflect the influence of science fiction and fantasy, as demonstrated most conspicuously by popular songs like the Rolling Stones' "Two Thousand Light Years from Home" (1967), David Bowie's "Space Oddity" (1969), and Elton John's "Rocket Man" (1973). Occasionally, musicians evolve their own fantastic visions, the best example of which is the painstakingly complex **mythology** of Sun Ra, who believed he had been sent to **Earth** from outer space, and his Arkestra.

Bibliography

Jeff Bond. *The Music of Star Trek*. Los Angeles, CA: Lone Eagle Publishing, 1999.

Tanya Brown. "The Music of the Spheres." *Vector*, No. 204 (March/April, 1999), 19–23.

Michel Delville. "The Moorcock/Hawkwind Connection." *Foundation*, No. 62 (Winter, 1994/1995), 64–69.

Charlene Engels. "Language and Music of the Spheres." Charles L. P. Silet, ed. *The Films of Steven Spielberg*. Lanham, MD: Scarecrow, 2002, 47–56.

Lenny Kaye. "Flying Saucers Rock and Roll." *Locus*, 5 (September 16, 1972), 6.

R.D. Larson, *Musique Fantastique*. Metuchen, NJ: Scarecrow, 1985.

Larry McCaffery. "Cutting Up." McCaffery, ed., *Storming the Reality Studio*. Durham: Duke University Press, 1991, 286–307.

John Shirley. "Science Fiction and Rock Music." *Metaphores*, 9/10 (April, 1984), 219–220.

Gary Westfahl. "The Sound of the City . . . and the Call of the Cosmos." *Interzone*, No. 153 (March, 2000), 48–50.

—*Pawel Frelik*

MUTATION

Overview

At the turn of the twentieth century it was speculated that the sudden, spontaneous mutation of life forms played a role in the **evolution** of species. In 1927, H.J. Muller used irradiation to bring about mutations in fruit flies. Since then, science fiction frequently dealt with the emergence of strange people or animals (see **Animals and Zoos**), often as a result of exposure to radiation.

Survey

For thousands of years, **mythology**, legends, and folktales have described bizarre anthropomorphic beings. Beings scarcely less bizarre appeared in ancient travel narratives and sophisticated fictional variations, such as Jonathan Swift's *Gulliver's Travels*. In the nineteenth century, Mary Shelley's *Frankenstein* first depicted the use of science to manufacture a humanoid being (see **Frankenstein Monsters**), thus exercising a power that was previously the domain of **gods and goddesses** or magicians. Nineteenth-century **fin de siècle** writers were fascinated by all kinds of transformation and degeneration of human forms (see **Decadence**), one example being Robert Louis Stevenson's *Strange Case of Dr. Jekyll and Mr. Hyde*.

In the twentieth century, science fiction began to emphasize the changing of human and other species through natural alteration of genes or the use of **genetic engineering** to alter form, size, and psychophysical abilities. James Blish's *The Seedling Stars* (1956) is a classic example of the latter kind of story (see **Pantropy**).

Stories of mutated humans first became common in the 1930s pulp magazines and in British scientific **romances** of the time, mutation often providing the justification for stories of **supermen**. Philip Wylie's *Gladiator* (1930), for example, describes a chemical that gives its protagonist great strength. Edmond Hamilton's "The Man Who Evolved" (1931) tells of a **scientist** who evolves himself with cosmic radiation. Olaf Stapledon's *Odd John* (1935), about a superintelligent mutant who finds he cannot to coexist in peace with **humanity**, is perhaps the best of these early superman tales. Arguably it was not equaled until the 1953 publication of *More than Human*, Theodore Sturgeon's tale of a group of mutants with **psychic powers** who merge minds and form a single "gestalt" being (see **Hive Minds**).

From the beginning, superior mutants were treated as important characters and presented sympathetically. A.E. van Vogt's *Slan* (1946) is among the first stories of superior mutants trying to survive among us, despite persecution. This scenario has continued, giving the theme of mutation much of its audience appeal. Another superior mutant, the Mule, plays a pivotal role in Isaac Asimov's *Foundation* series. He emerges as a galactic conqueror (see **Galactic Empire**) whose individual psychic powers were not foreseeable by Hari Seldon's psychohistory.

The explosion of atomic bombs in the 1940s led to an even greater focus on mutation, with mutated **monsters**, like the giant ants of *Them!* (1954) and giant spider of *Tarantula* (1954), **superheroes** and **villains**, and the appearance of mutated freaks after **nuclear wars**, as in John Wyndham's *Re-Birth* (1955) and Walter M. Miller, Jr.'s *A Canticle for Leibowitz* (see **Post-Holocaust Societies**). Radioactivity from nuclear explosions provided the basis for many stories of widespread or unexpected mutation.

Many of these themes come together in the *X-Men* comic book, television, and movie franchise, which commenced in 1963 with the first issues of the series now entitled *The Uncanny X-Men*. Here, superpowered mutants, who have apparently been brought into being by ambient nuclear radiation, are persecuted by "normal" society. Some fight back, seeking to conquer or even exterminate *homo sapiens*. Others devote themselves to protecting humanity and attempt to bring about a reconciliation. In this long-running storyline, mutants are analogous to many kinds of oppressed groups, or simply to social misfits and loners (see **Race Relations**).

More extreme mutation stories involve the morphing of **nature** as a whole, as in Poul Anderson's *Brain Wave* (1954), in which the **Earth** leaves a **force** field in space that had held back the functioning of human and animal nervous systems. Other examples are Greg Egan's *Teranesia* (1999), in which a new phase of evolution commences on an isolated Indonesian **island**, and Greg Bear's *Blood Music*, in which a freakish experiment triggers a rapid transformation of Earth's biosphere.

Discussion

Stories of mutation provide rationalized accounts of the **metamorphosis** of human beings and nature, a theme of timeless fascination that had previously emerged in other forms. Mutation stories can be divided into two categories. Some involve unexpected and uncontrolled alterations, often due to misused **technology** like nuclear testing or **nuclear war**, though sometimes due to natural causes. Others describe deliberate alteration of human or other beings by advanced human or extraterrestrial science. The latter can be more optimistic, like Blish's *The Seedling Stars* and other stories about reshaping humans for adaptation to life on **alien worlds**. More stories about the implications of deliberate genetic alteration can be expected in the future. Science fiction will continue to react to phenomena like the successful mapping of the human genome, controversies over genetic engineering and the cloning of plants and animals, and the prospect of genetically engineering humans for medical therapy or enhancement (see **Clones; Medicine**).

Bibliography

Brian Attebery. "Super Men." *Science-Fiction Studies*, 25 (March, 1998), 61–76.

Scott Bukatman. "X-Bodies." Bukatman, *Matters of Gravity*. Durham: Duke University Press, 2003, 48–78.

William A. Covino. "Grammars of Transgression." *Rhetoric Review*, 14 (Spring, 1996), 355–373.

R.J. Ellis. "Are You a Fucking Mutant?" *Foundation*, No. 65 (Autumn, 1995), 81–97.

Philip Harbottle. "March of the Mutants." *Vector*, No. 23 (December, 1963), 4–11.

Rob Latham. "Mutant Youth." Veronica Hollinger and Joan Gordon, eds., *Edging into the Future*. Philadelphia: University of Pennsylvania Press, 2002, 124–141.

Philip Nutman. "Gangsters vs. Mutants." Stephen Jones, ed., *Clive Barker's Shadows in Eden*. Lancaster, PA: Underwood-Miller, 1991, 271–278.

Domna Pastourmatzi, ed., *Biotechnological and Medical Themes in Science Fiction*. Thessaloniki, Greece: University Studio Press, 2002, 131–51.

Anne Simon. *Monsters, Mutants and Missing Links*. London: Ebury Press, 1999.

—Russell Blackford

MYSTERY

∎

Seek out mystery; what else is the whole cosmos but mystery?

—Poul Anderson
"Goat Song" (1972)

Overview

A sense of mystery is central to science fiction and fantasy, manifesting itself in simultaneous awareness of the ineffable and an urgent desire to find ways to explain the ineffable. Mystery relates to the clichéd **sense of wonder** and the idea of a **puzzle** or **riddle**, but the former can arise from any science fiction narrative, not merely the inexplicable, while in the latter the solution of an intellectual challenge forms either the heart or denouement of the story. In the history of fantastic fiction, mystery has moved almost inexorably from theological questions to problems and their resolutions.

Survey

Judeo-Christian traditions possess Christian mysteries (see **Christianity**): sacred cults granted membership only to the ritually initiated, and its triune God needed special cadres to justify His ways. Medieval dramas based on biblical stories were also known as mystery plays. When prose fiction developed in the Renaissance, the Christian deity was often a dominating figure, occasionally through His deliberate absence; a central mystery of Thomas More's *Utopia* is whether its religiously tolerant **utopia** is really an ideal society, while the devout Atlanteans of Francis Bacon's *The New Atlantis* (1627) (see **Atlantis**) presume to improve on His designs.

Narrative structure generates mystery in Mary Shelley's *Frankenstein*, which begins *in media res*. Continuing, one learns the motivations of Victor Frankenstein, who usurped one of **Heaven**'s mysteries, defying **death** to create sentient life. In the late nineteenth century, Jules Verne frequently explicated mysteries. *An Antarctic Mystery* (1898) concluded Edgar Allan Poe's mysterious *The Narrative of Arthur Gordon Pym*. Verne also explored the mysterious center of the **Earth** (*Journey to the Centre of the Earth* [1864]); beneath the sea (*Twenty Thousand Leagues under the Sea*); strange **islands** (*The Mysterious Island* [1875]); and even the heart of a comet (*Hector Servadac* [1877]) (see **Comets and Asteroids**).

Before science fiction became a genre, scientific **detective** stories depicted mysteries through narrative structure and exposition that provided backgrounds, motivations, and quasi-scientific rationales. One popular figure was Arthur B. Reeve's Craig Kennedy, who appeared in numerous stories beginning in 1910, and a short-lived magazine, Hugo Gernsback's *Scientific Detective Monthly* (1930), was devoted entirely to this subgenre. Pulp science fiction adopted this formula in more imaginative settings. John W. Campbell, Jr. used it in "Who Goes There?" (1938) to create **paranoia**, as men at an Antarctic base must deduce which one of them is really an alien in disguise (see **Aliens on Earth**). Curme Gray's *Murder in Millennium VI* (1951), one of the first science fiction mystery novels, describes murder in a futuristic matriarchal society. Alfred Bester's *The Demolished Man* depicts a murder deviously plotted and committed in a society of telepaths (see **Crime and Punishment; Psychic Powers**). Isaac Asimov paired human police officer Elijah Baley and **robot** R. Daneel Olivaw to investigate murders in *The Caves of Steel* (1954), *The Naked Sun* (1957), and *The Robots of Dawn* (1983) (see *I, Robot*). These novels are classic mysteries, with the murderer's identity revealed at the conclusion. Asimov follows the structure of the mystery story in other stories, including his *Foundation* trilogy, where the saga's focus becomes the search for the unknown location of the enigmatic Second Foundation.

Many stories feature mysteries involving strange artifacts or unusual future societies. Algis Budrys's *Rogue Moon* (1960) describes the investigation of a mysterious object on the dark side of the **Moon**. It thematically links to Stanley Kubrick's film *2001: A Space Odyssey*, suggested by Arthur C. Clarke's "The Sentinel" (1951), which features an equally puzzling lunar artifact. Frank Herbert's *Dune* series explores mysteries of life and **culture** on arid Arrakis. Lloyd Biggle's Jan Darzek series (beginning with *All the Colors of Darkness* [1963]) and William F. Nolan's Sam Space series (beginning with *Space for Hire* [1971]) blend hardboiled mystery and science fiction in outer space settings. Clarke's *Rendezvous with Rama* describes the discovery and exploration of a vast mysterious object, as does Greg Bear's *Eon* (1985). With *The Long ARM of Gil Hamilton* (1976) and *The Patchwork Girl* (1980), Larry Niven explored crime in a future society where organ transplantation is routine and healthy organs in great demand.

With Kubrick's breathtaking merger of genres, motion pictures became important purveyors of mystery, posing theological questions about the origins of the universe and existence, occasionally focusing on uncanny events on the margins of human existence. The doings of police and enforcement agencies remain endlessly mutable. *Soylent Green* (1973) presents police work in an overpopulated future (see **Overpopulation**). *Blade Runner* has little connection with Philip K. Dick's *Do Androids Dream of Electric Sheep?* but outstandingly depicts **near future** noir. *Robocop* (1987), which spawned two sequels, depicts a murdered policeman who becomes a **cyborg**. *Dark City* (1998) begins with a routine homicide investigation; *Signs* (2002) shows the exceptional intruding into the ordinary. A list of additional science fiction mysteries must include *The X-Files*, in which FBI agents Dana Scully and Fox Mulder investigate all sorts of mysterious and sinister phenomena.

Discussion

One reads genre fiction partially because it offers familiar structures and resolutions. Mystery is larger than the literary genres into which it is pigeonholed; it is an essential component in all human existence. We are bracketed by the mysteries of **birth** and death, and a search for answers to the mystery of life—the belief that "the truth is out there" (as stated in *The X-Files*)—can be said to compel and propel all creative acts. Mysteries are everywhere; their presence in fiction echoes their existence in life.

Bibliography

David Annan. *Cinema of Mystery and Fantasy*. London: Lorrimer, 1984.

John Dean. "Magic and Mystery in the Fiction of Ursula K. Le Guin." *Social Science Information*, 23 (1984), 143–153.

Elana Gomel. "Mystery, Apocalypse and Utopia." *Science-Fiction Studies* 22 (November 1995), 343–356.

W. Russell Gray. "Science Fiction Detectives." *Mid-Atlantic Almanack*, 2 (1993), 46–53.

Trevor Harris. "Measurement and Mystery in Verne." Edmund J. Smyth, ed., *Jules Verne: Narratives of Modernity*. Liverpool: Liverpool University Press, 2000, 109–121.

Mark S. Madoff. "Inside, Outside and the Gothic Locked-Room Mystery." Kenneth W. Graham, ed., *Gothic Fictions*. New York: AMS Press, 1989, 49–62.

Hazel Beasley Pierce. *A Literary Symbiosis*. Westport, CT: Greenwood, 1983.

Dorman T. Shindler. "Mind Over Matter." *Armchair Detective* (Spring 1997), 150–152.

R.J. Wilson. "Asimov's Mystery Story Structure." *Extrapolation*, 19 (May 1978), 101–107.

—*Richard Bleiler*

MYTHOLOGY

Overview

The current use of the word mythology to mean "something that people believe to be true that is demonstrably not true" is a by-product of **Christianity**'s conquest of the belief systems that came before it and obscures the nature of mythology for people today. Many feel that mythology was how people before Christianity and the scientific and technological revolutions explained the things that they did not understand. Mythology, however, is more subtle and complex than that. Mythology is somewhat like **poetry** in that it creates metaphors: a fiery chariot, for example, represents the **Sun** and its passage through the sky. Mythology is, therefore, a narrative method people developed to discuss things that they did not understand and could not explain. A significant segment of mythology dealt with sacred matters: creation of the world and the cosmos (see **Cosmology**), fertility, **gods and goddesses**, good and **evil**, and the destruction or end of the world (see **Eschatology**).

Survey

The simplest use of mythological materials by science fiction and fantasy writers is the borrowing of **names**. Robert E. Howard mostly looked to Scandinavian and Celtic mythologies to find names like Conan, but Howard's approach was eclectic, and the Cimmeria from which Conan was supposed to have come bears no resemblance to the historical Cimmeria. In books like *Day of the Minotaur* (1966) and *The Forest of Forever* (1971), Thomas Burnett Swann used a range of **supernatural creatures** from Greek mythology to people stories of his own devising about the end of an age. The most accomplished borrower was J.R.R. Tolkien. The names of **dwarfs** in *The Hobbit* come from *The Poetic Edda* (c. 1000) or from Snorri

Sturluson's *The Prose Edda* (c. 1220), and Gandalf's name, which can be translated "sorcerer elf," comes from there as well. Tolkien wove borrowings from Scandinavian mythology into a much larger tapestry that included borrowings from *Beowulf* (c. 800), the Icelandic sagas, the Finnish legends first compiled by Elias Lönnrot as *The Kalevala* (1835), and other northern European writings.

Many authors borrow and expand on specific mythological stories or entire pantheons of gods and goddesses. Science fiction and fantasy writers generally avoid Greek and Roman materials in favor of materials from Celtic and Scandinavian sources. In the last third of the twentieth century, a number of writers created fantasies based on Celtic materials. Lloyd Alexander's five-book Chronicles of Prydain, beginning with *The Book of Three* (1964), is probably the best known of these fantasies: it traces Taran's development from orphan to High King in a secondary world largely based on Welsh Celtic stories dating back to *The White Book of Rhydderch* (c. 1300) and *The Red Book of Hergest* (c. 1400). Other authors who also drew on Celtic materials include Nancy Bond, Susan Cooper, Tom Deitz, Kenneth C. Flint, Greg Frost, Alan Garner (see **The Owl Service**), and Louise Lawrence. Celtic-based novels by Kenneth Morris and Evangeline Walton from the first part of the twentieth century have returned to print decades after their first publication. Diana Paxson's Nibelungenlied trilogy, beginning with *The Wolf and the Raven* (1993), and Stephen Grundy's *Rhinegold* (1994) are based on the same Scandinavian/Teutonic mythology that provided the materials for Richard Wagner's Ring Cycle of operas. Charles de Lint's *Moonheart* (1984), set in eastern Canada, is a blend of Celtic and Native American myths. In the 1980s, Patricia Kennealy-Morrison began her Keltiad series, starting with *The Copper Crown* (1985), a tale set in the future featuring descendants of Celts who had left Earth in the early Middle Ages; and in the 1990s, Randy Lee Eickhoff began his Ulster series, starting with *The Raid* (1979), which was based on ancient Irish myths and legends from *The Mythological Cycle* and *The Ulster Cycle* (c. 1100).

Other writers have looked to the east, not the north. Roger Zelazny's **Lord of Light** and *Creatures of Light and Darkness* (1969) are respectively based on Indian mythology and Egyptian mythology (see **Egypt**). Some authors draw on Christian materials, usually the Old Testament rather than the New Testament, as a source, including C.S. Lewis' Narnia series (see **The Lion, the Witch and the Wardrobe**) and space trilogy (see **Out of the Silent Planet**); Madeleine L'Engle's *A Wrinkle in Time* (1962) and its sequels; and George MacDonald's *Phantastes* (1858) and *Lilith*, which present basic Christian conflicts and choices in new settings. Charles L. Harness's "The New Reality" (1950) poses a scientific origin for **Adam and Eve** while still following the basic outline from Genesis. Harlan Ellison's "The Deathbird" (1973) contrasts a sane Lucifer (see **Satan**) to an insane Jehovah (see **Deathbird Stories**), prefiguring Philip Pullman's His Dark Materials trilogy, beginning with *The Golden Compass* (1995). Michael Moorcock's "Behold the Man" (1966) is about a time traveler who goes back to find Jesus; and James Morrow's *Towing Jehovah* (1994) tells the story of a discredited ship's captain hired to tow the enormous corpse of Jehovah from the South Atlantic to the Arctic.

It has been said, notably by Joseph Campbell in *The Hero with a Thousand Faces* (1949), that mythology has given us the **Hero** Tale, the one story that underlies all fiction from the great epics, *Beowulf* and the rest, to the present. This is observable in popular culture; the Hero Tale is the basic structure of films like *Star*

Wars and *Independence Day* (1996) and television programs like **Wonder Woman,** **Hercules: The Legendary Journeys,** and **Xena: Warrior Princess.** The Hero Tale is also present in mythologically based fantasy and science fiction.

Discussion

In many ways, fantasy and science fiction struggle with the most important questions of all, what it means to be human and how to conduct oneself in the world (see **Ethics; Humanity**); these are topics that the ancient myths deal with as well, and incorporating mythology into science fiction and fantasy makes those literatures stronger and more resonant.

Bibliography

Joseph Campbell. *The Masks of God.* 4 volumes. 1959. New York: Viking Press, 1970.

H. Munro Chadwick. *The Heroic Age.* Cambridge: Cambridge University Press, 1926.

Linda Dégha. "Folk Narrative." Richard Dorson, ed., *Folklore and Folklife.* Chicago: University of Chicago Press, 1972, 53–83.

Casey Fredericks. *The Future of Eternity.* Bloomington: Indiana University Press, 1982.

Harry Slochower. *Mythopoesis.* Detroit: Wayne State University Press, 1970.

C.W. Sullivan III. *Welsh Celtic Myth in Modern Fantasy.* Westport, CT: Greenwood Press, 1989.

J.R.R. Tolkien. *Beowulf.* 1936. Oxford: Oxford University Press, 1977.

John Vickery, ed. *Myth and Literature.* Lincoln: University of Nebraska Press, 1966.

John White. *Mythology in the Modern Novel.* Princeton: Princeton University Press, 1971.

—C.W. Sullivan III

ℜ

NAMES

∎

Ged had neither lost nor won but, naming the shadow of his death with his own name, had made himself whole.

Ursula K. Le Guin
A Wizard of Earthsea (1968)

Overview

Names are a significant issue in science fiction and fantasy in two ways. First, from the perspective of characters in a story, the names of those around them may have special significance or even magical power (see **Magic**), and circumstances may require characters to change or conceal their names. Second, from the perspective of readers, the names chosen by authors can have a major impact on the persuasiveness and impact of characters, particularly in exotic or otherworldly settings where prosaic names like "John Smith" or "Mary Brown" might seem incongruous and deflating; thus, authors have learned to be extraordinarily careful in bestowing names upon various **heroes** and **villains**.

Survey

In some **cultures**, a person is given a "true name" that must be concealed from all but a few, since knowledge of that name would grant others a deeper understanding of or some power over, that person. This tradition influenced the classic **fairy tale** of Rumpelstiltskin and also figures in Ursula K. Le Guin's *A Wizard of Earthsea* and its sequels, wherein the **wizard** Ged zealously guards the secret of his true name for fear that **evil** opponents could defeat him if given that information. By the same principle, the revelation of his true name destroys the Horned King in Lloyd Alexander's *The Book of Three* (1964). Vernor Vinge's *True Names* (1981), which has been called the first **cyberpunk** story, extends the idea into **cyberspace**, where protagonists engage in a battle between **individuality and conformity**, protecting themselves by hiding their identities behind cyberspatial nicknames. Similarly, in Orson Scott Card's *Ender's Game*, Ender's brother and sister gain influence in that future world's version of cyberspace, despite their **youth** and vulnerability, by giving themselves the historical names of Demosthenes and Locke; and in *The Matrix*, an ordinary citizen named Thomas A. Anderson works against the system as a **computer** hacker known as Neo.

Protagonists may need more than one name for other reasons. **Superheroes** with **secret identities** need a name for heroism (***Batman, Wonder Woman***) and another name for everyday life (Bruce Wayne, Diana Prince). When they are **aliens on Earth,** they may have three names—birth name, heroic name, and everyday name; thus, different people may address ***Superman*** as Kal-El, Superman, or Clark Kent and Hawkman as Katar Hol, Hawkman, or Carter Hall. Characters in fantasy may take on new names to reflect a heightened status: in J.R.R. Tolkien's *The Lord of the Rings*, a man previously called Strider, once he joins Frodo's **quest**, is known by his royal name, Aragorn. In L. Frank Baum's *The Marvelous Land of Oz* (1904) (see *The Wonderful Wizard of Oz*) the boy Tip gets not only a new name, but a new **gender**, when he is revealed as Ozma, princess of Oz. In Gene Wolfe's *The Book of the New Sun*, men are named for animals or animal products, women for **plants,** and **robots** for minerals.

Authors may avoid naming their characters for a variety of reasons. In Frederik Pohl's "Day Million" (1966), simply calling the protagonists "boy" and "girl" conveys that their seemingly extraordinary **romance**, involving no actual contact, is simply a typical experience in their future world. Harkening back to the tradition of the medieval play *Everyman* (1500), whose title character is so identified, unnamed characters may hint at some allegorical significance (see **Allegory**), as in Michael Swanwick's *Stations of the Tide* (1991), which identifies its visitor to an **alien world** only as "the bureaucrat." In *The Prisoner*, authorities insist upon calling their captive "Number 6" as a deliberate assault upon his sense of **identity**, which he resists by proclaiming that "I am not a number" and "I am a free man."

Despite such protestations, people in the futures of science fiction are often quite happy to use numbers as names—one naming convention that writers employ to give their stories a distinctive "scientific" atmosphere. The practice does no psychological harm to future citizens in Harry Stephen Keeler's "John Jones's Dollar" (1915), Hugo Gernsback's *Ralph 124C 41+: A Romance of the Year 2660* (1925), and the film *Just Imagine* (1930), but in the later film *THX 1138* (1970), names instead of numbers, as in *The Prisoner*, function as one sign that these future people are trapped in a totalitarian **dystopia**. In contrast, other science fiction protagonists are given positively old-fashioned names: Robert A. Heinlein, for example, borrowed names from **history** for characters Woodrow Wilson Smith (aka Lazarus Long) in *Time Enough for Love* (1973) (see *The Past Through Tomorrow*) and Daniel Boone Davis in *The Door into Summer* (1957).

In fantasy, names are most often taken from ancient **mythologies** and legends: Tolkien famously drew names from Norse mythology, but Greek mythology and Celtic mythology have been mined for evocative names just as frequently. Another favorite practice is to give character names suggestive of their attributes, like Flay, Swelter, and Prunesquallor in Mervyn Peake's ***Titus Groan*** and its sequels. But some authors have a knack for inventing unusual and memorable names; one thinks, for example, of the name of Edgar Rice Burroughs's Tarzan (see *Tarzan of the Apes*), which purportedly means "white skin" in the language of **apes** but cannot be persuasively traced to any true antecedents.

Discussion

To be part of a strange world, arguably, a character requires a strange name, which suggests that the success of science fiction and fantasy stories may depend largely upon their characters' names. This explains why L. Sprague de Camp and Catherine Crook de Camp's "Plotting an Imaginative Story" spends a considerable amount of time advising aspiring writers about choosing good names for their characters, and why scholars and commentators devote so much attention to analyzing and interpreting those names.

Bibliography

John Algeo. "Magic Names." *Names*, 30 (June, 1982), 59–67.

Poul Anderson. "Nomenclature in Science Fiction." C.L. Grant, ed., *Writing and Selling Science Fiction*. Cincinnati, OH: Writers Digest, 1976, 77–90.

Marion Zimmer Bradley. "And Strange-Sounding Names." De Camp, L. Sprague, ed., *Blade of Conan*. New York: Ace, 1979, 293–299.

L. Sprague de Camp and Catherine Crook de Camp. "Plotting an Imaginative Story." De Camp and de Camp, *Science Fiction Handbook, Revised*. New York: McGraw-Hill, 1975, 103–132.

John Krueger. "Names and Nomenclatures in Science-Fiction." *Names*, 14 (December, 1968), 203–214.

Robert Plank. "Names and Roles of Characters in Science Fiction." *Names*, 9 (September, 1961), 151–159.

William A. Senior. "The Significance of Names." *Extrapolation*, 31 (Fall, 1990), 258–269.

John A. Stoler. "Christian Lore and Characters' Names in *A Canticle for Leibowitz*." *Literary Onomastics Studies*, 11 (1984), 77–91.

J.R.R. Tolkien. "Guide to the Names in *The Lord of the Rings*." Jared Lobdell, ed., *A Tolkien Compass*. New York: Del Rey, 1980, 168–216.

—*Joyce Scrivner*

NATIVE AMERICANS

Overview

Native Americans (also known as Indians), and characters that recall or resemble Native Americans, appear across the spectrum of science fiction and fantasy. Some stories also refer to Native American **mythology** or **gods and goddesses**. Works most typically involve the Native Americans who encountered white settlers on the nineteenth-century American **frontier**, the typical setting of **westerns** (see **America**). The indigenous peoples of **Latin America** are discussed in that entry.

Survey

Native Americans initially entered the consciousness of western culture as stereotypes—either bloodthirsty **barbarians** or "noble savages." In the first role, Native Americans were simply **villains** opposing virtuous whites; as such, they were attacked by armored airships and the other amazing **inventions** of Luis Senarens's Frank Reade, Jr. in dime novels of the nineteenth century, and despicable Apaches endeavored to kill Edgar Rice Burroughs's John Carter just before he was teleported to **Mars** in *A Princess of Mars*. More positive, though condescending, portrayals of Native American **culture** were epitomized by J.M. Barrie's *Peter and Wendy*, where the Indians of Neverland were first ruthless but principled enemies, and later Peter Pan's trustworthy allies.

In the early twentieth century, signalling a shift from stereotypes to sympathetic study, anthropologist Afred Kroeber researched and lived with the Native American Ishi, last living member of his tribe, and later wrote a book about his experiences, *Ishi of Two Worlds* (1961). His daughter, Ursula K. Le Guin, drew upon this heritage in writing *Always Coming Home* (1985), a novel about a **post-holocaust society** that harkens back to Native American culture and traditions. In a sense, Le Guin was revisiting the pattern of George R. Stewart's *Earth Abides*, which also predicted that a global **disaster**—here, a mysterious plague—might drive people back to ways of life recalling Native Americans; but Le Guin strived for an atmosphere of authenticity, even publishing the novel with an accompanying cassette of her people's **music**. Her work typifies the science fiction and fantasy of the twentieth century's final decades, which recoils from clichéd preconceptions (see **Cliché**) and endeavors to reflect actual Native American customs, beliefs, and values.

This shift in treatments of Native Americans is strikingly observed in the *Star Trek* universe. An episode of the original series, "The Paradise Syndrome" (1968), brought Kirk into contact with a Native American tribe relocated by ancient **aliens in space** to an **alien world**; awed by his ability to revive a seemingly dead person with artificial respiration, the ignorant savages revere Kirk as a god. Later, there is a vastly more sensitive portrayal in an episode of *Star Trek: The Next Generation*, "Journey's End" (1994), where Picard, while on a mission to relocate a colony of Native Americans who live too close to a contested border, must admit and accept the part his ancestor played in a similar, more violent relocation of Native Americans on the American frontier. And in *Star Trek: Voyager*, the first officer is a Native American, Chakotay, who as faithful servant and loyal confidant to Captain Janeway shares many similarities with the *sachem* or wise man. He also performs vision **quests** and tells **trickster** stories to crewmates in several episodes.

Other works of science fiction and fantasy reflected a new awareness of and sensitivity to Native American culture, some produced by Native American writers. A half-Pueblo Indian, Martin Cruz Smith wrote *Nightwing* (1977), a **horror** novel about a Native American on a reservation investigating a plague of attacking **vampire** bats, which seem to fulfill Native American prophecies about the **apocalypse**; and in *Stallion Gate* (1986), he retold the story of building the first atomic bomb from the perspective of a Native American character. A Choctaw–Cherokee writer, Owl Goingback, also blended Native American legends and horror in *Darker Than Night* (1999), while Misha drew upon her Metis heritage in creating a future **dystopia** in *Red Spider, White Web* (1990).

Relevant works by other writers include Orson Scott Card's *Seventh Son* (1987) and its sequels, which present an **alternate history** of nineteenth-century America with a self-governing Native American state peacefully co-existing with neighboring states dominated by European immigrants and S.P. Somtow's *Moon Dance* (1989), which involves the culture clash of Native American **werewolves** and their immigrant counterparts from **Europe**. In Allan Steele's *Clarke County, Space* (1990), a Native American living in a **space habitat** periodically visits and gains **wisdom** from Coyote, the Native American god, while S.L. Viehl's space physician Cherijo Grey Veil in *StarDoc* (2001) and its sequels is of Native American descent. The Walt Disney animated film *Pocahantas* (1995) generally adhered to the historical record, with fantasy embellishments limited to anthropomorphic animal friends. Comic books also introduced Native American **superheroes**: DC Comics' Super-Chief and Marvel's American Eagle and Thunderbird, a mutant who belonged to the X-Men until his tragic **death**.

Discussion

No longer associated with primitivism and **violence**, fictional Native Americans now embody positive values such as harmony with **nature**, wisdom, concern for the environment, magical powers, and spirituality (see **Ecology; Magic; Religion**). They often stand in favorable contrast to the capitalist and technologically advanced **civilizations** of America and Europe. However, not even the boldest visionaries of science fiction writers imagine Native Americans returning to a dominant or central role; instead, whether in the past, present, or future, they remain marginalized figures who effect change not by leading the charge but by encouraging other, more powerful peoples to follow their virtuous examples.

Bibliography

Diane Krumrey. "Subverting the Tonto Stereotype in Popular Fiction." Elizabeth Kraus and Carolin Auer, eds., *Simulacrum America*. Rochester, NY: Camden House, 2000, 161–168.

Howard E. McCurdy. *Space and the American Imagination*. Washington D.C.: Smithsonian Institute Press, 1997.

Darcee L. McLaren and Jennifer E. Porter. "(Re)Covering Sacred Ground." Porter and McLaren, eds., *Star Trek and Sacred Grounds*. Albany: State University of New York Press, 1999, 101–115.

Christine Morris. "Indians and Other Aliens." *Extrapolation*, 20 (Winter, 1979), 301–307.

Gregory M. Pfitzer. "The Only Good Alien is a Dead Alien." *Journal of American Culture*, 18 (1995), 51–67.

Shaun Reno. "The Zuni Indian Tribe." *Extrapolation*, 36 (Summer, 1995), 151–158.

Peter C. Rollins and John E. O'Connor, eds. *Hollywood's Indian*. Lexington: University Press of Kentucky, 1998.

Michael Sturma. "Aliens and Indians." *Journal of Popular Culture*, 36 (November, 2002), 318–334.

M.S. Weinkauf. "The Indian in Science Fiction." *Extrapolation*, 20 (Winter, 1979), 308–320.

—*Lincoln Geraghty*

NATURE

∎

He recalled another thing the old woman had said about a world being the sum of many things—the people, the dirt, the growing things, the moons, the tides, the suns—the unknown sum called nature, *a vague summation without any sense of the* now. *And he wondered:* What is the now?

—Frank Herbert
Dune (1965)

Overview

Despite the notorious difficulty of defining and delimiting the concept of nature—Raymond Williams called it, in *Keywords* (1976), "perhaps the most complex word in the language"—and because of the nearly ubiquitous presence of various manifestations of nature in fantasy and science fiction texts, this entry attempts to find common ground for the concept shared by both genres, noting how nature often serves as a source of aesthetic, moral, and epistemological authority or value. Attention will focus on nature on three levels: the personal, the surrounding environment, and the entire cosmos.

Survey

On the personal level, emphasis on nature as a source of aesthetic value is apparent in stories which celebrate the beautiful **hero** or heroine. One science fiction exploration of the dangers of enthrallment to surface **beauty** is James Tiptree, Jr.'s "The Girl Who Was Plugged In" (1973), wherein a spellbound world follows the exploits of a media celebrity without awareness of the ugly girl behind the public facade. At other levels, whether as primordial **forest**, an **alien world**, or an alien starscape, we find myriad natural **landscapes** in both fantasy and science fiction. The cozy charm of the Shire in J.R.R. Tolkien's *The Lord of the Rings* is far from the austere and dangerous beauty of the Martian landscapes of Kim Stanley Robinson's *Red Mars* and its sequels; both are in turn distant from the sublime stellar and intergalactic vistas from various manifestations of the *Star Trek* series, but all provide strong evidence of the aesthetic qualities of nature.

Fiction suggesting the moral authority of nature often describes human attempts to transform, exploit, or control nature. This often entails radically altering our bodies, or even creating new ones. The protagonists of Mary Shelley's *Frankenstein* and Robert Louis Stevenson's *Strange Case of Dr. Jekyll and Mr. Hyde* are foundational figures in this context, and countless cinematic **mad scientists** have followed in their footsteps. Science fiction often explores the ethical consequences of modifying the body in portrayals of **genetic engineering**, **cyborgs**, human-machine interfaces, and nanotechnology (see **Ethics**). With respect to the landscape, especially in fantasy, the decay and destruction of the natural world often signals that something **evil** is afoot, as in Robert Jordan's Wheel of Time sequence (see *The Eye of the World*). In some works, ecological harmony is only possible in **lost worlds** or other **pastoral** locations where nature is shown respect or even reverence, and people live in harmony with the natural world (see **Ecology**). Kurt Vonnegut, Jr., in *Galapagos*, suggests that we might be capable of living successfully with nature only by losing our **intelligence**. On a cosmic level are stories of evil beings or dangerous circumstances that may destroy not only the environment of one planet, but even the universe itself. Such is the case in Philip Pullman's *The Golden Compass* (1995) and its sequels. The power known as the Blight, in Vernor Vinge's *A Fire Upon the Deep* (1992), is such a threat. In Greg Egan's *Schild's Ladder* (2001), the deep structure of reality itself is in peril of irrevocable alteration.

Nature also possesses authority in fantasy and science fiction as a source of truth. In fantasy this may entail understanding what role **magic** plays in the natural world, while works of science fiction emphasize the truths of science, usually couched in terms of "laws of nature." Understanding and applying magical or scientific truths is a legitimate way to gain power, while careless or selfish misuse of natural **knowledge** is usually condemned. However, conflicts may arise between the **quest** for knowledge of nature, and the potential dangers of this unrestricted pursuit. Echoing myths of forbidden fruit as well as the story of Faust, some interesting fiction asks if there are things we were not meant to know. In C.S. Lewis's space trilogy (see *Out of the Silent Planet*), for instance, science and **technology** represent serious threats to the natural world, while more positive perspectives on the quest for knowledge can be found in works by Arthur C. Clarke, C.J. Cherryh, Larry Niven, and Nancy Kress.

Nature, like **Earth**, may also be personified as a character, as occurs in Piers Anthony's Incarnations of Immortality series, beginning with *On a Pale Horse* (1983). The concept crosses over into science fiction in Karl Schroeder's *Ventus* (2001), which describes an attempt to literally give nature a voice, using advanced nanotechnology and **terraforming**.

Discussion

When nature is a central concern in fantasy or science fiction, it is commonly, if sometimes implicitly, used to define a standard of values, and thus is portrayed as a basic source of beauty, justice, or truth. Both fantasy and science fiction use the theme of nature to deal with issues of **humanity**'s appropriate place in a larger scheme of things, asking what are the proper attitudes toward our own (human) natures and what is our fitting relationship to the natural world around us and the universe as a whole. Should we respect and honor nature, or is it ours to exploit at will? Finally, science fiction and fantasy texts about nature help us explore whether there are natural limits—and whether there should be ethical or social ones—to the quest for knowledge.

Bibliography

Peter Coats. *Nature*. Cambridge, UK: Polity, 1998.
Nigel Clark. "Panic Ecology." *Theory, Culture and Society*, 14 (February, 1997), 77–96.

William Cronon, ed. *Uncommon Ground*. New York: Norton, 1995.
Lorraine Datson and Fernando Vidal, eds. *The Moral Authority of Nature*. Chicago: University of Chicago Press, 2004.
Carol P. Hovanec. "Visions of Nature in *The Word for the World Is Forest*." *Extrapolation*, 30 (Spring, 1989), 84–93.
Scott Sanders. "Woman as Nature in Science Fiction." Marlene S. Barr, ed., *Future Females*. Bowling Green, OH: Bowling Green State University Popular Press, 1981, 42–59.
Kate Soper. "Realism, Humanism and the Politics of Nature." *Theoria* (December, 2001), 55–73.
———. *What Is Nature?* Oxford: Blackwell, 1995.
Raymond Williams. "Nature." Williams, *Keywords*. London: Croom Helm Ltd., 1976, 184–189.

—*Richard L. McKinney*

NEAR FUTURE

Overview

Focusing on the near future might seem an unwise decision for a science fiction writer, given that the genre's most spectacular tropes—such as **space travel** to the **stars** through **hyperspace, aliens in space, time travel,** and fantastic new **inventions**—are off limits. Instead, writers must restrict themselves to events that might plausibly occur in the next few decades, and there is the obvious danger that even such modest **predictions** will be rapidly overtaken by events, making the story seem quaintly obsolete. But there are benefits in such a decision as well. First, the familiarity of the near future world enables writers to appeal to readers who might otherwise be disinclined to sample works of "science fiction": thus, millions of people read **technothrillers** by Tom Clancy and watch James Bond movies (see *Doctor No*; **Espionage**) without recognizing that the modest scientific advances depicted in the stories are science-fictional. Such stories can also provide a pointed and provocative way to comment on current events without the distorting lens of a fantasy or **far future** setting.

Survey

Many stories of the near future naively imagine that new scientific discoveries can easily be lost or forgotten, so society is only temporarily disrupted before the disappearance of the new invention restores the *status quo*; an example would be the film **The Invisible Man,** based on H.G. Wells's 1897 novel, in which the secret of **invisibility** vanishes with the death of its inventor. Alternatively, the innovation may turn out to have a fatal flaw that negates its potentially revolutionary effects; thus, the fabric that never wears out in *The Man in the White Suit* (1951) is found to eventually fall apart, and the effects of an **intelligence**-increasing technique used in Daniel Keyes's *Flowers for Algernon* turn out to be temporary. Science fiction critics typically condemn such stories for dodging the difficult questions of how discoveries like invisibility, permanent fabrics, or enhanced intelligence might impact society once they were widely available, but *The Man in the White Suit* demonstrates that such questions can be satisfactorily explored even in the context of a story that ulti-mately eliminates the potential engine of change.

The *status quo* of the present or near future can also be maintained by paranoid assumptions that amazing inventions and discoveries are being deliberately hidden from all but a few, such as the secret Martian observers in Edgar Pangborn's *A Mirror for Observers* (1954) or the various conspiracies of *The X-Files* (see **Aliens on Earth**; **Paranoia**; **Secret History**). Stories of alien **invasions** in the near future are also com-mon, like Robert A. Heinlein's *The Puppet Masters* (1951) and the films *Invaders from Mars* and *Invasion of the Body Snatchers*.

Near future stories may involve large **disasters**, including the events leading up to a **nuclear war**, as in Eugene Burdick and Harvey Wheeler's *Fail-Safe* (1962) and the film *Dr. Strangelove*, or such a war's immediate aftermath, as in Philip Wylie's *Tomorrow!* (1954) or the film *The Day After* (1983). **Comets and asteroids** may strike the Earth, as in Larry Niven and Jerry Pournelle's *Lucifer's Hammer* (1977) and the films *Deep Impact* (1998) and *Armageddon* (1998). A new ice age threat-ens society in Anna Kavan's *Ice* (1967) and the film *The Day After Tomorrow* (2004), while catastrophic heating is the problem in the film *The Day the Earth Caught Fire* (1961).

For decades, a standard picture of future **civilization** prevailed, based largely on ideas of the early twentieth century: **cities** dominated by immense skyscrapers, with people **flying** around in personal vehicles or traveling by means of moving side-walks. As most famously observed in the animated series *The Jetsons* (1962–1963), this was a pristine, well-ordered future world. The era of **cyberpunk**, however, brought a dirtier, grittier look to near future science fiction, with dark slums con-trolled by underworld figures, as in the films *Blade Runner* and *Johnny Mnemonic* (1996). In a similar spirit, Bruce Sterling's *Islands in the Net* (1988) anticipated a world obsessed with Internet connections and dominated by multinational corpora-tions, while William Gibson's second trilogy of *Virtual Light* (1993), *Idoru* (1996), and *All Tomorrow's Parties* (1998) was set in a slightly advanced future world pop-ulated by a rogue's gallery of drifters and opportunists.

Finally, one might also classify as near future science fiction the stories about significant political developments that do not involve major disasters or technolog-ical innovations, like the threatened military coup in Fletcher Knebel and Charles Bailey II's *Seven Days in May* (1962), filmed in 1964, or the brainwashed assassin of Richard Condon's *The Manchurian Candidate* (1960), filmed in 1962 and 2004 (see **Politics**).

Discussion

Commentators are fond of saying that science fiction is the literature of change, yet near future science fiction typically appears to resist change: the world observed is much like our own, and the story concludes with nothing significantly changed about that world. Perhaps that is why works of this type often appeal more to gen-eral readers than to science fiction readers. Still, since many of science fiction's bolder predictions about our contemporary world—such as easy travel throughout the solar system or artificial intelligences more advanced than humans—have still not come to pass, anticipating and exploring a future that very much resembles today's world may well be fitting and prudent.

Bibliography

Marleen S. Barr. *Envisioning the Future*. Middletown, CT: Wesleyan University Press, 2003.

Christophe Canto amd Odile Faliu. *The History of the Future*. New York and Paris: Flammarion, 1993.

Marvin Cetron and Thomas O'Toole. *Encounters with the Future*. New York: McGraw-Hill, 1982.

Arthur C. Clarke. *Arthur C. Clarke's July 20, 2019*. New York: Macmillan, 1986.

Suzette H. Elgin. "Women's Language and Near Future Science Fiction." *Women's Studies*, 14 (1987), 175–182.

Russell Galen. "The Near Future Is Perfect." *Writer's Digest*, 74 (January, 1994), 49–50.

Geoffrey A. Landis. "Robots, Reality and the Future of Humanity in the 21st Century." *Analog*, 114 (June, 1994), 57–63.

Jose M. Mota. "Media, Messages, and Myths." George Slusser, Colin Greenland, and Eric S. Rabkin, eds., *Storm Warnings*. Carbondale: Southern Illinois University Press, 1987, 84–93.

Jonathan S. Taylor. "The Subjectivity of the Near Future." Rob Kitchin and James Kneale, eds., *Lost in Space*. London, New York: Continuum, 2002, 90–103.

—*Gary Westfahl*

NUCLEAR POWER

■

Overview

The infancy of science fiction was also the infancy of nuclear **physics**; as humans were probing the heart of the atom, they also were becoming more interested in fiction that looked to the future. Nuclear power stories in science fiction have gone through stages of promise, terror, **humor**, and near-apathy. Separate entries address **nuclear war** and **post-holocaust societies**.

Survey

The earliest nuclear power stories were enchanted with the prospect of a new power that, to many, represented **progress**. Even the **stars** were not the limit: the spaceships of G.P. Serviss's *A Columbus of Space* (1909) reached their destinations thanks to atomic power. Although nuclear scientists were not considered saints, as in Robert Williams Wood's 1915 novel *The Man Who Rocked the Earth*, the response to science run amok was more science, not a retreat from **technology**. Less optimistically, H.G. Wells's *The World Set Free* (1914) predicted a future nuclear war, albeit one that inspired a peaceful postwar world government.

John W. Campbell, Jr., under his pseudonym Don A. Stuart, was a staunch proponent of nuclear power and the triumph of the **scientist**, and his attitudes shaped the early years of science fiction more than anyone else. In 1934, his straightforwardly named "Atomic Power" showed a future in which atomic power was the only salvation of a world succumbing to entropy; in 1938, his novella "Who Goes There?" postulated that atomic power generators would be neutron-based. Campbell's scientists were largely peacemakers and positive figures.

Karel Capek's atomic tales were more ambivalent. He saw nuclear power as a source of chaos in the world; nor was he alone. Two novels questioned the safety of nuclear power plants: Robert A. Heinlein's "Blowups Happen" (1940) explained that even the best of technologies would be run by fallible human beings whose mistakes could be catastrophic. In 1942, Lester del Ray's "Nerves" described an accident at a nuclear power plant, tapping into public anxiety about nuclear power even further, and beyond that point it was impossible to consider nuclear power a cure-all, even before the first atomic bomb had been tested.

The bomb has overshadowed its more peaceful cousin in the years since its use. Even stories about nuclear power are often heavily bomb-influenced, inasmuch as the most common topic in nuclear power stories is nuclear power **disasters**. The word "nuclear" itself became associated with fear and danger, despair, and even **apocalypse**.

The dangers of nuclear power in fiction can be slow and creeping, such as radiation causing **mutations** that will suddenly spring up in the form of human or animal **monsters**. *Godzilla, King of the Monsters* epitomizes the subgenre of radioactive giant mutants, in which human beings' dangerous **intelligence** combines with the dangerous natural world for literally monstrous results. But the fictional dangers of nuclear power can also have immediate results. The movie *The China Syndrome* came out in 1979, after the Three Mile Island disaster. It postulated a nuclear plant disaster of literally Earth-shattering dimensions, with the voiced possibility of radiation going into the **Earth** and "burning a hole to China." Nuclear fears were amplified and dramatized in science fiction, but not beyond the actual horrific possibilities.

Nuclear power disasters are now historical fact rather than speculative curiosities. After the Chernobyl tragedy, German author Gudrun Pausewang wrote a nuclear holocaust novel for teenagers, *Fall-out* (1987); though it won the most prestigious prize for German children's books, the novel proved quite controversial. Science fiction writer Frederik Pohl wrote a realistic novel about the disaster, *Chernobyl* (1987), bringing a speculative sensibility to an historical topic. The pronuclear viewpoint, as expressed in novels like Larry Niven and Jerry Pournelle's *Lucifer's Hammer* (1977), has been more difficult to maintain since catastrophes like Three Mile Island and Chernobyl. The benefits of nuclear power are mostly quiet and ongoing, its disasters sudden and intense.

The realities of nuclear power make it clear to contemporary writers that nuclear power is not a panacea or wonderful source of unlimited energy. So, writers who wish to include an energy revolution in their stories must turn to other sources, such as the "Y-energy" in Nancy Kress's *Beggars in Spain* (1993). The continued existence and use of nuclear power in society has also made it the butt of jokes: Homer Simpson of **The Simpsons** works at the town's nuclear power plant. Homer's idiocy (particularly in his role as the plant's safety officer), and his boss's callous disregard for anything but a profit, make near-weekly appearances on the show, and supposed nuclear mutations like three-eyed fish are recurrent gags. Thus, the mutated monsters of the 1950s became political embarrassments and mild jokes in the 1990s (see **Politics**).

When nuclear power makes a positive or significant appearance in modern science fiction, its context is generally that of **space travel**, serving, for example, as the propulsion source for the spaceship *Discovery* in Arthur C. Clarke's ***2001: A Space Odyssey***. In space, no one needs to fear Godzilla's wrath or holes burnt through the

Earth, and nuclear waste disposal is not an issue without an ecosystem to pollute in the vacuum outside the atmosphere. Thus, the awesome power of mushroom clouds is safely removed from readers' backyards.

Discussion

No longer a sign of progress for most writers, nuclear power has assumed a secondary place, mostly in disaster novels and as a space-suitable technology. Nuclear hysteria has largely left science fiction as the general public becomes better informed about possible mutations and side-effects. Nuclear power remains a fearful topic, but giant mutant lizards are no longer required to get the point across.

Bibliography

Albert I. Berger. "Nuclear Energy." *Science-Fiction Studies*, 6 (July, 1979), 121–128.
M. Keith Booker. *Monsters, Mushroom Clouds, and the Cold War*. Westport, CT: Greenwood Press, 2001.
David Dowling. *Fictions of Nuclear Disaster*. Iowa City, IA: University of Iowa Press, 1987.
Amit Goswami, with Maggie Goswami. *The Cosmic Dancers*. New York: Harper & Row, 1983.
Peter Nicholls, David Langford, and Brian Stableford. "The Secret Is Energy." Nicholls, Langford, and Stableford, *The Science in Science Fiction*. New York: Alfred A. Knopf, 1983, 30–45.
Susan Tebbutt. "Doomsday Looms." Karen Sayer and John Moore, eds., *Science Fiction, Critical Frontiers*. London: Macmillan Press Ltd., 2000.
Spencer Weart. *Nuclear Fear*. Cambridge: Harvard University Press, 1988.
J. Mallory Wober. *Television and Nuclear Power*. Norwood, NJ: Albex Pub., 1992.

—Marissa Lingen

NUCLEAR WAR

Overview

From 1945 to the end of the Cold War, fiction set during or after a nuclear war was quite common. Only a minority of the stories were seriously intended as warnings against the use of such weapons. Far more common tales of sex and violence in the ruins resembled tales of **post-holocaust societies** not involving nuclear **weaponry**. A separate entry discusses **nuclear power**.

Survey

The first act of nuclear war, the dropping of the atomic bomb on Hiroshima in 1945, is examined in two **alternate history** stories that present opposite viewpoints: Kim Stanley Robinson's "The Lucky Strike" (1984) argues that the Hiroshima bomb need not have been dropped, but Alfred Coppel's *The Burning Mountain* (1983) makes the opposite case.

Among the "awful warning" novels about a worldwide nuclear war, the very first, H.G. Wells's *The World Set Free* (1914), came long before the first bombs were dropped, while Robert A. Heinlein's "Solution Unsatisfactory" (1940) anticipated the nervous stalemate that would result from a world of nations with nuclear weapons. Postwar stories about the immediate impact of atomic warfare on ordinary people include Judith Merril's *Shadow on the Hearth* (1950), filmed as *Atomic Attack* (1954), Philip Wylie's *Tomorrow!* (1954), and Nevil Shute's *On the Beach* (1957), filmed in 1959, though they were greatly surpassed in realism by Helen Clarkson's little-known *The Last Day* (1959). Noteworthy later works are Whitley Strieber and James Kunetka's *Warday* (1984) and films like *The Day After* (1983), the more thoughtful *Testament* (1983), and *Threads* (1984). In a class by itself is the Russian film *Letters from a Dead Man* (1986), which powerfully reflects the impact that nuclear winter theory had on the Soviet Union (see **Russia**). *Dr. Strangelove* is admired as an absurdist **satire** on the logic of nuclear deterrence. It is loosely based on a serious novel on the same subject, Peter George's *Red Alert* (1958), which is similar to Eugene Burdick and Harvey Wheeler's *Fail-Safe* (1962). Also effective is Raymond Briggs's graphic satire on civil defense, *When the Wind Blows* (1982).

Among the more thoughtful **far future** depictions of nuclear war, the most impressive are Walter M. Miller, Jr.'s *A Canticle for Leibowitz* and Russell Hoban's *Riddley Walker* (1980), both of which depict the deterioration of human society in the wake of a nuclear holocaust. Humanity is almost extinguished by such a war in Ray Bradbury's **The Martian Chronicles**, though many readers ignore its antinuclear message, enchanted by exotic Martians (see **Mars**).

Adam and Eve plots are rarer than is suggested in some criticism, but unbridled **sexuality** of all kinds is a prominent feature of much nuclear-war fiction, such as Piers Anthony's *Var the Stick* (1972). However, Suzy McKee Charnas in *Walk to the End of the World* (1974) and Sheri S. Tepper in **The Gate To Women's Country** give this theme a feminist twist to criticize male **violence** (see **Feminism**).

More often, nuclear war is a convenient device for stripping away the restraints of **civilization**. The struggle to survive justifies widespread mayhem (see **Survival**) in many popular "road" novels, of which the pioneer example is probably Roger Zelazny's *Damnation Alley* (1969), filmed in 1977, about the adventures of the world's last Hell's Angel; on its heels came **Mad Max** and its sequels. Starting with Jerry Ahern's *The Survivalist* (1981), a vast number of macho thrillers celebrating sex and violence poured out from Zebra Books and other publishers. Although *The Terminator* films, beginning with the original in 1984, belong roughly to this category, with "post-holocaust" violence being transported in time back to our own era (see **Time Travel**), *Terminator 2: Judgment Day* (1991) contains an effective depiction of a nuclear attack.

One of the more bizarre by-products of the nuclear age was the proliferation of stories depicting the radiation-induced **mutation** of animals and humans to give them super powers. Even in Daniel F. Galouye's serious *Dark Universe* (1961), his cave-dwelling survivors are given infrared vision. Telepathy (see **Psychic Powers**) is a common side-benefit of nuclear war, as in John Wyndham's *Re-Birth* (1955) and Leigh Brackett's *The Long Tomorrow* (1955). The latter novel also reflects a common fear in science fiction after 1945—that a backlash against science in a post-holocaust world would create an upsurge of superstition and bigotry. Neo-barbarian stories range from the frivolous (Robert Adams, *The Coming of the Horseclans* [1975]) to the more thoughtful Pelbar Cycle of Paul O. Williams, especially *The Dome in the Forest* (1981).

Discussion

Although a few plots before 1945 depicted wars involving atomic weapons, this theme was mainly a response to the American–Soviet nuclear arms race and was largely confined to the Cold War era. After the Gorbachev era and fall of the Berlin Wall, the vast majority of titles with postnuclear war plots were sequels in long-running survivalist thriller novels aimed at a specialized male market. Political **technothrillers** sometimes feature a Middle Eastern or South Asian regional nuclear exchange, but even they are strikingly rare, though the danger of such an exchange is perhaps greater than ever. Though many memorable works set after nuclear wars were written in the theme's heyday, nuclear war is now considered an outdated **cliché** in science fiction.

Bibliography

Martha A. Bartter. *The Way to Ground Zero*. Westport, CT: Greenwood Press, 1988.

Harold L. Berger. *Science Fiction and the New Dark Age*. Bowling Green, OH: Bowling Green State University Popular Press, l976.

M. Keith Booker. *Monsters, Mushroom Clouds, and the Cold War*. Westport, CT: Greenwood Press, 2001.

Paul Boyer. *By the Bomb's Early Light*. New York: Pantheon, 1985.

Paul Brians. *Nuclear Holocausts*. Kent, OH: Kent State University Press, 1987.

Mick Broderick. *Nuclear Movies*. Jefferson, NC: McFarland, 1991.

Joyce A. Evans. *Celluloid Mushroom Clouds*. Boulder, CO Westview, 1998.

David Seed. *American Science Fiction and the Cold War*. Edinburgh: Edinburgh University Press, 1999.

Spencer Weart. *Nuclear Fear*. Cambridge: Harvard University Press, 1988.

—Paul Brians

NUDITY

———————————————————■———————————————————

For a time Jack was angry; but when he had been without the jacket for a short while he began to realize that being half-clothed is infinitely more uncomfortable than being entirely naked. Soon he did not miss his clothing in the least, and from that he came to revel in the freedom of his unhampered state.

—Edgar Rice Burroughs
The Son of Tarzan (1916)

Overview

The **civilizations** of the West have adopted complex, even contradictory, attitudes to **sexuality** and the body, as is fully reflected in portrayals of nude or near-nude bodies in science fiction and fantasy.

Survey

Ancient civilizations accepted nudity, but **Christianity** considered the body shameful and insisted that it be hidden. Thomas More's *Utopia* is in the Christian tradition, describing a society in which monogamy is enforced harshly, but prospective brides and grooms do inspect each other naked before committing themselves to **marriage**. This is a relatively early example of the use of imaginative fiction to describe rationally reconstructed social mores.

Jonathan Swift's *Gulliver's Travels* deals with nudity and clothing in the context of an age-old question: what is it to be human? Gulliver encounters strange beings—**giants, intelligent horses**, and naked, brutish humans—whose bodies are always under scrutiny. He is often driven back to the resources of his own body and limited articles that he carries in his clothing.

In Charles Kingsley's nineteenth-century **fairy tale**, *The Water Babies*, a young chimneysweep is transformed into a tiny aquatic baby—evidently nude, though other water-babies wear white bathing suits. As in many narratives, naked immersion in **water** functions as a baptismal **rebirth**. Ordinary clothing signifies a fallen state, while nudity evokes purity, **freedom**, and a **pastoral** or Arcadian oneness with **nature** (see **Arcadia**). Similarly, the fantasy novels of William Morris often depict characters swimming naked or wearing little clothing—just one expression of the author's rejection of industrial society and its squalor. In George Orwell's **fable**, *Animal Farm*, clothes are despised as marks of human oppression.

Some twentieth-century science fiction uses nudity to suggest moral **decadence**. For example, the false Maria **robot** in Fritz Lang's movie *Metropolis* is displayed dancing almost naked. In Aldous Huxley's *Brave New World*, nudity and erotic play are encouraged even in young **children**, while adults have casual, and seemingly shallow, attitudes to nudity and sex. However, when science fiction and fantasy have not entirely avoided the subject of nudity, they have usually celebrated it.

There has always been an erotic element in fairy tales and other narratives about exotic times and places. Fairy tales have frequently been used for acceptable kinds of erotic **art**, and fantastic literature is well placed to take advantage of the convention that nudity is more acceptable if characters are distant from the reader's own society. Such nineteenth-century adventure novels as H. Rider Haggard's *She* involve naked or near-naked pagan women, and Edgar Rice Burroughs portrayed female characters, like Dejah Thoris in *A Princess of Mars*, as naked and sexually tantalizing (though his actual storylines are prudish). In his Tarzan books (see *Tarzan of the Apes*), nudity carries frequent connotations of oneness with nature and freedom from social restrictions.

In the pulp era, magazine covers often portrayed scantily clad women, though nudity was seldom emphasized in the stories themselves. Some did describe naked women whose strong bodies showed their sexual power. **Sword and sorcery** narratives, like Robert E. Howard's Conan stories (see *Conan the Conqueror*), emphasized the characters' bodies; and related fantasy art, notably that of Boris Vallejo, presents idealized nude, or near-nude, portrayals of both men and women.

The classic 1950s movie *Forbidden Planet* epitomizes the Arcadian and mildly erotic aspects of nudity in distant locations. Beautiful, young Altaira swims naked, wears scanty clothing, and keeps dangerous animals as pets. All this shows the Edenic nature of her life, and her essential innocence—but also her potential for sexual experience.

Comics, computer games, and movies continue the tradition of socially excused erotic display. **Superheroes**' costumes are scanty or skintight, revealing every contour of their physically perfect, sexually exaggerated, bodies. Hollywood action movies show the actors' sensationally "built" physiques, though instances of actual nudity usually have some plot justification. Movies about **aliens on Earth**, mutants, or robots who can pass for human sometimes display the characters nude to show their "inhuman" physical perfection, as in *The Terminator* and its sequels.

More intellectual justifications of nudity can be found in the fiction of Philip José Farmer, Poul Anderson, Robert A. Heinlein, Samuel R. Delany, and John Varley, though Farmer often lapses into parody and pornography. Heinlein's *Stranger in a Strange Land* satirizes prudery and monogamy (see **Satire**), and celebrates sex and the body. In Delany's *Triton*, people wear (and do) whatever they like, and some choose to go naked.

Discussion

Whether despised, glorified, or intellectually scrutinized, the nude body is a perennial source of fascination, with many connotations. Science fiction and fantasy have been well placed to explore those connotations, socially licenced by their non-mimetic storylines, strange characters, and remote locales.

Bibliography

Russell Blackford. "Debased and Lascivious?" James Sallis, ed., *Ash of Stars*. Jackson: University Press of Mississippi, 1996, 26–42.

Scott Bukatman. *Matters of Gravity*. Durham: Duke University Press, 2003.

Maureen Duffy. *The Erotic World of Faery*. London: Hodder and Stoughton, 1972.

Harry Harrison. *Great Balls of Fire!* New York: Grosset & Dunlap, 1977.

Linda Mizejewski. "Action Bodies in Futurist Spaces." Annette Kuhn, ed., *Alien Zone II*. London and New York: Verso, 1999, 152–172.

Richard Dale Mullen. "The Prudish Prurience of H. Rider Haggard and Edgar Rice Burroughs." *Riverside Quarterly*, 6 (August, 1973), 4–19; (April, 1974), 134–146.

Robin Roberts. "The Female Alien." Roberts, *A New Species*. Urbana and Chicago: University of Illinois Press, 1993, 40–65.

Vivian Sobchak. "The Virginity of Astronauts." Annette Kuhn, ed., *Alien Zone*. London and New York: Verso, 1990, 103–115.

Claudia Springer. *Electronic Eros*. Austin: University of Texas Press, 1996.

—Russell Blackford

OLD AGE

Old age is not an accomplishment; it is just something that happens to you despite yourself, like falling downstairs.

—Robert A. Heinlein
Podkayne of Mars (1963)

Overview

As forms of literature often associated with **children** and **youth**, science fiction and fantasy might be expected to have little to do with the elderly and their concerns. It is true that many stories follow the tradition of respecting older people as **mentors** possessing valuable **wisdom**, but there are also stories that express in various ways an aversion to the aging process and those affected by it. People who evade old age by attaining some form of **immortality and longevity**, perhaps involving **suspended animation and cryonics**, are discussed elsewhere.

Survey

Wise old men abound in fantasy. They are frequently **wizards**, like Merlin of the **Arthur** legends, Gandalf of J.R.R. Tolkien's *The Lord of the Rings*, and Dumbledore of J.K. Rowling's *Harry Potter and the Sorcerer's Stone*. Comparable figures in science fiction include Jubal Harshaw of Robert A. Heinlein's *Stranger in a Strange Land*, Obi Wan Kenobi of *Star Wars*, and Yoda of *The Empire Strikes Back* (1980). Less commonly, old women play this role, such as the diminutive clairvoyant of the film *Poltergeist* (1982). However, these sages rarely play a central role in the narrative; instead, they offer assistance and advice to a significantly younger **hero**. A rare work that employs a senior citizen as protagonist is Stephen King's *Insomnia* (1994), in which a seventy-year-old man joins forces with a woman of similar age to unravel a cosmic **mystery** involving the Three Fates of Greek **mythology** (see **Destiny**). Old people are also featured in the film *Cocoon* (1985) wherein they are first rejuvenated by an alien process before deciding to accompany their benefactors to an **alien world**.

Aged heroes like these may become more common in the future, given that the average age of the western world's population is gradually increasing as **medicine** lengthens human lifespans and more people choose to not have children. Brian W. Aldiss's *Greybeard* (1964) carries this trend to its ultimate conclusion by envisioning a future in which **nuclear war** has made it impossible for people to give **birth** to children; so, the entire population of **Earth** is soon made up of old people. Still, Aldiss introduces an element of hope with indications that somewhere, children are being born again.

More commonly, future **civilizations** are dominated by young people who seek to eliminate the elderly. In the film *Wild in the Streets* (1968), people over thirty-five are rounded up and sent to concentration camps to be constantly drugged with LSD (see **Drugs**), while in the film *Logan's Run* (1976), based on William F. Nolan and George Clayton Johnson's 1967 novel, all people are killed at the age of thirty—though the hero Logan, while fleeing to avoid this penalty, does encounter one old man who also escaped **death**. To Logan, who has never seen such a person, he is an object of wonder.

As another indication of abhorrence of the elderly, unnaturally rapid aging may be portrayed as the most horrific and catastrophic of fates. In the memorable conclusion of H. Rider Haggard's *She*, Ayesha's attempted rejuvenation in magical **fires** goes awry, causing her to rapidly age, shrivel, and die. In films, this is frequently the way that **vampires** die when opponents drive stakes into their hearts. In the *Star Trek* episode "The Deadly Years" (1967), Kirk and Spock are relieved of their duties on the *Enterprise* because an alien disease has turned them into old people, no longer considered capable of command.

Oddly enough, while stories like these might give someone every reason to seek to avoid growing old, there are also cautionary tales that warn against attempts to resist aging, one of them being *She*, wherein Ayesha's long efforts to remain perpetually young finally destroy her. In Oscar Wilde's **The Picture of Dorian Gray**, the dissolute Dorian long evades the wearing effects of his lifestyle because his portrait magically ages in his stead, but in the end he fittingly dies. In an episode of *The Twilight Zone*, "Long Live Walter Jameson" (1960), an alchemist gives a man immortality, but he only finds it depressing to watch those around him die. Eventually he gets shot and killed by a woman he abandoned, causing him—like Ayesha—to instantly age and wither into dust. In the film *Seconds* (1966), an elderly businessman pays for a secret process to make him look young and healthy again, but the results bring bitterness, not happiness. In another episode of *The Twilight Zone*, "The Trade-Ins" (1962), has an elderly couple seeking to purchase young new bodies decide, after learning they can only afford to buy one body, that it would be better, after all, for them to accept growing old together.

Discussion

With an aging readership amidst an aging population, it would be heartening to see science fiction and fantasy accepting older people as efficacious heroes, instead of so resolutely and repetitiously focusing on adolescents and young adults as protagonists and on futures that explicitly or implicitly exclude the elderly. At present, a novel like Nancy Kress's *The Prince of Morning Bells* (1981) conspicuously stands out for allowing its female hero to both grow old and continue adventuring, as does

Arthur C. Clarke's *2061: Odyssey Three*, with an aged but vigorous Heywood Floyd flying to rendezvous with Halley's Comet (see ***2001: A Space Odyssey***). As a condition that writers and readers will someday experience, old age surely merits more examination in science fiction and fantasy than it currently receives.

Bibliography

Carl Buchanan. "The Terrible Old Man." *Lovecraft Studies*, No. 29 (Fall, 1993), 19–30.

Arthur C. Clarke. "Life Meets Death and Twists Its Tail." Clarke, *Arthur C. Clarke's July 20, 2019*. New York: Macmillan, 1986, 229–247.

Susan Kray. "Jews in Time." Gary Westfahl, George Slusser, and David Leiby, eds., *Worlds Enough and Time*. Westport, CT: Greenwood Press, 2002, 87–101.

Tamar Lindsay. "Between the Lines: Older Men Who Want to Run With the Wolves." *Niekas*, No. 45 (1998), 95.

Barry N. Malzberg. "The All-Time, Prime-Time, Take-Me-to-Your-Leader Science Fiction Plot." Malzberg, *The Engines of the Night*. Garden City, NY: Doubleday, 1982, 147–158.

Miriam Y. Miller. "J.R.R. Tolkien's Merlin—An Old Man With a Staff." Jeanie Watson and Maureen Fries, eds., *The Figure of Merlin in the Nineteenth and Twentieth Centuries*. Lewiston, NY: Mellen, 1989, 121–142.

Charlotte Spivack. "Only in Dying, Life." *Modern Language Studies*, 14 (Summer, 1984), 43–53.

James Wade. "You Can't Get There From Here." Reynolds A. Morse, ed., *Shiel in Diverse Hands*. Cleveland, OH: Reynolds Morse Foundation, 1983, 195–203.

—Gary Westfahl

OMENS AND SIGNS

Overview

Humanity cannot resist seeing **magic** significance in the world's happenstances. Such things as comets (see **Comets and Asteroids**), **stars**, **weather**, and **birds** in flight surely offer guidance if subjected to proper **reading**. In fiction, especially fantasy, this is often true: authors play god and load their creation with cues for characters and readers alike. Elaborate systems for predicting the future are discussed under **Divination**.

Survey

In the nineteenth century, John Ruskin identified the projection of human emotion on to **landscape** and weather (popular in **Gothic** thrillers) as the "Pathetic Fallacy." Real storms rage only metaphorically; fantasy storms may indeed have emotions, like the stage-struck example awaiting its big entrance in Terry Pratchett's *Wyrd Sisters* (1988) (see ***The Colour of Magic***).

The "fallacy" is often made literal in J.R.R. Tolkien's ***The Lord of the Rings***. **Forests** and **caverns** arouse fear of the unknown: Tolkien peoples them with malign trees and **monsters**. Ominous dark birds overhead are literal spies. **Darkness**, associated with **evil**, becomes an expression of the arch-**villain**'s will when the smoke of volcanic activity—traditionally, the wrath of **gods and goddesses** or **demons**—hides the **Sun**.

Wrongness is indicated by an unnatural, pulsating brilliance of the sky in Alan Garner's *The Owl Service*. During **sea travel** in Ursula K. Le Guin's *A Wizard of Earthsea*, the **hero** realizes that a contrary wind is deliberately barring him from the **island** of **wizards**. When the lead character is crossed in **love** in Neil Gaiman's *Sandman: Brief Lives* (1994), his gloomy self-pity lashes the landscape with rain.

As Diana Wynne Jones remarks in *The Tough Guide to Fantasyland* (1996), fantasy characters' sensitivity to evil or wrongness amounts to a **talent** or **psychic power**. Examples are numerous. The opening of James Blish's *Black Easter* (1968) foreshadows the **apocalypse** to come with a (monastery) room that stinks of demons.

Portents are frequently ambiguous, Delphic **puzzles**, like the symbolic incident of a chameleon taken by a hawk in Pier's Anthony's *A Spell for Chameleon*. Fearing a prediction of the girl Chameleon's death, the hero eventually sees that the hawk represents himself and the capture is romantic. Other uncertain omens appear in the **mirror** of Avram Davidson's *The Phoenix and the Mirror* (1969), and through "dark **light**" photography in Terry Pratchett's *The Truth* (2000).

Signs may be solid **magical objects**, like the Signs of Light in Susan Cooper's *The Dark Is Rising* (1973). A wizard in Randall Garrett's *Too Many Magicians* (1967) remarks that in magic **ritual**, the best symbol is the thing itself—a sharp knife representing a sharp knife.

Science fiction prefers a rational reading of the world and tends to explain away apparent omens. Moments of portentous unease in Anne McCaffrey's *Dragonflight* are side effects of **time travel**—the sensed wrongness of existing twice at the same instant. Gene Wolfe's *The Book of the New Sun* includes an unnaturally extended night thanks to an eclipse of the Sun by a vast spaceship (see **Space Travel**). Biblical signs like plagues and **rivers** turning to **blood** are underpinned by solid **biology** in George R.R. Martin's *Tuf Voyaging* (1987).

Spectacular "shooting stars" in John Wyndham's *The Day of the Triffids* are harbingers of blindness (See **Vision and Blindness**) and may be misdirected space **weaponry**. Larry Niven's "Inconstant Moon" (1971) features the portent of a too-bright **Moon**, warning the knowledgeable of solar **disaster** on **Earth**'s far side. Light streaks in the sky of a **planetary colony** in Alastair Reynolds's *Absolution Gap* (2003), apparent side effects of **space war**, form the message LEAVE NOW.

More frivolously, an artificial-aurora experiment is sabotaged in Arthur C. Clarke's "Watch This Space" (1957), converting it to a colossal Coca-Cola ad (see **Advertising**). **First contact** is wrecked by ominous stars in Robert F. Young's "Written in the Stars" (1957): in alien language, our constellation Orion is an unspeakably offensive ideogram.

Less easily read science fiction signs include anomalies of the Moon's magnetic field, leading to the buried monolith of *2001: A Space Odyssey*; the beep of the Dirac communicator (see **Communication**), which unpacks to reveal all past and future Dirac messages in James Blish's "Beep" (1954); and, in Greg Egan's *Diaspora* (1997), a binary neutron star's tiny periodic discrepancy that flags the imminent arrival of an Earth-sterilizing gamma-ray flash. The ocean of Stanislaw Lem's

Solaris seethes with bewildering, portentous shapes whose significance **humanity** cannot grasp.

Discussion

Human superstition insists on reading meaning into the world, like the **barbarian** troops in Wolfe's *The Book of the New Sun*, who come under fire from advanced weaponry and defend themselves with "magic" invocations—each survivor increasingly convinced of the power of his magic while he survives. Fantasy, by contrast, is already riddled with meaning. The reader suspects that any seeming omen or sign is likely present for some purpose, and enters into a kind of metafictional complicity with the author. As in **detective** fiction, though, clues may be deliberately misleading. Even such default symbology as the identification of black with evil and white with good is fruitfully confused in Le Guin's Earthsea, where most people are dark-skinned and the "evil empire" is of whites; or L.E. Modesitt's Recluce series, beginning with *The Magic of Recluce* (1991), where black stands for order and white for chaos.

Bibliography

John A. Calabrese. "Dynamic Symbolism and the Mythic Resolution of Polar Extremes in *The Lord of the Rings*." Donald E. Palumbo, ed. *Spectrum of the Fantastic*. Westport, CT: Greenwood, 1988. 135–140.

Samuel R. Delany. "Of Sex, Objects, Signs, Systems, Sales, SF, and Other Things." *Australian Science Fiction Review*, Second Series, 7 (March 1987), 9–36.

Michael D.C. Drout. "Reading the Signs of Light." *Lion and the Unicorn*, 21(2) (Spring, 1997), 230–250.

Diana Wynne Jones. *The Tough Guide to Fantasyland*. London: Vista, 1996.

Paul Kincaid. "Cognitive Mapping 12: Clouds." *Vector*, No. 197 (January/February 1998), 16–17.

Nick Lowe. "The Well-Tempered Plot Device." *Ansible*, No. 46 (July 1986), 3–7.

Donald F. Theall. "On Science Fiction as Symbolic Communication." *Science-Fiction Studies*, 7(3) (November 1980), 247–262.

R.H. Wilson. "Some Recurrent Symbols in Science Fiction." *Extrapolation*, 2 (December, 1960), 2–4.

—David Langford

OPTIMISM AND PESSIMISM

∎

Overview

Optimism and pessimism are general attitudes toward the future, and hence are more relevant to science fiction than to fantasy. **Utopias** set in the future and other stories describing tremendous **progress** are effectively expressions of optimism, while **dystopias** and descriptions of future **decadence** necessarily convey pessimism.

Survey

In fantasies, individual characters may be optimistic or pessimistic about the outcome of their **quest**, but the genre's preference for happy endings suggests a pervading atmosphere of optimism regarding people's ability to resist **evil** and maintain a benevolent social order. Still, many fantasies—J.R.R. Tolkien's *The Lord of the Rings* being an obvious example—may convey the pessimistic sense that the story's idealized past of **magic** and **supernatural creatures** is doomed to die and be supplanted by our mundane, less desirable, world. An aura of unexpected grimness also pervades fantasies like Stephen R. Donaldson's *Lord Foul's Bane* and its sequels, as well as many works of **dark fantasy** and **horror.**

Writers not associated with science fiction generally have extreme views about the future of **humanity.** Some posit that reasonable men and women will eventually come together, achieve political or scientific solutions to basic human problems, and achieve a benign utopia. This society may be found today in an isolated enclave providing a pattern for the world to follow, as in Charlotte Perkins Gilman's *Herland* or B.F. Skinner's *Walden Two* (1948), or it may be in the future, as in Edward Bellamy's *Looking Backward, 2000-1887.* Others fear that governments will continue expanding their powers and, armed with new **technology,** become oppressive dystopias, as in Yevgeny Zamiatin's *We* or George Orwell's *Nineteen Eighty-Four.* Specific concerns that **computers** will someday seek to dominate or exterminate humanity surface in various works, such as D.F. Jones's *Colossus* (1966), *The Terminator* and its sequels, *The Matrix* and its sequels, and the film *I, Robot* (2004).

Considering the science fiction genre, Donald A. Wollheim's *The Universe Makers* (1971) interestingly argues that science fiction collectively presents a shared monomyth of the future, pessimistically envisioning **disasters** and crises in the **near future**—such as **nuclear war, overpopulation,** and other threats to Earth's **ecology**—but also projecting an optimistic conviction that humanity will in time overcome these problems, conquer space (see **Space Travel**), meet and develop harmonious relationships with **aliens in space,** establish a **galactic empire,** and advance toward an encounter with God. Many of the genre's greatest sagas—including E.E. "Doc" Smith's Lensman series (see *Triplanetary*), Robert A. Heinlein's Future History stories (see *The Past Through Tomorrow*), and Isaac Asimov's Robot and Foundation series (see *I, Robot; Foundation*)—can be fit into this pattern. Stories envisioning global nuclear wars that lead to primitive **post-holocaust societies** modify the picture only to place humanity's cosmic triumph further in the future; thus, works like Andre Norton's *Star Man's Son* (1952) and Walter M. Miller, Jr.'s *A Canticle for Leibowitz* conclude with humans planning to travel, or actually traveling, into space.

In works by the genre's greatest visionaries, however, this short-term pessimism and long-term optimism are overshadowed by an ultimate pessimism: humanity will achieve great heights but inevitably decline, perhaps doomed by the death of Earth's **Sun** or even the universe itself (see **Eschatology**). H.G. Wells's *The Time Machine* travels 800,000 years to the future to find humanity devolved into opposing races of gentle simpletons and subterranean savages; even farther in the future, Earth is dying and humanity is no more. Among the works influenced by Wells are William Hope Hodgson's *The House on the Borderland* (1908) and John W. Campbell, Jr.'s stories "Twilight" (1934) and "Night" (1935). Olaf Stapledon's *Last and First Men* describes humanity evolving into eighteen species over millions of years before finally confronting impending extinction. His *Star Maker* tells a similar story on a cosmic scale, with intelligent species throughout the universe merging into a **hive mind** that reaches out to its creator, is coldly rebuffed, and prepares for its own decline and death. George Zebrowski's *Macrolife* (1979) envisions group minds in **space habitats** merging into a gigantic entity that begins to break down as the universe approaches its end.

It remains possible to overlay on this dark picture a higher optimism that humans, or at least intelligent beings, might survive and advance beyond even such a cosmic **apocalypse**. The **hero** of Arthur C. Clarke's *Against the Fall of Night* (1953) learns that humanity did not really decline to decadence in two **cities** on Earth, but instead migrated out of the cosmos to some mysterious locale, presumably continuing to advance. In James Blish's *The Triumph of Time* (1958), concluding his Cities in Flight series, all humans die as the universe dies, but they hope to influence the creation of another universe. Stephen Baxter's sequel to *The Time Machine*, *The Time Ships* (1995), develops out of Wells's novel an expansive vision of innumerable **parallel worlds** and a universal pattern of perpetual progress and **exploration** into unknown realms.

Discussion

Arguably, both unalloyed optimism and unalloyed pessimism are unrealistic, given humanity's **history** of triumphs blended with tragedies, and some science fiction works envision future humanity as essentially continuing to muddle through, solving some problems while leaving others unresolved. Novels sometimes described as dystopias, like Frederik Pohl and C.M. Kornbluth's *The Space Merchants* and John Brunner's *Stand on Zanzibar*, might be better described in these terms, as future heroes confront nightmarish conditions but nevertheless achieve small victories and maintain a hopeful attitude. Alternately, works may envision a future paradise and future catastrophe as equally likely, contriving to present both possibilities: Olaf Stapledon's *Darkness and the Light* (1942) describes two contrasting futures for humanity, while Gregory Benford's *Timescape* leaves the original world of his **scientist** protagonist to be doomed while creating a parallel world that sidesteps disaster. Given the uncertainties of **prediction**, science fiction writers seemingly prefer to hedge their bets about the future.

Bibliography

W.C. Connelly. "Optimism in Anthony Burgess' *A Clockwork Orange*." *Extrapolation*, 14 (December, 1972), 25–29.

Leslie A. Fiedler. *Olaf Stapledon*. Oxford: Oxford University Press, 1983.

Howard Fink. "Orwell versus Koestler." Courtney T. Wemyss, ed., *George Orwell*. Westport, CT: Greenwood Press, 1987, 101–110.

Mark R. Hillegas. *The Future as Nightmare*. New York: Oxford University Press, 1967.

Ruth Levitas and Lucy Sargisson. "Utopia in Dark Times." Raffaella Baccolini and Tom Moylan, eds., *Dark Horizons*. New York: Routledge, 2003, 13–28.

Chris Morgan. *The Shape of Futures Past*. Exeter, England: Webb & Bower, 1980.

Lyman T. Sargent. "The Pessimistic Eutopias of H.G. Wells." *The Wellsian*, No. 7 (Summer, 1984), 2–18.

Gary Westfahl. "Gadgetry, Government, Genetics, and God." George Slusser, Paul Alkon, Roger Gaillard, and Danièle Chatelain, eds., *Transformations of Utopia*. New York: AMS Press, 1999, 229–241.
Donald A. Wollheim. *The Universe Makers*. New York: Harper, 1971.

—Gary Westfahl

OUTER PLANETS OF THE SOLAR SYSTEM

————————————————●————————————————

See Jupiter and the Outer Planets

OVERPOPULATION

————————————————●————————————————

POPULATION EXPLOSION Unique in human experience, an event which happened yesterday but which everyone swears won't happen until tomorrow.

—John Brunner
Stand on Zanzibar (1968)

Overview

Science fiction writers have frequently feared a Malthusian future, with massive numbers of individuals struggling over dwindling resources. Overpopulated worlds are most often depicted as **dystopias**, though there have been more positive portrayals such as James Blish and Norman L. Knight's *A Torrent of Faces* (1967).

Survey

Malthusian fears of masses in competition for resources appear as early as Mary Shelley's *Frankenstein*, published early in the nineteenth century. Victor Frankenstein refuses to create a mate for the **monster** that he created and animated (see **Frankenstein Monsters**), fearing an inevitable struggle for **survival** between its progeny and human beings.

However, the overpopulation of **Earth** did not become a major science fiction theme until the 1950s and 1960s. One of the first depictions of crowded megacities (see **Cities**) was Isaac Asimov's *The Caves of Steel* (1954) (see *I, Robot*). The 1960s saw increasing anxiety about the problem of an exponentially increasing global population, as expressed in Lester del Rey's *The Eleventh Commandment* (1962) and underscored by publication of Paul Ehrlich's nonfiction jeremiad, *The Population Bomb*, in 1968. In the same year, John Brunner's **Stand on Zanzibar** was published. This is perhaps the definitive overpopulation novel, employing complex narrative techniques, elaborate storylines, and a huge cast of characters to convey the scale and complexity of the global crisis it describes.

Science fiction narratives of overpopulation typically portray corporate rapacity, rationed resources, maddeningly crowded conditions, and environmental devastation (see **Ecology**). In Frederik Pohl and C.M. Kornbluth's **The Space Merchants**, manufacturers and advertisers encourage population growth to produce as many consumers as possible (see **Advertising**). Interplanetary colonization (see **Space Travel**) is employed, not to relieve crowding on Earth, but to provide room for even more consumers. Harry Harrison's *Make Room! Make Room!* (1966) emphasizes the extreme crowding of a future New York. Its cinematic adaptation, *Soylent Green* (1973), introduces a horrific twist: the problem of feeding the masses has been solved by the secret recycling of human bodies into a ubiquitous processed foodstuff. This movie epitomizes 1970s film depictions of ruined, overpopulated cities of the future.

Many stories, novels, and movies present societies that have adopted extreme responses to a population crisis. Along with the cannibalism of *Soylent Green*, science fiction has described a turn to **homosexuality**, as in Anthony Burgess's *The Wanting Seed* (1962); the use of pills to discourage sex, as in Kurt Vonnegut, Jr.'s "Welcome to the Monkey House" (1968); and the killing of all citizens when they reach the age of twenty-one, as in William F. Nolan and George Clayton Johnson's *Logan's Run* (1967), which became the basis for a 1976 film and a short-lived television series which more generously allowed adults to reach the age of thirty. Some overpopulated societies encourage **suicide**, as observed in *Soylent Green*; others propose a cull, as in George Turner's *Drowning Towers* (1987). The people of overcrowded futures are sometimes housed in immense buildings (see **Architecture and Interior Design**), while control of mind-bogglingly complex social logistics is handed over to powerful **computers**.

Though *The Space Merchants* depicts colonies in space as a cynical ploy to increase the population, other stories focus on migration to other worlds as an official response by authorities to crowded conditions on Earth—as portrayed in the movie **Blade Runner**, with its crowded city streets presenting enticements to join a colonization program. This contrasts with the situation in Philip K. Dick's **Do Androids Dream of Electric Sheep?**, on which the movie was based. In Dick's novel, human societies have decayed (see **Decadence**) following a **nuclear war**. Almost all animals (see **Animals and Zoos**) have died, and the world is polluted by radioactive fallout. Most survivors have fled to colonies on other planets, leaving behind an underpopulated, depressed world.

Many science fiction works present seemingly unending cities that sprawl across continents, tower into the sky, and plunge down to what seems like an underground level. By the 1980s, this image had lost some of its dystopian sting—becoming far more ambivalent, if not actually positive. The sprawling cities described in 1980s **cyberpunk** works, such as William Gibson's *Neuromancer*, are as remarkable for their energy and diversity as for their pollution, social inequality, and squalor.

Discussion

By the beginning of the twenty-first century, projections of a peaking global population in the middle of the century, combined with declining birthrates in European and western nations (see **Europe**), have intensified Malthusian fears. Though reduced birthrates, not global overpopulation, are a focus of political attention in the west, the Earth's carrying capacity remains under stress, huge conurbations continue to grow in developing nations, and there is the specter of massive unregulated migration to the industrialized First World. This opens the way for science fiction writers to explore possible futures of racial and cultural clashes, as demographic issues play themselves out through the twenty-first century.

Bibliography

Neal Bukeavich. "Are We Adopting the Right Measures to Cope?" *Science Fiction Studies*, 29 (March, 2002), 53–70.

Robert H. Canary. "Science Fiction as Fictive History." Thomas D. Clareson, ed., *Many Futures, Many Worlds*. Kent, OH: Kent State University Press, 1977, 164–181.

Joe De Bolt. "The Development of John Brunner." Thomas D. Clareson, ed., *Voices for the Future, Volume Two*. Bowling Green, Ohio: Bowling Green State University Popular Press, 1979, 106–135.

Maureen N. McLane. "Literate Species." *ELH*, 63 (Winter, 1996), 959–988.

Tom Moylan. "The Dystopian Turn." Moylan, *Scraps of the Untainted Sky*. Boulder, CO: Westview Press, 2000, 147–182.

B. Murdoch. "The Overpopulated Wasteland." *Revue des Langues Vivantes*, 39 (1973), 203–217.

W.M.S. Russell and Claire Russell. "Big Brother Antichrist." George Slusser, Colin Greenland, and Eric S. Rabkin, eds., *Storm Warnings*. Carbondale: Southern Illinois University Press, 1987, 159–171.

Vivian Sobchack. "Cities on the Edge of Time." Annette Kuhn, ed., *Alien Zone II*. London and New York: Verso, 1999, 123–143.

M.S. Weinkauf. "Theme for SF: Aesthetics and Overpopulation." *Extrapolation*, 13 (May, 1972), 152–164.

—Russell Blackford

P

PAIN

In the face of pain there are no heroes, no heroes, he thought over and over as he writhed on the floor, clutching use-lessly at his disabled left arm.

—George Orwell
Nineteen Eighty-Four (1949)

Overview

The narrative traditions of science fiction and fantasy demand that characters suffer more than their fair share of physical as well as psychological pain (the latter discussed under **Anxiety**). Endurance of pain is an heroic trait (see **Heroes**), and willful infliction of pain, particularly as **torture**, is generally the mark of villainy, or at least of considerable moral ambiguity (see **Villains**).

Survey

The ability to feel pain is what makes us human, according to science fiction and fantasy, and insensitivity to one's own pain (never mind that of others) isolates a character from **humanity**. Leprosy, a disease that involves nerve damage and loss of sensation, including pain, drives Thomas Convenant into bitter seclusion in Stephen R. Donaldson's ***Lord Foul's Bane***. The surgically altered Scanners in Cordwainer Smith's "Scanners Live in Vain" (1950) (see ***Norstrilia***) and the pain-immune physician in Andrew Miller's *Ingenious Pain* (2003) both struggle to retain connection. In Spider Robinson's *Callahan's Legacy* (1976), the one place Acayib, who was also born immune to pain, finds a sense of **community** is at Callahan's bar, a place with abundant welcome for the aberrant. Separation from humanity is literal in the case of James Tiptree, Jr.'s "Painwise" (1973), where **Earth** is the one thing that causes Tiptree's protagonist to suffer. Conversely, pain can reconnect characters to humanity. Personal experience of pain is one stimulus that starts the youthful torturer Sevarian on his long journey towards apotheosis in Gene Wolfe's ***The Book of the New Sun***.

Cultures that banish pain are suspect. The soma-soaked **dystopia** of Aldous Huxley's *Brave New World* so revolts the Savage that he turns to self-flagellation to free himself of it. The brave and moral flee the societies of Lois Lowry's *The Giver* (1993) and Ursula K. Le Guin's "The Ones Who Walk Away From Omelas" (1973), in which one individual assumes the pain of all. Even medical cures for pain should be distrusted (see **Medicine**), as in Kate Wilhelm's *The Clewiston Test* (1976).

Nevertheless, pain is frequently used dramatically and thematically as a test of character, conviction, or worth. The ability to endure pain makes Paul Atreides human in the eyes of the Bene Gesserit in Frank Herbert's **Dune** and makes John Sheridan and Delenn worthy, in the eyes of "the inquisitor" and the Vorlons, to lead their cause in the **Babylon 5** episode "Comes the Inquisitor" (1995). A painful ordeal marking the passage between child and adult is a staple feature of the science fiction and fantasy **Bildungsroman**, particularly if the young person comes into **magic** or **psychic powers**; Octavia E. Butler's Patternists, in *Patternmaster* (1976) and *Mind of My Mind* (1977), and Marian Zimmer Bradley's *leroni*, in *Heritage of Hastur* (1977) and *Stormqueen* (1978), pass through ordeals that are experienced as much physically as psychically, and Barbara Hambly's mercenary-turned-mage Sunwolf belatedly comes into power when he is fed agonizing poison in *The Ladies of Mandrigyn* (1984). Special abilities, whether magical or paranormal, often keep extracting a price in pain from their wielders, as in Diane Duane's *The Door into Fire* (1979) and Terry Brooks's *Running with the Demon* (1997).

The "problem of pain" is one question that bedevils those would believe in a benevolent deity. In Poul Anderson's "The Problem of Pain" (1973), a human struggling with this question encounters an alien answer. This is also the theme of several stories in Harlan Ellison's **Deathbird Stories**, notably "Paingod" (1964) and "The Deathbird" (1973). In the former, the deity responsible for inflicting pain on the universe must experience pain himself in order to grasp its meaning. Yet even as Christians ask this question, they embrace a **religion** whose central symbol is one of agonizing **death** (see **Christianity**). The first part of Dan Simmons's **Hyperion**, "The Priest's Tale," recapitulates but inverts that symbolism by underlining its cruelty, while later "The Scholar's Tale" directly addresses divine responsibility for suffering. In contrast, pain may be offered in willing service to one's god, as it is for the courtesan Phèdre nó Delauney in *Kushiel's Dart* (2001), born an anguisette, chosen victim of Kushiel, the **angel** of chastisement.

The literal sharing of pain is a theme largely unique to speculative literature. The conventional empath is someone (often a woman) of exquisite compassion and sensitivity, whose gift renders her helpless, as in the **Star Trek** episode "The Empath" (1968) and Zenna Henderson's *Pilgrimage: The Book of the People* (1961). However, the sharing of pain does not necessarily lead to compassion: in Robert Silverberg's *The Pain Peddlers* (1963), somatic recordings of surgery without anesthetic offer the ultimate in "reality TV." In Butler's *The Parable of the Sower* (1994), Lauren Olihima's hyper-empathy syndrome is not merely delusional, but a threat to her **survival** as her society descends into savagery. As others' pain-immunity isolates them, her empathy isolates her, and part of her progress involves forming and protecting a community of her own.

Discussion

The depiction of pain in science fiction and fantasy reflects the various cultural and religious traditions behind it: to experience pain is to be human and to endure it well is the mark of a hero. Pain is a necessary part of growth, and any privilege or special power must be paid for. People and mechanisms that would free us from pain are not necessarily to be trusted. However, science fiction and fantasy may also challenge and invert these assumptions.

Bibliography

Catherine Ahearn. "An Archetype of Pain." Sheila Roberts, ed., *Still the Frame Holds*. San Bernardino, CA: Borgo Press, 1993, 137–156.

Jayson Curry. "Formal Synthesis in *Deathbird Stories*." *Foundation*, No. 56 (Autumn, 1992), 23–35.

Arnold E. Davidson. "The Poetics of Pain in Margaret Atwood's *Bodily Harm*." *American Review of Canadian Studies*, 18 (Spring, 1988), 1–10.

Lillian M. Heldreth. "The Mercy of the Torturer." Robert A. Latham and Robert E. Collins, eds., *Modes of the Fantastic*. Westport, CT: Greenwood Press, 1995, 186–194.

Lisa A. Long. "A Relative Pain." *College English*, 64 (March, 2002), 459–483.

Robert Merchant. "The T-Shirt and the Psalm." *CSL: Bulletin of the New York C.S. Lewis Society*, 32 (January, 2001), 1–10.

Peter J. Reed. "Hurting 'Til It Laughs." Marc Leeds and Peter J. Reed, eds., *Kurt Vonnegut*. Westport, CT: Greenwood Press, 2000, 19–38.

R.C. Schlobin. "Thomas Burnett Swann's Nixies." *Extrapolation*, 24 (Spring, 1983), 5–13.

Ian Watson. "From Pan in the Home Countries to Pain on a Far Planet." *Foundation*, No. 43 (Summer, 1988), 25–36.

—Alison Sinclair

PANTROPY

Overview

Pantropy is a term coined by James Blish in the early 1950s to describe the process by which human beings are intentionally modified, by genetic or other means, to make it possible for them to survive, even flourish, in normally hostile environments, mainly those found in outer space or on **alien worlds**. Altering planetary environments to allow habitation is discussed under **Terraforming**.

Survey

In *The Seedling Stars* (1956), where Blish introduced the concept of pantropy and developed the theme, the "adapted men," as Blish termed modified humans, represented an alternative to terraforming, which would allow **humanity** to spread successfully across the cosmos. In the most memorable of the book's four stories, "Surface Tension" (1952), adapted men have been reduced to microscopic size (see **Miniaturization**). In *A Torrent of Faces* (1967), Blish and Norman L. Knight consider the creation of a race bioengineered to live in a different kind of alien environment—the Earth's oceans.

The first dangerous environment that humans will encounter after leaving **Earth** is outer space. Samuel R. Delany, in "Aye and Gomorrah" (1967), suggests that it might be necessary to engineer a new race to deal feasibly with space travel. In Vonda N. McIntyre's *Superluminal* (1984), successful spaceship pilots must be surgically restructured. "Scanners Live in Vain" (1948), from Cordwainer Smith's Instrumentality of Mankind series (see **Norstrilia**), portrays a future wherein the **pain** of **space travel** is only bearable to modified, desensitized people known as Scanners. In *Falling Free* (1988), Lois McMaster Bujold considers the ethical consequences of **genetic engineering** (see **Ethics**), which has produced people known as "quaddies," whose legs have been replaced by an extra pair of arms to better live and work in the zero-**gravity** environments of **space stations**. The "floaters" of Syne Mitchell's *Murphy's Gambit* (2000) are also physically and mentally adapted to life in free-fall, and they, like quaddies, are exploited by interstellar corporations.

In other stories, humans are altered to meet the challenges of strange alien worlds. The Seventh Men of Olaf Stapledon's *Last and First Men* are humans made smaller and less intelligent so as to become **flying** creatures on **Venus**. In Smith's "Alpha Ralpha Boulevard" (1961), reference is made to the so-called "hominids," who "had been changed to fit the conditions of a thousand worlds." In Robert Charles Wilson's *Bios* (1999), Zoe Fisher has been bioengineered from birth to function optimally on the planet Isis, all of whose alien **biology** is toxic to humans. In *The Children Star* (1999), Joan Slonczewski explores a process of genetic alteration termed life-shaping, which modifies humans to function in the deadly environment of the world of Prokaryon. Poul Anderson's "Call Me Joe" (1957) envisions creation of an artificial **superman**, remotely controlled by a handicapped person, to investigate the surface of Jupiter, while Arthur C. Clarke's "A Meeting with Medusa" (1971) assigns that task to a **cyborg**. Frederik Pohl's *Man Plus* (1976) is the detailed personal, social, and political story of the first man modified for life on **Mars** by both surgery and mechanical engineering. Cyborgs in space are found in Samuel R. Delany's *Nova* (1968) and Bruce Sterling's *Schismatrix* (1985).

Other works explore more exotic forms of pantropy. Nanotechnology is employed for radical human transformation in a number of **space operas**, including Tony Daniels's *Metaplanetary* (2001) and its sequels, Justina Robson's *Natural History* (2003), and Peter F. Hamilton's *The Reality Dysfunction* (1996) and its sequels. To meet with alien scientists, a character in Greg Egan's *Schild's Ladder* (2001) has herself transmitted to a space station 370 light years from Earth and installed in a body two millimeters high that is hermetically sealed against vacuum and feeds on nothing except **light**. In Stephen Baxter's *Flux* (1993), which is part of his Xeelee series, we have microscopic humans living inside of a neutron **star**.

The idea that, perhaps, humanity itself has already been technologically modified, possibly even created, by aliens at some point in the distant past, can also be seen as a variation of the pantropy theme, with Clarke's novel and the film *2001: A Space Odyssey* a prominent example. In David Brin's Uplift universe (see *Startide Rising*), certain aliens question whether human beings could have achieved their present state of **civilization** without the intervention of more advanced species, via a process of **uplift**. A character in Ursula K. Le Guin's *The Left Hand of Darkness* speculates that only human genetic modification by the mysterious Colonizers can explain the origins of the unique "ambisexuality" of the Gethenians.

Discussion

Although both pantropy and terraforming necessarily engage deeply with issues of **ecology**, they nonetheless represent the most extreme positions on what is in actuality a single continuum, concerning appropriate human attitudes to worlds we encounter as humankind expands outwards into space. Support for a policy of pantropy implies that it may be not only more technologically and economically feasible, but also more ethical, to change our own nature rather than that of entire planets. Pantropy narratives also explore questions of **identity**, asking just how radically we can transform our physical and biological selves—whether via nanotech, cyborg procedures, or biogenetic techniques—and still remain what can reasonably be called human.

Bibliography

Gardner Dozois, ed. *Supermen*. New York: St. Martin's, 2002.

Alan C. Elms. "Origins of the Underpeople." *Essays and Studies*, 43 (1990), 166–193.

Gregory Feeley. "Cages of Conscience from Seedling Stories." *Foundation*, No. 24 (February, 1982), 59–68.

N. Katherine Hayles. *How We Became Posthuman*. University of Chicago, 1999.

David Ketterer. "Change, Truth, and Sex in *The Seedling Stars* by James Blish." *Metaphores*, No. 9/10 (April, 1984), 145–160.

———. "Pantropy, Polyploidy, and Tectogenesis in the Fiction of James Blish and Norman L. Knight." *Science-Fiction Studies*, 10 (July, 1983), 199–218.

Tom Maddox. "The Wars of the Coin's Two Halves." *Mississippi Review*, 16 (1988), 237–244.

Peter Nicholls, David Langford, and Brian Stableford. "Pantropy: New Men for New Worlds." Nicholls, Langford, and Stableford, *The Science in Science Fiction*. 1982. New York: Alfred A. Knopf, 1983, 154–155.

—Richard L. McKinney

PARALLEL WORLDS

Overview

Parallel worlds resemble our own in most regards, whether they are located elsewhere in space or situated in another plane of existence. Worlds differing from ours due to divergent histories (see **Alternate History**) or those which are not necessarily analogous to ours (see **Dimensions**) are discussed elsewhere.

Survey

The roots of the parallel worlds concept can be found in **mythology**. Whether the "Otherworld" of Celtic mythology, an **Earth**-like realm accessible through various sacred spaces and portals, or the "other world" of the Hindu *Mahabharata* (c. 300), a celestial universe alongside our own, these mythological realms, where **nature** followed similar laws, were peopled by beings who resembled humans.

Parallel worlds in literature, by contrast, were first used for social commentary, **allegory**, or historical speculation. For example, though more properly considered an alternate history, Livy's *Ab Urbe Condita*, written in the first century BCE, can be seen as a prototypical parallel worlds story, in which the historian speculates about what might have happened had Alexander of Macedonia lived longer and attacked the Romans. In the modern era, the concept is found in George MacDonald's **Lilith**, in which the **hero** travels to another world where he encounters, in coded forms, characters representing **humanity**'s spiritual fall and possible redemption; in James Branch Cabell's *Jurgen*, in which the eponymous hero travels through different realms, including **Heaven** and **Hell**, in search of his perfect mate; and in H.G. Wells's *Men Like Gods* (1923), in which some Englishmen are mysteriously transported to another reality where the ills of our Earth have been eliminated.

Parallel worlds are often a setting for children's fantasies: **youth** from mundane, modern-day settings are transported, through one agency or another, to a more fantastic world. Preeminent examples include L. Frank Baum's ***The Wonderful Wizard of Oz*** and C.S. Lewis's ***The Lion, The Witch and the Wardrobe***.

Since the early days of pulp science fiction, parallel worlds have been a staple trope. In some instances, these reflective worlds are situated in our own solar system, typically sharing Earth's orbit on the opposite side of the **Sun**, often called "Counter-Earth," as in John Norman's Gor series, beginning in *Tarnsman of Gor* (1967); a similar duplicate Earth figures in the film *Journey to the Far Side of the Sun* (1969).

Other stories position parallel worlds elsewhere in our own galaxy or universe, but still within the confines of our own reality. Wells's *A Modern Utopia* (1905) placed a world virtually identical to Earth elsewhere in our galaxy, somewhere beyond Sirius, and Olaf Stapledon discussed a distant counterpart to Earth in *Star Maker*. The original *Star Trek* series was fond of this approach, with the *Enterprise* crew frequently encountering **alien worlds** that resembled some aspect of Earth **culture** or **history**, as in the episode "Bread and Circuses" (1968), set on a world where the Roman Empire never fell.

Most parallel worlds in science fiction, however, are in other dimensions or realms, often rationalized using theoretical physics, echoing the Many Worlds Theorem of Hugh Everett (which was itself prefigured by Murray Leinster's "Sidewise in Time" [1934]). In Andre Norton's *Witch World* (1963), a man is transported to a pseudo-medieval world (see **Medievalism and the Middle Ages**), recalling the Otherworld of Celtic mythology. Michael Moorcock introduced in *The Sundered Worlds* (1965) his concept of the "Multiverse," which would become the cornerstone of his creative output (culminating in the Second Ether series, beginning with *Blood: A Southern Fantasy* [1995]). Philip José Farmer's *The Gate of Time* (1966) features an American airman who inadvertently travels to a world where the North and South American continents did not exist (see **America; Latin America**), finding himself in a **Europe** dominated by descendants of proto-**Native Americans**. Clifford D. Simak's *Ring Around the Sun* (1953) presents the striking image of an infinite series of almost identical Earths, on different planes of existence, all orbiting the Sun, while Roger Zelazny's *Nine Princes in Amber* (1970) similarly reveals that our Earth is just one of many parallel worlds that are shadow reflections of a more fundamental reality.

In some stories, travel between parallel worlds is a key plot element, often involving a paramilitary policing agency. Examples include Jack Williamson's *The Legion of Time* (1938), Keith Laumer's *Worlds of the Imperium* (1962), H. Beam Piper's *Lord Kalvan of Otherwhen* (1965), and Robert A. Heinlein's *The Number of The Beast* (1980) (see **The Past Through Tomorrow**).

Discussion

Originally a tool used by historians and social commentators for hypothetical discourse or societal observation, parallel worlds became useful devices in early science fiction and have only increased in popularity since that time. By the end of the twentieth century, the concept, arguably something of a **cliché** in prose science fiction, gained new prominence outside the genre, serving as the basis for the television series *Sliders* (1995–2000), and big-budget action films like Jet Li's *The One* (2001). Michael Swanwick's story "Legions in Time" (2003), a clever reworking of concepts first mined by Williamson and Piper, suggests that the concept has some mileage left in the realm of prose science fiction as well.

Bibliography

John Brunner. "Parallel Worlds." *Foundation*, No. 3 (March, 1973), 6–14.
David Deutsch. *The Fabric of Reality*. New York: Penguin USA, 1995.
Nicholas Gevers. *Mirrors of the Past*. Cape Town: University of Cape Town, 1997.
Karen Hellekson. *The Alternate History*. Kent, OH: Kent State University Press, 2001.
J.L. Meikle. "Other Frequencies: The Parallel Worlds of Thomas Pynchon and H.P. Lovecraft." *Modern Fiction Studies*, 27 (Summer, 1981), 287–294.
Joseph D. Miller. "Parallel Universes." George Slusser and Eric S. Rabkin, eds., *Intersections*. Carbondale: Southern Illinois University Press, 1987, 19–25.
Paul J. Nahin, *Time Machines*. New York: American Institute of Physics, 1993.
Clifford A. Pickover. *Time*. Oxford: Oxford University Press, 1998.

—*Chris Roberson*

PARANOIA

Maybe all *systems—that is, any theoretical, verbal, symbolic, semantic, etc. formulation that attempts to act as an all-encompassing, all-explaining hypothesis of what the universe is about—are manifestations of paranoia. We should be content with the mysterious, the meaningless, the contradictory, the*

> *hostile, and most of all the unexplain-*
> *ably warm and giving.*
>
> —Philip K. Dick
> "The Android and the Human" (1972)

Overview

Paranoia, the suspicion that **evil** forces are conspiring to delude or manipulate the individual, is a common theme in fantasy and science fiction, especially variants influenced by the **Gothic**. A sense of paranoia is rife within **dark fantasy** and **horror**, while it is pronounced in science fiction that deals with problems of **perception** and **identity**, as well as **dystopias**. Other entries address the general topics of **Psychology** and **Madness**.

Survey

The **anxiety** that our experience may be merely a **game** or **dream**, that what we see and touch is an **illusion** controlled by invisible forces, has provided both specific plotlines and general atmosphere to many fantasy and science fiction texts. In the nineteenth century, Edgar Allan Poe crafted tales featuring paranoid narrators who, whether due to madness, **drugs**, or **magic**, could not trust the evidence of their senses: several of these stories feature sinister **doppelgängers** who manipulate narrators for inscrutable purposes. The heir of this tradition in the twentieth century was H.P. Lovecraft, whose Cthulhu Mythos stories elaborated a complex vision of lurking **elder races**; typically, an isolated protagonist, discovering the existence of these **supernatural creatures** from **omens and signs**, is driven mad with fear and loathing.

Absurdist and surrealist fantasy also flirts with paranoia (see **Absurdity; Surrealism**). Franz Kafka's stories are filled with hapless characters confronting unfathomable powers that seem geared primarily to make them miserable, while Jorge Luis Borges deploys **labyrinths** and conceptual **puzzles** to suggest elusive realms of being that challenge the capacities of **memory** and perception. In the later twentieth century, postmodern fantasy cultivated an air of paranoia by projecting political conspiracies involving hidden elites working behind the scenes (see **Secret History**); Kurt Vonnegut, Jr.'s *Slaughterhouse-Five* and Thomas Pynchon's *Gravity's Rainbow* (1973) converge with science fiction in depicting these elites as meddling extraterrestrials or posthuman immortals. Mass-media variants include television series like *The Twilight Zone, The Prisoner*, and *The X-Files*, which exploit the sense of helpless unease that derives from subjection to surreptitious control.

Science fiction's handling of the theme of paranoia takes three main forms, often occurring in combination: dystopias in which characters are hounded by pervasive authority; tales that capitalize on fears of inhuman "others," whether alien or technological; and stories about insidious agencies of control secretly guiding human consciousness.

George Orwell's *Nineteen Eighty-Four* is a classic projection of a suffocating tyranny that relentlessly monitors its garrisoned subjects, to the point that apprehensions of an omnipresent "Big Brother" corrode everyday experience. The film *Brazil* offers a similar portrait of a future state run by gray technocrats. Direct control of consciousness by a totalitarian system is extrapolated in Anthony Burgess's *A Clockwork Orange*, while a gentler hegemony in Frederik Pohl and C.M. Kornbluth's *The Space Merchants* takes the form of corporate **advertising** that inescapably channels consumer desire. These texts draw their paranoid charge from the tension between **individualism and conformity**: dystopian regimes constrain **freedom** and autonomy, producing a general sense of helpless manipulation.

A similar tone informs tales in which **aliens on Earth** or machines, rather than human governments, are the source of domination. Novels like Eric Frank Russell's *Sinister Barrier* (1939) and Robert A. Heinlein's *The Puppet Masters* (1951) feature humans subjected to degrading alien authority, the latter connecting with Cold War anxieties regarding Communist subversion. Science fiction films of the 1950s, like *Invaders from Mars* and *Invasion of the Body Snatchers*, followed similar scenarios, in which **monsters** from space secretly infiltrate human society, leading to widespread suspicion and **xenophobia**. Popular concerns about the unchecked powers of technology in the postwar period crystallized in stories of looming atomic **apocalypse**, as in *Dr. Strangelove*. Paranoia about the increasing influence of **computers** colored the work of **cyberpunk** authors like William Gibson, while the film *The Matrix* projects a grim collective immersion in a deceptive **virtual reality**.

When a tyrannical state, alien force, or scheming machine is the focus of paranoid fear, there is at least the possibility of resistance, but this is more difficult to muster when the mechanisms of control are less palpable. Philip K. Dick pioneered a form of paranoid science fiction in which protagonists are plagued with vague intuitions of the stage-managed falsity of their perceptual experience or delusory nature of their very identities. Novels like *The Three Stigmata of Palmer Eldritch* (1965), ***Do Androids Dream of Electric Sheep?***, and *A Scanner Darkly* (1977) deploy a paranoia so acute that the substance of reality itself is called into question. Films based on Dick's works, such as ***Blade Runner*** and ***Total Recall***, have brought this bleak vision to a wide popular audience.

Discussion

A sense of **mystery** lies at the heart of all fantasy, but this tone edges into paranoia in works concerned with the limits and fallibilities of human perception and memory. Paranoia in fantasy is connected to a tradition of the **sublime**, in which individuals confront huge, unknowable forces. Dark fantasy in particular draws its power from lingering doubts about our capacity to grapple with hidden immensities. In science fiction, paranoia is linked to the **sense of wonder** characteristic of the genre, but it puts a darker spin on the surprises and marvels of the universe, suggesting that **humanity** may be ill-prepared to deal with the epochal challenges of the future.

Bibliography

Michael J. Collins. "Version/Inversion." Michael A. Morrison, ed., *Trajectories of the Fantastic*. Westport, CT: Greenwood Press, 1997, 195–202.

Jodi Dean. *Aliens in America*. Ithaca, NY: Cornell University Press, 1998.

Neil Easterbrook. "Dianoia/Paranoia." Samuel J. Umland, ed., *Philip K. Dick*. Westport, CT: Greenwood Press, 1995, 19–42.

Carl Freedman. "Towards a Theory of Paranoia." *Science-Fiction Studies*, 11 (March, 1984), 15–24.

Cynthia Hendershot. *Paranoia, The Bomb, and 1950s Science Fiction Films*. Bowling Green, OH: Bowling Green State University Popular Press, 1999.

Alexei Panshin, James Blish, and Joanna Russ. *Paranoia and Science Fiction*. Baltimore: Science Fiction Writers Association, 1967.

Rachel Pollack. "Invasion of the Android Snatchers." *SFWA Bulletin*, 20 (Summer, 1986), 8–13.

George Turner. "A Case for Insomnia." *American Cinematographer*, 78 (March, 1997), 77–81.

Mark Wildermuth. "The Edge of Chaos." *Journal of Popular Film and Television*, 26 (Winter, 1999), 146–157.

—*Rob Latham*

PARASITES

Overview

Carl Zimmer's *Parasite Rex* (2000) traces the origin of "parasite" from its origin, a server at a temple feast, to its modern meaning as a creature that feeds off the bodily resources of others, as distinct from cooperative **symbiosis**. Parasites in science fiction tend to have material form or rational explanation, whereas in fantasy and horror, parasitism most often takes the form of nonmaterial **possession**. **Horror** and fantasy tell of **vampires**. Humans considered as parasites appear as an implicit, sometimes explicit, theme in **ecology**.

Survey

The broadest use of parasites in fantastic literature is in tales of alien **invasion**, in which the parasite progressively threatens the existence of the individual self, the **community**, and **humanity** itself. Episodes of *The X-Files* featured a variety of invertebrate parasites ("Ice" [1994], "The Host" [1995], "Firewalker" [1995], "F. Emasculata" [1995], and "Roadrunners" [2000]), writ large from natural models, and emerging (from space, the Antarctic ice, the depths of a volcano) to threaten the two protagonists. Communities under threat include spaceships, which are ideal for a tightly plotted contest in claustrophobic surroundings between humans and parasites as in A.E. van Vogt's *The Voyage of the Space Beagle* (1950). The hidden nature of parasitism heightens the suspense and **paranoia** as fundamental human relationships become untrustworthy. Finally, the threat to individual integrity may extend to the entire species, as in Robert A. Heinlein's *The Puppet Masters* (1951), the *Star Trek* episode "Operation: Annihilate" (1967), and the *Star Trek: The Next Generation* episode "Conspiracy" (1988). Little need be explained about the parasites' motivation, since it is a given that all parasites have a common urge to propagate their species.

Parasitism may bring with it secondary gains, as the parasite modifies the host to improve its own chances of survival. Thus parasitic infection in Octavia

E. Butler's *Clay's Ark* (1984) and Dean Asher's *The Parasite* (1996) gives the hosts superhuman powers and resistance to disease, but strips from them their humanity, while the hosts of the cruciform in Dan Simmons's *Hyperion* can be rebuilt despite mortal damage even as they progressively descend into senility. *Hyperion* portrays the initial tragic collision of religious symbolism between a Catholic missionary-priest and the worshippers/hosts of the parasitic cruciform. Later in the Hyperion Cantos, the human race must be freed from the stasis imposed by the cruciform. Controlled parasitic infection in G.C. Edmondson and C.M. Cotlan's *The Cunningham Equations* (1986) cures brain damage and augments **intelligence**. In keeping with the general tenor of moral parasite novels, those who would embrace the parasite for selfish or ignoble reasons come to a horrific end.

Despite its stigma, parasitism is a relationship, and science fiction and fantasy writers expand imaginatively upon that relationship by granting both host and parasite self-awareness, possibly letting them enter into a dialogue. Even Ripley has an evolving relationship with her nemeses: In *Alien* she learns of them; in *Aliens* (1986) her insight deepens when Ripley as **mother**-surrogate confronts the egg-laying alien queen; in *Alien3* (1992), she becomes a host herself; and in *Alien Resurrection* (1997), she (or her **clone**) becomes one (at least in part). The mother–child relationship offers the richest possibility for intimacy and ambivalence, with the young-as-parasite being another recurring theme. BBC Radio's 2003 adaptation of John Wyndham's *The Midwich Cuckoos* (1957), in which the women of a country village give birth to alien-germinated children, drew upon modern understanding of **family** dysfunctions to set motherly attachment against male rejection of and **violence** towards their alien "stepchildren." Though infant parasites are often represented as voracious and mindless larvae, drawn from natural models such as the botfly or parasitic wasp (as in *Alien*), their parents are not. Butler explores the ambivalence of the host–parasite relationship to its fullest in a novella, "Bloodchild" (1985), about the Tlic T'Gatoi and the young human who has been raised to host her young, without entirely knowing what that means until he witnesses a "birth" gone wrong. Critical interpretations range from a narrative of **slavery,** a commentary on male–female relations, power and **knowledge**, to an interspecies **love** story. Philip José Farmer's *The Lovers* (1954) offers another complex presentation of the host–parasite relationship. For the female protagonist's species, the mother's lot is to be devoured from within by her own young—a theme of "necrogenesis" that also figures in Brian W. Aldiss's Helliconia novels (see *Helliconia Spring*).

Discussion

Culturally, parasitism is viewed with distaste (unlike the more morally acceptable symbiosis) and, reflecting that, science fiction and fantasy portrayals range from horror to ambivalence. Parasites invariably have an extraterrestrial or unnatural origin (often as a result of **genetic engineering**); science fiction and fantasy does not acknowledge parasites as part of *our* **nature**. Parasitism is seldom a simple matter of physical infestation, particularly in works from the 1950s and 1960s, where it has been interpreted as expressing fears of communism, McCarthyism, or conformity (see **Individualism and Conformity**). More recently, parasitism has been used to express the complexities of mothering and worship.

Bibliography

Toni Cascio. "The Vampire's Seduction." *Journal of Poetry Therapy*, 15 (Fall, 2001), 19–28.

Elyce Rae Helford. "Would You Really Rather Die Than Bear My Young?" *African American Review*, 28 (Summer, 1994), 259–271.

Cyndy Hendershot. "The Invaded Body." *Extrapolation*, 39 (Spring, 1988), 26–39.

Jack Morgan. *The Biology of Horror*. Carbondale: Southern Illinois University Press, 2002.

Helen N. Parker. *Biological Themes in Modern Science Fiction*. Ann Arbor, MI: UMI Research Press, 1984.

Donna Pastourmatzi, ed. *Biotechnological and Medical Themes in Science Fiction*. Thessaloniki, Greece: University Studio Press, 2002.

David Seed. "Alien Invasions by Body Snatchers and Related Creatures." Victor Sage and Allen L. Smith, eds., *Modern Gothic*. Manchester UK: Manchester University Press, 1996, 152–170.

Chris West. "Queer Fears and Critical Orthodoxies." *Foundation*, No. 86 (Autumn, 2002), 17–27.

—*Alison Sinclair*

PASTORAL

∎

Overview

Critic Tom Shippey has endeavored to introduce the concept of science fiction as a "fabril" mode (from Latin "faber"—"maker" or smith). He distinguishes between the rural, nostalgic aspects of pastoral, and the urban, future-oriented iconography of science fiction that foregrounds the creator of artifacts rather than the shepherd. Science fiction is, arguably, the opposite of pastoral, which has been a strong influence on fantasy.

Survey

Shippey's distinction is useful, but pastoral, a mode associated with Classical and Elizabethan poets and later writers like John Milton and Percy Shelley, is also a particularly coded form. Like the enclosed worlds of science fiction and fantasy (with which it has surface similarities), pastoral enables writers to satirize their own worlds in emblematic settings. In Edmund Spenser's *The Faerie Queene* (1590, 1596), for example, contemporaries saw exaggerated versions of the court of Elizabeth I. Pastoral has its tropes and conventions and its own world, **Arcadia**. We revisit Arcadia in British fantasies like J.R.R. Tolkien's **The Lord of the Rings** and Lord Dunsany's **The King of Elfland's Daughter**, but also in the nostalgic worlds of the brands of science fiction and fantasy that celebrate American small-town or rural life (see **America**), like darkly whimsical Ray Bradbury stories or Clifford D. Simak novels like *Way Station* (1963) and **City**.

A sense of pastoral is also present in the deeply imagined invented countries or worlds of science fiction and fantasy, like Austin Tappan Wright's **Islandia**,

C.S. Lewis's Narnia (see *The Lion, the Witch and the Wardrobe*), and Ursula K. Le Guin's Earthsea (see *A Wizard of Earthsea*); it is even detected in works like Le Guin's *The Left Hand of Darkness* where pastoral's ability to create emblems of the reader's world can be observed. Arcadia can be found, transformed but ever-present, in the **cyberspace** of William Gibson's *Neuromancer*. The stylized, highly visual nature of the "alien environment," linked to common sets of reader expectations, allows writers to be inventive and imaginative in playing with and undermining those expectations.

Furthermore, pastoral is connected to utopian ways of thinking. This does not mean that science fiction **utopias** are pastoral, though some, like William Morris's *News From Nowhere* (1890), and W.H. Hudson's *A Crystal Age* (1887) clearly are, banishing the technological and urban. Le Guin's interrogation of utopia, *The Dispossessed*, contains the City/Country opposition of true pastoral, although the "rural" side of the equation is barren and infertile. The pastoral state has utopian overtones: it is a longed-for state of rest. This is more clearly seen in fantasy, where nostalgic rural medievalism is a default locale, and in science fiction with "medieval" settings like Anne McCaffrey's Pern series (see *Dragonflight*) (see **Medievalism and the Middle Ages**). There is a sense of longing and desire to retreat in such worlds. Other focuses of such desires are, like Jean Auel's *The Clan of the Cave Bear*, set in prehistoric times. Wright's *Islandia* is classically pastoral in that **love** is a fundamental motif and **magic** is avoided.

Both science fiction and fantasy differ most strongly from pastoral as *image*, but operate most effectively as pastoral as *emblem*, in their ability to express the **anxiety** of "ego in Arcadia sum"—"even in Arcadia there am I" (**Death**). Thus, the apparently idyllic world of Tolkien's Shire is imperiled by disruption by the world around it, while in *Neuromancer*, Case's fall from the exaltation of cyberspace into the prison of the "meat" (the body) spurs his **quest** to regain Arcadia—itself threatened by the growing self-awareness of an artificial intelligence. McCaffrey's Pern is endangered by "Thread" and Captain Hook menaces the childlike Arcadia of J.M. Barrie's *Peter and Wendy*. Enclosed worlds like Shangri-La (see James Hilton's *Lost Horizon*) and Islandia are threatened by exposure to the outside world. Even science fiction's most assured pastoral Arcadia, the **post-holocaust society** of George R. Stewart's *Earth Abides*, is, in the end, melancholy because the survivor's **children** reject a return to **civilization** and opt instead for tribal life.

Discussion

Pastoral is thus a complex set of patterns. In *The King of Elfland's Daughter*, Dunsany contrasts the attractiveness of both the eternal present of Faerie and the Mundane: the troll from Elfland delights in the changeability of Earthly realms, but these realms are significantly the rural, natural idyll of "traditional" pastoral. Bradbury's Mars (see *The Martian Chronicles*) is pastoral in both its traditional and more ambiguous settings. In "Mars Is Heaven" (1948), the re-creation of a small-town home environment dooms explorers from **Earth**, while in "The Million-Year Picnic" (1946) the colonists have "become" Martians as they see their reflections looking back at them from a canal. Also, in Bradbury's "The Emissary" (1947), images of rural boyhood, autumn leaves, and the love of a bedridden boy for his **dog** turn darkly sinister.

Bibliography

Holly B. Blackford. "The Writing on the Wall of *Redwall*." Carrie Hintz and Elaine Ostry, eds., *Utopian and Dystopian Writing for Children and Young Adults*. New York: Routledge, 2003, 89–106.

D.A. Burger. "Shire: A Tolkien Version of Pastoral." William Coyle, ed., *Aspects of Fantasy*. Westport, CT: Greenwood Press, 1986, 149–154.

Martin Delveaux. "From Pastoral Arcadia to Stable-State Mini-Cities." *Journal of the William Morris Society*, 13 (Autumn, 2000), 75–81.

Anita Moss. "Pastoral and Heroic Patterns." R.A. Collins and H.D. Pearce, ed., *The Scope of the Fantastic*: Westport, CT: Greenwood Press, 1985, 231–238.

John Ower. "'Aesop' and the Ambiguity of Clifford Simak's *City*." *Science-Fiction Studies*, 19 (July, 1979), 164–167.

David Pringle. "Aliens for Neighbours." *Foundation*, No. 11/12 (March, 1977), 15–29.

Salvatore Proietti. "Frederick Philip Grove's Version of Pastoral Utopianism." *Science-Fiction Studies*, 58 (November, 1992), 361–377.

Tom Shippey. "Introduction." Shippey, ed., *The Oxford Book of Science Fiction Stories*. Oxford: Oxford University Press, 1992, ix–xxvi.

Ernest J. Yanarella. "Machine in the Garden Revisited." Yanarella, ed., *Political Mythology and Popular Fiction*. Westport, CT: Greenwood press, 1988, 159–184.

—*Andy Sawyer*

PERCEPTION

The way you see things depends a great deal on where you look at them from.

—Norman Juster
The Phantom Tollbooth (1961)

Overview

Much literature of the fantastic concerns itself with the unreliable nature of perceived reality. It echoes modern **physics**, one of whose lessons is that things are not always as we perceive them to be, and indeed, at a fundamental level, are almost always quite other. Stories about **parallel worlds** or life after **death** may provide the moral that our perceptions of a superbly complex existence are cozily simplistic. Abilities to perceive beyond the normal senses are discussed as **psychic powers**. Straightforward **illusions** and invisible people or objects are likewise separately discussed (see **Invisibility**). Here the concern is more what might be termed "the fantasy of perception," fiction rooted in misperception—or at least a *different* perception—of reality.

Survey

At the heart of many fantasies of perception is a perceptual shift, where what was perceived before as truth is revealed to either protagonists or readers—most effectively, both—as a falsification or simplification. In the film *Hook* (1991), a middle-aged Peter

Pan returns to Neverland: burdened by his mundane perceptual mode, he sees only empty plates when the Lost Boys throw a banquet; only when he discovers how to see the plates as full of food do they become so, and is his return to Neverland truly effected. The opposite occurs at the end of John Fowles's *The Magus* (1965), which reveals that all we and the protagonist perceived as magical has been deliberate trickery (see **Magic**). The protagonist of the film *Mulholland Drive* (2001) sees its events as forming a sequence quite different from accepted reality. In many narratives it is left moot as to which perception of reality is valid, as in Henry James's *The Turn of the Screw* (1898), filmed as *The Innocents* (1961), whose ghosts (see **Ghosts and Hauntings**) may be actual, may be psychological projections of either the **children** or governess, or may be straightforward delusions.

Fictions may also involve the unreliability or pliability of **memory**. In Philip K. Dick's "We Can Remember It for You Wholesale" (1966), the basis for the film *Total Recall*, **technology** allows people to gain **memories** of experiences they never had—except that, once they possess those memories, in effect they *have* had those experiences. This links to tales in which an individual perceives a flood of experiences in a single instant, thus creating a reality loop. This was explored by Ambrose Bierce in "An Occurrence at Owl Creek Bridge" (1891), whose protagonist experiences hours of life in the instant of dying. Similarly, in Nikos Kazantzakis's *The Last Temptation of Christ* (1955), filmed in 1988, the crucified Christ in his own perception experiences the fullness of life before returning to his agonies. The eponymous protagonist of the film *Donnie Darko* (2001) undergoes weeks of surrealistic life in the instant of being killed by a falling airplane engine; those who played an important part in this reality loop find afterwards that they too have vague memories of it. The protagonist of *Femme Fatale* (2002) perceives a whole future life for herself while rinsing her hair in the bath; resurfacing, she manipulates events to create a better, but parallel, future. (The astronauts in *Mission to Mars* [2000] have their perceptions manipulated by crafty aliens.)

Similar to such loops are **dreams** or visions of futures that can be averted—as in Charles Dickens's *A Christmas Carol*, the film *It's a Wonderful Life*, Arthur Schnitzler's *Traumnovelle* (1926), filmed as *Eyes Wide Shut* (1999), and others. In *Naked Lunch* (1991), loosely based on William R. Burroughs's novel *The Naked Lunch* (1959), both reality loops and **drug**-influenced dreams play a part in the protagonist's perception of an alternate reality.

In Stanislaw Lem's *Solaris*, filmed in 1972 and 2002, and in *The Matrix* and its sequels, the deliberate manipulation of the perception of reality is central to the plot. The notion of *La Jetée*, elaborated in *12 Monkeys* (1995), is that **time** travel into the past is into a *perceived* past, not necessarily a consensus one. A related idea is at the heart of John Grant's "Wooden Horse" (2003), in which the past is viewed as not absolute but as a perception-based consensus that is as uncertain as the future; such consensus may create a present differing from the one we know.

Discussion

Finally, there are countless stories in which characters can perceive something inaccessible to the rest of the world. In W.P. Kinsella's *Shoeless Joe* (1982), filmed as *Field of Dreams*, dead baseball players can only be seen by those willing to let their grip on consensus reality slide. In *Angels in the Outfield* (1952), only a child sees the **angels** who assist the baseball players. In David Lindsay's *The Haunted Woman*

(1922) only a few see a flight of stairs leading to a reality that may or may not lie in the past. Most famously, in Mary Chase's play *Harvey* (1944), filmed in 1950, only Elwood sees the rabbit.

Bibliography

Robert A. Collins. "'Fantasy and 'Forestructures.'" George E. Slusser, Eric S. Rabkin, and Robert Scholes, eds., *Bridges to Fantasy*. Carbondale, IL: Southern Illinois University Press, 1982, 108–120.

Christian De Cock. "Of Philip K. Dick." Warren Smith, Matthew Higgins, Martin Parker, and Geoff Lightfoot, eds., *Science Fiction and Organization*. New York: Routledge, 2001, 160–176.

Tanya J. Gardiner-Scott. "Mervyn Peake: The Relativity of Perception." *Journal of the Fantastic in the Arts*, 1 (1988), 13–24.

A.R. Petrosky. "Effects of Reality Perception and Fantasy on Response to Literature." *Research in the Teaching of English*, 10 (Winter, 1976), 239–258.

Paul Saffo. "Viewpoint: Consensual Realities of Cyberspace." *Communications of the ACM*, 32 (June, 1989), 664–665.

Brian Spittles. "Twentieth Century Perception in *News From Nowhere*." *Journal of the William Morris Society*, 7 (Spring, 1988), 19–24.

Lawrence Sutin, ed. *The Shifting Realities of Philip K. Dick*. New York: Pantheon, 1995.

Robert J. Willis. "Dream on Monkey Mountain." Patrick D. Murphy, ed., *Staging the Impossible*. Westport, CT: Greenwood Press, 1992, 150–155.

—John Grant

PERSONIFICATION

Overview

The most common trope in literature, personification names the animation or embodiment of an abstraction, usually ascribing human qualities (such as speech or emotion) to animals or inanimate objects. Superficial understanding might limit it to childish **clichés**, superstitions, or primitive **mythology**, but personification is also an entrenched, essential element of literature.

Survey

We commonly use personification to identify a striking, exemplary, or paradigmatic instance of something: "he personifies evil," or "she personifies grace." But personification actually conflates two distinct tropes. One, *anthropomorphism*, transfers human characteristics to animals or inert objects, such as **birds**, **cats**, **flowers**, or **mountains**. Even sponges, toasters, or cabooses can impersonate or characterize. Familiar from **fables** and **fairy tales**, fiction and films for children feature **talking animals**—like rabbits in Richard Adams's *Watership Down* (1972) or **fish and sea** creatures in *Finding Nemo* (2003). The Cowardly Lion (see **Courage**) in L. Frank Baum's ***The Wonderful Wizard of Oz*** and wise lion in C.S. Lewis's ***The Lion, the Witch and the Wardrobe*** suggest ethical lessons, while personification in George Orwell's ***Animal Farm*** offers a political moral (see **Ethics; Politics**). Although such devices dominate **advertising**, anthropomorphism operates both insidiously and beautifully within **religions** (see **Adam and Eve**). Amos Tutuola's *My Life in the Bush of Ghosts* (1954) presents a powerful example, tracing the mythic unconscious across a **landscape** personifying both tribal tradition and the arrival of modernity in **Africa**. A related trope is the **trickster**, often configured as an animal, Coyote, as in Michael Chabon's *Summerland* (2002) and Neal Stephenson's *The Diamond Age* (1995).

In science fiction, simple anthropomorphism appears in the figure of the Old Man in the **Moon** in Georges Méliès's ***A Trip to the Moon***. More complex examples surface in ***The Matrix*** and its sequels, which personify **computer** programs (the Oracle, the Architect, the Keymaker), following a pattern established by *Tron* (1982) twenty years earlier. Most depictions of **cyberspace** abound with anthropomorphisms; **cyberpunk** tales, such as Stephenson's ***Snow Crash***, give human users **virtual reality** avatars. Computers themselves are frequently personified. While researchers in cybernetics and artificial intelligence (AI) seek to fabricate machine intelligence commensurable with human consciousness, whatever emerges probably will be unlike us. Nevertheless, science fiction depicts AI in those terms—HAL in ***2001: A Space Odyssey***, the master computer in Arthur C. Clarke's ***The City and the Stars*** (1956), or the **android** Data in ***Star Trek: The Next Generation***. Harlan Ellison's ***Deathbird Stories*** include several kinds of personifications. Further complications include the astonishingly paranoid personifications of Philip K. Dick's "Colony" (1953) (See **Paranoia**).

But since personification gives any abstract notion or object a face or mask from which to speak, it produces something more profound than talking **dogs** or toasters. When we say "this theory explains a trenchant problem," or "this painting speaks to me," we use personification; when pronouns attribute **gender** to inanimate objects, as they do in Romance languages, we use personification. Consequently, some critics prefer the original Greek term *prosopopoeia*, which captures both simple anthropomorphism and subtle conceptual complexities.

The varieties of prosopopoeia are astounding. In classical Greece, abstractions found incarnations as goddesses: Nike (victory), Nemesis (retribution), **Hubris** (pride), Themis (order), Dike (justice), Aphrodite (**love**), and others (see **Gods and Goddesses**). The Bible's *h'satan* (the adversary) personifies difficulty, resistance, chaos, or **evil**. Much medieval and Renaissance literature revolved around characterizations named **Beauty**, Love, **Sin**, or **Death**, a pattern replicated in **Gothic** fiction. Death continues to appear as a reaper in allegorical fantasies like the film *The Seventh Seal* (1957) (see **Allegory**) or **satires** like Terry Pratchett's Discworld series (see ***The Colour of Magic***) and ***The Simpsons***. In *Riddley Walker* (1980), Russell Hoban has death emerge as "Aunty." Other writers refuse broad representations but depict death individually, as in the ghostly "deaths" within Philip Pullman's *The Amber Spyglass* (2000). Even increasingly abstract notions can be personified. In Stanislaw Lem's *Solaris*, the alien ocean exemplifies alterity (see **Identity**), as do the strangers in ***The Brother from Another Planet*** and Karen Joy Fowler's *Sarah Canary* (1991). Marq in Samuel R. Delany's *Stars in My Pocket Like Grains of Sand* (1984) provides a general figure of **estrangement**. Italo Calvino's *Cosmicomics* (1965) treats modern scientific claims concerning the empirical universe—**cosmology**'s Big Bang, **physics**' elliptical planetary orbits, **biology**'s **evolution** of species—through the ancient device of animism.

In *Riddley Walker*, the doll Greenvine personifies the spirit of **nature**. Kurt Vonnegut, Jr.'s *Galápagos* calls Mary Hepburn "mother nature personified"—an especially uncanny figure because the personification ("Mother Nature") has a double articulation: Mary personifies a personification, a conceptual involution that is the most common form of literature's most common trope.

Discussion

Not mere ornaments of language (see **Language and Linguistics**), personifications are fundamental vectors of cognition (see **Knowledge**). All narratives illuminate and inform our experience, bringing the world "to life." In this sense, all **stories** revolve around *prosopopoeia*, the rhetorical device that animates narrative. As a text's "performative" aspect, it provides the means through which narratives **touch** us, and how we in turn touch the world. Postmodern theorist Paul de Man even calls it "the master trope of poetic discourse" and avers that to understand prosopopoeia is to understand understanding itself.

Paradoxically, even as personification ascribes voice and face, it de-faces, transforms the real into imaginary contrivance, exposes character as characterization, and unveils texts as fiction, not fact. Much fiction explicitly deploys the trope of the talking **book** (see Douglas Adams's *The Hitchhiker's Guide to the Galaxy*) or addresses something or someone absent, like the reader (a type of personification called apostrophe)—two significant examples of **metafiction and recursiveness**. Personification evokes narrative's **sublime** nature, and the terrible, wonderful stabilization of subjectivity it simultaneously affords and defers. Terribly, wonderfully, this paradox seems a fundamental fact of our discourse about the world.

Bibliography

Cynthia Chase. *Decomposing Figures*. Baltimore: Johns Hopkins University Press, 1986.

Paul de Man. *The Rhetoric of Romanticism*. New York: Columbia University Press, 1984.

Brent Fishbaugh. "Moore and Gibbon's Watchmen." *Extrapolation*, 39 (Fall, 1998), 189–198.

Samuel T. Joeckel. "In Search of Narnia on a Platonic Map of Progressive Cognition." *Mythlore*, 22 (Autumn, 1997), 8–11.

Sue Matheson. "C.S. Lewis and the Lion." *Mythlore*, 15 (Autumn, 1988), 13–18.

J. Hillis Miller. "Narrative." Frank Lentricchia and Thomas McLaughlin, eds., *Critical Terms for Literary Study*. Second Edition. Chicago: University of Chicago Press, 1995, 66–79.

James J. Paxson. *The Poetics of Personification*. New York: Cambridge University Press, 1994.

Emma Stafford. *Worshipping Virtues*. London: Classical Press of Wales, 2000.

—Neil Easterbrook

PESSIMISM

———————————◼———————————

See Optimism and Pessimism

PHILOSOPHY

———————————◼———————————

*I used to think that I was stupid, and then
I met philosophers.*

—Terry Pratchett
Small Gods (1992)

Overview

In contemporary literature, including science fiction and fantasy, it is often difficult to discern the direct influence of philosophy, though it has increasingly shaped critical perceptions of literature. Still, writers can often be observed wrestling with philosophical questions and, less frequently, employing philosophers as characters. A separate entry address the branch of philosophy known as **Ethics**.

Survey

If the intersection of philosophy and fantasy seems to invite little discussion, that may be because it is largely a literature of tradition, so that the ways fantasy confronts, say, the conflict of good versus **evil** or free will versus determinism will reflect patterns found elsewhere. The iconic object that transmutes **elements**, the Philosopher's Stone (featured in J.K. Rowling's *Harry Potter and the Sorcerer's Stone*), received its name centuries ago due to ancient perceptions of philosophers as masters of all forms of **wisdom**. One of the few fantasies featuring philosophers as characters, Terry Pratchett's Discworld novel *Small Gods* (1992) (see *The Colour of Magic*), suggests that they are generally idle and useless, though occasionally capable of providing practical ideas.

In science fiction, there are occasional appearances by actual philosophers: Aristotle in L. Sprague de Camp's "Aristotle and the Gun" (1958), and Socrates in Harry Turtledove's "The Daimon" (2002) and the film *Bill and Ted's Excellent Adventure* (1989), wherein he is one of the great figures from **history** brought to the present by time-traveling teenagers (see **Time Travel**). To have an impact on their future **civilization**, two teenagers in Orson Scott Card's *Ender's Game* hide behind the names of philosophers Demosthenes and Locke.

However, the potential for science fiction to serve as a vehicle for philosophical ideas—and for philosophy to provide fuel for science fiction—is better illustrated by a science fiction writer who was himself a philosopher, Olaf Stapledon. His *Last and First Men* is a two-billion-year history of successive races of **humanity**, concluding with a race whose wisdom far exceeds our own, while *Star Maker* extends its scale to one hundred billion years, concluding with a vision of the creative force behind the cosmos itself. Both works embody Stapledon's belief in the importance of **community** for individual fulfillment as well as a recognition of our limited capacity for comprehending truth.

One philosophical question posed by science's ability to predict the future is free will: do we live in a deterministic universe in which every event is fixed and unchangeable, or is there some **freedom** in an otherwise mechanistic universe? In his *Foundation* series, Isaac Asimov tackles this issue, envisioning a future in which the collective actions of human beings can be predicted by the science of psychohistory just as chemistry predicts the interactions of molecules. Asimov reconciles free will with psychohistory by asserting that such **knowledge** ultimately increases, rather than diminishes, human freedom.

Time travel raises similar questions of free will: can a time traveler murder his own grandfather before his father was conceived and eliminate himself from history? Science fiction writers have devised every conceivable answer to this question. Ward Moore's *Bring the Jubilee* suggests that observers of an historical event might alter their outcome simply by being there. However, Fritz Leiber's "Try and Change the Past" (1958) proposes that the "conservation of reality" will always return history to its original course; if you remove the bullet from a murderer's gun, a bullet-shaped meteor will strike the victim in its place.

While good stories must follow the rules of logic, one rarely finds a story focused on the subject of logic itself. A.E. van Vogt's *The World of Null-A* (1948) is an exception, wherein Gilbert Gosseyn ("Go Sane") develops his latent potential and becomes a kind of **superman** in part by escaping the limitations of Aristotelian logic. Tom Godwin's "The Cold Equations" (1954), however, relentlessly moves to its bitter conclusion—ejection of a stowaway into the depths of space—through the inescapable force of logic.

Another branch of philosophy is epistemology, the study of how we know what we know. *The Matrix* uses **virtual reality** to ask epistemological questions about the reliability of sensory **perceptions**. Philip K. Dick raised similar issues about our **memory** in "We Can Remember it for You Wholesale" (1966), wherein a clerk asking to be implanted with the false memory of having been a secret agent on **Mars** discovers that his actual experience of being one has already been erased from his mind. In the film *Blade Runner*, based on Dick's *Do Androids Dream of Electric Sheep?*, audiences question whether a **detective** is really a human being or an **android** with someone else's memories.

Discussion

A question that epitomizes the power of science fiction to explore philosophical ideas is, "What if you're really a brain in a jar, and your world is just a set of electronic impulses sent by some **mad scientist**?" To be sure, works of fantasy can play with such issues—in Robert A. Heinlein's "They" (1941), for example, a man correctly believes the world around him is an elaborate **illusion** staged by mysterious enemies—but the potential *reality* of such apparent delusions being achieved through technological advances may make the philosophical questions posed in science fiction seem especially powerful. Also, the scale of science fiction places humanity into a broader context, so that immediate concerns become less important and philosophical issues grow in significance. As scientific **progress** continues to raise philosophical issues—should human **clones** be permitted? Under what circumstances is **nuclear war** permissible? Should **computers** that seem to possess human **intelligence** have the legal rights of humans?—science fiction will continue exploring them in imaginative contexts.

Bibliography

Gregory Bassham and Eric Bronson. *The Lord of the Rings and Philosophy*. Chicago: Open Court, 2003.

Stephen R.L. Clark. *How to Live Forever*. London and New York: Routledge, 1995.

Michael Cobley. "The Ghost in the Pen." *Vector*, No. 136 (February/March 1987), 10–12; and No. 137 (April/May 1987), 12–13.

Justin Leiber. "On Science Fiction and Philosophy." *Philosophical Speculations on Science Fiction and Fantasy*, 1 (March, 1982), 5–11.

Robert E. Myers, ed. *The Intersection of Science Fiction and Philosophy*. Westport, CT: Greenwood Press, 1983.

Michael Philips, ed. *Philosophy and Science Fiction*. Buffalo, NY: Prometheus Books, 1984.

Mark Rowlands. *The Philosopher at the End of the Universe*. London: Ebury, 2003.

Nicolas D. Smith, ed. *Philosophers Look at Science Fiction*. Chicago: Nelson-Hall, 1982.

—*Ed McKnight*

PHYSICS

Overview

Many of the central ideas of science fiction come from the field of physics. As science fiction strives to encompass human possibilities from the Big Bang to the end of the universe (see **Cosmology; Eschatology**), physics is one of its best tools in doing so. Physics plays the role of a structure, an assumption, or a **puzzle** in many science fiction stories.

Survey

The modern science of physics has had virtually no impact on fantasy, one exception being the satirical references to contemporary theories scattered throughout Terry Pratchett's Discworld series (see ***The Colour of Magic*; Satire**). Rarely, quantum mechanics may be invoked as an excuse for strange activity, an analogy to **magic**, or a source of mysticism. However, from the earliest days of the genre, the ideas at the heart of many oustanding science fiction stories have involved physics. Even Cyrano de Bergerac's pioneering accounts of travel to the **Moon** and Mary Shelley's dreams of created life (see ***Frankenstein***) were based on the physics of their time—celestial mechanics and new experiments in electricity.

Jules Verne's *From the Earth to the Moon* takes readers on the trip described in its title via Isaac Newton's laws of motion. Verne's ballistics trace a classical arc through space, with a new explosive powering his Moon shot. Like many science fiction readers to come, Verne's readers were physics enthusiasts or became so under his tutelage. That enthusiasm, for some writers, goes even further, making physics symbolic of **progress**, science in general, or behavioral codes.

In the Newtonian rigidity of Tom Godwin's "The Cold Equations" (1954), physical reality implies social facts so obviously that no one can deny the equations are correct; thus there is only one solution to the story's problem. *Star Trek*'s engineer, Mr. Scott, protests that he cannot change the laws of physics. Physics stands for immutability or impossibility.

Yet the laws of physics have not been immutable, and quantum mechanics has infiltrated more and more stories. Heisenberg's Uncertainty Principle does not speak to human doubt, but in literary terms it provides authors with more flexibility than the classical viewpoint did. The fundamental physical **forces** are probabilistic, not deterministic, and science fiction, after some initial confusion or ignorance, has seized the opportunity.

Authors like Gregory Benford and Ken Wharton use their backgrounds as working physicists to write convincingly about quantum mechanical weirdness. Benford's *Timescape* tracks alternate timelines in a definitively quantum universe, each timeline featuring the research and personal trials of a working physicist. In *Timescape*, physics is not only daily labor and science-fictional conceit but also the way to a better world. This is the more positive of the three common views of physicists or other **scientists**: the savior scientist who, if not a **messiah**, at least points the way to something better than the current situation, either directly as in Benford's novel or by implication in improved, technically superior near-utopian societies.

The physicist, like other scientists, may also appear as a destructive force, too focused on the pursuit of **knowledge** to consider the social implications of their work. Kurt Vonnegut, Jr.'s *Cat's Cradle* is a classic example of this view of physicists, inspired in part by physicists' invention of **nuclear weapons**. In *Cat's Cradle*, **Earth** is literally left a frozen wasteland due to one scientist's unconstrained research into a substance called Ice-9. Here, physics unchecked by **politics** or **ethics** results in the destruction of the entire human race.

Ursula K. Le Guin's *The Dispossessed* and other works present a third view of physics and physicists: her physicist protagonist is a destabilizing force in his society, but is neither a savior nor a destroyer. His investigations can change his world, but whether it is for the better or for the worse is left as ambiguous as whether his society is a **utopia** or a **dystopia**.

The field of physics most frequently considered in science fiction is astronomy or astrophysics. Kim Stanley Robinson's Mars trilogy (see **Red Mars**) exemplifies how the work of scientists can support multiple, fascinating, human points of view; Robinson's trilogy proves that physics and related sciences are not on one political "side." Frederik Pohl is among the writers who have taken physics to its literal limits in their science fiction tales: to the end of the universe. While **eschatology** has never rivaled planetology or even relativity and quantum mechanics in popularity, books like Pohl's *The World at the End of Time* (1990) demonstrate the incredible range of the combination of physics and speculation.

Discussion

It is almost impossible to avoid physics in **hard science fiction**, as an underpinning to speculation, implicit component of a worldview, or explicit plot device. Even when contemporary physics-based speculation is not central, current knowledge of physics provides a framework around which science fiction authors must at least appear to work. Writers who want to include faster-than-light travel or **communication**, for example, must acknowledge that the current state of scientific knowledge deems these things impossible; so, they must invoke an advance in physics or some special condition like **hyperspace** to have some toehold on plausibility. Physics must be appeased.

Bibliography

Iain M. Banks. "Escape From the Laws of Physics." *New Scientist*, 138 (March 20, 1993), 38–39.

Russell Blackford. "Physics and Fantasy." *Journal of Popular Culture*, 19 (Winter, 1985), 35–44.

Amit Goswami with Maggie Goswami. *The Cosmic Dancers*. New York: Harper & Row, Publishers, 1983.

Lawrence Krauss. *Beyond Star Trek*. New York: Basic Books, 1997.

———. *The Physics of Star Trek*. New York: Basic Books, 1995.

Peter Nicholls, David Langford, and Brian Stableford. *The Science in Science Fiction*. London: Michael Joseph, 1982.

Paul Sporn. "The Modern Physics of Contemporary Criticism." Joseph W. Slade and Judith Y. Lee, eds., *Beyond The Two Cultures*. Ames: Iowa State University Press, 1990, 201–222.

M.T. Tavormina. "Physics as Metaphor." *Mosaic*, 13 (Spring/Summer 1988), 51–62.

Gregory L. Zentz. "Physics, Metaphysics, and Science Fiction." Michele K. Langford, ed., *Contours of the Fantastic*. Westport, CT: Greenwood Press, 1990, 173–184.

—*Marissa Lingen*

PIRATES

Overview

Pirates—broadly defined as seafaring bandits—have come to symbolize a variety of themes, including **revenge** on people who wronged them; **freedom** from the monotony of everyday life; **theft** of possessions, ideals, innocence, **money**, goods, or even **knowledge**; and **rebellion** against oppressive governments and their laws. Transplanted to fantastic settings, they commonly appear in science fiction and fantasy, particularly **space opera** and **heroic fantasy**.

Survey

Arguably, imaginative tales of pirates date to ancient Greece, since one might interpret independent, seagoing adventurers like Jason (see *Jason and the Argonauts*) and Homer's Ulysses as pirates. However, the profession of piracy came to prominence in the seventeenth century, as ships from **Europe** seized and returned plunder, such as **gold and silver**, and became tempting targets for legendary figures like Blackbeard. When pirates were actively feared, they were usually **villains**, but as modern advances in shipbuilding and changing patterns of trade began to make traditional piracy obsolete in the nineteenth century, writers reinvented pirates as exciting rogues or **heroes**.

The novel that established and popularized the iconography of pirates was Robert Louis Stevenson's *Treasure Island* (1883), wherein one finds such now-familiar tropes as peg-legged Long John Silver with a parrot on his shoulder (see **Birds**), victims forced to walk the plank, and **treasure maps** leading to buried gold. Along with other adaptations, Stevenson's story was ineptly transformed into science fiction in the animated *Treasure Planet* (2002). J.M. Barrie employed similar pirates, softened and sentimentalized, in his play *Peter Pan* (1904) (see **Peter and Wendy**). Stevenson's sinister Silver, and Barrie's foppish Captain Hook, have influenced all later depictions of pirates: the fantasy film *Pirates of the Caribbean: The Curse of the Black Pearl* (2003), for example, essentially contrasts Geoffrey Rush's version of Long John Silver with Johnny Depp's version of Captain Hook. That film's tale of dead pirates kept alive by a **curse** also reflects a common linkage between pirates and **ghosts and hauntings**, previously observed in the film *Blackbeard's Ghost* (1968).

Another influential character was Robert E. Howard's Conan (see **Conan the Conqueror**), who spent some of his career as a pirate, as titularly confirmed in the collection *Conan the Freebooter* (1968). Howard also wrote two stories about a more traditional pirate character, Black Vulmea, collected in *Black Vulmea's Vengeance* (1976). Edgar Rice Burroughs dabbled in pirate fiction with *Pirate Blood* (1970) but also depicted Carson Napier taking to seagoing piracy on **Venus** in *The Pirates of Venus* (1939). Children visiting Narnia are attacked by pirates in C.S. Lewis's *The Voyage of the Dawn Treader* (1952) (see **The Lion, the Witch and the Wardrobe**).

In the 1930s, as pirates hit the peak of their popularity in literature and film, science fiction writers embraced the notion that interplanetary spaceships with valuable cargo might be menaced by "space pirates." Jack Williamson's "The Prince of Space" (1931) is an early example of the space pirate as misunderstood hero, while Harry Bates and Jack Gilmore's Hawk Carse battle the implacably **evil** space pirate Ku Sui in numerous adventures beginning in 1931. In the 1940s and thereafter, more mature depictions of **space travel** avoided this now-clichéd figure (see **Cliché**), but space pirates lingered in juvenile science fiction like Jack Vance's *Vandals of the Void* (1953), Carey Rockwell's *On the Trail of the Space Pirates* (1953), and Isaac Asimov's *Lucky Starr and the Pirates of the Asteroids* (1954), while Murray Leinster reconsidered the profession of space piracy more knowingly and ironically in *The Pirates of Zan* (1958). Space pirates also became a staple of science fiction film and television: in the **Doctor Who** episode "The Space Pirates" (1969), the Doctor meets pirates while racing to find his lost spaceship; in the animated *Star Trek* episode "The Pirates of Orion" (1974) (see **Star Trek**), the *Enterprise* is menaced by the eponymous villains; and in the film *The Ice Pirates* (1984), alien pirates seize spaceships carrying valuable cargoes of ice.

For space pirates to figure in more recent science fiction, there must be elements of novelty or sophistication. Brigands of an ambitious nature are villains in Anne

McCaffrey's Space Pirates trilogy (*Sassinak* [1990], with Elizabeth Moon; *The Death of Sleep* [1990], with Jody Lynn Nye; and *Generation Warriors* [1991], with Moon). In David Weber's *Path of the Fury* (1992), after Alicia Devries's family is murdered by space pirates, she is possessed by the spirit of an ancient Greek fury (see **Possession**) and obtains her own spaceship to seek revenge. Space pirates also figure in two expansive space opera series: Iain M. Banks's Culture series, beginning with **Consider Phlebas**, and Stephen R. Donaldson's Gap series, beginning with *The Gap into Conflict: The Real Story* (1990).

Even as science fiction has marginalized the pirate, fantasy may make interesting use of the character. In William Goldman's recursive *The Princess Bride* (1973) (see **Metafiction and Recursiveness**), the hero masquerades as the Dread Pirate Roberts in order to rescue his long-lost **love**. Tim Powers mixes piracy and **voodoo** in *On Stranger Tides* (1987), which incorporates real-life pirates like Blackbeard who seek the legendary fountain of **youth**. In Michael Scott Rohan's *Chase the Morning* (1990), a modern-day businessmen enters a **parallel world** and gets involved with a band of fantastical pirates.

Discussion

Pirates appear to embody a captivating **dream** as they sail out over placid waters, under crimson skies and gentle sea breezes, searching for treasure and adventure. Paradoxically, recent efforts to revive the classic genre of pirate fiction in literature and film have been unsuccessful; perhaps it is doomed to extinction like the **western**. Still, the pirate seems likely to endure in the more exotic settings of science fiction and fantasy.

Bibliography

Robert H. Barrett. "Cloudland Revisited." *The Burroughs Bulletin*, No. 51 (Summer, 2002), 14–20.

David B. Bozarth. "A-Roving: An Analysis of *Pirate Blood*." *The Burroughs Bulletin*, No. 53 (Winter, 2003), 3–8.

David Cordingly. *Under the Black Flag*. New York: Random House, 1995.

Laurence G. Dunn. "Blood of a Pirate." *Burroughs Bulletin*, No. 53 (Winter, 2003), 9–11.

Michael Hague. *The Book of Pirates*. New York: HarperCollins, 2001.

Brian Lowry. "*Ice Pirates* Defrosted." *Starlog*, No. 82 (May, 1984), 44–46.

Jan Rogozinski. *Pirates!* New York: Facts onFile, 1995.

Barbara Sjoholm. *The Pirate Queen*. Emeryville, CA: Seal Press, 2004.

Jo Stanley. *Bold in Her Breeches*. London and San Francisco: Pandora, 1995.

—*Michael Penncavage*

PLAGUES AND DISEASES

All England slept; and from my window, commanding a wide prospect of the star-illumined country, I saw the land

stretched out in placid rest. I was awake,
alive, while the brother of death pos-
sessed my race.

—Mary Shelley
The Last Man (1826)

Overview

Biomedical fiction, in which plagues and diseases play prominent roles, falls into two categories. The first features plague or disease as a natural phenomenon threatening **humanity** with extinction; with human drama in the foreground, plague functions as an environmental **disaster** equivalent to famine, **war**, or earthquake. The second portrays plague as an alien or **monster**, originating from humanity's failure to respect the boundaries and laws of **nature**. A separate entry addresses the general topic of **Medicine**.

Survey

Novels of near extinction, like Mary Shelley's *The Last Man*, Jack London's *The Scarlet Plague* (1912), George R. Stewart's *Earth Abides*, Stephen King's *The Stand* (1978), and Greg Bear's *Darwin's Radio* (1999) portray worlds in which ecological imbalances or evolutionary processes give rise to deadly infections (see **Ecology; Evolution**). Two interconnected themes appear in these works: the vulnerability of humanity to pathogens that emerge from the external world or from the human genome itself, and humanity's irrepressible instinct for **survival**, manifested in the efforts of health-care workers to stem the disease and peregrinations of survivors. Shelley features an air-borne contagion that annihilates the human race but for one survivor. The atmospheric desolation of her fiction contrasts with the survival theme in London's novel. *The Scarlet Plague* anticipates the influenza pandemic of 1918 by describing a virulent outbreak in 2013; **civilization** deteriorates rapidly before the plague, and survivors reconsruct a society in California. *Earth Abides* exemplifies the sociology of reconstruction: survivors in a depopulated **America** set up a **community** overlooking San Francisco Bay. An eschatological atmosphere pervades *The Stand* (See **Eschatology**): erupting in 1990, the devastating disease is catalyst for the fulfillment of biblical prophecy in the Book of Revelation, as survivors struggle against an opposing, diabolic remnant. In *Darwin's Radio*, an endogenous retrovirus, incipient in the human genome, causes miscarriages and spreads like influenza. The origin of this potentially extinctive disease is traced back to Neanderthal remains preserved in a frozen **cavern**.

Human trespass into nature, through unethical pharmacology or **genetic engineering**, is another important theme, often linked to the motif of the alien microbe, either extraterrestrial or terrestrial in origin. Michael Crichton's *The Andromeda Strain* (1969) criticizes aggressive impulses and scientific **hubris**. A satellite, designed to retrieve pathogenic microbes from space for use in war, is contaminated with a lethal organism. Sophisticated containment measures are subverted by human error, and the germ frustrates efforts to neutralize it. Only the random mutation of the organism to a benign form provides humanity with a reprieve. The invader may also be a terrestrial organism from the past. In Frank Slaughter's *Plague Ship* (1976), a geological expedition disinters a prehistoric bacterium from a five-thousand-year-old Peruvian tomb. The organism has survived the ages in spores insulating it from the elements. Modern medicine strives but fails to make headway against the disease, but nature randomly intervenes: brine splashed on a culture plate transforms the microbe from a lethal to an innocuous form.

The most frightening alien microbe of all is the chimera, a genetically engineered monster. Chimera research is an historical fact, the most notorious practitioners of which were the Soviets who, in the 1980s, devised for military use microbial cross-breeds such as Ebola-smallpox. The release of a chimera on a small scale is the topic of Richard Preston's *The Cobra Event* (1997): a **mad scientist** genetically engineers a neurological agent, smallpox, and the common cold. A microbiologist with an eschatological mania uses weapons-grade anthrax in John S. Marr and John Baldwin's *The Eleventh Plague* (1998), as does a former Soviet technician in league with neo-Nazis in Robin Cook's *Vector* (1999). In these novels, epidemiologists systematically defeat terrorists, maniacs, and cunning murderers (see **Crime and Punishment**). On one hand, the great strength of plague fiction has been adherence to contemporary biomedical theory. If readers have general knowledge of the pathogen in question, and if the content is scientifically accurate and credibly presented, a novel can have frightening immediacy. On the other hand, a plague fantasy, foregoing scientific plausibility, separates itself from readers' experience and cultural **memory**—since some may have actually experienced a terrible outbreak firsthand.

Discussion

The human experience of plagues and diseases has been filled with unheeded lessons and life-saving insights into humanity's place in the world. One lesson is that humanity is vulnerable to microbes and should not let its guard down in the perpetual struggle against pathogens. Understanding man's relationship with dangerous germs is important if we are to appreciate the fiction. The theme of man's intrusion into nature, a staple of plague fiction, reflects the scientific fact that disturbing ecological systems through deforestation, uncontrolled hunting, or urban development causes unexpected mutations and brings settlers into contact with dangerous germs (one theory for the origin of AIDS, Ebola, and Lyme disease). How health-care professionals and scientists pre-empt and control outbreaks is another significant theme in plague fiction. Yet another is the misuse of science and **technology** in the creation of pathogenic monsters, designed for profit and war.

Bibliography

P.S. Alterman. "Neuron and Junction." Thomas P. Dunn, ed., *The Mechanical God*. Westport, CT: Greenwood Press, 1982, 109–115.

Greg Bear. "A Short Biological Primer." Bear, *Darwin's Radio*. New York: Ballantine Books, 1999, 527–529.

D. Donlan. "Experiencing *The Andromeda Strain*." *English Journal*, 63 (September, 1974), 72–73.

Steven E. Kagle. "Beyond Armageddon." Tony Magistrale, ed., *A Casebook on The Stand*. San Bernardino, CA: Borgo Press, 1992, 189–209.

William Lomax. "Epic Reversal in Mary Shelley's *The Last Man*." Michele K. Langford, ed., *Contours of Fantasy*. Westport, CT: Greenwood Press, 1990, 7–17.

Anne McWhir. "Mary Shelley's Anti-Contagionism." *Mosaic*, 35 (June 2002), 22–38.

Donna Pastourmatzi, ed. *Biotechnological and Medical Themes in Science Fiction*. Thessaloniki, Greece: University Studio Press, 2002.

Gary Westfahl and George Slusser, eds. *No Cure for the Future*. Westport, CT: Greenwood Press, 2002.

—*Charles De Paolo*

PLANETARY COLONIES

Overview

As **humanity** steps onto planets other than **Earth,** we examine the nature of our newest **frontiers** and explore the challenges of **alien worlds**. How humans deal with the demands of existence beyond the safety of our planet speaks of our will to walk untrodden pathways and settle and survive in unknown places. Stories about planetary colonies involving massive transformations of worlds, or of those settling them, are discussed under **Terraforming** and **Pantropy**.

Survey

Early works of science fiction usually posited that other planets were inhabited, most likely by beings as advanced as or more advanced than humans, so the task of visitors from Earth was not colonization but integration into a existing **civilization**— which is what happens to the **scientist** Cavor in H.G. Wells's *The First Men in the Moon* (1901) and John Carter in Edgar Rice Burroughs's *A Princess of Mars* and its sequels. It was the gradual realization that the **Moon** and **Mars**, and other worlds like them, were either uninhabited, or inhabited only by simple lifeforms, that inspired more stories about planetary colonization.

Today, the novels of Robert A. Heinlein and Arthur C. Clarke are probably the most familiar representatives of the flood of stories about planetary colonies that began appearing in the 1950s. Both wrote about the problems of settlers on the Moon (Heinlein's "The Menace from Earth" [1957] and *The Moon Is a Harsh Mistress* [1966], Clarke's *Earthlight* [1955] and *A Fall of Moondust* [1961]); on Mars (Heinlein's *Red Planet* [1949], Clarke's *Sands of Mars* [1952]); and on the distant moons of **Jupiter and the Outer Planets** (Jupiter's Ganymede in Heinlein's *Farmer in the Sky* [1950], Saturn's Titan in Clarke's *Imperial Earth* [1975]). Both authors, like others, strove for an atmosphere of realism in describing planetary conditions and human efforts to adapt to them, though they occasionally posited the discovery of indigenous aliens (see **Aliens in Space**), which posed no threat to the colonization process. Less concerned with science were works like Ray Bradbury's poetic *The Martian Chronicles* and Philip K. Dick's **surrealistic** *Martian Time-Slip* (1964).

Stories about planetary colonies in other solar systems tend to seem less realistic, since they invariably must posit either faster-than-light travel (see **Hyperspace**) or **teleportation** to get humans there in a single lifetime. On the basis of such assumptions, however, Heinlein did produce persuasive accounts of people settling on distant worlds in *Time Enough for Love* (1973) (see *The Past Through Tomorrow*) and *Tunnel in the Sky* (1955). (Stories about **generation starships** designed to eventually establish planetary colonies after hundreds of years in transit generally have passengers settle into permanent residence in space.) Most stories about planetary colonies throughout the galaxy take place long after they have been settled, as is usually the case with worlds inhabited by humans visited in **Star Trek** and its successor series; Isaac Asimov's *The Naked Sun* (1957) (see *I, Robot*) involves a planetary colony that has become overly dependent on **robots**.

Sometimes, stories about faraway planetary colonies even take on the atmosphere of fantasy, which is the case with Anne McCaffrey's *Dragonflight* and its sequels, wherein a lost colony of humans evolve a lifestyle of harmonious coexistence with genetically engineered **dragons**. It is also speculated that the hermaphroditic civilization in Ursula K. Le Guin's *The Left Hand of Darkness* emerged from a planetary colony that was an experiment in **genetic engineering**.

Recent stories about colonizing other worlds display a realization that settlement will involve political problems as well as scientific ones. While Kim Stanley Robinson's **Red Mars** does involve the hard sciences of **physics** and **biology** needed for successful terraforming, he devotes increasing attention to the political struggles that arise as more and more people inhabit the planet in the sequels *Green Mars* (1994) and *Blue Mars* (1966). Also discussing colonization from a more political perspective is Ken MacLeod's *The Stone Canal* (1996), which employs a planetary colony to examine the future **politics** of capitalist and socialist states. Returning to a more fantastic style of writing, Michael Carroll's *The Dead Colony* (2001) speaks of insurrection and political intrigue on the future world of Pelicos, while Scott Reeve's *Colony* (2002) tells the story of how opposing political visions can have devastating effects upon newly established groups of settlers.

Also relevant to this topic are stories speculating that Earth itself may be a planetary colony; for example, in James P. Hogan's *Inherit the Stars* (1977), scientists discover that humans are the descendents of beings who inhabited a planet between Mars and Jupiter and colonized Earth before their world was destroyed.

Discussion

Although there are stories about humans living in the vacuum of outer space (see **Space Stations; Space Habitats**), living on the surface of another planet remains the most attractive dream. Since humans have historically chosen to settle in some of the most inhospitable regions on Earth, it is plausible to assume that inhospitable planets may someday become **homes** as well, so stories about planetary colonies could serve as **predictions**. However, the concept of colonizing a planet other than our own can also function metaphorically as a way to examine many of our deepest compulsions and fears—another sort of story about people struggling to transform the unfamiliar into the familiar.

Bibliography

K.V. Bailey. "Life, Mars and Everything." *The Third Alternative*, No. 14 (1997), 40–43.

Karl S. Guthke. *The Last Frontier*. Ithaca, NY: Cornell University Press, 1990.

Joe Haldeman. *Vietnam and Other Alien Worlds*. Framingham, MA: NESFA, 1993.

Frank Herbert. "Men on Other Planets." Reginald Bretnor, ed., *The Craft of Science Fiction*. New York: Harper, 1976, 121–135.

Ivan Millett. "Colonisation: Beyond the Earth." *The Zone and Premonitions*, No. 5 (Spring, 1997), 23–24.

Peter Nicholls, David Langford, and Brian Stableford. "Colonizing Other Planets." Nicholls, Langford, and Stableford, *The Science in Science Fiction*. 1982. New York: Alfred A. Knopf, 1983, 26–27.

Robert A. Zubrin. "The Martian Frontier." *Analog*, 115 (November, 1995), 70–83.

Robert M. Zubrin and David A. Baker. "Mars Direct." *Analog*, 111 (July, 1991), 77–99.

—Patricia Kerslake

PLANTS

■

Overview

In the everyday world, plants, **flowers**, trees (see **Forests**), and fungi are unmoving, unintelligent (see **Intelligence**) organisms that are most often used to invoke images of natural **beauty** and serenity, and perhaps to inspire a craving for a salad (see **Food and Drink**). Thus it seems only natural that speculative fiction writers strive to turn readers' expectations upside-down and portray plants as active, smart, and even ferocious.

Survey

H.P. Lovecraft employs such a reversal in his story "The Colour Out of Space" (1927): a meteorite lands in Nahum Gardner's orchard, and afterward the plants and trees that grow on his lands suck the life out of everything around them. In Ursula K. Le Guin's "Vaster Than Empires and More Slow" (1971), an intergalactic survey team sets down on a planet whose only lifeforms are non-moving vegetation. However, the interconnected plant life covering the planet is aware, and the vast plant mind (see **Hive Minds**) reacts with terror to the presence of humans. The plant mind's terror in turn affects the lone telepath (see **Psychic Powers**) among the explorers.

Other stories detail human fascination with normal plants. In Edmond Hamilton's "Alien Earth" (1949), a young scientist visiting the tropics can slow his metabolism down so much that he can observe plants at their own pace. The scientist can then see the truly dynamic nature of plants' growth and interactions, and he becomes entranced.

Plants play an important role in many fantasy stories as ingredients for spells and magical potions. The use of plants in **magic** is grounded in **mythology** and folklore, since every human **culture** has discovered the medicinal properties of certain plants (see **Medicine**) and as a consequence has attributed magical or spiritual properties to others. For example, in *The Mummy's Hand* (1940) and later sequels, tana leaves have the power to bring the Egyptian mummy Kharis back to life (see **Egypt**).

Plants are radically different from animals, and as such can seem quite alien, especially if given unexpected attributes. Edgar Rice Burroughs's *Thuvia, Maid of Mars* (1920) features an encounter with the horrific, bloodthirsty Plant Men of Barsoom (see ***A Princess of Mars***). In John Wyndham's ***The Day of the Triffids*** and its adaptations, the titular triffids are unleashed experimental plants that can walk, sting, and kill to feast on human flesh. Killer plants appear in other works such as William Hope Hodgson's *The Boats of the 'Glen Carrig'* (1907), which features human-devouring plant life. The black comedy *The Little Shop of Horrors* (1960) focuses on a young employee of a flower store who nurtures an intelligent, carnivorous plant he names Audrey. As Audrey grows to monstrous proportions, it forces the young man to kill people to feed it. Other antagonistic plants are a bit more subtle. In the film ***Invasion of the Body Snatchers*** (based on Jack Finney's 1955 novel *The Body Snatchers*), plant-like aliens grow human **doppelgängers** from pods. The plant-like nature of the aliens is more apparent in the 1978 film remake, in which the aliens spread by way of flowerlike blossoms. And the film ***The Thing (from Another World)*** features a **monster** alien that is officially a plant, memorably described as "an intellectual carrot."

Not all plant-like aliens are villainous. Stanley G. Weinbaum's "The Lotus Eaters" (1935) is a classic story about the discovery, on **Venus**, of highly intelligent but fatally apathetic plants. In the ***Farscape*** series, the seductive humanoid priestess Zhaan is revealed to be an evolved plant near the end of the first season. Her unique needs for light and soil provide the basis for the plots of many episodes, and her photogasmic reaction to solar flares provides comic relief. Another sexy, mobile plant appears in John Boyd's science fiction **satire** *The Pollinators of Eden* (1969).

In Pat Murphy's story "His Vegetable Wife" (1986), a farmer (see **Farms**) **terraforming** a distant world plants and grows a wife for himself among his other crops; Murphy uses the farmer's assumptions of his wife's vegetative nature to explore rape and domestic **violence**. Another sympathetic anthropomorphic plant is portrayed in the *Swamp Thing* comics, which debuted in 1972 and were later adapted for television and film. The Swamp Thing is created when a scientist is exposed to plant growth chemicals during an explosion; he becomes a huge plant–human hybrid who can regenerate lost limbs and (in later versions of the comic) exercise supernatural control over plant life. Jeff Noon's novel *Pollen* (2001) provides a different science-fictional take on plant–human hybrids while it weaves a plot in which pollen threatens to make the world sneeze itself to death. Poison Ivy, a villainous opponent of *Batman* who appeared in the film *Batman and Robin* (1997), also displays extraordinary powers over plants.

Discussion

Plants are often used merely as part of world building in science fiction and fantasy, like the genetically engineered plants (see **Genetic Engineering**), which are planted on **Mars** to thicken its atmosphere in Kim Stanley Robinson's ***Red Mars***.

However, many works move plants into the foreground as antagonistic forces or sympathetic, intelligent characters. Writers will undoubtedly continue to do interesting things with plants as science continues to reveal what fascinating organisms they truly are.

Bibliography

Clark A. Brady. "Plant Men of Barsoom." Brady, *The Burroughs Cyclopedia*. Jefferson, NC: McFarland, 1996, 256–266.

Leroy W. Dubeck, Suzanne E. Moshier, and Judith E. Boss. "*The Day of the Triffids.*" Dubeck, Moshier, and Boss, *Science in Cinema*. New York: Teacher's College Press, 1988, 109–115.

Tom Fischer. "Green Mythology." *Horticulture*, 99 (May/June 2002), 26.

David Ketterer. "'Vivisection': Schoolboy' John Wyndham's' First Publication?" *Science Fiction Studies*, 26 (July, 1999), 303–311.

Candace R. Miller. *More Tales From the Plant Kingdom*. Lima, OH: Pourquoi Press, 1998.

Linda H. Schneekloth. "Plants: The Ultimate Alien." *Extrapolation*, 42 (Fall, 2001), 246–254.

J.A. Schulp. "The Flora of Middle Earth." Gisbert Kranz, ed., *Inklings*. Lüdenscheid, Germany: Stier, 1985, 129–186.

Brian Taylor. *Gardens of the Gods*. Shropshire, England: Clun Valley Publications, 1996.

—*Lucy A. Snyder*

POETRY

■

The life of a poet lies not merely in the finite language-dance of expression but in the nearly infinite combinations of perception and memory combined with the sensitivity to what is perceived and remembered.

—Dan Simmons
Hyperion (1989)

Overview

Today, science fiction poetry is a thriving tradition, as poems involving science fiction topics and themes are regularly published in magazines and journals, and the annual Rhysling Awards honor outstanding science fiction poems. However, this entry focuses on various interactions between poetry and the prose narratives of science fiction and fantasy, as well as rarer connections to film and television. Separate entries discuss playwright and poet William **Shakespeare** and the general subject of **Writing and Authors**.

Survey

The first poet to appear as a character in a work of fantasy is arguably Vergil, the guide through **Hell** and Purgatory in Dante's *Inferno* and *Purgatorio* (c. 1306–1321). Much later, a Vergil portrayed as a magician was the protagonist of Avram Davidson's *The Phoenix and the Mirror* (1969) and *Vergil in Averno* (1987) (see **Magic**). Recent writers have shown special interest in British poets of the Romantic period. Percy Blythe Shelley and Lord Byron were living with Mary Shelley when she wrote *Frankenstein*, and all three mysteriously coexist with Shelley's Frankenstein and his **monster** in Brian W. Aldiss's *Frankenstein Unbound* (1973), filmed in 1990. William Blake, renamed Talespinner, roams the **frontier** of an **alternate history** version of nineteenth-century America in Orson Scott Card's Alvin Maker series, beginning with *Seventh Son* (1987); a recreated John Keats is a recurring presence in the future universe of Dan Simmons's *Hyperion*; and William Wordsworth makes an appearance in John Myers Myers's eclectic fantasy *The Moon's Fire-Eating Daughter* (1981), which also features, among numerous writers, the Greek poet Homer, Roman poet Martial, and Renaissance poet Edmund Spenser.

Fictional poets are rarely protagonists of science fiction or fantasy stories but are occasionally significant characters. A poet figures prominently in Samuel R. Delany's **far future** Fall of the Towers trilogy, beginning with *Captives of the Flames* (1963), and the future solar system of his "Time Considered as a Helix of Semi-Precious Stones" (1968) features a group of "Singers" renowned and cherished for their ability to spontaneously create poetry in the streets. One pilgrim in Simmons's *Hyperion* is a poet, famous for composing an elegy about, and entitled, *The Dying Earth*.

In addition to using poets as characters, writers often reflect the influence of famous poems. The fantasy world of Myers's *Silverlock* (1949) includes characters from Homer's *Odyssey* (c. 750 BCE), the medieval poem *Sir Gawain and the Green Knight* (c. 1370), and Spenser's *The Faerie Queene* (1590, 1596). Henry Kuttner's and C.L. Moore's "Mimsy Were the Borogoves" (1943) explains Lewis Carroll's poem "Jabberwocky," which first appeared in *Through the Looking Glass* (1871) (see *Alice's Adventures in Wonderland*), as a formula for traveling through **time** and space, accessible only to **children**. Edgar Allan Poe's poems "The Conqueror Worm" (1843) and "The Raven" (1845) have inspired **horror** films, though there are only tenuous connections between those poems and the films *The Raven* (1935), *The Raven* (1963), and *The Conqueror Worm* (1968). Critic Robin Roberts explored how Matthew Arnold's "Dover Beach" (1867) inspired and shaped a number of science fiction stories, including Kuttner and Moore's "Clash by Night" (1943), George R.R. Martin's "A Song for Lya" (1974), Robert Silverberg's *Tom O'Bedlam* (1985), and Michael Swanwick's *Vacuum Flowers* (1987).

Writers may borrow phrases from poems as story titles. Ray Bradbury does this frequently: his chilling tale of an automated house without residents, "There Will Come Soft Rains" (1950), incorporates the 1920 Sara Teasdale poem that gives the story its title (See **The Martion Chronicles**) his episode of *The Twilight Zone* about a **robot** grandmother, "I Sing the Body Electric" (1962), adapted as a story in 1969, borrows the title of Walt Whitman's 1890 poem; and his story about space travelers exploring the **Sun**, "The Golden Apples of the Sun" (1953), takes its title from the final lines of W.B. Yeats's "The Song of Wandering Aengus" (1899).

Many modern stories follow the pattern of Carroll's Alice books by incorporating passages of original poetry; one ingenious example is the fourteen chapter titles of Hal Clement's *Fossil* (1993), which form a perfectly rendered sonnet. However, the most common convention is to ostensibly present song lyrics being sung by characters—though readers, lacking access to melodies, will necessarily relate to them as poems. Perhaps the most famous poem within a story is Robert A. Heinlein's "The Green Hills of Earth" in the story of that name (1947), which is the ostensible biography of Rhysling, "the Blind Singer of the Spaceways" who **sacrifices** his life to save his fellow crewmen; the Rhysling Award is named after this character. A space traveler who writes songs in his spare time also provides lyrics in Lee Correy's juvenile *Starship Through Space* (1954), and Eleanor Arnason's "The Warlord of Saturn's Moon" includes a bit of poetry about Saturn's moon Titan. Two prominent works of fantasy filled with poems presented as song lyrics are J.R.R. Tolkien's **The Lord of the Rings** and Myers's *Silverlock*; some of Tolkien's lyrics were officially set to music by Donald Swann in *The Road Goes Ever On: A Song Cycle* (1967), while Karen Anderson's afterword to the 1966 edition of *Silverlock*, "The Songs of *Silverlock*," describes the ongoing efforts of science fiction fans to provide music for Myers's words. Other fantasy writers have continued the tradition of filling their novels with poems, one example being Guy Gavriel Kay's *A Song for Arbonne* (1992).

Discussion

Based on sales of poetry books and circulation figures for poetry journals, one might conclude that few people read poetry today. Still, there seems to remain some hunger for such writing, albeit one preferentially satisfied by occasional snippets of poetry embedded within prose—a few poems scattered through science fiction magazines or fantasy novels. Few readers complain about these poems, and many readers manifestly appreciate them. It may be, then, that poetry is destined to endure as an occasional and pleasurable respite in an everyday diet of prose; and since science fiction and fantasy may contain more instances of poetry than other fields of literature, these imaginative genres may play an important role in keeping poetry alive.

Bibliography

Karen Anderson. "The Songs of *Silverlock*." John Myers Myers, *Silverlock*. New York: Ace Books, 1966, 515–516.

K.V. Bailey. "Alien or Kin? Science Fiction and Poetry." *Fantasy Commentator*, 8 (Winter, 1993, 1994), 32–39.

Dainis Bisenieks. "Power and Poetry in Middle-Earth." *Mythlore*, 3 (1975), 20–24.

Joe R. Christopher. "Tolkien's Lyric Poetry." Verlyn Flieger and Carl F. Hostetter, eds., *Tolkien's Legendarium*. Westport, CT: Greenwood Press, 2000, 143–160.

Mary Q. Kelly. "The Poetry of Fantasy." Neil D. Isaacs and Rose A. Zimbardo, eds., *Tolkien and the Critics*. Notre Dame: University of Notre Dame Press, 1968, 170–200.

Jane M. Lindskold. "The Pervasive Influence of Poetry in the Works of Roger Zelazny." *Extrapolation*, 33 (Spring, 1992), 41–58.

William Reynolds. "Poetry as Metaphor in *The Lord of the Rings*." *Mythlore*, 4 (June, 1977), 12–16.

Robin Roberts. "Matthew Arnold's 'Dover Beach,' Gender, and Science Fiction." *Extrapolation*, 33 (Fall, 1992), 245–257.

—Gary Westfahl

POLAR REGIONS

━━━━━━━━━━━━━━━━━━━━━━■━━━━━━━━━━━━━━━━━━━━━━

Overview

The Earth's polar regions represent extremes and, prior to Robert Peary's and Roald Amundsen's expeditions, they were considered unattainable. As such, explorers were lionized, **explorations** were limited in scope, and there was rampant speculation about climates, geographies, and possible flora and fauna. When the polar regions were imagined as inhabited, isolated residents generally represented either an ideal society (see **Utopia**) or a **lost world**; at times, the lost race developed into an ideal society. In crank literature, the polar regions often represented the **habitat** of superior beings and the terrestrially unattainable (see **Elder Races; Gods and Goddesses**); they also represented openings into a **hollow Earth**, where there were worlds contained within the shell of the Earth, as in *Symzonia* (1820) by "Adam Seaborn." In dime novels, reaching the poles and polar regions was but an exercise in technological application. In this, the authors were prescient.

Survey

At the start of the nineteenth century the Arctic was surmised to be inhospitable, and Mary Shelley's *Frankenstein* opens on a ship trapped in ice while attempting to find a northwest passage, a quest motivated by the untenable belief that the northern seas would ultimately open and the climate become subtropical. Robert Ames Bennett's lost race adventure *Thyra* (1901) utilizes this motif, occurring in a tropical land filled with **dinosaurs** and Vikings. At late as the 1930s, when the North Pole had long been reached and its territory mapped, writers still posited the existence of hidden temperate regions: thus, the 1935 film adaptation of H. Rider Haggard's *She* moved Ayesha's African kingdom to a hidden valley in the Arctic, and Max Brand's *The Smoking Land* (1937) places a lost race in a mysterious Arctic region shrouded by perpetual fog.

Other writers were more willing to embrace an endlessly cold Arctic, such as Jules Verne, whose *The Purchase of the North Pole* (1889) portrays a failed attempt to melt the paleocrystic ice for economic purposes. M.P. Shiel likewise accepted the frigidity of the north, rejected lost races and new beings, and postulated in *The Purple Cloud* that reaching the North Pole demonstrated deadly, unforgivable **hubris**. In George Allan England's "The Thing from—Outside" (1923), an inhospitable Arctic environment hides horrific beings. Robert McCammon's *Baal* (1978), which details the coming of the anti-Christ (see **Christianity**), is perhaps the last significant fantastic work to make use of the arctic regions, though one would be remiss not to mention Doc Savage and Superman (see **Superheroes;** *Superman*), both of whom have Fortresses of Solitude housed in the Arctic, and Santa Claus, who makes his home at the North Pole and appears in numerous **Christmas** fantasies. The Arctic also figures in Margaret Wise Brown's children's fantasy *The Peppermint Family* (1950), in which a man temporarily abandons his family to fish and hunt for polar bears at the North Pole.

The South Pole and Antarctica have been used less frequently as settings. In one early work, Thomas Erskine's *Armata: A Fragment* (1817), it is discovered that the Earth is physically attached to another spherical world at the South Pole. A novel that proved more influential is Edgar Allan Poe's *The Narrative of Arthur Gordon Pym,* which concludes abruptly with South Pole explorers approaching a mysterious figure. Verne's *An Antarctic Mystery* (1897) continues and resolves Poe's work, as does Howard Waldrop and Steven Utley's "Black as the Pit from Pole to Pole" (1977), which also uses Frankenstein's **monster** as its protagonist. Poe himself is a character in Rudy Rucker's *The Hollow Earth* (1990), which involves a mirror Earth (see **Parallel Worlds**) accessible through an opening in the Antarctic. H.P. Lovecraft's "At the Mountains of Madness" (1930) references Poe but concentrates its narrative elsewhere, describing the Antarctic discovery of technologically advanced Old Ones.

In John W. Campbell, Jr.'s "Who Goes There?" (1938), a small group of Antarctic explorers is preyed upon by a malevolent alien **shapeshifter** (see **Aliens on Earth**) they have inadvertently awakened. The film adaptation *The Thing (from Another World)* moved the story to the Arctic, perhaps to be closer to **America** and heighten audience's **paranoia** about alien **invasion**, and featured a standard alien monster who arrived in a flying saucer (see **UFOs**). A work that may have inspired Campbell is John Martin Leahy's "In Amundsen's Tent" (1928), wherein a malign extraterrestrial lifeform is found in a tent left by Amundsen's expedition. John Taine's *The Greatest Adventure* (1929) likewise does not reference Poe but recounts the discovery of the remnants of elder races and their legacy, a malign genetically engineered and parasitic **plant** (see **Parasites**).

Discussion

The polar regions are now accessible to tourists and have lost much of their **mystery** and **romance**. They no longer conceal dinosaurs, lost races, or northwest passages, nor does their ice routinely imprison ships, but their extreme isolation and inhospitable **weather** permits them to figure as threatened areas in eco-thrillers (see **Ecology**) and as the location for remote military and scientific bases. One writer fascinated with today's real Antarctica is Kim Stanley Robinson, who had his Martian colonists train there in *Red Mars* and employed it as the setting of his **near future** novel *Antarctica* (1998).

Bibliography

J. Lasley Dameron. "Poe's Pym and Scoresby on Polar Cataracts." *Resources for American Literary Study*, 21 (1995), 258–260.

Jason C. Eckhardt. "Behind the Mountains of Madness." *Lovecraft Studies*, 6 (Spring, 1987), 31–38.

Elana Glansberg. "Refusing History at the End of the Earth." *Tulsa Studies in Women's Literature*, 21 (Spring, 2002), 99–121.

Paul N. Hyde. "Philologist at the North Pole." *Mythlore*, 15 (Autumn, 1988), 23–27.

Elizabeth Leane. "Antarctica as a Scientific Utopia." *Foundation*, No. 89 (Autumn, 2003), 27–34.

Tom Moylan. "The Moment is Here . . . And It's Important." Raffaella Baccolini and Moylan, eds., *Dark Horizons*. New York: Routledge, 2003, 135–154.

Kim Stanley Robinson and Charles N. Brown. "Kim Stanley Robinson: Antarctica and Other Alien Landscapes." *Locus*, 39 (September, 1997), 4–6, 83–84.

Paul Voermans. "Scripts Deep Enough." *New York Review of Science Fiction*, No. 125 (January, 1999), 1, 4–5.

—Richard Bleiler

POLITICS

―――――――――――――――――――■―――――――――――――――――――

> *[Vir:] I thought the purpose of filing*
> *these reports was to provide accurate*
> *intelligence.*
> *[Londo:] Vir, intelligence has nothing to*
> *do with politics.*
>
> —J. Michael Straczynski
> "Point of No Return," episode of *Babylon 5*
> (1996)

Overview

By one standard distinction, science fiction is a literature devoted to change, while fantasy is a literature devoted to upholding traditions and resisting change. Frederik Pohl argues that, because it involves change, all science fiction is necessarily about politics; it would follow, then, that all fantasy is necessarily apolitical. Though there are exceptions in each case, the generalization seems defensible enough to serve as a basis for discussion. Ways of setting up **governance systems** that in a sense precede politics are discussed elsewhere, as are the often political underpinnings of **alternate history**.

Survey

In stressing the primacy of politics in science fiction, Pohl may be drawing on his own experience during the Great Depression, when he and other members of the Futurians destined to become major writers furiously discussed writing and politics. This era of turbulent events—like the Spanish Civil War and the rise of Nazism— surely influenced other developing writers as well, perhaps accounting for the genre's ongoing fascination with politics.

H.G. Wells toyed with Fabian socialism early in his career and wrote *A Modern Utopia* (1905) to illustrate the role of personal voice and large complexity in political systems (see **Utopia**). This emphasis on change and continuing revolution when an open "speech community" prevails has extended throughout the twentieth-century expression of political ideas in science fiction. Politics thrives on dialectic or opposing argument. Robert A. Heinlein, Ursula K. Le Guin, and Samuel R. Delany each make use of the image of satellites or moons to represent the dialectic of political systems. Philosophical anarchy where government becomes as slight as possible, as in Heinlein's *The Moon is a Harsh Mistress* (1966), foreshadowed an abundance of libertarian ideas in science fiction (and fantasy, such as Stephen R. Donaldson's **Lord Foul's Bane** and its sequels). Le Guin's "ambiguous utopia," *The Dispossessed*, was also presented in images of a pioneering satellite opposing an established world. Delany's "heterotopia" on the satellite of Nepture named *Triton* is the most complex example of diverse peoples and political systems that combine **freedom** of expression for individual voices with schemes of government.

Stressing a variety of voices leads to narratives about the politics of special interest groups such as gender politics (see **Homosexuality**) and **feminism** in Delany's works and Marge Piercy's *Woman on the Edge of Time*. At the opposite pole, Heinlein's *Starship Troopers* startlingly yokes democratic institutions with militarism (see **Class Systems**) where good citizenship is tied to government service. Analogies to practical political situations in the mundane world have been dramatized in episodes of *Star Trek* and its sequels as well as, less subtly, in *Star Wars*. More recent, with libertarian principles working in dialectic with Marxism, are Kim Stanley Robinson's ideas about how to govern in *Red Mars* and its sequels. Across the Atlantic, Ken MacLeod brings a British perspective to novels about **planetary colonies** that focus heavily on political issues.

But the key fascination, perhaps, in science fiction has been the politics of large general systems, often imagined as empires or political ideologies that are somehow omniscient about human **destiny**. Isaac Asimov's theory about, and **technology** to implement, psychohistory (see **Psychology**) is a twentieth-century version (projected into future **history**) of Enlightenment thinker Jeremy Bentham's utiliarianism. The vitality of stories about his **galactic empire** first described in his *Foundation* series, even continued by other hands after Asimov's death, speaks to the appeal of general and imperial systems of political organizations. Similarly, the baroque politics of the feudal Houses in Frank Herbert's *Dune* and its sequels and continuing insurgency of the Fremen—another series carried on by other writers after the author's death—illustrate how eager readers are for large, general systems of order even as the diversification inherent in personal voice appeals as well.

In contrast, fantasy appears content, when it deals with politics at all, to focus on events in small arenas: the petty courtroom intrigues of the **Ruritanian romance**, or the urban politics of corrupt officials and dissolute aristocrats shrewdly observed in Glen Cook's Garrett novels, beginning with *Sweet Silver Blues* (1987). Large empires are typically **evil** and poorly managed, undone by the errors of ill-governed underlings, as in J.R.R. Tolkien's *The Lord of the Rings*, where incompetent orcs allow Frodo to complete his **quest** and thus destroy Sauron's dominion.

Discussion

Pohl is probably correct that science fiction is always political: even the most technological writers devoted to **hard science fiction** and world building, where planetary colonies are less important than speculations about **ecology**, support by implication the Heinleinian philosophical anarchism wherein governmental systems are best when they do not get in the way of the individual scientist or explorer. In Gregory Benford's *Timescape*, for example, things seem to be falling apart politically, but science is still freely supported by a government hoping for a technological solution to its political problems. Thus, by looking at texts carefully, one can extract political statements from even the most seemingly apolitical of science fiction writers.

Bibliography

Brian Attebery. "The Politics of Fantasy." Robert A. Latham and Robert A. Collins, eds., *Modes of the Fantastic*. Westport, CT: Greenwood Press, 1995, 1–13.

Martin H. Greenberg and Joseph D. Olander. "Teaching Political Science Fiction." Jack Williamson, ed., *Teaching Science Fiction*. Philadelphia: Owlswick, 1980, 145–156.

Donald M. Hassler and Clyde Wilcox, eds. *Political Science Fiction*. Columbia: University of South Carolina Press, 1997.

David Hughes. "The Mood of *A Modern Utopia*." *Extrapolation*, 19 (December, 1978), 59–67.

Ken MacLeod. "Politics and Science Fiction." Edward James and Farah Mendlesohn, eds., *The Cambridge Companion to Science Fiction*. Cambridge: Cambridge University Press, 2003, 230–240.

Frederik Pohl. *The Way the Future Was*. New York: Ballantine Books, 1978.

L.D. Rossi. *The Politics of Fantasy*. Ann Arbor: UMI Research Press, 1984.

David Seed. *American Science Fiction and the Cold War*, London: Routledge, 1999.

Clyde Wilcox. "Governing Galactic Civilization." *Extrapolation*, 32 (Summer, 1991), 111–123.

—Donald M. Hassler

POSSESSION

Overview

Stories of possession feature the mind of an individual being "possessed," or taken over, by another mind or other active agency. Certain aspects of possession are discussed in entries devoted to **demons** or **Satan**. Outside the religious framework (see **Religion**) possession can be considered a form of **invasion**, while the physical takeover may involve forms of parasitism (see **Parasites**). Related entries are **Ghosts and Hauntings** and **Hypnotism**.

Survey

In western culture, the phenomenon of possession is part of the Christian worldview—its occurrences are a work of Satan or demons (see **Christianity**). Contemporary fictions, some allegedly based on real-life cases, draw on that paradigm, the most famous being William Peter Blatty's *The Exorcist* (1971), filmed in1973. Additionally, the novel and the screen adaptation exemplify the superhuman character of the phenomenon—possession is frequently not only an individual loss of control or **identity** but an enactment of the conflict between larger forces of good and **evil** or stability and chaos, in which humans are mere pawns. Such possessions are commonplace in supernatural and **horror** fiction; among the variations is Stephen King's *The Shining*, in which the protagonist is possessed by the **evil** spirit of the hotel where he works as a caretaker. A whole range of possessions figure in episodes of the *Buffy the Vampire Slayer* series, including one in which Faith, Buffy's fellow slayer, takes over her body.

Vampirism (see **Vampires**) and lycanthropy (see **Werewolves**) can also be considered forms of possession—the former permanent and the latter temporary though usually irreversible—in which it is not only the mind but the body that is hijacked and conforms to the requirements and form of the invading agency. While any relevant text (see Bram Stoker's *Dracula*) provides examples, the movie *Blade* (1998) problematizes the struggle of the protagonist's organism with the vampiric nature striving to take over.

Typical possessions are not common in genre fantasy. Possessed individuals are rarely protagonists; the passivity of their controlled minds makes it hard to identify with characters, a psychological mechanism that is central to fantasy as escapism. However, a number of minor possessions can be found; examples include the Nazgul in J.R.R. Tolkien's *The Lord of the Rings*, the Ravers in Stephen R. Donaldson's Chronicles of Thomas Covenant the Unbeliever (see *Lord Foul's Bane*), and the Ten Who Were Taken of Glen Cook's *The Black Company* (1984) and its sequels. This category may include characters who remain possessed only some of the time or who actively fight the possessing force. In Tolkien's epic Frodo and others fall under the temporary spell (see **Magic**) of the One Ring while Elric in Michael Moorcock's series, beginning with *The Stealer of Souls* (1963), constantly struggles with the pervasive influence of his **sword** Stormbringer.

Despite being predominantly spiritual and thus antithetical to rationality, the motif of possession has found several interesting variations in genre science fiction. During the Cold War stories about aliens taking over human minds became potent metaphors for the threat of Communist spies. Fears of invisible foes and its attendant **paranoia** loom large in movies like *Invaders from Mars* and *Invasion of the Body Snatchers*, the latter being probably the best cinematic vision of the loss of individual identity and feelings. A relevant literary example is Robert A. Heinlein's *The Puppet Masters* (1951).

Other forms of possession in science fiction include a voluntary or forced exchange of minds between two bodies, or a mind's takeover of an "empty" body. Examples of such switches are found in Damon Knight's *Mind Switch* (1965) and Thomas M. Disch's *Camp Concentration* (1968). In the late twentieth century this particular topos received a new lease of life. Grounded in the assumption that a mind can be digitized and transferred between containers, **cyberpunk** narratives postulate a reality in which a mind can be overlaid—temporarily or permanently—with another, possibly without the host's knowledge or consent. Such techno-possessions are present in Michael Swanwick's *Vacuum Flowers* (1987) and Walter Jon Williams's *Hardwired* (1986). Additionally, several texts re-integrate a spiritual dimension into a wholly technological world; for example, in William Gibson's *Count Zero* (1986) (see **Neuromancer**) some cyberspace operators become "horses" for **voodoo** deities hijacking their minds while connected. Outside cyberpunk, the build-up of voodoo-related possession incomprehensible for the character possessed occurs in Lucius Shepard's *Floater* (2003).

Discussion

Traditionally possession was associated with religion and the presence of nonphysical entities inside one's mind. Defined in this way, possession remains a popular motif for fiction writers but near the end of the twentieth century the concept acquired an entirely new dimension. Many texts featuring various forms of control over one's mind and/or body can be treated as not only imaginative stories recycling Christian notions but expressions of an emerging cultural condition. They imaginatively channel one of the biggest fears of contemporary western culture—the loss of agency to forces not completely comprehended by individuals who find themselves in their midst and discover themselves to be incapable of influencing them (see **Individualism and Conformity**).

Bibliography

Robert F. Geary. "The Exorcist: Deep Horror?" *Journal of the Fantastic in the Arts*, 5 (1993), 55–63.

Joan Gordon and Veronica Hollinger, eds. *Blood Read*. Philadelphia: University of Pennsylvania Press, 1997.

Burton Hatlen. "Good and Evil in Stephen King's *The Shining*." Anthony Magistrale, ed., *The Shining Reader*. Mercer Island, WA: Starmont, 1990, 81–104.

Cosette N. Kies. "Voodoo Visions." Karen P. Smith, ed., *African-American Voices in Young Adult Literature*. Metuchen, NJ: Scarecrow, 1994, 337–368.

Clayton Koelb. "Inspiration and Possession." George Slusser and Eric S. Rabkin, eds., *Aliens*. Carbondale: Southern Illinois University Press, 1987, 157–167.

Arthur Kroker. *The Possessed Individual*. London: Macmillan Press, 1992.

Theodore Schick. "The Cracks of Doom." Gregory Bassham and Eric Bronson, eds., *The Lord of the Rings and Philosophy*. Chicago: Open Court, 2003, 21–32.

David Seed. "Conspiracy Narratives." Seed, *American Science Fiction and the Cold War*. Edinburgh: Edinburgh University Press, 1999, 132–144.

—*Pawel Frelik*

POSTCOLONIALISM

Overview

Conservative science fiction has extrapolated a colonial discourse, racism (see **Race Relations**), and **sexism** into space by usurping planets (see **Planetary Colonies**), exterminating alien populations, bringing the "gift of civilization"—i.e., imperialist **culture**—to less intelligent aliens, and recoiling from alien **invasions**. Similarly, conservative fantasy openly embraces past colonizing **civilizations** as idealized models for imagined worlds. Postmodern, feminist, and nonEuropean science fiction and fantasy rewrite these topics (see **Feminism; Postmodernism**), often from a shared postcolonial and feminist angle of marginality, and reposition the colonial/patriarchal object as subject.

Survey

With the closed Western **frontier** in the New World and the end of colonialism, science fiction shifted to the open frontiers of outer space. **Space operas** of the early twentieth century focus on the imposition of American and European values on other planets (see **America**), as seen in Edgar Rice Burroughs's **Mars** novels (see *A Princess of Mars*) wherein a visitor from **Earth** eventually becomes ruler of Mars.

Other science fiction **westerns** founded **galactic empires** and subjugated or elimi-nated **aliens in space,** who generally figured only as foils or as the cultural, ethnic, and sexual *other*: in *Return to Tomorrow* (1954), for example, L. Ron Hubbard notoriously promoted total genocide of all alien races to guarantee human hege-mony, whereas John W. Campbell, Jr.'s stories, published in the 1920s and 1930s, express a mentality that seems supportive of **social Darwinism** and even **slavery.**

Some science fiction stories project imperialistic desires onto aliens who become genocidal colonizers of Earth. Taking the colonial history of the British Empire as a model for the Martian invasion on Earth, H.G.Wells's *The War of the Worlds* pro-vides one of the earliest critiques of colonial history in science fiction. However, it also exemplifies human **xenophobia.** Alien invasion and the subjugation of humankind is a dominant topic in Robert A. Heinlein's *The Puppet Masters* (1951), while Arthur C. Clarke's *Childhood's End* depicts a less common and benign alien colonization. Jack Finney's *The Body Snatchers* (1955) and its film versions (see *The Invasion of the Body Snatchers*) express fears of an alien physical and psychological usurpation of the human body.

From the late 1950s on, critical views of such colonial attitudes of oppression, slavery, and outright genocide proliferate; examples include Robert Silverberg's *Invaders from Earth* (1958) and Thomas M. Disch's *The Genocides* (1965). Other novels like Poul Anderson's *Virgin Planet* (1959), Joanna Russ's *And Chaos Died* (1970), and Gene Wolfe's *The Fifth Head of Cerberus* (1972) satirize terrestrial colonialist behavior and enact sociological experiments on **alien worlds** that reveal the atrocities of our colonial history. In her feminist **dystopia** *The Word for World Is Forest* (1972), Ursula K. Le Guin satirizes from an ecological perspective the colo-nial exploitation of (human) resources (see **Ecology; Satire**).

The era of these revisionist works, paradoxically, is also the time when fantasy became established as a genre, with works usually building upon the example of J.R.R. Tolkien's *The Lord of the Rings* to celebrate discredited European values, with the alien other, represented here by the orcs, re-inscribed as **monsters** meriting only ruthless extermination. Not surprisingly, then, works of this period that mingle sci-ence fiction and fantasy, like Marion Zimmer Bradley's Darkover novels, beginning with *The Sword of Aldones* (1962) and Anne McCaffrey's Pern novels, beginning with *Dragonflight,* attempt to ameliorate the traditional and revisionist in romantic visions of human colonizers and colonized aliens peacefully coexisting in exotic but **pastoral** environments. The native (alien) population may rebel against colonizers, but more commonly human adaptation to alien environments works well.

Since the late 1970s feminist science fiction has rewritten stock conventions and connected postcolonial and feminist criticism to critiques of the colonization and exploitation of women's, alien's, and the ethnic other's mind and body. Significant texts include Joan Slonczewski's *A Door into Ocean* (1986) and its sequels; Octavia E. Butler's reworking of slave narratives in the Patternist series, beginning with *Patternmaster* (1976); Suzette Haden Elgin's *Native Tongue* (1984) and its sequels; and Suzy McKee Charnas's Holdfast tetralogy, beginning with *Walk to the End of the World* (1974). Sometimes **gender** relations are provokingly depicted in terms of human contact with aliens, as in Ursula K. Le Guin's *The Left Hand of Darkness.* Fantasy writers revisited traditional sagas from fresh perspectives, an example being Marion Zimmer Bradley's feminist approach to the Arthurian legends, *The Mists of Avalon* (see **Arthur**).

Since the late 1990s, science fiction, utopian and dystopian writing from African Americans, as represented in Sheree R. Thomas's anthology *Dark Matter* (2000), and from outside the Western hemisphere—such as Amitav Ghosh's *The Calcutta Chromosome* (1995) from India or Buchi Emecheta's *The Rape of Shavi* (1985) from Nigeria—has increasingly received attention. However, postcolonial **utopias** share many features with critical utopias and transgressive dystopias; generally, the detested colonial/patriarchal rule is depicted as a **dystopia**, but, as the narrative progresses, the evolved postcolonial/post-patriarchal society is equally questioned, as the emerging utopia privileges an ongoing process of transculturation and fluid state of hybridity.

Discussion

In the past, the spaceships of science fiction have all too often been populated with monastic fraternities of **scientists**, engineers, and space explorers eager to invade, conquer, and subjugate, while fantasy **heroes** embark upon **quests** with similarly questionable motives. A postcolonial perspective allows these works to be fruitfully re-examined, both in fiction and critical studies, and encourages readers and critics, in this age of **globalization**, to pay more attention to the science fiction and fantasy of nonEuropean writers who in their own imaginative ways seek to escape the confines of colonialist thought.

Bibliography

Cassie Carter. "The Metacolonization of Dick's *The Man in the High Castle*." *Science-Fiction Studies*, 22 (November, 1995), 333–342.

Claire Chambers. "Postcolonial Science Fiction." *Journal of Commonwealth Literature*, 38 (Spring, 2003), 57–72.

Jane L. Donawerth and Carol Kolmerten, eds. *Utopian and Science Fiction by Women.* Syracuse: Syracuse University Press, 1994.

David Galef. "Tiptree and the Problem of the Other." *Science Fiction Studies*, 28 (July, 2001), 201–222.

Elisabeth A. Leonard, ed. *Into Darkness Peering.* Westport, CT: Greenwood Press, 1997.

Dunja M. Mohr. *Worlds Apart?* Jefferson, NC: McFarland, 2005.

Diane M. Nelson. "A Social Science Fiction of Fevers, Delirium and Discovery." *Science Fiction Studies*, 30 (July, 2003), 246–266.

Ralph Pordzik. *The Quest for Postcolonial Utopia.* New York: Peter Lang, 2001.

—Dunja M. Mohr

POST-HOLOCAUST SOCIETIES

We who were meant to roam the stars
go now on foot upon a ravaged earth.
But above us those other worlds still
hang, and still they beckon. And so is the

promise still given. If we make not the
mistakes of the Old Ones then shall we
know in time more than the winds of this
earth and the trails of this earth.

—Andre Norton
Star Man's Son (1952)

Overview

Narratives set after a world-wrecking catastrophe may provide warnings against possible **disasters**, justifications for bizarrely transformed societies, or excuses for tales of anarchistic **sexuality** and **violence**. After Hiroshima and until the end of the Cold War, most post-holocaust works were set after **nuclear war**, but environmental disasters—both natural and artificially created—are also common (see **Ecology**).

Survey

World-ending disasters often reduce the number of human survivors to a bare minimum. There are **Adam and Eve** stories like John Christopher's "Two" (1952); but some go further, as in Mary Shelley's *The Last Man* (see **Last Man**). The threatened extinction of the human race is often used to justify **taboo** sexual couplings, as in Ward Moore's "Lot" (1953). Fighting over rare fertile women is a frequent theme in such tales and films like *28 Days Later* (2002). A few aging survivors seem doomed to live out the twilight of **humanity** in a world irreparably damaged by a reactor disaster in Brian W. Aldiss's *Greybeard* (1964).

J.G. Ballard wrote a number of evocative novels vividly depicting the end of the world from various causes, like *The Drowned World*, that almost rapturously embrace human extinction. Other less drastic catastrophes catapult society back into the Middle Ages (Edgar Pangborn's *Davy* [1964]) (see **Medievalism and the Middle Ages**), or into **barbarian** dark ages, as in Paul O. Williams's Pelbar Cycle, beginning with *The Breaking of Northwallt* (1981). Walter M. Miller, Jr. included the whole **cycle** of barbarism to feudalism to **civilization** in *A Canticle for Leibowitz*. The best of the neo-Medieval post-holocaust novels is Russell Hoban's *Riddley Walker* (1980), set in an age in which humanity has become a crippled shadow of its former self. The cruder sort of neo-barbarian fiction, like Robert Adams's *The Coming of the Horseclans* (1975) and its sequels, and movies like the *Mad Max* series, use the collapse of civilization as an excuse for wild orgies of violence.

Utopias are commonly constructed from the ashes of destroyed societies, as in H.G. Wells's *The Shape of Things to Come* (1933), filmed as *Things to Come*. Philip K. Dick presents an urban society in which war-caused radiation threatens not only humans but all life, and people make a cult of raising animals, in the dystopian *Do Androids Dream of Electric Sheep?* (see **Dystopia**).

War-caused radiation is frequently used to rationalize the emergence of super-powered humans, as in John Wyndham's *Re-Birth* (1955), but **evolution** takes a more sardonic turn in Kurt Vonnegut, Jr.'s *Galápagos*, in which humans devolve into simple seal-like creatures. Better known is the film *Planet of the Apes* and its sequels and adaptations, in which radiation-induced evolutionary changes transpose the positions of **apes** and humans.

Alien **invasions** may create the world-wrecking holocaust, the pioneering work being Wells's *The War of the Worlds*, which created the model for subsequent works in realistic modern settings, such as John Wyndham's *The Day of the Triffids*, where previously unproblematic **plants** become menaces when the world's population goes blind. Whereas Wells's novel allegorized British conquests of people like the Tasmanians, films like *Independence Day* (1996) exalt American power and **courage**. In Octavia E. Butler's Xenogenesis series (beginning with *Dawn*), peace-loving aliens attempt to breed self-destructive combativeness out of humanity.

Sometimes our own **technology** threatens the survival of humanity, as in the Terminator films (see *The Terminator*) and *The Matrix* and its sequels. Human ingenuity and courage triumph over impossible odds amid spectacular special effects.

Novels of global environmental catastrophe include George R. Stewart's *Earth Abides* and Margaret Atwood's *The Handmaid's Tale*, in which human fertility is threatened by environmental pollution and a neo-Christian cult forces fertile women to bear **children** while depriving them of sexual pleasure. Kate Wilhelm's *Where Late the Sweet Birds Sang* (1976) movingly depicts a dying environment. Ursula K. Le Guin created a complex agrarian culture in the aftermath of a global environmental collapse in *Always Coming Home* (1985).

Brian W. Aldiss's *Helliconia Spring* and its sequels depict a planet whose orbit is influenced by two **stars** in ways that produce eons-long seasons, which in turn create periodic waves of extinction, with variations on the dominant race being adapted to either winter or summer conditions. He works in the nuclear winter theory that emerged just as he was writing the novel (see **Seasons**).

Apocalyptic fiction is not always allegorical. A large readership of fundamentalist Christians has made bestsellers of Tim Lehaye and Jerry B. Jenkins's *Left Behind* (1996) and its sequels, depicting the chaos and destruction wrought by sinners left behind when Christ takes the saved up to **Heaven** in the Rapture.

Discussion

Despite potentially grim themes, post-holocaust tales are seldom serious warnings against avoidable dangers. Rather, their authors use the ensuing chaos to revel in abundant scenes of sex and violence. The long tradition of the radiation-induced evolution of superbeings is a particularly frivolous example of the trivialization of **apocalypse** in science fiction.

Bibliography

Harold L. Berger. *Science Fiction and the New Dark Age*. Bowling Green, Ohio: Bowling Green State University Popular Press, l976.

Paul Brians. *Nuclear Holocausts*. Kent, OH: Kent State University Press, 1987.

David Dowling. *Fictions of Nuclear Disaster*. London: Macmillan, 1987.

Brooks Landon. "Eve at the End of the World." Donald E. Palumbo, ed. *Erotic Universe*. Westport, CT: Greenwood Press, 1986, 60–74.

Chris Morgan. "The End of the World as We Know It." Morgan, *The Shape of Futures Past*. Exeter, England: Webb & Bower, 1980, 17–35.

Kim Newman. *Apocalypse Movies*. New York: St. Martin's, 1999.
Eric S. Rabkin, Martin H. Greenberg, and Joseph D. Olander, eds. *The End of the World*.
    Carbondale: Southern Illinois University Press, 1983.
David Seed. *Imagining Apocalypse*. New York: Saint Martin's, 2000.

—Paul Brians

POSTMODERNISM

∎

Overview

"Postmodernism" refers to a wide array of understandings about social, political, economic, and cultural relations developed in Westernized post-industrial societies since the mid-twentieth century. The term identifies the features of a fragmented and hybridized way-of-being in a world understood to be open to multiple and contradictory interpretations. "Postmodernism" describes a particular socio-political moment and condition shaped by multinational capitalism and economic and cultural **globalization**, and identifies a broad range of cultural productions shaped by ironically self-reflexive aesthetic themes and forms. The postmodern literary fantastic ranges from Latin American **magic realism** like Gabriel García Márquez's *One Hundred Years of Solitude* (1970) (see **Latin America**) to metafiction like Margaret Atwood's feminist dystopian novel, *The Handmaid's Tale* (see **Dystopia; Feminism**). Fantastic literature demonstrates a particularly complex relationship to the postmodern.

Survey

As a social condition, "postmodernity" is often read as a philosophical and/or political break with, or swerve away from, the long project of Enlightenment modernity whose origins are historically associated with the eighteenth-century rise of the humanist subject in the context of political liberalism, secularism, and the triumph of scientific method. The unselfconscious Golden Age science fiction of writers like Isaac Asimov and Arthur C. Clarke can be understood as textual analogues of this version of modernity. Post-Einsteinian shifts in scientific paradigms, however, and developments in fields as disparate as quantum physics and **genetic engineering** are more accurately represented in the chaotic and heterogeneous universes of the New Baroque **space opera** exemplified by Iain M. Banks's *Consider Phlebas* and of **hard science fiction** novels like Greg Egan's *Diaspora* (1997).

Postmodernist tendencies appear in genre fantasy in a variety of guises, for example, in the creation of increasingly diverse and mature **imaginary worlds** in works like Stephen R. Donaldson's *Lord Foul's Bane* and its sequels. Perhaps even more significant is the postmodern shift of perspective in some fantasy and **horror** away from the human center and toward "monstrous" margins. This is one of the most striking features of Anne Rice's popular *Interview with the Vampire* and its sequels. Marion Zimmer Bradley's *The Mists of Avalon* demonstrates both these postmodern tendencies in constructing a dense, sophisticated version of the world of Arthurian fantasy (see **Arthur**) that recounts its events through the revisionary feminist perspectives of its female characters. In all popular genres, the proliferation of writing by women—as well as queer writers and writers of color—is a positive outcome of the crises of authority which, in part, define the postmodern.

The fantastic genres tend to produce individual works that are postmodern, not as a result of formal and literary strategies, but because of the particularly postmodern perspectives upon which they draw upon to create their imagined worlds. Noteworthy exceptions like Joanna Russ's lesbian–feminist *The Female Man* and Samuel R. Delany's heterotopian *Triton*, however, demonstrate how even science fiction, whose closest textual relative is the realist novel, can produce works of impressive self-reflexivity and formal originality. Meanwhile, more and more mainstream literary works draw upon fantastic genres for ideas and images, exemplifying another feature of postmodernism: the blurring of boundaries between mainstream fiction and various genres of fantastic fiction that yields works sometimes referred to as "slipstream." Richard Powers's self-consciously literary *Galatea 2.2* (1995), which recounts the construction of an Artificial Intelligence (see **Computers**), is a good example of such slipstream fiction.

Boundaries have also blurred between and among the subgenres of the fantastic, evidenced in the increasing generic hybridity of works like Sheri S. Tepper's *Beauty* (1991), which combines the **fairy tale** with elements drawn from fantasy, historical fiction, and science fiction. The term "weird fiction" is sometimes used to identify generic hybrids like China Miéville's *Perdido Street Station* and *The Scar* (2002), novels that incorporate elements of science fiction, fantasy, and horror to create fictional universes of incredible complexity and richness. Kim Stanley Robinson's *The Years of Rice and Salt* is an **alternate history** that is also a self-reflexive meditation on the continuing relevance of utopian fiction at the beginning of the twenty-first century (see **Utopia**).

Philip K. Dick's science fiction, including *Do Androids Dream of Electric Sheep?* and *Ubik* (1969), is often read as exemplary of science fiction's increasing awareness of the pressures of global capitalism and pervasive technologization on everyday life, while his classic alternate history, *The Man in the High Castle*, undertakes the kind of ontological disruption of apparently stable realities often associated with the postmodern. The pervasive influence of technoscience on human life is acutely thematized in the **cyberpunk** writing of the 1980s and 1990s, most memorably in William Gibson's first novel, *Neuromancer*; not coincidentally, Ridley Scott's film *Blade Runner*, based on Dick's *Androids*, is steeped in the imagery that came to be associated with cyberpunk and which continues to circulate in the Wachowski brothers' *The Matrix* and its sequels. The wide variety of posthuman characters—**clones**, artificial intelligences, **cyborgs**, **androids**, downloaded intelligences, holograms, and others—that inhabit the worlds of science fiction demonstrate one crucial way in which a postmodern sensibility shaped by biotechnoscientific globalization is also shaping the popular imagination.

Discussion

Some critics suggest that the ultimate expression of the technological postmodern is found, not in the imagined worlds of print science fiction, fantasy, or horror, but in the spectacular special effects used to produce films such as the **Alien** series, the **Star Wars** series, and *The Matrix* trilogy. Most of these films, combining elements from science fiction, fantasy, and horror, also demonstrate the generic hybridity that is central to fantastic cultural production in the context of postmodernism.

Bibliography

Scott Bukatman. *Terminal Identity*. Durham, NC: Duke University Press, 1993.

Andrew M. Butler. "Postmodernism and Science Fiction." Edward James and Farah Mendlesohn, eds., *The Cambridge Companion to Science Fiction*. Cambridge: Cambridge UP, 2003, 137–148.

Veronica Hollinger. "Fantasies of Absence." Joan Gordon and Hollinger, eds., *Blood Read*. Philadelphia: University of Pennsylvania Press, 1997, 199–212.

Fredric Jameson. *Postmodernism or, The Cultural Logic of Late Capitalism*. Durham, NC: Duke University Press, 1991.

Larry McCaffery, ed. *Storming the Reality Studio*. Durham, NC: Duke University Press, 1991.

Brian McHale. *Constructing Postmodernism*. New York: Routledge, 1992.

Lance Olsen. *Ellipse of Uncertainty*. Westport, CT: Greenwood Press, 1987.

Gary K. Wolfe. "Evaporating Genre." Veronica Hollinger and Joan Gordon, eds., *Edging into the Future*. Philadelphia: University of Pennsylvania Press, 2002, 11–29.

Jenny Wolmark. *Aliens and Others*. Hemel Hempstead, Herts: Harvester Wheatsheaf, 1993.

—Veronica Hollinger

PREDICTIONS

■

Is there anything to add to that preface now? Nothing except my epitaph. That, when the time comes, will manifestly have to be: "I told you so. You damned fools." (The italics are mine.)

—H.G. Wells
"Preface to the 1941 Edition,"
The War in the Air (1941)

Overview

Science fiction writers often make predictions about the future based on technological, cultural, moral, religious and sociological tendencies of the day. While **hard science fiction** writers base predictive fiction on cutting-edge science, others look to the past for insight into the future, because the **history** of **humanity** is filled with repeating **cycles** of **war** and valor, **wisdom**, and stupidity, kingdoms and ruins. They predict whether human life will be better or worse in the years ahead, and whether **technology** will make our lives easier or have harmful effects on our lives. Stories about people making predictions within narratives are discussed under **Divination**.

Survey

Jules Verne made many astounding predictions. In *From the Earth to the Moon*, he accurately predicts the first trip to the **Moon** over a century ahead of time, from the size of the crew and command module to the use of retro-rocketry, right down to basing the launch out of Florida. Then in *Twenty Thousand Leagues under the Sea*, Verne's Nautilus is an example of a self-propelled submarine capable of maneuvering and traveling at high speeds underwater (see **Underwater Adventure**). Verne's writings also predicted divers' wetsuits and aqualungs, and devices such as electrical clocks, stoves, generators and motors, and electrical lights. Of course, some of Verne's predictions have not yet come to light, such as seaweed cigarettes and the discovery of **Atlantis**.

H.G. Wells also made many successful predictions. As early as 1899 in *When the Sleeper Wakes*, Wells foresaw such technological advances as air conditioning, video recordings, automatic doors, portable televisions, and fighter aircraft. Some say that Winston Churchill was inspired by Wells's description of ironclad fighting machines in "The Land Ironclads" (1903) to initiate a program to build such **weaponry**, and soon tanks appeared on the World War One battlefield. But like Verne, Wells also made predictions that have not been realized, such as automatic clothes-making machines, moving conveyor roadways (see **Transportation**), and super **cities** that encompass all of Earth's population.

However, Hugo Gernsback, not Wells nor Verne, is considered the father of science fiction. Gernsback was also a master at predicting the future. His 1925 novel, *Ralph 124C 41+: A Romance of the Year 2660*, predicts remote-control power transmission, video phone calls, transcontinental air service, sky-writing, solar power, microfiche, fax machines, synthetic foods (see **Food and Drink**), artificial cloth, tape recorders, radar, and spaceflight. *Ralph 124C 41+* also makes other predictions that may still come true, like instantaneous translation devices, complete **weather** control, stainless steel streets, **invisibility** cloaks, and anti-**gravity** machines. Gernsback foresaw that by the year 2660 it will be possible for instruction to be absorbed through **sleep**-learning, that restaurants will have gases to stimulate appetites, that radium solutions will restore dead humans to life (see **Immortality and Longevity**), and that **first contact** with aliens will have occurred.

As exciting as some predictions are, many authors worry that technology could enslave humanity, as occurs in the **dystopia** in Aldous Huxley's *Brave New World*. George Orwell's *Nineteen Eighty-Four*, with its dark warnings about a disturbing future that many thought was possible, is the standard example of fiction that had the effect of counter-predictions in helping to ensure that the predicted future did not develop.

In Robert A. Heinlein's predictions for the future, he provided dates for when new **inventions** and social changes would arise. His collection *The Past Through*

Tomorrow predicted that a gas shortage for cars would result in the creation of a system of mechanized roadways around the year 2000, which did not transpire. Heinlein also forecast that the weather will be controlled by 2070, prolonged existence will be attained through selective breeding and organ transplants by 2125, and **suspended animation and cryonics** for **space travel** will be perfected by 2125. Murray Leinster's "A Logic Named Joe" (1946) pioneeringly predicted home **computers** linked to a network resembling the Internet. Joe Haldeman also made specific predictions in *The Forever War*, such as the regeneration of amputated limbs by 2189, establishment of individual force fields by 2189, and eradication of most diseases by 2458.

Perhaps the most prescient of all has been John Brunner, whose *Stand on Zanzibar* predicts interactive TV, laser printers, semi-sentient computers, **clones**, and the moral debate over **genetic engineering**. Perhaps the first true **cyberpunk** author, Brunner preceded Vernor Vinge's prediction of the Internet in *True Names* (1981) by thirteen years. Yet the most celebrated cyberpunk book is William Gibson's *Neuromancer*, which popularized the term **cyberspace** three years after Vinge nailed the details with descriptions of online gathering places. Given the track record of these authors, the time may come when people upload their consciousnesses into the Net to wage **war** against **evil** artificial intelligences.

Discussion

Although science fiction looks to the future, it is linked to concerns of the present day. Consequently, its predictions can actually influence the future, whether through inspiring underwater **exploration** or warning against the dangers of **overpopulation** and pollution. And so science fiction writers will continue to predict the future to better the present, with topics that include genetic engineering, humans on **Mars**, **miniaturization**, and **virtual reality**.

Bibliography

Paul D. Aligica. "Prediction, Explanation and the Epistemology of Future Studies." *Futures*, 35 (December, 2003), 1027–1040.

Isaac Asimov. "Science Fiction, an Aid to Science, Foresees the Future." *Smithsonian*, 1 (May, 1970), 41–47.

Ben Bova. "The SF Game." Bova, *Viewpoint*. Cambridge, MA: NESFA Press, 1977, 89–96.

J.J. Corn and Brian Harrigan. *Yesterday's Tomorrows*. New York: Summit, 1984.

Howard V. Hendrix. "The Thing of Shapes to Come." George Slusser, Colin Greenland, and Eric S. Rabkin, eds., *Storm Warnings*. Carbondale: Southern Illinois University Press, 1987, 43–54.

Chris Morgan. *The Shape of Futures Past* Exeter: Webb & Bower, 1980.

Brian M. Stableford. "Science Fiction and the Image of the Future." *Foundation*, No. 14 (September, 1978), 26–34.

W. Warren Wagar. *The Next Three Futures*. Westport, CT: Greenwood Press, 1991.

George Zebrowski. "The Importance of Being Cosmic." Damien Broderick, ed., *Earth Is But a Star*. Crawley: University of Western Australia Press, 2001, 130–137.

—Nick Aires

PREHISTORIC FICTION

Overview

Since *The Oxford English Dictionary* defines prehistory as an "account of events or conditions prior to written or recorded history," prehistoric fiction would therefore concern human experiences before the advent of writing in 6000 BCE. Although the genre deals with ancient subject matter, its value, inherent in its diversity, is undiminished: **biology, anthropology, evolution, psychology, technology, civilization, race relations, religion,** and **history** are some recurrent topics.

Survey

A controversial literary tradition (comprising more than 300 titles), prehistoric fiction has, in some contexts, misrepresented early humans while, in others, it has challenged traditional ideas about the origin and place of **humanity** in **nature**. Post-Darwinian fiction often debates evolution, science, and theology. Jules Verne in *The Village in the Treetops* (1901) and Edgar Rice Burroughs in *The Land That Time Forgot* (1924) support medieval concepts of **nature** while weaving modern science into their fiction. Although Verne drew on contemporary sources, like the discovery of *Homo erectus*, his description of prehistoric humanity identified these creatures as the genetic ancestors of non-white humans only. Since the prevailing evolutionary view was that non-whites descended from primitive forms, the fiction reinforced racial hierarchies of the times. Supporting an arcane view of man's place in nature, Burroughs positioned prehistoric forms of man on a continuum ranging from most primitive to most advanced, with white Europeans at the highest level and people of color at lower levels.

Prehistoric fiction has conveyed not only racial stereotypes, but also scientific misinformation about early humans. In Jules Verne's *Journey to the Center of the Earth* (1864) and Arthur Conan Doyle's **The Lost World,** dinosaurs and archaic humans are presented as contemporaries of each other. Later films like *One Million Years B.C.* (1940, remade 1966) and *When Dinosaurs Ruled the Earth* (1970) perpetuated similar myths. Jack London's *Before Adam* (1906) contradicts fossil records by rendering certain hominid sub-species as contemporaries of each other. H.G. Wells, in "The Grisly Folk" (1921), portrays Neanderthals as man-eating **apes** and Cro-Magnons as civilized forerunners of modern Europeans, following the now-discredited science of his day.

Authors have tried, with varying results, to rehabilitate the image of early humanity, clear away racial assumptions, and find common traits that unite the human **family**, past and present. In "The Day Is Done" (1939), Lester del Rey creates a pathetic but dignified Neanderthal whose murder at the hands of intrusive moderns comments on prejudice and misanthropy. William Golding's *The Inheritors* (1955) sought to correct misconceptions of primitive humans but sacrificed credibility by basing his portrayal of the dignified Neanderthal on pseudo-scientific interpretations of **intelligence**. Arthur C. Clarke's *2001: A Space Odyssey* portrays human ancestors stereotypically, endorsing the questionable theory of the killer ape as the genetic forebear of modern humans. The intervention of alien intelligence allows primitive people to develop the naturally selective advantage of tool use to avoid extinction; paradoxically, the birth of **technology** culminates in the threat of **nuclear war**. The theme of historical crisis is central to prehistoric fiction. In works like *2001: A Space Odyssey*, J.H. Rosny-Aine's *The Quest for Fire* (1911), Johannes V. Jensen's *The Long Journey* (1908, 1923), and Bjorn Kurten's *Dance of the Tiger* (1978), the plot turns on climactic events, like the acquisition of **fire**, the use of tools and weapons, or fossil evidence of aggression. Michael Bishop's *No Enemy but Time* (1982) describes a modern man's **time travel** to join a prehistoric tribe.

Rejecting dogmatic preconceptions, some writers try to reconstruct human prehistory in terms consistent with scientific **knowledge**, with noteworthy success as in Stephen Baxter's *Evolution* (2002). Authors who carefully explore scientific theory have anticipated actual discoveries. Rosny-Aine extrapolates from science in his depiction of fire acquisition by *Homo erectus* to suggest that this technology facilitated the evolution of this early form into modern humanity. Paleo-anthropologists now theorize that **fire** may indeed have brought early people a naturally selective advantage. In *The Clan of the Cave Bear*, Jean Auel's inclusion of interbreeding between European Neanderthals and modern humans may have been authenticated by a 1999 fossil discovery.

Discussion

Reading prehistoric fiction from complementary viewpoints can develop critical skills. Readers can determine the degree to which an author used contemporary science carefully and whether it influenced the depiction of early humanity. Such reading would help rectify distorted images of prehistoric humanity in popular culture. Important sociological themes are explored in prehistoric fiction, like the clan and tribe as family, along with issues of **gender** and race relations, particularly as it pertains to western concepts of Third World people. Prehistoric fiction should be read both in and out of context, to see if it adumbrates new discoveries of the past and reflects attitudes about contemporary life.

Bibliography

Marc Angenot and Nadia Khouri. "An International Bibliography of Prehistoric Fiction." *Science-Fiction Studies*, 8 (March, 1981), 38–53.
G.B. Chamberlain. "Angenot-Khouri Bibliography of Prehistoric Fiction: Additions, Corrections, and Comment." *Science-Fiction Studies*, 9 (November, 1982), 342–346.
Charles De Paolo. *Human Prehistory in Fiction*. Jefferson, NC: McFarland & Company, 2003.
Loren Eisley. "Epilogue: Jack London, Evolutionist." Jack London, *Before Adam*. Lincoln: University of Nebraska Press, 2000, 243–251.
Langdon Elsbree. "The Language of Extremity." *Extrapolation*, 40 (Fall, 1999), 233–243.
Carol Mason, Martin Harry Greenberg, and Patricia Warrick, eds., *Anthropology through Science Fiction*. New York: St. Martin's Press, 1974.
J.M. Walker. "Reciprocity and Exchange in William Golding's *The Inheritors*." *Science-Fiction Studies*, 8 (November, 1981), 297–310.
Gary Westfahl. "Prehistory Lessons." *Interzone*, No. 157 (July, 2000), 49–50.
Clyde Wilcox. "Prehistoric Gender Politics." *Extrapolation*, 40 (Winter, 1999), 325–333.

—*Charles De Paolo*

PRISONS

Overview

Ever since Jeremy Bentham devised the panopticon, a supposedly model prison we would now recognize as psychological **torture**, prisons have constituted a problem for liberal philosophers. Would there still be crime in **utopia**, and if so how could criminals be dealt with in ways consistent with the society's moral principles? Pondering this question, writers have generated many different types of prisons and approaches to broader issues of **crime and punishment**. Few represent serious contributions to debates about how to deal with criminals, and those that do usually suggest that, however liberal the intention, prisons are illiberal in execution or effect. More commonly, writer employ prisons as **microcosms** to reflect social mores.

Survey

The prison of fantasy is the medieval dungeon, a gloomy underground structure of stone walls and iron bars where the unlucky may be locked up and forgotten. One such facility is described in L. Sprague de Camp and Fletcher Platt's "The Roaring Trumpet" (1940), with the protagonist tormented by an insane captive (see **Madness**) constantly screaming "Yngvi is a louse!" More modern prisons may be settings for **ghosts and hauntings**; for example, in an episode of *The Twilight Zone*, "Death's-Head Revisited" (1961), a former Nazi officer visiting a concentration camp is confronted by ghosts of people he tortured.

In science fiction, one common way to deal with future criminals, following the model of eighteenth-century convict settlements, is to transport them offworld. The **heroes** in *Blakes 7* are being transported to a prison planet before they **escape**. Prison colonies may be on **Mars**, as in D.G. Compton's *Farewell, Earth's Bliss* (1966); a Jovian moon, as in Christopher Evans's *Mortal Remains* (1995) (see **Jupiter and the Outer Planets**); a **space station**, as in Patricia McKillip's *Fool's Run* (1987); or a distant planet, as in *Alien3* (see *Alien*). Prisoners are often forced to perform meaningless hard labor, as on the prison world in *Barbarella* (1968). The revenge the new world or its inhabitants might extract is just a part of the punishment, like the surreal **pains** suffered by prisoners on Cordwainer Smith's "A Planet Named Shayol" (1961). Most stories of space prisons concern ingenious escapes, not the nature of the colony, though occasionally we get glimpses of dysfunctional societies, as in Robert Sheckley's *The Status Civilization* (1960) and Philip K. Dick's *Clans of the Alphane Moon* (1964); in the latter, a planetary asylum becomes a society structured upon models of psychological disorder.

Prison worlds represent one way to physically separate criminals from society, but science fiction writers find other methods. Robert Silverberg's *Hawksbill Station* (1968) uses **time travel** to establish a prison colony in the distant past (see **Prehistoric Fiction**). Others use **drugs, cryonics and suspended animation**, or **virtual reality** to suspend the prisoner outside **time**, as happens in Jonatham Lethem's *Gun, with Occasional Music* (1994), whereas Steve Aylett's *Slaughtermatic* (1998) has criminals suspended within **computer** simulations where they continue committing crimes until the simulation runs out of power.

The notion that imprisonment can be within the mind opens up new areas for prison stories. Bob Shaw's *Night Walk* (1967) combines the physical prison—a labyrinthine swamp—with a psychological prison—the prisoner's eyes are removed—though while escaping the hero finds new ways of seeing. Other authors identify blindness with imprisonment (see **Vision and Blindness**). In "To See the Invisible Man" (1962), Robert Silverberg's prisoner is condemned to be treated as if invisible by the rest of society, an extrapolation from Nathaniel Hawthorne's *The Scarlet Letter* (1850). Initially this seems to be no real punishment, as the narrator exploits his "**invisibility**" voyeuristically, but it is revealed as a state of terrifying vulnerability. In a variation on this theme, Gardner Dozois's "The Visible Man" (1975) can be seen but cannot see those around him, an enforced alienation that is highly destructive.

Such stories present the prison of the mind as an **allegory** for alienation, also a feature of more conventional prison stories like Evans's *In Limbo* (1985). In *The Prisoner* the surroundings are designed to look as unlike a prison as possible, but increasingly surreal irruptions into this "village" emphasize the increasing alienation of the nameless prisoner, Number 6, from those controlling his society. Significantly, in science fiction and fantasy, prisoners are more likely rebels than criminals; the prison embodies their struggle against their authoritarian masters. Building on this idea, many writers use the prison to represent **dystopia**. Sometimes, as in Geoff Ryman's "Oh, Happy Day!" (1985) or Octavia E. Butler's *The Parable of the Talents* (1998), the model of the concentration camp represents society's repression on the grounds of **sexuality** (Ryman) or race and **gender** (Butler). Others use less identifiable prisons to express formless rage against the world: Harlan Ellison's "I Have No Mouth, and I Must Scream" (1967) uses the helplessness of prisoners to represent the horrors of **nuclear war**.

Discussion

Prisons are places apart, which make them symbolically convenient settings for science fiction and fantasy. The prison is equated with authority and restriction. It may seem like utopia, but as we come to understand its true nature we must escape, as in Ursula K. Le Guin's "The Ones Who Walk Away from Omelas" (1973). The prisoner, meanwhile, is the rebel who rejects authority, strives for **freedom**, or suffers exclusion from **civilization** as a martyr. The fantastic panopticon does not rehabilitate prisoners but looks deep into what isolates them from society.

Bibliography

Russell Blackford. "Tiger in the Prison House." *Science Fiction*, 13 (1996), 3–9.

M. Keith Booker. *Strange TV*. Westport, CT: Greenwood Press, 2002.

E. Shaskan Bumas. "Fictions of the Panopticon." *American Literature*, 73 (March, 2001), 121–146.

Sheila Finch. "Paradise Lost." *Extrapolation*, 26 (Fall, 1985), 240–249.

Mike Gold. "*The Prisoner*." *Fantastic Films*, 3 (July, 1980), 66–71.

Fiona Kelleghan. "Hell's My Destination." *Science-Fiction Studies*, 21 (November, 1994), 351–364.

Tom Soter, "Uncaging *The Prisoner*." *Starlog*, No. 135 (October, 1988), 37–43, 59.
Matthew White and Jaffer Ali. *The Official Prisoner Companion*. New York: Warner Books, 1988.

—*Paul Kincaid*

PROGRESS

—•—

> *Every passing hour brings the Solar System forty-three thousand miles closer to Globular Cluster M13 in Hercules C and still there are some misfits who insist that there is no such thing as progress.*
>
> —Kurt Vonnegut, Jr.
> *The Sirens of Titan* (1959)

Overview

Science fiction has always been obsessed with the scientific and technological progress that would significantly change the quality of human life. Fantasy remains generally unenthusiastic about scientific advances, but in science fiction, the constant upward progress of **humanity** has become an article of faith.

Survey

The classical world had no concept of progress, though Athenian Greeks had an idea of "pushing forward" (*prokope*) that Romans rendered as "progressio." In medieval **Europe**, where theories concerning world **history** were determined by **religion** and tied to **eschatology**, humanity was considered fallen from an earlier Golden Age when we existed in a state of grace. Concepts of progress developed during the Enlightenment, best represented by three philosophers. The earliest theorist of progress, Jean Marie Condorcet believed that humanity would be progressively liberated from servile ignorance through scientific advances. G.W.F. Hegel saw **history** as a progressive dialectic leading to a fully self-conscious human spirit purged from superstition and myth. Auguste Comte articulated the position, called *positivism* (or *scientism*)—that empirical science provides the only source of true **knowledge**(see **Philosophy**).

Along with concrete developments in scientific research, these abstractions crystallized into practical discoveries and **inventions**, especially in **America**, where technoscientific optimism flourished. **Machines and mechanization** transformed **economics**, **education**, and industry. Thomas Edison became a national hero. Frederick Winslow Taylor designed the assembly line of modern manufacturing satirized in Yevgeny Zamiatin's *We* (see **Satire**), which by increasing productivity not only made millions for **business** barons but also raised workers' standards of living.

The wonder and awe of technological change created a powerful myth about miraculous progress that was central to the birth of science fiction. Arguably, all science fiction concerns progress by identifying some novel change in scientific or technological conditions. The "March of Progress" appealed especially to writers of pulp magazines and early "Edisonades"; Howard R. Garis's Tom Swift stories were popular, and space operas like E.E. "Doc" Smith's *Triplanetary* and Isaac Asimov's *Foundation* forecast fantastic progress in the far future. Early science fiction editors Hugo Gernsback and John W. Campbell, Jr. were technophiles—enthusiastic proponents of progress who thought science fiction would both outline and precipitate a better future.

Science fiction understands progress positively, negatively, and neutrally: optimistic dreams of progress producing a better society; pessimistic fears of technological developments destroying our way of life (see **Optimism and Pessimism**); and the impartial ambivalence of technological progress producing only more of the same. These attitudes figure respectively in **utopias** that, from the perspective of progressive futures, offer insights into the "primitive" present (see Edward Bellamy's *Looking Backward, 2000–1887*); in **dystopias** that, from the perspective of decadent futures, offer insights into a dangerous direction of the present (see Aldous Huxley's *Brave New World*); and in numerous texts suggesting that however much progress occurs, serious cultural, social, and ethical issues will persist (see Joanna Russ's *The Female Man*; Marge Piercy's *Woman on the Edge of Time*).

The dominant strain in science fiction regards technoscience as *always* progressive. The various *Star Trek* series argue that technological developments will trigger ethical progress. In Arthur Clarke's *The City and the Stars* (1956), *The Hammer of God* (1994), and *3001: The Final Odyssey* (1997) (see *2001: A Space Odyssey*) **technology** produces social progress by supplanting false superstitions. While conceptual breakthroughs may have unanticipated results (see Mary Shelley's *Frankenstein*; Greg Bear's *Blood Music*), technophiles generally embrace the continually increasing **speed** of technological change. Some writers see a rapidly approaching watershed moment whereafter "everything" will differ. Dubbed by Vernor Vinge as the "singularity," this moment becomes central in much science fiction after 1980. Following the singularity, humanity will become *posthumanity* (see **Identity**), a term used frequently since the emergence of **cyberpunk**, as in Bruce Sterling's *Schismatrix* (1985) and Dan Simmons's *Ilium* (2003). In *Singularity Sky* (2003) and *Iron Sunrise* (2004), Charles Stross deploys economic, cultural, and evolutionary singularities, suggesting that many current social concerns (like poverty or hunger) will be rendered moot by future technologies such as cornucopia machines, similar to *Star Trek*'s miraculous *replicators*.

Yet a counter-dominant strain sees progress more as a nightmare than a **dream**, suggesting that our **destiny** threatens devolution as much as **evolution**. This attitude characterizes attacks on **social Darwinism** in H.G. Wells's work, especially *The Time Machine*, where descendants of the intellectual aristocracy literally feed humanity's moribund corporeality; or Kurt Vonnegut, Jr.'s *Galápagos*, which blames the human brain for our social woes, **predicting** that *Homo sapiens* will one million years hence become small, unimportant, seal-like creatures. *Things to Come* and William Gibson's *Neuromancer* nicely represent the third strain of ambivalence: while Case's engagement with progress produces **sublime** transcendence, street punks are "nihilistic technofetishists," grotesque parodies of Enlightenment ideals.

Discussion

Fantasy usually remains skeptical about progress, especially of the technological kind, instead offering romanticized nostalgia, rejecting modernity in favor of epistemological models of **medievalism and the Middle Ages, magic,** and the supernatural. J.R.R. Tolkien's *The Lord of the Rings* characterizes Mordor, and Peter Jackson's *The Lord of the Rings: The Fellowship of the Ring* and its sequels depict Saruman's Isengard, as industrial factories. Rather than proffering stories of technoscientific ascent, fantasy frequently prefers a "falling" or cyclical model of history (see **Cycles**).

Though few writers remain unequivocally positive or negative about technology, an implicit hope in progress stays constant. Ironically, while our health, education, and standard of living indicate that technoscientific progress has made our lives better, many remain unhappy, still searching and hoping for more. Perhaps science fiction is an ideal medium for humanity to explore such paradoxes.

Bibliography

Gregg Easterbrook. *The Progress Paradox*. New York: Random, 2003.

Mark R. Hillegas. "Science Fiction and the Idea of Progress." *Extrapolation*, 1 (May, 1960), 25–28.

Rosemary Jackson. *Fantasy*. New York: Methuen, 1981.

Fredric Jameson. "Progress Versus Utopia." *Science-Fiction Studies*, 9 (July, 1982), 147–159.

Don Riggs. "Future and Progress in *Foundation* and *Dune*." Donald E. Palumbo, ed., *Spectrum of the Fantastic*. Westport, CT: Greenwood Press, 1988, 113–117.

Brian Stableford. "Science Fiction and the Mythology of Progress." Stableford, *Opening Minds*. San Bernardino, CA: Borgo Press, 1995, 29–36.

Vernor Vinge. "Technological Singularity." *Whole Earth Review*, No. 76 (Winter, 1993), 81–88.

W. Warren Wagar. *The Idea of Progress Since the Renaissance*. New York: Wiley, 1969.

—Neil Easterbrook

PROMISE

Overview

Many works of science fiction and fantasy embody the idea of promise on a broad scale: scientific advances may promise a better future, or fulfillment of a **quest** may promise a return to a simple, happy life. Tales also center around literal promises, which may be given, granted, or uttered as threats. Prophecies made with systems of **divination**, which may seem like promises, and **curses**, a negative promise with magical force (see **Magic**), are discussed elsewhere.

Survey

Promises made to **heroes** may inspire them to take action, setting stories in motion. In J.R.R. Tolkien's *The Hobbit*, Bilbo is promised an equal share of a **dragon's** treasure if he joins the **dwarfs** on their journey to reclaim it. In the **fairy tale** filmed as *Beauty and the Beast*, a loyal daughter promises to live with a hideous beast to save her **father**'s life. And in the film *Field of Dreams*, a mysterious voice promises a farmer, "If you build it, he will come," prompting him to create a baseball field that attracts dead baseball stars eager to play their favorite game (see **Farms; Sports**), including his own deceased father. A subgroup of these stories involve outlaws or criminals who are persuaded by promises to perform worthwhile tasks: in the film *Escape from New York* (1981), a convict is promised **freedom** if he rescues the United States President from an anarchic New York City, while in William Gibson's *Neuromancer*, the streetwise rogue Case undertakes a mission in exchange for a promise to restore his access to **cyberspace**.

Promises may also keep a story going when it has apparently reached a conclusion: in L. Frank Baum's *The Wonderful Wizard of Oz*, Dorothy and her companions believe their adventures are over when they reach the Emerald City; instead of granting their wishes immediately, however, the Wizard promises to do so only after they kill the Wicked Witch of the West, thus sending them on another mission. Similarly, promises may be a necessary device to launch sequels to seemingly completed narratives; in the film *Jurassic Park III* (2001), Dr. Grant had sworn (reasonably enough, in light of his experiences) that he would have nothing more to do with **dinosaurs**, but he is persuaded by the promise of a large fee to fly back to the forbidden **island**, where events force him to virtually repeat his previous adventure (see Michael Crichton's *Jurassic Park*).

Some fantasies may begin with heroes solemnly swearing an oath to fulfill certain responsibilities, a promise that invariably has terrible consequences when broken. In the legends of King **Arthur**, recounted in texts ranging from Thomas Malory's *Le Morte d'Arthur* (1485) to Marion Zimmer Bradley's *The Mists of Avalon*, Lancelot, like other Knights of the Round Table, vows to be faithful to Arthur and Guinevere; when he and Guinevere begin their illicit relationship, it inexorably leads to the fall of Camelot and the **deaths** of Arthur and Lancelot. In Tolkien's *The Lord of the Rings*, members of the Fellowship of the Ring vow to assist Frodo in his quest to destroy the **ring**, but Boromir breaks his promise and attempts to seize the ring, resulting in his own death.

Broken promises in science fiction may also have terrible results. In Mary Shelley's *Frankenstein*, Frankenstein at one point promises the **monster** he created that he will construct him a female partner for him; in exchange, the monster promises to permanently withdraw from human **civilization** with his mate. However, Frankenstein reneges on his promise and destroys the second monster before she is completed, prompting the monster to kill Frankenstein's bride as an act of **revenge**. In Isaac Asimov's "Liar!" (1941), a story included in *I, Robot*, a mind-reading **robot** (see **Psychic Powers**) feels compelled by the Three Laws of Robotics to falsely promise Dr. Susan Calvin that another scientist **loves** her; feeling betrayed when she learns the truth, she takes sadistic pleasure in driving him to **madness**. More broadly, **scientists** who construct **Frankenstein** monsters and fail to nurture them, with examples ranging from Frankenstein and H.G. Wells's Dr. Moreau (see *The Island of Doctor Moreau*) to the manufacturer of **androids** in the film *Blade Runner*, break an implicit promise to be good parents to their **children** and hence properly face tragic fates.

Discussion

Interpreted at their broadest possible level, promises might be regarded as the foundation of storytelling: writers implicitly promise readers to provide entertaining narratives that adhere to generic expectations, and readers respond positively or negatively depending upon whether writers fulfill those promises. Such bargains are maintained so regularly that, paradoxically, there can be a thrill of pleasure when storytellers deliberately violate them. A celebrated example is the film *Psycho* (1960), which shocked audiences by killing off its viewpoint character in the first thirty minutes, removing the figure they were sure would be central to the entire story. Still, enthralled by the unexpectedly different narrative that followed, audiences forgave Alfred Hitchcock for spectacularly breaking a promise.

Bibliography

Gorman Beauchamp. "The Frankenstein Complex and Asimov's Robots." *Mosaic*, 13 (Spring/Summer, 1980), 83–94.

Robert C. Goldbort. "How Dare You Sport Thus With Life?" *Journal of Medical Humanities*, 16 (Summer, 1995), 79–91.

Jane Goodall. "Frankenstein and the Reprobate's Conscience." *Studies in the Novel*, 13 (Spring, 1999), 19–43.

Donna Haraway. "The Promises of Monsters." Jenny Wolmark, ed., *Cybersexualities*. Edinburgh: Edinburgh University Press, 1999, 314–366.

Ron Heckelman. "The Swelling Act." George Slusser and Eric S. Rabkin, eds., *Mindscapes*. Carbondale: Southern Illinois University Press, 1989, 16–33.

Dominic Manganiello. "History as Judgement and Promise in *A Canticle for Leibowitz*." *Science-Fiction Studies*, 13 (July, 1986), 159–169.

Arthur P. Patterson. "Frankenstein's Self-Centeredness Leads Inevitably to Self-Destruction." Don Nardo, ed., *Readings on Frankenstein*. San Diego, CA: Greenhaven, 2000, 90–100.

Jean Pfaelzer. "The Sentimental Promise and the Utopian Myth." *ATQ*, 3 (March, 1989), 85–99.

—Stephen D. Rogers

PSYCHIC POWERS

A shallow rectangular pool held gold-fish, who gulped hopefully as they swam to the surface and flipped down again. The little minds of the fish lay open to Cody, minds thoughtless as so many bright, tiny, steady flames on little birthday candles, as he walked past the pool.

—Henry Kuttner and C.L. Moore
"Humpty Dumpty" (1953)

Overview

Powers of the mind, a cherished belief throughout **history**, were long the province of **magic** and the occult. Since the nineteenth century, attempted laboratory investigation of such "wild talents" gave them some scientific respectability. That **humanity** would develop psychic abilities through **evolution** became a popular science fiction assumption. Fantasies about people with such powers are discussed under **Talents**.

Survey

Psychic powers are traditionally linked to matters of life, **death**, and **religion**. **Hypnotism**, in Edgar Allan Poe's "The Facts in the Case of M. Valdemar" (1845), preserves life in a corpse despite decay. Arthur Conan Doyle's faith that psychic mediums could contact the dead led him to force the same belief on his hard-headed **scientist** Professor Challenger (see Arthur Conan Doyle's *The Lost World*) in *The Land of Mist* (1926). **Divination** is as old as history but takes on new interest when given a science fiction rationale in Robert A. Heinlein's "Life-Line" (1939) (see *The Past Through Tomorrow*), or when its deterministic consequences are scrutinized in Philip K. Dick's *The World Jones Made* (1956); prophecy aided by **drugs** is a vital thread in Frank Herbert's *Dune*.

Among talents grouped as ESP or extra-sensory **perception**, telepathy is most popular; clairvoyance or remote vision is sometimes included. A.E. van Vogt's *Slan* (1946) established the **cliché** of persecuted telepathic **supermen**, whose **paranoia** is more gently handled in Henry Kuttner's *Mutant* (1953). The 1950s science fiction vogue for psychic or psi powers owed much to magazine editor John W. Campbell, Jr., who was fascinated by fringe scientific notions like mind–machine interaction through "psychic electronics" or psionics. Authors, like Murray Leinster with "The Psionic Moustrap" (1955), targeted Campbell's enthusiasm.

Space operas by E.E. "Doc" Smith (see *Triplanetary*) and James H. Schmitz play with telepathic probes and thought screens; Smith's *First Lensman* (1950) adds a nontelepath who extracts information via muscle-reading (see **Psychology**). The telepath hero of Wilson Tucker's science fiction **espionage** thriller *Wild Talent* (1954) develops more physical talents under pressure of circumstances, as does the protagonist in James Blish's *Jack of Eagles* (1952), who not only grapples with a scientific rationale for psi but makes understanding **physics** essential in controlling the talent.

Alfred Bester's *The Demolished Man*, with its crime-solving telepathic minority, is a mature treatment. John Wyndham's *Re-Birth* (1955) deals sensitively with persecuted telepathic **children** in a **post-holocaust society**. John Brunner's *The Whole Man* (1966) features a master telepathic healer who tackles patients' **madness** head-on but, ironically, is physically deformed.

Telepathy may be a **curse**: Brunner's "Protect Me from My Friends" (1962) assumes that the mass uproar of human mentation will drive telepaths to **madness**, while Bester's *The Stars My Destination* features a "projective telepath" unable to stop broadcasting thoughts to others. A **hive mind** emerges in Arthur C. Clarke's *Childhood's End* as telepathic children become unable to distinguish between their and others' feelings. On the contrary, the gestalt-mind components linked by telepathy in Theodore Sturgeon's *More Than Human* are enhanced rather than diminished, as in the same author's *The Cosmic Rape* (1958).

Hypnotic power is tacitly subsumed into telepathy on the assumption that strong minds can dominate weaker ones via mental contact: Smith's and Schmitz's stories involve such control, which in van Vogt's *The Book of Ptath* (1947) becomes full-scale **possession**. The same effect is achieved with a psionic machine in Frederik Pohl's *A Plague of Pythons* (1965).

Psi powers affecting the material world include **teleportation** (see *The Stars My Destination*) and telekinesis, the ability to lift and move objects at a distance. Jack Vance's "Telek" (1952) shows a world ruled by a telekinetic elite; Stephen King's *Carrie* (1974) features a more typical loner. The supermen of Colin Wilson's *The Mind Parasites* (1967) become telekinetically able to hurl the **Moon** from its orbit.

A natural resulting talent of psychic power is levitation, **air travel** under one's own mental power, as in Michael Harrison's *Higher Things* (1945) and Isaac Asimov's "Belief" (1953). The black **wizard** in James Blish's *The Day After Judgment* (1971) achieves this feat by **magic**. A logical spinoff—since speeding up molecular movement increases temperature—is pyrokinesis or fire-starting, as seen in King's *Firestarter* (1980). Pyrotics and levitators (and "hypnos") are among the talented humans produced by **mutation** in Eric Frank Russell's *Sentinels from Space* (1953).

Discussion

The importation into science fiction of talents formerly regarded as magic chiefly involves taxonomy and terminology: polysyllables with a scientific flavor. Instead of "mindspeech" or "far-seeing," one speaks of telepathy and clairvoyance; Cordwainer Smith uses *hier* and *spiek* for mental equivalents of hearing and speaking in *Norstrilia*. Levitation is common in Asian martial-arts fantasy movies like *Zu: Warriors of the Magic Mountain* (1982) and *Crouching Tiger, Hidden Dragon* (2000).

Telepathy remains a convenient device to ease **communication** with **aliens in space** or **aliens on Earth**, though it seems implausible that an alien's mentality would be less inscrutable than its language. Elsewhere, the allure of psi powers has faded in the light of modern communications, with cellphones and **cyberspace** replacing the unrealized **dream** of telepathy.

Bibliography

Eric Bentcliffe. "Psionics Fiction." *Vector*, No. 6 (January, 1960), 25–27.

H.L. Drake. "Introduction: On Psi Powers." *Journal of the Fantastic in the Arts*, 9 (1998), 257–267.

Harry Harrison. "How to Sell to John W. Campbell, or Psionics in One Easy Lesson." *SFWA Bulletin*, 7 (August, 1969), 17–23.

Peter M. Lowentrout. "PsiFi." *Extrapolation*, 30 (Winter, 1989), 388–403.

Peter Nicholls, David Langford, and Brian Stableford. "Powers of the Mind." Nicholls, Langford, and Stableford, *The Science in Science Fiction*. 1982. New York: Knopf, 1983, 168–175.

Idella Purnell Stone, ed. *14 Great Tales of ESP*. New York: Fawcett, 1969.

Susan Stratton. "Time and Some Mysteries of Mind." Gary Westfahl, George Slusser, and David Leiby, eds., *Worlds Enough and Time*. Westport, CT: Greenwood Press, 2002, 77–85.

Robert Thouless. *From Anecdote to Experiment in Psychical Research*. London: Routledge & Kegan Paul, 1972.

Nancy H. Traill. *Possible Worlds of the Fantastic*. Toronto: University of Toronto Press, 1996.

—David Langford

PSYCHOLOGY

■

Warning: Therapy can be dangerous to your health. Especially if you are the therapist.

—Suzy McKee Charnas
"The Unicorn Tapestry" (1980)

Overview

Science fiction is often referred to as a "literature of ideas," emphasizing ideas from the physical sciences and **biology**. But central themes in science fiction since World War II often come from psychological sources. Even the defining response to science fiction sought by writers and readers, a **sense of wonder**, is an intense psychological experience, not intellectual contemplation. Fantasy fiction is also nourished by deep psychological roots. Of the many psychological concepts used in science fiction and fantasy, the most frequent can be summarized in terms of motives, symptoms and syndromes, theories, and therapy. Separate entries discuss **madness, paranoia,** and **mad scientists.**

Survey

Science fiction stories often rest on assumptions about general human motives: that we as a species are explorers, ultimately aiming "ad astra" even if we must do it "per aspera" (see **Exploration**); that we are basically good at heart, as in Ivan Yefremov's "Heart of the Serpent" (1959); or that conversely we are basically destructive, even **evil**, as in James Tiptree, Jr.'s "The Last Flight of Dr. Ain" (1968). Individual human motives, like personal guilt (see Frederik Pohl's *Gateway*; **Guilt and Responsibility**) or suppressed maternal feelings (see *Alien*; **Mothers**), may be central to resolution of interstellar events. Nonhuman animal motives may provide a story's core, as in Clifford D. Simak's exploration of **dog** psychology, *City*, and Cordwainer Smith's equivalent treatment of **cats**, "The Game of Rat and Dragon" (1956). Motives of alien species may be simple—Martians (see **Mars**) coveting **Earth**'s water and warmth in H.G. Wells's *War of the Worlds*, or aliens that look and think like elephants in Larry Niven and Jerry Pournelle's *Footfall* (1985)—or complex and unknowable, such as the sentient **alien world** of Stanislaw Lem's *Solaris*.

Mad scientists are so populous in science fiction and horror films as to become **clichés**, but psychological symptoms short of insanity may provide essential characterizations or plot elements. Psychological defenses like denial may be depicted, as in Judith Merril's "That Only a Mother" (1948). The distinctive **perception** and convictions characteristic of near-**death** experiences are explored by a research psychologist and a neurologist in Connie Willis's *Passage* (2001). Individuals and entire societies are beset by agoraphobia and acrophobia in many of Isaac Asimov's stories, like "Nightfall" (1941) and *The Caves of Steel* (1954) (see *I, Robot*). The belief

Sigmund Freud referred to as "omnipotence of thought"—common in early childhood and characteristic of adult obsessive-compulsive neurotics—is reified in **superhero** stories like *The Matrix* as well as more serious works like Ursula K. Le Guin's *The Lathe of Heaven* (1971). Depression at less than psychotic levels is pervasive in J.G. Ballard's **disaster** novels like *The Drowned World*, while splitting or multiple personality syndromes provide a basis for stories like Robert Louis Stevenson's *Strange Case of Dr. Jekyll and Mr. Hyde* and Marion Zimmer Bradley's "Elbow Room" (1980). The narcissistic personality syndrome has figured both in solipsistic stories like Robert A. Heinlein's "They" (1941) and stories like Philip K. Dick's "We Can Remember It for You Wholesale" (1966) where individuals learn that the fate of humanity/the world/the universe rests on their shoulders. A loosely defined character disorder termed "borderline personality"—moving back and forth across the border between functioning psyche and out-and-out psychosis—appears endemic among protagonists of stories in which fantasy elements insistently intrude into the mundane world, like James Thurber's "The Secret Life of Walter Mitty" (1939), filmed in 1946.

The current influence of Freudian theory on science fiction and fantasy is most often indirect, but applications of Freud are explicit in Philip José Farmer's "Mother" (1953) and *Forbidden Planet*. Jack London used Jungian theory in "The Red One" (1918). Jung's ideas still inform works like Ursula K. Le Guin's *A Wizard of Earthsea* and Frank Herbert's *Dune*, as well as *Star Wars* (via Joseph Campbell). Behaviorist theories have been less pervasive, though B.F. Skinner's own **utopia**, *Walden Two* (1948), and Anthony Burgess's *A Clockwork Orange* are prime examples.

Science fiction and fantasy writers have been personally and professionally ambivalent about psychotherapy. In Jack Williamson's "scientific **werewolf**" novel *Darker than You Think* (1948), the therapist is an egotistical hypocrite; but the **hero**'s gradual acceptance of his own werewolfness was (according to Williamson's autobiography) a disguised version of the author's therapy-supported self-acceptance as a genre writer. In Roger Zelazny's *The Dream Master* (1966), a therapist enters the **dreams** of a patient to seek a cure, while Greg Bear's *Queen of Angels* (1990) elaborates upon the therapist-enters-patient's-psyche process, offering a society where the "haves" are "therapied" and the have-nots live in untherapied ghettoes. In Suzy McKee Charnas's "The Unicorn Tapestry" (1980), a therapist treats a **vampire**. In Frederik Pohl's *Gateway*, the narrator benefits from treatment by a **computer**-simulated Sigmund Freud; in Barry N. Malzberg's *The Remaking of Sigmund Freud* (1985), a simulated Sigmund is less successful.

Discussion

A few science fiction and fantasy writers have had advanced psychological training, including David H. Keller, Alice B. Sheldon (Tiptree), Jerry Pournelle, and Walker Percy. Others developed their own forms of psychological expertise, notably Paul M.A. Linebarger (Cordwainer Smith), who became an expert in psychological warfare, and L. Ron Hubbard, creator of Dianetics and Scientology. Even more have experienced psychotherapy first-hand—perhaps explaining why science fiction and fantasy stories convincingly portray psychotherapists more often than psychological researchers.

Bibliography

Greg Bear. "Doctors of the Mind." Gary Westfahl and George Slusser, eds., *No Cure for the Future*. Westport, CT: Greenwood Press, 2002, 119–126.

Alan C. Elms. *Uncovering Lives*. New York: Oxford University Press, 1994.

———. "The Psychologist Who Empathized with Rats." *Science Fiction Studies*, 31 (March, 2004), 81–96.

James Kirsch. "Jack London's Quest: 'The Red One.'" *Psychological Perspectives*, 11 (1980), 137–154.

Russell Miller. *Bare-Faced Messiah*. New York: Henry Holt, 1987.

Robert Plank. *The Emotional Significance of Imaginary Beings*. Springfield, IL: Thomas, 1968.

Lawrence Sutin. *Divine Invasions: A Life of Philip K. Dick*. New York: Harmony Books, 1989.

Jack Williamson. *Wonder's Child*. New York: Bluejay Books, 1984.

—Alan C. Elms

PUNISHMENT

See Crime and Punishment

PUPPETS

See Dolls and Puppets

PUZZLES

Overview

Distinctions drawn between **mysteries**, puzzles, and **riddles** may never be precise or inarguable, but these general principles might be advanced: a puzzle is a type of mystery especially devised by one person to test another person, but not one merely stated in words to be answered in a few words, which is the essence of a riddle. Separate entries address aspects of **detective** and **espionage** fiction related to solving puzzles.

Survey

A work of fiction itself might be a puzzle created by authors for readers to solve, found in varieties both sublime and ridiculous. At one extreme, authors may follow the example of James Joyce's *Finnegans Wake* (1938) by producing novels written in such a complex and enigmatic style that readers must repeatedly study the text simply to figure out what is going on or what the author intends to convey. Note-worthy science fiction novels emulating *Finnegans Wake* include Brian W. Aldiss's *Barefoot in the Head* (1969) and Samuel R. Delany's *Dhalgren* (1975).

At the opposite end of the literary spectrum are "game books" or "multiple ending books," written in the second person and aimed at younger readers, which offer a series of passages that, in the manner of programmed learning, ask readers to select one of two courses of action, then to turn to one of two different pages, read the results of that choice, and make another similar decision. In the first game-book, Edward Packard's *The Cave of Time* (1979), readers who are told that they are in a **cavern** providing access to different periods of the past and future (see **Time Travel**) succeed by making choices leading to a happy ending or fail by making choices leading to **exile** in some undesirable era or **death**. Martin Gardner also wrote brief science fiction stories, many collected in *Puzzles from Other Worlds* (1986), that were primarily mathematical puzzles (see **Mathematics**).

Within a narrative, a puzzle may be a physical object that one must manipulate in certain ways to achieve desired results, a sort of puzzle that is visually interesting and attractive to filmmakers. Unlocking a puzzle box unleashes **horror** in the film *Hellraiser* (1987) and its sequels; figuring out how to open an ancient Egyptian chest is crucial in the film *The Mummy* (1999) (see **Egypt**); and *Johnny Mnemonic* (1996) must correctly manipulate an array of symbols in the **virtual reality** of **cyberspace** to break into a database.

A related sort of challenge is the need to find and assemble various pieces of a puzzle that together have special powers: in an episode of ***The Outer Limits***, "Demon with a Glass Hand" (1964), an unknowing **robot** must find and reattach the fingers of his glass hand to obtain the information he needs, and in an episode of ***Star Trek: The Next Generation***, "The Chase" (1993), Captain Picard vies with Klingons and Cardassians to track down scattered samples of ancient DNA which, when put together, produce a message from the deceased race that was their common ancestor.

Another tangible puzzle is a structure from which **heroes** must **escape**, like a maze (see **Labyrinth**) or **prison**. Stories about **ghosts and hauntings** may hinge on discovery of a secret passage or doorway, often a bookcase against the wall that rotates to provide access to a room on the other side where answers to the mystery lie. In narratives derived from stage melodramas of the nineteenth century, **villains** may construct elaborate deathtraps, requiring heroes to devise ingenious escapes. Such deathtraps were sometimes employed as the "cliffhanger" endings of chapters of film serials like *Flash Gordon* (1936); later, the same format was followed by the *Batman* series (1966–1968) (see ***Batman***), as the first of each two-part episode con-cluded with Batman and Robin in a bizarre deathtrap. These were also recurring hazards for secret agent James Bond (see ***Doctor No***); in *Goldfinger* (1964), for example, the villain straps him down and projects a laser beam slowly moving toward his body, threatening to slice him into two.

Another standard pattern is a series of tests designed by now-deceased people that may lead clever heroes to a **treasure**; examples in film include the **comedy** *It's a Mad Mad Mad Mad World* (1963) and *National Treasure* (2004), a **secret history** positing that **America**'s founding fathers left clues to the location of a vast fortune in iconic objects like the Declaration of Independence. Arguably, Isaac Asimov's original *Foundation* trilogy follows this structure, with Hari Seldon guiding his First Foundation to proper actions by means of periodically revealed recorded messages.

Discussion

Narrowly defined, puzzles as central features in narratives are associated with lesser texts, with the focus of attention on, say, how a hero contrives to break some glass to obtain a sliver enabling him to cut ropes binding him, not more profound moral, ethical, or philosophical dilemmas (see **Ethics; Philosophy**). Still, the trope of the puzzle can be employed to evocative effect. In Carl Sagan's *Contact* (1985), an enigmatic alien message is a deliberate puzzle, which when solved provides instructions for humans to build a machine allowing them to meet the advanced **aliens in space** who sent the message. Later, following up on a hint the aliens provide, **scientists** discover that within the seemingly random sequence of digits generated by calculating pi is a visual pattern, evidence of intelligent design suggesting that the universe itself is a puzzle knowingly constructed by higher beings for both humans and aliens to solve. A more significant sort of puzzle cannot be imagined.

Bibliography

Peter Atkins. *The Hellraiser Chronicles*. London: Titan, 1992.

William C. Cline. *Serials-ly Speaking*. Jefferson, NC: McFarland, 1994.

Deborah D'Agati. "The Problem with Solving." *Lovecraft Studies*, Nos. 42/43 (Autumn, 2001), 54–60.

Martin Gardner. *Puzzles from Other Worlds*. Oxford: Oxford University Press, 1986.

Patrick Gonder. "Like a Monstrous Jigsaw Puzzle." *Velvet Light Trap*, No. 52 (Fall, 2003), 33–44.

Roy Kinnard. *Science Fiction Serials*. Jefferson, NC: McFarland Press, 1998.

Richard A. Slaughter. "*The Matrix*: A Disturbing Postmodern Puzzle." *Futures*, 33 (March, 2001), 209–211.

Gary Westfahl. "Giving Horatio Alger Goosebumps." Westfahl, *Science Fiction, Children's Literature, and Popular Culture*. Westport, CT: Greenwood Press, 2000, 37–48.

—Gary Westfahl

QUEENS

Overview

The figure of the princess or queen appears in a variety of fantastic literature, from **mythology** and works by William **Shakespeare** to modern epics and retellings of **fairy tales**. Since the advent of **feminism**, she has become a figure of controversy and a target for revision.

Survey

In early fantasy, the character of a royal female more often depended on her actions in the familial sphere, not the political. Euripides's villainous *Medea* (430 BC) (see **Villains**), for example, slaughters her own **children** as **revenge** when her husband abandons her for a more powerful royal daughter. Over a millennium later, Shakespeare makes farce of a power struggle between Titania, queen of **fairies**, and her husband in *A Midsummer Night's Dream* (1594). Titania's desire to keep a mortal child is deemed unacceptable by Oberon, who wants the boy for himself. In consequence, Titania is bewitched and made to look the fool, and Oberon tricks her into giving him the child. Though one queen is tragic and the other comedic, they, along with many queens between them, are depicted primarily as wives and **mothers**, not rulers (see **Kings**).

A shift occurred when the Grimm Brothers published their *Household Tales* in 1812. In these stories, too, the queen acted in the personal sphere rather than the political, but as maiden or dutiful daughter. Plucky heroines like "Ashputtel," guided by a ghostly mother, acted to better their situation through **marriage** to a prince. Fairy tale maidens were queens-in-waiting. In such situations, marrying to become a princess was often, though not always, the end of their story. In "The Maiden Without Hands," the heroine's adventures continue after her marriage, when she is separated from her husband through the machinations of a villain. Recognition by her spouse restores her to her rightful place.

Fairy tale princesses were rarely shown, however, after becoming queens. Although occasionally, as in "The Maiden Without Hands," a dowager or ghostly queen might help the princess, queens who sought to use their power as rulers were more often villains. In the Grimm Brothers' story later adapted as *Snow White and the Seven Dwarfs*, the "good" queen dies giving **birth**, and is replaced by a second woman who is jealous of her stepdaughter, the beautiful princess Snow White (see **Beauty**), and orders a huntsman to kill her. Snow White ultimately ensures her safety by marrying a prince.

The queen experienced another major shift in the twentieth century, as fantasy and science fiction codified as genres. The limits of the personal sphere began to crumble, and royal women began to appear as warriors (see **Amazons**) and figures of prophecy, like Eowyn in J.R.R. Tolkien's *The Lord of the Rings*. Romance remained a strong driving force, as John Carter's courtship of the powerful Martian princess Dejah Thoris (see **Mars**) in Edgar Rice Burroughs's *A Princess of Mars*, but motherhood or, inversely, daughterhood, began to take a back seat.

As the century wore on, feminism strengthened the role of the queen in science fiction, making her stronger and more political than her predecessors. However, increasing the power and effectiveness of female rulers could not negate writers' concerns about the **evils** of monarchy itself, as in Joan D. Vinge's *The Snow Queen* (1980) and its sequels, an epic saga where galactic **politics** and personal greed dominate the conflict between a vicious queen and her **clone**. In science fiction, figures of female empowerment proved less likely to be rulers than rebels, perhaps as a result of the genre's predilections for **freedom**.

Monarchies fared better in fantasy, as did queens. The feminist movement spawned books of revisionist fantasy focusing on the contributions of women, like *The Mists of Avalon*, in which Marion Zimmer Bradley retells Arthurian legend as a conflict between Queen Gwenhwyfar and sister-in-law Morgaine (see **Arthur**). Historical queens and fairy tale princesses have also been reinvented (see **History**), as modern writers imagine them without the limitations of **sexism**.

Queens of old have been joined by new creations. Ysandre, the savvy politico in Jacqueline Carey's *Kushiel's Dart* (2001) and its sequels, balances power and personality, duty and desire. The prophesied savior of Lynn Flewelling's *The Bone Doll's Twin* (2001) is transformed into a boy for most of her childhood, causing much personal anguish. The **cliché** of the lady in distress is reversed and played out to the extreme in Anne Bishop's Black Jewels trilogy, beginning with *Daughter of the Blood* (1998), where handsome men in bondage await the arrival of a prophesied queen (see **Role Reversals**). In Nalo Hopkinson's Caribbean-inspired *Midnight Robber* (2000), the heroine, a woman of color, achieves personal fulfillment and survival by becoming the mythical Robber Queen.

Discussion

As feminism became a driving force in world politics, the complexity and range of the queen increased, and a broader **cultural** dialogue surrounding the place of women in public and private spheres resonated in the figure of the queen, who has proven particularly fascinating to women writers. Perhaps this fascination stems from the fact that the queen represents the ultimate female empowerment, ruling her environment rather than being ruled by it. Though politics have impacted her depiction for good or ill, she remains a staple in the lexicon of fantastic literature.

Bibliography

Deborah Byrd. "Gynocentric Mythmaking in Joan Vinge's *Snow Queen*." *Extrapolation*, 27 (Fall, 1986), 234–244.

Janice Crosby. "The Snow Queen and the Goddess in the Machine." *Femspec*, 2 (2000), 5–10.

Maureen Duffy. "The Fairy Queen." Duffy, *The Erotic World of Faery*. 1972. New York: Avon, 1980, 111–130.

Vishwas R. Gaitonde. "On the Lives and Deaths of Kings and Queens." *Burroughs Bulletin*, No. 48 (Fall, 2001), 5–10.

Barbara A. Gordon-Wise. *The Reclamation of a Queen*. Westport, CT: Greenwood Press, 1991.

Elizabeth Wanning Harries. *Twice upon a Time*. Princeton, NJ: Princeton University Press, 2003.

Ann F. Howey. "Queens, Ladies, and Saints." *Arthuriana*, 9 (Spring, 1999), 23–38.

Ruth Morse. "Sterile Queens and Questing Orphans." *Quondam et Futurus*, 2 (Summer, 1992), 41–53.

Susan A. Walsh. "Darling Mothers, Devilish Queens." *Victorian Newsletter*, No. 72 (Fall, 1987), 32–35.

—*Shannan Palma*

QUESTS

Overview

The journey of the **hero** across strange **landscapes**, encountering many adventures, is one of the most basic narrative strategies in all literature. Quests may be to obtain **magical objects** or **knowledge**, or the focus may be on shaping the character of the quester, the story becoming a **Bildungsroman**.

Survey

"When you start on your journey to Ithaca, pray that the road is long," wrote the early twentieth-century Greek poet C.P. Cavafy, reflecting on one of literature's earliest quests, Homer's *Odyssey* (c. 750 BCE)—but the advice also applies to the first extant quest story, *Gilgamesh* (c. 2500 BCE), in which the eponymous hero seeks but fails to obtain the secret of immortality (see **Immortality and Longevity**) and in the process learns the limitations of the human condition. The purpose of the quest, says Cavafy, is not the end of the journey but the transformative nature of the journey itself. Gilgamesh begins as a wild man; by the end, he is tamed. Odysseus at the beginning is proud and clever; once he regains Ithaca, he is wise and ready to assume his responsibilities as husband, **father**, and **king**. Similar quests occur in the *Argonautica* of Apollonius of Rhodes (c. 250 BCE), the story of Jason and the Golden Fleece, and Vergil's *Aeneid* (c. 19 BCE), about the founding of Rome. The tradition continued into the Middle Ages with Geoffrey of Monmouth, whose *History of the Kings of Britain* (c. 1135) may have introduced the story of Brutus, son of Aeneas, who founded Britain after ridding the country of **giants**. More significantly, Geoffrey's book was a major wellspring of the Arthurian mythos (see **Arthur; Chivalry**), which, by incorporating Grail legends, becomes another major realm of quest literature.

The allegorizing tendencies of medieval literature were ideally suited to the Holy Grail story (see **Allegory**). Grail quests are almost always transformative. The Grail is no mere lost piece of tableware, but the object of a spiritual journey. Chrétien de

Troyes's *Perceval* (c. 1182) has the mystery of the Grail displayed before him, but fails to ask the right question, and so fails. Only Galahad, son of Lancelot, as heroic as his father but without **sin** and therefore the perfect knight, can attain the goal. Once he has, he cannot continue on **Earth** and is assumed into **Heaven**. T.H. White's *The Once and Future King* (1958) includes the interesting observation that the perfect knight would be insufferable company. In White's tetralogy, as in Thomas Malory's *Le Morte d'Arthur* (1485), the Grail quest otherwise proves ruinous for the Round Table by raising the moral bar too high. Most knights are destroyed, not improved, by the experience.

In modern fantasy, the most famous quest is that of Frodo Baggins in J.R.R. Tolkien's **The Lord of the Rings**, which reverses most traditional motifs. Frodo's quest is not to obtain something, but to get rid of something. As the book darkens into nightmare, his inner struggle is to stave off moral corruption caused by the One Ring's baleful influence. If he dallies too long, he will become **evil** himself and forgo his purpose. It is a near thing at the end, as, tottering on the edge of the fiery abyss (see **Fire**), he cannot find the strength to complete his mission and providence must intervene. Frodo returns from the quest like one of Arthur's less than perfect knights, honored but shattered. A more upbeat transformative quest is that of the **apprentice wizard** Ged in Ursula K. Le Guin's **A Wizard of Earthsea**, in which, seeking redemption for his own sin, he must confront and absorb the literal and allegorical shadow of his pride to become a complete person.

In post-Tolkien fantasy, the quest may only be a simple-minded excuse to extend the plot. In Terry Brooks's slavishly imitative **The Sword of Shannara** the author apes the trappings of Tolkien's story but removes its original elements. Brooks's quest is to find a magic **sword**. In John Jakes's Brak the Barbarian stories (see **Barbarians**), first collected in *Brak the Barbarian Versus the Sorceress* (1969), the hero's quest for his homeland merely moves him from one story to the next, without character or thematic development. Science fiction writer E.C. Tubb carried this to the ultimate extreme, stringing out Dumarest of Terra's quest for the lost planet Earth, which began in *The Winds of Gath* (1967), over more than thirty volumes before finally concluding in 1992.

The quest for lost Earth remains a potent theme in **space opera**, with examples including Keith Laumer and Rosel George Brown's *Earthblood* (1966) and Algis Budrys's *The Amsirs and the Iron Thorn* (1967). In such stories, the quest for the homeworld is a quest for the understanding of origins. The truth, when discovered, may be disheartening, as in Isaac Asimov's *Foundation and Earth* (1986) (see **Foundation**), wherein it is learned that the long-forgotten Earth was deliberately made uninhabitable. A quest for knowledge, also transformative, is common in stories about **post-holocaust societies**, in which heroes seek the forbidden redoubt of ancient science, as in John Wyndham's *Re-Birth* (1955), Poul Anderson's *Vault of the Ages* (1952), Leigh Brackett's *The Long Tomorrow* (1955), and Jack McDevitt's *Eternity Road* (1997).

Discussion

Quests, when they are more than mere plot-extenders, are about the journey of life itself, which as we mature leads to discovery and transformation, or, if things go badly, failure and degeneration. But to stop questing is to stop living.

Bibliography

W.H. Auden. "The Quest Hero." Neil D. Isaacs and Rose A. Zimbardo, eds., *Tolkien and the Critics*. Notre Dame: University of Notre Dame Press, 1968, 40–61.

Annie Combes. "From Quest to Quest." *Arthuriana*, 12 (Fall, 2002), 7–30.

Robert Ellwood. *Frodo's Quest*. Wheaton, IL: Theosophical/Quest, 2002.

Sylvia Engdahl. "Prospective on the Future." Millicent Lentz, ed., *Young Adult Literature*. Chicago: ALA, 1980, 425–433.

Jorge J.E. Gracia. "The Quests of Sam and Gollum for the Happy Life." Gregory Bassham and Eric Bronson, eds., *The Lord of the Rings and Philosophy*. Chicago: Open Court, 2003, 61–71.

Robin Hobb. "A Bar and A Quest." Karen Haber, ed., *Meditations on Middle Earth*. New York: St. Martin's, 2001, 85–100.

Sue Jenkins. "Love, Loss, and Seeking." *Children's Literature in Education*, 15 (Summer, 1984), 73–83.

Anne Wilson. *Magical Quest*. Manchester: Manchester University Press, 1988.

—Darrell Schweitzer

R

RACE RELATIONS

Racism was not a problem on the Disc-world, because—what with trolls and dwarfs and so on—speciesism was more interesting. Black and white lived in per-fect harmony and ganged up on green.

—Terry Pratchett
Witches Abroad (1991)

Overview

Race can be a troubled subject in science fiction and fantasy, as in the real world. Science fiction may take on issues of race directly—logically enough, because race has been imagined through the discourses of science for centuries. Fantasy tends to allegorize race relations (see **Allegory**) using fantastical species, like the hobbits, **elves, dwarfs**, orcs, and people in J.R.R. Tolkien's *The Lord of the Rings*.

Survey

Awareness of racial issues in science fiction dates back to Mary Shelley's *Frankenstein*, wherein the **monster** is notably Asian in appearance, with yellow skin and lustrous black hair. While Shelley's sympathies lie with the monster, the foreign racial char-acteristics of Bram Stoker's *Dracula* and his minions bespeak nineteenth-century fears of the reverse colonization of **Europe** by "inferior" races. In contrast, H.G. Wells's *The War of the Worlds* displays a postcolonial awareness of the destruction of indigenous races, like Tasmanian aborigines, which he compares to the colonization of England by advanced Martians (see **Mars; Postcolonialism**). Similarly, Wells's *The Time Machine* hypothesizes a future in which class distinctions cause humans to evolve into two separate species (see **Class System**).

In the early twentieth century, race played an uninterrogated role in delineating "good guys" from "bad guys." The heroes of E.E. "Doc" Smith's *The Skylark of Space* (1928) and its sequels are blue-eyed blonds, while the **villain** is a stereotyp-ical, dark-haired French-Canadian. Worse still were "Yellow Peril" novels depicting white fears of being overrun by "Asian hordes," sentiments represented in M.P. Shiel's *Yellow Danger* (1898) and Robert A. Heinlein's *Sixth Column* (1949).

From the 1950s onward, American science fiction primarily focused on black/white relations, sometimes in allegorical fashion, as in Clifford D. Simak's "How-2" (1954), where **robots** stood in for African-Americans. Heinlein's *Farnham's Freehold* (1964) transports a rugged survivalist to a nightmarish **far future** ruled by African-Americans, while Philip K. Dick and Ray Nelson's *The Ganymede Takeover* (1967) envisions troubled relationships between blacks and whites continuing in the aftermath of an alien **invasion**. When not focusing on racial matters, white authors gestured toward progressive attitudes by including nonwhite characters. The first **Star Trek** series notably featured a black woman, even if her role was that of glorified secretary; *Star Trek* also dealt with racism directly in "Let That Be Your Last Battlefield" (1969), which allegorized the **absurdity** of racism in a battle between sole survivors of a racial war that destroyed their planet; the combatants are half-white and half-black, but with reversed colors, a distinction that is meaningless to the *Enterprise* crew. Similar racial allegories permeated *Planet of the Apes* and its sequels, with race differences represented by devolved humans and the evolved **apes** dominating them.

It is debatable whether including limited numbers of visible minorities was an effective antiracist strategy or mere tokenism. Still, some novels began presenting blackness as normal: for instance, all characters in Ursula K. Le Guin's *The Left Hand of Darkness* are dark and the human is black. Dark skin is the norm in the world of Le Guin's *A Wizard of Earthsea*, with white characters regarded as **barbarians**. Such depictions in science fiction literature do not necessarily carry over into film; thus, the television movie *A Wizard of Earthsea* (2004) depicts Ged as white, not dark-skinned. Racial stereotyping remains common in science fiction films, as demonstrated, for example, by the Jewish and African-American characters in *Independence Day* (1996).

In the 1960s and 1970s, there also emerged authors like Samuel R. Delany and Octavia E. Butler writing from an African-American perspective. Delany's **Triton** depicts a utopian future in which race, like sex, is a matter of choice (see **Utopia**); while the protagonist transforms himself from an unhappy white man into an unhappy white woman, another major character, a black male politician, transforms herself both racially and sexually. Butler also focuses on black protagonists. In **Dawn** and its sequels, the issue of race is interrogated as humans are genetically transformed by their encounter with an alien race that trades genetic materials. Butler's **Kindred** takes on American racial history (see **America**), with a black protagonist repeatedly swept into the past to save the white slaveowner who will become her great-grandfather (see **Time Travel**). The novel depicts both the **evils** of **slavery** and the complicity and **violence** it enforces on slaveholders and slaves.

Since the 1990s, there has been an upsurge in the numbers of racialized writers drawn to science fiction and fantasy. Delany and Butler were once the only well-known African-American genre authors, and few could identify a single writer of Asian or **Native American** descent; today, authors of color are more numerous and more visible. Anthologies like Sheree Thomas's *Dark Matter* (2000) and Nalo Hopkinson and Uppinder Mehan's *So Long Been Dreaming* (2004) highlight the growing importance of racialized writers in the field. Moreover, writers of color have won major awards, notably Hopkinson for *Brown Girl in the Ring* (2001) and

Hiromi Goto for *The Kappa Child* (2001), the latter distinguished by evocative use of western fantasy and Japanese **mythology** (see **Japan**) to explore issues of **gender**, race, and **sexuality**.

Discussion

The trope of the alien (see **Aliens in Space; Aliens on Earth**) has always had allegorical power to represent abjected others in western society, whether women, homosexuals, or people of color (see **Homosexuality**). Science fiction's aliens have been deployed to both criticize racism and denigrate the other. However, as the ethnographic make-up of science fiction and fantasy expands and diversifies, the genres will reflect these changes in new and unexpected ways.

Bibliography

Samuel R. Delany. *Silent Interviews*. Hanover: Wesleyan University Press, 1994.

Elyce Rae Helford. "Would You Really Rather Die than Bear My Young?" *African American Review*, 28 (1994), 259–271.

Elisabeth Anne Leonard, ed. *Into Darkness Peering*. Westport, CT: Greenwood Press, 1997.

Burton Raffel. "Genre to the Rear, Race and Gender to the Fore." *The Literary Review*, 38 (1995), 454–461.

Gregory E. Rutledge. "Futurist Fiction and Fantasy." *Callaloo*, 24 (2001), 236–252.

James R. Sallis, ed. *Ash of Stars*. Jackson: University Press of Mississippi, 1996.

Ziauddin Sardar and Sean Cubitt, eds. *Aliens R Us*. London: Pluto Press, 2002.

Paul Youngquist. "The Space Machine." *African American Review*, 37 (2003), 333–343.

—Wendy Pearson

RADIO

See Television and Radio

RATS AND MICE

Overview

The ubiquity of rats and mice in world literature reflects their long and close association with human activity. They are significant characters in fantastic literature, often endowed with the power of speech (see **Talking Animals**) and human or superhuman **intelligence**. Although they may appear as companions or helpers to **gods and goddesses**, humans, and other animals, because of their natural destructiveness and their historical association with **plagues and diseases** (particularly rats), rats and mice may be accorded negative attributes and linked to **sin** (see **Christianity**), **death**, underworld denizens, and **evil**.

Survey

The folklore of rats and mice is similar, but because of their larger size and aggressiveness, rats are less well regarded. Their fecundity and resourcefulness have contributed to their association with Asian gods of **wisdom**, success, and prosperity. In some cases, their perceived wisdom is associated with death and the underworld; the belief that rats have foreknowledge of doomed ships is an example of their posited **knowledge**. Mice were used in **divination** in some cultures, while in others, mice are regarded as souls of the dead. Many of these traditional associations have been translated into fantastic literature. In Stephen King's *The Green Mile* (1996), the appearance of a strangely intuitive mouse in a death row cellblock coincides with a series of supernatural occurrences that challenges ordinary assumptions about good and evil.

In modern fantasy and science fiction, rats and mice may achieve human or superhuman intelligence in laboratory settings through human intervention, as in Daniel Keyes's *Flowers for Algernon* and Robert O'Brien's *Mrs. Frisby and the Rats of NIMH* (1971) (filmed as *The Secret of NIMH* [1982]), or, in the case of Terry Pratchett's *The Amazing Maurice and His Educated Rodents* (2001), by foraging in a dump outside a university for **wizards**. Secret **civilizations** of rats or mice figure in Margery Sharp's *The Rescuers* (1959) and its sequels and film adaptations and in Fritz Leiber's *The Swords of Lankhmar* (1968). An unusual example of rodent intelligence occurs in Douglas Adams's *The Hitchhiker's Guide to the Galaxy* (1979), wherein **Earth** is revealed to be a **computer** run by hyper-intelligent mice.

Though the mouse is a common symbol of timidity and ineffectiveness, it may also symbolize **courage** and perseverance in the face of great odds. In one of Aesop's **fables**, a mouse frees a lion caught in a hunter's net by gnawing through the ropes. Modern versions of the fable occur in L. Frank Baum's *The Wonderful Wizard of Oz*, where the Queen of the Field Mice rescues Dorothy and the Cowardly Lion from a deadly poppy field, and C.S. Lewis's *The Lion, the Witch and the Wardrobe*, in which the great lion Aslan, bound by infernal creatures, is set free by gnawing mice. An heroic mouse, Reepicheep, who figures in Lewis's *The Voyage of the Dawn Treader* (1952), later provided a model for the giant talking rats of Mary Gentle's *Rats and Gargoyles* (1990).

In **fables** and folktales advocating pragmatism, mice may be overcome by larger enemies, but in children's fantasy and science fiction, they regularly overcome their foes. Through didactic stories, young readers are encouraged to overcome insecurities and identify with brave and resourceful mouse characters like Abelard in William Steig's *Abel's Island* (1976), who develops **survival** skills while stranded, like Robinson Crusoe, on a deserted **island**, and Matthias, the young warrior who defends Redwall Abbey against the depredations of rats, stoats, weasels, ferrets, and foxes in Brian Jacques's *Redwall* (1986). Kindly and heroic mice are standard figures (see **Heroes**) in animated films, including *Cinderella* (1950), *An American Tail* (1986), and *The Great Mouse Detective* (1986), and one cannot forget Mickey Mouse, first featured in *Steamboat Willie* (1928).

Rats and mice frequently assist **children**, adults, and other animals as companions, confidants, or familiars. The rat Melchisedec is a witness to orphan Sara's cruel treatment in a London boarding school in Frances Hodgson Burnett's *A Little Princess* (1905), while the amiable Rat in Kenneth Grahame's *The Wind in the Willows* (1908) campaigns to restore Toad to his ancestral hall when it is invaded

by uncouth weasels, stoats, and ferrets. Templeton, the barnyard rat in E.B. White's
Charlotte's Web (1952), is disagreeable but essential to Charlotte's plan to save
Wilbur the pig. A particularly sinister relationship between humans and rats is portrayed in the film *Willard* (1971; remade 2003) in which a pathologically unstable
man trains rats to kill his employer. Once the deed is done, the rats, commanded by
one of their own, turn on their former master. The scenes of hundreds of scurrying
rats recalls the sudden appearance of hordes of rats in a room housing boxes of polluted soil in Bram Stoker's **Dracula**.

Discussion

Apart from Charlotte Maria Tucker's *The Rambles of a Rat* (1857), a didactic fantasy that promotes kindness to rats and poor children, and O'Brien's *Mrs. Frisby
and the Rats of NIMH*, in which super-rats establish a self-sufficient rat **utopia**,
attempts to defend rats in fantastic literature are rare. The predominant association
of rats with dark forces is graphically represented in the remarkable rat-faced,
serpent-tailed **goblin** designed by Dante Gabriel Rossetti for the frontispiece of
Goblin Market (1862), Christina Rossetti's tale of temptation and seduction. Mice,
by contrast, have lost their original negative associations by way of Beatrix Potter-
like illustrations of mice in aprons and vests and frequent portrayals of mice as
doughty role models in children's fantasy.

Bibliography

Mark Bailey. "The Honour and Glory of a Mouse." *Mythlore*, 5 (Autumn 1978), 35–36, 46.
Paula T. Connolly. "Frisby-Turned-Brisby." Lucy Rollin, ed., *The Antic Art*. Fort Atkinson,
    WI: Highsmith, 1993, 73–82.
Bonnie Gaarden. "The Inner Family of *The Wind in the Willows*." *Children's Literature*,
    22 (1994), 43–57.
John Gilbert. "Horror of The Rats." Stephen Jones, ed., *James Herbert*. London: New
    English Library, 1992, 105–107.
Daniel Keyes. *Algernon, Charlie and I*. Boca Raton, FL: Challcrest, 1999.
Anita Moss. "The Spear and the Piccolo." *Children's Literature*, 10 (1982), 124–140.
Cynthia C. Rostankowski. "The Monastic Life and the Warrior's Quest." *The Lion and the
    Unicorn*, 27 (January 2003), 83–98.
Jack Zipes. "Introduction." L. Frank Baum, *The Wonderful World of Oz*. New York:
    Penguin, 1998, ix–xxix.

—*Janis Dawson*

READING

Overview

The fundamental fact of our engagement with literature is that we read texts; the
fundamental act is that we interpret as we read. Science fiction and fantasy make
much of both the common fact of reading and its uncommon significance, for reading

is not just written **communication**, but a general trope for interpretation and cognition—how we make meaning of our experience in the world. Other entries address the related topics of **Books, Libraries,** and **Writing and Authors**.

Survey

Many are surprised to discover that reading has a history. In classical Greece, silent reading was rare, both because **books** were very expensive and because language was written without punctuation, vowels, or spacing between words. Reading usually involved public performances by a professional called a *rapsode*. Since 1967, when the French critic Roland Barthes declared the "death" of the author and "birth" of the reader, reading has been heavily theorized and thematized. Postmodern criticism distinguishes between old models of reading, which understand reading as decoding authorial intention, and new models, which conceptualize readers as active agents in constructing meaning, not passive receptors, and thus implies that acts of reading are never definitive or complete, since different readers read differently (see **Postmodernism**).

Science fiction and fantasy depict reading in three ways. The first is as literal act. In the middle of Stanislaw Lem's *Solaris*, Kelvin goes to the library, where he reads for the novel's next twenty-five pages—slightly more than ten percent of the book. (Having characters read allows writers to provide large quantities of exposition—so-called "infodumps.") Russell Hoban's *Riddley Walker* (1980) centers on reading: in a **post-holocaust society** where almost no one is literate, reading past documents is the secret to recovering lost **knowledge**. *Riddley Walker* is a veritable museum of reading practices, protocols, and problems: Riddley reads several texts, reads to the audience, and receives a lesson in reading (also a paradigmatic instance of misreading). In Mary Shelley's *Frankenstein*, the **monster's** sole **education, ethics,** and **philosophy** come from reading three **books** valued by English Romantics. In Neal Stephenson's *The Diamond Age* (1995), the heroine happens upon an interactive book that teaches her precisely what she must know. The society of Ray Bradbury's *Fahrenheit 451* outlaws books as dangerous, since they contain subversive knowledge and produce idle imaginings; rebel readers resourcefully devote their lives to memorizing entire books.

The second type of reading concerns metaphors of interpretation or cognition. In Ursula K. Le Guin's *The Left Hand of Darkness*, Genly Ai reports to the Ekumen his reading of Gethenian **culture** (and provides misreadings). William Gibson makes the protagonists of *Idoru* (1996) and *Pattern Recognition* (2003) into semioticians—readers of cultural signs surrounding them. In *Solaris*, the alien ocean "reads" humanity "like a book"; Kelvin also seeks out two special books, hoping to detect the truth of his conditions. Indeed, the motif of detection connects textual readers or readings with empirical readers holding real books.

Clever writers transform empirical readers into characters, bridging boundaries between fictional text and physical world, which identifies the third type of reading: the *real* reader as reader. Robert A. Heinlein's *The Moon Is a Harsh Mistress* (1966) makes the empirical reader a future member of the book's society. In *Frankenstein*, the reader is Robert Walton's sister, since the novel comprises a series of letters written by him to her. Yevgeny Zamiatin's *We* is a diary written by D-503 to be read by aliens. Such metafictional devices engage ancillary concerns, especially writing; D-503 and Winston Smith in George Orwell's *Nineteen Eighty-Four* write the text readers hold. Libraries appear with great frequency and importance, as in Jorge Luis Borges's stories.

Much fantasy embeds within its text other texts, especially of invented **mythologies**; J.R.R. Tolkien filled *The Lord of the Rings* with moments of reading (traditional **poetry**, ancient stories): the Fellowship cannot pass Moria's gate (see **Threshold**) until properly reading its inscription. Reading not only parallels the plot's larger **mysteries**, but underscores the world's historical past, enlarging and enriching its fictional world. Fantasies may configure literacy as marking the difference between the civilized and primitive, as in Edgar Rice Burroughs's *Tarzan of the Apes*.

Discussion

Trying to trace the theoretical relation of reading to interpretation may seem ridiculous, a postmodern game of recursion. One device in Douglas Adams's *The Hitchhiker's Guide to the Galaxy* is a book, also entitled *The Hitchhiker's Guide to the Galaxy*, continually consulted by befuddled characters who, like readers, need information about the unfolding story. Such **satire** foregrounds the **allegory** of reading implicit in every text. Novelist and critic Samuel R. Delany argues that the very definition of science fiction concerns a set of reading protocols—to read science fiction or fantasy, one must recognize the *megatext* of historical traditions and conventions within which particular texts are coded and read.

Reading literature or watching films, therefore, always means re-reading: interpreting, arguing, reworking. Thousands of scholarly articles have titles that include "a reading of," synonymous with "an interpretation of." However, works of fiction themselves provide re-readings of their intellectual debts within the larger megatext. Philip Pullman's His Dark Materials series, beginning with *The Golden Compass* (1995), rereads and reworks John Milton's *Paradise Lost* (1667) and a host of other texts within and outside the fantastic genres.

Finally, fantasy and science fiction love the image of the reader, whether introverted loner or extroverted fan. More than **rockets** or ray guns, **magic rings** or **swords**, the bookish geek—the reader—remains the fantastic's central emblem.

Bibliography

Roland Barthes. "On Reading." *The Rustle of Language*, trans. Richard Howard. New York: Hill & Wang, 1986, 33–46.

Damien Broderick. *Reading By Starlight*. New York: Routledge, 1995.

Samuel R. Delany. *Silent Interviews*. Hanover: Wesleyan University Press, 1994.

Michael D.C. Drout. "Reading the Signs of Light." *The Lion and the Unicorn*, 21 (April, 1997), 230–250.

Marc Leeds. "Beyond the Slaughterhouse." Leeds and Peter Reed, eds., *The Vonnegut Chronicles*. Westport, CT: Greenwood Press, 1996, 91–102.

Alberto Manguel. *A History of Reading*. New York: Penguin, 1996.

Peter Rabinowitz. *Before Reading*. Ithaca: Cornell University Press, 1987.

Peter Stockwell. "Isomorphic Relations in Reading Science Fiction." *Language and Literature*, 1 (1992), 79–99.

—*Neil Easterbrook*

REBELLION

■

*Revolutions are not won by enlisting the
masses. Revolution is a science only a
few are competent to practice. It depends
on correct organization and, above all, on
communications.*

—Robert A. Heinlein
The Moon Is a Harsh Mistress (1966)

Overview

Uprisings against oppressive or outright **evil** governments and authority figures
occur frequently in science fiction and fantasy. A revolution translates a desire for
freedom into dramatic conflict that drives a story, with tyrants as recognizable and
unambiguous **villains**—particularly when they are aliens or **computers**. Stories of
rebellion also provide vehicles for discussions of **politics** and **governance systems** as
rebels discover that, having overthrown a tyranny, they must construct a new government that will not replicate the tyranny they fought to destroy.

Survey

Rebellions offer powerful dramatic imagery, like the crowd revolt scenes in
Metropolis, inspired by Sergei Eisenstein's docudrama *Battleship Potemkin* (1925).
The battles between the Imperial forces and the outnumbered but doughty Rebels
are crucial scenes of *Star Wars* and its sequels, with the gross imbalance of forces
helping to reinforce audience sympathy with the Rebels. Similarly, the crew of the
Liberator on *Blakes 7* fights in the face of the overwhelming force of the oppressive
Federation. The Fremen of Frank Herbert's *Dune* were a despised and hunted people before they found a leader in Paul Atreides and revolted against the tyranny of
the Harkonnens.

In some stories, oppressors began as good leaders, even **heroes**, until they forget their responsibilities to the governed and begin regarding their privileges as due
deference. President Clark in *Babylon 5* came to set Earthgov back in order, but
overstepped himself and became a tyrant. In Larry Niven's *A Gift from Earth*
(1968), the Crew of the original "slowboat" to Mount Lookitthat and their descendents have come to treat the ordinary colonists as little more than walking organ
farms, until a new ship from **Earth** brings medical knowledge that promises to
render those privileges meaningless. Similarly, the Pilots' Guild of C.J. Cherryh's
Foreigner (1994) received special privileges to honor their ancestors' **sacrifices**
while mining fuel in a deadly radiation cloud, but when they became arrogant,
the colonists left, taking drop capsules to the planet below.

Tyrants in science fiction are not necessarily human. In *Planet of the Apes*
and its sequels, humans have become slaves to the chimps and gorillas they uplifted
as a cheap labor force (see **Uplift**). Whereas French author Pierre Boulle's original
novel (1963) envisioned no efforts to oppose the apes' domination, American film

adaptations predictably emphasize **humanity**'s struggles to regain its lost liberty (see **America**). Aliens may take over the Earth, as in the miniseries *V* (1983), inspiring fierce human resistance. Computers designed to watch over humanity may instead become tyrants, as in D.F. Jones's *Colossus* (1969), filmed as *Colossus: The Forbin Project* (1969) and two later film series. In *The Matrix* and its sequels, computers feed humans **illusions** of twentieth-century normalcy while they are milked of vital energy, and in *The Terminator* and its sequels, computers strive to exterminate all humans. In both cases, a small group of knowledgeable people seeks to bring down the computers, by moving outside of **virtual reality** and subverting it in *The Matrix*, and traveling backward in time to prevent computer conquest in *The Terminator* (see **Time Travel**).

While many stories of rebellion end when oppressors are overthrown, some authors treat the success of the rebellion as a problem, confronting rebels with the necessity of setting up a government that will not become another tyranny. George Orwell's *Animal Farm*, which begins with animals rebelling against a farmer, is a **fable** about what happens when rebels evolve into the sorts of overlords they originally opposed and a **satire** of the **history** of Soviet **Russia**, as Bolshevik idealism gave way to the brutality of Joseph Stalin. In both *The Moon is a Harsh Mistress* (1966) and " 'If This Goes On—' " (1940) (see *The Past Through Tomorrow*), Robert A. Heinlein describes both a rebellion and subsequent establishment of a new government. Similarly, Sherwood Smith's fantasy *Crown Duel* (2002) brings down the wicked **king** at midpoint, with the second half involving court intrigues of the provisional government as the next king is decided upon. Walter Jon Williams's *Metropolitan* (1995) and *City on Fire* (1997) make two characters' efforts to establish a working government part of an ongoing meditation on the nature of responsibility (see **Guilt and Responsibility**).

Discussion

Many science fiction revolutions are little more than retellings of historical revolutions in space. Since many science fiction writers are American, the Revolutionary War has been a most common model. However, other writers draw upon the French Revolution, Russian Revolution, or even England's Civil War and Glorious Revolution. While some stories have clear one-to-one correlations with one or another historical revolt, others reference them only in a general sense as they celebrate or analyze the phenomenon of rebellion and its consequences.

Bibliography

Joe Abbott. "They Came from Beyond the Center." *Literature/Film Quarterly*, 22 (1994), 21–27.

Arthur A. Berger. *"The Terminator."* Berger, ed., *The Postmodern Presence*. Walnut Creek, CA: Altamira Press, 1998, 157–165.

Lorenzo DiTommaso. "History and Historical Effect in Frank Herbert's *Dune*." *Science-Fiction Studies*, 19 (November, 1992), 311–325.

Edward James. "Violent Revolution in Modern American Science Fiction." Philip J. Davies, ed., *Science Fiction, Social Conflict, and War*. Manchester: Manchester University Press, 1990, 98–112.

John Newsinger. "Rebellion and Power in the Juvenile Science Fiction of John Christopher." *Foundation*, No. 47 (Winter, 1989/1990), 46–54.

Carol S. Pearson. "Of Time and Revolution." Ruby Rohrlich, ed., *Women in Search of Utopia*. New York: Schocken, 1984, 260–268.

J.A. Perkins. "MYCROFTXX Is Alive and Well." *Notes on Contemporary Literature*, 5 (January, 1975), 13–15.

Curtis C. Smith. *Welcome to the Revolution*. San Bernardino, CA: Borgo Press, 1995.

Carolyn Wendell. "Responsible Rebellion in Vonda N. McIntyre's *Fireflood, Dreamsnake*, and *Exile Waiting*." Tom Staicar, ed., *Critical Encounters II*. New York: Ungar, 1982, 125–144.

—*Leigh Kimmel*

REBIRTH

Overview

The term "rebirth" can apply to instances when a dead person is brought back to life, or when one is significantly transformed in a manner suggesting a new start or new beginning. Cases of **metamorphosis** without such connotations, like the activities of **shapeshifters** or persons transformed into **vampires** or **werewolves**, are discussed elsewhere. Science fiction often focuses on rebirths involving an evolutionary progression of human into **superman** (see **Evolution**).

Survey

The death and resurrection of Jesus Christ (see **Christianity**) is the rebirth that most influenced literature. Two prominent Christ figures in fantasy and science fiction are the lion Aslan of C.S. Lewis's *The Lion, the Witch and the Wardrobe*, who dies to defeat the **evil witch** afflicting Narnia before being reborn, and Klaatu of the film *The Day the Earth Stood Still*, the **alien on Earth** who is killed while attempting to bring his message of peace to a suspicious **humanity** but is scientifically restored to life to complete his mission. Significantly, Klaatu assumes the name of Mr. Carpenter, referencing Jesus's traditional profession. Not quite a Christ figure, but a significant benefactor, is the **wizard** Gandalf the Grey of J.R.R. Tolkien's *The Lord of the Rings*, who **sacrifices** his life to protect other members of the Fellowship of the Ring before returning to life as the more ethereal Gandalf the White. One might also mention in this context *E.T.: The Extra-Terrestrial*, who seemingly dies when captured by human investigators but later returns to life; *Buffy the Vampire Slayer*, who is twice killed in the course of her television series but is revived to carry on with her heroic deeds (see **Heroes**), and *Superman*, who died in comic books of the 1990s but was eventually revived.

Beings who are reborn may also be **monsters**—like **zombies** brought back to life as mindless slaves by **voodoo magic**, or the Egyptian mummy Kharis (see **Egypt**) of the film *The Mummy's Hand* (1940) and its sequels, revived by tana leaves to menace the world. The rebirth of a monster, however implausibly accomplished, may be a necessary device to generate profitable sequels to popular films; thus, the Universal films that followed the original *Frankenstein* each began with the

Frankenstein monster restored to life, just as Godzilla was reborn in the early sequels to *Godzilla, King of the Monsters*. H. Rider Haggard's sinister *She* periodically employs magical **fires** to restore her **youth**, though the process finally goes horribly wrong and instantly accelerates her through **old age** to **death**.

Today, humans possess one simple technique for restoring life to the apparently deceased—mouth-to-mouth resuscitation—and its use in less advanced **cultures** can make a visitor seem a miracle worker or even a god—which is how Kirk is regarded when he saves a member of a Native American tribe in the *Star Trek* episode, "The Paradise Syndrome" (1968) (see **Native Americans**). However, in Octavia E. Butler's *Kindred*, the time-traveling Dana (see **Time Travel**) is greeted with suspicion and fear when she uses the same method to revive the nineteenth-century child who is her distant ancestor.

Science fiction routinely assumes that, in the future, there will exist scientific methods to revive dead people, perhaps involving **suspended animation and cryonics**, though the process may not require preparation: in Neil R. Jones's "The Jameson Satellite" (1931), a dead **astronaut** in space is restored to life in the **far future** when advanced **robots** transplant his frozen brain into a robot body, and in Arthur C. Clarke's *3001: The Final Odyssey* (1997), Frank Poole, killed by renegade **computer** HAL in the original *2001: A Space Odyssey*, is found floating in deep space and revived a thousand years later. Cloning represents another way to achieve rebirth (see **Clones**), two examples being Michael Crichton's *Jurassic Park*, wherein scientists use the preserved DNA of **dinosaurs** to bring them back to life, and the film *Alien Resurrection* (1997), in which a cloned Ripley returns to again confront her adversaries (see **Alien**). The most complex scientific revival is that of Mr. Spock in the film *Star Trek III: The Search for Spock* (1984), wherein the regenerative powers of the Genesis Project reanimate his body, while his personality, transferred to McCoy's brain by Vulcan **psychic powers**, is eventually restored to his body in a Vulcan **ritual** (see *Star Trek: The Motion Picture*).

Evolution reveals that species often evolve by retaining juvenile features, the process termed neoteny, which explains why evolved humans of the future may resemble **babies**, with large bald heads balanced on small bodies, suggesting rebirth; a person achieves this state by scientifically accelerated evolution in an episode of *The Outer Limits*, "The Sixth Finger" (1963). But at the conclusion of *2001: A Space Odyssey*, Dave Bowman is literally transformed into an immense baby, the Star Child, a superman with the power to instantly remove all nuclear weapons from the Earth (though this is only revealed in Clarke's novel and its sequels) (see **Nuclear Power; Nuclear War**).

Discussion

Since **nature** itself goes through seasonal **cycles** of **birth**, death, and rebirth, human reawakening, renewal, and rejuvenation can suggest a closeness to **nature** (see **Seasons**), an implicit hopefulness, or attainment of, or **quest** for, a purer transcendental self. Rebirth expresses aspirations to perpetual life but also reflects societal concerns about **technology** and **anxieties** about a monstrous Other or a reprehensible inner self ready to emerge from beneath the surface. As science seemingly progresses toward a literal power to bring the dead back to life, science fiction and fantasy will surely continue to consider the **dream**, and nightmare, of rebirth.

Bibliography

Carl Boem. "Superman." *Journal of the Fantastic in the Arts*, 11 (2001), 236–244.
Carrol Fry. "From Technology to Transcendence." *Extrapolation*, 44, (Fall, 2003), 331–343.
David Hoch. "Mythic Patterns in *2001: A Space Odyssey*." *Journal of Popular Culture*, 4 (Spring, 1971), 961–965.
Constance Markey. "Birth and Rebirth in Current Fantasy Films." *Film Criticism*, 7 (1982), 14–25.
Caroline J. Picart. *The Cinematic Rebirths of Frankenstein*. Westport, CT: Praeger, 2002.
Lane Roth. "Death and Rebirth in *Star Trek 2: The Wrath of Khan*." *Extrapolation*, 28 (Summer, 1987), 159–165.
George Slusser, Gary Westfahl, and Eric S. Rabkin, eds. *Immortal Engines*. Athens: University of Georgia Press, 1996.
Elisabeth Vonarburg. "Birth and Rebirth in Space." *Foundation*, No. 51 (Spring, 1991), 5–28.

—Frances Pheasant-Kelly

RECURSIVENESS

■

See Metafiction and Recursiveness

REINCARNATION

■

Overview

According to Hinduism, every living creature is reborn after **death** in the body of another creature, higher or lower in the hierarchy of life, according to how well they behaved in their previous lives; one's goal is to reach the highest level of **humanity**, the Brahmin caste, before ascending further to the ultimate state of nirvana. Many people in western **cultures** have embraced the concept of reincarnation without the Hindu element of spiritual advancement, sometimes claiming to recall experiences from their own earlier lives; the now-discredited case of Virginia Tighe—a woman who under **hypnosis** purportedly described her previous existence as a nineteenth-century woman named Bridey Murphy—popularized the idea in the 1950s. Other forms of **rebirth** in science fiction and fantasy are discussed elsewhere.

Survey

Stories about reincarnation often embody the themes of **love** and **destiny**. Reincarnation may provide the opportunity for past lovers to reunite when one or both come back to life in new bodies: in H. Rider Haggard's *She*, Ayesha is drawn to Leo Vincey because he is the reincarnation of her ancient lover; in **horror** stories about reanimated Egyptian mummies (see **Egypt**), beginning with *The Mummy* (1932), the mummy typically seeks out a modern woman who is the reincarnation of his beloved; and the film *The Curse of the Faceless Man* (1958) tells a similar story about a revenant from the buried Roman city of Pompeii. In Nell Gavin's *Threads: The Reincarnation of Anne Boleyn* (2002), the reincarnations of Henry VIII and Anne Boleyn meet in modern times and reexamine their experiences in Renaissance England and other past lives. A more complex love story involving reincarnation is an episode of ***The Twilight Zone***, "Her Pilgrim Soul" (1985), which author Alan Brennert adapted as a story in 1989: a **scientist** encounters a beautiful woman who rapidly ages from infancy to adulthood in a holographic projection; she eventually reveals that she is his wife from a previous life who died in childbirth and has returned in this form to grow old with him and thus ease his lingering **pain** about her loss.

People may also discover that they are the reincarnations of ancient **heroes** and, hence, are destined to achieve greatness themselves. Edwin L. Arnold's *Phra the Phoenician* (1890) involves a Phoenician from Egypt's glorious past who is continually reborn through **history** as a capable warrior. In Steve Lawhead's *Avalon: The Return of King Arthur* (1999), a modern man learns that he is the reincarnation of legendary King **Arthur**. In the film *The Swordsman* (1992), a contemporary **detective** learns that he is the reincarnation of a Greek warrior and companion of Alexander the Great. Thomas Covenant of Stephen R. Donaldson's ***Lord Foul's Bane*** and its sequels is welcomed in the Land as the reincarnation of a renowned hero. Katherine Kerr's Devenny series, beginning with *Daggerspell* (1996), involves a **wizard** who is continually reincarnated to assist other reincarnated colleagues, while Julie D'Arcy's *Time of the Wolf* (1999) features a woman who discovers that she is the reincarnation of a warrior's wife.

Of course, not only heroes, but **villains** may be reincarnated: in Max Ehrlich's *The Reincarnation of Peter Proud* (1974), filmed in 1974, a professor slowly realizes that he is the reincarnation of a murderer, and in Anne Stuart's *Break the Night* (1996), Jack the Ripper is reincarnated to terrorize the streets of twentieth-century Los Angeles.

Reincarnation may also be a device to tell stories about the distant past or the **far future**. Jack London's *Before Adam* (1906) and Haggard's *Allan and the Ice Gods* (1927) involve contemporary men who recall the experiences of ancestors who lived in prehistoric times (see **Prehistoric Fiction**), while in William Hope Hodgson's *The Night Land* (1912) and Jack Williamson's *After World's End* (1939), present-day men mentally inhabit the bodies of their heroic reincarnations in the future.

Science fiction rarely takes reincarnation seriously, though the hero of Robert A. Heinlein's *Beyond This Horizon* (1948), seeking answers to life's ultimate questions, eventually comes to believe in reincarnation, regarding his son as the reincarnation of a great thinker. And in Andrew J. Offutt's "Population Implosion" (1967), people begin dying early for no apparent reason because there are only a finite number of endlessly recycled souls, all of them now being used in an overpopulated **Earth**, so one person must die every time a new **baby** is born (see **Birth; Overpopulation**).

In films and television, reincarnation may be played for laughs: in *Defending Your Life* (1991), souls awaiting reassignment to either another life on Earth or passage to a higher plane of existence can visit Shirley MacLaine's "Past Lives Pavillion" to find out about their previous lives; the hapless hero learns that he has always been a bumbler and a coward. In the series *My Mother, the Car* (1965–1966), a man is bedeviled by his dead **mother**, who returned to life as his antique car, and in the film *Oh, Heavenly Dog!* (1980), a detective returns to life as an adorable **dog**, still intent upon solving his case.

Discussion

It is easy to understand why the concept of reincarnation is appealing: not only does it promise an afterlife, eliminating fears of death, but it offers an endless series of new lives in comfortably familiar environments, not a distant **Heaven** or astral plane. In Arthur C. Clarke's *The City and the Stars* (1956), future scientists, seeking an ideal human condition, developed a system of reincarnation: people are periodically reborn, first enjoying **youth** as apparently new beings but later remembering previous existences. This process, it is suggested, is more interesting and satisfying than the constant, unchanging life of immortals (see **Immortality and Longevity**). Might this have been the Creator's intent?

Bibliography

P.B. Ellis. *H. Rider Haggard*. London: Routledge & Kegan Paul, 1978.

Andrew Gordon. "Play It Again, Sam." Gary Westfahl, George Slusser, and David Leiby, eds., *Worlds Enough and Time*. Westport, CT: Greenwood Press, 2002. 139–148.

Lieselotte E. Kurth-Voigt. *Continued Existence, Reincarnation, and the Power of Sympathy in Classical Weimar*. New York: Camden House, 1999.

Lynn Kear. *Reincarnation*. Westport, CT: Greenwood Press, 1996.

Constance Markey. "Birth and Rebirth in Current Fantasy Films." *Film Criticism*, 7 (Fall, 1982), 14–25.

Gloria S. Melendez. "Reincarnation and Metempsychosis in Amado Nervo's Fiction of Fantasy." Michael Collings, ed., *Reflections on the Fantastic*. Westport, CT: Greenwood Press, 1986, 41–50.

Catherine Storr. "H. Rider Haggard's *She*." *Children's Literature In Education*, 22 (September, 1991), 161–168.

Gary Westfahl. "Zen and the Art of Mario Maintenance." George Slusser, Gary Westfahl, and Eric S. Rabkin, eds., *Immortal Engines*. Athens: University of Georgia Press, 1996, 211–220.

—Gary Westfahl

RELIGION

Religion is but the most ancient and honorable way in which men have striven to make sense out of God's universe.

—Frank Herbert
Dune (1965)

Overview

Religion is seminal to human existence. In science fiction and fantasy, it can be utilized as polemic, providing a tale's underlying metaphor. Religion may also be seen as antithetical to worlds of fantasy or scientific drives to truth. Often, it is a key component of richly crafted **imaginary worlds**. The religions of **Christianity, Islam,** and **Judaism** are discussed elsewhere.

Survey

In western literature, debates about and uses of religion almost invariably involve Christianity in some fashion, although there are works rooted in other traditions, including Greek **mythology** (see *Jason and the Argonauts; Hercules: The Legendary Journeys; Xena: Warrior Princess*), Hinduism (see Roger Zelazny's *Lord of Light*), Egyptian mythology (Zelazny's *Creatures of Light and Darkness* [1969]) (see **Egypt**), and Buddhism (Hermann Hesse's *Siddhartha* [1922]).

Science fiction and Christian apologetics are mirrored in C.S. Lewis's *Out of the Silent Planet*, a tale of an Earthman kidnapped by unethical **scientists** as a **sacrifice** for Martians incapable of understanding such an offering (see **Mars**). Here, other worlds of our **Sun** are in constant contact while Earth, the only fallen planet, is silent. Lewis's fantasy series, begun with *The Lion, the Witch and the Wardrobe*, recasts the crucifixion of Christ in the form of the lion Aslan, slain by a wicked **witch** as surrogate for a young boy's obligation. Conversely, Philip Pullman's His Dark Materials trilogy, beginning with *The Golden Compass* (1995), is purposeful propaganda for the other side.

Walter M. Miller, Jr.'s *A Canticle for Leibowitz* presents a special order of the Catholic Church, charged with the task of preserving the remnants of human **knowledge** after a nuclear **apocalypse**. The novel traces the order's mission to its cynical conclusion, presenting a struggle to safeguard a **secret history** and **knowledge** for a **humanity** ultimately undeserving, doomed by its own impulses. The novel owes much to the end of the world scenario of Mary Shelley's *The Last Man*.

Sometimes, science fiction and religion are seen as antithetical. One tenet of the *Star Trek* series, conveyed in episodes like "Who Mourns for Adonais?" (1967) and "The Apple" (1967), was that religion is a primitive superstition that humanity must outgrow to achieve lasting peace and prosperity. In that worldview, the logical, atheist Vulcan race served as wiser role models for comparatively immature humans. Despite this, the series *Star Trek: Deep Space Nine* reintroduced religion when the atheist Federation found their far outpost hosted by a race of ancestor-worshippers. This was further complicated when the station's captain was revealed as a **messiah** of this alien race, with the divided loyalties such a situation necessitated.

In fantasy, the magical nature of the world is frequently under threat from organized religion, as is clearly presented in Marion Zimmer Bradley's *The Mists of Avalon*, wherein Bradley employs goddess worship to reinterpret the Arthurian legend apart from the patriarchal Christianity of earlier versions (see **Arthur**). Pagan **magic** also dwindles when Christianity emerges in Tom Robbins's *Jitterbug Perfume* (1984) and Neil Gaiman's *American Gods* (2001).

Sometimes, a character or society's particular religious convictions provide metaphors for understanding a phenomenon that is otherwise beyond human comprehension. In William Gibson's *Count Zero* (1986) (see **Neuromancer**), a fractured artificial intelligence seeks sympathetic alliances and finds in the practitioners of **voodoo** a population prepared to relate to it according to its needs. Other times, a science fiction element in a story gives rise to circumstances later granted a religious (mis)interpretation. The **aliens on Earth** in Arthur C. Clarke's *Childhood's End* are revealed by their demonic appearance to have been the instigators in human pre-history of religious notions of **Satan** (see **Demons**). A single instance of **time travel** in *Babylon 5* gives the Minbari race the mysterious Valen, their chief religious figure and founder of the monastic, military order known as the Rangers, who later play a crucial role in the galaxy's climactic war against dark forces (see **Space Wars**).

Writers frequently extrapolate entirely new religions for the (often alien) inhabitants of other times and places. In Robert A. Heinlein's *Stranger in a Strange Land*, an alien **philosophy** provides the basis for a new religious movement on Earth, essentially a revival of Dionysian **love** cults. The *Star Wars* series welded a western tale of good versus evil with eastern philosophical notions of **yin and yang**. Meanwhile, one of the most sophisticated treatments of the power of belief was presented in Frank Herbert's *Dune*, which describes a religion—originally manufactured as a means of population suppression—becoming fulfilled and thus a powerful tiger by the tail that reaches back to control its controllers.

Discussion

Religion parallels science as a means by which humans explore the nature of our existence. As a source of comfort and reassurance, religion unsurprisingly has had an often-combative relationship with the ever-evolving field of science and, more recently, with science fiction. In presenting a world in which the moral laws are anchored to natural ones, religion shares an affinity with much of fantasy. Sometimes, this is expressed in the outgrowth of magical epics from religious themes, as in the work of Lewis and J.R.R. Tolkien. At other times, the fantasy impulse supplants the religious one, with religious institutions depicted as being antithetical to magical realms and wonders. Finally, as an outgrowth of the basic human drive to ask the question "Why?" it is only natural to conjecture that this staple of human existence should be a staple of nonhuman, pre-human, and future human existence as well.

Bibliography

John Allan. *The Gospel According to Science Fiction*. London: Falcon, 1975.

Mike Alsford. *What If? Religious Themes in Science Fiction*. London: Darton, Longman, Todd, 2000.

Norman Beswick. "Glimpses of Ecclesiastical Space." *Foundation*, No. 53 (Autumn, 1991), 24–36.

Robert Galbreath. "Fantastic Literature as Gnosis." *Extrapolation*, 29 (Winter, 1988), 330–337.

Andrew Greeley. *God in Popular Culture*. Chicago: Thomas More, 1988.

J.N. King. "Theology, Science Fiction, and Man's Future." Thomas D. Clareson, ed., *Many Futures, Many Worlds*. Kent, OH: Kent State University Press, 1977, 237–259.

Frederick A. Kreuziger. *Apocalypse and Science Fiction*. Chico, CA: Scholars Press, 1982.

C.S. Lewis. "Religion and Rocketry." Lewis, *The World's Last Night and Other Essays*. New York: Harcourt, 1960, 83–92.

—Lou Anders

RESPONSIBILITY

■

See Guilt and Responsibility

REVENGE

■

Overview

Revenge is a central theme in western literature, giving shape and life to foundational literary characters. Revenge has had particular appeal for fantasy, science fiction, and **horror** writers as a desire that is inescapably human but also potentially monstrous. The revenge narrative is thus particularly adaptable to literary investigations of boundaries between the human and inhuman and between **civilization** and barbarism (see **Barbarians**).

Survey

The negative consequences of vengeance are emphasized in ancient works derived from Greek **mythology**. A key text is Aeschylus's trilogy of plays, the Oresteia: *Agamemnon, The Libation Bearers*, and *The Eumenides* (all 458 BCE). Angry because he sacrificed their daughter to launch the Trojan War, Clytemnestra murders her husband Agamemnon upon his return; their son Orestes then kills Clytemnestra, though this matricide causes him to be tormented by vengeful Furies; but Athena, goddess of **wisdom**, intervenes to spare Orestes in a decision reached by trial, signalling the need to replace individual acts of vengeance with systems of justice.

In the centuries that follow, people who sought revenge were primarily **villains**. In the **Arthur** legends, the illegitimate son of King Arthur, Mordred, seeks revenge for his illegitimacy by inciting civil **war** in Britain and precipitating the destruction of Camelot. John Milton's *Paradise Lost* (1667) casts **Satan** as an avenging antihero who seeks retribution against the just God who cast him out of **Heaven**. Milton gives us a Satan whose vengeful desires, while momentarily compelling, are inextricably linked to pride, chief of the seven deadly **sins**. Milton's Christian perspective (see **Christianity**) provides another reason for believing that revenge serves only the self, not the common good. A more recent example of the exiled avenger narrative is *Star Trek II: The Wrath of Khan* (see *Star Trek: The Motion Picture*). Khan is a latter-day Satan seeking to exact revenge by hunting down and punishing Kirk, whom Khan blames for his **exile** and the **death** of his wife. Significantly, the original *Star Trek* episode that introduced Khan, "Space Seed" (1967), featured a quotation from *Paradise Lost*, and in the film, a copy of *Paradise Lost* is seen on Khan's bookshelf.

Another recurring figure is the good person whose overpowering desire for revenge results in **madness**. In Alexander Dumas's *The Count of Monte Cristo* (1844), Edmond Dantes plots elaborate revenge against those who imprisoned him, but revenge makes him dark and obsessive, leading to doubt, remorse, and serious questions about whether the end justifies the means. Alfred Bester's *The Stars My Destination* puts a science fiction spin on Dumas's novel, with Gully Foyle using his desire for revenge against the spaceship that would not stop to save him as motivation for surviving and making himself one of the world's most powerful men. Sympathy for Foyle erodes, however, as his **quest** for revenge leads to megalomania and narcissism and ultimately threatens the world's safety. The film *Memento* (2000) dramatically depicts the dehumanizing effects of revenge, as the sympathetic hero is radically transformed by vengeful desires from a noble truth-seeker into a *de facto* serial killer.

Even the heroic Batman (see **Heroes**), who becomes a righteous "avenger of evil" in response to his parents' murders, is occasionally overcome by dark, nihilistic, and even criminal impulses brought on by the primal desire for revenge, as explored in Frank Miller's graphic novel *Batman: The Dark Knight Returns* (1986) and the film *Batman*. Still, he remains sympathetic, as does the protagonist of Stephen King's *Carrie* (1974), filmed in 1976: the focus here is the revenge of the outcast, as a persecuted teenager with **psychic powers** unleashes supernatural vengeance on those who wronged her.

In science fiction, seeking revenge can seem justifiable in response to scientific transgressions of **nature**'s laws. In Mary Shelley's **Frankenstein**, Frankenstein's **monster** goes on a vengeful rampage after being denied a mate, ultimately killing Frankenstein's own fiancée. Frank Herbert picks up this theme: in *The Dosadi Experiment* (1977), a human–alien people are subjects of a cruel experiment in forced **evolution** that results in their becoming powerful, escaping, and avenging themselves on their creators and the galaxy; and in *The White Plague* (1982), a **scientist** seeking to avenge the death of his **family** unleashes a genetically modified virus against countries he holds responsible, but the plague does not recognize national boundaries and threatens to spread worldwide. The films *The Toxic Avenger* (1985) and *Robocop* (1987) respectively feature a mutant and **cyborg** who exact revenge on those responsible for their transformations (see **Mutation**).

Villainous, despicable revenge has remained the norm in **horror** films. Monsters like Jason of *Friday the 13th* (1980) and its sequels, and Freddy Krueger of *Nightmare of Elm Street* (1984) and its sequels, were first motivated by a desire for revenge, as were serial killers in *Scream* (1996) and *I Know What You Did Last Summer* (1997).

Discussion

The primal force of the desire for revenge can reveal certain aspects of a character's **identity**, or human nature in general. The way that revenge threatens or alters the avenger's personality is evidenced by the prevalence of anonymity (or pseudonymity) as a motif in revenge narratives. In Jules Verne's **20,000 Leagues under the Sea**, the mysteriously vengeful Captain Nemo, revealed as an Indian prince in *The Mysterious Island* (1875), chooses an alias that in Latin means "no one"; Edmond Dantes and Gully Foyle take on new **names**; and Batman struggles to conceal his real name. Part of this name-hiding is strategic, but symbolically it represents the powerful capacity of the quest for revenge to overcome and change the very nature of the avenger.

Bibliography

Carol J. Clover. *Men, Women, and Chainsaws*. Princeton: Princeton University Press, 1992.

Laura Grindstaff. "Sometimes Being a Bitch Is All a Woman Has to Hold on To." Martha McCaughey and Neal King, eds., *Reel Knockouts*. Austin: University of Texas Press, 2001, 147–171.

Bengt af Klintberg. "Why Are So Many Modern Legends about Revenge?" Gillian Bennett and Paul Smith, eds., *Contemporary Legend*. New York: Garland, 1996, 261–266.

Michael M. Levy. "*The Duchess of Malfi* Revisited." *Extrapolation*, 43 (Winter, 2002), 456–464.

Jeffrie G. Murphy. *Getting Even*. Oxford: Oxford University Press, 2003.

Annie Nocenti. "Christopher Nolan's Revenge Redux." *Independent Film and Video Monthly*, 24 (2001), 32–35.

Jin Sunwoo. "Cycle of Revenge in John Milton's Major Poems." *Milton Studies*, 12 (2002), 103–122.

David S. Werman. "Edgar Allan Poe, James Ensor, and the Psychology of Revenge." *The Annual of Psychoanalysis*, 21 (1993), 301–314.

—*Michael Sharp*

RIDDLES

Overview

The tradition of riddling questions with tricky or impossible answers has roots in **mythology** and **fairy tales**, and regularly reappears in genre fantasy. Hard questions in science fiction generally involve universal principles, not the classic riddle's specific allusiveness, wordplay (see **Language and Linguistics**), or concealment of **names**.

Survey

The riddle of the Sphinx from the Oedipus story is frequently re-examined. "What goes on four legs in the morning, two legs at noon, and three legs in the evening?" The answer is "man." Terry Pratchett subjects this metaphorical timescale to critical analysis in *Pyramids* (1989) (see *The Colour of Magic*). John Sladek reduces the answer to **absurdity** in "One Damned Thing after Another . . ." (1973). The **hero** of Piers Anthony's *A Spell for Chameleon*, transformed into a sphinx, is impelled to ask its riddle—which goes unanswered for fear that, like the Sphinx, he will commit **suicide**. John Barnes's metafictional *One for the Morning Glory* (1996) complicates the riddle, observing that "the answer is always yourself."

In **fairy tales** like "Rumpelstiltskin" or "Tom Tit Tot," the impossible task of guessing the eponymous riddler's name is traditionally solved by eavesdropping while he gloats. The similar riddle of the Master Doorkeeper, who guards the **threshold** in Ursula K. Le Guin's *A Wizard of Earthsea*, baffles overly subtle applicants who fail to simply *ask* for his name. That this should be freely given is unexpected, because the name grants power over the person. **Courage** and trust are required to answer the Doorkeeper's second "riddle," in which he asks newly graduated **wizards** to reveal *their* names.

Tolkien's riddle-game in *The Hobbit* draws on traditional sources like the Norse Sagas, nursery rhymes and the Anglo-Saxon *Exeter Book* (c. 975–1000); it nods to the Sphinx with a different "legs" riddle. Bilbo's unanswerable question "What have I got in my pockets?" echoes Odin's trick, in the *Elder Edda* (c. 1090), of demanding an answer that only Odin can know.

In *Alice's Adventures in Wonderland*, the Mad Hatter's riddle "Why is a raven like a writing desk?" has no obvious answer, though Lewis Carroll later devised one. **Children**'s nonsense riddles baffle a **giant** in Poul Anderson's *Three Hearts and Three Lions* (1961). The simple **poetry** and gestures of childish folklore in Barry Hughart's *Bridge of Birds* (1984) (see **China**) are riddles holding keys to ancient **mysteries**. Other fantasy predictions may be couched in riddle form, requiring careful interpretation (see **Divination**).

A darker riddle-game counterpoints a duel of electronic **weaponry** in Michael Swanwick's *The Iron Dragon's Daughter* (1993). Pamela Dean's *Juniper, Gentian and Rosemary* (1998) features a character who may be **Satan** in **disguise** and who—as though under a **curse** against speaking truly or informatively—speaks in riddles and quotations.

Mentors and other authority figures often test rivals or pupils with riddles. Merlin requires Ransom in C.S. Lewis's *That Hideous Strength* (1945) (see *Out of the Silent Planet*) to prove himself thus. Children must do the same in Susan Cooper's *The Grey King* (1975), where "What is the shore that fears the sea?" is punningly answered as beech, a wood easily damaged by salt water.

Riddle-gaming is elevated into a ramified academic discipline with its own college (see **Education**) in Patricia McKillip's Riddle-Master trilogy, beginning with *The Riddle-Master of Hed* (1976). The scholarly principle that one should always "answer the unanswered riddle" (normally by research), and infer its "stricture" or moral, becomes literally deadly as the hero confronts a clutch of riddles that are keys to **magic** and a transformation of the world.

In film, the Bridge of Death sequence in *Monty Python and the Holy Grail* (1975) spoofs the traditional fantasy need to answer riddles before passing a threshold. The Riddler is one of *Batman*'s long-established foes, constantly challenging him with tricky **puzzles**.

More science-fictionally, the heroine of Anne McCaffrey's *Dragonflight*, after **time travel** into the past, commissions the riddling "Question Song" whose answers she already unravelled four hundred years hence. One round of competitive **games** in Piers Anthony's *Blue Adept* (1981) requires the hero to swap riddles in **mathematics** with an alien opponent. A riddling description that allows various interpretations conceals the galactic location of the Second Foundation in Isaac Asimov's *Foundation* series.

Discussion

Some riddling questions are inherently unanswerable or, as in John Brunner's *The Traveler in Black* (1971), cannot even be formulated. Paradoxes and self-referential statements—like Epimenides the Cretan's "All Cretans are liars"—highlight the limits of reason and logic, and are traditionally employed in science fiction to baffle and disable troublesome **computers**. However, the supposed paradoxes of Louise Cooper's fantasy *The Book of Paradox* (1973) are mere verbal quibbles resembling children's catch-question riddles.

In Zen **philosophy**, a conceptual leap to insight is sought through riddling "koans" ("What is the sound of one hand clapping?") which have no logical answer and are intended to "break the mind of logic." Rudy Rucker's *White Light* (1980) suggests that comprehending the riddles of infinity requires stepping outside logic and mathematics into the white light of transcendence. In *Star Wars* terms, the message is to close your eyes and use the Force.

Bibliography

Douglas A. Anderson, ed. *The Annotated Hobbit*, by J.R.R. Tolkien. London: Unwin Hyman, 1988.

Mark Bryant. *Riddles*. New York: Peter Bedrick, 1984.

Kevin Crossley-Holland, trans. and ed. *The Exeter Riddle Book*. London: The Folio Society, 1978.

Bob Garcia. "Batman: The Riddler." *Cinefantastique*, 24/25 (February, 1994), 15–16.

Patrick Hughes and George Brecht. *Vicious Circles and Infinity*. London: Jonathan Cape, 1976.

Francis Huxley. *The Raven and the Writing Desk*. London: Thames and Hudson, 1976.

Gwendolyn A. Morgan. "Dualism and Mirror Imagery in Anglo-Saxon Riddles." *Journal of the Fantastic in the Arts*, 5 (1992), 74–85.

Iona and Peter Opie. *The Oxford Dictionary of Nursery Rhymes*. New York: Oxford University Press, 1951.

Archer Taylor. *English Riddles from Oral Tradition*. Berkeley and Los Angeles: University of California Press, 1951.

—*David Langford*

RINGS

∎

> *He had some wits, as well as luck and a magic ring—and all three are very useful possessions.*
>
> —J.R.R. Tolkien
> *The Hobbit* (1937)

Overview

The **magic** ring—conferring powers like **invisibility** (see J.R.R. Tolkien's *The Hobbit*) or, as is supposedly the case with the Ring of King Solomon, the ability to understand the speech of animals—is a staple of folklore and fantasy. As a symbol of the linkages of **eternity** (the circle), commitment (the exchange of rings in **marriage**), or power (the rings traditionally worn by popes and prelates), the ring lends itself to emblematic use in fiction. In the physical world, rings of stones, so-called "fairy rings" of fungal growth, and other physical manifestations like planetary "rings" and artificial structures like Larry Niven's *Ringworld* (1970), exemplify the numinous power of the ring or circle, although rings are only one class of the many **magical objects**.

Survey

Rings offer status and talismanic protection in numerous medieval **romances**, and these uses shift easily into **fairy tales** and fantasy. One striking example of the ring in folklore is the "Ring of the Nibelung," the subject of legends dramatized in opera by Richard Wagner. Forged by the **dwarf** Alberich, the ring confers limitless power upon its owner. Tom Holt spoofs Wagnerian themes in *Expecting Someone Taller* (1987) where the Ring falls into the possession of the hapless Malcolm. The ring Bilbo discovers in *The Hobbit* turns out to be the "One Ring," the focus of Sauron's power over men, dwarfs, and **elves**, in Tolkien's *The Lord of the Rings*. By destroying it, Frodo can eliminate the Dark Lord, but he also runs the risk of being corrupted by it, as was Gollum. The Ring is attractive on several levels: it is beautiful, it gives supernatural power, and its soul-destroying bondage to a greater **evil** is masked by fantasies of being able to combat and replace the current "Dark Lord." More than a mere "magic ring" it is a Faustian symbol of power, greed, and obsession.

The rings devised by Uncle Andrew in C.S. Lewis's *The Magician's Nephew* (1955) (see *The Lion, the Witch and the Wardrobe*) allow magical travel into **parallel worlds**, including Narnia. Stone circles are sometimes portals from one **dimension** into another, or locations of **sacrifices** to summon **demons** or deities, used as such in the *Doctor Who* episode "The Stones of Blood" (1978). The fourth Quatermass series, *Quatermass* (1979) (see *The Quatermass Experiment*), sees a stone circle as the focus of destructive alien energy. H.P. Lovecraft features stone circles as locations for unholy **rituals** in stories like "The Dunwich Horror" (1929) and *The Lurker at the Threshold* (1945), the latter co-authored by August Derleth. Terry Pratchett satirizes the theory that megalithic circles like Stonehenge were forms of "astronomical calendars" by having druid-like characters, speaking like Information Technology obsessives, use them as **computers** in *The Light Fantastic* (1986) (see *The Colour of Magic*). A ring of stones bars the portal to a world of inimical elves in his *Lords and Ladies* (1992).

The traditional "magic ring" appears in science-fictional form as the "power rings" used by the almost god-like beings in Michael Moorcock's Dancers at the End of Time series, beginning with *An Alien Heat* (1972), to create anything they desire. The comic book hero Green Lantern also possesses a power ring, given to him by alien Guardians to defend **humanity**. A ring can be a surveillance device: in Piers Anthony and Robert E. Margroff's *The Ring* (1968) rings are attached to criminals, delivering punishments if they transgress (see **Crime and Punishment**).

Planetary rings and "rings" in space bear some of the same symbolism. The rings of Saturn (see **Jupiter and the Outer Planets**) are natural locales for juvenile adventures like Donald A. Wollheim's *The Secret of Saturn's Rings* (1954) and Isaac Asimov's *Lucky Starr and the Rings of Saturn* (1958). Ice from Saturn's rings is towed to **Mars** to water **deserts** in Isaac Asimov's "The Martian Way" (1952). Ice-rings are placed around Earth to capture solar energy in Piers Anthony's *Rings of Ice* (1974); the experiment goes wrong, leading to a **flood**. *Artificial* rings exist, including Niven's immense *Ringworld*, which suggests the power of their creators not only in the "ring" symbolism but also in the implications of the advanced **technology** required to construct them.

Discussion

Rings may appear in fantasy simply as adornment; a symbol of status. Moorcock's Elric wears a ring to show that he is rightful ruler of Melniboné, not an outcast mercenary. Here they reflect fantasy as, simply, *desire*, but fantasy explores desire in a more complex way than wish-fulfilment. Thus, rings may almost have their own personalities, which are untrustworthy. But the natural symbol of the ring is the serpent that eats its own tail: the image of recurring **cycles** that provides the title of E.R. Eddison's *The Worm Ouroboros*. Here is an emblem of **eternity** and that most challenging of science fiction concepts, **time**.

Bibliography

Jessica Cook. "The Lady's 'Blushing' Ring in *Sir Gawain and the Green Knight*." *Review of English Studies*, 49 (1998), 1–8.

Virginia Dabney. "On the Natures and Histories of the Great Rings." Glen Goodknight, ed., *Mythcon I*. Los Angeles: Mythopoeic Society, 1971, 8–10.

David Day. *Tolkien's Ring*. London: HarperCollins, 1994.

James R. Edwards. "Magic Rings in C. S. Lewis and J. R. R. Tolkien." *CSL: The Bulletin of the New York C. S. Lewis Society*, 30 (September, 1999), 1–7.

Flieg Hollander and Jay Freeman. "Cosmology and Ringworld." *Is*, No. 6 (1972), 13–16.

Alison Milbank. "My Precious." Gregory Bassham and Eric Bronson, eds., *The Lord of the Rings and Philosophy*. Chicago: Open Court, 2003, 33–45.

R.E. Morse. "Rings of Power in Plato and Tolkien." *Mythlore*, 7 (Autumn, 1980), 38.

Melanie Rawls, "Rings of Power." *Mythlore*, 11 (Autumn, 1984), 29–32.

—*Andy Sawyer*

RITUALS

Overview

Rituals are structured patterns of behavior normally associated with **religions**, that is, activities designed to worship or placate a deity. However, they may also be a series of actions necessary to achieve some magical outcome (see **Magic**). Most rituals observed in fantasy and science fiction derive from, or are based on, those of **Christianity**, though rituals associated with pagan **mythology**, **Judaism**, and **Islam** may also appear.

Survey

In **horror** fiction, many rituals are associated with worshiping **Satan** such as the Black Mass, a blasphemous parody of the Catholic Mass carried out by **witches** and warlocks, and other elaborate rituals designed to summon **demons**. In Nathaniel

Hawthorne's "Young Goodman Brown" (1835), an idealistic young man is shocked to discover that, at night, the good citizens of his town gather in the **forest** to celebrate **evil** and practice witchcraft. *The Devils of Darkness* (1965) and *The Devil's Rain* (1974) are among the innumerable films featuring sinister Satanic ceremonies. Rituals recalling Christianity also figure in the series *Buffy the Vampire Slayer*, where **vampires** of the brethren of Aurelius function like a religious sect, employing candles, incantations, and an altar in their rituals while drinking **blood** in the manner of Holy Communion.

Sinister rituals may also involve human **sacrifice**, as is attempted by the natives of Kong Island in the film *King Kong*. In *The Wicker Man* (1973), an isolated Scottish **island community**, untouched by modern society, pursues pagan ideals that result in the sacrificial burning of a virgin police officer sent to investigate a child's disappearance. Christopher Marlowe's *Doctor Faustus* (1604) was one of the first to master the rituals necessary to summon a demon, Beelzebub, with tragic results (see **Tragedy**), while in film, one impressive ceremony that brings forth a demon is observed in *The Devil's Bride* (1968).

In opposition to Satan and his minions, there is the official Catholic ritual of exorcism, designed to remove the demons possessing some victim. The most famous exorcism is that in the film *The Exorcist* (1973), based on William Peter Blatty's 1971 novel. Father Karras and Father Merrin perform an exorcism on Regan, a young girl possessed by the Devil; eventually, Karras commands the Devil to leave Regan's body and enter his own in a sacrificial gesture resulting in his **death** (see **Possession**).

Of course, many rituals have pleasant or positive overtones, like baptism or **marriage**. The ritual of being officially knighted by a **king** holding a **sword** is central to legends of King **Arthur**. J.K. Rowling's *Harry Potter and the Sorcerer's Stone* and its sequels are filled with magical variations of traditional rituals associated with British boarding schools (see **Education**). The future world of *Star Trek* retains many traditional rituals, including the honor guard assembled to greet the purported Abraham Lincoln in "The Savage Curtain" (1969) and the solemn space funeral for Mr. Spock in the film *Star Trek II: The Wrath of Khan* (1982) (see *Star Trek: The Motion Picture*). In **alternate histories**, the different nature of the society under consideration can be conveyed with wry **humor** by describing the different sorts of rituals practiced therein; for example, in Esther M. Friesner's *Druid's Blood* (1988), set in a nineteenth-century Britain where magic is part of everyday life, readers enjoy pondering the traditionally prim and proper Queen Victoria following the long-established customs of this alternate **culture** by periodically participating in a public, and scandalous, pagan fertility ritual.

When new societies are formed in a **wilderness**, people must develop their own rituals. In William Golding's *Lord of the Flies*, stranded schoolboys evolve the ritual of formally assembling whenever they hear the blowing of the conch; the bearer of the conch also holds the power to speak at the assembly. This rite of **civilization**, unfortunately, is eventually replaced by another: the ceremony of the pig's slaughter, accompanied by a ritualistic chanting of "kill the pig, cut her throat," ultimately followed by human slaughter. In another *Star Trek* episode, "The Omega Glory" (1967), Kirk finds savages on a backwards planet ritualistically reciting the words of an ancient text; when Kirk reads it himself and discovers that it is the United States Constitution, he realizes that he is in a **parallel world** where the United States was devastated by a **nuclear war**, leading to this primitive **post-holocaust society** held together by ritualistic kinship with a document whose meaning they have forgotten.

Discussion

It is easy to understand why societies and groups develop rituals: they promote bonding and provide reassurance that the universe is an orderly place where proper performance of certain actions will lead to desired results. Still, rituals can also reflect a stubborn determination to cling to tradition, even when changing conditions make that unwise; this is why rituals are often associated with ancient evils and cruel practices (like human and animal sacrifice) that most contemporary people now abhor. All humans need their rituals, then, but they must also recognize that there comes a time when certain rituals should be abandoned.

Bibliography

K.V. Bailey. "Play and Ritual in Science Fiction." *Foundation*, No. 27 (February, 1983), 5–24.

Anna Clemens. "Art, Myth, and Ritual in Le Guin's *The Left Hand of Darkness*." *Canadian Review of American Studies*, 17 (Winter, 1986), 423–436.

Walker Evans. "Monster Movies and Rites of Initiation." *Journal of Popular Film and Television*, 4 (1975), 124–142.

Sharon Russell and James Backes. "The Rites of Passage in Contemporary Vampire Films." C.W. Sullivan III, ed., *The Dark Fantastic*. Westport, CT: Greenwood Press, 1997, 129–136.

Theresa Thompson. "Rituals of Male Violence." Kathleen M. Lant and Theresa Thompson, eds., *Imaging the Worst*. Westport, CT: Greenwood Press, 1998, 47–58.

David Tomas. "Old Rituals for New Space." Michael Benedikt, ed., *Cyberspace: First Steps*. Cambridge: MIT Press, 1991, 31–48.

Louis Tremaine. "Ritual Experience in *Odd John* and *Sirius*." Patrick McCarthy, ed., *The Legacy of Olaf Stapledon*. Westport, CT: Greenwood Press, 1989, 67–86.

J.R. Wytenbroek. "Rites of Passage in *The Hobbit*." *Mythlore*, 13 (Summer, 1987), 5–8, 40.

—*Frances Pheasant-Kelly*

RIVERS

Overview

Natural waterways in real or **imaginary worlds**, rivers figure prominently in fantasy and science fiction as both topographical indications of **landscape** and mythopoeic symbols representing transformation and **rebirth**. The roots of such symbolism lie in various **mythologies** and **religions**, including **Christianity**, as well as works of speculative literature. **Quests** often involve journeys on, across, or to rivers. The possible existence of rivers or canals on **Mars** has long provoked speculation. Related entries include **Flood, Sea Travel, Undersea Adventure,** and **Water**.

Survey

In mythic tradition, rivers sometimes serve as boundaries between realms, like the rivers Styx and Acheron, which in Greek mythology were entrances to the underworld. Roman mythology envisioned the river Lethe flowing through the Paradise of Elysium, whose waters offered forgetfulness for reincarnated souls (see **Memory**). John Milton's *Paradise Lost* (1667) features the river Lethe as a symbol of forgetfulness, indicating a strong, archetypal function of rivers in myth and literature as symbols of rebirth and regeneration. These rivers may play similar roles in more recent depictions of classical underworlds; for example, John Kendrick Bangs's charming account of dead people engaging in amiable conversation during a pleasant afterlife is entitled *A Houseboat on the Styx* (1895). The regenerative symbolism of rivers is manifest in the story of the Greek **hero** Hercules, who harnessed the power of two rivers to clean the filth of the Augean stables in one day. It is also a strong element in the biblical story of Moses, rescued as an infant from the Nile River—a story echoed in Paul K. McAuley's *Child of the River* (1997).

Although rivers may seem insignificant compared to vast seas and oceans, they also suggest immensity and great power—such as "Alph, the sacred river" in Samuel Taylor Coleridge's poem "Kubla Khan" (1797)—so they may appropriately be centerpieces of expansive imaginary landscapes. When Philip José Farmer envisioned an immense world where millions of humans were mysteriously reborn, he named it Riverworld and made an extended river its chief geographical feature; the series' first volume was *To Your Scattered Bodies Go* (1971). Dave Duncan's Seventh Sword trilogy, beginning with *The Reluctant Swordsman* (1988), depicts a world of variable geography where an all-encompassing River randomly transports travelers to different destinations. A river is the defining image of S.P. Somtow's surrealistic Riverrun trilogy (see **Surrealism**), which began with *Riverrun* (1991), involving ordinary humans embroiled in a cosmic struggle for control of the universe ranging across various **parallel worlds**.

In contrast, events on a small scale involving rivers can also be important. In J.R.R. Tolkien's **The Hobbit** and **The Lord of the Rings**, the transformation of an entire world starts with the discovery of the One Ring of Power in the muck of a river bottom, as visualized in the film *The Lord of the Rings: The Return of the King* (2003) (see **The Lord of the Rings: The Fellowship of the Ring**). Octavia E. Butler's **Kindred** begins with a modern-day woman who suddenly travels back in time and saves a distant ancestor from drowning in a river (see **Time Travel**). Rivers may also take adventurers on quests into unknown realms to encounter **monsters**, like the horrific Gill Man lurking in the Amazon River which attacks explorers in *The Creature from the Black Lagoon* (1954).

On **alien worlds**, the presence of rivers would imply the existence of indigenous lifeforms, which is why there is much current interest in possible evidence of dried-up riverbeds on **Mars**. In the late nineteenth century, American astronomer Percival Lowell drew upon observations by Giovanni Schiaparelli to suggest that there were vast networks of canals on Mars, constructed by Martians to transport water across their drought-stricken planet. These speculations, reported in his books *Mars* (1896) and *Mars as the Abode of Life* (1908), influenced innumerable stories about a decadent Martian **civilization** of ancient **cities** (see **Decadence**) linked by canals, with examples including Edgar Rice Burroughs's **A Princess of Mars** and its sequels and

Leigh Brackett's "Queen of the Martian Catacombs" (1949). One of these works, Ray Bradbury's *The Martian Chronicles*, hauntingly concludes with human **children**, told by their **father** that they were going to see Martians, observing their reflections in a Martian canal and realizing that, with the original inhabitants now extinct, they—the human settlers—are now the Martians.

Discussion

Rivers serve multiple functions in speculative literature: as allegorical symbols of regeneration and power, settings for key events and quests, and evidence of life. The ability to travel along a river can also suggest **freedom**, so the absence of rivers conversely suggests confinement. Thus, in *Star Wars*, living on the **desert** planet of Tattoine, Luke Skywalker longs to **escape**; and in *The Empire Strikes Back* (1980), when he travels to another world to be trained as a Jedi Knight, he significantly finds his teacher Yoda himself in a moist swamp. And it is after immersion in this realm of slowly flowing waters that Luke finds himself reborn as a mighty warrior.

Bibliography

Michael Baigent, Richard Lee, and Henry Lincoln. *Holy Blood, Holy Grail*. New York: Delacorte Press, 1982.

Clark A. Brady. "Barsoomian Canals." Brady, *The Burroughs Cyclopedia*. Jefferson, NC: McFarland, 1996, 57–58.

Kerry Dearborn. "The Bridge Over the River Why." *North Wind*, No. 16 (1997), 29–40, 45–46.

W.B. Johnson and Thomas D. Clareson. "The Interplay of Science and Fiction: The Canals of Mars." *Extrapolation*, 5 (May, 1964), 37–39.

Gianni Guadalupi and Alberto Manguel, eds. *The Dictionary of Imaginary Places*. New York: MacMillan 1980.

Anton Polarion and R.E. Prindle. "Tarzan and the River." *Burroughs Bulletin*, No. 53 (Winter, 2003), 13–18; No. 54 (Spring, 2003), 3–9; No. 57 (Winter, 2004), 11–19.

Brian Stableford. "The River Mallory" and "Riverworld." Stableford, *The Dictionary of Science Fiction Places*. New York: Wonderland Press, 1999, 263.

Jesse L. Weston. *From Ritual to Romance*. Cambridge: Cambridge University Press, 1920.

—*Daniel E. Blackston*

ROBOTS

∎

1—A robot may not injure a human being, or, through inaction, allow a human being to come to harm.
2—A robot must obey the orders given it by human beings except where such orders would conflict with the First Law.

3—A robot must protect its own exis-
tence as long as such protection does not
conflict with the First or Second Law.

—Isaac Asimov
I, Robot (1950)

Overview

Mechanical imitations of **humanity** have a persistent fascination, offering the **hubris** of creation without the complexities of **biology**; the child-like joy of seeing **dolls and puppets** come alive; greater dramatic possibilities than sedentary **computers**; and endless scope for **satire** on the human makers they **mirror**. Organic robots resembling humans are discussed as **Androids**, and human/machine hybrids are discussed as **Cyborgs**.

Survey

The first proto-robot was the **giant** brass man Talus, who in Greek **mythology** was forged by the god Hephaestus and defended Crete by heating his body and hugging invaders to death; fearsome robot guards are called taluses in Gene Wolfe's *Nightside the Long Sun* (1993) (see *The Book of the New Sun*). Another early avatar is the **golem**. Automata appear in E.T.A. Hoffmann's "The Sandman" (1817), Edgar Allan Poe's "Maelzel's Chess Player" (1835), Ambrose Bierce's "Moxon's Master" (1899) (see **Chess**), L. Frank Baum's *Ozma of Oz* (1907)—with an animated, axe-wielding metal giant—Gerald Kersh's "The King Who Collected Clocks" (1947), and Philip Pullman's ingeniously metafictional *Clockwork* (1996). The Tin Man in Baum's *The Wonderful Wizard of Oz* is a former human with body parts entirely replaced by metal.

Modern science fiction robots take their name from the Czech word *robota* (indentured laborers), made famous by Karel Capek's 1920 play *R.U.R.—Rossum's Universal Robots*. **Mad scientists** might create **Frankenstein monster** robots, and defective models may be murderous, as in Idris Seabright's blackly comic "Short in the Chest" (1964), but others have been sympathetic, like Eando Binder's Adam Link in the stories collected as *Adam Link: Robot* (1965). Neil R. Jones, beginning with "Time's Mausoleum" (1933), wrote twenty stories about a race of alien robots who put the brain of Professor Jameson's frozen brain into a robot body and roamed the galaxy. Jack Williamson's robot invaders in *The Humanoids* (1949) are so solicitous that they prohibit most human activities for our own good. Clifford D. Simak's robots tend to be perfect servants, like Jenkins in *City*.

Most famously, Isaac Asimov (with assistance from editor John W. Campbell, Jr.) produced the Laws of Robotics governing robots' "positronic brains" in *I, Robot*. The first law prevents robots from killing or injuring humans, overriding lesser rules of obedience and self-preservation. Asimov devised ingenious loopholes and paradoxes in his laws, generating **puzzles** in stories resembling **detective** fiction.

Robot women constitute a subgenre of their own. The false Maria of *Metropolis* was followed by the metal woman of Lester del Rey's "Helen O'Loy" (1938), who makes a perfect wife—a relationship whose darker implications drive *The Stepford*

Wives (1974; remade 2004) and are examined from the robot's viewpoint in Amy Thomson's *Virtual Girl* (1993) (see **Feminism**). The robotized dancer-heroine of C.L. Moore's "No Woman Born" (1944) loves her new, sinuous body but subtly loses **humanity**. Piers Anthony's science-fantasy *Split Infinity* (1980) provides its **wizard** hero with a robot lover.

Famous movie robots include the eight-foot emissary of enforced peace in *The Day the Earth Stood Still* and Robby of *Forbidden Planet*, who was the first robot cult hero, prefiguring the cute droids of *Star Wars*. *The Terminator*, like *Westworld* (1973), reverts to older traditions of implacable robot menaces, while *A.I.: Artificial Intelligence* is more sentimental (see **Children**). Douglas Adams's *The Hitchhiker's Guide to the Galaxy* introduced the hilariously gloomy Marvin the Paranoid Android, another cult figure, like the admirable Kryten in *Red Dwarf*.

As **mirrors** of humanity, robots imitate our vices. The self-admiring Joe of Henry Kuttner's comic *Robots Have No Tails* (1952) exhibits both vanity and sloth. Abner J. Gelula's "Automaton" (1931) lusts for its creator's daughter; more plausibly, John Sladek's sex-crazed robot in "Machine Screw" (1975) commits outrages like raping a Cadillac. Sladek's fascination with robots ranges from the innocent, Candide-like machine of his **satire** *Roderick* (1980) to his genial murderer in *Tik-Tok* (1983), whose "asimov circuits" failed.

Elaborately comic robot **fables** are gathered in Stanislaw Lem's *The Cyberiad* (1965), which derides the plausibility of Asimov's laws. Creaky, malfunctioning, conversationally irritating robots abound in the science fiction of Ron Goulart and Robert Sheckley. This is also true of Philip K. Dick, whose deeper concern is **identity**, the blurring of distinctions between flesh and machine, man and robot, as conveyed in the simple confusion in "Impostor" (1953) and the tortuous **paranoia** of *Do Androids Dream of Electric Sheep?*

Several stories consider self-sustaining robot **evolution**, usually in a posthuman context: examples include James White's *Second Ending* (1962), Stephen Baxter's *Evolution* (2002), and the **far future** scenario of Poul Anderson's "Epilogue" (1962), where machine life has inherited the **Earth**.

Discussion

Classic robots are humanoid, but Anthony Boucher's "Q.U.R." (1943) challenged this **cliché** with "Quimby's Usuform Robots," functionally built and happier for it; such sentient appliances make up the **hive mind** of "Constructs" in China Miéville's *Perdido Street Station*. Robert L. Forward's *The Flight of the Dragonfly* (1984) features "bush robots" branching with ever-smaller manipulators, the whole being endlessly reconfigurable—like A. Merritt's *The Metal Monster* (1946). Robots in Iain M. Banks's *Consider Phlebas* are designed for **flying**: examples include spaceships with AI "Minds," autonomous, sassy "drones," and tiny "knife missiles" (see **Weaponry**). *Doctor Who* has its loved and hated robot **dog**, K-9.

Oddities from Gene Wolfe's *The Book of the New Sun* sequence include a reverse cyborg—a robot partly repaired with flesh—and a hollow robot wearable like armor. Eric Frank Russell's "Mechanistria" (1942) depicts an alien robot **ecology** with a bizarre diversity of design. Overall, the "Q.U.R." **philosophy** seems a better **prediction** than humanoid form.

Bibliography

Isaac Asimov, Martin H. Greenberg, and Charles Waugh, eds. *Robots*. New York: Signet, 1989.

John Cohen. *Human Robots in Myth and Science*. South Brunswick, NJ: Barnes, 1967.

Damon Knight, ed. *The Metal Smile*. New York: Belmont, 1968.

Stanislaw Lem. "Robots in Science Fiction." Thomas D. Clareson, ed., *SF: The Other Side of Realism*. Bowling Green, OH: Bowling Green State University Popular Press, 1971, 307–325.

Donald G. Lloyd. "Renegade Robots and Hard-Wired Heroes." Paul Loukides and Linda K. Fuller, eds., *Beyond the Stars III*. Bowling Green, OH: Bowling Green State University Popular Press, 1993, 216–228.

Noel Perrin. "Robots." George Slusser and Eric S. Rabkin, eds., *Aliens*. Carbondale: Southern Illinois University Press, 1987, 102–112.

Jasia Reichardt. *Robots*. New York: Viking Press, 1978.

Jeff Rovin. *Aliens, Robots, and Spaceships*. New York: Facts on File, 1995.

Sue Short. "The Measure of a Man?" *Extrapolation*, 44 (Summer, 2003), 209–223.

—*David Langford*

ROCKETS

The rocket lay on the launching field, blowing out pink clouds of fire and oven heat. The rocket stood in the cold winter morning, making summer with every breath of its mighty exhausts. The rocket made climates, and summer lay for a brief moment upon the land . . . .

—Ray Bradbury
"Rocket Summer" (1950)

Overview

Observed from the surface of **Earth,** a rocket flying upward with human passengers symbolizes technological **progress** and **escape** from the mundane world, although it is often denigrated as a mere phallic symbol. Further advances in traveling into and through space are discussed under **Space Travel** and **Hyperspace,** while people who make such travel their profession are discussed as **Astronauts.**

Survey

The small rockets first developed in medieval **China** were used as fireworks and **weaponry.** Cyrano de Bergerac, in *The Comical History of the States and Empires of the Moon and Sun* (1687), was apparently the first to envision rockets as a way to travel into space, but during the next two centuries, fictional space flights generally employed versions of balloons or airships (see **Air Travel**). However Jules Verne famously envisioned a gigantic cannon in *From the Earth to the Moon,* as visually replicated in the film *A Trip to the Moon.*

By the early twentienth century, rockets emerged as the best way to reach space in the minds of three advanced thinkers: Konstantin Tsiolkovsky in Russia, Hermann Oberth in Germany, and Robert Goddard in the United States. Tsiolkovsky created rockets only in thinly fictionalized tracts like *Beyond the Planet Earth* (1920) which garnered little attention, though he may have influenced the planned rocket launch that is the focus of activity in Yevgeny Zamiatin's **We**. However, Oberth and Goddard actually built and tested experimental rockets, work that attracted the attention of the young American science fiction community. Hugo Gernsback republished a nonfiction book about rocketry by a colleague of Oberth named Hermann von Noordung, *The Problems of Space Travel*, in his magazine *Science Wonder Stories* in 1929; in 1930, Goddard contributed a brief response to a "Symposium" on the topic "Can Man Free Himself from Gravity?" in the same magazine. The realistic rocket in Fritz Lang's *Woman in the Moon* (1929)—which employed Oberth as its technical advisor and introduced the idea of a backwards numerical "countdown" before a rocket launch—and a similar vehicle in **Things to Come** further established the rocket as the best method to reach outer space.

Around that time, rocketry was also popularized as a possible means of personal human flight (see **Flying**), especially in science fiction aimed at juvenile audiences. Heroes who flew with rockets on their backs included Buck Rogers in his comic strip, the comic-book space hero Adam Strange, and later, the hero of the film *The Rocketeer* (1991), adapted from a graphic novel.

The end of World War II, and nascent space programs in America and Russia, led to a host of science fiction stories that endeavored to realistically portray how humans might construct rockets to carry them into space. Examples include Arthur C. Clarke's *Prelude to Space* (1951), Murray Leinster's *Space Platform* (1954), J. Lloyd Castle's *Satellite E-One* (1954), and Lester del Rey's *Step to the Stars* (1954). The film *Destination Moon* (1950), loosely based on but more plausible than Robert A. Heinlein's juvenile novel *Rocket Ship Galileo* (1947), established a parallel tradition of "documentary" style science fiction films that prominently featured tall, streamlined rockets, held erect by framing structures, that lifted up into the sky; others included *Project Moonbase* (1953), *Riders to the Stars* (1954), *Conquest of Space* (1955), and the television series *Men into Space* (1959–1960). *When Worlds Collide* (1951) visualized the alternate plan of a rocket that accelerates horizontally on a long runway.

While these novels and films focused on hardware, Ray Bradbury considered rockets more poetically in stories like "I, Rocket" (1947), in which a rocket tells its own story. Bradbury's **The Martian Chronicles** includes a charming vignette, "Rocket Summer," describing how the roaring flames from a rocket launch briefly bring warm **weather** to chilly environs. More cynical views of the rocket also emerged: Edmond Hamilton's classic "What's It Like Out There?" (1952) calls a rocketship a "prison-cell that flew," while Judith Merril's "So Proudly We Hail" (1953) describes a rocket ready to be boarded and launched as a "metal dragon" that is "hungering for the living flesh that would feed it this night."

By the 1960s, writers and filmmakers largely abandoned the large monolithic rocketship in favor of the multi-stage rockets being used to launch NASA's astronauts, activity that engendered near-future **technothrillers** borrowing the hardware and ambience of America's space program. Examples include Jeff Sutton's *Apollo at Go* (1963), Martin Caidin's *Marooned* (1964), adapted as a film in 1969, the film

Countdown (1968), and the television movie *Stowaway to the Moon* (1972). Now that rockets capable of carrying humans into space existed, much of the excitement associated with the icon dissipated, since rockets could now figure in realistic portrayals of actual events, like the television movie *Return to Earth* (1976), about Buzz Aldrin's experiences during and after the Apollo 11 mission, and the film *Apollo 13* (1995), about that catastrophic flight. J.G. Ballard waxed eloquent about lifeless landscapes of abandoned rockets and launching pads in *Memories of the Space Age* (1986) and elsewhere, as rockets seemingly evolved into not only everyday symbols of the present but nostalgic relics from the past.

Discussion

While the phrase "rocket science" endures as a synonym for tasks requiring great **intelligence**, one cannot deny that, in literature and life, rockets are no longer important icons in the popular imagination. In the contexts of both current events and the extravagant space vehicles of **Star Trek** and **Star Wars**, the rocket seems oldfashioned, featured prominently only in retro-futures like the **alternate history** 1939 of *Sky Captain and the World of Tomorrow* (2004). Still, perhaps ironically, the icon of the rocketship remains a common symbol for science fiction, retaining a faint aura of futurism and unlimited technological possibilities.

Bibliography

Paul A. Carter. "Rockets to the Moon 1919–1944." *American Studies*, 15 (Spring, 1974), 31–46.

Vincent di Fate and Ian Summers. *Di Fate's Catalog of Science Fiction Hardware*. New York: Workman Publishing, 1980.

Harry Harrison and Malcolm Edwards. *Spacecraft in Fact and Fiction*. New York: Exeter Books, 1979.

Steve Higgins. "Descending on a Point of Flame." *Vector*, No. 85 (January/February, 1978), 13–17.

Patrick Lucanio and Gary Coville. *Smokin' Rockets*. Jefferson, NC: McFarland, 2002.

Robert Malone with J. C. Suares. *Rocketship*. New York: Harper & Row, 1977.

Ron Miller. "Evolution of the Spaceship." *Starlog*, No. 58 (May, 1982), 26–27; No. 59 (June, 1982), 56–57; No. 60 (July, 1982), 54–55.

Ron Miller. *The Dream Machines*. Malabar, FL: Krieger, 1993.

Jeff Rovin. *Aliens, Robots, and Spaceships*. New York: Facts on File, 1995.

—*Gary Westfahl*

ROLE REVERSALS

Overviews

Various sorts of role reversals occur in science fiction and fantasy. The governor and the governed, the hunter and the hunted, parents (see **Mothers; Fathers**) and **children**, men and women—all may switch places with results ranging from the comic to the horrific. These scenarios can be boiled down to one basic sort of reversal—the powerful become the powerless and/or the powerless become the powerful—so stories on this theme, whether humorous or serious, are invariably meditations on the nature of power: Who has it, who does not have it, and how it affects those who do and do not have it.

Survey

By ancient tradition, **carnival** days should involve temporary elevation of a lower-class citizen to a position of power, as observed in Victor Hugo's *The Hunchback of Notre Dame* (1831) and its film adaptations. One favorite theme is the royal person and commoner who resemble each other and hence can trade places, as in Mark Twain's *The Prince and the Pauper* (1881). A variant story line involves the commoner who temporarily impersonates an imprisoned ruler; examples include Anthony Hope Hawkins's **Ruritanian romance** *The Prisoner of Zenda* (1894) and Robert A. Heinlein's *Double Star* (1956), in which an actor named Lorenzo Smythe impersonates (and ultimately becomes the permanent replacement for) an interplanetary political leader (see **Politics**). Also relevant is Philip K. Dick's *Solar Lottery* (1955), about a future society in which random events may suddenly elevate an ordinary citizen to supreme power, making the previous ruler powerless.

Perhaps reflecting guilt about the way that humans treat animals (see **Animals and Zoos**), many stories envision people unhappily placed in the position of animals. In Richard Connell's "The Most Dangerous Game" (1924), people are hunted like animals; a science fiction version is Robert Sheckley's "The Seventh Victim" (1953), about a game played in the future involving assassins pursuing human targets. Martians treat people like animals in Leslie F. Stone's "The Human Pets of Mars" (1936) and an episode of **The Twilight Zone**, "People Are Alike All Over" (1960), where human explorers end up in a Martian zoo (see **Mars**). Kurt Vonnegut, Jr.'s *Slaughterhouse-Five* also depicts a man spending time in an alien zoo. Pierre Boulle's *Planet of the Apes* (1963) and its film adaptations (see *Planet of the Apes*) envision humans as dumb beasts under the thumb of intelligent **apes**. A children's story about people treated like animals is Helen Hill and Violet Maxwell's "How Charley Made Topsy Love Him" (1922), in which a boy learns to treat his **cat** gently by being transported to a world where he is manhandled by a **giant** girl.

F. Anstey's *Vice Versa* (1882) introduced the theme of a boy and his father switching places; a corresponding tale about a mother and daughter is Mary Rodgers's *Freaky Friday* (1972). The 1970s and 1980s saw a flurry of films about children becoming adults and adults becoming children, including adaptations of *Freaky Friday* (1976) (remade in 2003) and *Vice Versa* (1988) (which had been previously filmed in 1947), *Big* (1988), *Eighteen Again!* (1988), and *Young Again* (1986). **Miniaturization** and **enlargement** can have the effect of making children seem like adults and adults seem like children: Gulliver is treated like a child in a land of **giants** in *Gulliver's Travels*, a fate that also afflicts *The Incredible Shrinking Man*; an enlarged Alice can take control of the courtroom in *Alice's Adventures in Wonderland*; and gigantic children become powerful figures in films like *Village of the Giants* (1965) and *Honey, I Blew Up the Kid* (1992).

A tale of men and women exchanging roles is Walter Besant's *The Revolt of Man* (1922), depicting a future in which women rule society and men are trapped in subservient roles; the same scenario is explored in August Anson's *When Woman Reigns* (1938). Alfred Coppel's "Defender of the Faith" (1952) is a dystopian portrayal of a brutal matriarchy in the future (see **Dystopia**). It is noteworthy that feminist **utopias**, while granting women authority, rarely involve subjugating men (see **Feminism**). On a more personal level, men pretending to be women and women pretending to be men are conventions of theatrical farces and film comedies; a related fantasy is Lawrence Watt-Evans and Esther M. Friesner's *Split Heirs* (1993), about a girl brought up as a man and left unaware of her true gender. Thorne Smith's *Turnabout* (1931), about a husband and wife who magically exchange identities, was the basis of a 1979 television series of that name (see **Magic**).

Discussion

As the proverb says, "The grass is always greener on the other side," so it is not surprising that poor people might dream of becoming **kings**, while kings might long for the simple life of commoners—the desires that motivate the switch in *The Prince and the Pauper*. Most of these stories end conservatively, with people returning to their original roles, chastised to discover that their inherited or designated position is the best place to remain. Since science fiction is generally more open to change, some stories predictably argue that people can adapt to and thrive in any role, even one completely opposite to their background and character. Vonnegut's 1966 introduction to *Mother Night* (1961) famously notes that "We are what we pretend to be" in reference to his story about a loyal American who pretends to be a Nazi propagandist and effectively becomes one, just as Heinlein's Smythe first pretends to be, then becomes, an effective politician. In science fiction, role reversals are more likely to become permanent.

Bibliography

D.L. Ashliman. "Symbolic Sex-Role Reversals in the Grimms' Fairy Tales." Jan Hokenson, ed., *Forms of the Fantastic*. Westport, CT: Greenwood Press, 1986, 193–198.

Stephanie Demetrakopoulos. "Feminism, Sex Role Exchanges, and Other Subliminal Fantasies in Bram Stoker's *Dracula*." *Frontiers*, 2 (Fall, 1977), 104–113.

Peter Fitting. "So We All Became Mothers." *Science-Fiction Studies*, 12 (July, 1985), 156–183.

Darby Lewes. "Gender-Bending: Two Role-Reversal Utopias by Nineteenth-Century Women." Monica Elbert, ed., *Separate Spheres No More*. Tuscaloosa: University of Alabama Press, 2000, 158–175.

Daphne Patai. "When Women Rule." *Extrapolation*, 23 (Spring, 1982), 56–69.

Michelle Persell. "It's All Play-Acting." Marc Leeds and Peter J. Reed, eds., *Kurt Vonnegut*. Westport, CT: Greenwood Press, 2000, 39–50.

Batya Weinbaum. "Sex-Role Reversal in the Thirties." *Science-Fiction Studies*, 24 (November, 1997), 471–482.

Batya Weinbaum. "Sex-Role Reversals in *Star Trek*'s Planets of Women as Indices of Second Wave Media Protest." *FemSpec*, 1 (1999), 9–27.

—Gary Westfahl

ROMANCE

———————————————— ∎ ————————————————

I wanted Prester John, and Excalibur held by a moon-white arm out of a silent lake. I wanted to sail with Ulysses and with Tros of Samothrace and eat the lotus in a land that seemed always after-noon. I wanted the feeling of romance and the sense of wonder I had known as a kid. I wanted the world to be what they had promised me it was going to be— instead of the tawdry, lousy, fouled-up mess it is.

—Robert A. Heinlein
Glory Road (1963)

Overview

In the nineteenth century, the term "romance" referred to prose narratives involving unusual events in exotic realms, in contrast to novels, prose narratives about every-day life in familiar settings. For that reason, one early name for science fiction was the "scientific romance," novels occurring in imaginary European principalities were termed **Ruritanian romances**, and one name for **sword and sorcery** adventures on other planets is the "planetary romance." To persons untrained in literary stud-ies, the term is now inextricably associated with **love** stories, particularly the for-mulaic texts aimed at female readers, now known as romance novels.

Survey

Northrop Frye's *Anatomy of Criticism: Four Essays* (1957) argues that there are four basic genres associated with the four **seasons: comedy**, romance, **tragedy**, and irony and **satire**. While comedy involves **youth** overthrowing the old social orders to replace them with better ones, romances feature older protagonists seeking to maintain or restore benevolent social orders already in place. Historically, the term was first associated with medieval narratives about noble **heroes** valiantly battling **evil** forces on an epic scale; examples include *The Song of Roland* (c. 1100), Thomas Malory's *Le Morte d'Arthur* (1485) (see **Arthur**), Ariosto's *Orlando Furioso* (1516), and Edmund Spenser's *The Faerie Queene* (1590, 1596). Ironically, the work in this tradition most familiar to modern readers, Miguel de Cervantes's *Don Quixote* (1605, 1615), was an affectionate **satire** of such epics.

    While the eighteenth century was dominated by the novel, this sort of romance was revived in the nineteenth century by writers like Walter Scott and James Fenimore Cooper, who transplanted the romance to American settings (see **America**). Later, H. Rider Haggard wrote romances about **lost worlds** in **Africa**, although he also told similar tales about ancient Egyptians (*Cleopatra* [1889]) (see **Egypt**), the Vikings (*Eric Brighteyes* [1891]), and the Mayans of Central America (*Heart of the*

World [1895]) (see **Latin America**). Mark Twain was of two minds regarding this revival, writing a respectful novel about Joan of Arc, *Personal Recollections of Joan of Arc* (1896), but also lampooning Arthurian legends in *A Connecticut Yankee in King Arthur's Court*. As stories shifted to imagined pasts rather than historical settings and were infused with **magic**, the **heroic fantasy** was born, one early example being William Morris's *The Well at the World's End* (1896).

As for romance in the other sense, the heroes of science fiction and fantasy often rescue and marry beautiful damsels in distress, or are accompanied by female companions serving as romantic interests. Still, especially in science fiction, the focus of attention is adventure, not romance, with little in the way of passionate love scenes or character development. In the 1920s, Hugo Gernsback editorially campaigned to distinguish his serious, substantive science fiction stories from frivolous love stories in other magazines, and writers generally followed his lead by downplaying romance and foregrounding science and spectacle. Still, there have been memorable romantic stories in science fiction, including Lester del Rey's "Helen O'Loy" (1938), about the love between a man and a self-sacrificing female **robot** (see **Sacrifice**); Leigh Brackett's "The Woman from Altair" (1951), about an alien woman who marries a human and returns with him to **Earth**; and an episode of Robert A. Heinlein's *Time Enough for Love* (1973) (see *The Past Through Tomorrow*) about the **marriage** between the immortal Lazarus Long and a mortal woman, who settle on a **frontier** planet. Episodes of *Star Trek*, including "The Paradise Syndrome" (1968), "This Side of Paradise" (1967), and "For the World Is Hollow, and I Have Touched the Sky" (1968) featured doomed romances between beautiful women and series regulars Kirk, Spock, and McCoy. Love stories are more common in fantasy, including various recountings of the doomed affair between King Arthur's wife Guinevere and Lancelot, like Marion Zimmer Bradley's *The Mists of Avalon*, and the classic **fairy tale**, *Beauty and the Beast*.

Finally, there is one form of romance novel that involves science fiction and fantasy: the **time travel** romance typically involving a woman transported by unspecified means to a glamorous historical setting to be romanced by a handsome rogue. Diana Gabaldon's *Outlander* (1991) and its sequels are the most celebrated examples of the subgenre.

Discussion

Today, with larger numbers of female readers and writers, romance in the modern sense plays a larger role in science fiction and fantasy than it once did, when readers and writers were predominantly male. Still, the romantic elements of greatest significance to these genres arguably harken back to the term's older meaning—the romance of distant lands, **magical objects**, strange beings, and advanced **technology**—since these, unlike well-crafted love stories, are unavailable in other forms of literature.

Bibliography

Lloyd Alexander. "High Fantasy and Heroic Romance." *Horn Book*, 47 (December, 1971), 577–584.

Allienne R. Becker. *The Lost Worlds Romance*. Westport, CT: Greenwood Press, 1992.

D.S. Brewer. "*The Lord of the Rings* as Romance." Mary Salu and Robert T. Farrell, eds., *J.R.R. Tolkien: Scholar and Storyteller*. Ithaca, NY: Cornell University Press, 1979, 249–264.

Patrick R. Burger. *The Political Unconcious of the Fantasy Subgenre of Romance*. Lewiston, NY: Edwin Mellen, 2001.

Amanda Hodgson. *The Romances of William Morris*. Cambridge: Cambridge University Press, 1987.

Kathryn Hume. "Medieval Romance and Science Fiction." *Journal of Popular Culture*, 16 (Summer, 1982), 15–26.

Anne McCaffrey. "Hitch Your Dragon to a Star." Reginald Bretnor, ed., *Science Fiction, Today and Tomorrow*. New York: Harper, 1974, 278–294.

Michael Moorcock. *Wizardry and Wild Romance*. London: Gollancz, 1987.

R.H. Thompson. "Modern Fantasy and Medieval Romance." Roger C. Schlobin, ed., *The Aesthetics of Fantasy Literature and Art*. Notre Dame: University of Notre Dame Press, 1982, 211–225.

—*Gary Westfahl*

RURITANIAN ROMANCE

Overview

A Ruritanian romance involves adventure, **romance**, and occasional social criticism in an imaginary European principality, usually featuring a British or American visitor who hobnobs with royalty (see **Kings; Queens**) and takes part in political intrigues (see **Politics**). The subgenre is named after Ruritania, the setting of the novel which established its conventions: Anthony Hope Hawkins's *The Prisoner of Zenda* (1894). Stories involving actual European countries are discussed under **Europe**.

Survey

The Ruritanian romance might be regarded as a transformation of the **lost worlds** story, since it also features outsiders who penetrate unknown areas, battle hostile hierarchies, and sometimes marry princesses. However, there is an air of comforting familiarity, even domesticity, in the genre's settings and characters, engendering the atmosphere of a mimetic society novel. At its heyday, then, the Ruritanian romance was a story that could appeal to readers of both H. Rider Haggard and Anthony Trollope.

The prototypical *The Prisoner of Zenda* involves Rudolph Rassendyll, an Englishman with connections to lesser nobility, who ventures into Ruritania, a small kingdom somewhere south of Saxony. Rassendyll, because of an ancestor's amorous affairs, looks exactly like the King of Ruritania, so he takes the place of the king during a crisis and foil the plans of a villainous usurper (see **Villains**). Although he and the princess fall in love, Rudolph makes a noble renunciation. The adventures consist of swordplay, pistol fights, and midnight rides in locales like **castles**, moats, and dungeons.

The Prisoner of Zenda was enormously popular, inspiring stage and screen adaptations, and remains in print today. Hawkins wrote other novels of this sort, including the sequel *Rupert of Hentzau* (1898) and *The Heart of Princess Osra* (1896), and other writers followed in his footsteps, including Harold McGrath (*Arms and the Women* [1898]) and Winston Churchill (*Savrola* [1900]); Bret Harte considered the novel worthy of a devastating parody, "Rupert the Resembler" (1902).

However, Hawkins's most prominent successor was George Barr McCutcheon, who wrote six novels set in Graustark, a principality somewhere between **Russia** and Austria. In the first, *Graustark* (1901), Grenfall Lorry, an American playboy who is infatuated with a beautiful woman he meets in Denver, follows her to Graustark, where he learns that she is Yetive, princess of the land. Lorry and a friend save the realm politically and economically, and Lorry weds Yetive. Here the same trinity of ideas holds as in Ruritania: romance, **sword**-and-cloak adventure, and conservative social thought. In later novels other characters enter after Lorry and Yetive die in an **automobile** accident.

Another noteworthy example of the form, Edgar Rice Burroughs's *The Mad King* (1926), follows Hope's precedent more closely: Barney Custer is a gentleman farmer from Nebraska whose mother was a runaway princess from Lotha, a kingdom squeezed in among Russia, Serbia, and Austria. On visiting Lotha, Barney rescues beautiful Princess Emma and impersonates King Leopold, who is not really mad, only nasty. The king is eventually killed, and Barney, who has royal blood, becomes king and marries the princess.

After World War I, the Ruritanian romance became less popular, but examples still appeared, like John Buchan's *The House of the Four Winds* (1935). However, a crucial shift occurred: whereas previous Ruritanian romances were entirely in earnest, later works were humorous, even satirical (see **Humor; Satire**). There is a sardonic tone, for example, in Dashiell Hammett's "This King Business" (1928), wherein a **detective** becomes kingmaker in Steffania, a small state near Serbia. Even more farcical was the film *Duck Soup* (1933), featuring Groucho Marx's Rufus T. Firefly as the unlikely prime minister of the principality of Freedonia. Peter Ustinov's play *Romanoff and Juliet* (1957), filmed in 1961, comically recasts the Romeo and Juliet story as the romance of a Russian man and American girl in the tiny country of Concordia. And in Leonard Wibberley's *The Mouse That Roared* (1955), filmed in 1959, the minuscule principality of Grand Fenwick ludicrously declares **war** on the United States in order to lose and receive generous foreign aid, although incredible events bring about its victory instead; sequels were *The Mouse on the Moon* (1962) and *The Mouse on Wall Street* (1969).

In the 1950s and 1960s, the Ruritanian romance was also transplanted to space, as colorful rogues traveling through space found themselves on backwards planets whose petty monarchs and palace intrigues recalled Ruritania and Graustack. Thus, despite exotic settings and science-fictional props, many adventures featuring Jack Vance's Magnus Ridolph, collected in *The Many Worlds of Magnus Ridolph* (1966), and Keith Laumer's Jaime Retief, first collected in *Envoy to New Worlds* (1963), could be considered Ruritanian romances; indeed, Gary Westfahl suggests calling such tales "Ruritanian space opera."

Discussion

In pure form, the Ruritanian romance is a fantasy only because its setting is not an actual nation; everything else is realistic. Yet in mood and atmosphere, the subgenre nostalgically recalls a colorful and simpler past lifestyle that somehow endured in an isolated pocket of modern society. Today, in a crowded, interconnected world making the survival of such quaint **microcosms** unlikely, most readers prefer stories along these lines that are frankly set in ancient times or **parallel worlds**, which also allows for expansive adventures beyond the confines of palaces and courtyards. Perhaps the Ruritanian romance has faded because it has been replaced by the **heroic fantasy**.

Bibliography

Vesna Goldsworthy. *Inventing Ruritania*. New Haven: Yale University Press, 1998.

Anthony Hope. *Memories and Notes*. Garden City, NY: Doran, 1928.

A. L. Lazarus and Victor H. Jones. *Beyond Graustark*. Port Washington, NY: Kennikat, 1981.

Charles Mallett. *Anthony Hope and His Books*. 1935. Port Washington, NY: Kennikat, 1968.

Nikita Nankov. "Revisiting Ruritania and Vulgaria." *Slavic and East European Journal*, 46 (Summer, 2002), 363–368.

Tony Thomas. *The Great Adventure Films*. Secaucus, NJ: Citadel Press, 1976.

Raymond P. Wallace. "Cardboard Kingdoms," *San Jose Studies,* 13 (Spring, 1987), 23–34.

Gary Westfahl. "Space Opera." Edward James and Farah Mendlesohn, eds., *The Cambridge Companion to Science Fiction*. Cambridge: Cambridge University Press, 2003, 197–208.

—Gary Westfahl

RUSSIA

∎

Overview

The Bolshevik Revolution made average Americans aware of Russia and the former Soviet Union, not as a distant, exotic land, but as a threat to our way of life. Cold War fears made Russians the **villains** in stories involving **espionage** or **nuclear war**. Writers sympathetic to socialism employed the Russian model for idealistic **utopias** before glasnost revealed the bankruptcy of the Soviet system.

Survey

With two major "Red Scares"—immediately following the Bolshevik Revolution and during the 1950s at the instigation of Senator Joseph McCarthy—science fiction writers could readily characterize Russians as villains. Once the Soviet Union had nuclear weapons, Russians were enemies in post-apocalyptic novels like Pat Frank's *Alas Babylon* (1959) or the movie *Red Dawn* (1984) (see **Apocalypse; Post-Holocaust Societies**). The Klingons of *Star Trek* appeared to represent Russians, locked into cold war with the Federation. Given this symbolism, it is unsurprising that *Star Trek: The Next Generation,* produced as Mikhail Gorbachev was moving toward rapprochement with the United States, featured Klingons allied with the Federation and a Klingon in the *Enterprise* crew.

George Orwell's ***Animal Farm*** had coded references to the Soviet Union for a serious purpose. Orwell thought the Soviet government had betrayed its own ideals and wrote his **fable** as a **satire**, complete with the rivalry of Leon Trotsky and Joseph Stalin. Orwell's *Nineteen Eighty-Four* can also be read as a comment on Soviet society, with Big Brother as Stalin, not a prognostication of the future.

Within the Soviet Union, writers found science fiction a useful vehicle for social criticism, beginning with Yevgeny Zamiatin, whose *We* showed a sterile future where perfect equality had been attained at the cost of human feelings. Vladimir Mayakovsky's play *The Bedbug* (1929) used **time travel** to deliver his human protagonist into a perfect socialist future where he could find no place except as an exhibit in a zoo (see **Animals and Zoos**). Mikhail Bulgakov wrote a satirical fantasy, *The Master and Margarita* (1967), in which **Satan** comes to Moscow and rips away the tissue of lies covering the brutal realities of Soviet society.

With Nikita Khrushchev's repudiation of Stalinism, a new generation of Soviet writers found science fiction less heavily censored, because it was regarded as a genre of escapist fluff incapable of political content (see **Politics**). Boris Strugatsky and Arkady Strugatsky wrote several novels with such content behind apparently simplistic adventure plots, like *Prisoners of Power* (1969), in which a Terran **hero** lands on a distant planet whose vices satirize Soviet bureaucracy, disguised with fantastical **technologies** like mind-control rays. Vasili Aksyonov dabbled in science fiction as a vehicle for social commentary in his **alternate history**, *The Island of Crimea* (1981), wherein the Crimean Peninsula, cut off from the Soviet mainland, develops a democratic, capitalistic society with all the strengths and weaknesses of the **America** Aksyonov had visited and enjoyed in an academic exchange program. The film *Solaris*, adapted by Soviet director Andrei Tarkovsky from Stanislaw Lem's novel, makes veiled reference to the **hubris** of the Soviet government, particularly in the Terrans' reliance upon technology to separate themselves from a world they are purportedly exploring.

The Thaw and attempted rapproachments between the United States and the Soviet Union led to more positive portrayals of Russians in western science fiction. Arthur C. Clarke's novel and the film ***2001: A Space Odyssey*** are ambivalent toward Russians, with guarded exchanges between American and Soviet space travelers, but in Clarke's sequel *2010: Odyssey Two* (1982), filmed in 1984 as *2010: The Year We Make Contact*, the protagonist travels in a Russian spaceship, and his cosmonaut crewmates are sympathetic characters. The slang of the narrator in Anthony Burgess's ***A Clockwork Orange*** is heavily Russified, though the anti-**violence** conditioning he undergoes seems based on the worst of Soviet psychiatric abuse. The communalistic utopian society in Ursula K. Le Guin's ***The Dispossessed*** draws upon the ideals of Russian thinkers like Peter Kropotkin, although the creeping growth of bureaucracy nods to the **horror** that Soviet Communism actually became.

In the times before and after the 1991 fall of the Soviet Union, rogue elements in Russian society might still function as villains, as in the James Bond film *GoldenEye* (1995) (see **Doctor No**), but fears of Russia were declining. Norman Spinrad's *Russian Spring* (1991) forecast a dominant but democratic Russia in the future, while Eugene Byrne and Kim Newman even wrote a satirical alternate history, *Back in the USSA* (1997), in which the United States is a Communist tyranny and Russia a prosperous constitutional monarchy—a **role reversal** of the Cold War. In fantasy,

C.J. Cherryh's *Rusalka* (1989) and its sequels are set in a magical medieval Russia (see **Magic**), while Orson Scott Card used Russian legends to create his contemporary version of the Sleeping Beauty story, *Enchantment* (1998).

Discussion

Absent the Bolshevik Revolution and the Soviet Union's subsequent emergence as a world power under Stalin, Russia might have remained unimportant to most westerners. Instead it became a bogeyman for some and fountain of hope for others, depending upon their political leanings. All these positions were reflected in science fiction and fantasy, whether openly or covertly. The Soviet Union also developed its own science fiction writers, often working under strong political constraints.

Bibliography

Keith Alldritt. *The Making of George Orwell*. New York: St. Martin's Press 1969.

Anindita Banerjee. "Electricity." *Science Fiction Studies*, 30 (March, 2003) 49–71.

Frank M. Bartholomew. "The Russian Utopia." E.D.S. Sullivan, ed., *The Utopian Vision*. San Diego, CA: San Diego University Press, 1983, 69–92.

Vitalli Kaplan. "A Look Behind the Wall." *Russian Studies in Literature*, 38 (Summer, 2002), 62–84.

Mary Mayer. "Russia in the Shadows and Wells Under a Cloud." *Wellsian*, No. 15 (1992), 16–24.

Halina Stephan. "Fairy Tale and Folklore in Soviet Science Fiction." *Mosaic*, 16 (Summer, 1983), 1–10.

Andrey Stolyarov. "The Red Dawn." *New York Review of Science Fiction*, No. 90 (February, 1996), 1, 8–12.

Adam Weiner. *By Authors Possessed*. Evanston, IL: Northwestern University Press, 1998.

George Zebrowski. *Beneath the Red Star*. San Bernardino, CA: Borgo Press, 1996.

—Leigh Kimmel

S

SACRIFICE

Overview

Sacrifices were originally **ritual** offerings to **gods and goddesses**—typically, slaughtered animals—designed to elicit divine favors, like rain or bountiful harvests. Many early **cultures** and **religions** practiced human sacrifice for such purposes: there are traces of such traditions in the biblical story of Abraham, who is asked by God to sacrifice his son Isaac, and Greek legends about the beginning of the Trojan War, when Agamemnon had to sacrifice his daughter Iphigenia before sailing for Troy; Mexico's Aztec culture was also noted for bloody human sacrifices. The term now applies more broadly to freely offered **gifts** of anything valuable, ranging from one's life to valuable possessions, in order to achieve a worthwhile goal.

Survey

In science fiction and fantasy, human sacrifice is encountered only in **lost worlds**, where the practice serves to both brand the **civilization** as barbaric and menace the story's **heroes**; an example in film is *King Kong*, where Kong Island's natives prepared to sacrifice the blond American actress to the giant **ape** they worship (see **Barbarians**). The killing of Piggy in William Golding's *Lord of the Flies* is a sort of human sacrifice signalling the shipwrecked boys' descent into barbarism. Some **horror** stories posit the survival of human sacrifice to ensure good crops in isolated small towns dependent upon agriculture, as occurs in Thomas Tryon's *Harvest Home* (1974); Shirley Jackson's "The Lottery" (1948) apparently represents a similar case, although the purpose of the ritual killing in that story is left unstated.

The sacrificial act reverberating throughout western culture is the crucifixion of Jesus Christ, who allowed himself to be killed to redeem **humanity** from **sin**, and was reborn after three days (see **Christianity**). Works of science fiction may retell the Christ story ironically: in Michael Moorcock's *Behold the Man* (1969), based on a 1966 novella, a time traveler goes to observe Christ's life, discovers that he is actually a congenital idiot, and decides to take his place in launching a religious movement and dying on the cross; Gore Vidal's *Live from Golgotha* (1992) satirically imagines modern media coverage of the crucifixion (see **Satire**; **Time Travel**). The Christ story is retold symbolically in C.S. Lewis's *The Lion, the Witch and the Wardrobe*, in which the lion Aslan dies to save Edmund but comes back to life (see

Lions and Tigers), and in the film *The Day the Earth Stood Still,* in which alien visitor Klaatu experiences **death** and **rebirth** to save humanity from destruction.

People who give up their lives to save another person are common figures in popular fiction, with Sydney Carton in Charles Dickens's *A Tale of Two Cities* (1859)—who is alluded to in Tim Powers's *Earthquake Weather* (1987)—providing the pattern. Examples range from Tinker Bell drinking poison to save Peter Pan in J.M. Barrie's *Peter and Wendy* to Spock sacrificing himself to save the *Enterprise* crew in *Star Trek II: The Wrath of Khan* (1982) (see **Star Trek: The Motion Picture**)—though both characters are restored to life. But there is no resurrection for Tarzan's ape-**mother**, who dies while protecting her adopted son in *Tarzan of the Apes*, or Jor-El and La-Ra of Krypton, who employ their experimental **rocket** to save their son Kal-El instead of themselves in all versions of the *Superman* story.

Some sacrifices do not involve loss of life, but nonetheless extract a great toll. After his perilous **quest** to destroy the life-draining **ring** he carries, Frodo of J.R.R. Tolkien's *The Lord of the Rings* not only has lost a finger, but is left a shell of his former self, unable to settle into the happy domesticity of his friend Sam. Dr. Archibald Graham in the film *Field of Dreams* briefly fulfills his dream of playing baseball again as a **youth,** but gives it up to return to **medicine** and save a choking child. To atone for his unknowing destruction of alien Buggers, Ender of Orson Scott Card's *Ender's Game* travels through the galaxy to speak on behalf of dead people and find a **home** for the last surviving Bugger, as recounted in *Speaker for the Dead* (1986) and later novels. The **robot** Jenkins in Clifford D. Simak's *City* devotes himself to millennia of selfless service to the Webster family and the uplifted animals that succeed them (see **Uplift**) though he is finally persuaded to abandon his outpost on **Earth** and pursue his own **destiny** in the saga's belated "Epilog" (1973).

Discussion

Stories of people sacrificing themselves appeal to people's deepest emotions; few scenarios have the impact of people giving up their lives, or everything they value, to bring about some desired outcome. In their own lives, people usually could not bring themselves to make such ultimate sacrifices, no matter how worthy its purpose, but can at least vicariously experience the **pain** and satisfaction of such sacrifices through stories and films.

Bibliography

Bernadette L. Bosky. "Choice, Sacrifice, Destiny, and Nature in *The Stand.*" Tony Magistrale, ed., *A Casebook on The Stand*. San Bernardino, CA: Borgo Press, 1992, 123–142.

Marjorie J. Burns. "Eating, Devouring, Sacrifice and Ultimate Just Desserts." *Mythlore*, 21 (Winter, 1996), 108–114.

Matthew A. Fike. "Hero's Education in Sacrificial Love." *Mythlore*, 14 (Summer, 1988), 34–38.

Gwenyth Hood. "Nature and Technology." *Mythlore*, 19 (Autumn, 1993), 6–12.

Larry Kreitzer. "Suffering, Sacrifice and Redemption." Jennifer E. Porter and Darcee L. McLaren, eds., *Star Trek and Sacred Ground*. Albany: State University of New York Press, 1999, 139–164.

Jay Ruud. "Aslan's Sacrifice and the Doctrine of Atonement in *The Lion, The Witch and The Wardrobe.*" *Mythlore*, 26 (Spring, 2001), 15–23.

Gregory J. Sakal. "No Big Win." James B. South, ed., *Buffy the Vampire Slayer and Philosophy*. Chicago: Open Court, 2003, 239–253.

Michelle Spedding and Katherine Ramsland. "The Price of Perfection." Ramsland, ed., *The Anne Rice Reader*. New York: Ballantine, 1997, 225–236.

—Gary Westfahl

SATAN

I have given myself to the devil, because the devil is the only god in whom all the tribes believe.

—Walter M. Miller, Jr.
"The Soul-Empty Ones" (1951a)

Overview

Originally an **angel**, Satan led an unsuccessful **rebellion** against God and, along with his cohorts, was consequently cast out of **Heaven** into **Hell**, where he now reigns over and torments sinners after their **deaths** (see **Sin**). His other names include the Devil, Old Nick, Lucifer, Beelzebub, and Mephistopheles (spellings vary), although sometimes these are distinguished as separate beings: John Milton's epic poem *Paradise Lost* (1667) describes Beelzebub as Satan's assistant, while Christopher Marlowe's play *Doctor Faustus* (1604) presents a Satanic trinity of Lucifer, Beelzebub, and Mephistopheles. A separate entry discusses **demons**.

Survey

The Old Testament of the Bible has no references to Satan, though **Christianity** identifies him with the serpent (see **Snakes and Worms**) that tempts **Adam and Eve** in the Garden of Eden and the "Adversary" who prods God to test Job; modern retellings of these stories, like Jerry Bock, Sheldon Harnick, and Jerome Coopersmith's musical *The Apple Tree* (1966) and Archibald MacLeish's play *J.B.* (1956), feature Satan as a character. The most extensive account of the biblical Satan is Milton's *Paradise Lost*, wherein Satan almost becomes an heroic figure (see **Heroes**) as he defiantly establishes his capital of Pandemonium in Hell and methodically works to thwart God by tempting Adam and Eve. Another noted author, Daniel Defoe, provided a comprehensive portrait of Satan in *History of the Devil* (1726).

Among other activities, Satan serves as **king** of Hell, though this role is not always emphasized; Dante's *Inferno* (c. 1306–1321), for instance, depicts Satan as an immense three-headed face endlessly chewing the bodies of the arch-sinners Judas, Cassius, and Brutus, seemingly not involved in administrative duties. Satan is often depicted as greeting newly arrived souls and explaining, or escorting them to, their punishment, as in an episode of ***The Twilight Zone***, "A Nice Place to Visit" (1960).

When Satan visits **Earth**, one thing on his mind may be emulating God and having a son by a mortal woman—who would grow up to be the Anti-Christ. While such encounters are rarely depicted, their results are ominously visible in stories like Ira Levin's *Rosemary's Baby* (1967), filmed in 1968, and the film *The Omen* (1976) and its sequels. The film *End of Days* (1999) involves an effort to bring such a **birth** about. Sons of the Devil normally bring nothing but trouble, but one of them, Marvel Comics' Son of Satan, rebelliously defies his father and employs his demonic powers to oppose Satan, becoming a **superhero**.

However, Satan's standard reason for visiting Earth is to lure people into selling their souls in exchange for some magical but ephemeral boon (see **Magic**). The two major versions of the Faust story—Marlowe's *Doctor Faustus* and Goethe's *Faust* (1808–1832)—illustrate the two ways such stories end: the foolish victim is forced to honor his bargain and descend into Hell, like Marlowe's Faustus, or he contrives to evade his just punishment, like Goethe's Faust—a scenario generally more appealing to modern tastes. Examples of these stories include Stephen Vincent Benet's "The Devil and Daniel Webster" (1937), filmed in 1941, in which a farmer avoids damnation when he persuades orator Daniel Webster to argue on his behalf before a jury of dead Americans (see **America**); Robert Bloch's "The Hell-Bound Train" (1958), in which a man given a watch that stops **time** finally uses it while riding with Satan on the train to Hell, permanently postponing his arrival; and Joe Haldeman's "I of Newton" (1970), filmed as an episode of *The Twilight Zone* in 1985, in which a man granted the right to escape his fate if he can name something Satan cannot do succeeds by telling the Devil to "get lost." Also, in Stephen King's *Needful Things* (1991), filmed in 1993, a mysterious shopkeeper not explicitly identified as Satan tempts residents of a small town in Maine with unique solutions to their problems. Sometimes, Satan delegates the task of garnering souls to subordinates: in a Swedish television series, *13 Demon Street* (1959), episodes show Satan sending his female assistant to lure people to Hell (three episodes were edited together as the film *The Devil's Messenger* [1962]), and in the film *The Devil and Max Devlin* (1970), Satan offers a dead landlord the chance to return to Earth if he agrees to persuade three people to give up their souls.

When Satan himself is not around to bedevil humanity, cults of his devoted worshippers may be centers of attention, engaged in nefarious behaviors. A classic story is Nathaniel Hawthorne's "Young Goodman Brown" (1835), in which an innocent young man discovers that the seemingly virtuous citizens of his town secretly go into the **forest** to worship the Devil and celebrate **evil** as "the nature of mankind." Less memorable are the antics of sinister Satanists in films like *The Devil's Bride* (1968), *Satan's Black Wedding* (1971), and *The Devil's Rain* (1975).

Discussion

The figure of Satan has not lost his power to awe and terrify, as evidenced by his continuing presence in **horror** films. Still, the manner in which the Satan seeking souls has devolved into a demure, even comical character suggests a shift in attitudes: people worry more about the evil Satan might inspire in this world than the **pain** and **torture** he might inflict in the next world. To put the point another way, many still believe in Satan as the embodiment of evil but are less inclined to believe in his residence, Hell.

Bibliography

Basil Davenport, ed. *Deals with the Devil*. New York: Dodd, Mead, 1958.

Andrew Delbanco. *The Death of Satan*. New York: Farrar, Straus, and Giroux, 1995.

Marshall William Fishwick. *Faust Revisited*. New York: Seabury Press, 1963.

Edward Langton. *Satan, a Portrait*. London, Skeffington & Son, Ltd., 1946.

Mike Resnick, Martin H. Greenberg, and Loren D. Estleman, eds. *Deals with the Devil*. New York: DAW Books, 1994.

Maxmilian J. Rudwin. *The Devil in Legend and Literature*. Chicago: Open Court Publishing Co., 1931.

Maxmilian J. Rudwin, ed. *Devil Stories*. New York: Alfred A. Knopf, 1921.

Nikolas Schreck. *The Satanic Screen*. London: Creation, 2001.

Hannes Vatter. *The Devil in English Literature*. Bern: Francke, 1978.

—*Gary Westfahl*

SATIRE

Overview

Satire is a literary form that uses **humor**—sometimes gentle, but often biting and sarcastic—to illustrate human foibles and social injustices, usually with the ultimate objective of improving society or human behavior. To the satirist, laughter and ridicule are weapons against brutality and ignorance. A separate entry addresses **Comedy**.

Survey

Two early satirists were Aristophanes and Lucian of Samosata, who wrote of **cities** in the air or voyages to the **Moon** to gain unique perspectives on human folly. In modern times, Thomas More's *Utopia* blends subtle satire with the story of an imaginary **island** where reason prevails. More satirizes the materialism of his own society through foreign visitors who covet the gold that Utopians themselves use only to make shackles and chamber pots.

Two centuries later Jonathan Swift made full use of the extraordinary voyage's potential for satire in *Gulliver's Travels*. On the island of Lilliput, with its minuscule inhabitants, Swift reduces the religious struggles of eighteenth-century England to a debate between two factions who break their eggs on opposite ends. The monstrous residents of Brobdingnag, on the other hand, serve Swift's satirical purposes by exaggerating familiar human foibles to gigantic scale. Swift also satirizes **scientists** with the distracted, impractical residents of Laputa, whose idea of language reform is to carry with them everything they might ever wish to discuss, so that instead of relying on words to communicate they need only point at the objects themselves.

Whereas fantasy has always served the satirist's need to exaggerate a subject's actual imperfections to unrealistic proportions, the development of science fiction in the nineteenth and early twentieth centuries allowed satirists to take current social conditions and extrapolate them into absurd or nightmarish visions of the future. Aldous Huxley's **Brave New World** extends the industrialization of his own time into a dystopian future (see **Dystopia**) that manufactures human beings like **automobiles**. George Orwell's *Nineteen Eighty-Four* extrapolates the political oppression of the early twentieth century into a technologically advanced future, but the novel is less satirical than his earlier *Animal Farm*, in which Communism is portrayed as a revolution of **farm** animals ultimately betrayed by Stalinist pigs.

The **advertising** industry of the 1950s is the target of Frederik Pohl and C.M. Kornbluth's satire *The Space Merchants*, originally entitled *Gravy Planet*, which describes an advertising campaign to "sell" the hellish planet **Venus** to potential colonists. From subliminal advertising to laser-like beams that transmit advertisements directly onto the eyes, Pohl and Kornbluth anticipate the unrelenting encroachment of advertising into every nook and cranny of modern life.

An author who frequently employs science-fictional themes and motifs for the purpose of satire is Kurt Vonnegut, Jr. His first novel, *Player Piano* (1952), describes the devastating impact of automation on a small industrial town, while *The Sirens of Titan* (1959) self-consciously satirizes the conventions of science fiction itself. The "chrono-synclastic infundibulum" that allows the novel's protagonist to exist simultaneously at all points in the solar system is a deliberately unbelievable narrative device, as is "The Universal Will to Become," the cosmic principle that allows the alien Tralfamadorians to manipulate human **history** simply to provide a spare part for a stranded spaceship. Another of Vonnegut's favorite satirical targets is **religion**. *The Sirens of Titan* features a new religion, "The Church of God the Utterly Indifferent," through which Vonnegut attacks the notion that material success signals God's favor; *Cat's Cradle* offers another fictional religion, Bokononism, which declares itself to be nothing but "foma," or harmless untruths.

Religion is also a favorite target of James Morrow, who follows in Vonnegut's satirical tradition with *Only Begotten Daughter* (1990), the story of a late twentieth-century sister of Jesus Christ, and *Towing Jehovah* (1994), which describes a **quest** to retrieve the body of God from the middle of the Atlantic and preserve it in an Arctic cave.

Science fiction films often turn to satire to comment on contemporary trends. *Dr. Strangelove* satirizes the politicians and scientists who plot **nuclear war**; Woody Allen's *Sleeper* (1973) brings a slapstick sensibility to the story of a contemporary man who awakens to find himself in a strange future world (see **Suspended Animation and Cryonics**); and Paul Verhoeven's *Robocop* (1987) satirically comments upon the casual **violence** and corruption of its future world even as it indulges in a violent spectacle of its own.

Discussion

Fantasy and satire frequently overlap, as in Swift's *Gulliver's Travels*, largely because satire depends on exaggeration to make plain the imperfections it seeks to reveal, exaggeration that often extends into the realm of the fantastic. Both science fiction and fantasy also lend themselves to satire by providing more objective perspectives on the human condition, not limited to the realistic present.

Science fiction's capacity to extrapolate current trends into the distant future, as in Huxley's *Brave New World* and Pohl and Kornbluth's *The Space Merchants*, also makes it an ideal vehicle for satire. Indeed, the strongly dystopian tradition in science fiction, in which the future always seems to appear darker than the present, arises in part from the fact that the genre lends itself so well to satire.

Bibliography

Isaac Asimov. "Satire." Asimov, *Asimov's Galaxy*. New York: Doubleday, 1989, 45–48.

Laura K. Egendorf. *Satire*. San Diego: Greenhaven Press, 2002.

R.C. Elliott. "Saturnalia, Satire, and Utopia." *Yale Review*, 55 (June, 1966), 535–536.

Conrad Festa. "Vonnegut's Satire." Jerome Klinkowitz, ed., *Vonnegut in America*. New York: Delacorte, 1977, 133–149.

Gilbert Highet. "Out of This World." Highet, *Anatomy of Satire*. Princeton: Princeton University Press, 1962, 159–177.

Robert Kiely. "Satire as Fantasy." *Summary*, 1 (1971), 41–43.

Donald E. Palumbo. "Science Fiction as Allegorical Social Satire." *Studies in Contemporary Satire*, 9 (1982), 1–8.

Jean Pfaelzer. "Parody and Satire in American Dystopian Fiction of the Nineteenth Century." *Science-Fiction Studies*, 7 (March 1980), 61–72.

—*Ed McKnight*

SCIENTISTS

■

Why can't scientists leave things alone? What about my bit of washing when there's no washing to do?

—Roger MacDougall, John Dighton, and
Alexander Mackendrick
The Man in the White Suit (1951)

Overview

Images of scientists, alchemists, or natural philosophers in literature since the sixteenth century still influence characterizations of scientists in fiction and film. Although most scientists today work as teams in institutions, they are frequently presented as isolated and uncommunicative. Besides inventors and **mad scientists** (see **Inventions**), recurrent stereotypes are evil alchemists, wise scientists, inhuman researchers, adventurers, and irresponsible scientists.

Survey

With their protective devices of secrecy, obscure language, and symbols, alchemists embodied medieval suspicions about **knowledge** and prefigure the arcane image of science. Alchemy also fascinated due to its **promises** of wealth, perpetual motion, **immortality and longevity,** and creation of life. Because science still offer such allurements, alchemist stereotypes survive in both fantasy and science fiction. Robert Louis

Stevenson's *Strange Case of Dr. Jekyll and Mr. Hyde* suggests that such characteristics are intrinsically human, but usually they are portrayed as abnormal.

Francis Bacon's **utopia** *The New Atlantis* (1627) introduced the concept of a scientific elite, promoting experimental method, internationalism, **communication**, and social responsibility. Bacon's ideals were actualized in the Royal Society of London, and Isaac Newton later epitomized the noble scientist, reducing chaos to physical laws. H.G. Wells's scientific utopias pioneered the belief that scientists could be entrusted with world government. This concept died with Hiroshima, but noble scientists may still rule **galactic empires** or save Earth from **monsters**, aliens, or ecological or medical **disaster**. During the Cold War fictional scientists averted **nuclear war** or protested against weapons research (see **Weaponry**). Isaac Asimov's scientists in *I, Robot* and the *Foundation* series were social benefactors. *Star Trek* and Stanislaw Lem's *Solaris* support communication with alien civilizations, and Carl Sagan's novel *Contact* (1985) posits an encounter between an astronomer and a disembodied intelligence.

Utopias governed by scientists were criticized in Yevgeny Zamiatin's *We* and Aldous Huxley's *Brave New World*; later, Ursula K. Le Guin and Marge Piercy attacked the *Star Trek* series as extraterrestrial sexist imperialism (see **Sexism**). Le Guin's *The Dispossessed* offers an alternative vision of a scientist bridging political divides.

The most enduring stereotype is the emotionless researcher sacrificing human relationships for science. Statements of unconcern by atomic weapons developers revived this stereotype of scientists totally preoccupied with their research in **physics**, **mathematics**, **biology** or **computer** science, motivated only by utilitarian rationalism. Wells's *The Island of Doctor Moreau*, filmed as *Island of Lost Souls*, focuses on an amoral biologist attempting to humanize animals (see **Uplift**), while in C.S. Lewis's *Out of the Silent Planet*, Weston's utilitarian foundation employs vivisection, eugenics, racism, and behaviorism to achieve social "efficiency." Hoenikker of Kurt Vonnegut, Jr.'s *Cat's Cradle* ignores the apocalyptic consequences of his research.

Scientist-adventurers appear first in Jules Verne's novels, crossing geographical and intellectual **frontiers** to demonstrate optimism about **progress** and **technology**. *Twenty Thousand Leagues under the Sea* and *From the Earth to the Moon* (filmed as *A Trip to the Moon*) were models for heroic scientists in Hugo Gernsback's *Ralph 124C 41+: A Romance of the Year 2660* (1925) and Arthur Conan Doyle's *The Lost World*. Their descendants are the space traveling **heroes** of pulp magazines, *Star Trek*, and the *Doctor Who* series (see **Space Travel**).

Scientists whose experiments become uncontrollable express common fears of disasters resulting from **nuclear power**, nuclear war, **genetic engineering**, artificial **intelligence**, or organ transplants (see **Medicine**). Mary Shelley's *Frankenstein* provided the prototype, but Karel Capek's play *R.U.R.* (1920) elicited a subgenre of stories where **robots**, computers, **androids**, or **cyborgs** overpower humans. Films of **post-holocaust societies**, like *Planet of the Apes* and *The Terminator*, implicitly blamed scientists not only for the planet's devastation, but also its potential biological and social degeneration, embodied in many post–1945 **horror** films involving **monsters**, like *The Beast from 20,000 Fathoms* (1953) and *Godzilla, King of the Monsters*. Nuclear accidents in *The China Syndrome* (1979) and *Silkwood* (1984) implied that, even in peacetime, physicists could not guarantee the safety of power plants, while *The Fly* (1958, 1986) and Michael Crichton's *Jurassic Park* and its film adaptations extended the range of uncontrolled experiments to biology, conveying fears of **mutations, clones,** and genetic engineering.

Discussion

Despite the prestige of science in western culture, surveys of scientists in fiction and film show that **evil** or flawed scientists are a clear majority. These archetypal scientists not only mirror a selected actuality but allow imaginative exploration of complex or subversive ideas, wild hopes, and suppressed fears that transcend time, place, and race—hopes of surmounting human limitations, and fears of the power of **knowledge** by those who cannot influence its direction or control its consequences. The enormous gender disparity in depictions of scientists reflects a real (though decreasing) imbalance but also a perception of the general disempowerment of women. Only in utopian fantasy like Charlotte Perkins Gilman's *Herland* do women fully control scientific power. Fictional treatments can also influence attitudes to real science. The surprising new concept of an alien **messiah** replacing alien invaders was introduced through films from *The Day the Earth Stood Still* through *Close Encounters of the Third Kind, E.T.: The Extra-Terrestrial* and *The Terminator*. Their message of apocalyptic comfort elicited support for research into extraterrestrial intelligence.

Bibliography

John Cohen. *Human Robots in Myth and Science*. London: Allen and Unwin, 1966.

Anne Cranny-Francis. "Sexuality and Sex-Role Stereotyping in *Star Trek*." *Science-Fiction Studies*, 12 (July, 1985), 274–284.

Eva Flicker. "Between Brains and Breasts." *Public Understanding of Science*, 12 (July, 2003), 307–318.

Donna Harraway. *Simians, Cyborgs and Women*. New York: Routledge, 1991.

Roslynn D. Haynes. *From Faust to Strangelove*. Baltimore: Johns Hopkins University Press, 1994.

———. "From Alchemy to Artificial Intelligence." *Public Understanding of Science*, 12 (July, 2003), 243–254.

George Levine and U.C. Knoepflmacher, eds. *The Endurance of Frankenstein*. Berkeley and Los Angeles: University of California Press, 1979.

Tom Shippey. "Starship Troopers, Galactic Heroes, Mercenary Princes." Alan Sandison and Robert Dingley, ed., *Histories of the Future*. Basingstoke, Hampshire and New York: Palgrave, 2000, 168–183.

Spencer Weart. *Scientists in Power*. Cambridge, MA: Harvard University Press, 1979.

—Roslynn Haynes

SEA CREATURES

See Fish and Sea Creatures

SEA TRAVEL

Overview

Sea travel features prominently in both fantasy and science fiction literature, as a plot device and metaphor. In some stories, ocean voyages are a metaphor for separation or alienation; in others, they follow a **quest** pattern, facing down **monsters** or searching **islands** for the thing most needed. The tropes of sea voyages also provide familiarity in tales of **space travel**.

Survey

Sea travel stories included mythic or fantastic elements from their earliest days. The tale of Jason and the Golden Fleece, retold in *Jason and the Argonauts*, and Homer's *Odyssey* (c. 750 BCE) both feature long sea voyages, quests for **treasure**, or simply a search for a route **home**. Celtic and Norse myths include tales of long sea voyages, with **heroes** crossing oceans to explore new islands and continents. The **mythology** of the **South Pacific**, too, is heavily based on sea voyages, for obvious reasons. Contemporary fabulists regularly draw on these old stories.

Among the most famous of fantastic sea explorers was Gulliver in Jonathan Swift's *Gulliver's Travels*. Swift portrayed adventures for his hero but also satirized his own society's foibles with the other countries he envisioned as part of Gulliver's **explorations** (see **Satire**). From Thomas More's time (see *Utopia*) to Swift's, sea voyagers came home with tales of new lands so often that audiences for these books were used to envisioning strange and wondrous places they had never heard of across the sea.

Equally renowned is Jules Verne's *Twenty Thousand Leagues under the Sea*, with the **underwater** adventures of Captain Nemo and his crew. Though Verne's submarine was not the first to travel beneath the waves, it is the best remembered of its type, exploring strange **fish** and **sea creatures** and providing captain and crew an **escape** from societies with which they disagreed.

The quest and exploration theme carried into speculative sea stories as different as C.S. Lewis's *The Voyage of the Dawn Treader* (1952) (see *The Lion, the Witch and the Wardrobe*) and James Morrow's *Towing Jehovah* (1994). The former is a Christian children's fantasy, the latter a satirical speculative novel wherein God's corpse must be hauled up to the Arctic by sea, but both contain elements of quests for personal development and physical achievement.

In *The Voyage of the Dawn Treader*, as in many volumes before it and since, sailors must contend with a sea serpent. Other such creatures can be more benevolent or more similar to humans, like dolphins, **mermaids**, and selkies (see **Shapeshifters**). For benevolent, gentle animal adventures by sea, Hugh Lofting's *The Story of Doctor Dolittle* is an excellent example, as are its sequels and adaptations. The doctor's closeness with **nature** extends to land, sea, and air creatures.

Robin Hobb's Liveship Traders series, beginning with *Ship of Magic* (1998), focuses entirely on sea travelers—both humans and, with the flexibility fantasy offers, sentient ships. Her portrayals of people living at sea range from those who love it and find it exhilarating to those who see it as a painful duty, a life sentence of **exile** from the work and people they love on land. Hobb's characters engage in **trade** and **transportation**, and even have run-ins with **pirates**.

Many stories use the sea to emphasize separation, isolation, or **estrangement**. In Ursula K. Le Guin's *A Wizard of Earthsea* and its sequels, the archipelago provides a **pastoral** way of life for simple fishers, farmers, and magicians, separated from each other by water and yet comfortable with it and land alike. In David Brin's *Glory Season* (1993), sea travel is a barrier between the male sailors and the more numerous female land-dwellers. The difference between their societies is underscored— and deliberately reinforced—by the long sea voyages the men take.

In Mary Shelley's *The Last Man*, the title character is left in a sailboat at the end, but his journey is not portrayed as meaningful. While he travels, he has no particular destination, there being no one else with whom to share the world. In this way, sea travel once again emphasizes isolation. Nor is this the only time Shelley did so: Frankenstein's monster is left on an ice floe at the end of his story, traveling without volition on an icy sea (see Shelley's *Frankenstein*).

The language of sea travel has made its way into air and space throughout the history of science fiction. **Air travel** stories employed sailing ship conventions when air travel was still fictional or rare, and space travel has followed suit. There is little doubt that the real-life naval experience of writers like Robert A. Heinlein and A. Bertram Chandler influenced their depictions of military space fleets. No one has taken this correspondence further than David Weber, whose Honor Harrington series, beginning with *On Basilisk Station* (1993), is a spacefaring homage to C.M. Forester's Horatio Hornblower sea stories. Some episodes of *Star Trek: The Next Generation* took this influence for a final inversion: space travelers in a navy-influenced Star Fleet used the holodeck to play at being sailors in the nineteenth-century British Navy.

Discussion

In both science fiction and fantasy, sea travel is as variable as the sea itself, taking on tones of exploration, escape, estrangement, or almost any other theme authors care to consider. While sea travel is less common in science fiction than space travel, its assumptions and preoccupations have shaped the genre.

Bibliography

Michele Barrett and Duncan Barrett. "The Starry Sea." Barrett and Barrett, *Star Trek: The Human Frontier*. New York: Routledge, 2001, 9–51.

John Boardman. "Ocean Trade in the Hyborian Age." L. Sprague de Camp, ed., *Blade of Conan*. New York: Ace, 1979, 45–50.

A. Bertram Chandler. "Sea and Science Fiction." *Owlflight*, 3 (1982), 25–31.

Eleanor M. Farrell. "And Clove the Wind from Unseen Shores." *Mythlore*, 12 (Spring, 1986), 43–47, 60.

Gwyneth Jones. *Deconstructing the Starships*. Liverpool: Liverpool University Press, 1999.

Patrick A. McCarthy. "Allusions in Ballard's *The Drowned World*." *Science-Fiction Studies*, 24 (July, 1997), 302–310.

Warren G. Rochelle. *Communities of the Heart*. Liverpool: Liverpool University Press, 2001.

Frederik M. Smith, ed. *The Genres of Gulliver's Travels*. Newark: University of Delaware Press, 1990.

—Marissa Lingen

SEASONS

■
---

*He never gave up his search for the Door
into Summer.*

—Robert A. Heinlein
The Door into Summer (1957)

Overview

The **cycle** of four seasons long imposed a pattern on human lives, ameliorated only recently as people developed improved methods of avoiding or moderating the effects of **weather**. Indeed, in *Anatomy of Criticism* (1957) Northrop Frye persuasively argues that all human narratives are aspects of one basic monomyth, with four basic genres sequentially corresponding to the seasons: irony and **satire**, the genres of winter, give way to **comedy**, genre of spring, followed by **romance**, genre of summer, and **tragedy**, genre of autumn. It is also common to describe human experience from **youth** to **old age** in terms of the seasons; so, for example, Persia Woolley retells the life of **Arthur**'s Guinevere from first **romance** to final downfall in novels entitled *Child of the Northern Spring* (1987), *Queen of the Summer Stars* (1990), and *Guinevere, the Legend in Autumn* (1991). Thus, all literary works reflect seasonal imagery in some way, although some science fiction and fantasy texts foreground the seasons.

Survey

The cold season of winter is almost always regarded as unpleasant; only in **Christmas** stories might the arrival of frigid weather and snow be a boon, as in the film *White Christmas* (1953), where an almost magical snowfall on Christmas Eve saves a ski resort from bankruptcy. For most characters, however, winter is a condition to dislike and to **dream** of escaping (see **Escape**). Robert A. Heinlein begins *The Door into Summer* (1957) with a fictionalized description of an actual experience: during a Colorado winter, one of Heinlein's **cats** went to a door, waited for someone to open it, eyed the harsh winter, and walked away to stand at another door; when that door was opened, the cat again looked out and went to stand by a third door. To explain the cat's behavior, Heinlein's wife said that the cat was looking for "the door into summer"—which became the governing metaphor of Heinlein's story, as a plucky inventor does everything he can, including suspended animation (see **Suspended Animation and Cryonics**) and **time travel**, to find happiness for himself and loved ones.

One daunting situation in fantasy is a world where seasonal change stops, freezing everyone in winter. In C.S. Lewis's ***The Lion, the Witch and the Wardrobe***, an **evil witch** afflicts Narnia with perpetual winter, and Patricia McKillip's *Winter Rose* (1996) involves characters trapped in a horrible realm where winter never ends. Ursula K. Le Guin's ***The Left Hand of Darkness***, by naming her frigid planet Winter, conveys the concept metaphorically, suggesting the long-isolated planet of hermaphrodites is unhealthily frozen in a static pattern and must open itself to the liberating influences of other worlds. Another science fiction equivalent to tales of perpetual winter is visions of a future **Earth** trapped in an ice age, as in Anna Kavan's *Ice* (1967), Poul Anderson's *The Winter of the World* (1976), and Richard Moran's *Empire of Ice* (1994) and *Earth Winter* (1995).

The arrival of spring is a joyous time, as seen in the conclusion of Lewis's novel, when the witch's defeat brings Narnia a long-delayed spring. The season is regularly associated with forms of **rebirth**, as in Norman Spinrad's *Russian Spring* (1992), about a reformed, resurgent **Russia**, and Robert Silverberg's *At Winter's End* (1988) and *Queen of Springtime* (1989), describing the future reemergence of **humanity**.

Summer is generally the happiest season, especially for **children**, since this is their time off from school. Given his perpetually child-like outlook, Ray Bradbury is especially inclined to celebrate summer: in "The Sound of Summer Running," a section of *Dandelion Wine* (1957) later published separately, a boy eager for a new pair of summer tennis shoes magically communicates his enthusiasm to an old shoe salesman, while "Rocket Summer," a vignette from **The Martian Chronicles**, implausibly but poetically imagines that a rocket launch might briefly bring summer weather to its surroundings. In books for younger readers, summer can be time for magical events, as in Penelope Farmer's *Summer Birds* (1985), about children learning to fly, and Brenda Clough's *An Impossible Summer* (1992), about children finding a talking opossum (see **Magic; Talking Animals**). However, **horror** writers may deliberately juxtapose the brightness of summer with dark events, as in Dan Simmons's *Summer of Night* (1991), about an evil force killing children, and Robert Hawks's *Summers End* (1994), about children victimized by **vampires**.

Still, autumn is usually the season associated with horror, the time of **Halloween** and dark **rituals** associated with harvests, as in Thomas Tryon's *Harvest Home* (1973); this is why Bradbury entitled a collection of his horror stories adapted for comic books *The Autumn People* (1965). But Bradbury also delights in Halloween activities, celebrating them fondly in *The Halloween Tree* (1972) and elsewhere.

Fantasy writers sometime envision interesting variations in seasonal patterns: in Clive Barker's *Thief of Always* (1992), a boy travels to another **dimension** where each season passes in one day, and Terry Pratchett's Discworld (see *The Colour of Magic*) has eight seasons instead of four. In creating **alien worlds**, science fiction writers may include unusual seasonal patterns: Hal Clement's *Cycle of Fire* (1957) features a planet with an unusual orbit that causes a regular season of extreme heat, requiring unusual adaptations in planetary lifeforms, while Brian W. Aldiss's **Helliconia Spring** and its sequels meticulously describe the biosphere and complex **civilization** of a planet where seasons last for thousands of years.

Discussion

While fantasy, committed to tradition, remains tied to the four seasons, the artificial future **habitats** of science fiction—whether in space or on Earth—interestingly include cycles of night and day but no seasonal variations. The utopian dream they convey is a world of one constant season with consistent, predictable weather. Since humans living near the Arctic Circle or the Equator have thrived in such conditions, we know such existence is possible; still, an absence of seasons is one reason why visions of apparently idyllic technological futures may seem sterile and unpalatable.

Bibliography

Margaret L. Carter. "Perpetual Winter in C. S. Lewis and Patricia McKillip." *Mythlore*, 16 (Autumn, 1989), 35–36, 57.

Gail Gibbons. *The Reasons for Seasons*. New York: Holiday House, 1995.

Heidi Goennel. *Seasons*. Boston, MA: Little, Brown, 1986.

Michael G. Kammen. *A Time to Every Purpose*. Chapel Hill: University of North Carolina Press, 2004.

David Ketterer. "Ursula K. Le Guin's Archetypal Winter Journey." Harold Bloom, ed., *Ursula K. Le Guin*. New York: Chelsea House, 1986, 11–22.

Joanne C. Letwinch. *Soaring Through the Universe*. Englewood, CO: Teacher Ideas Press, 1999.

Nancy-Lou Patterson. "Always Winter and Never Christmas." *Mythlore*, 18 (Autumn, 1991), 10–14.

Joe L. Sanders. "Breaking the Circle: Heinlein's *The Door into Summer*." *New York Review of Science Fiction*, No. 60 (August, 1993), 1, 10–13.

—Gary Westfahl

SECRET HISTORY

Overview

A secret history describes events that conflict with commonly accepted views of **history**, but which have been deliberately suppressed or forgotten. It differs from historical fiction in its divergence from historical fact, and from **alternate history** in that present-day reality is not changed, only our perception of it.

Survey

An early experiment in secret history is Argentine writer Jorge Luis Borges's "Tlön, Uqbar, Orbis Tertius" (1941), in which a secret society attempts to change the world by means of a fictional encyclopedia, the gradual influence of which leads **humanity** to replace our own history with the fictional history of a mythological world called Tlön.

A secret conspiracy—benevolent or otherwise—to suppress historical fact has become a nearly indispensable element of the secret history genre. While Borges's story depicts the fabrication of an elaborate fictional history and its gradual substitution for our own, a secret history more commonly describes the process by which an investigator (or a group of investigators) uncovers the "true" history buried beneath our commonly accepted views.

Thomas Pynchon's *The Crying of Lot 49* (1963) centers on such a discovery made by the novel's protagonist, Oedipa Maas. What begins as the tedious job of executing the will of her former employer turns into the paranoid pursuit of Tristero (see **Paranoia**), a medieval postal service that may or may not still operate in contemporary Los Angeles. Defeated by its rival, Thurn und Taxis (a medieval mail delivery service that actually existed), the Tristero organization has been transformed into an underground society, signs of which Oedipa finds encoded within medieval revenge dramas, scrawled on bus windows and lavatory walls, and displayed on ubiquitous mail receptacles deceptively labeled WASTE (which she learns actually stands for We Await Silent Tristero's Empire).

Whether Oedipa's conspiracy theory is factual or merely a product of her own paranoid search for meaning remains unresolved at the novel's conclusion. Either interpretation remains within the realm of scientific realism, but secret history also merges into the realm of fantasy, as in John Crowley's *Little, Big* and Tim Powers's *The Anubis Gates* (1983). In the former, Smoky Barnable discovers that Edgewood, the upstate New York mansion of the Drinkwater family, intersects with the supernatural realm of Faerie, a source of magical power through which the loosely-organized conspiracy known as the Noisy Bridge Rod and Gun Club seeks to stave off a resurgent Holy Roman Empire, led by the reawakened Emperor Barbarossa. In the latter, a time-traveling academic is stranded in a nineteenth-century London (see **Time Travel**) of secret guilds and underground **monsters**, where a conspiracy of Egyptian sorcerers seeks to strike back at colonial rulers by restoring the ancient **gods and goddesses** (see **Egypt**). The presence of anachronistic **inventions**, and appearances by historical figures like Lord Byron and Samuel Taylor Coleridge, makes *The Anubis Gates* a prototype for the literary subgenre of **steampunk**.

Italian author and scholar Umberto Eco brings his expertise in the field of semiotics (the study of signs and sign systems) to secret history in *Foucault's Pendulum* (1989). What begins as an intellectual parlor game among three friends becomes a life-or-**death** struggle when they attempt to weave every known conspiracy theory into one ridiculous, all-encompassing Plan involving (among other things) the Knights Templar, the Holy Grail, the Gregorian calendar and plate tectonics. When they unify these conspiracy theories by inventing a secret society called the Tres, they either stumble into an actual conspiracy or inadvertently bring one into being. Ironically, those who believe they are members of the Tres pursue the conspiracy theorists because they seem to know more about their own group and its secret agenda than they themselves do.

While there have been other examples, like R.A. Lafferty's *Fourth Mansions* (1969) and Mary Gentle's *Ash: A Secret History* (1999), the secret history achieved its greatest commercial success with Dan Brown's *The Da Vinci Code* (2003). Premised on a conspiracy to suppress the role of women in the early church, particularly that of Mary Magdalene in the life and ministry of Christ, *The Da Vinci Code* presents a series of **puzzles**, supposedly encrypted into the work of Leonardo da Vinci, that contain the secrets of the Priory of Sion, a secret society dedicated to restoring the status of women in the Catholic Church. Like all secret histories, *The Da Vinci Code* captivates readers by challenging their assumptions about history and their place within it.

Discussion

Coleridge wrote that for readers to enjoy works of fantasy they must experience "a willing suspension of disbelief." If a story contradicts what the reader already knows (or thinks she knows) about the world, this conflict can interrupt the reader's suspension of disbelief and ruin the story. Science fiction often aids the reader's suspension of disbelief by setting the story in the future (as in Frank Herbert's **Dune**), when science and **technology** has developed beyond the limitations of the present day. Fantasy achieves the same goal by setting the story in the mythic past (as in J.R.R. Tolkien's *The Lord of the Rings*), or in a **parallel world**. Secret history rejects both these options, choosing instead to risk the reader's disbelief by openly contradicting elements of the historical past within an otherwise realistic historical setting. The secret history inverts reality, substituting its own fiction for historical fact.

Bibliography

Jon Adams. "Science Fiction in Pursuit of History." Bernd Engler and Kurt Muller, eds., *Historiographic Metafiction in Modern American and Canadian Literature*. Munchen: Schoningh, 1994, 147–161.

R.H. Canary. "Science Fiction as Fictive History." *Extrapolation*, 16 (December, 1974), 81–93.

David Cowart. *History and the Contemporary Novel*. Carbondale, Illinois: Southern Illinois University Press, 1989.

L. Sprague De Camp. "Pseudohistory." De Camp, *Rubber Dinosaurs and Wooden Elephants*. San Bernardino, CA: Borgo Press, 1996, 63–67.

Karen Hellekson. *The Alternate History*. Kent, Ohio: Kent State University Press, 2001.

Edward James. "The Historian and SF." *Foundation*, No. 35 (Winter, 1985/1886), 5–13.

D. Roselle. "Teaching About World History through Science Fiction." *Social Education*, 37 (February, 1973), 94–150.

Pamela Sargent. "Science Fiction, Historical Fiction, and Alternate History." *SFWA Bulletin*, 29 (Fall, 1995), 3–7.

T.A. Shippey. "Science Fiction and the Idea of History." *Foundation*, No. 4 (July, 1973), 4–19.

—Ed McKnight

SECRET IDENTITIES
■

Overview

The term "secret identity" is most frequently applied to **superheroes** who carry on normal existence under another name when not doing heroic deeds. A secret identity can also result from a **metamorphosis** into another being given a different name or a manifestation of a side of one's personality obscured to other people. Secret identities can be also assumed to carry out **espionage** in **technothrillers** or to **escape** from some unpleasant situation.

Survey

Stories of secret identities have roots in ancient **mythologies** as disguised deities (see **Gods and Goddesses**) frequently descended to walk among mortals. Ovid's *Metamorphosis* (c. 8 CE), for example, tells of Jupiter and Mercury traveling in disguise to meet, and magically reward, a kindly couple. Old gods living in banishment in the mundane world are principal characters in Neil Gaiman's *American Gods* (2001).

In medieval times stories circulated about kings (and sometimes **queens**) moving in secrecy among their peoples, often assuming identities of destitute subjects, as later occurred in Mark Twain's *The Prince and the Pauper* (1881).

Perhaps reacting against the normative spirit of the era, the nineteenth century marked the publication of numerous stories involving doubles (see **Doppelgänger**) and secret identities. Among them are E.T.A. Hoffmann's *The Devil's Elixirs* (1815–1816) and Theophile Gautier's "Chevalier Double" (1840), but the most famous is Robert Louis Stevenson's ***Strange Case of Dr. Jekyll and Mr. Hyde***, in which the protagonists are two polarized aspects, good and **evil**, of one human psyche, with the new name of Mr. Hyde concealing the fact that he represents the darker side of Dr. Jekyll.

In the twentieth century secret identities became the domain of superheroes. Typically, one of their double lives is as an average and inconspicuous, albeit possibly wealthy or intelligent person. The other is as a superhero who, equipped with special powers and distinguished by a dramatic costume, fights crime and injustice. The superhero persona may represent the person's original identity—the Krypton-born ***Superman*** masquerades as Clark Kent and the **Amazon** ***Wonder Woman*** masquerades as Diana Prince—or it may be a second role assumed after acquisition or development of special powers—teenager Peter Parker becomes Spider-Man and millionaire Bruce Wayne becomes ***Batman***. Since almost all superheroes come from **America**, their double nature can be partly read in terms of the traditional American notion of the possibility of one's reinvention and the lack of restrictions on re-making one's identity.

Although superheroes' secret identities are predominantly integrated parts of their personalities and their transformations—either literal or metaphorical—are conscious and controlled, it is possible for characters to have *alter egos* that they are unaware of. This may result from amnesia—which may be natural or induced by some external factors or agents. In the movie ***Total Recall***, the protagonist discovers that his memories are not his own but he has no idea who tampered with them. Recovery of his original identity brings him to **Mars**, where he joins the **rebellion** against the oppressive establishment. A more complex treatment of the theme of technologically mediated identities comes in Greg Bear's *Slant* (1997), which features a mysterious mercenary figure, Carl Black/Jack Giffey, the latter being an artificial persona deactivated by a password. Further, there is a distinct albeit unresolved possibility that behind the two is Colonel Sir John Yardley, an ex-dictator from Bear's *Queen of Angels* (1990).

In fantasy or fantasy-oriented fiction, characters may be unwitting avatars of deities, slowly realizing who they really are. The gradual uncovering of a secret identity may be connected with acquisition or restoration of supernatural powers. This occurs in Jack Williamson's *Darker Than You Think* (1948) and Roger Zelazny's *Creatures of Light and Darkness* (1969), in which characters discover that they are respectively the dark **messiah** of a primordial race of **shapeshifters** and the defeated Egyptian god Set (see **Egypt**).

Science fiction works in which secret identities are assumed for purposes of espionage are too numerous to list, particularly in technothrillers and **cyberpunk**. One early example is *Children of the Lens* (1954) (see ***Triplanetary***), where E.E. "Doc" Smith temporarily casts, tongue-in-cheek, Kimball Kinnison as Sybly Whyte, an author of particularly bad **space operas**.

Discussion

Stories of secret identities, usually characterized by features radically different from those of "ordinary" identities, can be viewed as reflections of people's desires and fears. In older literature doubles were manifestations of rebellion against social restrictions (see **Individualism and Conformity**) or incarnations of one's darker side. In the twentieth century such fictions can be additionally regarded as a channeling of the **anxiety** connected with the pressures of life and omnipresence of constructed official selves, and an admission that modern personality is not as coherent as often believed. Within the framework of **postmodernism**, which views inconsistency in character as natural, literary secret identities can be read as reflections on multifaceted identity, some part of which is too weak or too radical to be manifested publicly.

Bibliography

Thomas Andrae. "From Menace to Messiah." *Discourse*, 2 (Summer 1980), 84–111.

Will Brooker. *Batman Unmasked*. London: Continuum, 2000.

Brian A. Hollerback. "Devining Neil Gaiman: An Exegesis of *American Gods*." *Strange Horizons* (October, 2001), 29–41.

Mark Jancovich. "Identity and Repression in *Dr. Jekyll and Mr. Hyde*." Michael Stuprich, ed., *Horror*. San Diego, CA: Greenhaven Press, 2001, 143–147.

Donna Lance. "Science Fiction and Mythology." Judith Kellogg and Jesse Crisler, eds., *Literature and Hawaii's Children*. Honolulu: University of Hawaii at Manoa, 1994, 125–132.

Lawrence McCallum. "The Many Faces of Evil." *Eldritch Tales*, 7 (1990), 31–36.

Salvatore Mondello. "Spider-Man." Jack Nachbar, Deborah Weiser and John L. Wright, eds., *Popular Culture Reader*. Bowling Green, OH: Bowling Green State University Popular Press, 1978, 216–224.

Gary Westfahl. "The Three Lives of Superman—and Everybody Else." Westfahl, *Science Fiction, Children's Literature, and Popular Culture*. Westport, CT: Greenwood Press, 2000, 13–17.

James S. Whitlark. "Superheroes as Dream Doubles." William Coyle, ed., *Aspects of Fantasy*. Westport, CT: Greenwood Press, 1986, 107–112.

—Pawel Frelik

SENSE OF WONDER

All this long human story, most passionate and tragic in the living, was but an unimportant, a seemingly barren and negligible effort, lasting only for a few moments in the life of the galaxy. When it was over, the host of the planetary systems still lived on, with here and there a

casualty, and here and there among the
stars a new planetary birth, and here and
there a fresh disaster.

—Olaf Stapledon
Star Maker (1937)

Overview

One of the core effects of science fiction is the "sense of wonder": the thrill of being forced into new ways of seeing things. Often associated with a vastness of scale, in which an object like a huge spaceship or a detailed, plausible picture of an **alien world** causes readers to reflect upon their own positions as inhabitants of a universe stranger than they imagined, it is sometimes ironized by fans as the "gosh-wow!" effect. This effect can be achieved through paradigm shifts, reconsiderations of the universe and **humanity**'s place in it, and as such is associated with the **sublime**. It can also be achieved—at least in young and/or naïve readers of science fiction—by technological effects like huge planet-busting **weaponry** and "big dumb objects."

Survey

The early effects of wonder appear in **space operas** like E.E. "Doc" Smith's *Triplanetary* and *Star Wars*, where the props instilling it are imaginative representations of bigger and bigger spaceships or (carefully sanitized) **space war** on a larger and larger scale. Such props are reinforced by the tendency of blockbuster science fiction films to go for spectacle at the expense of rational plot or character (as in the film *Independence Day* [1996]). This is not necessarily to disparage such effects, and in *2001: A Space Odyssey*, extended contemplation of humanity's early days, faced with either developing **intelligence** or becoming extinct, and spacecraft almost dancing in space to a soundtrack of classical music, go far beyond spectacle. A more numinous sense of wonder exists in the way Arthur C. Clarke contemplates the universe as something that both inspires awe and can be understood. There is a poetic melancholy in *Childhood's End* as we watch humanity transcend and consider its Guardians who cannot. Clarke's sense of immensities comes from the epic future **histories** of Olaf Stapledon, *Last and First Men* and *Star Maker*, in which the spirit of humanity is celebrated but the essential fragility of the human condition is emphasized. Time and again, the human race is all but brought to extinction. In the latter novel, we see the different kinds of life possible in the universe: science fiction's encounter with **aliens in space** is often less a metaphor for how we deal with social otherness but more exhilaration at the idea of Otherness itself. Stories like Terry Carr's "The Dance of the Changer and the Three" (1968) attempt to describe something truly alien. Such impulses occur in fantasy as well, in Sam's naïve astonishment at the "oliphaunt" and Frodo's wonderment at the elf-queen Galadriel (see J.R.R. Tolkien's *The Lord of the Rings*).

Wonder leads to the conceptual breakthrough, the progression from astonishment at the novelty presented before us to critical consideration of its potential. The *idea* of the creature in Mary Shelley's *Frankenstein*, or the **robot** in Capek's *R.U.R.* (1920), leads to almost immediate consideration of what such symbols mean. Although the hero of Hugo Gernsback's *Ralph 124C 41+: A Romance of the Year*

2660 (1925) rarely moves beyond astonishment, science fiction opened up ways of using popular fiction to tell stories about the future and began debates with the more skeptical **utopias** of H.G. Wells that continue to this day. Wells's championing of **technology** in polemics like *A Modern Utopia* (1905) and explorations of **time** and **evolution** in *The Time Machine* stem in part from his visionary sense of the wonders of the future, and much utopian fiction is, at heart, wonderment. We "wonder" both at the physical **Mars** presented by Kim Stanley Robinson's *Red Mars* and at the potential for utopian and political speculations such a location offers. The same impulse is at the heart of the neo-space opera exemplified by Iain M. Banks's *Consider Phlebas*, where the desire for action, technology and loud adventure is fueled by a humanistic passion for morality.

Discussion

The sense of wonder is linked, above all, to the idea of science fiction, and some kinds of fantasy, as literatures of ideas or effect, rather than character. This is where problems arise. The significantly titled magazines *Astounding Stories* and *Wonder Stories* featured writers like Nat Schachner, whose stories like "Crystallized Thought" (1937) were full of ideas but lacking in simple exploration of commonplace humanity. But "wonder" is also linked to the *speculative*, extrapolative undercurrents of science fiction: "what if?" and the thought-experiment. It is scientific inquiry at its most basic ("What happens if I do *this*?") and its most urgent ("How do I *understand* the universe and my place in it?"). In fantasy, it often arises from the contemplation of place, the Romantic awe at **landscape, mountains**, and **rivers,** and is especially close to its antecedents in the sublime: the "infinite spaces" that so terrified Blaise Pascal. In both modes, it concerns the description of the indescribable, the charting of places no one has ever been, and the encounter with aliens. In science fiction, especially, it is where desire fuses with the intellect in a passionate quest to explore and *understand*.

Bibliography

Gregory Benford. "Effing the Ineffable." *Foundation*, No. 38 (Winter, 1986/1987), 49–57.

James Blish. "A Question of Content." Blish, *The Issue at Hand*. Chicago: Advent, 1964, 138–149.

Istvan Csicsery–Ronay, Jr. "On the Grotesque in Science Fiction." *Science Fiction Studies*, 29 (March, 2002), 71–99.

Eric L. Davin. "Hugo Gernsback, Sense of Wonder, and the Birth of Science Fiction." Davin, *Pioneers of Wonder*. Amherst, NY: Prometheus Books, 1999, 13–26.

Thomas M. Disch. "Science Fiction as a Church." *Foundation*, No. 25 (June, 1982), 53–58.

David Hartwell. *Age of Wonders*. Revised Edition. New York: Tor, 1996.

Cornel Robu. "A Key to Science Fiction: The Sublime." *Foundation*, No. 42 (Spring, 1988), 21–37.

———. "The Sense of Wonder Is 'a Sense Sublime.'" *SFRA Review*, No. 211 (May/June, 1994), 43–64.

David Sandner. "Habituated to the Vast." *Extrapolation*, 41 (Fall, 2000), 283–297.

—Andy Sawyer

SEXISM

∎

Overview

Science fiction and fantasy have historically reflected sexism, favoring men and denigrating women. This occurs by ignoring women; representing female symbols as **evil**; portraying women only as objects to be rescued; and limiting them to roles as assistants and subordinates. More enlightened representations of women are discussed under **Feminism** and **Gender**.

Survey

Science fiction "has been considered a predominantly masculine field which, through its focus on science and technology, 'naturally' excludes women," Helen Merrick notes. Early science fiction, as Eric S. Rabkin observes, maltreated women by simply ignoring them, as men conquered **nature** on other planets with the use of machines. Similarly, **utopias** like Edward Bellamy's *Looking Backward, 2000–1887* offer only the male view. A study of utopian literature indicates that with rare exceptions like Charlotte Perkins Gilman's *Herland*, women are largely eclipsed until the feminist utopias of the 1970s. Women may even be excluded from future human **cultures**: in Thomas Gardner's "The Last Woman" (1932), all women but one have died out. The all-male Science Civilization keeps her alive in a cage, displayed like an animal in a zoo, and finally executes her.

Many fantasies exclude women as well. J.R.R. Tolkien's *The Lord of the Rings* is one of the innumerable fantasies with an almost entirely male cast of characters: on a bonding **quest**, one group of males battles other males in a predominantly masculine world. However, an evil female symbol, a **ring**, corrupts and destroys the wearer. When women play a prominent role in fantasies, it is often as evil **temptresses** whom **heroes** resist and overcome, a prominent example being Ayesha in H. Rider Haggard's *She*.

When women were featured in science fiction, they were generally plot foils, beautiful objects that men could rescue from rape by male **villains** of various species. Edgar Rice Burroughs is one of the writers who treated woman in this fashion. He popularized the image of the exotic princess in early interplanetary novels like *A Princess of Mars*: a woman on some distant planet must be saved from sundry scoundrels, and in the course of his adventures the hero triumphs and marries her. Jane Porter of Burroughs's *Tarzan of the Apes* is the contemporary American version of this figure (see **America**). Fritz Burg's "The Silicon Empire" (1933) exemplifies the theme of women in need of rescue by featuring a beautiful nude on a marble slab kept in suspended animation fifteen miles underground until the hero saves her.

If heroes cannot find a women to rescue and cherish, they may create one. In a classic **robot** story, Lester del Rey's "Helen O'Loy" (1938), Dave, an ingenious inventor, creates a female robot, programming her with the emotional qualities he identifies with females of the species. The metallic Helen falls in love with and marries her creator, illustrating a sexist desire that robs creativity from women and makes women products and possessions of men. Decades later, another scientist dominating a coded romantic relationship with a beautiful female robot figured in the television series *My Living Doll* (1964–1965).

Women in science fiction may also serve as assistants to heroes, sometimes help-ing out but more often becoming objects to be rescued, one example being Dale Arden of the serial *Flash Gordon* (1936) and its sequels. Women might appear as daughters of **scientists** or professors, primarily there to listen to men's theories, make coffee, get rescued, and eventually marry the hero. This binary depiction at the core of sexism, with men as the scientists and women as helpless, often endan-gered companions, carried over into science fiction films like *It Came From Outer Space* (1953). Fiancée Ellen supports amateur astronomer John Putnam, who has no need to explain his avocation; when Ellen vanishes in the grasp of an **alien on Earth**, he rescues her. The 1986 video release of *It! The Terror from Beyond Space* (1958) boasts a cover reminiscent of covers in the pulps, a large alien **monster** holding up a terrified woman. Sexism sets the tone of the movie as women serve seated male astronauts, and the only woman scientist confesses that her devotion to science entirely resulted from a love affair with a man gone awry—her involvement with science presented as problematic.

Discussion

In science fiction and fantasy of recent decades, given more enlightened social attitudes and growing numbers of women readers and writers, one would expect to encounter sexism only as an archaic attitude to be scathingly criticized. This is the case, for example, in Joanna Russ's **The Female Man**, in which one of the depicted worlds is a sexist **dystopia** where **war** between men and women is actively waged. Still, others argue that sexism is still rampant, albeit in more sub-tle forms: women may be given more active roles but remain supporting charac-ters, as in J.K. Rowling's Harry Potter series (see **Harry Potter and the Sorcerer's Stone**), or stories may foreground female heroes who mimic masculine behavior and attitudes (like Ripley in **Alien** and its sequels). Certainly, progress has occurred, but one cannot say that science fiction and fantasy are entirely free of the ancient taint of sexism.

Bibliography

Brian Attebery. *Decoding Gender in Science Fiction*. New York: Routledge, 2002.

Angelika Bammer. *Partial Visions*. New York: Routledge, 1991.

Sarah Lefanu. *In the Chinks of the World Machine*. Bloomington: Indiana University Press, 1988.

Ursula K. Le Guin. "American SF and the Other." Le Guin, *The Language of the Night*. New York: Putnam, 1979, 97–100.

Helen Merrick. "Gender in Science Fiction." Edward James and Farah Mendelsohn, eds., *The Cambridge Companion to Science Fiction*. Cambridge: Cambridge University Press, 2003, 241–252.

Eric S. Rabkin. "Science Fiction Women before Liberation." Marleen Barr, ed., *Future Females*. Bowling Green, OH: Bowling Green State University Popular Press, 1981. 9–25.

Robin Roberts. *A New Species*. Urbana: University of Illinois Press, 1993.

Gary Westfahl. "Superladies in Waiting." *Foundation*, No. 58 (Summer, 1993), 42–62.

Jenny Wolmark. *Aliens and Others*. Hemel Hempstead, Herts: Harvester, 1994.

—*Batya Weinbaum*

SEXUALITY

—■—

I'm just a sweet transvestite
From Transexual
Transylvania.

—Richard O'Brien
"Sweet Transvestite," *The Rocky Horror*
Show (1973)

Overview

Sexuality refers to erotic relationships between one person and one or more other beings, or toward or from objects. This is a controversial subject because on one hand it seems missing from many genre narratives, yet on the other it is present as a subtext within many others—and indeed within the same narratives. Other entries address the topics of **gender** and **homosexuality**.

Survey

In the eighteenth and nineteenth centuries it was impossible to directly represent sexual acts, although sexuality is implicit in any narrative dealing with romantic attachments and **marriage**. In the **Gothic** novel there were even areas where this might stray into nonheterosexual sexuality (though the word "heterosexual" was not coined until 1869). In Mary Shelley's *Frankenstein* the eponymous protagonist usurps the traditionally female role of reproduction, demonstrates sexual attraction to his dead mother, avoids his conjugal rites after his wedding, and chases his creation several hundred miles across hostile **landscapes**. The narrator, meanwhile, has gone in search of a special friend on an Arctic sea journey.

The neo-Gothic classics—including Robert Louis Stevenson's *Strange Case of Dr Jekyll and Mr Hyde*, Oscar Wilde's *The Picture of Dorian Gray*, and Bram Stoker's *Dracula*—depict the often furtive sexual predilections of late Victorian bachelors. The latter also depicts female sexuality, with Lucy Westenra unable to decide between three suitors and rather wishing she had even more. Jonathan Harker, meanwhile, has been unmanned by his seduction by three female **vampires** and rescue by a male vampire. This was not the first vampire narrative to deal with (and punish) sexuality of various kinds, and not the last.

Science fiction was initially heteronormative—with the Time Traveller in Wells's *The Time Machine* telling his tale to a group of bachelors but having an Eloi woman to fall in love with. Women largely disappeared from written science fiction for sixty years, largely playing token roles as beautiful daughters and love interests (see **Sexism**). Most narratives centered on a group of men, offering scope for slippage from homosociality to an unacknowledged homosexuality. Fantasy was equally uninterested in sexuality—desire being largely absent from, for example, the surface of J.R.R. Tolkien's *The Lord of the Rings*.

On screen, despite the Hays Code from the early 1930s, sexual subtexts were common. Precisely what the Eighth Wonder of the World could get up to with the screaming blonde in *King Kong* remained unclear, but the great **ape** was clearly attracted to her. Equally, the scene in which Nikki ties up Captain Patrick Hendry slips a mild form of bondage into *The Thing (from Another World)*; the Thing can also be taken to represent dangerous male desire.

In the 1950s some pioneering fiction explored sexuality: Philip José Farmer's *The Lovers* (1952) scandalously featured an **Earth** society that banned sexual activity and a man who fell in love with a female alien; and Theodore Sturgeon, having sensitively explored homosexuality in "The World Well Lost" (1953), critiqued sexual relationships in the neutrally sexed **utopia** of Ledom in *Venus Plus X* (1960).

From the 1960s the genres became more permissive and James Bond (from *Doctor No* onwards) and James Kirk in *Star Trek* proved their masculinity by bedding a series of women. Robert A. Heinlein, in *Stranger in a Strange Land*, applied his libertarianism to sexuality, allowing for threesomes and group sex—although these had been subtly present in early books. In later novels the menu was expanded to include incest between different generations and, in *I Will Fear No Evil* (1970), an old man is transferred into a young woman's body, remaining sexually active.

It is only with novels like Ursula K. Le Guin's *The Left Hand of Darkness* that sexuality was really addressed as an issue: the Gethen are sexually neutral until they come into season, when they become male or female. Joanna Russ's *The Female Man* features a controversial scene in which a woman uses a man (with a monkey's brain) as a **cyborg** sextoy. The novel also questions "commonsensical" male notions about women. Only in the mid-1970s could Samuel R. Delany openly represent homosexuality and other forms of sexuality, also presenting in *Triton* a world where people routinely changed their sex. In his Nevèryon sequence beginning with *Tales of Nevèrÿon* (1979) Delany related sexuality to **slavery**, **economics** and **governance systems** and addressed issues surrounding AIDS.

Discussion

Although there are feminist and gay critics addressing issues of sexuality, there is much work still to be done, and heterosexuality is still rarely discussed from a male perspective. Twenty-first century writers like China Miéville in *Perdido Street Station* are addressing interspecies sexuality, as well as putting the implications of rape at the hearts of narratives. The sense by producers that science fiction is primarily aimed at children means that sexuality is still sidelined in telefantasy—the liberated universe of *Star Trek* is heterosexual and sex in the first three seasons of *Buffy the Vampire Slayer* was almost always punished—with Angel turning **evil** after sleeping with Buffy and Xander facing a series of monstrous women.

Bibliography

Albert I. Berger. "Love, Death and the Atomic Bomb." *Science-Fiction Studies*, 8 (November, 1981), 280–296.

Russell Blackford. "Sexuality in Science Fiction." *Science Fiction*, 6 (1984), 41.

Anne Cranny-Francis. "Sexuality and Sex-Role Stereotyping in *Star Trek*." *Science-Fiction Studies*, 12 (November, 1985), 274–284.

Kelly Hurley. *The Gothic Body*. Cambridge: Cambridge University Press, 1996.

Donald E. Palumbo, ed. *Eros in the Mind's Eye*. Westport, CT: Greenwood Press, 1986.

Donald E. Palumbo, ed. *Erotic Universe*. Westport, CT: Greenwood Press, 1986.

Warren G. Rochelle. "Dual Attractions." *Foundation*, No. 76 (Summer, 1999), 48–62.

Vivian Sobchack. "The Virginity of Astronauts." George Slusser and Eric S. Rabkin, eds., *Shadows of the Magic Lamp*. Carbondale: Southern Illinois University Press, 1985, 41–57.

Chris West. "Queer Fears and Critical Orthodoxies." *Foundation*, No. 86 (Autumn, 2002), 17–27.

—*Andrew M. Butler*

SHAKESPEARE

Overview

William Shakespeare's unique place in English literature—he is not only acknowledged as the greatest playwright and poet in the language, but was long regarded as an embodiment of the English national spirit, a figure of supreme moral **wisdom** and **political** insight—has lent themes in his canon an extraordinary authority, although few of his plots were original with him. Since the eighteenth century, English fiction and **poetry**—especially fantastic literature—have been deeply influenced by Shakespearian themes and motifs.

Survey

The first fantasies to employ Shakespearean themes were dramatic rather than literary, of which Henry Purcell's opera *The Fairy Queen* (1692) may be the earliest. Shakespeare began appearing as a character in novels in the early nineteenth century. This convention remains popular, and is sometimes employed by novelists better known for literary than historical fiction: examples include Anthony Burgess's *Nothing like the Sun* (1964) and Leon Rooke's *Shakespeare's Dog* (1983). While novelists of *belles lettres* have retold Shakespearean tales, usually to ironic effect—examples include James Branch Cabell's *Hamlet Had an Uncle* (1940) and John Updike's *Gertrude and Claudius* (2000)—the use of Shakespearian themes (as opposed to his plots or person) in contemporary literature remains uncommon. A rare exception is Jane Smiley's *A Thousand Acres* (1991) in which the family dynamics of *King Lear* are replayed in the American Midwest.

Since the 1940s, however, Shakespeare's plays—frequently but not exclusively those with supernatural elements, like *A Midsummer Night's Dream* (c. 1594), *Macbeth* (c. 1606), and *The Tempest* (c. 1611)—have served as sources for fantasy and science fiction novels, stories, and films. What W.H. Auden called Shakespeare's mythopoeic imagination seems in some respects more amenable to fantastic genres (which includes lyric verse) than the realistic and Modernist traditions that the contemporary novel long favored.

Although neither Fritz Leiber's novel *Gather, Darkness!* (1943) nor any stories in his collection *The Night's Black Agents* (1947) make explicit references to *Macbeth*,

Leiber dealt with themes from that play—especially **witches**, as in his *Conjure Wife* (1953)—throughout his career. Interestingly, motifs from *Macbeth* continued to recur throughout Leiber's science fiction, as in *The Big Time* (1958), which employs an epigraph from the play, and (again notwithstanding its title) "Four Ghosts in Hamlet" (1965). For Leiber, Shakespeare offers imaginative inspiration, rather than a discrete source for themes or story-lines.

Other authors tend to adapt Shakespeare more explicitly. *The Tempest* has proven amenable for both science fiction and fantasy, as its locale can remain an **island** or another world (see **Alien Worlds**) and Prospero can be a scientist—as in H.G. Wells's *The Island of Doctor Moreau* and the film *Forbidden Planet*—or a magus (see **Magic**). Caliban—who since the nineteenth century has been conceived more sympathetically than in Shakespeare—may be an alien (see **Aliens in Space**) or aborigine who encounters Prospero and his kin as figures of colonial hegemony (see **Postcolonialism**). Works of science fiction or fantasy that emphasize a revisionist Caliban or morally dubious Prospero include Brian W. Aldiss's "Else the Isle with Calibans" (1994), Tad Williams's *Caliban* (1994), John Fowles's *The Magus* (1965), Auden's "The Sea and the Mirror" (1944), and the Prospero poems in Eric Pankey's *The Late Romances* (1997).

A Midsummer Night's Dream, involving as it does both figures from Greek **mythology** and **fairies** (with **Amazons** only incidentally present), has been an especially rich source for modern fantasy. Fiction involving Greek gods rarely owe anything to Shakespeare, but the faerie **cosmologies** dramatized in John Crowley's *Little, Big*, Emma Bull's *War for the Oaks* (1987), Lisa Goldstein's *Strange Devices of the Sun and Moon* (1993), and Kara Dalkey's *Steel Rose* (1997) are deeply informed by Shakespeare's play. Most of the modern fantasies that include fairies show Shakespeare's influence (sometimes mediated through Victorian pictorial representations of the fairy world), as do works that include the imp figures Robin Goodfellow or Puck (whom Shakespeare conflated).

Although fantasy elements exist in other Shakespeare plays—*Richard III* (c. 1594), *Julius Caesar* (c. 1599), and *Hamlet* (c. 1601) include ghosts, while *Pericles* (c. 1608), *Cymbeline* (c. 1610), and *The Winter's Tale* (c. 1611) feature magical transformations—their themes appear less frequently in fantasy and science fiction. However, Poul Anderson's *A Midsummer Tempest* (1974) employs elements from the **history** plays (as well as the works implicit in its title), while the figure of Falstaff has inspired numerous bluff rogues in genre fiction, including Nicholas Van Rijn in Poul Anderson's Polesotechnic novels, beginning with *War of the Wing-Men* (1958), and Harvey Mudd in the television series *Star Trek*. More generally, various incarnations of *Star Trek* have employed so many references to Shakespeare that a special issue of the science fiction journal *Extrapolation* was devoted to the topic "Shakespeare and *Star Trek*."

Discussion

The presence of *Love's Labour's Lost* (c. 1594) in John Crowley's *Aegypt* (1987) and *Twelfth Night* (c. 1600) in Gene Wolfe's *The Book of the New Sun* are immensely subtler than the genre's earlier use of Shakespearean themes. This suggests that the self-consciousness that long characterized literary allusion in prose fantasy now belongs—even for so daunting as figure as Shakespeare—to its past history.

Bibliography

Brian W. Aldiss. "If Hamlet's Uncle Had Been a Nicer Guy." Allienne R. Becker, ed., *Visions of the Fantastic*. Westport, CT: Greenwood Press, 1996, 21–24.

Matthew S.S. Davis. "The Words of Mercury are Harsh . . ." *Foundation*, No. 89 (Autumn, 2003), 35–46.

Gregory Feeley. "The Evidence of Things Not Shown." *New York Review of Science Fiction*, No. 31 (March, 1991), 1, 8–10; No. 32 (April 1991), 12–16.

Giles Gordon, ed. *Shakespeare Stories*. London: Hamish Hamilton, 1982.

Katharine Kerr and Martin H. Greenberg, eds. *Weird Tales from Shakespeare*. New York: DAW Books, 1994.

S. Schoenbaum. *Shakespeare's Lives*. New York: Oxford University Press, 1970, 1991.

Gary Taylor. *Reinventing Shakespeare*. New York: Weidenfeld and Nicolson, 1989.

Deborah Willis. "Shakespeare's *Tempest* and the Discourse of Colonialism." Gerald Graff and James Phelan, eds. *The Tempest*. New York: Bedford/St. Martin's, 2000, 256–268.

—Gregory Feeley

SHAPESHIFTERS

∎

Overview

The term "shapeshifting" might be applied to all forms of **metamorphosis**: a single magical transformation of human into animal or vice versa, or a **curse** that periodically changes people into different forms, like **werewolves**. Ovid's *Metamorphoses* (c. 8 CE) includes many tales of shapeshifting from classical **mythology**. However, as the term is used today, shapeshifters are usually beings who can transform themselves at will into various shapes and creatures. These shapeshifters are also rooted in myth and legend, though their powers may now be explained in scientific terms.

Survey

The prototypical shapeshifter was the Greek god Proteus, who could also foretell the future (see **Divination**). After the Trojan War, Menelaus seizes Proteus, holds him firmly while he repeatedly transforms himself, and finally forces him to provide the information that he needs. Another significant figure is Homer's **temptress** Circe, who does not change her own appearance but turns Odysseus's men into swine, as described in Homer's *Odyssey* (c. 750 BCE); a similar figure appears in Edmund Spenser's *The Faerie Queene* (1590, 1596), wherein Guyon confronts Circe's sister enchantress, Acrasia (incontinence), who is surrounded by ex-lovers changed into wild beasts with minds and "figures hideous." In Greek myth and Spenser, ambiguous, transformational beings like Proteus and Circe are untrustworthy, immoral, and willful **gods and goddesses**.

In later centuries, shapeshifters continued to appear in European folklore and literature. Irish legends regarded stags and deer as otherworldly, so shapeshifting between deer and humans frequently occurs in Irish lore: Fionn's wife, Sadb, is turned into a fawn by druidic **magic** and their son, Ois'n, is considered half deer, half human. Another example is *Leabhar Gabhala* (c. 1150), which offers the curious account of Tuan, a man who loses his human shape for nine hundred years, spending three hundred years as a wild ox, two hundred as a stallion, three hundred as a solitary **bird**, and another hundred as a salmon, eventually eaten, before finally fathering himself. Scottish legends include the selkies, people who transform themselves into seals. Some versions of the **vampire** myth, including Bram Stoker's *Dracula*, grant vampires the power to transform themselves into various animals, particularly bats and wolves, although in the film *Van Helsing* (2004) Dracula's women also become **flying** harpies.

Contemporary **horror** stories and films remain fascinated with humans transformed into animals: in addition to werewolves, there is the film *Cat People* (1942), remade in 1986, wherein a young girl, if kissed, becomes a devouring panther. Also relevant is Robert Louis Stevenson's *Strange Case of Dr. Jekyll and Mr Hyde*, in which the more bestial human self beneath Jekyll's civilized veneer is released by a scientifically brewed potion. Jekyll befriends lawyers and conforms socially while Hyde treads on **children**, beats up infirm old people with a walking stick, and abuses, rapes, and dismembers prostitutes. Hyde—representing the unleashed sexual and **violent** energies cooped up in constrained civilized man—is rendered as furry and animal-like in film adaptations (see *Dr. Jekyll and Mr. Hyde*). Such shapeshifters embody fears of the **invasion** of the unfamiliar into familiar, safe, **family** relationships, partnerships, and our sense of wholeness and dignity.

In science fiction, a common theme is the **alien on Earth** who employs shapeshifting abilities to look human, as in the film *I Married a Monster from Outer Space* (1958) and episodes of the series *The X-Files*, in which police officers and bureaucrats reveal themselves to others momentarily, the **evil** within them suddenly glimpsed as they shapeshift into alien forms before reverting to human appearance.

In comic books, unlimited powers of shapeshifting may be found in **superheroes**, like DC Comics' Chameleon Boy of the Legion of Super-Heroes and Metamorpho. The alien security officer of *Star Trek: Deep Space Nine*—the figure who did the most to popularize the term "shapeshifter"—is also an heroic figure who employs shapeshifting abilities to protect a Federation **space station**. More frequently, though, shapeshifting is an attribute of **villains** or **monsters**. In John W. Campbell, Jr.'s "Who Goes There?" (1938), an alien with the ability to assume any form menaces an Antarctic base; while the first film version, *The Thing (from Another World)* eliminated the element of shapeshifting, it reemerged in the remake *The Thing* (1982). In an episode of *Star Trek*, "The Man Trap" (1966), the *Enterprise* is threatening by a shapeshifting alien who desperately craves the salt in human bodies. The evil Mystique, a shapeshifting mutant, opposes the X-Men in comic books and the films *X-Men* (2000) and *X2: X-Men United* (2003).

Discussion

In western civilization, the notion that our external shape is only a civilized veneer concealing our untamed, animal natures can be disturbing and frightening, so many shapeshifters are characterized as monsters. However, in eastern civilizations and among indigenous peoples, shapeshifting may relate positively to the myths and power of shamanism, the recognition of a spiritual self and what Marina Warner terms a "seductive invitation" that is fascinating in contrast to the Christian commitment to an embodied self (see **Christianity**). Shapeshifting may offer **escape** from **humanity's** limitations and positive alternatives to one's conformist, everyday self (see **Individualism and Conformity**); Donna Haraway theorizes shapeshifting as the basis for an empowering feminist re-reading of the body (see **Feminism**). Imagining transformations thus functions as an enlightening, liberating way to question what it means to be human.

Bibliography

Ernest L. Fontana. "Metamorphoses of Proteus: Calvino's *Cosmicomics*." *Perspectives in Contemporary Literature*, 5 (1979), 147–154.

Donna Haraway. "A Cyborg Manifesto." 1985. Haraway, *Simians, Cyborgs, and Women*. New York: Routledge, 1991, 149–181.

P.M.C. Forbes Irving. *Metamorphosis in Greek Myths*. Oxford: Oxford University Press, 1992.

Anna L. Kaplan. "*Star Trek: Deep Space Nine*: Rene Auberjonois, Odo." *Cinefantastique*, 29 (November, 1997), 32–34.

Robert Simpson. "Children of the Night." *Twilight Zone*, 7 (December, 1987), 22–25, 84–86.

Lisa Tuttle. "Pets and Monsters." Lucie Armitt, ed., *Where No Man Has Gone Before*. London, New York: Routledge, 1991, 97–108.

Marina Warner. *Fantastic Metamorphoses, Other Worlds*. New York: Oxford University Press, 2002.

Marina Warner. *No Go the Bogeyman*. London: Chatto and Windus, 1998.

Pat Wheeler. "Metamorphoses of the Female Subject." *Foundation*, No. 84 (Spring, 2002), 36–47.

—Gina Wisker

SHARED WORLDS

Overview

Imaginary worlds developed jointly by multiple authors are now a mainstay of fantasy and science fiction publishing, and many talented authors have participated in shared world projects. Critical assessments of shared world fiction tend to be harsh, as reviewers dismiss "sharecropper" or "franchise" books as wastes of resources that would be better spent on fiction fueled by individual, not collective vision. Still, even the strongest condemnations cannot dim the enthusiasm for shared world titles with both readers and publishers.

Survey

The roots of shared world fiction lie in the story papers and dime novels of the late nineteenth century. To appeal to the newly emerging mass market, publishers offered sensational but formulaic adventures undertaken by series characters like

Nick Carter (see **Detectives**). Since it was all but impossible for individual authors to meet the demand for stories linked to popular characters, publishers controlling these creations employed several writers to generate the necessary prose. They bought all rights to each work for a flat fee and usually ran a house name as the byline, making the actual author secondary to the intellectual property promoted by the story.

This strategy of minimizing authorial identity became the norm for shared world projects in the early twentieth century. Operations like the Stratemeyer Syndicate, originator of the science fiction series featuring boy inventor Tom Swift, functioned like fiction factories, with a stable of anonymous authors churning out stories as fast as they could be sold. The pulp magazines of the 1930s adopted the same model, with various writers chronicling the adventures of Doc Savage, Captain Future, and other series characters.

By the 1980s, house names became less prevalent, and book lines tied to *Star Wars* and *Star Trek* boasted high-profile contributors like Terry Brooks (see *The Sword of Shannara*) and Greg Bear (see *Blood Music*). Shared worlds connected to role-playing **games** allowed for more creative freedom, with settings less fixed in fans' minds than those from television or films. R.A. Salvatore introduced the scimitar-wielding dark **elf**, Drizzt Do'Urden, to the pre-existing Forgotten Realms **heroic fantasy** setting in *Homeland* (1990), but Drizzt and Salvatore came to so dominate the line that the publisher promoted his authorial identity.

Authorial identity is promoted in a different way with shared world works that continue a famous writer's creation. After the death of L. Frank Baum (see *The Wonderful Wizard of Oz*), Ruth Plumly Thompson extended the Oz series with nineteen books, five more than Baum himself, before yielding to additional Oz authors. Robert E. Howard (see *Conan the Conqueror*) published only seventeen Conan stories in his lifetime, but beginning in the 1950s, L. Sprague de Camp and others completed Howard's unfinished stories, rewrote non-Conan stories to feature Conan, and created dozens of new novels featuring the **barbarian** icon. A trilogy of novels by Gregory Benford, Greg Bear, and David Brin continued the *Foundation* series after Isaac Asimov's passing. Questions have arisen regarding the legitimacy of these works, since the original author's intent for a series is difficult to ascertain. The new writers also face the daunting task of producing entertaining stories without being able to substantially alter the given imaginary world.

Questions of legitimacy are lessened when living authors invite other writers to participate in their imaginary worlds. Marion Zimmer Bradley (see *The Mists of Avalon*) allowed a wide circle of fans and authors to pen stories filling in the **history** of her **alien world** of Darkover. Larry Niven invited authors like Poul Anderson and Jerry Pournelle to chronicle the Man-Kzin War in his Known Space universe, the setting of *Ringworld* (1970). Such shared world projects work more as collaborations, with original creators participating directly in the project and letting secondary authors more actively contribute to the world's development.

For other shared world projects, a core group of authors creates a broad setting outline, then invites other creators to join them. These collective efforts give authors the chance to maintain copyright to their stories and a modicum of creative control over their characters. Robert Lynn Asprin and Lynn Abbey's anthology *Thieves' World* (1979) and its sequels, an heroic fantasy series, kicked off a wave of these collaborative efforts, including George R.R. Martin's anthology *Wild Cards* (1987) and its sequels, featuring various **superheroes**.

Other works identified as shared worlds have even less centralized creative control. In the 1930s, H.P. Lovecraft informally opened up elements of his Arkham Cycle of stories to other writers, who developed the setting into a loose canon later known as the Cthulhu Mythos. Though Lovecraft commented upon tales, he did not exert formal control over their contents. *The Petrified Planet*, released in 1952, was the first in the short-lived Twayne Triplets series. Using an introductory scientific essay as the starting point for an imaginary world, Fletcher Pratt, H. Beam Piper, and Judith Merril crafted individual stories that emphasized individual perspective over tightly maintained continuity. Harlan Ellison (see *Deathbird Stories*) took a similar approach when putting together *Medea: Harlan's World* in 1985.

At its most extreme, this lack of centralized content control results in books that are shared world in name only. James Lowder's trilogy of **zombie** anthologies, beginning with *The Book of All Flesh* (2001), featured the logo for a role-playing game on their covers, but individual stories did not involve a coordinated imaginary world and presented radically diverse variations on the zombie theme. Such projects utilize the marketing appeal of shared worlds but avoid the restrictions on creativity that accompany them.

Discussion

The demand for shared world fiction can be explained by the appeal of the familiar. Readers find comfort in revisiting familiar imaginary worlds through action-packed tales that thrill, but do not substantially alter the setting or its major characters. Not all shared world fiction offers up such safe fare, however, and series that allow authorial control can generate stories that explore characters and themes from a variety of perspectives, just as a multitude of authors have intriguingly explored **Arthur** and the Matter of Britain across the centuries.

Bibliography

Isaac Asimov. "Sharing Universes." *Isaac Asimov's Science Fiction Magazine*, 14 (August, 1990), 4–8.
Peter S. Beagle. "Authors in Search of a Universe." *Omni*, 10 (November, 1987), 40, 106.
Gregory Benford. "Beyond the Fall of Snobbery." *Vector*, No. 157 (October, 1990), 3.
Patricia Monk. "The Shared Universe." *Journal of the Fantastic in the Arts*, 2 (1990), 7–46.
Frederik Pohl and Elizabeth A. Hull. "The Sharing of Worlds." *Extrapolation*, 30 (Winter, 1989), 339–349.
Faye Ringel. "The Scribblies." *Extrapolation*, 35 (Fall, 1994), 201–210.
Pamela Sargent. "In the Tradition of." George Zebrowski, ed., *Synergy Science Fiction*. New York: Harcourt, 1989, 246–260.
Peter Wright. "The Shared World of Doctor Who." *Foundation*, No. 75 (Spring, 1999), 78–96.

—James Lowder

SIN

■

Even the most evil of men and women, if you understand their hearts, had some generous act that redeems them, at least a little, from their sins.

—Orson Scott Card
Speaker for the Dead (1986)

Overview

A sin is a violation of a **religion**'s moral code, an important concept in **Christianity**. Although sins are **evil** actions, sinners are not necessarily evil; rather, they may simply be weak and susceptible to temptation, and realizing the wrongness of their deeds, may be burdened with a tremendous guilt (see **Guilt and Responsibility**). By Christian doctrine, all humans inherited original sin from their ancestors **Adam and Eve** and can evade punishment for their sins only because Jesus Christ died on the Cross as the surrogate recipient of their just punishment (see **Messiahs**). Sin therefore becomes a major issue in science fiction stories that symbolically retell the story of Christ, like C.S. Lewis's *The Lion, the Witch and the Wardrobe,* or science fiction works examining alien societies that may lack original sin, like Lewis's *Perelandra* (1942) (see *Out of the Silent Planet*) and James Blish's *A Case of Conscience* (1958).

Survey

Early Christians classified all sins into seven categories—the Seven Deadly Sins of Pride, Envy, Gluttony, Lust, Wrath, Greed, and Sloth—which sometimes figure in older works of fantasy: in *The Purgatorio* (c. 1306–1321), Dante envisioned Purgatory as a mountain with seven levels, each designed to purge sinners of one sin to gradually become worthy to enter **Heaven**—and a pageant of the Seven Deadly Sins is presented to amuse the fallen Faustus in Christopher Marlowe's play *Doctor Faustus* (1604). The Seven Deadly Sins also provide a convenient organizing principle for a discussion of sin in science fiction and fantasy.

Pride is often the downfall of misguided **kings** and **queens** of fantasy who refuse to admit they are wrong, like the Steward of Gondor in J.R.R. Tolkien's *The Lord of the Rings,* and alien invaders of Earth who have superior **technology** but underestimate the ingenuity and determination of outmatched human opponents, as in the film *Independence Day* (1996). Pride is lampooned in Edwin A. Abbott's *Flatland* by describing the absurd pretensions of the King of Lineland, overweeningly proud of a realm that appears pitifully limited to outside observers.

Envy may be displayed by the wicked stepmothers of fantasy who resent the superior **beauty** of their stepdaughters, like the wicked **queen** in *Snow White and the Seven Dwarfs* and Cinderella's stepmother. Aliens are also victimized by envy; as expressed in the memorable opening passage of H.G. Wells's *The War of the*

Worlds, it was envy of Earth's bountiful natural resources that motivated inhabitants of a barren **Mars** to invade Earth and doom themselves.

Gluttony today may be viewed as more a foible than a sin, though the film *Willy Wonka and the Chocolate Factory* (1970) inflicts surprisingly severe punishment upon a young glutton, and a voracious overeater is satirized in the film *Monty Python's The Meaning of Life* (1983) (see **Satire**). Sometimes it is feared that future humans will become enormously fat due to gluttony, as occurs in a **space station** in Jack Vance's "Abercrombie Station" (1952).

Lust characterizes **villains** who seek to take beautiful women away from virtuous **heroes** they **love**, a recurring crisis in the works of Edgar Rice Burroughs and other science fiction and fantasy adventures influenced by melodrama; and Thomas Covenant's rape of a young woman in Stephen R. Donaldson's *Lord Foul's Bane* seems a shocking violation of the Land's moral order. The classic bug-eyed **monsters** lusting after scantily clad human females appeared more often on covers of science fiction magazines than in their stories, but the pattern is observed in science fiction films like *The Creature from the Black Lagoon* (1954).

An irrational wrath may motivate villains to perform particularly evil deeds: wrath drives the offended Paul Lozano to obsessively hunt down and kill Billy Pilgrim in Kurt Vonnegut, Jr.'s *Slaughterhouse-Five*, and wrath inspires a vengeful **computer** to inflict grotesque punishment on the man who thwarted its goals in Harlan Ellison's "I Have No Mouth, and I Must Scream" (1967).

Greed for **gold and silver** is often attributed to **dwarfs**, as in J.R.R. Tolkien's *The Hobbit*, and is displayed by most villains who confront **superheroes**; in the film *Superman*, for example, Lex Luthor's scheme to sink California into the ocean is motivated by a desire to get rich by selling the new oceanfront properties that will be created by the **disaster**.

Given fantasy's keen interest in opposing evil at all costs, and science fiction's characteristic commitment to unending human **progress** in the future, sloth in pursuing such goals may be the most despised sin; one readily finds heroes who are proud or lustful or greedy, but rarely one who is lazy. There is a particular fear that scientific progress and **evolution** will make our descendants weak, helpless people, as exemplified by the gentle Eloi of Wells's *The Time Machine*, the people who have lost the ability to move on their own accord in David H. Keller's "The Revolt of the Pedestrians" (1928), and the passive dwarfs pampered by machines in John W. Campbell, Jr.'s "Twilight" (1934).

Discussion

Sins are not always opposed in science fiction and fantasy, since some works embrace forms of behavior usually regarded as sinful and decadent (see **Decadence**) or thoughtfully question traditional moral codes. A short list of examples might include Oscar Wilde's *The Picture of Dorian Gray*, Robert A. Heinlein's *Stranger in a Strange Land* (originally titled, interestingly, *The Heretic*), and *The Rocky Horror Picture Show* (1975). Overall, though, the moral values expressed in science fiction and fantasy are typically conventional, especially in recent decades as books and movies aspire to reach as wide an audience as possible. Of course, appealing to popular tastes to gain wealth and high status is hardly an original sin.

Bibliography

Isaac Asimov. "Unforgivable Sin." Asimov, *Asimov's Galaxy*. New York: Doubleday, 1989, 41–44.

Isaac Asimov, Charles G. Waugh, and Martin Harry Greenberg, eds. *The Seven Deadly Sins of Science Fiction*. New York: Fawcett, 1980.

I.F. Clarke. "20th Century Future-Think." *Futures*, 24 (May, 1992), 388–396.

Gary W. Crawford. "The Landscape of Sin." Darrell Schweitzer, ed., *Discovering Classic Horror Fiction I*. Mercer Island, WA: Starmont, 1992, 74–99.

Don King. "Narnia and the Seven Deadly Sins." *Mythlore*, 10 (Spring, 1984), 14–19.

Michael H. Macdonald and Mark P. Shea. "Saving Sinners and Reconciling Churches." David Mills, ed., *The Pilgrim's Guide*. Grand Rapids, MI: Eerdmans, 1998, 43–52.

Charles W. Nelson. "The Sins of Middle-Earth." George Clark and Daniel Timmons, eds., *J.R.R. Tolkien and His Literary Resonances*. Westport, CT: Greenwood Press, 2000, 83–94.

Ellen M. Pedersen. "John Norman's Seven Sins." *Vector*, No. 141 (December, 1987/January, 1998), 15–16.

Anne E. Tanski. "The Sins of the Innocent." Val Gough and Jill Rudd, eds., *A Very Different Story*. Liverpool, UK: Liverpool University Press, 1998, 68–80.

—*Gary Westfahl*

SKELETONS

Overview

A human skeleton may be observed in a doctor's office or professor's classroom, signalling the person's serious interest in the science of human anatomy; this is why doctors, like *Star Trek*'s Dr. McCoy, are nicknamed "Bones." More frequently, skeletons are associated with **horror** and the macabre. Unexpected discovery of a skeleton may represent a **mystery** to solve (see **Crime and Punishment**), and a frightening **monster** in literature and film is an ambulatory skeleton. To this day, skeleton costumes remain popular **disguises** to wear on **Halloween**.

Survey

Skeletons found in strange places can be intriguing beginnings to science fiction stories. Three examples are Rex Gordon's *First Through Time* (1962), in which a woman **scientist** working on **time travel** views a film taken by a camera sent into the **near future** and shockingly observes her own skeleton; James P. Hogan's *Inherit the Stars* (1977), wherein discovery on the **Moon** of an ancient skeleton in a spacesuit inspires a scientific search for evidence of an earlier race of spacefaring humans; and Michael Libling's "Timmy Gobel's Bug Jar" (2001), inside of which some children discover a tiny human skeleton.

Skeletons are standard features of haunted houses (see **Ghosts and Hauntings**). For example, a skeleton on a rope is employed to frighten people in the film *House on Haunted Hill* (1958), and the Hardy Boys investigate mysterious doings in

Franklin W. Dixon's *The Ghost at Skeleton Rock* (1957). Sometimes a skull is the center of attention: in **King Kong**, the sight of a huge cliff shaped like a skull ominously warns of horrors to come when adventurers approach Kong's home, Skull Island; in *Psycho* (1960), one shocking scene reveals that Norman Bates's mother as a dessicated corpse with a skull for a face—an image imposed on the insane Bates's face at the end of the film; and in the film *The Skull* (1965), based on Robert Bloch's "The Skull of the Marquis de Sade" (1945), a man purchases the Marquis de Sade's skull and learns it is possessed by his spirit, forcing him to become a murderer.

The allegorical figure of **Death** is often represented as a walking skeleton (see **Allegory**) cloaked in a black hood and carrying a scythe. This is how he appears in Terry Pratchett's Discworld novels (see *The Colour of Magic*), sometimes accompanied by his diminutive companion, a rat skeleton known as the Death of Rats (see **Rats and Mice**). In the silent film *Phantom of the Opera* (1926), the Phantom disrupts a ball by appearing dressed as a skeletal Death.

Villains often resemble skeletons, with examples including the Red Skull, the Nazi enemy of Marvel Comics' Captain America during World War II; the Horned King of the film *The Black Cauldron* (1984), who wears a skull mask; and Skeletor, who opposes the **heroic** He-Man from his headquarters in Castle Grayskull in the animated series *He-Man and the Masters of the Universe* (1983–1985) and later films and series. Defying expectations, a Marvel Comics hero, the **demon**-possessed Ghost Rider, has the face of a skeleton. The hapless protagonist of Thorne Smith's *Skin and Bones* (1933), due to a chemical accident, becomes an animated skeleton at inconvenient moments. Sinister **aliens in space** may resemble skeletons, an example being the Morgors of Edgar Rice Burroughs's John Carter story "Skeleton Men of Jupiter" (1943) (see *A Princess of Mars*), while Fritz Leiber's fantasy *Swords of Lankhmar* (1968) features "Ghouls" with invisible flesh but visible bones.

Since the earliest days of the cinema, making skeletons walk has been a favorite special effect. An early Walt Disney cartoon, *The Skeleton Dance* (1929), animated four dancing skeletons; it was remade as *Skeleton Frolic* in 1937. Ray Harryhausen employed stop-motion animation to have Jason battle **sword**-wielding skeletons in the film *Jason and the Argonauts*; similar skeletons designed as a homage to Harryhausen appear in an episode of *The Adventures of Sinbad*, "Little Miss Magic" (1996). *Army of Darkness* (1992) features sinister skeleton soldiers, and a badly animated walking skeleton is the menace in the satirical film *The Lost Skeleton of Cadavra* (2001) (see **Satire**).

Another horrific motif is a process of removing people's bones, thus making them into immobile blobs. In George Méliès's *A Novice at X-Rays* (1897), a scientist takes an x-ray of a man, but the image of his skeleton immediately walks away, causing the now-boneless man to collapse. In David H. Keller's "The Boneless Horrors" (1929), a chemical that dissolves bones destroys the rulers of ancient **Atlantis**. A similar idea was employed to better effect in Ray Bradbury's "Skeleton" (1945), in which a man obsessed and horrified by the notion that he has a skeleton inside his body eventually contrives to have it removed, leaving him a grotesque "jellyfish" lying on the ground.

A developing piece of **technology** is the exo-skeleton, a mechanical framework worn on the outside of the body to assist in movement or amplify human power. One of them is employed in Fritz Leiber's *A Specter Is Haunting Texas* (1968) to allow a tall, thin inhabitant of a **space habitat** to walk on the surface of the **Earth** despite weak, atrophied muscles.

Discussion

Skeletons inspire fear because they represent the ultimate **destiny** of every human—to be reduced, over time, to a lifeless assemblage of bones. To scientists, however, skeletons are respected and valued as treasure troves of information about people, especially those in the distant past; every newly unearthed skeleton of a human ancestor further enriches our incomplete picture of how we evolved from simple primates to intelligent masters of a complex **civilization** (see **Evolution**). In these ways, skeletons are evocative emblems of both **humanity**'s future and its past.

Bibliography

Clark A. Brady. "Morgors." Brady, *The Burroughs Cyclopedia*. Jefferson, NC: McFarland, 1996, 224–225.

Stanley Manders. "*Lost Skeleton of Cadavar*." *Cinefantastique*, 36 (February/March, 2004), 56.

Neil Pettigrew. "Skeleton Battle." *Cinefantastique*, 31 (February, 1999), 30–31.

Jeff Rovin. "The Red Skull" and "Skeletor." Rovin, *The Encyclopedia of Supervillains*. New York: Facts on File, 1987, 296–297, 320.

Marc Shapiro. "Red Skull With the Right Stuff." *Starlog*, No. 157 (August, 1990), 59–61, 72.

George Turner. "Sailing Back to Skull Island." *American Cinematographer*, 73 (August, 1992), 67–71.

Tim Underwood and Chuck Miller. "Skull Beneath the Skin." Underwood and Miller, *Kingdom of Fear*. Columbia: Underwood Miller, 1986, 255–267.

James Van Hise. "Skull-Face." Van Hise, ed., *The Fantastic Worlds of Robert E. Howard*. Yucca Valley, CA: James Van Hise, 1997, 76–81.

—*Gary Westfahl*

SLAVERY

Overview

Slavery frequently appears in science fiction and fantasy to dramatize the perennial search for **freedom** and **rebellion** against unjust authority. Some works involve outright chattel slavery, while others involve less blatant forms of unfree labor like oppressive labor contracts. **Technology** may produce new forms of quasi-slaves such as mechanical **robots, androids.** or genetically modified animals. Encounters with alien intelligences might lead to questions about their personhood, and the possibility of their enslavement.

Survey

The most obvious treatments of slavery in science fiction and fantasy often deal with variations on **America**'s antebellum South, often through **alternate history** and **time travel**. Ward Moore's *Bring the Jubilee* features a protagonist, from a world in which the South won the Civil War and maintained slavery, whose actions during a trip to the past lead to a change that allows the North to triumph, thus creating our own world. More recently, Harry Turtledove reversed that situation in *The Guns of the South* (1992), in which modern racists deliver assault rifles to the Confederate army to create a world in which racially based chattel slavery continues to be practiced. The protagonist of Octavia E. Butler's *Kindred* is constantly aware of the perils of changing history in her travels to her ancestors' time, but still undertakes small acts of subversion like teaching slaves to read (see **Reading**).

However, not all alternate historical explorations of slavery involve time travelers. Harry Turtledove has also written a series in which the South wins the Civil War by their own efforts. In *How Few Remain* (1997), the South has retained chattel slavery, but is pressured by European allies to manumit its slaves. In succeeding volumes, African-Americans are legally free but remain in constrained social situations little better than slavery. Another alternate history of slavery is S.M. Stirling's Draka series, beginning with *Marching Through Georgia* (1988), in which exiled Loyalists settle in **Africa** and create a slave-based society that ultimately conquers the world and takes slavery into space.

The reappearance of slavery in space has been a familiar motif, from the notorious Gor novels of John Norman, beginning with *Tarnsman of Gor* (1966), to Robert A. Heinlein's thoughtful *Citizen of the Galaxy* (1957). In the future solar system of Charles L. Harness's *The Paradox Men* (1953), a society of idealistic rebels steals with the sole intention of gaining money to purchase people out of slavery. In **Dune**, the Fremen recall having been slaves on Salusa Secundus for nine generations. David Weber's Honor Harrington series, beginning with *On Basilisk Station* (1993), has its genetic slavers of Mesa, and they become primary **villains** in *Crown of Slaves* (2003), cowritten with Eric Flint. The film *Stargate* and spinoff series *Stargate: SG1* (1997–) feature slaveowning alien villains who pose as ancient Egyptian deities (see **Egypt**). Slaveholding may also reappear in **post-holocaust societies**, like the one depicted in Heinlein's *Farnham's Freehold* (1964).

Even in societies that reject traditional chattel slavery, technology may produce new forms of unfree labor. Heinlein's "Logic of Empire" (1941) and Frederik Pohl and C.M. Kornbluth's *The Space Merchants* describe forms of contract labor that effectively amount to virtual slavery. Robots and androids have been frequent slaves, as seen in Karel Capek's play *R.U.R.* (1920) and the film *Metropolis*, in which the beautiful robot woman leads a rebellion of the oppressed. In the film *Blade Runner*, replicants created to labor in dangerous off-world situations **escape** to hide among humans in a polluted Earth, while the highly intelligent droids of the *Star Wars* movies are programmed to accept their status as property, as are robots in Isaac Asimov's *I, Robot*. But not all created slaves are necessarily mechanical. Biotechnical manipulation can also create intelligent but rightless beings, like the lower castes of Aldous Huxley's *Brave New World* or the uplifted underpeople (see **Uplift**) in Cordwainer Smith's *Norstrilia*. Heinlein's "Jerry Was a Man" (1948) is a classic story of a bioengineered being who gains freedom from slavery in a court of law. In the *Planet of the Apes* films, the situation has been reversed, as genetically enhanced **apes** become owners of human slaves.

Relations between naturally occurring intelligent species can involve slavery, particularly if the stronger species thinks of personhood primarily in terms of membership in their own species. In Larry Niven's *World of Ptavvs* (1966), the telepathic

Thrintun (see **Psychic Powers**) consider all people who lack their dominating Power as natural slaves. In later books of Niven's Known Space series, the catlike Kzinti enslave their conquests, including the humans of Wunderland. Even **children**'s fantasy can raise serious questions about our relations with other intelligent species, like the house **elves** whom Hermione Granger sets out to liberate in *Harry Potter and the Goblet of Fire* (2002) (see **Harry Potter and the Sorcerer's Stone**).

Discussion

Slavery is a recurring theme in science fiction and fantasy because it stands in direct opposition to freedom, providing opportunities for dramatic conflict. Chattel slavery may serve as a metaphor for other oppressive relationships like wage slavery, while stories about robots, androids, and genetically engineered animals can be thought-experiments, exploring possible consequences of technological advancement.

Bibliography

Pamela Bedore. "Slavery and Symbiosis in Octavia Butler's *Kindred*." *Foundation*, No. 84 (Spring, 2002), 73–81.

Brycchan Carey. "Hermione and the House-Elves." Giselle L. Anatol, ed. *Reading Harry Potter*. Westport, CT: Praeger, 2003, 103–115.

Alex Comfort. "The Warrior and the Suffragette." *Paunch*, No. 48/49 (1977), 6–17.

Alan C. Elms. "Origins of the Underpeople." Tom Shippey, ed., *Fictional Space*. Atlantic Highlands, NJ: Humanities Press, 1991. 166–193.

Johan Heje. "On the Genesis of *Norstrilia*." *Extrapolation*, 30 (Summer, 1989), 146–155.

William Lanahan. "Slave Girls and Strategies." *Algol*, 12 (November, 1974), 22–26.

Angelyn Mitchell. "Not Enough of the Past." *Melus*, 26 (Fall, 2001), 51–70.

Robert Reginald. "A Stitch in Time." Reginald, *Xenograffiti*. San Bernardino, CA: Borgo Press, 1996, 19–23.

Maria Varsam. "Concrete Dystopia." Raffaella Baccolini and Tom Moylan, eds., *Dark Horizons*. New York: Routledge, 2003, 203–224.

—Leigh Kimmel

SLEEP

It was only in their waking hours, Quentin let me know, that men allowed themselves to be separated by the artificial barriers of color, ethnics, politics, ideology, hunger, territorial imperatives. In their repose all men were one because all slept, and slept alike. Sleep, you might almost say, was humanity's least common denominator, because most

*common, indeed, universal. Sun makes
men aliens to each other and, thus,
themselves. Night unites. Mankind could
open itself to, and assert, its true physio-
logical community only with eyes closed.*

—Bernard Wolfe
"The Girl with Rapid Eye Movements"
(1972)

Overview

For all its universality, sleep is rather absent in science fiction and fantasy. True, **suspended animation and cryonics** are found throughout science fiction, but these cases should be differentiated from uses of sleep without technological aids. Sleep, as a necessary biological state, a period of rest, can generally be construed to fit into generic categories, with some exceptions. Within fantasy, and particularly **fairy tales**, going to sleep is used to establish the liminal time between daytime and dreaming (see **Dreams**), and, as such, is susceptible to reality-bending experiences; within science fiction, sleep is generally perceived as a biological necessity that might be overcome or enhanced through scientific **progress**. In both cases, however, sleep is seen as possibly allowing individuals to overcome the constraints of daily life, either in the sense of social norms or the case of unconscious abilities of their bodies that manifest themselves at night.

Survey

Fantasies written for young **children** may betray a realization that the covert purpose of the story, in the eyes of parents, may be to put the children to sleep. Margaret Wise Brown's *Goodnight, Moon* (1942) lullingly records a young rabbit's bedtime **rituals**, and Dr. Seuss's *Dr. Seuss' Sleep Book* (1962) describes various strange creatures going to sleep and concludes by asking readers to do the same. Stories may be presented within the framework of someone reading a bedtime story to a child, like William Goldman's *The Princess Bride* (1973) and its 1987 film adaptation, or as tales told at night around the campire, which is the format of the **horror** anthology series *Are You Afraid of the Dark?* (1992–1996, 1999–2000). Stories may also involve events that occur while children are supposedly sleeping (and without their parents' care), as is the case with J.M. Barrie's *Peter and Wendy* and C.S. Lewis's Narnia series, begun in *The Lion, the Witch and the Wardrobe*.

In fantasy there are a number of cases where sleep extends past its normal limits (Rip Van Winkle, Sleeping Beauty, and *Snow White and the Seven Dwarfs*). Unlike suspended animation, these extended periods of sleep in fantasy may be magically induced (i.e., the poison apple that Snow White eats, given by her wicked stepmother) (see **Magic**), and are often challenges to be overcome. For Washington Irving's "Rip Van Winkle" (1819), sleeping is a means of moving him into the future (see **Time Travel**) without the conceit of **technology**, where he is confronted with changes that occur in his **community** over **time**, as well as his role in that community.

In the case of Bernard Wolfe's "The Girl with Rapid Eye Movements" (1972), sleep is seen as a period where extra-sensory communication can occur (see **Psychic Powers**), in this case between two college students who communicate dream images to one another, inspiring, in one of them, song lyrics. More interesting is the rhetoric of the researchers studying the possibilities of sleep, which is steeped in universal humanism: because sleeping is something that every human must do, they argue, it should be better understood for its ability to bring people together.

This humanism is in conflict with stories about characters that do not require sleep. Examples in fantasy include the Scarecrow and the Tin Woodman of L. Frank Baum's *The Wonderful Wizard of Oz*, who wait idly while Dorothy and the Cowardly Lion sleep and do not succumb to the sleep-inducing odors of the poppy field. In science fiction, people who do not sleep may be viewed as the next stage of human **evolution**, like the superhuman children of Nancy Kress's *Beggars in Spain* (1993). A better-known example is the DC Comics **superhero** *Superman*, who, because his alien physiology is powered by the yellow sun of Earth (see **Aliens on Earth**), does not need to eat or sleep. His all-too-human colleague *Batman*, however, is often shown battling the need to sleep, and in Denny O'Neill's graphic novel *Knightfall* (1995) he is purposefully deprived of sleep by his nemesis Bane to induce a psychotic break. The Marvel Comics character Sleepwalker, who starred in a short-lived eponymous series, is named for his possession by an alien who takes over his body while he sleeps and prowls New York City as a superhero.

The DC Comics superhero Sandman, in his original incarnation in the 1940s, employs a gun that dispenses a sleep-inducing gas, a common form of **weaponry** within science fiction; a similar device is employed by **villains** in Hugo Gernsback's *Ralph 124C 41+: A Romance of the Year 2660* (1925) and John W. Campbell, Jr.'s first Arcot, Wade, and Morey story, "Piracy Preferred" (1930). The humane weaponry of Gene Roddenberry's *Star Trek* universe, "phasers" that can be set to "stun" people instead of harming them, might be seen as an extrapolation from these earlier devices.

Discussion

As a biological need, sleep is sometimes seen as an element of human life that needs to be overcome or capitalized upon, as in the case of *Ralph 124C 41+*, where a "hypno-bioscope" pumps novels into the brains of sleepers. It should also be mentioned that sleeping is often perceived as a highly vulnerable state, hence the popularity of **horror** stories that take place at night, when humans are vulnerable to nocturnal predators, especially such creatures as **vampires**, **zombies** and **werewolves**. The sleep researchers in Wolfe's "The Girl with Rapid Eye Movements" are correct: sleep is an essential bodily function, and it unifies not just human life, but animal life on **Earth**. As such, it may be too commonplace to play a central role in much science fiction and fantasy, but its infrequent highlighting, especially in science fiction, may raise questions about what it means to be human and to be a body, and what surprises await beyond the veil of waking life.

Bibliography

Hugo Gernsback. "The Wonders of Sleep." *Wonder Stories*, 2 (June, 1930), 5.
Peter Huston. "Hypnosis and Society's Plague of Forgotten Horrors." *Expanse*, 1 (Summer 1994), 77–81.

Darek Jarrett. *The Sleep of Reason*. London: Weidenfeld & Nicholson, 1988.

Sharon Packer. *Dreams in Myth, Medicine, and Movies*. Westport, CT: Praeger, 2002.

Martin Riccardo. "Vampires as Sleepwalkers." *The Ultimate Unknown*, No. 6 (Winter, 1997), 63–64.

Midori Snyder. "Folkroots." *Realms of Fantasy*, 6 (October, 1999), 26–33, 78.

P.L. Travers. "About the Sleeping Beauty." John Matthews and Caitlin Matthews, eds., *A Fairy Tale Reader*. New York: Harper/Aquarian, 1993, 58–66.

Bernard Wolfe. "Afterword." Harlan Ellison, ed., *Again, Dangerous Visions 1*. 1972. New York: Signet Books, 1973, 391–397.

—*Matthew Wolf-Meyer*

SNAKES AND WORMS

Overview

Biologically, snakes and worms have little in common: they are respectively reptiles and lower-order invertebrates, which independently evolved limbless bodies and slithering styles of movement. But they are often regarded as similar, particularly when depicted as the vastly enlarged **monsters** often observed in science fiction and fantasy (see **Enlargement**). In western **culture**, snakes and worms owe much of their duplicitous and **evil** reputation to the Bible (see **Christianity**; **Judaism**; **Religion**), especially the story of **Adam and Eve**, wherein a serpent—later identified as **Satan**—tempts **humanity** into **sin**. Other cultures and myths view serpents more ambiguously: snakes slew Laocoon and thus (indirectly) permitted the sacking of Troy (see **Gods and Goddesses; Mythology**); the Midgard Serpent (Jormangund) surrounds the world, biting its own tail and forming the Worm Ouroboros. Indian cultures have worshipped snakes, and the staff of Aesculapius features two snakes, which represent his healing powers (see **Medicine**). Nevertheless, for every positive depiction of snakes and worms, there are at least two negative ones. Sea serpents are discussed under **Fish and Sea Creatures**.

Survey

Snakes and worms appear throughout premodern literatures. The *Enuma Elish* (c. 1200 BCE) claims that Tiamat, mother goddess of the Babylonians, was a cosmic serpent. In classical Greek literature, Ophion with his fish-like serpent tail was the first ruler of the Titans, supplanted by Kronos. Ophiuchus is a physician who uncovered the mysteries of life and death through studying serpents and was killed by Zeus for fear that the **knowledge** would convey immortality to humans (see **Immortality and Longevity**). Large, fiery, and occasionally airborne serpents appeared in the Bible in Deuteronomy and Isaiah, and the Book of Job includes seven mentions of worms.

In the nineteenth and early twentieth century, snakes and worms figured in various works. Oliver Wendell Holmes's *Elsie Venner* (1861) sees a rattlesnake bite transform a pregnant woman's child into a snake woman, graceful but cold-bloodedly unsociable until, little by little, **love** makes her human again. Rudyard Kipling's *The Jungle Book* (1894) exploits the common belief that snakes possess the power of **hypnotism**; also relevant is Bram Stoker's *Lair of the White Worm* (1911), which features a gigantic were-snake with hypnotic powers who may also be Lady Arabella March. Other works in the early twentieth century utilized snakes and worms, including Edwin L. Sabin's *The City of the Sun* (1924) and Bassett Morgan's "Laocoon" (1926), the latter of which involves brain transplants into a gigantic sea serpent. The best-known of these works is A. Merritt's *The Face in the Abyss* (1931), which involves a Snake Mother, the remnants of **Atlantis**, and lost races. Gigantic snakes appeared repeatedly in the stories of Robert E. Howard, who also utilized **identity**-stealing serpent men in his King Kull series. The giant reptile **king** of the Whoomangs in Ralph Milne Farley's "The Radio Planet" (1926) controls beings by inserting moth larva into their brains.

More recent fantasy and science fiction stories employ snakes more imaginatively. Clark Ashton Smith's "Coming of the White Worm" (1941) used a worm to symbolize glaciation and treachery, and Michael Moorcock's "Sojan and the Sons of the Snake God" (1958) describes the **hero** Sojan deceived by a snake cult. A sexless and deadly snake woman appears briefly but memorably in Cordwainer Smith's "The Ballad of Lost C'Mell" (1962). Frank Herbert's *Dune* and its sequels utilize gigantic sandworms, whose complex lifecycles produce the valuable melange; the sandworms are potentially immortal, and *God Emperor of Dune* (1981) describes a human attempt at co-opting that immortality. Quieter and more heartfelt, Vonda N. McIntyre's "Of Mist, and Grass, and Sand" (1973) is narrated by a healer who utilizes genetically engineered snakes; the superstitions and **violence** of those she assists lead to their killing her healer snake (see **Tragedy**) and inspire her search through a post-holocaust **city** for a replacement. The post-feminist stories of this world, collected as *Dreamsnake* (1978) (see **Feminism**), probably represent a high point in depictions of human-ophidian relations.

Other works largely fail to do anything unusual with snakes. Enlarged monsters include the gigantic *Anaconda* (1997) and the immense burrowing earthworms that menace desert residents in the film *Tremors* (1990) and its sequels. In J.K. Rowling's Harry Potter series (see ***Harry Potter and the Sorcerer's Stone***), devious children are assigned to the House of Slytherin, whose emblem is a snake and whose most notable alumnus is the alliteratively named Severus Snape; and in Lemony Snicket's *The Reptile Room* (1999), the Incredibly Deadly Viper proves anything but.

Discussion

Legless yet ambulatory, snakes and worms can be endlessly fascinating. They are occasionally venomous and frequently represent **death**, though their ability to shed their skins speaks to ideals like rejuvenation and **reincarnation**. Although snakes and worms are universally recognized, relatively few authors have explored their potential. It is easy to rely upon **clichés** and generalizations when describing snakes and worms, and it takes an exceptional writer to see beyond these.

Bibliography

Jorge Luis Borges with Margarita Guerrero. "The Uroboros." Borges with Guerrero, *The Book of Imaginary Beings*, rev., enl., and trans. Norman Thomas di Giovanni. 1970. New York: Penguin, 1974, 150–151.

William Hughes and Andrew Smith, eds., *Bram Stoker*. New York: St. Martin's, 1998.

Paula Parisi. "*Anaconda*." *Cinefex*, No. 70 (June, 1997), 61–68, 161–162.

Inge-Lise Paulsen. "Can Women Fly?" *Women's Studies International Forum*, 7 (1984), 103–110.

Roger B. Salomon. *Mazes of the Serpent*. Ithaca, NY: Cornell University Press, 2002.

Estelle Shay. "Aftershocks." *Cinefex*, No. 66 (June, 1996), 13–16, 119–120.

James Van Hise, ed. *The Fantastic Worlds of Robert E. Howard*. Yucca Valley, CA: James Van Hise, 1997.

Carolyn Wendell. "Responsible Rebellion in Vonda N. McIntyre's *Fireflood*, *Dreamsnake*, and *Exile Waiting*." Tom Staicar, ed., *Critical Encounters II*. New York: Ungar, 1982, 125–144.

Diane S. Wood. "Breaking the Code." *Extrapolation*, 31 (Spring, 1990), 63–72.

—Trent Walters

SOCIAL DARWINISM

■

Overview

Social Darwinism is the logical fallacy, derived from Charles Darwin's theory of **evolution**, that the process of natural selection can function within the brief times-pan of a few generations, or even one generation, so a person who becomes rich while others remain poor, or a nation that conquers other nations, purportedly demonstrates "survival of the fittest" and superiority over bested competitors. In fact, Darwin explained that it would take many, many generations for meaningful differences between species to result in one's **survival** and another's extinction, so the ephemeral triumphs and failures of individuals and groups are not necessarily related to their merits. Still, while this idea is discredited, it remains a powerful influence on science fiction and fantasy.

Survey

Considering individuals in a society, social Darwinism can justify rule by royalty, or any **class system**, so fantasy novels that accept such hierarchal structures could be said to espouse social Darwinism. There are fantasies like Glen Cook's Garrett novels, beginning with *Sweet Silver Blues* (1987), wherein virtuous poor people struggle to get by while corrupt, decadent nobles and officials retain positions of power; but one more often observes **youth** with **courage** and conviction rising to the top, where they find that most members of the ruling class welcoming them thoroughly deserve their lofty status—though an occasional bad egg is killed or dethroned. Elizabeth Moon's Paksenarrion series, beginning with *Sheepfarmer's Daughter* (1988), is one of innumerable fantasies following this Horatio Alger-like pattern, here with a poor but determined woman warrior who lifts herself up from poverty to lead the masses and consort with royalty.

The only system in which social Darwinism might be valid for individuals would be a perfect meritocracy, designed to guarantee that the worthy would achieve power and prominence while the unworthy would not. This idea is at the heart of H.G. Wells's utopian schemes (see **Utopia**), as described in *A Modern Utopia* (1905), *Men Like Gods* (1923), and elsewhere. Future societies, as in George Turner's *Drowning Towers* (1987), may administer tests to young people to locate and elevate the best and brightest; or people may engage in brutal competitions to win special status, like the "Land Race" in the overpopulated world of Robert Sheckley's "The People Trap" (1968) (see **Overpopulation**). People perhaps find **post-holocaust societies** attractive because, they believe, a return to rugged anarchy will end domination by effete elites and allow strong, resourceful individuals to reclaim their rightful places as leaders. This attitude is conveyed in Larry Niven and Jerry Pournelle's *Lucifer's Hammer* (1977), wherein only those individuals courageous and intelligent enough to seize control of a nuclear power plant survive and prosper when Earth is devastated by the impact of a comet (see **Comets and Asteroids; Nuclear Power**). But William Golding's *Lord of the Flies* suggests that, under such harsh conditions, it may be the worst, not the best, people who prevail.

In the context of conflicts between nations, social Darwinism would explain European colonization of the world (see **Europe**) as a natural consequence of the white race's superiority, potentially threatened only by a resurgence of Asian countries—the "Yellow Peril" that M.P. Shiel warned of in novels like *The Yellow Danger* (1898) and *The Yellow Wave* (1905) (see **Race Relations**). As people gradually stopped regarding world **history** as a competition between races, the concept of social Darwinism was applied to the political struggle between capitalism and Communism during the Cold War (see **Politics**): by means of success in **war** or economic development, one **governance system** was destined to achieve decisive victory over the other and thus prove its superiority. However, even as politicians' rhetoric and films like *Invasion U.S.A.* (1953) reflected this attitude, science fiction writers generally resisted visions of one-sided triumph, preferring to predict that the two sides would learn to live together in peace and eventually develop a world government that would blend features of both systems.

When **Earth** becomes or is considered unified, social Darwinism is then applied to the inevitable competition between **humanity** and **aliens in space**. Robert A. Heinlein repeatedly argues that humans will dominate the universe because of their unique ingenuity and determination, an idea expressed most forcefully in *The Puppet Masters* (1951) and *Have Space Suit—Will Travel* (1958). Again, however, science fiction more generally embraces the position that future humans and aliens will learn to cooperate with each other and form productive alliances, which is the message incessantly driven home in *Star Trek* and its successor series.

Discussion

As an ideology, social Darwinism is appealing to people who have succeeded and abhorrent to people who have failed. So, one may only need to examine the differing backgrounds of science fiction and fantasy writers to explain different attitudes toward social Darwinism. Many might fervently hope that this dubious concept would permanently disappear. Still, the very persistence of social Darwinism in ongoing battles between ideas—if one applies the concept of social Darwinism to social Darwinism itself—might suggest that this belief has demonstrated some value, and thus that it is fit to survive.

Bibliography

Joseph Carroll. *Literary Darwinism: Evolution, Human Nature and Literature*, New York: Routledge, 2004.

Peter Fitting. "Eating Your Way to the Top: Social Darwinism in SF." Gary Westfahl, George Slusser, and Eric S. Rabkin, eds., *Foods of the Gods*. Athens: University of Georgia Press, 1996, 172–187.

Matthew Hartman. "Utopian Evolution: The Sentimental Critique of Social Darwinism in Bellamy and Pierce." *Utopian Studies*, 10 (1999), 26–41.

Leo J. Henkin. *Darwinism in the English Novel, 1860–1910*. New York: Russell & Russell, 1963.

Arthur E. Jones. *Darwinism and Its Relationship to Realism and Naturalism in American Fiction 1860–1900*. Madison, WI: Drew University, 1950.

Rafeeq O. McGiveron. "'Starry-Eyed internationalists' versus the Social Darwinists: Heinlein's Transnational Governments." *Extrapolation*. 40 (Spring, 1999), 53–70.

Peter Morton. *The Vital Science: Biology and the Literary Imagination, 1860–1900*. London: Allen & Unwin, 1984.

P.E. Smith, II. "The Evolution of Politics and the Politics of Evolution." Joseph D. Olander and Martin H. Greenberg, eds., *Robert A. Heinlein*. New York: Taplinger, 1978, 137–171.

Jeanne M. Walker. "Survival of the Fittest in Alexei Panshin's *Rite of Passage*." *Extrapolation*, 27 (Spring, 1986), 19–32.

—*Gary Westfahl*

SOUTH PACIFIC

Overview

The Pacific Ocean was among the last areas settled by humans and explored by westerners: For example Hawaii was reached by Polynesians only around 500 CE, and by James Cook in 1778. Life beneath its surface, especially the deepest trenches, remains mysterious to this day. Thus, Pacific waters provide perfect locations for **lost worlds**, utopian **communities**, dangerous scientific experiments, secret alien visitations, and **underwater adventure** although one can argue that this fascinating region of the world has largely been underutilized in the genres of science fiction and fantasy. There is a separate entry addressing the topic of the continent of **Australia**.

Survey

Early western fantasies set on Pacific **islands**, predating Cook's voyages and the Romantic fascination with exotic **landscapes** and local habitations, made little effort to describe actual flora, fauna, or topography. This was true for **utopias** and **satires** whose goal, after all, was to comment on domestic issues. Thomas More's *Utopia* gives few geographical clues, though Francis Bacon's *The New Atlantis* (1627) is set in the North Pacific. The voyages of Jonathan Swift's **Gulliver's Travels** are arguably entirely in the Pacific, with Lilliput northeast of Tasmania and Brobdingnab a vast land in the far North.

Modern authors also employ South Pacific settings for social commentaries. Robert A. Heinlein and Elma Wentz's "Beyond Doubt" (1941) farcically explains statues on Easter Island as relics of an ancient political campaign (see Politics). Austin Tappan Wright's utopia *Islandia* is located near Antarctica, while "New Athens," the artists' colony in Arthur C. Clarke's *Childhood's End*, offers inhabitants welcome isolation along with beaches and the Pacific's gentle climate. Societies are sometimes built on artificial islands such as the utopian/anarchist community Stateless in Greg Egan's *Distress* (1998); the Neo-Venice built on wrecked ships in Jon Courtenay Grimwood's *Lucifer's Dragon* (1998); and the floating dystopia in the film *Waterworld* (1995).

New Zealand frequently features utopias, dystopias, and satires, notably Samuel Butler's *Erewhon* (1872), whose "nowhere" is beyond a mountain range. Butler only lived briefly in New Zealand, but native-born writers have continued exploring themes of communal living, feminism, and environmentalism in science fiction and fantasy. Janet Frame's *Intensive Care* (1970) and Vernon Wilkinson's *After the Bomb* (1984) take place after future wars, while Fiona Farrell's *The Skinny Louie Book* (1992) and Rachel McAlpine's *The Limits of Green* (1985) have elements of magic realism.

A remote island is ideal for "forbidden" science, like the Pacific jungles employed for dark experiments in H.G. Wells's *The Island of Doctor Moreau* and film adaptations (see *Island of Lost Souls*). Brian W. Aldiss's *Moreau's Other Island* (1980) is a modern variation on Wells's tale, while Egan's *Teranesia* (1999) involves rapid genetic mutation on an Indonesian island without a mad scientist.

A century ago, Pacific islands were still plausible locations for lost worlds like Edgar Rice Burroughs's *The Land That Time Forgot* (1924), where western explorers find not only dinosaurs but people who metamorphose in one lifetime from ape-creatures to advanced humans (see Metamorphosis). A. Merritt's *The Moon Pool* (1919) opens with haunting evocations of tropical seas before characters visit the underground realm of superhumans. *King Kong*'s Skull Island, with dinosaurs and ape-worshipping "natives," is officially in the Indian Ocean but still deserves mention here.

Such remoteness is also suitable for extraterrestrial visitations (see Aliens on Earth). An early landmark is Jack London's "The Red One" (1918), in which "natives" worship the remnant of a spaceship, while Michael Crichton's *Sphere* (1987) has scientists investigating another spaceship underwater. In G. Harry Stine's Starsea Invaders trilogy, beginning with *First Action* (1993), a military submarine pursues aliens, while "Metamartians" are found in a trench off Tonga in Rudy Rucker's *Realware* (2000).

Whether aliens or only giant squids lurk beneath the surface, the Pacific is a popular setting for underwater adventures. Jules Verne's *Twenty Thousand Leagues under the Sea*, much of which takes place in Pacific waters, remains the most famous submarine tale. Clarke's *The Deep Range* (1957) is one of many modern novels to portray future submarine technology, in this case along with marine mining and food harvesting. Not all underwater living requires mechanical devices: many stories feature humans who are genetically engineered for aquatic life, intelligent dolphins—or killer whales, as in Vonda McIntyre's *Starfarers* (1989), with early scenes in Pacific waters (see **Fish and Sea Creatures**).

Atomic experiments in the Pacific inspired film allegories of nuclear devastation, including *Godzilla, King of the Monsters*, with its awakened dinosaur demolishing Tokyo, and *It Came From Beneath the Sea* (1955), where a giant octopus from the ocean attacks San Francisco. *Godzilla* inspired many sequels like *Mothra* (1961), featuring a giant moth worshipped (once again) by "natives" of its island.

Relatively few stories are rooted in the history and cultures of Pacific peoples. One notable exception is Kathleen Ann Goonan's *The Bones of Time* (1996), whose time traveling narrative (see **Time Travel**) involves **clones** of the first Hawaiian **king** and the politics of Hawaiian sovereignty. In more of a fantasy vein, Dan Simmons's *The Fires of Eden* (1994) depicts supernatural **revenge** upon a Hawaiian resort, while Carol Severance's *Reefsong* (1992) and Island Warrior trilogy (beginning with *Demon Drums* [1992]) feature shark gods and other Pacific Island myths (see **Mythology**). Polynesian-influenced cultures on **alien worlds** figure in Isaac Asimov's *Foundation and Earth* (1986) (see **Foundation**) and Orson Scott Card's *Children of the Mind* (1996) (see **Ender's Game**).

Discussion

In its vastness, the Pacific has played a role analogous to outer space in speculative fiction—with islands like planets and vessels of **exploration** that are predecessors to "ships" facing unplumbed "oceans" of space. For some writers, Pacific isolation allows for unhindered experiments, whether scientific or social, often with tranquil beaches in contrast to savage or sophisticated interiors. For others, the appeal is almost purely that of the unknown—hence those lost worlds and strange **cultures** and creatures.

Bibliography

Arthur E. Case. "The Geography and Chronology of *Gulliver's Travels*." Case, *Four Essays on Gulliver's Travels*. Princeton: Princeton University Press, 1945, 50–68.

David D. Combs. "Confrontation in Paradise." *The Ultimate Unknown*, No. 1 (Fall, 1995), 24.

Suzanne Kosanke and Todd H. Sammons, eds. *Literature and Hawaii's Children*. Honolulu, HI: Children's Literature Hawaii, 1996.

Geoffrey A. Landis. "The Demon Under Hawaii." *Analog*, 112 (July, 1992), 76–87.

Bill Patterson. "A Study of 'Beyond Doubt.'" *Heinlein Journal*, No. 11 (July, 2002), 38–48.

Lyman Tower Sargent. "Utopianism and the Creation of New Zealand National Identity." *Utopian Studies*, 12 (2001), 1–18.

Thomas Schnellbächer. "Has the Empire Sunk Yet?" *Science Fiction Studies*, 27 (November, 2000), 382–396.

O.H.K. Spate. "The Pacific." Eugene Kamenka, ed., *Utopias*. Melbourne: Oxford University Press, 1987, 20–34.

—Joseph Milicia

SPACE HABITATS

The great human summer of time to come, he realized, would be lived out of the cradle, in free space, around the sun in space habitats, and out among the stars.

—George Zebrowski
Macrolife (1979)

Overview

Space habitats are artificial constructs, designed to provide **homes** for inhabitants and protect them from the hostile environment of space. Unlike **space stations**, they tend to be larger, more complex structures, often gigantic cylinders with attractive **landscapes** on interior surfaces. Although **generation starships** are literally habitats in space, they are distinguished from space habitats by an emphasis on travelling toward a particular destination.

Survey

The first story about of an artificial **Earth** satellite, Edward Everett Hale's "The Brick Moon" (1869), was also the first depiction of a space habitat, since inhabitants of the satellite, though launched into orbit by mistake, were able to settle down on their man-made world to build a happy, functioning society. The first true science-fictional space habitat, however, came in Jack Williamson's "The Prince of Space" (1931).

As scientific and technological advances made living in space more feasible, science fiction writers envisioned space habitats in the iconic shape of a wheel or doughnut. More eclectically, in his Cities in Flight series beginning with *Earthman, Come Home* (1955), James Blish envisioned **cities**, thanks to development of anti-aging drugs and an anti-**gravity** drive, literally leaving **Earth** for a nomadic existence in space.

In the 1970s, Gerard O'Neill argued that people could live safely and comfortably in space in huge rotating spheres or cylinders, complete with elaborate landscaping and **mirrors** to provide solar energy. Thereafter, fictional space habitats were often either modeled on O'Neill's designs or located in hollowed-out asteroids, an idea favored by Freeman Dyson (see **Comets and Asteroids**). Examples include the *Babylon 5* station, Island One in Ben Bova's *Colony* (1978), Freeside in William Gibson's *Neuromancer*, and the alien spacecraft in Arthur C. Clarke's *Rendezvous with Rama* and its sequels. Peter F. Hamilton's *The Reality Dysfunction* (1996), its sequels, and stories in *A Second Chance at Eden* (1997) feature the O'Neill Halo, a **ring** of 974 asteroid settlements orbiting Earth.

C.J. Cherryh examines space habitats extensively in her Alliance-Union series, including *Downbelow Station* (1981) and *Cyteen* (1988). In Cherryh's future, life in space habitats is often considered more practical and desirable than life on planetary surfaces. Tensions between space dwellers and planet-based residents recur in numerous narratives, including Bova's *Colony*, where terrorists must be dealt with; Larry Niven and Jerry Pournelle's "Spirals" (1979), in which Earth authorities threaten to shut down an orbital habitat; and Jane Fancher's *Groundties* (1991) and its sequels, wherein planet-based Ethnic Reconstructionists contest the power and values of people from off-planet environments. In George Zebrowski's *Macrolife* (1979), **humanity** has developed into a star-faring, asteroid-based **civilization**, allowing for **evolution** beyond anything possible for planet-bound species, a theme approached differently in Bruce Sterling's *Schismatrix* (1985).

Space habitats may function as points of contact with **aliens in space**. Jocasta Station in Maxine McArthur's *Time Future* (1999) and *Time Past* (2002), the **Gateway** asteroid in Frederik Pohl's Heechee series, Plenty in Colin Greenland's *Take Back Plenty* (1990) and its sequels, and the eponymous habitat of **Star Trek: Deep Space Nine** were all built by alien species. On *Deep Space Nine*, *Babylon 5*, and the stations of Cherryh's future, humans and aliens attempt (sometimes with difficulty) to understand each other and work together. One successful result of human–alien cooperation is a multi-environmental space habitat and medical facility, Sector Twelve General Hospital, showcased in James White's works (see **Hospital Station**). Further glimpses of everyday life in space are found in Alexei Panshin's *Rite of Passage* (1968), Joe Haldeman's *Worlds: A Novel of the Near Future* (1981) and its sequels, Allen Steele's Near Space series, beginning with *Clarke County, Space* (1990), and Karl Schroeder's *Permanence* (2002).

Several stories, often **space operas** set in the **far future**, describe space habitats built on immense scales, like the title artifact of Larry Niven's *Ringworld* (1970) and its sequels; the Dyson spheres in Bob Shaw's *Orbitsville* (1975) and its sequels and in Frederik Pohl and Jack Williamson's *Farthest Star* (1975) and its sequels; the fantastic construct in Paul J. McAuley's *Child of the River* (1997) and its sequels; and the mysterious, capricious world of Linda Nagata's *Memory* (2003). Perhaps the largest space structure of all appears in Greg Bear's *Eon* (1985): an alien-modified asteroid that is larger on the inside than the outside, with one portion of the structure apparently infinite, extending into not only space, but also time.

Discussion

The most interesting space habitat narratives provide a taste of life on such structures, exploring the impact their distinct environments might have on the **perceptions** and values of someone born, growing up, or residing there. By immersing readers in details of habitat life, and considering the potential personal, social, and ethical consequences of permanent residence in space, works encourage us to question previously self-evident truths from new perspectives and realize how important context is for all our evaluations.

Bibliography

Gregory Benford and George Zebrowski, eds. *Skylife*. New York: Harcourt, 2000.

Freeman Dyson. *Disturbing the Universe*. New York: Harper, 1979.

Ben R. Finney and Eric M. Jones, eds. *Interstellar Migration and the Human Experience*. Berkeley: University of California, 1985.

T.A. Heppenheimer. *Colonies in Space*. New York: Warner, 1977.

De Witt Douglas Kilgore. *Astrofuturism*. Philadelphia: University of Pennsylvania, 2003.
Marshall T. Savage. *The Millennial Project*. Boston: Little, Brown, 1994.
Norman Spinrad. "Dreams of Space." Spinrad. *Science Fiction in the Real World*. Carbondale: Southern Illinois University Press, 1990, 122–135.
Gerard O'Neill. *The High Frontier*. New York: Bantam, 1977.
Gary Westfahl. *Islands in the Sky*. San Bernardino, CA: Borgo Press, 1996.

—*Richard L. McKinney*

SPACE OPERA

∎

Overview

This subgenre of science fiction has been significantly redefined. A term coined by Wilson Tucker in 1941 to denote bad, routine science fiction, "space opera" later epitomized nostalgia for the genre's supposed Golden Age and **sense of wonder**. Today it means any fast-moving, colorful science fiction with galactic scope and exuberant action.

Survey

Much early magazine science fiction, long on **clichés** and short on literary merit, satisfied a particular appetite and was fondly remembered by those who read it at impressionable ages. Such nostalgia, coupled with the grandiose, dramatic associations of "opera," helped shift the meaning to encompass large-scale science fiction adventure in general.

Edgar Rice Burroughs's Barsoom adventures (see **A Princess of Mars**) are precursors of space opera, making up for lack of interstellar scope with exotic color and melodrama. Classic examples include E.E. "Doc" Smith's Skylark series, beginning with *The Skylark of Space* (1928), and his Lensman sequence (see **Triplanetary**). Edmond Hamilton wrote in a similarly crude but energetic vein, producing the quintessential space opera title in "Crashing Suns" (1928). Jack Williamson's *The Legion of Space* (1934) was another early landmark. Leigh Brackett began contributing her own stylish swashbuckling in 1940, and Philip Francis Nowlan's *Armageddon 2419 AD* (1928–1929) brought space opera into popular culture when adapted as the *Buck Rogers* comic strip in 1929.

Space opera's essential ingredients include casual **space travel** (preferably interstellar, at superlight **speed**), daring escapades by reckless **heroes**, and destructive **weaponry**. **Sword and sorcery** extravagance and/or **Ruritanian romance** provides seasoning: the **far future** societies of both A.E. van Vogt's *The Weapon Shops of Isher* (1951) and Charles L. Harness's *The Paradox Men* (1953) are ruled by empresses, and the latter anticipates **Dune** in justifying swordplay in a milieu of advanced small arms (see **Swords**). Males of **superman** stature appear in both novels, and in Alfred Bester's pyrotechnic **The Demolished Man** and **The Stars My Destination**. They recur throughout Gordon R. Dickson's Dorsai military-science fiction series, which began with *The Genetic General* (1960). In Poul Anderson's

Dominic Flandry saga, beginning with *We Claim These Stars* (1959), the merely competent Flandry battles unendingly to preserve **humanity**'s corrupt, doomed **galactic empire**. Samuel R. Delany added a slant of **mythology** to the subgenre in *Nova* (1968).

Although *Star Trek* strayed into this mode, the classic media space opera is *Star Wars*, which serves up all the standard elements with glowing color and special effects. Linking to the subgenre's pulp-magazine roots, its sequel *The Empire Strikes Back* (1980) was co-scripted by Brackett.

With space-operatic imagery brought to wider audiences, all traces of the term's derogatory sense has faded, assisted by works by authors who playfully, selectively, and intelligently used its props: Orson Scott Card's *Ender's Game*; C.J. Cherryh's Alliance/Union series, beginning with *Brothers of Earth* (1976); David Brin's *Startide Rising*; Iain M. Banks's Culture novels, beginning with *Consider Phlebas*; Lois McMaster Bujold's Miles Vorkosigan series, beginning with *Shards of Honor* (1986); Stephen R. Donaldson's deliberately Wagneresque Gap series (space *grand* opera), beginning with *The Gap into Conflict: The Real Story* (1990); Colin Greenland's *Take Back Plenty* (1990); and Vernor Vinge's *A Fire Upon the Deep* (1992). Dan Simmons's **Hyperion** knowingly embeds science fiction modes in a space opera framework.

Other British authors joined Banks and Greenland in the perceived space opera renaissance, arousing interest since Britons had rarely worked in this mode: Bob Shaw's *The Palace of Eternity* (1969) was a rare exception. In the early 1990s there came Paul J. McAuley's *Eternal Light* (1991) and others; Stephen Baxter's Xeelee sequence, including *Ring* (1994); Peter F. Hamilton's **horror** elements imported into his massive Night's Dawn trilogy, beginning with *The Reality Dysfunction* (1996); and Alastair Reynolds opening his Inhibitors saga with *Revelation Space* (2000). John Clute, a London-dwelling Canadian, embraced space opera wholeheartedly and with unstinting linguistic richness in *Appleseed* (2001), and M. John Harrison—whose sardonic, nihilistic anti-space opera *The Centauri Device* (1974) had seemed a farewell to the genre—fused widescreen galactic action with haunting imagery in *Light* (2002).

Some authors began deliberately "retro" space-opera series with an old-fashioned science fiction flavor, like Kevin J. Anderson's *Hidden Empire* (2002). The failing galactic empire of Walter Jon Williams's *The Praxis* (2002) has banned research into AI, nanotechnology, and other "modern" science fiction preoccupations.

Discussion

Space opera's reclamation of the science fiction mainstream seems driven partly by the lure of success—**space war** having captivated filmgoers—and partly by reaction against "literary" assumptions that the best science fiction avoids familiar genre imagery. It has proved possible to blend galactic grandeur with literate and moving narration.

Space opera has its own subgenres. Military science fiction emphasizes strategy and tactics rather than vision: Larry Niven's *Man-Kzin Wars* anthology (1988) and its sequels, based on his Known Space sequence, are examples. Space-navy stories paying homage to C.S. Forester's Horatio Hornblower include David Weber's Honor Harrington novels, beginning with *On Basilisk Station* (1993) and David

Feintuch's Seafort series, beginning with *Midshipman's Hope* (1994). Space opera **humor** includes Harry Harrison's *Star Smashers of the Galaxy Rangers* (1973), parodying Smith, and Robert Sheckley's "Zirn Left Unguarded, the Jenghik Palace in Flames, Jon Westerly Dead" (1972), a bittersweet elegy for all space opera.

Bibliography

Brian W. Aldiss. "The Flight into Tomorrow." Aldiss, *This World and Nearer Ones*. London: Weidenfeld & Nicolson, 1979, 194–197.

Brian W. Aldiss, ed. *Space Opera*. London: Weidenfeld & Nicolson, 1974.

Leigh Brackett. "Introduction: Beyond Our Narrow Skies." Brackett, ed., *The Best of Planet Stories No. 1*. New York: Ballantine, 1975, 1–8.

M. John Harrison, Gwyneth Jones, Russell Letson, Ken MacLeod, Paul McAuley, and Gary K. Wolfe. "The New Space Opera." *Locus*, 151 (August, 2003), 40–44.

Patricia Monk. "Not Just Cosmic Skullduggery." *Extrapolation*, 33 (Winter, 1992), 295–316.

Lawrence Person. "The Culture-D Space Opera of Iain M. Banks." *Science Fiction Eye*, 2 (February, 1990), 33–36.

Joe L. Sanders. "Space Opera Reconsidered." *New York Review of Science Fiction*, No. 82 (June, 1995), 1, 3–6.

Gary Westfahl. "Beyond Logic and Literacy." *Extrapolation* 35 (Fall, 1994), 176–185.

Gary Westfahl, ed. *Space and Beyond*. Westport, CT: Greenwood Press, 2000.

—*David Langford*

SPACE STATIONS

Overview

Space stations are artificial constructions in space, usually relatively small, intended primarily for utilitarian purposes, with crews serving limited periods of time. **Space habitats**, in contrast (though there is overlap between the categories), are larger, more complex structures, designed as permanent **homes** for residents.

Survey

Influenced by pioneering space enthusiasts like Konstantin Tsiolkovsky, Willy Ley, and Wernher von Braun, much science fiction of the 1950s and 1960s depicted what would become a central icon of the genre: the space station as a torus or wheel. A space wheel painted by Chesley Bonestell for a 1952 issue of *Collier's* magazine is among the most important pieces of space art ever produced. The station from the film *2001: A Space Odyssey* is a famous wheel-shaped construction, while the eponymous habitat of *Star Trek: Deep Space Nine* is a descendant of these designs. Other interesting visual representations of space stations are found in television series like *Star Trek*, *Babylon 5*, and *Farscape*, and movies like *Silent Running* (1971) and the *Star Wars* films.

Much **near future** science fiction depicting **humanity**'s expansion into space features one or more space stations, like the "future history" epitomized in Robert A.

Heinlein's *The Past Through Tomorrow*. Later examples are Allen Steele's Near Space series, begun with *Clarke County, Space* (1990), and Michael Flynn's *Firestar* (1996) and its sequels. An early portrayal of the dangers of living in space is James Gunn's *Station in Space* (1958).

Space stations display a broad spectrum of uses. Thanks to low **gravity**, they may provide health benefits for the ill or elderly, as suggested in Arthur C. Clarke's "Death and the Senator" (1961) and Dean Ing's "Down and Out on Ellfive Prime" (1980). They are often important to **business** or industry, as in William Gibson's **Neuromancer** and its sequels, Ben Bova's *Privateers* (1985), and C.J. Cherryh's *Heavy Time* (1991) and *Hellburner* (1992) from her Alliance-Union series. S.P. Somtow's *Mallworld* (1984) is a giant shopping and recreation center, while Mike Resnick's *Eros Ascending* (1984) and its sequels and Philip K. Dick's *The Crack in Space* (1966) present space bordellos. **Prisons** are sometimes on stations, as in Patricia. McKillip's *Fool's Run* (1987). In Ben Bova's *Exiled from Earth* (1971), the world's genetic engineers are imprisoned in a space station to avoid the instability to which their work might lead. Stations built to observe **alien worlds** are prominent in Stanislaw Lem's *Solaris*, the films made from it, and Brian W. Aldiss's Helliconia Trilogy (see **Helliconia Spring**).

Works involving military functions of space stations include C.M. Kornbluth's *Not this August* (1955), Ben Bova's *Peacekeepers* (1988), and David Weber's Honor Harrington series, begun in *On Basilisk Station* (1993). Walter Jon Williams, in *Hardwired* (1986) and its sequels, tells of an **Earth** devastated by use of orbital **weaponry**, and the Death Star from *Star Wars* is a kind of space station. Space stations as the last hope of humanity, should Earth be ravaged by **war**, are central in Thomas N. Scortia's *Earthwreck!* (1974), Charles Sheffield's *Between the Strokes of Night* (1985), and Kevin J. Anderson and Doug Beason's *Lifeline* (1990).

Space stations as port or docking facilities are encountered in **space operas** set against the **far future** background of a **galactic empire** or interstellar confederation, like the series begun in Catherine Asaro's *Primary Inversion* (1995), Julie E. Czerneda's *In the Company of Others* (2001), and Peter F. Hamilton's *Pandora's Star* (2004).

Among the more unusual space stations is the space elevator, introduced into science fiction almost simultaneously by Arthur C. Clarke in *The Fountains of Paradise* (1979) and Charles Sheffield in *The Web Between the Worlds* (1979). A space elevator consists of a long material link, like a superstrong cable, that physically connects the surface of a planet to a station in geosynchronous orbit. Space elevators figure in David Gerrold's *Jumping Off the Planet* (2000) and, linked to **Mars**, in Kim Stanley Robinson's **Red Mars**. In Sean Williams and Shane Dix's *Echoes of Earth* (2002), mysterious variants of space elevators unexpectedly appear in orbit above an uninhabited planet.

Discussion

Space stations are common in science fiction narratives, but are rarely a primary focus of stories. Although they can serve as intertextually significant symbols or provide iconic identifications, they are usually relegated to the status of futuristic prop, or backdrop against which actions take place. They are seldom centrally important in and of themselves. One reason is that true space stations are intrinsically temporary things, points of transition in the lives of provisional residents and visitors, or way stations for a human race heading for **alien worlds** or distant **stars**. Consequently, the most intriguing engagements with the space station theme are in stories focused on exploring that process of transition.

Bibliography

Gregory Benford and George Zebrowski, eds. *Skylife*. New York: Harcourt, 2000.
Martin H. Greenberg and John Helfers, eds. *Space Stations*. New York: DAW, 2004.
Albert A. Harrison. *Spacefaring*. Berkeley: University of California, 2001.
Roger D. Launius. *Space Stations*. Washington: Smithsonian, 2003.
Howard E. McCurdy. *Space and the American Imagination*. Washington: Smithsonian, 1997.
Jerry Pournelle, ed. *The Endless Frontier*. New York: Ace, 1979.
Jerry Pournelle and John F. Carr, eds. *The Endless Frontier, Volume II*. New York: Ace, 1982.
———. *Cities in Space*. New York: Ace, 1991.
Gary Westfahl. *Islands in the Sky*. San Bernardino, CA: Borgo Press, 1996.

—*Richard L. McKinney*

SPACE TRAVEL
∎

"It is good to renew one's wonder," said the philosopher. "Space travel has again made children of us all."

—Ray Bradbury
The Martian Chronicles (1950)

Overview

In defining space travel, one defines what constitutes "space" for a given **culture**. For westerners, space from the beginning has been an expansive medium: an early **dream** is **flying** above **Earth**, as in Socrates's myth of the soul as chariot in Plato's *Phaedrus* (c. 360 BCE) (see **Air Travel**). For Greeks and Christians, limited **cosmologies** held space travel back (see **Christianity**); even Christopher Marlowe's *Doctor Faustus* (1604), who achieves some science fiction "firsts"—**invisibility** and an aerial view of Earth—finally falls back to **Hell** and everlasting punishment. The seeds, however, of later, defiant flight are there, and we have consequently seen flying machines reach what we now call "outer space"—ever since Cyrano de Bergerac's *The Comical History of the States and Empires of the Moon and Sun* (1656)—and take people to the **Moon, alien worlds**, and **stars**.

Survey

Space travel, primarily a science fiction trope, rarely occurs in fantasies, including works for **children** like J.M. Barrie's *Peter and Wendy* and Antoine de Saint-Exupéry's *The Little Prince* (1943); C.S. Lewis's *Perelandra* (1942), with its **angel**-assisted flight to **Venus**; the film *The Adventures of Baron Munchausen* (1989), wherein the Baron fancifully flies to the Moon to visit its **king** and **queen**; and Diana Wynne Jones's *The Year of the Griffin* (2000), in which a magical Moon flight goes awry and reaches another planet instead.

If one discounts works like de Bergerac's adventure or Edgar Allan Poe's "The Unparalleled Adventures of One Hans Pfaall" (1835), science fiction space travel, powered by physical means and obeying natural laws, begins with Jules Verne's *From the Earth to the Moon* and *Around the Moon* (1870). Verne painstakingly describes construction and operation of a moon ship, a ballistic projectile fired from a giant cannon, along with an account (if erroneous) of what life would be like in transit and the discovery via spaceflight of new realms, here the dark side of the Moon. These features, accompanied by illustrations, became staples of science fiction space stories. Though in Verne we only orbit the Moon, H.G. Wells's *The First Men in the Moon* (1901) puts a man on the Moon, using an anti-**gravity** propellant, Cavorite, which Verne rejected as "invention."

Early stories of space flight are limited to the Moon and **Mars**, but soon further voyages are envisioned. In the **space operas** of Edmond Hamilton (*Outside the Universe* [1929]) and E.E. "Doc" Smith (*The Skylark of Space* [1928]), readers travel to distant universes at greater-than-light **speeds** without plausible explanation. The era of space opera culminates in Hubert Rogers's cover for the October, 1939 issue of *Astounding Science-Fiction* displaying Smith's Grey Lensman: lantern jaw, jump suit, hand on ray gun (see *Triplanetary*).

As is often the case in science fiction, extravagant **dreams** inspired real-life endeavors. The technological advances of World War II ushered in the world of Arthur C. Clarke, the British Interplanetary Society, and Apollo spaceflights. There had been earlier nonfictional speculations on space travel from Konstantin Tsiolkovsky in the 1920s and Hermann Oberth and Willy Ley in the 1930s, the latter discussed in the science fiction pulps. But with Clarke's early works, fiction and reality merged: *Islands in the Sky* (1952) demonstrated working **space stations**, and *The Sands of Mars* (1951) described a flight to Mars and a permanent base there. Innovative yet feasible space vessels were unveiled, like the solar sails of Clarke's "The Wind from the Sun" (1964), a concept also developed in Gérard Klein's *The Sailing Ships of the Sun* (1961), and revisited by Robert L. Forward's *Future Magic* (1988), which debates their technological merits.

Some writers also accepted the limitations of relativity: the **generation starship** of Heinlein's "Universe" (1941) makes a story out of the light speed barrier, as does Brian W. Aldiss's *Starship* (1958). There is speculation about near-light-speed drives, like the Bussard drive of Poul Anderson's *Tau Zero* (1970), which is an electromagnetic scoop that collects interstellar gases and converts them to fuel. **Hyperspace** and hyperdrives are employed; for example, intergalactic travel in Heinlein's *Starman Jones* (1953) is effected by computing "folds" in space. **Scientists** vie with science fiction writers in hyperspace speculations. Frank Tipler's "Rotating Cylinders and the Possibility of Global Causality Violation" (1974) posits the use of space warps or **black holes** as time machines—the "jumps" soon observed in Joe Haldeman's *The Forever War*.

The science fiction of the 1980s and 1990s collapses from cosmic to known space. In William Gibson's **Neuromancer** the Tessier-Ashpool **space habitat** literally "downloads" into the "matrix" of **cyberspace**, trading vast expanses for claustrophobic "inner space," a mind-womb. The 1990s see Gregory Benford pull in from the intergalactic sweep of *Great Sky River* (1986) to the nearer space of Mars, the colonization of which is also the locus of Kim Stanley Robinson's **Red Mars**. Overall, science fiction space travel since World War II has mirrored the United States space program: anticipation in the 1950s and early 1960s, euphoria into the 1970s, modulating into skepticism and gradual withdrawal since the 1980s.

Discussion

The **rocket** was arguably the major icon of the twentieth century, demanding attention to the visual aspect of space travel. First came Georges Méliès's *A Trip to the Moon*, the film that linked special effects to depictions of spaceflight. Films like *Woman in the Moon* (1929) and *Things to Come* were constructed around rockets and space flight. Heinlein, as technical advisor for *Destination Moon* (1950), insisted upon a "realistic" depiction of space flight, not improved upon until *2001: A Space Odyssey*, which revolutionized how film presented space flight. Finally, there is the *Star Trek* series, the true epic of the space flight century: as the *Enterprise* was unveiled in *Star Trek: The Motion Picture*, this revered ship passed from fetish to object of genuine awe. Clearly, the theme of space travel is as central to twentieth-century science fiction as science fiction is central to twentieth-century literature, film, and **art**.

Bibliography

Arthur C. Clarke. *The Promise of Space*. London: Hodder & Stroughton, 1968.

T.D. Crouch. "To Fly to the World in the Moon." Eugene M. Emme, ed., *Science Fiction and Space Futures*. San Diego: Univelt, 1982, 7–26.

Jack Dann and George Zebrowski, eds. *Faster Than Light*. New York: Ace, 1976.

Thomas M. Disch. "From the Earth to the Moon—in 101 Years." Disch, *The Dreams Our Stuff Is Made Of*. New York: Simon & Schuster, 1998, 57–77.

George Locke. *Voyages in Space*. London: Ferrett, 1975.

Sam Moskowitz. "Two Thousand Years of Space Travel." *Fantastic Universe*, 11 (October, 1959), 80–88, 79.

Frederik Pohl. "Where Space Travel Went Wrong." *Amazing Stories*, 69 (Spring, 1994), 88–99.

Donald Ruehrwein. "A History of Interstellar Space Travel (As Presented in Science Fiction)." *Odyssey*, 5 (May 1, 1979), 14–17.

Gary Westfahl, ed. *Space and Beyond*. Westport, CT: Greenwood Press, 2000.

—George Slusser

SPACE WAR

∎

Overview

War in space would require enormously advanced **technology** and would occur at such **speeds** and distances that it would be hard for humans to comprehend. Depiction of space war reflects the varying levels of optimism authors have about contact with **aliens in space**: space wars may also be revisions of wars on **Earth**.

Survey

Space war can be divided into four different types: "Hornblower in space"; interstellar war; attacks by aliens; and the intergalactic United Nations. Following the example of C.S. Forester's novels about naval officer Horatio Hornblower, several science fiction series track the careers (often in extended **Bildungsroman**) of military men and women as they pass from callow youth to age and **wisdom**. Examples are Gordon R. Dickson's Dorsai books, beginning with *The Genetic General* (1960), though their action often takes place in **planetary colonies**; Lois McMaster Bujold's Miles Vorkosigan series, beginning with *Shards of Honor* (1986); David Feintuch's Seafort novels, beginning with *Midshipman's Hope* (1994); and David Weber's Honor Harrington books, beginning with *On Basilisk Station* (1993). Each series depicts spacecraft in fleets of space navies fighting with futuristic **weaponry** but often using strategies and tactics Forester would recognize. The books focus on honorable people who act humanely; texts are as much lessons in comportment and maturity as they are about space war.

Interstellar war tends to be more varied: texts as diverse as David Brin's Uplift saga (see *Startide Rising*), Iain M. Banks's Culture novels (see *Consider Phlebas*), and George Lucas's *Star Wars* trilogies fall into this category. In each text there is war between humans, or humans and aliens: Brin sets half the action in *Startide Rising* in a months-long space battle; Banks casts large portions of the Culture novels on board fighting spacecraft; and Lucas's *Star Wars* films render space fighting most graphically (in the manner of **space opera**), creating scenes sometimes explicitly modeled on World War II air battles. Space-faring armadas still seem like ocean-going vessels with added energy shields, ion or photon cannons, and lasers.

Attacks by aliens tend to overlap the previous category. The tradition of alien space assault (see H.G. Wells's *The War of the Worlds*) has been continued in A.E. van Vogt's Space Beagle stories, beginning with "Black Destroyer" (1939), whose human spacecraft is infiltrated and attacked by several aliens (parts of this narrative were later acknowledged as an influence on *Alien*). Fred Saberhagen's Berserker stories, beginning with "Fortress Ship" (1963), explore the idea of intelligent, uninhabited **computer** spacecraft that seek out and destroy human life. The gritty quality of Saberhagen's Berserker battles gives them a sense of authenticity and grimness not found in *Star Wars* films (thoughtful consideration is also given to the problem of collaboration with known enemies). Alien menaces fight humans in Robert A. Heinlein's *Starship Troopers*, Orson Scott Card's *Ender's Game*, and Joe Haldeman's *The Forever War*, although Haldeman discusses only the computer's overall strategy, abandoning the idea that humans react quickly enough to fight space battles. Larry Niven and Jerry Pournelle offer a detailed picture of humans confronting aliens in space in *The Mote in God's Eye* (1974).

A sort of intergalactic United Nations appears most strikingly in the *Star Trek* series (and its various sequels) where once again we see Horatio Hornblower (Captains Kirk, Picard, Janeway) on patrol, making the galaxy safe for humans and their allies. David Brin's Uplift trilogies move in the same direction, while Iain M. Banks's more problematic Culture rights perceived wrongs across the known universe. Banks novels also offer nuanced consideration of the reasons people go to war. These texts are markedly different from many others in seeking peaceful means to resolve differences, privileging tolerance over anger. Because of these qualities such texts may be dismissed as utopian, but they show science fiction's strength in imagining ways to avoid conflict, to reason, communicate, and negotiate. These texts display a fundamental optimism that humans are capable of living and cooperating with each other, and aliens, in space.

Discussion

One should consider what message space navy series give readers: do they natural-
ize the militarization of space? Do they propose that the only way to explore is to
join the military and "see the galaxy"? Equally problematic are romantic visions of
war in space, shown as bloodless and painless, where only the nameless die. Few
authors or filmmakers question what war in space would cost a planetary economy:
Haldeman suggested it would take all the resources the human race has to pursue
such an endeavor. Readers or viewers, entertained by space wars in works like the film
The Last Starfighter (1984), should also ponder the cautionary tales of Saberhagen,
Haldeman, Card, and Banks. War in space continues to be war on the Earth reimag-
ined in a different environment—the questions we ask of texts about war and violence must be asked of these texts as well.

Bibliography

Martha A. Bartter. *The Way to Ground Zero*. Westport, CT: Greenwood, 1988.
Tim Blackmore. "Is This Going to Be Another Bug Hunt?" *The Journal of Popular Culture*,
     29 (1996), 211–226.
Jeanne Van Buren Dann and Jack Dann, eds. *In the Field of Fire*. New York: Tor, 1987.
Joe Haldeman, ed. *There Won't Be War*. New York: Tor, 1991.
David Langford. *War in 2080*. New York: William Morrow, 1979.
John Newman and Michael Unsworth. *Future War Novels*. Phoenix, AZ: Oryx Press, 1984.
Jerry Pournelle, ed. *There Will Be War*. New York: Tor, 1983.
George Slusser and Eric S. Rabkin, eds. *Fights of Fancy*. Athens, GA: University of Georgia
     Press, 1993.
Norman Spinrad. "Must There Be War?" Spinrad, *Science Fiction in the Real World*.
     Carbondale: Southern Illinois University Press, 1990, 139–148.

—Tim Blackmore

SPEED

■

> *Speed, is that progress? Anyway, why*
> *progress? Why not enjoy what one has?*
> *Men have never exhausted present*
> *pleasures.*

> —Austin Tappan Wright
> *Islandia* (1942)

Overview

In Austin Tappan Wright's *Islandia*, a resident asks, "Speed, is that progress?" In
the past two centuries, most would answer yes," since much technological **progress**
involved efforts to achieve greater and greater speed—in **transportation**, **communication**, manufacturing (see **Work and Leisure**), and athletics (see **Sports**)—and science fiction consistently envisions further advances in the future. Still, as suggested

by Wright's sedate **utopia**, many dislike the ever-increasing pace of life and perhaps find solace and support in the **pastoral** atmosphere of fantasy.

Survey

One ancient **dream** has been the person who runs at extraordinary speeds. Hermes, the Greek messenger god (Mercury to the Romans), possessed great speed, as did Boreas's winged sons, Calais and Zetes, who won races at Pelias's funeral after joining Jason's **quest** for the Golden Fleece. In modern times, while a remarkably fast runner figures in the film *The Adventures of Baron Munchausen* (1989), most speedsters are comic book **superheroes**: the "M" in the **magic** word "Shazam!" gives Captain Marvel the "speed of Mercury"; **Earth**'s yellow **Sun** provides Superman with sufficient super-speed to fly faster than the speed of **light** and achieve **time travel**; the Whizzer implausibly gains super-speed by a transfusion of mongoose **blood**; Johnny Quick relies on the magic formula "3X2(97Z)4A"; and the two versions of the Flash respectively gained their powers by inhaling "heavy water" fumes and being bathed in chemicals. The latter Flash starred in the series *The Flash* (1989–1990) and had a sidekick, Kid Flash, who replaced him when he died. In films, people who suddenly run more quickly than usual (an easily achieved special effect) were a convention in **comedies** not normally considered fantasies, though the super-fast feats of television's **cyborg** *The Six Million Dollar Man* (1974–1978) were unusually depicted in slow motion.

Humans can also achieve great speeds in advanced vehicles, which nineteenth-century **technology** increasingly introduced. Railroads and steamships naturally suggested even faster vehicles to writers like Jules Verne, whose *Around the World in Eighty Days* (1872) announced in its title an awareness that global transportation was becoming more rapid. Verne's submarine (in *Twenty Thousand Leagues under the Sea*) and airship (in *Robur the Conqueror* [1886]) were celebrated for their speed, as was Edward Sylvester Ellis's *The Steam Man of the Prairie* (1876), a robotic steam engine traveling 60 miles per hour (see **Robots**). In *From the Earth to the Moon* Verne also employed a gigantic cannon to achieve the velocity needed for **space travel**. As the telegraph, telephone, and radio increased the speed of communication, Hugo Gernsback envisioned further improvements like picturephones and television in *Ralph 124C 41+: A Romance of the Year 2660* (1925).

After the 1920s, when E.E. "Doc" Smith's novels (see *Triplanetary*) extended science-fictional space travel beyond the solar system, writers had to overcome Albert Einstein's stipulation that nothing could travel faster than light in order to transport characters to the **stars**. The most common justification was **hyperspace** or "warp drive," using the fourth **dimension** to travel more rapidly than the third dimension allowed, though there were other solutions like Smith's "inertia-less drive."

When Ernest Rutherford's atomic theory briefly sanctioned the notion that atoms were miniature solar systems (see **Microcosm; Miniaturization**), stories like R.F. Starzl's "Out of the Sub-Universe" (1928) recognized that life in tiny worlds would proceed at a greater pace than life in our world. The idea re-emerged in Theodore Sturgeon's "Microcosmic God" (1941), wherein a **scientist** creates a miniature world where inhabitants rapidly progress toward technological **civilization**. Occasionally, beings of normal size move more rapidly than humans: a man gains this ability in H.G. Wells's "The New Accelerator" (1901); aliens living at blinding speed figure in the *Star Trek* episode "Wink of an Eye" (1968); and the *Star Trek: Voyager* episode "Blink of an Eye" (2000) depicts an **alien world** that lives through several generations while the *Voyager* experiences a few weeks. Accelerated **evolution** of a different sort occurs in Edmond Hamilton's "The Man Who Evolved" (1931), about a man scientifically advanced to various levels of super-humanity (see **Superman**) before reverting to protoplasm; an episode of *The Outer Limits*, "The Sixth Finger" (1963), tells a similar story.

Ongoing advances in the speed of transportation inspired science-fictional variations, including an ultra-fast *Supertrain* in the series of that name (1979); advanced aircraft (see **Air Travel**); and faster submarines (the film *Voyage to the Bottom of the Sea* [1961], its successor series (1964–1968), and the series *SeaQuest DSV* [1993–1995]) (see **Undersea Adventure**). Factory assembly lines sparked fears that humans were being forced to work too quickly and too mechanically, as expressed in Charlie Chaplin's *Modern Times* (1936) and Kurt Vonnegut, Jr.'s *Player Piano* (1952) (see **Machines and Mechanization**). Alfred Bester's *The Stars My Destination* envisioned **teleportation** as the ultimate rapid-transit system. The advent of **computers** and the Internet created the possibility of incredibly fast existence as a human consciousness downloaded into a computer, as in Frederik Pohl's *The Annals of the Heechee* (1987) (see **Gateway**).

Discussion

Contemporary fantasy visibly lacks our society's, and science fiction's, obsession with speed: novels harken back to past times when lives moved more slowly, and most characters travel on foot or horseback and employ no forms of communication faster than letters or carrier pigeons. Significant alterations in speed usually involve long suspensions of **time**: magically timeless places like *Brigadoon* (play, 1947; film 1954) or characters who **sleep** for decades like Washington Irving's "Rip Van Winkle" (1819). Still, the emergence of **urban fantasy** and edgy novels like China Miéville's *Perdido Street Station* suggest that even stately fantasy may succumb to western civilization's need for speed.

Bibliography

Isaac Asimov. "Faster Than Light." Asimov, *Asimov's Galaxy*. New York: Doubleday, 1989, 181–185.

Les Daniels. "*Flash Comics*" and "Flashback." Daniels, *DC Comics*. Boston and New York: Little, Brown, 1995, 50–51, 116–117.

Jack Dann and George Zebrowski, eds. *Faster Than Light*. New York: Harper & Row, 1976.

David Langford. "Through the Dark Cold—." Langford, *War in 2080*. New York: William Morrow, 1979, 168–186.

John McGervey. "The Art and Science of Leaping Tall Buildings." Dennis Dooley and Gary Engle, eds., *Superman at Fifty*. Cleveland, OH: Octavia, 1987, 130–136.

Robert A. Metzger. "State of the Art: Speed of Thought." *SFWA Bulletin*, 31 (Winter, 1997), 13–17.

Peter Nicholls, David Langford, and Brian Stableford. "The Limits of the Possible." Nicholls, Langford, and Stableford, *The Science in Science Fiction*. 1982. New York: Alfred A. Knopf, 1983, 66–87.

Dennis O'Neill. "The Flash." O'Neill, ed., *Secret Origins of Super DC Heroes*. New York: Warner Books, 1976, 90–92.

Alen Vitas. "Warp 9 to Hyperreality." Elizabeth Kraus and Carolin Auer, eds., *Simulacrum America*. Rochester, NY: Camden House, 2000, 122–135.

—Lynne Lundquist

SPORTS

Overview

Sports, or organized athletic events, play a prominent role in many **cultures** and hence regularly figure in science fiction and fantasy. Separate entries discuss **Games, Toys,** and **Work and Leisure.**

Survey

The oldest sport is the race, a contest of **speed**, though two Greek stories demonstrate that the fastest runner may not always win: in Aesop's fable about the tortoise and hare, the hare loses because he does not take the challenge seriously, and the mythical Atalanta loses a race by pausing to pick up golden apples. Some modern fantasies involve **horse** races, like D.H. Lawrence's "The Rocking-Horse Winner" (1933) and the film *Mary Poppins* (1964), wherein Mary Poppins rides a carousel horse to victory in a magical world within a chalk drawing. Exotic races in science fiction involve futuristic sleds in Gary Wright's "Mirror of Ice" (1967) and solar-powered spacecraft in Arthur C. Clarke's "The Wind from the Sun" (1964).

In American literature, baseball most fascinates writers and filmmakers, serving as the subject of Philip Roth's surrealistic *The Great American Novel* (1973) (see **Surrealism**). Baseball fantasies include Douglas Wallop's *The Year the Yankees Lost the Pennant* (1954), about a man who sells his soul to **Satan** to become a star outfielder for his favorite team (the novel inspired the Broadway musical *Damn Yankees* [1955], filmed in 1958), and Robert Coover's *The Universal Baseball Association, J. Henry Waugh, Prop.* (1968), involving a man obsessed with the imaginary baseball league he created. W.P. Kinsella has written tales of **magic realism** involving baseball, notably *The Iowa Baseball Confederacy* (1986), about an endless baseball game involving famous people, and *Shoeless Joe* (1982), in which a mysterious voice urges a man to build a baseball field that attracts dead baseball legends, filmed as *Field of Dreams*. Other fantasy films about baseball include *It Happens Every Spring* (1949), in which a chemical that repels wood makes a **scientist** an unhittable pitcher; *Angels in the Outfield* (1952, remade 1994), wherein **angels** help a baseball team; an episode of *The Twilight Zone*, "The Mighty Casey" (1960), about a **robot** pitcher; and *Cooperstown* (1992), about a man visited by the ghost of an ex-teammate (see **Ghosts and Hauntings**). Stories about baseball include George Alec Effinger's "Naked to the Invisible Eye" (1973), about a pitcher with **psychic powers**; Michael Bishop's *Brittle Innings* (1994), wherein the Frankenstein **monster** discovers baseball; and Kim Stanley Robinson's *Pacific Edge* (1990), where baseball is regularly played in a future **utopia**, and "Arthur Sternbach Brings the Curveball to Mars" (1999), whose title is self-explanatory (see *Red Mars*). Nostalgia for the abandoned game of baseball is a recurring theme in the series *Star Trek: Deep Space Nine*.

Sports like football, basketball, and hockey attract less attention, though the **gravity**-defying substance flubber leads hometown basketball and football teams to victory in the films *The Absent Minded Professor* (1961) and its sequel *Son of Flubber* (1963). In Clifford D. Simak's "Rule 18" (1938), humans win a football game against **Mars** by employing **time travel** to assemble an all-star team of past greats; the incorrectly killed man in *Heaven Can Wait* returns to life as a star quarterback; and the sequel to *Angels in the Outfield*, *Angels in the Endzone* (1997), involves angels helping a football team. **Aliens on Earth** take up basketball in Effinger's "Downtown at the Buzzer" (1977) and the animated film *Space Jam* (1996). The game of cricket is a warped recollection of a **space war** in Douglas Adams's *Life, the Universe and Everything* (1982) (see *The Hitchhiker's Guide to the Galaxy*). Numerous fantasy films for children involve animals that become star players: a football-playing donkey kicks field goals in *Gus* (1976); *Matilda* (1978) is a boxing kangaroo; a **dog** takes up basketball in *Air Bud* (1997) and later dabbles in football (*Air Bud: Golden Retriever* [1998]), soccer (*Air Bud: World Pup* [2002]), baseball (*Air Bud: Seventh Inning Fetch* [2002]), and volleyball (*Air Bud: Spikes Back* [2003]); and a monkey is a hockey goalie in *MVP: Most Valuable Primate* (1999) before taking up skateboarding (*MVP 2: Most Vertical Primate* [2002]) and snowboarding (*MXP: Most Extreme Primate* [2003]) (see **Apes**). An episode of *The Twilight Zone*, "Steel" (1963), involves an **android** boxer, while Brian W. Aldiss's *The Dark Light Years* (1964) and William R. Burkett, Jr.'s *Bloodsport* (1997) describe hunting strange animals on **alien worlds**.

Stories may envision new future sports employing advanced **technology** to achieve thrills and excitement; one example is rollerball, introduced in William Harrison's "Roller Ball Murder" (1973) and featured in two films entitled *Rollerball* (1975, 2002), but high-speed futuristic sports also figure in the film *Starship Troopers* (1997) and S.L. Viehl's *Shockball* (2001), and vicious competitions between teams of children in a **space station** are part of the training in Orson Scott Card's *Ender's Game*. Frederik Pohl and C.M. Kornbluth's *Gladiator-at-Law* (1955) posits a revival of Roman gladiatorial battles, and similar contests involving powerful robots figure in the film *Robojox* (1990). Robert Sheckley's "The Seventh Victim" (1953) and Stephen King's *The Running Man* (1982) predict globally observed hunts for human victims. Stories also posit new sports developed for zero-**gravity** conditions, like "space diving" in Fritz Leiber's "The Beat Cluster" (1961) and "Skyball" in Chris Claremont's *FirstFlight* (1987), while Robert A. Heinlein's "The Menace from Earth" (1958) and Isaac Asimov's "For the Birds" (1980) describe the sport of human-powered **flying** in the low gravity of, respectively, the **Moon** and a **space habitat**.

Sports are rarely important in the **far future**, although Mike Resnick's epic *Birthright: The Book of Man* (1982) describes a time in **humanity**'s future when people were obsessed with staging and winning athletic competitions against alien races.

Discussion

Until television made sporting events accessible to all households, realistic sports fiction was a vibrant genre, but there have been relatively few stories and films of this nature in recent decades. By describing sports with unusual rules and participants that cannot be observed on television, however, science fiction and fantasy are helping to keep the tradition of sports fiction alive.

Bibliography

Isaac Asimov, Martin H. Greenberg, and Charles G. Waugh, eds. *Isaac Asimov's Wonderful Worlds of Science Fiction #2: The Science Fictional Olympics*. New York: Signet Books, 1984.

Arthur C. Clarke. "A Day at the Ballpark." Clarke, *July 20, 2019*. New York: Macmillan, 1986, 155–169.

Don D'Ammassa. "Sporting Blood." *Niekas*, No. 46 (February, 2001), 23.

David Drake, Charles G. Waugh, and Martin H. Greenberg, eds. *Space Gladiators*. New York: Ace Books, 1989.

George Alec Effinger. *Idle Pleasures*. New York: Berkley, 1983.

Gary Genosko. "Sports." *Borderlines*, No. 44 (1997), 13–15.

Elizabeth A. Hull. "Merging Madness." Richard D. Erlich, ed., *Clockwork Worlds*. Westport, CT: Greenwood Press, 1983, 163–180.

Nan C. Scott. "The Sports Section." *Niekas*, No. 46 (February, 2001), 19–21.

—*Gary Westfahl*

STARS

■

"Look," whispered Chuck, and George lifted his eyes to heaven. (There is always a last time for everything.) Overhead, without any fuss, the stars were going out.

—Arthur C. Clarke
"The Nine Billion Names of God" (1952)

Overview

Many stories of **space travel** involve stars, although they may also function as **sublime** objects in earthbound fantasies. Separate entries discuss the **Sun** and stars that become **black holes**.

Survey

Isaac Asimov's classic "Nightfall" (1941), expanded into the novel *Nightfall* (1990) with Robert Silverberg as co-author, is the story of a planet always in sunlight in a system of multiple suns, where night comes only once every two millennia, with devastating consequences: the darkness and the terrifying sight of stars drive people to **madness**. When stars begin vanishing from the sky in Arthur C. Clarke's "The Nine Billion Names of God" (1953), it signals the end of the world (see **Apocalypse**). Mysterious or strange stellar conditions play important roles in Vernor Vinge's *A Deepness in the Sky* (2000) and Peter F. Hamilton's *Pandora's Star* (2004) and sequel. Vinge's novel, a kind of prequel to his *A Fire Upon the Deep* (1995), depicts an unusual variable star whose irregular behavior has drastic consequences for both humans visiting the system and spider-like aliens on one of its planets. In Hamilton's novels, a space mission investigating how a distant star suddenly disappeared from the heavens discovers that something unknown has sealed off an entire stellar system.

A star that explodes is known as a nova or supernova, and several science fiction tales deal with such phenomena, which threaten anything near the explosion. Because of the sudden, excessive brightness of the **Moon**, the protagonists of Larry Niven's "Inconstant Moon" (1971) fear that our own sun has become a nova, although it turns out that there has only been an extremely large solar flare, albeit one sufficient to bring about the collapse of contemporary **civilization**. Clarke's classic "The Star" (1955) highlights the religious and ethical implications of the discovery that the star of Bethlehem was a supernova which destroyed an alien race. Poul Anderson's "Day of Burning" (1967), from his Technic Civilization series, tells of attempts by a technologically advanced human civilization to mobilize the still-feudal alien inhabitants of a planet that will soon be struck by the wavefront of a supernova. Works in which **Earth** is endangered by the explosions of distant stars include Roger MacBride Allen and Eric Kotani's *Supernova* (1991) and Charles Sheffield's *Aftermath* (1998). Robert Silverberg's "The Iron Star" (1987) involves not only two supernovae, but also a neutron star and a black hole.

Neutron stars are featured in a number of science fiction stories. These are the small remnants of supernovae, a few kilometers in diameter, which are made up exclusively of neutrons. Larry Niven's "Neutron Star" (1966) describes the dangers of flying a spaceship too close to such an object, and Niven's novel *The Integral Trees* (1984) and its sequel take place in a thick **ring** of gas, stripped from a Jovian planet, orbiting a neutron star. In Robert L. Forward's *Dragon's Egg* (1980) and its sequel, tiny aliens live on the surface of a neutron star, while in Stephen Baxter's *Flux* (1993), part of his Xeelee series, we have microscopic humans living inside of one.

Conjectures about life-forms that might exist in or on more normal stars, including the Sun, are found in Olaf Stapledon's *Star Maker*, Hal Clement's "Proof" (1942), Frederik Pohl and Jack Williamson's *The Reefs of Space* (1964) and its sequels, Gregory Benford and Gordon Eklund's *If the Stars Are Gods* (1977), and David Brin's *Sundiver* (1980) (see *Startide Rising*).

Space operas, especially those set in the **far future**, sometimes portray **technologies** that can manipulate or even destroy stars. Two examples are Larry Niven's Known Space series, begun with *The World of Ptavvs* (1966), and Peter F. Hamilton's the Night's Dawn Trilogy, begun in *The Reality Dysfunction* (1996). In Robert J. Sawyer's *Calculating God* (2000) the star Betelgeuse may have been deliberately turned into a supernova by **aliens in space**.

Discussion

A further subtle and subjective dimension to the function of stars in fantasy and science fiction is that they evoke the kind of sublimity described by Edmund Burke in his *Philosophical Enquiry into the Origin of Our Ideas of the Sublime and Beautiful*

(1757). While approaching Mount Doom in J.R.R. Tolkien's *The Lord of the Rings*, Sam gets a new feeling of hope when he observes a star. The very term *stars* is itself highly charged, as indicated by its use in emotively rich titles like Fredric Brown's *The Lights in the Sky Are Stars* (1953), Clarke's *The City and the Stars* (1956), Alfred Bester's *The Stars My Destination*, and Samuel R. Delany's *Stars in My Pocket Like Grains of Sand* (1984). Not all these novels deal directly with the astrophysical objects we designate as stars, but all call forth an emotional reaction to a significant and influential icon.

Bibliography

John Dean. "Use of Stars in the Literature of Science Fiction and Fantasy." *Metaphores*, Nos. 9–10 (April, 1984), 91–100.

G. Gale. "The Stars Above and the Very Idea of Philosophy." *Vistas in Astronomy*, 39 (1995), 547–551.

Susan Glicksohn. "A City of Which the Stars Are Suburbs." Thomas D. Clareson, ed., *SF: The Other Side of Realism*. Bowling Green, OH: Bowling Green State University Popular Press, 1971, 334–347.

Alexander Nedelkovich. "The Stellar Parallels: Robert Silverberg, Larry Niven, and Arthur C. Clarke." *Extrapolation*, 21 (Winter, 1980), 348–360.

R.L. Poss. "Whitman's 'Learn'd Astronomer' and the Poetry of Stars." *Vistas in Astronomy*, 39 (1995), 615–622.

Cornel Robu. "A Key to Science Fiction: The Sublime." *Foundation*, No. 42 (Spring, 1988), 21–37.

David Sandner. "Habituated to the Vast." *Extrapolation*, 41 (Fall, 2000), 282–297.

William A. Wheaton. "In the Deeps of Time, Amongst the Innumerable Stars." *Vector*, No. 197 (January/February, 1998), 9–11.

—*Richard L. McKinney*

STATUES

Overview

Images of living creatures carved in stone, statues naturally give rise to notions that they represent beings that were once alive or might come to life, as occurs in the two principal sorts of fantasies where they appear. As three-dimensional works of **art**, statues may also possess and project an aura of power unrelated to their possible past or future life. Smaller objects resembling human beings are discussed under **Dolls and Puppets**.

Survey

Statues may be the few surviving representatives of ancient **civilizations** and thus the past. In *La Jetée*, one of the first things the time-travelling narrator (see **Time Travel**) sees upon entering the past is a series of statues, suggesting—as does the film itself—that we can only envision the past as a series of still images. Less poetically, the famous statues on Easter Island are disappointingly explained as political caricatures in Robert A. Heinlein and Elma Wentz's "Beyond Doubt" (1941) (see **Politics**). Famous American statues often appear in films: in *Planet of the Apes*, the **hero**'s concluding glimpse of the half-buried Statue of Liberty evocatively communicates that this **ape**-dominated world is in fact the future of his own **Earth**; in Tim Burton's 2002 remake, the statue the hero sees upon returning to Earth—an ape replacing Abraham Lincoln in the Lincoln Memorial—less effectively conveys that the world has experienced the same tragic transformation; and the presidential sculptures on Mount Rushmore provide a surrealistic backdrop (see **Surrealism**) to the conclusion of Alfred Hitchcock's *North by Northwest* (1959).

In the future, space explorers may discover statues of extinct aliens, as in Arthur C. Clarke's "Jupiter Five" (1953) (see **Aliens in Space**). Sam Moskowitz's "Man of the Stars" (1941) imagines future statues on Earth honoring space pioneers, but in *Star Trek: First Contact* (1996) (see *Star Trek: Generations*), one of those pioneers is unhappy to learn that there will someday be a statue of him at the site where his **rocket** is launched.

Most fantasies involving statues derive from two tales from Greek and Roman **mythology**. First is the story of Perseus, who cuts off the head of Medusa, whose visage turns people into stone, and then uses her head as a weapon—as visualized in the film *Clash of the Titans* (1980). People are petrified by evildoers in C.S. Lewis's *The Lion, the Witch and the Wardrobe* and the film *Return to Oz* (1986) (see *The Wizard of Oz*), which borrowed the idea from L. Frank Baum's *The Marvelous Land of Oz* (1906) (see *The Wonderful Wizard of Oz*). J.R.R. Tolkien's *The Hobbit* includes a scene in which a troll is turned to stone when exposed to sunlight. In the horror film *Waxwork* (1988), teenagers who touch statues in a wax museum are killed and become lifeless parts of the exhibit.

The other archetypal statue story is Pygmalion and Galatea, about a sculptor whose statue becomes a living woman. In James Branch Cabell's *Figures of Earth* (1921) (see *Jurgen*), a man mimics stories of God's creation of **humanity** by making clay figures and bringing them to life. Stories focusing on animated statues may portray them sympathetically, as in Thorne Smith's *The Night Life of the Gods* (1931), filmed in 1935, which involves statues of Greek **gods and goddesses** coming to life and humorously tormenting New Yorkers. Quasimodo enjoys the lively company of talking gargoyles adorning his church in Walt Disney version of *The Hunchback of Notre Dame* (1995), and the plastic statues used to display clothes in department stores, mannequins, may come to life as likable characters, as in the film *One Touch of Venus* (1948); an episode of *The Twilight Zone*, "The After Hours" (1960); and the films *Mannequin* (1987) and *Mannequin Two* (1991).

However, statues brought to life may also be fierce avengers, reflecting the influence of legends of the **golem**. In Lorzeno da Ponte and Wolfgang Amadeus Mozart's classic opera *Don Giovanni* (1787), derived from a seventeenth-century play by Tirso de Molina, the amoral Don Juan is ultimately dragged into **Hell** by the awakened statue of one of the men he wronged. Statues with murder on their minds also figure in the films *Burn, Witch, Burn* (1961) and *The Norliss Tapes* (1974), while sinister gargoyles brought to life by pollution are featured in Harlan Ellison's "Bleeding Stones" (1973) (see *Deathbird Stories*). Statues of famous murderers in a wax museum contrive to carry out new crimes in another episode of *The Twilight Zone*, "The New Exhibit" (1963).

Discussion

As holograms and other realistic three-dimensional images become easier to produce (see **Virtual Reality**), statues will probably become less important as artworks and artifacts. Perhaps this is why one so rarely encounters statues in stories about humanity's future; stories as far back as Edmond Hamilton's "The Dead Planet" (1946) assumed that advanced humans would be capable of creating machines that could indefinitely continue to project realistic images of themselves to visiting aliens, eliminating the need for something as crude as a statue to convey what humans looked like. In showing sculptors of the **far future** shaping clouds instead of stone, J.G. Ballard's "The Cloud-Sculptors of Coral D" (1967) also suggests that sculpture might become a matter of ephemeral pleasure, not an essential way to preserve information. Still, it is dangerous to predict the extinction of a longstanding form of art, and it remains possible that humans will long continue to create, observe, and write stories about statues.

Bibliography

Brian Arkins. "Sexy Statues." *Classical and Modern Literature*, 18 (Spring, 1998), 247–250.
Steve Biodrowski. "*Waxwork*." *Cinefantastique*, 19 (January, 1989), 102–103.
———. "*Waxwork II: Lost in Time*." *Cinefantastique*, 22 (June, 1992), 48–49.
Naomi Greene. "Deadly Statues." *The French Review*, 61 (May, 1988), 890–898.
Kenneth Gross. *The Dream of the Moving Statue*. Ithaca, NY: Cornell University Press, 1992.
Elwira Grossman. "Witkacy and Shaw's Stage Statues." Milton T. Wolf, ed., *Shaw and Science Fiction*. University Park: Pennsylvania State University Press, 1997, 39–52.
Anne McCaffrey, ed. *Alchemy and Academe*. New York: Ballantine, 1980.
Deborah Steiner. *Images in Mind*. Princeton: Princeton University Press, 2001.

—*Gary Westfahl*

STEAMPUNK

Overview

Although rarely applied to all science fiction set in the past, steampunk specifically refers to stories occurring in the nineteenth century that focus on that century's **technology** as other science fiction stories focus on future technology—steam engines rather than **cyberspace**. Even steampunk fiction by American writers usually focuses on Victorian and Edwardian England, particularly the Dickensian image of London as a capital of technology, shrouded in fog and rooted in dirt and squalor. Steampunk intersects with the concerns of **alternate history**, the **Gothic, cities, machines and mechanization, landscape**, and, increasingly, **illustration and graphics**, sometimes also involving **metafiction and recursiveness**.

Survey

Once established, literary subgenres usually suggest predecessors; regarding steampunk, various earlier texts can be retrofitted with the steampunk label: works by Edgar Allan Poe, Jules Verne, and H.G. Wells; Mark Twain's *A Connecticut Yankee in King Arthur's Court*; Charles Dickens's novels (in terms of aesthetics if not content); Keith Roberts's *Pavane* (1968), in which the Spanish Armada defeats Elizabethan England and Britain retains a preindustrial technology, memorably represented by long-distance communication with networks of semaphore towers; Harry Harrison's *A Transatlantic Tunnel, Hurrah!* (1972), wherein a failed American Revolution leads to a twentieth-century British Empire still relying on nineteenth-century hardware (see **America**); Philip José Farmer's *The Other Log of Phileas Fogg* (1973) and *The Adventures of the Peerless Peer* (1974), reexamining Verne's Phileas Fogg, Arthur Conan Doyle's Sherlock Holmes, and Edgar Rice Burroughs's *Tarzan of the Apes*; Richard A. Lupoff's *Into the Aether: Being the Adventures of Professor Thintwhistle and His Incredible Aether Flying on the Moon* (1974); Manly Wade Wellman and Wade Wellman's *Sherlock Holmes' War of the Worlds* (1975); and Michael Moorcock's Nomad of the Time Streams series, beginning with *The Warlord of the Air* (1971).

However, K.W. Jeter reportedly coined the term **steampunk** in the 1980s to describe novels by him, Tim Powers, and James P. Blaylock. Jeter's *Morlock Night* (1979) is a **time travel** novel invoking both Wells and King **Arthur**'s Merlin in late-Victorian London; the protagonist of Powers's *The Anubis Gates* (1983) travels back to 1810 London to confront not only an early industrial landscape but also ancient Egyptian **magic** (see **Egypt**); and in Blaylock's *Homunculus* (1986), nineteenth-century London intersects with another old tradition, alchemy.

Although these authors published other works regarded as steampunk (like Jeter's *Infernal Devices: A Mad Victorian Fantasy* [1987]), the best-known steampunk novel is William Gibson and Bruce Sterling's **The Difference Engine**, in which the mechanical **computers** proposed by Charles Babbage in the 1820s actually succeed and the computer revolution arrives a century and a half early. Equally important is Paul Di Filippo's *The Steampunk Trilogy* (1995), a collection of three novellas that expand the steampunk landscape to nineteenth-century America: "Hottentots" confronts famed scientist Louis Agassiz with **monsters** out of H.P. Lovecraft, while "Walt and Emily" imagines an encounter between Walt Whitman and Emily Dickinson. 1995 also brought Stephen Baxter's *The Time Ships*, a sequel to Wells's **The Time Machine**.

Other science fiction stories in Victorian settings include Connie Willis's *To Say Nothing of the Dog* (1998), Jan Lars Jensen's "The Secret History of the Ornithopter" (1997), and Ted Chiang's reconsideration of the **golem** legend, "Seventy-Two Letters" (2000). Neil Gaiman's "A Study in Emerald" (2003) conflates Lovecraft and Sherlock Holmes. The steampunk aesthetic is also observed in fantasies like Kim Newman's *Anno Dracula* (1992), wherein Bram Stoker's **Dracula** marries Queen Victoria. In addition, China Miéville's **Perdido Street Station**, though set in an imaginary city, vividly presents a gaslit, industrial urban landscape recalling nineteenth-century London.

Given its memorable landscape and costumes, steampunk would seem ideal for visual media, and it has thrived in graphic novels like Alan Moore's *From Hell* (1991–1996) and *The League of Extraordinary Gentlemen* (1999–2003), and Joe Kelly and Chris Bachalo's inarguably titled *Steampunk* (2000–2002). Moore's *League* provides a definitive steampunk scenario, bringing together well-known characters from fantastic fiction, including Verne's Captain Nemo and H. Rider Haggard's Allan Quatermain, to fight a super-scientific **villain** in Victorian London.

Surprisingly, steampunk has fared less well in film and television. The series *The Wild, Wild West* (1965–1969), which equipped two nineteenth-century secret service agents with high-tech devices for novel **western** adventures, is cited as proto-steampunk and remains a cult favorite. However, film versions of the series (1999) and *The League of Extraordinary Gentlemen* (2003), while visually sumptuous, were critical and commercial failures. More aesthetically successful, though barely noticed, was the Canadian series *The Secret Adventures of Jules Verne* (2001), which combined striking visuals, intelligent scripts, and engaging performances to describe a young Verne's adventures with Phileas Fogg and his cousin Rebecca, first female agent of the British Secret Service.

Discussion

Paul Di Filippo has observed that the past is "like an alien world out in space . . . a strange other dimension," a statement encapsulating the appeal of steampunk. While some might see this as a failure of imagination—looking backward, not forward—there is much in steampunk to reward both astute readers and ambitious writers. The best steampunk, like the best **cyberpunk**, immerses readers in a dense, convincing landscape combining conceptual audacity with familiar ways of storytelling and familiar characters. There are excellent reasons, then, for science fiction and fantasy to continue visiting the alien past.

Bibliography

Paul Di Filippo. "A La Modes." *Locus*, 51 (September, 2003), 76–78.

Nick Gevers. "A Steampunk of the Trailer Parks: Paul di Filippo Interviewed." *Interzone*, No. 155 (May, 2000), 25–29.

Steffen Hantke. "Difference Engines and Other Infernal Devices." *Extrapolation*, 40 (Fall, 1999), 244–254.

Peter J. Heck. "Trends and Genres in Science Fiction." David G. Thompkins, ed., *Science Fiction Writer's Market Place and Source Book*. Cincinnati, OH: Writer's Digest Books, 1994, 2–12.

Fiona Kelleghan. "No Refuge Any More." *New York Review of Science Fiction*, No. 143 (July, 2000), 1, 4–6.

Andy Lane. "Steampunk Timmy: Tim Powers." *Skeleton Crew*, No. 4 (April, 1991), 5–6.

Andy Watson and J.B. Reynolds. "Interview with Tim Powers and James P. Blaylock." *Science Fiction Review*, 15 (May, 1986), 18–26.

Janeen Webb. "Simmons and Powers: Postmodernism to Postromanticism." Allienne R. Becker, ed., *Visions of the Fantastic*. Westport, CT: Greenwood Press, 1996, 139–148.

—*F. Brett Cox*

STORIES

■

*When I used to read fairy tales, I fancied
that kind of thing never happened, and
now here I am in the middle of one!*

—Lewis Carroll
Alice's Adventures in Wonderland (1865)

Overview

Stories are often about the practice of telling stories, narrators who tell stories, and the influence of **fables, fairy tales,** and **mythology** on audiences' beliefs and behavior. The act of **reading** stories in **books** and concerns of **writing and authors** are discussed elsewhere.

Survey

Many works of science fiction and fantasy are presented as stories narrated to an audience. Mary Shelley's *Frankenstein* relates his story in the supposed writings of an Arctic explorer, while the **time travel** adventures of the inventor of H.G. Wells's *The Time Machine* are told to a friend who records them. Shelley's *The Last Man* and Wells's *The Island of Doctor Moreau* are the purported contents of discovered manuscripts. Anne Rice's *Interview with the Vampire* is narrated to a journalist, while William Goldman's *The Princess Bride* (1973) is a **fairy tale** being told as a bedtime story. Nor are such framing devices outdated; voiceovers in films like *Blade Runner* serve a similar purpose.

Stories recounted by characters raise questions about truth and **perception.** The reporting of events afterwards rather than as they occur reinforces the status of J.R.R. Tolkien's *The Lord of the Rings* as a **history** of Middle-earth, while the **talking animals** of the **far future** in Clifford D. Simak's *City* debate whether stories about **humanity** are mythology or fact. In *Star Trek: Voyager,* **children** hearing a ghost story in "The Haunting of Deck Twelve" (2000) argue about how much of it to believe (see **Ghosts and Hauntings**). Storytelling also serves a moral purpose; in *The Terminator,* the **hero** from a future **post-holocaust society** warns not only the **mother** of the future **rebellion**'s leader but also audiences about the consequences of relying on **machines and mechanization.** Sometimes books are constructed as collections of stories told by several characters with different views about their world, as in Dan Simmons's *Hyperion* and Peter S. Beagle's *Giant Bones* (1997).

The **art** or practice of storytelling is a concern in many works (see **Metafiction and Recursiveness**). Bilbo reflects on the similarity of his adventures to stories he has heard in Tolkien's *The Hobbit,* while characters in Beagle's *The Last Unicorn,* John Crowley's *Little, Big,* and Michael Ende's *The Neverending Story* (1979) are aware of their participation in a story. A **father**'s inability to tell stories provides the impetus for the **quest** in Salman Rushdie's *Haroun and the Sea of Stories* (1990), while in an episode of *Star Trek: Deep Space Nine,* "Far Beyond the Stars" (1998), Sisko **dreams** that he is a 1950s author writing about a **space station.**

Stories about storytelling reflect on the power of narrative to create **imaginary worlds**. In Marion Zimmer Bradley's *The Mists of Avalon*, stories told by practitioners of **religions** determine the world's fate, while mythology comes to life in Patricia McKillip's *Sorceress and the Cygnet* (1991) and Robert Holdstock's *Mythago Wood* (1984). The protagonists of *Mad Max Beyond Thunderdome* (1985) (see **Mad Max**) and Frank Herbert's *Dune* are transformed into legends, a form of **immortality and longevity** not always appreciated. Stories are also essential in the construction of **identity**; the **robot** David is driven by the tale of Pinocchio in *A.I.: Artificial Intelligence* and the protagonists of Alan Garner's *The Owl Service*, caught in a story **cycle**, fight to control their **destiny**. Stories provide **education**, helping **youth** to learn appropriate behavior in their **community**. The rabbits of Richard Adams's *Watership Down* (1972) imitate the actions of the **trickster** whose stories they hear (see **Gods and Goddesses**), and the rats of Terry Pratchett's *The Amazing Maurice and His Educated Rodents* (2001) (see **Rats and Mice**), viewing tales of Mr. Bunnsy as a guidebook, are dismayed to learn that the stories are not true.

Because stories are powerful and fictions may be regarded as forms of **illusion** or deceit, some communities exercise control over storytelling. In the **parallel world** of Neal Stephenson's *The Diamond Age* (1995), a stolen children's storybook is actually a **computer** containing **knowledge** that brings **freedom** from oppression. In the **dystopias** of Ray Bradbury's *Fahrenheit 451* and Aldous Huxley's *Brave New World*, literature is forbidden; the banning of stories drives the narrator of "Usher II" to **madness** and **revenge** in Bradbury's *The Martian Chronicles*.

Discussion

The practice and conventions of storytelling are central concerns in science fiction and fantasy because those genres are especially concerned with the creation of imaginary worlds. Stories help to form and change belief systems and influence the behavior of individuals and societies, which is often the storyteller's goal. When fictional worlds and characters inhabiting them are more than reflections of the actual world inhabited by storytellers and their audience, when those worlds are displaced in space and time and possibility, the art of creating fiction is as involving as the resulting stories. As **technology** changes the ways stories are circulated, it will be interesting to see how storytelling practices are depicted in the future.

Bibliography

Andrew M. Butler. "A Story About Stories." *Vector*, No. 227 (Jan/Feb, 2003), 10–11.
Robert Crossley. "Taking It as a Story." George Slusser, Patrick Parrinder, and Danièle Chatelain, eds., *H.G. Wells's Perennial Time Machine*. Athens: University of Georgia Press, 2001, 12–26.
Colin Duriez. "Sub-creation and Tolkien's Theology of Story." K.J. Battarbee, ed., *Scholarship and Fantasy*. Turku, Finland: University of Turku, 1993, 133–150.
Marilyn Jurich. *Scheherazade's Sisters*. Westport, CT: Greenwood Press, 1998.
Frank McConnell. "You Bet Your Life." George Slusser, Gary Westfahl, and Eric S. Rabkin, eds., *Immortal Engines*. Athens: University of Georgia Press, 1996, 221–230.
Marge Piercy. "Telling Stories About Stories." *Utopian Studies*, 5 (1994), 1–3.

Peter Schakel and Charles A. Huttar, eds., *Word and Story in C.S. Lewis*. Columbia: University of Missouri Press, 1991.
Thelma J. Shinn. "Fable of Reality." *Extrapolation*, 31 (Spring, 1990), 5–14.
Naomi Wood. "Paradise Lost and Found." *Children's Literature in Education*, 32 (December, 2001), 237–260.

—Christine Mains

SUBLIME

—————————■—————————

Overview

The sublime and the beautiful are two central categories of aesthetics, the study of art's essence and effects on human emotion (see **Beauty**). Frequently compared to and conflated with **sense of wonder**, the sublime specifies the profound feelings associated with extreme **perception** and exalted intellection—whether positive or negative, lovely or terrible.

Survey

Longinus, Edmund Burke, and Immanuel Kant offered three influential definitions of the sublime. Longinus's *On the Sublime* (c. 50 CE) addressed literary style and rhetoric, arguing that poems produce sudden, singular moments of *ekstasis*, "elevation" or ecstasy—transport outside the self, a vital if fleeting feeling. Despite this early articulation, the sublime only returned to prominence in the seventeenth century. Burke and Kant articulated elements of what would be called the romantic sublime, though neither were romantics. Burke's concern was sensation, especially the feeling generated in the mind by strong emotions responding to empirical objects or events; his principal example was terror or danger, which he linked to the concept of powerful feeling. Kant's concern was judgment, but, like romantic philosophers, he associated the sublime with **nature**; using examples like Mont Blanc (see **Mountains**), which Kant thought apt since it was really big. He linked physical grandeur to the conceptually grandiose, ideas like "infinity" or "God." But since the infinite cannot be captured by finite systems of language, painting, or **music**, sublime images "present the unpresentable," as Kant phrased it.

These definitions agree that the sublime lifts us up, transports us to another state, and such moments of elevation structure large parts of science fiction and fantasy. In *Solaris*, Stanislaw Lem complies a veritable textbook on the sublime: Kelvin's terror at his dead lover's reappearance, the unpresentable dread of Snow's phi-creature, or Kelvin's dream-like encounter with the alien in the contact scene. The sublime names the moment when, in Isaac Asimov's "Nightfall" (1941) the stars appear or, in Arthur C. Clarke's "The Nine Billion Names of God" (1953), they vanish. The sublime names Sam's awe at the ethereal beauty of the **elf** Galadriel in J.R.R. Tolkien's *The Lord of the Rings*; the narrator's epiphany, in Bob Shaw's

"Light of Other Days" (1966), when he realizes he has seen the farmer's dead wife through slow glass; the dramatic irony of Ray Bradbury's "There Will Come Soft Rains" (1950) (see *The Martian Chronicles*); and Riddley's encounter with the terrifying gnosis of female divinity in Russell Hoban's *Riddley Walker* (1981).

The sublime names what William Gibson's Case (in *Neuromancer*) or Bobby (in *Mona Lisa Overdrive* [1988]) feel by transport (see **Escape**) into the **virtual reality** of **cyberspace**. Indeed, in science fiction the technological sublime has been important since the nineteenth century. People were inspired by the grandeur and power not only of Mont Blanc and the Grand Canyon but also the railroad and the Brooklyn Bridge. Some natural objects became mechanical miracles: Niagara Falls became a source of the electricity that transformed America. The most current cognate of the technological sublime concerns special effects in film. When done well, they are spectacular, as in *2001: A Space Odyssey*; when done poorly, they are ridiculous, like the fatuous attempt to represent "god" in *Star Trek V: The Final Frontier* (see *Star Trek: The Motion Picture*).

Because Burke emphasized the sublimity produced by terror, there are suitable applications to H.P. Lovecraft, Stephen King, Clive Barker, and other writers of **Gothic** or **horror**. Some readers find the more subtle terrors expressed by Edgar Allan Poe's *The Narrative of Arthur Gordon Pym* or Oscar Wilde's *The Picture of Dorian Gray* evocative of the sublime. Mary Shelley's *Frankenstein* demonstrates how the sublime follows either the ardor of intellectual breakthrough or the horrific consequences of radical change. Great scale can also delight and terrify, so grandiose projects like Olaf Stapledon's *Last and First Men* or *Star Maker* capture qualities of the sublime. Sometimes stories of mannered or baroque metaphysical discovery, like David Lindsay's *A Voyage to Arcturus*, are said to produce the sublime, since they align emotion with the higher faculty of cognition. The term may also describe stories where a character or species evolves to a transcendent state, as happens in Clarke's *Childhood's End* (see **Evolution**).

Discussion

Two important matters merit additional discussion. First is the distinction between the true sublime and false sublime, which Longinus excoriates: the sentimental, pallid, or bombastic (a phenomenon common in "sci-fi" or **sword and sorcery** fantasy). The beautiful can be light or comic, delicate or sweet, emotionally moving but finally transient (only *skin deep*); the sublime—serious, indelibly deep, sometimes even grave—is not produced by the facile **clichés** or ephemeral thrills of commercial horror films. Instead, the sublime signals a severe disjunction with quotidian experience, of the sort represented when, in Yevgeny Zamiatin's *We*, the extraordinary power of the human imagination overwhelms D-503.

The second regards correlations between the sublime and sense of wonder in science fiction or fantasy. Cornel Robu argues that, at least in science fiction, the sublime and sense of wonder designate the same faculty; science fiction's aesthetic pleasures are peculiarly sublime, a specificity matched only by **tragedy**. Robu thinks the key to understanding science fiction is to link its use of science and novel concepts to the sublime. When speaking of wonder or awe in fantasy, we address an important but not the only feature transporting us to ever higher qualities of contemplation.

Bibliography

Scott Bukatman. "The Artificial Infinite." Annette Kuhn, ed., *Alien Zone II*. London: Verso, 1999, 249–275.

Neil Easterbrook. "The Sublime Simulacra." *Critique*, 36 (Spring, 1995), 177–194.

Francis Ferguson. *Solitude and the Sublime*. New York: Routledge, 1992.

Nancy Fredricks. "On the Sublime and Beautiful in Shelley's *Frankenstein*." *Essays in Literature*, 23 (Fall, 1996), 178–189.

Steffen H. Hantke. "The Function of the Sublime in Contemporary Horror." *Foundation*, No.71 (Autumn, 1997), 45–63.

Dale J. Nelson. "Lovecraft and the Burkean Sublime." *Lovecraft Studies*, No. 24 (Spring, 1991), 2–6.

Cornel Robu. "A Key to Science Fiction." *Foundation*, No. 42 (Spring, 1988), 21–37.

———. "'The Sense of Wonder' Is 'Sense Sublime.'" *Science Fiction Research Association Review*, No. 211 (May/June, 1994), 43–64.

Bart Thurber. "Toward a Technological Sublime." R.E. Myers, ed., *The Intersection of Science Fiction and Philosophy*. Westport, CT: Greenwood Press, 1983, 211–224.

—*Neil Easterbrook*

SUICIDE

■

Overview

The act of taking one's own life usually results from extreme physical or mental **pain** and can be emotionally wrenching to persons acquainted with the suicide. A separate entry addresses **Violence**, and people who allow themselves to die so others may live are discussed under **Sacrifice**.

Survey

The Catholic Church regards suicide as a serious **sin**, which is why Dante's *Inferno* (c. 1306–1321) torments suicides in the seventh circle of **Hell**, and why Catholic **cemeteries** refuse to allow burials of suicides. Extending this attitude into a **near future** dominated by Christian fundamentalism (see **Christianity**), James Stevens-Arce's *Soulsaver* (2000) envisions the "Suicide Prevention Corps of America" employing cryonics (see **Suspended Animation and Cryonics**) to revive suicides so they can be punished. However, religious fanatics may also commit suicide if urged to do so by a charismatic leader (see **Religion**), as occurred in Jim Jones's Guyana community in 1979 and the San Diego **home** of **UFO** cultists in 1996; a similar event is imminent on an **alien world** in Simon Spurrier's *Strontium Dog: Prophet Margin* (2005).

Suicides are often caused by despair: in J.R.R. Tolkien's *The Lord of the Rings*, the Steward of Gondor seeks to kill himself in the funeral pyre prematurely arranged for his dying son; in Philip K. Dick's *Dr. Bloodmoney* (1964), a man on a **space station** after a **nuclear war** was accompanied by his wife, but she suffered from "suicidal depression" and took her own life; in Octavia E. Butler's *Kindred*, Alice commits suicide when she believes that her slaveowner has sold her **children**, removing the only happiness in her life; in Don Sakers's "Tarawa Rising" (1990), an aging, washed-up transvestite performer plans to kill himself; and in Kurt Vonnegut, Jr.'s satirical "Requiem for a Dreamer" (2004), inept science fiction writer Kilgore Trout (see **Writing and Authors**) commits suicide because of President George W. Bush's predicted reelection.

Suicide may also result from **madness** caused by an enigmatic encounter with **aliens in space**: in Stanislaw Lem's *Solaris*, a **scientist** commits suicide because he is maddened by mysterious visitors generated by the sentient **alien world**, and in William Gibson's "Hinterlands" (1981), solitary travelers into a mysterious space warp often commit suicide upon their return. People with extremely long lifespans (see **Immortality and Longevity**) may contemplate suicide because they are tired of living: Robert A. Heinlein's *Time Enough for Love* (1973) begins with the attempted suicide of Lazarus Long, thwarted by citizens eager to keep this famous man alive (see *The Past Through Tomorrow*).

However, people may commit suicide to achieve some worthwhile goal. Drawing upon the Japanese tradition of honorable suicide, Pierre Boulle's *Garden on the Moon* (1965) envisions **Japan** winning the race to the **Moon** because a Japanese **astronaut** is willing to land on the lunar surface without a way to return to **Earth**, dying so Japan can have the glory of being the first nation to reach the Moon. In the film *I, Robot* (2004), a **detective** determines that a scientist staged his own suicide to spark an investigation into a **computer**'s plans to assume world control.

Stories may begin with investigations of apparent suicides that often turn out to be murders: in Michael A. Burstein's "The Quantum Teleporter" (2000), a man investigates the suicide of a scientist working on **teleportation**. However, suicides generate no concern when **villains**, their **evil** designs thwarted, choose the option of suicide; in several episodes of the television series *Mission: Impossible* (1966–1973), ingeniously framed evildoers are handed revolvers by deceived colleagues so they can commit suicide.

In future **dystopias**, suicide may be a common reaction to unpleasant conditions, as in John Varley's *Millennium* (1983), filmed in 1989. Societies bedeviled by **overpopulation** may encourage citizens to commit suicide in facilities that make killing oneself a pleasant experience, termed "Municipal Lethal Chambers" in Max Beerbohm's *A Christmas Garland* (1912) and "suicide parlours" in S.P. Somtow's *Mallworld* (1981). Such facilities are also part of future worlds in Robert Sheckley's *Immortality, Inc.* (1959), the film *Soylent Green* (1973), and the series *Futurama*.

The concept of suicide can be applied to entire species, frequently in arguments that **humanity** may soon effectively commit suicide through self-inflicted problems like nuclear war, overpopulation, and pollution. Still, like individual suicide, racial suicide may also be a justifiable method to bring about a greater good: Edmond Hamilton's "The Dead Planet" (1946) reveals that the future human race voluntarily destroyed its own **Sun**, and itself, to eliminate sinister energy beings threatening the cosmos.

Discussion

Suicides are arguably uncommon in fantasy and science fiction because these are fundamentally optimistic genres (see **Optimism and Pessimism**), believing that good will inevitably triumph over evil and **humanity** is destined to **progress** toward a better future, while suicide reflects pessimism about such desirable outcomes. Still, suicide is a problem science fiction must address, particularly involving the question of how humans might become and remain immortal without succumbing to desires for death—an issue raised, but not resolved, in Heinlein's *Time Enough for Love*.

Bibliography

Harry S. Abram. "Death Psychology, Science Fiction, and the Writings of Stanley G. Weinbaum." *Suicide*, 3 (Summer, 1975), 93–97.

Paul K. Alkon. "Shall We All Commit Suicide?" *Foundation*, No. 74 (Autumn, 1998), 38–47.

John Allett. "The Durkheimian Theme of Suicide in *Tono-Bungay*." *Wellsian*, No. 13 (1990), 35–42.

John F. Desmond. "Language, Suicide, and the Writer." Jan N. Gretlund, ed., *Walker Percy*. Jackson: University Press of Mississippi, 1991, 131–154.

Barbara T. Gates. "Blue Devils and Green Tea." *Studies in Short Fiction*, 24 (Winter, 1987), 15–23.

Patrick D. Murphy. "Suicide, Murder, Culture, and Catastrophe." Nicholas Ruddick, ed., *State of the Fantastic*. Westport, CT: Greenwood Press, 1992, 121–132.

Bettina T. Pederson. "Suicidal Logic." Karen Sayer and Rosemary Mitchell, eds., *Victorian Gothic*. Trinity and All Saints, UK: Leeds Centre for Victorian Studies, 2003, 110–123.

Dan Persons. "*The Love Suicides At Sonezaki*." *Cinefantastique*, 19 (March, 1989), 50–51.

—*Gary Westfahl*

THE SUN

If you have only lived on Earth, you have never seen the Sun.

—Arthur C. Clarke
"Out of the Sun" (1958)

Overview

The Sun is a typical **star**, an immense gas globe generating energy via nuclear fusion. It occupies a central place in the **mythologies** and legends of all cultures. In fantastic fiction, the Sun has been visited occasionally, and its potential exhaustion, extinction, destruction, and sentience have inspired the development of new beings and **cultures** and discussions of **religion**. Solar flares and sunspots may disrupt vital **communication** and are staples in **disaster** fiction.

Survey

Although the **Moon** was visited early and often in science fiction, the fictive potential of the Sun was not explored until relatively late. The most significant early work to make use of it was Cyrano de Bergerac's *The Comical History of the States and Empires of the Moon and Sun* (1687), in which the imprisoned narrator condenses the Sun's rays via a **mirror** and is blown there, where he lands on a sunspot and converses with a humanoid inhabitant before entering the Sun and finding it is an avian kingdom (see **Birds**). Later explorers find the Sun inhabited by giant spiders (Donald Horner, *By Aeroplane to the Sun* [1910]), God and various spiritual beings (Wladislaw Lach-Szyrma's "The Portals of the King of Day" [1888] and John Mastin, *Through the Sun in an Airship* [1909]), and brunettes (George Fowler's *A Flight to the Moon* [1813]). Lizardlike flame beings originally from the Sun inhabiting igneous rocks in Olaf Stapledon's *The Flames* (1947) want humans to create a radioactive belt around the equator.

Authors of two important nineteenth-century works utilizing the Sun had scientific backgrounds and, perhaps coincidentally, chose to present worlds in which the Sun could no longer be taken for granted. Camille Flammarion's *Omega* (1893–1894) speculates about the Sun's extinction, and near the conclusion of *The Time Machine* H.G. Wells visualized a red Sun over a dying **Earth**. Wells later provided the introduction to the English edition of Gabriel de Tarde's *Underground Man* (1904), which likewise utilizes a diminishing Sun. William Hope Hodgson's *The House on the Borderland* (1908) describes the Sun's extinction, and *The Night Land* (1912) features a mad world of monsters on a darkened Earth. These directly link to the works of Clark Ashton Smith, whose vicious fantasies of Zothique, beginning with "The Empire of the Necromancers" (1932), are set in a distant future, "when the sun is dim and tarnished." Jack Vance's stories of *The Dying Earth* (1950) utilize the same milieu. Gene Wolfe's ***The Book of the New Sun*** series partially concerns the reignition of the dying Sun, an accomplishment involving a white hole (see **Black Hole**) that has undisguised theological overtones.

A dying Sun is a cooler one, and decreased sunlight causes glaciation and other environmental changes in numerous pulp stories, including Nat Schachner's "When the Sun Dies" (1935) and Fritz Leiber's "A Pail of Air" (1951), a superior description of life in a sunless world.

When not gradually dying, the Sun may quickly doom the Earth. Threats can be generated or manipulated by **aliens in space,** as in Clare Winger Harris's "The Menace of Mars" (1928), or manmade, as in *The Day the Earth Caught Fire* (1961), when simultaneous polar atomic bombs (see **Nuclear Power; Polar Regions**) knock the Earth from its orbit. Most commonly, the Sun can destroy the world by going nova, a situation explored in dozens of stories like Olaf Stapledon's ***Last and First Men*** and Larry Niven's "Inconstant Moon" (1971); the latter ends on a cautiously upbeat note. In Arthur C. Clarke's "Rescue Party" (1946), aliens arrive to save **humanity** from a nova and discover it is unnecessary.

Though typically used for illumination and destruction, the Sun has also shielded. Counter-Earths may lurk on the other side of the Sun in orbits diametrically opposite this Earth. Sometimes they evolved along largely parallel lines, as in Edgar Wallace's *Planetoid 127* (1929). Occasionally, as in the film *Journey to the Far Side of the Sun* (1969), beings from one Earth interact with the beings from the other Earth. When the shielding Sun is removed to show a Counter-Earth, the setting may also be Burroughsian, with repetitive battles and dreary action, as in John Norman's interminable Gor series, beginning with *Tarnsman of Gor* (1966).

In a plot device that oddly recapitulates the mythological use of the Sun, some fantastic fiction makes use of the Sun as a theological construct. Gregory Benford and Gordon Eklund's *If the Stars Are Gods* (1977) describes aliens who are determined to know the Sun, which they claim is sentient and divine. More euhemeristically, an insecure Sun frets about her spots in Alasdair Gray's "The Problem" (1983).

Discussion

Perhaps because it is generally taken for granted, the fictive potential of the Sun has barely been tapped. It can offer something different to all writers of fantastic fiction, and its future is literally and metaphorically a bright one.

Bibliography

Isaac Asimov. "The Sun and the Moon." Asimov, *Asimov's Galaxy*. Garden City, NY: Doubleday, 1989, 154–157.

Arthur C. Clarke, ed. *Project Solar Sail*. New York: New American Library, 1990.

David Heuring. "*Solar Crisis*." *American Cinematographer*, 71 (December, 1990), 34–42.

David Ketterer. "*Solaris* and the Illegitimate Suns of Science Fiction." *Extrapolation*, 14 (December, 1972), 73–89.

Alexis Glynn Latner. "Catching the Wind from the Sun." *Analog*, 118 (November, 1998), 34–42.

Marjorie Hope Nicolson. "Flying Chariots." Nicolson, *Voyages to the Moon*. New York, Macmillan, 1948, 150–200.

John Pennington. "Solar Mythology in George MacDonald's 'Little Daylight' and 'The Day Boy and the Night Girl.'" *Journal of the Fantastic in the Arts*, 10 (1999), 308–320.

Brian Stableford. "The Sun." Stableford, *The Dictionary of Science Fiction Places*. New York: Wonderland Press, 1999, 295.

—*Richard Bleiler*

SUPERHEROES

Overview

Superheroes are **heroes** with extraordinary abilities who fight, usually in **cities**, against criminals (see **Crime and Punishment**), super-**villains**, **mad scientists**, **monsters**, and other **evil** forces. Superheroes may be **gods and goddesses**, wizards, **aliens on Earth**, **robots**, **androids**, **cyborgs**, or mutants (see **Mutation**). They may rely on **psychic powers**, **inventions**, and advanced **weaponry**. Superheroes typically have **secret identities** and operate in **disguise**.

Survey

Precursors of superheroes are found in **mythology**, folklore, and pulp-magazine crimefighters who concealed their identities. Another influence has been science fiction treatments of the **superman** theme like Philip Wylie's *Gladiator* (1930). But proper superheroes only emerged in the comic books of the 1930s (see **Illustration and Graphics**).

Superman was the first superhero. His alien anatomy granted him extraordinary strength and **speed**; he later gained additional powers, like **flying**, explained as the effects of Earth's **Sun** on his alien physique. Following the character's success, comic-book publishers introduced dozens of superheroes. One of the most significant is *Batman*, a normal man who trained himself to fight crime to **revenge** his parents' murder. A **detective** who employs numerous devices and vehicles along with physical skills, he was also one of the first superheroes to adopt a young sidekick, intended to give **children** someone to identify with. Other important Golden Age superheroes included the Sub-Mariner, a prince of **Atlantis** seeking vengeance against **humanity** before siding with the Allies during World War II; the Human Torch, an android; Captain Marvel, a boy who gained god-like powers with a **magic** word; Captain America, a superman created by the military through **drugs**; and *Wonder Woman*, an **Amazon** princess.

The popularity of superhero comics and others brought them to the attention of both Congress and psychologist Frederic Wertham, whose *The Seduction of the Innocent* (1954) charged comics, including superhero titles, with corrupting America's **youth**. In response, the industry created the Comics Code Authority, which severely limited comics' content.

In the late 1950s publishers launched the Silver Age by updating older superheroes and introducing new ones. In the atomic age, superheroes' powers were more likely scientific than supernatural. For instance, in the Golden Age Hawkman was a reincarnated Egyptian prince (see **Egypt; Reincarnation**), but in the Silver Age he became an alien police officer. In contrast, both versions of the Flash achieved great speed through laboratory accidents, but the latter's powers were expanded, with accompanying scientific explanations; and the Atom, formerly a small, pugnacious fighter, could shrink himself (see **Miniaturization**) thanks to stellar radiation. Radiation created many new superheroes, like the Fantastic Four, whom **space travel** mutated in different ways and who often dealt with **aliens in space**; the Hulk, a **scientist** transformed into a monster (see **Metamorphosis**); Spider-Man, given his abilities by a bite from a radioactive arachnid; and the X-Men, a team of powerful mutants. Other common powers of Silver Age superheroes were **enlargement**, shapeshifting, and **teleportation** (see **Shapeshifters**). Not all were the creations of science, however; Thor was a god straight from Norse mythology.

As comics marketing changed with the proliferation of specialty shops and rise of the graphic novel in the 1980s, superheroes also changed. In both Alan Moore's *Watchmen* (1987), an **alternate history** caused by the existence of superheroes, and Frank Miller's *Batman: The Dark Knight Returns* (1986), superheroes became darker and more realistic, while Neil Gaiman's *Sandman* (1989) revised an older hero into part of a pantheon of god-like beings whose experiences Gaiman detailed in one of comics' greatest artistic achievements. **Violence**, always connected with superheroes, became more extreme, with characters like the Punisher and Spawn.

Although comics readership was never immense, superheroes have been popular in radio shows, television, and movies. Significant television shows include *The Adventures of Superman* (1951–1957), *Batman* (1966–1968), *Wonder Woman*, *The Incredible Hulk* (1978–1983), *Lois and Clark: The New Adventures of Superman* (1993–1997), and *Smallville* (2001–). Major movies include *Superman*, *Batman*, *X-Men* (2000), *Spider-Man* (2002), and *The Incredibles* (2004).

Superheroes have also appeared in prose, either with comic-book characters—as with Andrew Vachss's *Batman: The Ultimate Evil* (1995)—or as original characters, as in *Superheroes* (1995), edited by John Varley, and the **shared-world** series beginning with *Wild Cards* (1987), edited by George R.R. Martin.

Discussion

Although superhero comics have been produced internationally, superheroes are largely an American phenomenon (see **America**), and the motif of vigilante justice is a long American tradition dating back to **westerns**. Young readers enjoy the power fantasy of superheroes, and for teens, superheroes' secret identities connect to common feelings of alienation, while mutation among the X-Men, typically manifesting in adolescence, becomes a metaphor for puberty. The black-and-white morality of some superhero comics may appeal to young readers, while the more ambiguous morality of others may explain their attraction to adults. Superheroes also possess a strong visual appeal, from the men's colorful costumes to well-endowed female superheroes wearing skin-tight costumes or next to nothing. Superhero comics have always straddled science fiction and fantasy. Superman, for instance, is an alien who is powerless before magic; Wonder Woman is an Amazon flying an invisible plane (see **Invisibility**). In the Avengers, the android Vision and the Scarlet Witch (a mutant) have partnered with the god Thor. Thus superhero comics have always existed between the two genres.

Bibliography

Mike Benton. *Superhero Comics of the Golden Age*. Dallas: Taylor, 1992.
———. *Superhero Comics of the Silver Age*. Dallas: Taylor, 1991.
Mila Bongco. *Reading Comics*. New York: Garland, 2000.
Jules Feiffer, ed. *The Great Comic Book Heroes*. New York: Dial, 1965.
Gerard Jones and Will Jacobs. *The Comic Book Heroes*. Rev. ed. Rocklin, CA: Prima, 1997.
Richard Reynolds. *Superheroes*. London: Batsford, 1992.
Trina Robbins. *The Great Women Super Heroes*. Northampton, MA: Kitchen Sink Press, 1996.
Jeff Rovin. *The Encyclopedia of Superheroes*. New York: Facts on File, 1985.
Bradford W. Wright. *Comic Book Nation*. Baltimore: Johns Hopkins University Press, 2001.

—*Darren Harris-Fain*

SUPERMAN

∎

Overview

The concept of the superman—an individual or race of vastly superior power and ability—is thoroughly steeped in the science fiction tradition, but not confined to the genre. "What's next beyond *Homo sapiens*?" is a question often asked, and possible answers have had as profound an impact on human **history** as any other speculative concept.

Survey

Achilles, Beowulf, and Gilgamesh are among the earliest examples of the superman concept in ancient human **cultures** (see **Mythology**). **Heroes** of great physical prowess, they were sometimes **gods and goddesses** with magical powers (see **Magic**). While such larger-than-life or divine figures endure in contemporary fantasy, as in *Hercules: The Legendary Journeys*, the scientific concepts of **genetic engineering, evolution** and **mutation** have foregrounded science fiction speculations about the emergence of a new species of human. Friedrich Nietzsche described the concept as *Übermensch*; others referred to the supplanting race as *Homo superior*. George Bernard Shaw explored the concept in his plays *Man And Superman* (1903) and *Back to Methuselah* (1921).

Olaf Stapledon's *Last and First Men* is a genetic engineering *tour de force*, with humans creating not just one, but *seventeen* successor species over the course of several billion years. Each human species designs its successor, allowing the genus to survive **Earth**'s destruction by first colonizing **Venus** (see **Planetary Colonies**), and later Neptune (see **Jupiter and the Outer Planets**). Such human-directed evolution—eugenics—was popular subject matter in early twentieth-century fiction like Aldous Huxley's *Brave New World* and played prominent roles cinematically in *Star Trek II: The Wrath of Khan* (see **Star Trek: The Motion Picture**) and *Gattaca* (1997). Orson Scott Card's *Ender's Game* features a made-to-order superman in the form of a boy, bred specifically to become **humanity**'s savior. Placing such unbearable responsibility on a child, and tricking him into annihilating an alien species, casts doubts on whether humans deserve to survive. Nancy Kress's *Beggars in Spain* (1993) and its sequels address the complex discriminatory and social consequences of the seemingly innocuous elimination of the "sleep" gene" in select individuals. Greg Egan's "The Moat" (1991) raises the specter of proactive genetic separatists against the ominous backdrop of rising racism in **Australia**.

Stapledon's *Odd John* (1935) features mutant supermen who boast tremendous **intelligence** and mental powers, but whose lack of empathy and compassion make them enemies of the human race—a trait shared with mutants in Clifford D. Simak's *City*. Henry Kuttner's *Mutant* (1953) takes a similar premise but makes telepathic mutants the victims of harsh persecutions, as does A.E. van Vogt in *Slan* (1946) (see **Psychic Powers**). So pervasive is the idea of the hyper-intelligent mutant that Kurt Vonnegut, Jr. satirized it in *Slapstick* (1976) (see **Satire**) with a pair of incestuous, idiot-savant twins who access phenomenal abilities while in the throes of passion.

Theodore Sturgeon represents the next phase of human evolution with **children** that form a communal organism in *More Than Human*. In each other's presence, they ultimately function with unparalleled efficiency and a heightened sense of **ethics**, creating what Sturgeon terms *Homo gestalt*. Children are also pivotal in Arthur C. Clarke's *Childhood's End*, when they attain a form of group consciousness (see **Hive Minds**), shedding all vestiges of humanity to follow their **destiny** and merge with the alien, god-like Overmind (see **Metamorphosis**). Clarke revisits alien intervention in human evolution in *2001: A Space*

Odyssey. **Astronaut** David Bowman is subjected to forced evolution by mysterious aliens, experiencing **rebirth** as a god-like "Star Child." Another alien probe subjects astronaut John Crichton to evolutionary experiments in an episode of *Farscape*, "My Three Crichtons" (2000), but they not only produce a cold, intellectually superior *Homo superior*, but also a dim, emotional *Homo neanderthalensis*.

Other devices have been used to create supermen. In Frederik Pohl's *Man Plus* (1976), the protagonist undergoes surgical enhancement to become a **cyborg** capable of survival on **Mars** (see **Pantropy**), superior to normal humans in that harsh environment. In Frank Herbert's *Children of Dune* (1976) (see **Dune**), Leto II, already an extraordinary human, infects himself with sand trout to gain phenomenal abilities. Ironically, the **superhero** known as *Superman* is not human at all, but an **alien on Earth** from the doomed planet Krypton whose powers derive from Earth's lesser **gravity** and radiation of our yellow **Sun**. Reversing that situation, Edgar Rice Burroughs's John Carter, in *A Princess of Mars*, gains superhuman powers in the lesser gravity of the planet **Mars**, and Michael Valentine Smith comes to Earth boasting psychic powers learned on Mars in Robert A. Heinlein's *Stranger in a Strange Land*.

Discussion

Superman is a powerful theme within science fiction because it is one of the few genre concepts aggressively pursued and shaped by modern society outside the bounds of speculation. In the early decades of the twentieth century, science fiction reflected western society's fascination with the promise of eugenics, which led to Nazi Germany's eugenics-inspired **horrors**. Reflecting the fears and insecurities of *Homo sapiens*, most depictions of *Homo superior* are that of a hostile, supplanting threat. While the intellectually advanced, emotionally challenged *Homo superior* and eugenics have become **clichés**, science fiction literature has turned its critical, cautionary eye towards the twenty-first century's equivalents in gene therapy and other emerging biotechnologies.

Bibliography

Thomas Andrae. "From Menace to Messiah." *Discourse*, 2 (Summer, 1980), 84–111.

Brian Ash. "Beyond Humanity." Ash, *Faces of the Future*. London: Elek Books Ltd., 1975, 129–143.

R.C.W. Ettinger. *Man Into Superman*. New York: St. Martin's Press, 1972.

Beverly Friend. "The Sturgeon Connection." Thomas D. Clareson, ed., *Voices for the Future, Volume 1*. Bowling Green, OH: Bowling Green State University Popular Press, 1976, 153–166.

Elizabeth Anne Hull. "On His Shoulders." *The Annual of Bernard Shaw Studies*, 17 (1997), 107–117.

David A. Kirby. "The New Eugenics in Cinema." *Science Fiction Studies*, 27 (July, 2000), 193–215.

Stanislaw Lem. "On Stapledon's *Last and First Men*." *Science-Fiction Studies*, 13 (November, 1986), 272–291.

Elaine Radford. "Ender and Hitler." *Fantasy Review*, 10 (June, 1987), 11–12, 48–49.

—*Jayme Lynn Blaschke*

SUPERNATURAL CREATURES

■

Overview

Supernatural creatures are common in fantasy and sometimes observed in science fiction; they are usually derived from the **mythology** and folklore of **Europe**, but writers also draw upon the traditions of other **cultures** or offer original creations. Separate entries discuss **dwarfs, elves, fairies, giants, goblins, mermaids, monsters, unicorns, vampires,** and **werewolves.**

Survey

One type of supernatural creature imagined by ancient peoples was a combination of humans and one or more animals, including the mermaid (half-woman, half-fish) and the centaur (half-man, half-horse) (see **Horses**). Two such beings—the satyr (half-man, half-goat) and minotaur (half-man, half-bull)—figure in Thomas Burnett Swann's *Day of the Minotaur* (1966). Another is the sphinx (half-woman, half-lion) (see **Lions and Tigers**) who asked Oedipus her famous **riddle**; she turns up in Atlantic City as a modern businesswoman in Esther M. Friesner's *Sphynxes Wild* (1989). Harpies, vicious eagles with women's heads who attack people, appear in Friesner Tim Desmond trilogy, beginning with *Gnome Man's Land* (1991). A griffin (half-lion, half-eagle) (see **Birds**) was adapted as a symbol for Jesus Christ (the mixture of landbound and **flying** animal signifying His human and divine nature) (see **Christianity**) and as such appears in a vision in Dante's *Purgatorio* (c. 1306–1321). A griffin shorn of allegorical import is encountered in Lewis Carroll's ***Alice's Adventures in Wonderland.*** One of the strangest of these creatures was the chimera, usually described as a combination of lion, goat, and serpent (see **Snakes and Worms**) and mentioned in Homer's *Iliad* (c. 750 BCE) and Virgil's *Aeneid* (19 BCE); today, the term usually refers to exotic animal mixtures created by **genetic engineering.**

A favorite supernatural creature is the diminutive human being, sometimes endowed with magical powers (see **Magic**). Gnomes are related to dwarfs—small, stocky, bearded figures often said to live underground. Upton Sinclair wrote a children's book about **forest** gnomes, *The Gnomobile* (1936), filmed in 1967 as *The Gnome-Mobile*; in Henry Kuttner's "A Gnome There Was" (1941) a contemporary man is transformed into a gnome (see **Metamorphosis**) and put to work as a miner; but gnomes were popularized by Wil Huygen and Rien Poortvliet's *Gnomes* (1977). H.L. Gold's "Trouble with Water" (1939) involves a man **cursed** by a "water gnome," but commentators agree that the being would have been better termed a sprite—a tiny creature more commonly associated with **water**. In Irish folklore, leprechauns were tiny men prone to malicious mischief but, if captured, they could lead people to pots of gold at the end of the rainbow (see **Gold and Silver**). Leprechauns along traditional lines—troublesome but basically benign—figure in fantasy film *Darby O'Gill and the Little People* (1959), but a monstrous, homicidal leprechaun figures in the **horror** film *Leprechaun* (1992) and its sequels. Gremlins are also mischievous little creatures, the subject of Roald Dahl's *The Gremlins* (1943) (which was the product of an abandoned Walt Disney plan to make a gremlin movie), but they are now better known for appearances in the films *Gremlins* (1984) and *Gremlins II: The New Batch* (1991). A gremlin is observed sabotaging an airplane's wing in an episode of *The Twilight Zone*, "Nightmare at 20,000 Feet" (1963). Gremlins contrast with brownies, amicable little beings who help people with household chores, as described in Juliana Ewing's "The Brownies" (1865).

Cultures were also inventive in imagining monstrous, frightening creatures. Gorgons, women with snakes instead of hair who turned anyone looking at them into **statues**, menaced the Greek **hero** Perseus, as visualized in the film *Clash of the Titans* (1980). The bogeyman is a traditional figure cited to terrify **children** into obedience, though there is a more sympathetically portrayed bogeyman in Raymond Briggs's *Fungus the Bogeyman* (1977). The banshee, a terrifying figure from Irish folklore, is an ominous harbinger of **death** in the final scenes of *Darby O'Gill and the Little People* and the horror film *Cry of the Banshee* (1970); however, a beautiful female banshee becomes Tim Desmond's friend and guide in Friesner's Tim Desmond trilogy. Trolls are lanky figures related to goblins, said to prefer dark places, who prey on unwary travelers in J.R.R. Tolkien's *The Hobbit* and menace the contemporary world in the film *Troll* (1986); they may be conflated with ogres. Gnolls (half-gnomes, half-trolls) are characters in the Dungeons and Dragons roleplaying **game** who also appear in Glen Cook's Garrett novels, beginning with *Sweet Silver Blues* (1987). Another invented monster is Carroll's Jabberwock in the poem "Jabberwocky" introduced in *Through the Looking Glass* (1871).

Genies are supernatural beings from Arabian folklore who live inside magic lamps and grant wishes to people who rub the lamps to release them. They appear in adaptations of the Aladdin story, including the animated film *Aladdin* (1991) and its sequels, but writers prefer genies discovered in contemporary society whose powers lead to comic misadventures, the plot of F. Anstey's *The Brass Bottle* (1900), adapted as a film in 1964, and an episode of *The Twilight Zone*, "I Dream of Genie" (1963). The situation comedy *I Dream of Jeannie* (1965–1970) involves a beautiful female genie who serves, and eventually marries, an **astronaut**.

One science fiction novel involving supernatural creatures is Clifford D. Simak's *The Goblin Reservation* (1968), wherein a future **Earth** learns that folkloric beings actually exist, though they long hid from humans, and as the title suggests has brought them to live in special areas to preserve them from extinction.

Discussion

One reason that supernatural creatures are usually not found in science fiction is that they have been replaced by aliens (see **Aliens in Space**; **Aliens on Earth**), portrayals of which may harken back to folkloric images: friendly little aliens like Yoda from the *Star Wars* films and *E.T.: The Extra-Terrestrial* recall elves and gnomes, just as horrific monsters like *Alien* and *Predator* (1987) recall goblins and banshees. Thus, although belief in such creatures has all but vanished in the modern world, they in a sense remain alive in popular visions of **humanity**'s future.

Bibliography

Margaret Blount. *Animal Land*. New York: Morrow, 1975.

Jorge Luis Borges, with Margarita Guerrero. *The Book of Imaginary Beings*. Revised, enlarged, and trans. Norman Thomas di Giovanni. 1970. New York: Penguin, 1974.

Maureen Duffy. *The Erotic World of Faery.* 1972. New York: Avon Books, 1980.

David D. Gilmore. *Monsters.* Philadelphia: University of Pennsylvania Press, 2002.

Elliott Gose. *Mere Creatures.* Toronto: University of Toronto Press, 1988.

Wil Huygen and Rien Poortvliet. *Gnomes.* New York: Abrams Publishing, 1977.

Malcolm South, ed. *Mythical and Fabulous Creatures.* Westport, CT: Greenwood Press, 1987.

Tom Weaver. *Monsters, Mutants, and Heavenly Creatures.* Baltimore, MD: Midnight Marquee Press, 1996.

—Gary Westfahl

SURREALISM

The doorknob opened a blue eye and looked at him.

—Henry Kuttner and C.L. Moore
"The Fairy Chessmen" (1946)

Overview

Surrealism was a style of **art** promoted in the early twentieth century that juxtaposed realistic and fantastic images in the manner of **dreams**; the best-known artist associated with the movement was Salvador Dali. Works overtly referencing surrealism like Lisa Goldstein's *The Dream Years* (1985), John Sladek's "Stop Evolution in Its Tracks!" (1988), and Robert Irwin's *The Exquisite Corpse* (1995) are uncommon, but the term may be applied to other texts and films that combine realism and fantasy in illogical or dreamlike fashions, including works considered **magic realism**. A related topic is **absurdity**.

Survey

Any story that is dream-like in nature might be deemed surrealistic, like Lewis Carroll's ***Alice's Adventures in Wonderland***, which depicts events like a perfectly ordinary tea party with guests including a dormouse (see **Talking Animals**). John Myers Myers's fantasy *Silverlock* (1949) takes a man to a realm called the Commonwealth, wherein characters from **mythology** and literature randomly appear; Myers's *The Moon's Fire-Eating Daughter* (1981) similarly involves a man who meets noteworthy authors along a mysterious Road. In science fiction, A.E. van Vogt's novels often lurch in unexpected directions, as **villains** become **heroes** and protagonists' **perceptions** of themselves and their universe keep changing, in a style that might be called surrealistic.

In the absence of a better term, one might also consider the unique novels of William S. Burroughs as surrealistic. In *The Wild Boys: A Book of the Dead* (1971), exemplifying his "cut-up" technique, a narrative involving a dystopian **near future** (see **Dystopia**) dominated by bands of young outlaws is broken up by seemingly random passages depicting sexual encounters (see **Homosexuality; Sexuality**) and graphic **violence**. Allegorical stories may seem surrealistic, as events are driven more by symbolic necessities than realistic motives (see **Allegory**). The atmosphere may be particularly evident in stories where the author's allegorical intentions are unclear, like David Lindsay's *A Voyage to Arcturus* and Esther M. Friesner's *Yesterday We Saw Mermaids* (1992), which recasts the story of Christopher Columbus's first voyage to **America** as a fantastic journey involving **supernatural creatures**. Plays in the tradition of the Theatre of the Absurd can be regarded as surrealistic, one example being Michel de Ghelderode's *Christopher Columbus* (1927), another extravagantly unrealistic retelling of Columbus's adventures.

Still, given its artistic origins, surrealism is more frequently associated with films and television programs. Dali himself produced films like the short film *Un Chien Andalou* (1929), with its stunning image of a sliced eyeball, and the bizarre dream sequence of Alfred Hitchcock's *Spellbound* (1945). Another filmmaker influenced by surrealism, Jean Cocteau, strikingly included human arms as part of the decor in the Beast's **castle** of *Beauty and the Beast*. Animated films may recall surrealism, like the "Pink Elephants on Parade" dream sequence in *Dumbo* (1941).

A few television series have employed visible sets in place of a convincing background and unusual set decoration to suggest a world that both is and is not real. In an episode of *Star Trek*, "Spectre of the Gun" (1968), an **alien in space** transports the *Enterprise* crew to an imperfect re-creation of a **western** town, consisting of setpieces on a barren plain, where they must re-enact the Gunfight at the O.K. Corral, with themselves as the doomed victims. The series *The Avengers* (1961–1969) evolved a style of storytelling featuring incomplete sets and events unrelated to realistic people in the everyday world. The Village of the series *The Prisoner* resembles a quaint resort, but there are bizarre touches like immense balloons that capture fugitives and signs with enigmatic slogans like "A still tongue makes a happy life."

Filmed adaptations of comic books may seem surrealistic if they consciously emulate the stylized appearance of the comics: the television series *Batman* (1966–1968) overlaid carefully choreographed fight scenes with descriptive interjections like "Pow!" and "Splat!" after each blow, and the film *Dick Tracy* (1990) takes place in a stark fantasy **city** limited to primary colors. In contrast to these bright visions, the film *Batman* was set in a dark, imposingly **Gothic** Gotham City unlike any actual metropolis.

Discussion

Since science fiction values logic above all else, readers resist the anarchic illogic of surrealism; thus, while van Vogt was popular in the 1940s, a process of destroying his reputation began with Damon Knight's 1945 article "Cosmic Jerrybuilder," which discounted the energy and excitement of his works and instead complained that none of his future worlds or storylines ultimately made any sense. Even fantasy readers prefer cohesive settings, with **magic** adhering to clearly established rules, relegating novels like Myers's *Silverlock* to the status of little-known cult favorites. Thus, instead of the juxtaposition of the real and unreal characteristic of surrealism, science fiction and fantasy usually prefer unreal worlds developed and presented in a spirit of realism, combining the real and unreal in a different way.

Bibliography

P.S. Alterman. "The Surreal Translations of Samuel R. Delany." *Science-Fiction Studies*, 4 (March, 1977), 25–34.

Janice Bogstad. "SF as Surrealism." *Janus*, No. 12/13 (Summer/Autumn, 1978), 31–33.

Jill Carrick. "Creation Playing Solitaire." *Arena*, No. 92 (Spring, 1990), 74–95.

James J. Devon. "Beneath the Surface." Walter Irwin and G.B. Love, eds., *The Best of the Best of Trek*. New York: Roc, 1990, 260–268.

Mike Gold. "*The Prisoner.*" *Fantastic Films*, 3 (July, 1980), 66–71.

James Gunn. "Inner Concerns in Outer Space." *Fantasy Newsletter*, 5 (January, 1982), 5–7.

Terry Hale and Andrew Hugill. "The Science Is Fiction." Edmund J. Smyth, ed., *Jules Verne*. Liverpool, UK: Liverpool University Press, 2000, 122–141.

W.F. Touponce. "Some Aspects of Surrealism in the Work of Ray Bradbury." *Extrapolation*, 25 (Fall, 1984), 228–238.

Ian Watson. "Science Fiction, Surrealism, and Shamanism." *New York Review of Science Fiction*, No. 130 (June, 1999), 1, 8–12.

—*Gary Westfahl*

SURVIVAL

Staying alive is as good as it gets.

—Alex Garland
28 Days Later (2002)

Overview

The urge to survive is an instinct within every human and a common theme in science fiction and fantasy. Science fiction, in particular, can place people in situations where their ability to survive is put to the test. Outer space, **alien worlds**, unknown machinery—everything unfamiliar tests the protagonist's ability to understand and survive it. Apocalyptic, post-apocalyptic and dystopian stories are tales of the survival in changed conditions (see **Apocalypse; Dystopia**).

Survey

One of the earliest post-apocalyptic stories is Mary Shelley's **The Last Man**. After a plague destroys humanity (see **Plagues and Diseases**), the hero who survived in the Arctic must endure until he discovers another survivor, a woman with whom he can re-establish the human race (see **Last Man**). Edgar Allan Poe's **The Narrative of Arthur Gordon Pym** is a **Gothic** fantasy which transforms an ordinary tale of **sea travel** into an epic of one man surviving cannibalism, ghost-ships, premature burial, and **barbarians**.

The **fin de siécle** seemed to bring an attitude of pessimism. Jules Verne's *An Antarctic Mystery* (1897) re-visited Poe's story and found it to be real, and once more survivable. In 1901 M.P. Shiel's **The Purple Cloud** had the world destroyed by gas, with a lone survivor once more questing for a partner in the lonely **cities** of a deserted **Earth**. Not long after this, Arthur Conan Doyle tested the ability of his **heroes** in a hidden land filled with primeval **monsters** in *The Lost World* and threatened the world with passage through a strange ether in *The Poison Belt* (1914).

After World War II, surviving an apocalypse became a common motif in science fiction. In George R. Stewart's *Earth Abides*, ecological and social **disaster** forces survivors to live without the modern world they knew and retain some of its **knowledge**. They fail, returning to a simpler, more agrarian way of life.

A different sort of ecological disaster occurs in John Wyndham's *The Day of the Triffids*: walking **plants** take over England after a freak storm of meteors blinds everyone (see **Vision and Blindness**). The few survivors who keep their sight band together, but social and health problems break up the group. The protagonist and his partner go to a **farm** where they develop methods to fight off the Triffids, a fight they are losing when they are rescued and taken to an **island** which has been totally cleared, where they plan to regain the world. In John Christopher's *No Blade of Grass* (1956), a virus destroys every type of grass, including those used for food, like rice and wheat. Survivors of the mass starvation must invade a farm that was prepared for the catastrophe.

In the film *The Incredible Shrinking Man* the protagonist, exposed to radioactive mist, begins to shrink. Eventually, he is locked in a basement, the prey of **insects** and spiders. He survives, but at the end of the film is becoming smaller and smaller. Still, his successful efforts, physical and mental, to accept what is happening to him make the film a poignant classic.

J.G. Ballard's *The Drowned World* is set in a future where the icecaps have melted and London is a primeval swamp. An expedition to monitor its developing flora and fauna must come to terms with this new environment. The novel explores the metaphors by which people live, and how a change in physical systems can challenge the meaning made from the world. Eventually, some of the party adapt to the changes and adopt the swamp as their new way of life.

Do Androids Dream of Electric Sheep?, the Philip K. Dick novel that inspired the film *Blade Runner*, revolves around the idea of **androids** with limited lifespans. They return to Earth to discover how to overcome this limited life and Deckard, a **detective**, is charged with hunting them down and killing them. He succeeds, and they do not survive, but their attempts to do so and the emotional stress of falling in love with another android lead Deckard to question the system in which he lives.

In the film *The Terminator* a man is sent back from a future (see **Time Travel**) in which there has been a **war** against machines to protect Sarah Connor, **mother** of their future victorious leader. This is necessary because the machines have sent a Terminator, a human-like **robot**, back in time to kill her and prevent the birth of her son. The robot pursues Connor relentlessly but is evaded every time until a climactic final battle in a factory. Her protector dies, but the robot is destroyed by another machine.

Discussion

Survival, in most cases, is a question of adaptation to circumstances that threaten the character, be they giant plants, melted icecaps, robots, or **miniaturization**. If the adaptation is successful, the character survives; if it is not, they do not. In many cases the challenge to adapt is a simple physical one, but often there are mental and emotional changes to consider as well. A different way of seeing a changed world (see **Perception**) is often the first step to survival.

Bibliography

Judith Bogert. "Survival." Donald E. Palumbo, ed., *Erotic Universe*. Westport, CT: Greenwood Press, 1986, 25–43.

Mick Broderick. "Surviving Armageddon." *Science-Fiction Studies*, 20 (November, 1993), 362–382.

Gloria Cowan and Margaret O'Brien. "Gender and Survival vs. Death in Slasher Films." *Sex Roles*, 23 (August, 1990), 187–196.

Peter Freese. "Surviving the End." *Critique*, 36 (Spring, 1995), 163–176.

Judith B. Kerman. "J. G. Ballard." Carl B. Yoke, ed., *Phoenix from the Ashes*. Westport, CT: Greenwood Press, 1987, 133–144.

Michael M. Levy. "Ophelia Triumphant." *Foundation*, No. 72 (Spring, 1998), 34–41.

Victoria Middleton. "Exile, Isolation and Accomodation in *The Last Man*." Mary Lowe–Evans, ed., *Critical Essays On Mary Wollestoncraft Shelley*. New York: G. K. Hall, 1998, 166–182.

John J. Pierce. "Apres les Deluge, Nous." *Fantasy Commentator*, 5 (Fall, 1986), 228–240.

George Slusser. "Pocket Apocalypse." David Seed, ed., *Imagining Apocalypse*. New York: St. Martin's, 2000, 118–135.

—Ian Nichols

SUSPENDED ANIMATION AND CRYONICS

Overview

Suspended animation and cryonics are modern **technology**'s answer to the resurrection problem (see **Rebirth**). Christ's resurrection and its eschatological apparatus are no longer feasible after the humanist renaissance (see **Eschatology**). We have instead "little resurrections" (like the "bringing to life" of Hermione's **statue** in William **Shakespeare**'s *A Winter's Tale* [1611]) and what Steven B. Harris calls "mal-resurrections," reflecting Frankensteinian fears that suspension and subsequent reanimation of life will diminish its original power and form. In neither case do we escape **time**. Cryonics hopes, through preservative and restorative technologies, to allow humans to **sleep** through bad times and awake in better days, thus fulfilling old **dreams** of **immortality and longevity**.

Survey

These dreams might be traced back to Charles Perrault's **fairy tale** "Sleeping Beauty" (1696) and similar legends, but Americans proved distinctively interested in this process. Benjamin Franklin wished he and select friends could be preserved in a cask of Madiera wine to awaken in America's glorious future. Through long sleep, Washington Irving's "Rip Van Winkle" (1819) escapes **war** and a shrewish wife, but at the price of eliding his adult life, waking up in **old age**. In contrast, Henry David Thoreau at the end of *Walden* (1854) hopes for miracles to emerge from sleeping forces at the heart of this same oppressive society: "Who knows what beautiful and winged life" may unexpectedly emerge "from amidst society's most trivial and handselled furniture, to enjoy its perfect summer life at last." This optimistic millennial sleep is at work in works like Edward Bellamy's **Looking Backward, 2000–1887**, where a man from the "bad" present is projected by hibernation into a utopian Boston of the future (see **Utopia**). Mark Twain's **A Connecticut Yankee in King Arthur's Court** propels Hank Morgan back in time to sixth-century England (see **Time Travel**) to decimate knighthood with Gatling guns; then, put into a long sleep by Merlin's spell, he awakens back in his nineteenth century. Across the Atlantic, H.G. Wells's *When the Sleeper Wakes* (1899) tells of another sleeper who wakes two hundred years in the future, to find himself rich from accrued interest on his bank account.

All these stories preceded the birth of twentieth-century cryonics as a real-life movement, inspired by science fiction stories and a "prophet" born of them. Neil R. Jones's "The Jameson Satellite" (1931), the pulp starting point, involves a dead **astronaut**, frozen in space, who is revived by **far future** aliens who transfer his brain to a machine body. On its heels came Robert Ettinger's seminal story, "The Penultimate Trump" (1948), in which cryonics is named. His subsequent book *The Prospect of Immortality* (1964) inspired the founding of the Cryonics Society of America, a movement still thriving as the Alcor Foundation.

If suspended animation held utopian promise for the nineteenth century, later science fiction appears more skeptical of cryonics, as movement and business venture. In René Barjavel's *Ravage* (1942), future high-rise dwellers freeze their ancestors in tanks in their living room walls, but when Armageddon brings a power failure, this cozy arrangement comes crashing down. In A.E. van Vogt's "Far Centaurus" (1944), voyagers in suspended animation on a long space journey awaken at their destination to find that humans, in the meantime, have discovered better means of spaceflight and are there to greet them. Larry Niven's *World of Ptavvs* (1966) and Vernor Vinge's *The Peace War* (1984) ponder the use of "stasis fields" to preserve human life. Arkady Strugatsky and Boris Strugatsky's "Candles Before the Control Board" (1953) reflects on awareness of Jones's message: where one cannot preserve the body, one transfers the brain to another medium to preserve life. Here, the rush to "download" the mind of a "great scientist" into an immense **computer** is 98% complete when **death** occurs—an effort anticipating the cybertechnology of William Gibson's *Count Zero* (1986) and *Mona Lisa Overdrive* (1988) (see **Neuromancer**), wherein the goal is to transfer individual minds to **cyberspace**. Though the Stragatskys' task seems absurd, it might succeed next time. But, the authors ask, to what end?

Other works focus on the commercial aspect of cryonics. Philip K. Dick's *Ubik* (1969) portrays beings suspended in "half-life" imposing their personal physical "world" on other sleepers. Following the lead of Robert A. Heinlein's *The Door into Summer* (1957), Clifford D. Simak's *Why Call Them Back from Heaven?* (1966) and Norman Spinrad's *Bug Jack Barron* (1968) treat cryonics as a morally dubious, socially destructive enterprise. Michael Coney continues the brain transplant theme in *Friends Come in Boxes* (1974), displaying the ravages of this practice on something as basic as the natural birthrate. Successful cryonics leads to moral dilemma or ecological **disaster**. Who should benefit from this technology? And why?

Discussion

In today's age of "simulations" and hologramic reconstructions, dead beings are better considered clusters of information, awaiting reanimation. In Robert Silverberg's "Enter a Soldier. Later: Enter Another" (1996), future specialists in crafting holograms of French **kings** for public spectacles create more complex constructs—Francisco Pizarro and Socrates. These Frankensteinian resurrections prove fortuituous rather than monstrous, as they find themselves in a new time, where each evolves in new directions through fruitful dialogue, overcoming one posited barrier to cryonic re-awakening—culture shock. Old, closed books and lives can be re-opened and allowed to grow, creating better timelines. For Frankenstein's creature and its cyronic cousins, there is finally a mate.

Bibliography

R.C.W. Ettinger. *The Prospect of Immortality*. Garden City, NY: Doubleday, 1964.

Steven B. Harris. "The Immortality Myth in Technology." George Slusser, Gary Westfahl and Eric S. Rabkin, eds. *Immortal Engines*. Athens: University of Georgia Press, 1996, 45–67.

Amiee Louise Lester. "Cryonics: DOA." *Midnight Graffiti*, No. 6 (Winter, 1990/1999), 56–59.

Peter Nicholls, David Langford, and Brian Stableford. "Cryonics." Nicholls, Langford, and Stableford, *The Science in Science Fiction*. 1982. New York: Alfred A. Knopf, 1983, 147.

Joe L. Sanders. "Breaking the Circle." *New York Review of Science Fiction*, No. 60 (August, 1993), 1, 10–13.

George Slusser. "Cryonics as Bodily Utopia." George Slusser, Paul Alkon, Roger Gaillard and Danièle Chatelain, eds., *Transformations of Utopia*. New York: AMS Press, 1999, 139–152.

Carl D. Yoke and Donald M. Hassler, eds. *Death and the Serpent*. Westport, CT: Greenwood Press, 1985.

Frederick Yuan. "Immortality and Robert Silverberg." M.J. Tolley, ed., *The Stellar Gauge*. Carleton, Australia: Norstrilia, 1980, 239–258.

—*George Slusser*

SWORD AND SORCERY

Overview

Sword and sorcery is a fantasy subgenre that emphasizes physical conflict between **heroes** and **supernatural creatures** like **gods and goddesses, demons, witches,** or **wizards**. Some stories feature **monsters** or survivors of **elder races**, but seldom **elves, dwarfs,** or **fairies**. Heroes are usually **barbarians**, at least in that they are less moral and altruistic than other fantasy protagonists; they are also bigger than life, violent and wield **swords** or axes. The setting is generally a recognizable version of **Earth** where **magic** works, either in the distant past or **far future**.

Survey

The term "sword and sorcery" was coined by Fritz Leiber but the genre was pioneered by Robert E. Howard, a Texas pulp writer who combined fantasy, **history**, **horror**, and the **Gothic** to create the Hyborian Age and such characters as **Conan the Conqueror** and Kull. Howard did not create in a vacuum. Sword and sorcery elements existed in *Gilgamesh* (c. 2500 BCE), *The Odyssey* (c. 750 BCE), *Beowulf* (c. 800), *The Song of Roland* (c. 1050), the Norse Eddas, and *The Arabian Nights Entertainment* (c. 1450), each of which depicted heroes with edged weapons in conflict with gods and monsters. Later writers also had influence. H. Rider Haggard's *She* is considered the first western novel to feature **lost worlds**, which became sword and sorcery staples. William Morris began the modern tradition of adult **heroic fantasy** set in quasi-medieval (see **Medievalism and the Middle Ages**) imaginary worlds. E.R. Eddison's *The Worm Ouroboros* provided a lush, archaic-sounding prose and fantastic **landscapes**. (It also influenced J.R.R. Tolkien's *The Hobbit* and *The Lord of the Rings* trilogy.) Eddison included an historical timeline for his characters as an appendix, common practice in today's fantasy.

A short list of other sword and sorcery influences includes Lord Dunsany (see *The King of Elfland's Daughter*), Mervyn Peake (see *Titus Groan*), Arthur Conan Doyle (see *The Lost World*), and David Lindsay (see *A Voyage to Arcturus*), but the most immediate influences on Howard were *A Princess of Mars* and *Tarzan of the Apes* by Edgar Rice Burroughs. *A Princess of Mars* established the prototype for "planetary romance," wherein an earthman transported to another world must use his wits, muscles, and sword against human and nonhuman foes. There is a princess to rescue and fall in **love** with; the hero is chivalrous and **sexuality** is kept offstage (see **Chivalry**); the setting is an exotic **alien world** populated by strange **plants**, animals, and intelligent humanoids; the emphasis is on swordfights, wild **escapes**, and daring deeds. Burroughs later launched similar series set in a **hollow Earth**, beginning with *At the Earth's Core* (1922), and on **Venus**, beginning with *Pirates of Venus* (1934).

Many writers modeled their works on Burroughs's Martian books, including Howard, though he introduced more explicit sexuality. But Burroughs's Tarzan was a greater influence on Howard's first sword and sorcery hero, Kull, who was raised by tigers just as Tarzan was raised by **apes**. Kull in turn was a prototype for Conan; indeed, the first published Conan story was rewritten from an unpublished Kull tale. Conan, also closer to Tarzan than to John Carter, is a barbarian who once drops a woman in a cesspool. While he follows his own rough code, he has little use for **civilization**. He lusts for **treasure, gold and silver**, and beautiful women and is seldom concerned with "fair play." He verges on being an antihero. Other major characters were Leiber's Fafhrd and the Gray Mouser, introduced in "Two Sought Adventure" (1939).

The Conan stories were republished as books in the 1960s with cover paintings by Frank Frazetta (see **Illustration and Graphics**), and their success ignited a boom that attracted many writers to sword and sorcery. Michael Moorcock created Elric, a more complex but less human character than Conan who first appeared in *The*

Stealer of Souls (1963). John Norman's Gor novels, beginning with *Tarnsman of Gor* (1966), became notorious for scenes of **torture**. Karl Edward Wagner created Kane, a character based upon the Biblical "Cain" who was introduced in *Darkness Weaves with Many Shadows* (1971). Charles Saunders developed an alternate **Africa** and a black hero named *Imaro* (1981).

Discussion

Sword and sorcery entered mainstream consciousness with the films *Conan the Barbarian* (1982) and *Conan the Destroyer* (1984), starring Arnold Schwarzenegger; *Kull the Conqueror* (1997) starred Kevin Sorbo from **Hercules: The Legendary Journeys**, which also qualifies as sword and sorcery and spawned a spinoff, **Xena: Warrior Princess**. While both series were often light-hearted and comical, *Xena* could be darker and more realistically violent, making it closer to the roots of sword and sorcery. A problem with sword and sorcery films has been the failure of directors and actors to take the form seriously. Characters are thrown in for comic relief, and there is incessant winking at the audience. Peter Jackson took J.R.R. Tolkien seriously when directing **The Lord of the Rings: The Fellowship of the Ring** and its sequels, receiving critical and popular acclaim. The same could be done with sword and sorcery.

Bibliography

L. Sprague de Camp. *Literary Swordsmen and Sorcerers*. Sauk City WI: Arkham House, 1976.

Malcolm Edwards and Robert Holdstock. *Realms of Fantasy*. Garden City, NY: Doubleday, 1983.

Casey Fredericks. "In Defense of Heroic Fantasy." Fredericks, *The Future of Eternity*. Bloomington: Indiana University Press, 1982, 91–120.

Patrice Louinet. "Introduction." Robert E. Howard, *The Coming of Conan the Cimmerian*. New York: Del Rey, 2003, xix–xxv.

Michael Moorcock. *Wizardry and Wild Romance*. London: Victor Gollancz, 1987.

Baird Searles, Beth Meacham, and Michael Franklin. *A Reader's Guide to Fantasy*. New York: Facts on File, 1982.

Karl Edward Wagner: "Foreword." Robert E. Howard, *The Hour of the Dragon*. New York: Berkley, 1977, 1–12.

Paul Zweig. *The Adventurer*. New York: Basic Books, 1974.

—Charles Gramlich

SWORDS

■

He woke in sunlit morning, lying on his side, looking at the swords, cavalry sabres, hung crossed on the chimney-piece. They were tools, he thought,

*expressing purpose as simply as a nee-
dle or a hammer, their purpose, their
reason or meaning, being death; they
were made to kill men with; the slightly
curved and still unpolished blades were
death, were in fact his own death, which
he saw with clarity and relaxation.*

—Ursula K. Le Guin
"Two Delays on the Northern Line" (1979)

Overview

Swords, especially magical or marvelous ones (see **Magic**), are among the great symbols and themes of traditional and mythic narratives. From the swords of ancient
mythology to the light sabers in *Star Wars*, these weapons, symbols or proof of
authority and mystical power, have pervaded the world's stories (see **Weaponry**).
The subgenre most closely associated with swords, **sword and sorcery**, is discussed
separately.

Survey

The sword in fantasy and science fiction has its inspirations in the mythic
antecedents of oral narratives and legends, later written down, originating in the
dim past. One of the "Four Treasures" of the Tuatha De Danaan in Irish myth,
Fragarach is the Sword of Nuada (variously, the Sword of "Air" or "Fire"), a
weapon that cleft enemies in half. Later given to Cuchulainn by Lugh, eventually in
the hands of Conn of the Hundred Battles, it granted power over the winds, and no
foe could resist it in battle.

Norse mythology gives us two famous swords. Tyrfing, given by Andvari
(German, Alberich) to Odin, was a cursed weapon: every time it was drawn from
its scabbard a man must die (see **Curses**). In the Norse legend "The Waking of
Agantyr," the dead Agantyr is summoned awake by his daughter Hervor (one of
mythic literature's first sword-maidens) and forced to give her the sword. Tyrfing
proved the bane of most who bore it, the curse extending through whole family lines.

The sword Gram, influential in medieval and modern fantastic narrative,
seems to foreshadow or echo the Sword in the Stone (see **Arthur**) and inspired
more than one of J.R.R. Tolkien's imaginative creations in *The Lord of the Rings*.
Gram's story is recorded in both prose and epic verse by the man often regarded
as the founder of mythopoeic fantasy, William Morris. Morris and Eirikr
Magnusson's translation of *The Saga of the Volsungs* (1888), as well as Morris's
poetic epic *The Story of Sigurd the Volsung and the Fall of the Niblungs* (1876), tell
the tale of Gram. A mysterious one-eyed stranger, the god Odin in his usual guise
among men, enters the great hall of king Volsung and buries a sword up to its hilt
in the great central tree, the Branstock (the name in Norse means "Sword Tree").
He challenges the company to attempt to draw the weapon from the tree. He who
does so shall have the sword as a **gift**. All fail except for Sigmund, Volsung's son and

eventual **father** of the title character. Gram, whose name means "Wrath" and which by some accounts glows along its edge when drawn, is later broken into shards by Odin himself, again appearing as the one-eyed stranger in the midst of battle, when it is Sigmund's time to die bravely. Sigmund is thus honored by Odin himself, both chosen in life and gathered in death. The shards are retained and the sword is remade for Sigmund's son Sigurd by the **dwarf**-smith Regin, on the promise that Sigurd will slay the **dragon** Fafnir, once Regin's brother but changed into a dragon by his greed and hoarding of gold. Of course Sigurd succeeds at this labor of dragon-slaying.

If these motifs seem familiar from Tolkienian fantasy and other stories, one need not wonder. In *The Lord of the Rings*, the shards of the sword Narsil are remade for Aragorn as symbolic proof of his kingship. Lusting after material things—a hoard of **gold and silver** or a precious **ring**—is depicted as **evil**, both in Tolkien and his Norse-Germanic antecedents. Of course other swords in Tolkien's fiction are important. Gandalf's sword Glamdring ("Foe Hammer") figures in the tale, in both the stand against the Balrog in Moria and later battles. Bilbo's and later Frodo's short sword, Sting, glows magically when orcs are near to warn of impending danger.

Elsewhere in fantasy, while the story of the Sword of the Stone figures in innumerable stories about King Arthur and Camelot, it receives special emphasis in T.H. White's *The Once and Future King* (1958), the story of Arthur's **youth**, and its animated film adaptation *The Sword in the Stone* (1963). Sword and sorcery tales tend to foreground **heroes'** swords by giving them colorful names, like Graywand and Scalpel in Fritz Leiber's Fafhrd and the Gray Mouser stories beginning with "Two Sought Adventure" (1939), The Lady Vivamus in Robert A. Heinlein's *Glory Road* (1963), and Grayswandir in Roger Zelazny's *Nine Princes in Amber* (1970) and its sequels. The idea of the sword destined to kill, perhaps even said to possess its own homicidal personality, recurs in Poul Anderson's *The Broken Sword* (1954), Michael Moorcock's Elric stories, beginning with *The Stealer of Souls* (1963), and Glen Cook's *The Swordbearer* (1982). Swordplay is regularly featured in **Ruritanian romances** like Anthony Hope Hawkins's *The Prisoner of Zenda* (1894), and is common in Edgar Rice Burroughs's Mars novels (see *A Princess of Mars*) and similar planetary **romances**, despite the incongruity of such primitive weapons coexisting with remnants of alien **technology**.

Discussion

Due to the nature of the weapon itself, one rarely finds it in science fiction, although an enjoyable exception is Anderson's *The High Crusade* (1960), in which sword-wielding medieval Europeans (see **Europe; Medievalism and the Middle Ages**) defeat an alien **invasion** and, gaining access to their spaceship, conquer the galaxy. The executioner in Gene Wolfe's **far future** world of *The Book of the New Sun* wields a memorable sword named Terminus Est. Another exception, the light sabers of the *Star Wars* films, remind us that George Lucas is essentially presenting a time-shifted medieval romance, replete with damsel in distress, a "Black Knight," the hero of **destiny**, and an inherited marvelous sword. Perhaps, no matter whether it appears on an **alien world** or the far future, a sword may always signal that we are only reading a saga of humanity's bloody **history** in disguise.

Bibliography

L. Sprague de Camp. *Literary Swordsmen and Sorcerers*. Sauk City WI: Arkham House, 1976.

J.T. Freyberg. "Hold High the Cardboard Sword." *Psychology Today*, 8 (February, 1975), 63–64.

Justin Leiber. "Fritz Leiber." *Riverside Quarterly*, 8 (August, 1991), 236–240, and 9 (August, 1992), 36–44.

Sandra Miesel. "Sword-play." Fred Saberhagen, ed., *First Book of Swords*. New York: Tor, 1983, 289–309.

Andrew J. Offutt, ed. *Swords against Darkness*. New York: Zebra, 1977.

Katherine Roberts. "Scientific Swords to Magic Realism." *Vector*, No. 205 (May/June, 1999), 12–14.

Jessica A. Salmonson. "Fantasy with Swordplay." *Martial Arts Movies*, 2 (June, 1982), 46–50.

Thom Sciacca. "Sword and Sandal." *Filmfax*, No. 22 (September, 1990), 44–49, 94.

—*Frank Coffman*

SYMBIOSIS

■

Overview

Symbiosis is a special case of commensalism—the close physical association of different species in **biology**—in which both parties benefit from the relationship. This is distinct, though not always entirely, from **parasites'** one-sided exploitation of hosts. Genre fiction also offers nonbiological analogues of symbiosis, mediated by **psychic powers**.

Survey

Symbiosis informs many biological **puzzle** stories, often requiring a **detective** approach. Hal Clement's *Needle* (1950) stars a jellylike alien symbiont that lives co-operatively within oxygen breathers: stranded on **Earth** and inhabiting a human boy, this "Hunter" must locate and defeat a similarly positioned criminal of his species. James White's *Star Surgeon* (1963) (see **Hospital Station**) features a "disease" that proves to be a Hunter-like internal doctor (see **Medicine**) that has misunderstood its patient's needs; White explores this situation further in *Final Diagnosis* (1997).

Similar symbionts in Walter M. Miller, Jr.'s "Dark Benediction" (1951) and Algis Budrys's "Silent Brother" (1956), though benevolent, are feared as contagious diseases. Another hidden symbiont features in **Star Trek: Deep Space Nine**, whose Trill species comprises long-lived vermiform beings inhabiting successive humanoid hosts. Alien "cruciforms" that attach themselves to humans in Dan Simmons's **Hyperion** confer a kind of immortality that some recipients find undesirable (see **Immortality and Longevity**).

Humanoid aliens live in beneficial symbiosis with **forests** of the planetary ecosystem in Eric Frank Russell's "Symbiotica" (1943); but sentient alien trees in James H. Schmitz's "The Pork Chop Tree" (1965) and "Compulsion" (1970), though welcoming to human partners, reduce them through psychic **genetic engineering** to mindlessly happy parasites. Conversely, the deadly helico virus in Brian W. Aldiss's *Helliconia Spring* brings symbiotic benefits to survivors.

Robert Sheckley's "Specialist" (1953) imagines **space travel** in a ship, which is a joyful symbiosis of various **aliens in space**: to fill a vital role in this gestalt is the forgotten **destiny** of **humanity**. Aliens in Poul Anderson's "Hiding Place" (1961) are combinations of two different creatures which, separated, prove difficult to identify among nonsapients in a multispecies zoo (see **Animals and Zoos**). As similar partnership between arachnoids and crustaceans features in Olaf Stapledon's *Star Maker.*

A complex, triple alien symbiosis is central to John Barnes's *Sin of Origin* (1988). Greg Bear's *Blood Music* radically transforms the human condition by making blood lymphocytes into intelligent symbiotes, whose explorations redefine their relationship with the body. David Langford and John Grant's tasteless **horror** spoof *Guts* (2001) supposes the human digestive system is a potentially independent symbiote, capable of separatist revolt.

Biological **technology** or nanotechnology may produce artificial symbiotes like the living spacesuits that protect life in a vacuum in John Varley's "Equinoctial" (1977) and Spider Robinson and Jeanne Robinson's *Stardance* (1979). Another artificial symbiosis, involving alien biota, is inflicted by a **mad scientist** upon the human heroine of Tricia Sullivan's *Dreaming in Smoke* (1998).

Psychic symbiosis with intangible beings is offered as an explanation or equivalent of the soul in Clifford D. Simak's *Time and Again* (1951) and Bob Shaw's *The Palace of Eternity* (1969). The mental bond between rider and **dragon** in Anne McCaffrey's *Dragonflight* is so strong that dragons invariably and humans usually choose **suicide** upon losing their other-species partner. But this bond remains endlessly rewarding, unlike the potentially dangerous linkage to **horse**-like alien "nighthorses" which C.J. Cherryh describes, as though rebutting McCaffrey's wish-fulfilment, in *Rider at the Gate* (1995).

Other telepathic commensals are the alien "wind" that speaks within the **hero's** head in Brian Stableford's Hooded Swan series, beginning with *The Halcyon Drift* (1972), and the elusive occupier of successive human bodies in Christopher Evans's *The Insider* (1981) (see **Possession**). The intangible "nopal" brain-parasites of Jack Vance's *The Brains of Earth* (1966), though repulsive to **perception**, are nevertheless benevolent since they protect against something worse.

Large-scale psychic symbiosis offers the possibility of gestalt minds, as in Arthur C. Clarke's *Childhood's End*, Theodore Sturgeon's *More Than Human* and *The Cosmic Rape* (1958), and Keith Roberts's *The Inner Wheel* (1970) (see **Hive Minds**). Humanity ultimately enters mental symbiosis with the omnipotent **computer** Multivac in Isaac Asimov's "The Last Question" (1956), rather as some religious theorists believe that souls will merge into the continuum of God.

Discussion

Biological symbiosis has little place in fantasy, but its psychic analogue—as in McCaffrey's *Dragonflight*—can occur. The hero of L.E. Modesitt's *The Towers of the Sunset* (1994) joins himself and his woman in such a dangerous and irrevocable "life-link," like dragon and rider. A similarly unwise bond grows between the pro-tagonist of Robin Hobb's *Assassin's Apprentice* (1995) and his **dog**. Traditional **witches** and their familiar animals live in quasi-symbiosis, with the witch suckling the familiar with **blood** as payment for use of its **talent**. This situation is reflected in the fake (technology-backed) witch cult of Fritz Leiber's *Gather, Darkness!* (1950). In Philip Pullman's His Dark Materials trilogy, opening with *The Golden Compass* (1995), familiars are physical externalizations of the soul—initially **shapeshifters** but later stable reflections of the adult persona. Should the magical link be broken, terrible dehumanization results.

Speculative fictional portrayals of symbiosis evoke a tension between the wish-fulfilment of inbuilt companionship and healing, and the **anxiety** associated with invasiveness and erosion of the self.

Bibliography

Athena Andreadis. *To Seek Out New Life*. New York: Crown Books, 1998.

James Brown. "Cyborgs and Symbionts." Edward James and Farah Mendlesohn, eds., *The Parliament of Dreams*. Reading, UK: Science Fiction Foundation, 1998, 110–129.

David Langford. "The Essential Hal Clement, Volume 1." *New York Review of Science Fiction*, No. 130 (June, 1999), 6–7.

Peter Nicholls, David Langford, and Brian Stableford. "Alien Life-styles." Nicholls, Langford, and Stableford, *The Science in Science Fiction*. 1982. New York: Knopf, 1983, 60–61.

Michael Okuda, Denise Okuda, and Debbie Mirek. "Host," "Symbiont," and "Trill." Okuda, Okuda, and Mirek, *The Star Trek Encyclopedia*. New York and London: Simon & Schuster, 1994, 130, 328, 352–353.

Helen M. Parker. *Biological Themes in Science Fiction*. Ann Arbor: UMI Research Press, 1984.

David Pringle. "*The Palace of Eternity*." Pringle, *Science Fiction: The 100 Best Novels*. New York: Carroll and Graf, 1985, 141–142.

Claire Squires. *Philip Pullman's His Dark Materials Trilogy*. New York: Continuum, 2003.

—*David Langford*

T

TABOOS

Overview

The term "taboo"—a Tongan word meaning a social prohibition or restriction—applies to science fiction and fantasy in two ways. First, violations of taboos within narrative worlds can serve as plot devices for getting **heroes** into trouble (see **Evil; Sin**)—as a casual remark almost provokes a deadly duel in the complex future society of Robert A. Heinlein's *Beyond This Horizon* (1948). More interestingly, one can discuss taboos applicable to science fiction and fantasy stories themselves. For many years neither science fiction nor fantasy possessed the necessary cultural awareness to acknowledge the existence of such taboos. Robert Bloch was one of the first to decry their existence, stating that one "won't find him [the science fiction hero] fighting in defense of incest, homosexuality, free love, nihilism, the Single Tax, abolition of individual property rights, euthanasia or the castration of the tonsils of Elvis Presley." Times have changed, but the taboos Bloch described in 1959 remain reasonably intact today.

Survey

Although capable of exploring ideas better than other literary genres, fantastic fiction has been surprisingly conservative in approaching these ideas. In American pulp magazines, protagonists were invariably young, with **old age** an unconsidered subject except when it involved **immortality and longevity**. **Race relations** were not explored, most characters and almost all **heroes** being white, male, and implicitly Christian (see **Christianity**). **Civilization** was always considered in Judeo–Christian terms; an innate sense of manifest **destiny** led to exploitation of the environment; and apart from heterosexual relations, **sexuality** (including **homosexuality**, incest, and sex with **aliens in space, androids**, animals, **children, monsters**, and **robots**) was absent. **Virginity** was the norm, though male **villains** often possessed a sexual awareness that displayed itself in reprehensible attitudes towards the hero's presumably platonic girlfriends (see **Clichés**). These generalizations also held true for British fantastic fiction, though gadflies like John Collier occasionally recognized and deliberately violated taboos; *His Monkey Wife* (1930) parodies the traditional shopgirl **romance** and cheerfully concludes with bestiality.

The dominant science fiction magazine during the 1930s and 1940s had been *Astounding Science-Fiction*, whose editor (John W. Campbell, Jr.) believed that sex had no place in science fiction and had copyeditor Kay Tarrant blue-pencil anything objectionable. During the 1950s and 1960s, however, a new generation of American science fiction writers—the so-called New Wave—began questioning assumptions. New and viable magazines came into existence, eliminating *Astounding*'s hegemony. Philip José Farmer's "The Lovers" (1952) speculated about sex between a human and an alien resembling a human female. Theodore Sturgeon's "The World Well Lost" (1953) made use of homosexuality and so incensed Campbell that after rejecting it he called other editors to warn them against it. Sturgeon's "The Silken-Swift" (1953) was one of the first genre works to observe that true virginity was of the spirit, not the flesh. Still, the genre remained a generation behind the rest of the world: John Steinbeck had made the same point fifteen years earlier in "Saint Katy the Virgin" (1938).

Harlan Ellison's landmark anthologies *Dangerous Visions* (1967) and *Again, Dangerous Visions* (1972) deliberately collected stories challenging these taboos, though several contributors noted that the stories were exceptional only within the genre; restrictions governing fantastic fiction were largely absent in mainstream literature. Many writers have since gone out of their way to identify and violate existing taboos. **Judaism** and **Islam** were featured in fiction, and writers recognized the inevitability of old age and the necessity of **death**, with Joanna Russ's *We Who Are about To* (1977) arguing in favor of swift, self-induced termination. Sexual identity was explored by Ursula K. Le Guin (see *The Left Hand of Darkness*) and Russ (see *The Female Man*), and Samuel R. Delany explored not only sexual **identity** but sexuality in an astounding variety of forms (see *Triton*). British writers Michael Moorcock and J.G. Ballard considered sexuality and the very concepts that governed the telling of **stories** and creation of narrative, drawing from (among others) the works of Alfred Jarry.

The Vietnam War challenged longstanding taboos against pacifism and nonviolence. Previously, Clifford D. Simak's *City* provided the only major depiction of pacifism, with sentient **robots** as utter pacifists willing to abandon **Earth** rather than kill an ant. Le Guin's *The Word for World Is Forest* (1972) and Joe Haldeman's *The Forever War* used the Vietnam War to show the messiness, inhumanity, and **horrors** of **war**. Pacifistic attitudes have since generally prevailed in science fiction, though by a curious twist, those who write glowingly or exclusively of war and **weaponry** are now seen as taboo breakers in their own right. The same holds with the acceptance of Christianity: it is now the taboo-breaking writer who conceives of Christianity positively.

Discussion

At this point, almost no taboo is off limits to fantastic fiction. Writers have explored virtually all forms of sexuality, examined virtually all cultural assumptions, and strived to challenge readers' beliefs and attitudes. Such writers, however, are only a gifted minority and hardly represent the norm. Fantastic fiction remains generally conservative, and writers with the strongest sales tend not to question the norms that were in place by the first half of the twentieth century.

Bibliography

Robert Bloch. "Imagination and Modern Social Criticism." Basil Davenport, ed., *The Science Fiction Novel*. Chicago: Advent: Publishers, 1959, 97–121.

Reginald Bretnor, ed. *Modern Science Fiction*. New York: Coward McCann, 1953.

Frank Cioffi. *Formula Fiction?* Westport, CT: Greenwood Press, 1982.

Harlan Ellison, ed. *Again, Dangerous Visions*. Garden City, NY: Doubleday, 1972.

Ursula K. Le Guin. *The Language of the Night*. New York: HarperCollins, 1992.

Barry N. Malzberg. *The Engines of the Night*. Garden City, NY: Doubleday, 1982.

Paul Neimark, ed. *Taboo*. Chicago: New Classics House, 1964.

Roger Schlobin, ed. *The Aesthetics of Fantasy Literature and Art*. Notre Dame, IN: University of Notre Dame Press, 1982.

George E. Slusser and Eric S. Rabkin, eds. *Aliens*. Carbondale, IN: University of Southern Illinois Press, 1987.

—*Richard Bleiler*

TALENTS

Overview

Talents are the **psychic powers** of fantasy—magical powers that are inborn, do not require **magical objects,** and are not explained in scientific or pseudo-scientific terms (see **Magic**); in Orson Scott Card's Alvin Maker series, beginning with *Seventh Son* (1987), such abilities are more colloquially called "knacks." "Talents" is also the term regularly used for the helpful attributes acquired by characters in video **games,** **computer** games, and role-playing games.

Survey

One useful talent is precognition, or the ability to predict the future, although for Cassandra of Greek **mythology,** the gift had little value, since her prophetic powers were balanced by the **curse** that nobody would believe her predictions (see **Divination**). A boy in Diana Wynne Jones's *Power of Three* (1976) faces the same predicament. Some stories about King **Arthur** grant Merlin the power of prophecy, while Irene Radford's *Guardian of the Balance* (1999) and its sequels focus on Merlin's daughter, who inherited that talent. In Card's Alvin Maker series, a "torch" looks at people's hidden "heartfire" and tells how long they are likely to live; an episode of *The Twilight Zone*, "The Purple Testament" (1960), involves a similar ability: a man can tell when people are about to die by looking in their faces, and eventually looks in the **mirror** to observes his own impending **death**. In Joan Aiken's *The Cockatrice Boys* (1996), a young girl can predict the imminent arrival of the **monsters** that will invade Britain (see **Invasion**). The ability to see only a few seconds into the future may not seem useful, but it helps one character of Randall Garrett's *Too Many Magicians* (1967) in his swordfights (see **Swords**).

Other talents involve influencing other people's emotions—as observed in Dave Duncan's *The Cursed* (1995) and Sharon Green's *Challenges* (1998) and its sequels—or detecting them with unfailing accuracy—as in Kristine Kathryn Rusch's *Heart Readers* (1993). Phobia, a female **villain** who battles DC Comics' Teen Titans, has the innate ability to make other people feel afraid. Card's Alvin Maker series attributes Napoleon's success to his "knack" for making other people loyal to him.

Mindreading is also useful: in Robert E. Howard's "The People of the Black Circle" (1934), an enemy of **Conan the Conqueror**, the Master of Yimsha, can read people's minds. In Glen Cook's Garrett novels, beginning with *Sweet Silver Blues* (1987), **detective** Garrett values the company of the Dead Man because he can to an extent tell him what guests are thinking. The ability to project thoughts is called "bespeaking" in Diane Duane's *The Door into Fire* (1979), but "mindspeech," the term used in Mercedes Lackey's Valdemar novel *By the Sword* (1991), is more common.

An unusual rapport with animals may qualify as a talent, as observed in the films *The Beastmaster* (1982) and *Beastmaster 2: Through the Portal of Time* (1990), which feature a **hero** who mentally communicates with wild animals and makes them follow commands. Another villain encountered by Howard's Conan, Zogar Sag, has the magical power to control animals, as described in "Beyond the Black River" (1935).

Some youthful heroes discover they have powers that directly affect the world around them: in David Lubar's *Hidden Talents* (1999), a boy can start **fires** with a thought, which is also what a "spark" does in Card's Alvin Maker stories. Michael Harrison's *Higher Things* (1945) involves a man who discovers that he can levitate his own body to immense heights. In Rita Murphy's *Harmony* (2002), a girl learns that she can move objects and cause a microwave oven to explode. The power of magical healing is conspicuously displayed by Elizabeth Moon's woman warrior Paksennarion in *Sheepfarmer's Daughter* (1988) and its sequels; Mary Taffs's *Healing Magick* (2004) also features a Healer.

A few talents are harder to classify. A man in Piers Anthony's *A Spell for Chameleon*, when told of a destination, can immediately point in its direction; and in Colin Wilson's *The Philosopher's Stone* (1969), a man **touches** an object from the lost continent of Mu and learns its story. A talent believed in and highly valued by many in real life—"dowsing," the ability to locate underground sources of **water**—is surprisingly inconspicuous in fantasy, although this is another power of Card's Alvin Maker.

One science fiction work unusually employing the term "talents" is Anne McCaffrey's Pegasus series, beginning with *To Ride Pegasus* (1973): people in the future who have psychic powers like telepathy and **teleportation** are recruited by the government to assist in achieving **space travel** and other activities. It is characteristic of science fiction to institutionalize and perpetuate the use of talents through several generations, whereas fantasy is content to focus on stories of talented individuals who make a difference in the lives of other individuals.

Discussion

Stories about talents clearly reflect in part a fulfillment of childhood wishes for magical powers, and although science fiction stories may associate such abilities with mutants who are feared, disliked, or hunted down, people with talents are usually respected and appreciated for their contributions. (There are only a few exceptions: Mickey Zucker Reichart's "Nightfall's Promise" (2002) occurs on a world where people born with special abilities must keep them secret to avoid persecution). Thus, while having a psychic power might be a burden and affliction, having a talent is most often a blessing.

Bibliography

Mara E. Donaldson. "Prophetic and Apocalyptic Eschatology in Ursula K. Le Guin's *The Farthest Shore* and *Tehanu*." *SEMELA*, 60 (1992), 111–122.

Vic Ghidalia, ed. *The Oddballs*. New York: Manor Books, 1973.

Andrew Greeley. "Anne McCaffrey." Greeley, *God in Popular Culture*. Chicago: Thomas More, 1988, 201–209.

Deidre Greene. "Higher Argument." Patricia Reynolds and Glen H. GoodKnight, eds., *Proceedings of the J.R.R. Tolkien Centenary Conference, Keble College, Oxford, 1992*. Altadena, CA: Mythopoeic Press, 1995, 45–52.

A.O.H. Jarman. "The Merlin Legend and the Welsh Tradition of Prophecy." Rachel Bromwich, Jarman, and Brynley F. Roberts, eds., *The Arthur of the Welsh*. Cardiff: University of Wales Press, 1991, 117–146.

Susan Stone-Blackburn. "Feminist Nurturers and Psychic Healers." Milton T. Wolf and Daryl F. Mallett, eds., *Imaginative Futures*. San Bernardino, CA: Jacob's Ladder Books, 1995, 167–178.

Raymond H. Thompson. "Rationalizing the Irrational." *Arthuriana*, 10 (Spring, 2000), 116–126.

Paul Walker. "Anne McCaffrey." Walker, *Speaking of Science Fiction*. Oradell, NJ: Luna Publications, 1978, 253–262.

—*Gary Westfahl*

TALKING ANIMALS

The creatures outside looked from pig to man, and from man to pig, and from pig to man again; but already it was impossible to say which was which.

—George Orwell
Animal Farm (1945)

Overview

Talking animals are popular motifs in fantasy fiction. Either communicating with others of their species or breaking species boundaries and speaking to other animals and/or humans, speaking animals represent and comment on human behavior or allow animals to speak for themselves. Animals without human characteristics are discussed in **animals and zoos**, while animals scientifically raised to human **intelligence** are considered under **Uplift**.

Survey

The value of animals as tellers of tales began to be tapped with Dorothy Kilner's *The Life and Perambulations of a Mouse* (1783), believed to be the first full-length story in which animals narrate their own life history—the first "animal autobiography." The last quarter of the nineteenth century, however, demonstrated the growing popularity and multiplying uses of talking animals. Anna Sewell's *Black Beauty* (1877), written from a **horse**'s perspective, attempted to educate people about rampant cruelty to working horses and other domestic animals. Margaret Marshall Saunders's **dog** autobiography *Beautiful Joe* (1894) also preached against cruelty to animals while promoting animal rights. Other Victorian and Edwardian authors like Lewis Carroll (see *Alice's Adventures in Wonderland*), Kenneth Grahame (*The Wind in the Willows* [1908]), and Beatrix Potter (*The Tale of Peter Rabbit* [1901]) created idealized animal worlds symbolizing the era's romantic nostalgia for times past. Animals that interacted with humans, like Carroll's Cheshire **cat** and Potter's Mrs. Tiggy-winkle, often acted as guides to aid **children** on journeys of self-discovery.

Talking animals in literature can be divided into four main categories: beast tales, pourquoi tales, "true" animal fantasy, and "anthropomorphic" fantasy. Beast tales (see **Fables**) which directly descend from Aesop's *Fables* (c. 6th century BCE), employ animals to depict **humanity**'s virtues and flaws. Folk tales like "The Three Billy Goats Gruff," "The Little Red Hen," "The Story of Chicken Little," "The Three Little Pigs," and "The Bremen Town Musicians" use animal speech to preach didactic moralism. Other beast tales like Jonathan Swift's "A Voyage to the Country of the Houyhnhnms" in *Gulliver's Travels*, Rudyard Kipling's *The Jungle Book* (1894), George Orwell's *Animal Farm*, Pierre Boulle's *Planet of the Apes* (1963) (see *Planet of the Apes*), and Will Self's *Great Apes* (1997) employ beast tales as social **satires**; animal speech and behavior illustrate people's inhumanity, hypocrisy, and innate speciesism.

Grounded in the folktale tradition, pourquoi tales explain aspects of nature; the most famous of these is Rudyard Kipling's *Just So Stories* (1902), including "How the Leopard Got His Spots," "The Cat that Walked by Himself," and "The Elephant's Child."

True animal fantasy involves animals behaving naturally in natural environments such as **forests** and meadows (Felix Salten's *Bambi* [1923], Richard Adams's *Watership Down* [1972], William Horwood's *Duncton Wood* [1980] and its sequels) or **farms** (E.B. White's *Charlotte's Web* [1952], Dick King-Smith's *Babe* [1983]); intelligent animals may also appear in human surroundings (George Selden's *A Cricket in Times Square* [1960]). In these tales, animal speech is rarely heard by humans. If particular humans understand animals, the characters are usually children, like Fern in *Charlotte's Web*, not yet socialized to understand that animals cannot speak.

Anthropomorphic fantasy exhibits animal characters who are "animal" in name only. These animals, exhibiting human characteristics and behaviors, are not confined by the abilities of their species. Tales like Grahame's *The Wind in the Willows*,

John Masefield's *The Midnight Folk* (1927), E.B. White's *Stuart Little* (1945), William Steig's *Abel's Island* (1976) and the film *Cats and Dogs* (2001) exemplify this genre.

In science fiction, talking animals usually are technologically altered or uplifted. H.G. Wells's **The Island of Doctor Moreau**, Clifford D. Simak's **City**, Dean Koontz's *Watchers* (1987), and Kirsten Bakis's *Lives of the Monster Dogs* (1997) use these hybrid animals to comment not only on **culture** and humans' belief in their eminence but also to recognize the significance of **evolution** and animals' inherent natures. Other works, like Douglas Adams's **The Hitchhiker's Guide to the Galaxy** and its sequels, hypothesize that animals like mice (see **Rats and Mice**) and dolphins (see **Fish and Sea Creatures**) are actually highly intelligent while simultaneously commenting on man's **barbarian** practices.

Popular on television and in film, talking animals have starred in the 1950 film *Francis the Talking Mule* and its sequels, directed by Arthur Lubin (who also created the television series *Mister Ed* [1961–1966], about a talking horse); the series *Lancelot Link: Secret Chimp* (1970), a chimpanzee spoof of human **espionage** shows; and *Babe* (1995), a film based on King-Smith's book about a pig who learns to herd sheep, which inspired the sequel *Babe: Pig in the City* (1998). Talking animals abound in Disney animated feature films like *Dumbo* (1941), *Cinderella* (1950), *Lady and the Tramp* (1955), *The Aristocats* (1970), *The Fox and the Hound* (1981), and *The Lion King* (1994). Disney primarily uses talking creatures as lovable, humorous commodities who can be placed in jeopardy without fear for human life.

Discussion

As the parrot Polynesia tells Dr. Dolittle in Hugh Lofting's **The Story of Dr. Dolittle** and Fern's **father** tells her **mother** in *Charlotte's Web*, animals speak; it is humans who are unwilling or unable to hear or understand them. Literature, film, and television remain filled with talking beasts, denoting society's fascination with the possibility of animal speech. Talking animals posit fantasies of cross-species **communication** and reflect desires to comprehend animal minds and be invited into animal worlds.

Bibliography

Steve Baker. "Of Maus and More." Baker, *Picturing the Beast*. Urbana: University of Illinois Press, 1993, 120–161.

Margaret Blount. *Animal Land*. London: Hutchinson & Co., Ltd., 1974.

Humphrey Carpenter. *Secret Gardens*. Boston: Houghton Mifflin Co., 1985.

Sheila Egoff. *Worlds Within*. Chicago: American Library Association, 1988.

Erica Fudge. *Animal*. London: Reaktion Books, 2002.

John Goldthwaite. *The Natural History of Make-Believe*. New York: Oxford University Press, 1996.

Elliott Gose. *Mere Creatures*. Toronto: University of Toronto Press, 1988.

Jennifer Ham and Matthew Senior. *Animal Acts*. New York: Routledge, 1997.

—Cat Yampell

Taverns and Inns

Overview

The role of taverns and inns as fictional locales and narrative motifs is longstanding in western literature, dating back to the first vernacular writing in medieval France, and represented in the fabliaux, short *dits* and contes, Rutebeuf, dramas, and poetry of the twelfth century, coinciding with the emergence of a secular literary **culture**. The tavern became the narrative model for a new vision of the identity and social function of literature, a place allowing new interests in profit and play to confront older ecclesiastical traditions and serving as "the privileged point of contact between the sacred and the secular," as described in Andrew Cowell's *At Play in the Tavern* (1999). Taverns became settings of cultural **rebellion** and associated illicit activities like gambling, prostitution, usury, and carousing. While the social forces inspiring this use of the motif have faded, echoes of these themes still resonate, especially in fantasy.

Survey

The basic features of rustic inns—particularly for **heroic fantasy**—were established by J.R.R. Tolkien's *The Lord of the Rings*, though other antecedents exist in literature, folklore, and **fairy tales**. The tavern provides a communal, convivial meeting place to share the news and **stories** that provide background information while authors indulge in descriptions of **food and drink**. It is a place for meetings between different races, danger, intrigue, Frodo's first use of the **ring**, and Tolkien's **poetry** presented as songs. The overall tone suggests **romance** and nostalgia, an idealized remembrance of times when taverns were gathering places and country inns provided rest along overland routes. Tolkien's description—crowded common rooms dominated by large fireplaces, tables, and partial lighting, where strangers lurk unseen in shadows; lodging, stables, and fare whose quality is a moral compass; an overweight, jovial, and harried innkeeper—became a model for numerous writers.

Tolkien imitator Terry Brooks minimally expands upon his conceit in *The Sword of Shannara*, using a tavern as the place where the **hero's quest** both begins and ends. In Dennis L. McKiernan's *The Dragonstone* (1996), a similar inn is a seedy den of thieves (see **Theft**). But the author relying most upon the tavern is Robert Jordan (see *The Eye of the World*): the inn is not only a conventional plot device and **threshold** for quests but also, by means of its recurring presence and descriptive detail, almost a character in itself, allowing protagonists to seek sanctuary, measure their travel, and establish and renew relationships. Characters support themselves there as gleemen or itinerant musicians. Inns become a prominent setting for conspiracy and rebellion, and gambling is a significant feature (see **Games**).

Science fiction, especially in movies and television, has appropriated this image of the tavern, most prominently in the first *Star Wars* movie and television series *Star Trek: The Next Generation* and *Star Trek: Deep Space Nine*. The Mos Eisley Cantina in *Star Wars* recalls Tolkien's tavern: an intersection of races, if alien, where deals are made in shadowy corners. Granted, the musician playing tambor or lute is replaced by a full-scale jazz band, and the tavern's thieves and **pirates** now work in space (see **Space Travel; Theft**); but as far as its use as plot device and locale, only its planetary setting and decor have been altered. A similar situation prevails for *Star Trek: Deep Space Nine*. Here, while transferred to a **space station**, the tavern remains a gathering spot for residents and travelers, though there are new elements: holosuites for sexual recreation (see **Sexuality**) and the exploration of labor union relations (see **Business; Work and Leisure**). The motif's role in *Star Trek: The Next Generation* is also conventional, with a focus on the *Enterprise*'s barkeeper, Guinan, a mysterious alien who possesses an unusual sense extending beyond linear space-time (see **Time Travel**).

Other science fiction novels use this setting as a stage for **violence** and interaction with artificial intelligence (Richard K. Morgan, *Altered Carbon* [2002]), whereas two fantasy works—Steven Brust's *Jhereg* (1983) and Terry Pratchett's Discworld series (see *The Colour of Magic*)—emphasize **humor**, thus parodying the motif. George Alec Effinger's "The City on the Sand" (1973) utilizes a streetside cafe to describe the **city** of Budayeen and meditate on the **estrangement** of a failed writer and expatriate, whereas in "Marîd Throws a Party" (2003), a dissolute bar-owner is inconvenienced by a **death** during his birthday party.

Others use the locale as a setting for narration of poetry (Alfred Noyes, *Tales of the Mermaid Tavern* [1913]) or telling **stories** (L. Sprague de Camp and Fletcher S. Pratt, *Tales from Gavagan's Bar* [1953]). The Old Phoenix Tavern in Poul Anderson's *A Midsummer's Tempest* (1974) serves as a threshold to **parallel worlds**. The Gaff and Slasher in Peter S. Beagle's *The Innkeeper's Song* (1993) opens similarly onto another **dimension**, while also elevating and subverting the traditional inn to elaborate multiple storylines incorporating death, **rebirth, dreams, love, gender, shapeshifters** and a **talking animal**.

Discussion

The theme of taverns and inns is dominated by Tolkien's pattern, imitated to varying degrees by later writers. The basic concept, similarly utilized in science fiction, is an important recurring prop, notable perhaps for its very familiarity. Its relevance is demonstrated by its long use as motif, dating back to our earliest vernacular literature. And since that literature arose alongside secular **culture**, sharing its concerns for profit and play as well as ambience of dissent, it is unsurprising that it still appears today within genres broadly associated with entertainment, popular culture, and dissidence.

Bibliography

John Gregory Betancourt. *Slab's Tavern and Other Uncanny Places*. Buffalo, NY: W. Paul Ganley, 1990.

Clark A. Brady. "Barsoomian Inns." Brady, *The Burroughs Cyclopedia*. Jefferson, NC: MacFarland, 1996, 152.

Andrew Cowell. *At Play in the Tavern*. Ann Arbor: University of Michigan Press, 1999.

Diana W. Jones. *The Tough Guide to Fantasyland*. London: Vista, 1996.

Jonathan Langford. "Sitting Down to the Sacramental Feast." Gary Westfahl, George Slusser, and Eric S. Rabkin, eds., *Foods of the Gods*. Athens: University of Georgia Press, 1996, 117–141.

Suzanne Rahn. "Life at The Squirrel Inn." *Lion and the Unicorn*, 12 (December, 1988), 224–239.

George Scithers and Darrell Schweitzer, eds. *Tales from the Spaceport Bar*. New York: Avon, 1987.

Margaret Weis and Tracy Hickman, eds. *Leaves From the Inn of the Last Home*. Lake Geneva, WI: TSR, 1993.

—*William Thompson*

TECHNOLOGY

———————————————————■———————————————————

Overview

Modern fantasy has tended to react with abhorrence to the accelerating technological change that was experienced in the nineteenth and twentieth centuries, and to embrace a *faux* medievalism (see **Medievalism and the Middle Ages**)—although forms of medieval technology sometimes figure in works like Michael Scott Rohan's Winter of the World trilogy, beginning with *The Anvil of Ice* (1986), and L.E. Modesitt's *The Magic of Recluce* (1991) and its sequels. Science fiction, by contrast, has displayed more ambivalence. There has been deep conflict within the field between the respective proponents of technological **optimism and pessimism**.

Survey

In medieval and renaissance **Europe**, there was a tradition of suspicion toward "impious" inquiries into nature that was expressed in hostile literary depictions of **magic** and alchemy. Jonathan Swift's *Gulliver's Travels* includes merciless **satire** of Enlightenment-era **scientists**, and hostility to science and technology increased in the Romantic period around the beginning of the nineteenth century, as in Mary Shelley's *Frankenstein*. However, in the later nineteenth century, technological **progress** became a popular value in industrialized nations. Science fiction showed optimism in the imaginary voyages described in Jules Verne's early novels, which postulated devices like Nemo's submarine in *Twenty Thousand Leagues under the Sea*. This period's techno-optimism culminated in futuristic **utopias**, including Edward Bellamy's *Looking Backward, 2000–1887* and H.G. Wells's *A Modern Utopia* (1905).

Wells was more than a "Wellsian" techno-utopian, and his great scientific romances of the 1890s, like *The Time Machine*, contained dark elements. However, the utopian component of his output produced a backlash—first seen, perhaps, in E.M. Forster's cautionary tale of a machine-dependent future, "The Machine Stops" (1909). Thereafter, Yevgeny Zamiatin, Aldous Huxley, and George Orwell described **dystopias** in which technology is an instrument for totalitarian enslavement, or enforcement of a decadent and repugnant form of social stability (see **Decadence**; Zamiatin's *We*; Huxley's *Brave New World*; Orwell's *Nineteen Eighty-Four*).

In contrast with these developments, the science fiction pulp magazines of Hugo Gernsback's era valorized science, scientists, and technology. So-called "Golden Age" science fiction (from the late 1930s to the late 1940s) was only slightly more cautious in its optimism about technology and the future, exemplified by Isaac

Asimov's concentration on solving intellectual **puzzles** and sympathetic portrayals of **robots** (see *I, Robot*).

However, widespread intellectual rejection of technology followed the destruction of Hiroshima and the atrocities of the Nazi death camps. Postwar science fiction began to express fears of decay or destruction, produced by over-reliance on technology or the use of immensely powerful **weaponry** (see **Nuclear War**). In works like *The Drowned World*, J.G. Ballard, the dominant figure the 1960s British New Wave, expressed visions of a doomed society.

Meanwhile, cinematic science fiction was Frankensteinian or dystopian from the beginning, as with *Metropolis*, Fritz Lang's portrait of a mechanized, dehumanizing future **city** (see **Machines and Mechanization**). Some early movies were more optimistic, notably *Just Imagine* (1930) and *Things to Come* (surely the high-water mark of technocratic Wellsianism), but 1950s science fiction cinema showed a strong anti-technological bias, most markedly in many American and Japanese films about scientific **monsters**, like *Them!* (1954), and *Godzilla, King of the Monsters*.

A common theme at this time was that human beings are psychologically incapable of handling technological power (see **Psychology**). In *Forbidden Planet*, "monsters from the id" are unleashed when Dr. Morbius subconsciously gains control of an alien **civilization**'s vast power source (the same power with which the aliens destroyed themselves). Similar ideas frequently emerged in the 1960s television series, *The Outer Limits*. In the late decades of the twentieth century, the technophobic imagination focused increasingly on **computers** and artificial **intelligence** (as in *The Terminator*, *The Matrix*, their sequels, and *A.I.: Artificial Intelligence*), and biotechnology (as in the *Jurassic Park* movies) (see **Biology; Cloning; Genetic Engineering**).

Throughout this time, however, an optimistic tradition was maintained in literary science fiction, especially on television. *Star Trek*, and its successors and imitators, expressed hope for **humanity**'s survival and increased maturity, wise use of advanced technology, and eventual colonization of space. In the 1980s, **cyberpunk** portrayed advanced technologies as inevitable, adaptable, and exciting—but also potentially damaging to societies and individuals. This ambivalence continued in post-cyberpunk science fiction, while science fiction cinema increasingly associated technology with special effects and sheer spectacle.

Discussion

Most forms of actual or postulated technology receive both positive and negative portrayals in science fiction. The predicted technology of molecular engineering (or nanotechnology) is one example. While in some works it offers a world of plenty, it is a threat in Michael Crichton's *Prey* (2002), where escaped "clouds" of tiny nanotech devices commence bizarre parasitism on human victims (see **Parasites**). A fascinating genre phenomenon is exemplified by Robby the Robot's co-option into the spaceship's crew at the end of *Forbidden Planet*, and the way the **dinosaurs** come to seem more admirable than monstrous as the *Jurassic Park* series of movies continues. Similarly, *The Terminator*'s sequels introduce "good" killer **cyborgs**, and the audience of the original movie largely identified with its antihero. Seemingly antitechnological narratives frequently show technological devices and products as alluring—as irresistibly *cool*—and they are accommodated within the narratives' value systems.

Bibliography

Scott Bukatman. *Terminal Identity*. Durham and London: Duke University Press, 1993.

Roslynn D. Haynes. *From Faust to Strangelove*. Baltimore and London: Johns Hopkins Univ. Press, 1994.

Mark R. Hillegas. *The Future as Nightmare*. 1967. Carbondale and Edwardsville: Southern Illinois University Press, 1974.

T.J. Matheson. "Marcuse, Ellul, and the Science-Fiction Film." *Science-Fiction Studies*, 19 (November, 1992), 326–339.

Joseph D. Miller. "From Dr. Frankenstein to Dr. McCoy." Gary Westfahl and George Slusser, eds., *No Cure for the Future*. Westport, CT: Greenwood Press, 2002, 53–64.

Michael Ryan and Douglas Kellner. "Technophobia." Annette Kuhn, ed., *Alien Zone*. London: Verso, 1990, 58–65.

J.P. Telotte. *Replications*. Urbana and Chicago: University of Illinois Press, 1995.

Patricia S. Warrick. *The Cybernetic Imagination in Science Fiction*. Cambridge, MA: MIT Press, 1980.

Gary Westfahl. *Cosmic Engineers*. Westport, CT: Greenwood Press, 1996.

—Russell Blackford

TECHNOTHRILLERS

Overview

The technothriller, a loosely defined subgenre of the thriller, is arguably not science fiction or fantasy. However, it has numerous aspects of interest to science fiction—especially **hard science fiction**—and many science fiction authors have produced technothrillers. In film, technothrillers are a Hollywood staple that may be regarded as a Trojan Horse of science fiction, using science-fictional tropes to attract audiences who would never consider themselves open to science fiction itself; an example is *Broken Arrow* (1996), in which **theft** of top-secret advanced nukes prompts a standard action plot.

Survey

Most tales of **superheroes** are, almost by definition, technothrillers, in that the world where superheroes operate must be ours (or a similar **parallel world**) for the **heroes'** superpowers to have full dramatic effect. The same can be said of the James Bond movies—begun with *Doctor No*—whose general template is that an arch-**villain** has obtained sophisticated technological gadgets to allow him to conquer the world; Bond, surrounded with gadgetry of his own and seemingly unkillable, is effectively a superhero. The television series *The Avengers* (1961–1969) took this cocktail and added a copious dash of **surrealism**. *The Terminator*, although rooted in science fiction, can be read as a technothriller in which superpowers are given to the villain, not the hero.

Advances in **computer** technology frequently generate technothriller plots. In Ira Levin's *Sliver* (1991), filmed in 1993, a computerized surveillance system permits a voyeuristic psychopath to spy on, seduce, and murder female residents of a condominium. Philip Kerr's *Gridiron* (1996) takes this further: the computerized security system, Abraham, of an automated Los Angeles office building becomes so sensitive to perceived threats that it begins exterminating occupants. In the film *WarGames* (1983) the U.S. military's supercomputer cannot distinguish between real life and the video **game** a teenager thinks he is playing with it, so it threatens the world. Bruce Sterling's *The Zenith Angle* (2004) uses technothriller tropes to portray a man transformed from innocuous cyber-geek into ruthless spy boss by the forces of U.S. *faux*-patriotism prevalent in the wake of the September 11 attacks.

The technothriller can cross over into genres other than science fiction, notably **horror**. In Dean R. Koontz's *Demon Seed* (1973), filmed in 1977, a domestic computer tyrannizes a woman and eventually rapes her—via its quasi-**robot** peripheral—with the implausible aim of creating a new super-race blending human and machine. In Greg Bear's *Dead Lines* (2004), a sort of super cellular telephone, drawing on a sub-real energy level, inadvertently conjures up an epidemic of ghosts (see **Ghosts and Hauntings**). The same author's *Vitals* (2003) less successfully derives horror from a bioterrorism plot.

A separate category of technothrillers concerns **medicine**. The paramount names in commercial terms are Michael Crichton and especially Robin Cook. In Cook's *Coma* (1977), filmed by Crichton in 1978, wicked doctors plunge patients into terminal comas so their bodies may be harvested for transplant surgery. A string of similar novels followed from Cook's hand. Crichton himself displays more versatility; among his technothrillers are *The Terminal Man* (1972), filmed in 1974, in which electronic brain implants are used to control a man, and *Prey* (2002), in which swarms of medical nanobots develop a form of **intelligence**. His 1973 film *Westworld* is a nonmedical technothriller. A more accomplished novelist in this field than either is Tess Gerritsen. In her *Life Support* (1997), medics inseminate prostitutes with packages of tailored genes to grow quasi-fetuses with supernumerary pituitary glands, which are harvested to rejuvenate ultra-rich elderly clients. *Gravity* (1999) combines the medical technothriller with the more orthodox form: a ferociously destructive man-made disease strikes a **space station**; to rescue astronauts while protecting **Earth** from havoc, a hero uses a private-enterprise space shuttle.

Technothriller authors of note who cannot be imagined as science fiction writers include Larry Bond, Dale Brown, Tom Clancy, Stephen Coonts, Clive Cussler, Bob Langley, R.J. Pineiro, and Craig Thomas. Science fiction authors better known for technothrillers are Dean Ing, Frank M. Robinson, and William H. Keith, Jr. (who writes science fiction under that name but writes technothrillers as Keith William Andrews, Robert Cain, Keith Douglass, and H. Jay Riker).

Discussion

The world of the technothriller is essentially our own world, perhaps displaced into the nearest of **near futures**. Into this world is introduced a technological advance that drives the plot. The device or development in question may be merely a McGuffin or may be integral to unfolding events, but rarely is it permitted to have a large-scale effect upon its world—though the threat of worldwide devastation, should our heroes not prevail, is a common element. It is easy to see why **espionage** frequently characterizes the technothriller: one way of insuring the world remains unchanged by plot's end is to keep everything safely in the realm of the clandestine, so the reader's **paranoia**—this could be happening *now* and I would be none the wiser—can be added to the tools in the thriller writer's kit.

Bibliography

Stephen Coonts, ed. *Combat*. New York: Tor, 2001.

D.K. Fischer. "Michael Crichton on Robots, Writing and Directing, and *Runaway*." *Ciné-fantastique*, 15 (May, 1985), 6, 59.

Neil Frude. *The Robot Heritage*. London: Century, 1984.

Helen S. Garson. *Tom Clancy*. Westport, CT: Greenwood Press, 1996.

Martin H. Greenberg, Ed Gorman and Bill Munster, eds. *The Dean Koontz Companion*. New York: Berkley, 1994.

Abbe Mowshowitz. *Inside Information*. Reading, MA: Addison-Wesley, 1977.

Lorena L. Stookey. *Robin Cook*. Westport, CT: Greenwood Press, 1996.

Elizabeth A. Trembley. *Michael Crichton*. Westport, CT: Greenwood Press, 1996.

Gary Westfahl. "Claremont, California: Notes from the Home Front." *Interzone*, No. 174 (December, 2001), 52–53.

—*John Grant*

TELEPORTATION

He jaunted up the geodesic lines of space-time to an Elsewhere and an Else-when. He arrived in chaos. He hung in a precarious para-Now for a moment and then tumbled back into chaos.

—Alfred Bester
The Stars My Destination (1956)

Overview

"Teleportation" describes instantaneous or near-instantaneous transfer of matter from one point in space to another, usually without concern for intervening barriers. Science fiction teleportation invokes imaginary **physics** and **technology**, such as matter transmitters, gateways, or wormholes (see **Black Holes; Space Travel**). Individuals may supposedly achieve the effect through **psychic powers**.

Survey

Personal teleportation generates most narrative interest as an isolated, constrained talent rather than part of a panoply of superheroic powers. Thus the **superman** hero of A.E. van Vogt's *The World of Null-A* (1948) requires considerable training to harness his teleporting power and finds that reference points "memorized" as jump destinations are usable for only a limited time. An entire teleporting society in Alfred Bester's *The Stars My Destination* is similarly restricted by the need to visualize one's target before "jaunting" (entrance mazes are used to conceal house interiors), and by an apparent maximum leap of 1,000 miles. In Theodore Sturgeon's *More Than Human*, teleporting twin girls form part of a gestalt entity whose initial flaws include a lack of competent controlling **intelligence**.

The wish-fulfillment aspect of teleportation is inverted in stories like Daniel F. Galouye's "The Last Leap" (1960) and Philip E. High's *Blindfold from the Stars* (1979), in which novice teleporters struggle *not* to flash instantly to any imagined destination—such as the **Sun**. The hazard in John Brunner's *The Stardroppers* (1972) is the ease of jumping into interplanetary vacuum.

Individual teleporters' power is harnessed for commercial cargo **transportation** in Kevin O'Donnell Jr.'s *Caverns* (1981) and sequels, and in Anne McCaffrey's *Pegasus in Space* (2002). Teleporting aliens include the **dragons** of McCaffrey's *Dragonflight*, certain gifted humanoids in Vernor Vinge's *The Witling* (1976), and the "mind hound," which in James H. Schmitz's *The Lion Game* (1973) follows its prey telepathically and teleports to kill.

Roger Zelazny's science-fantasy *Creatures of Light and Darkness* (1969) poses a question in **cosmology**, with a character able to teleport anywhere he can imagine: does he create his weirder destinations or discover them in **parallel worlds**? Teleportation is rarely an appropriate term for fantasy's magical transitions, but Charles Williams's *Many Dimensions* (1931) discusses the blasphemy (see **Religion**) of using a numinous, holy **magical object** for mundane transport purposes, while Phyllis Eisenstein's *Born to Exile* (1978) interestingly depicts a teleporting elite in a fantasy world.

Mechanical teleportation or matter transmission is frequent in science fiction, the most familiar example being the *Star Trek* transporter (spoofed in the 1999 film *Galaxy Quest*). Iain M. Banks's Culture novels (see **Consider Phlebas**) achieve this effect by "displacer" technology involving a small element of risk, whereas the literal **mirrors** of Gene Wolfe's *The Book of the New Sun* provide not only transport but a seeming link with realms of **supernatural creatures**.

The impact of teleportation on **Earth** society would be immense. Bester offers many ideas in *The Stars My Destination*, including a teleporting criminal population following the night (see **Darkness**) around the world. Larry Niven's "Flash Crowd" (1973) shows public transmitter booths allowing mass convergence on scenes of interest, fomenting instant riots. In *All the Colors of Darkness* (1963), Lloyd Biggle, Jr. examines the initial upheaval as a global transmitter network undercuts **air travel** and threatens road and rail **transportation**. The sequel *Watchers of the Dark* (1966) shows an alien **city** in partial decay because transmitters make it unnecessary to venture outdoors, a situation also explored in Isaac Asimov's claustrophobic "It's Such a Beautiful Day" (1954).

Biggle's spaceships are receiverless matter transmitters that also can transmit themselves. This is reduced to absurdity in Bob Shaw's comic *Who Goes Here?* (1977), with a 200-meter ship shifted millions of times per second by its own rear-end transmitter to a receiver at its front.

Large, temporary matter-transmission portals facilitate interstellar **planetary colonies** in Robert A. Heinlein's *Tunnel in the Sky* (1955). "Springer" transmitters in John Barnes's *A Million Open Doors* (1992) and sequels catalyze social chaos as isolated worlds meet galactic **culture**. Clifford D. Simak's interstellar network in *Way Station* (1963) involves matter *duplicators*; supposedly the passenger's unique essence or soul is transmitted, leaving behind a corpse for disposal. Algis Budrys's *Rogue Moon* (1960) explores this disquieting issue of **identity**, using successive duplicates as disposable explorers of a deadly alien **puzzle**. Duplicates created by transmission in Thomas Disch's *Echo Round His Bones* (1967) are fully human but intangible, like ghosts.

Discussion

Few aspects of society would remain untouched by widespread teleportation or matter transmission. Uses range from the frivolous, like Niven's beer glass that refills itself via transmitter, to ultimate emergency services, which in Banks's Culture can instantly "displace" useful assistance from far away to save, for instance, falling mountaineers before impact.

Houses of many transmitter-linked rooms, perhaps on different **alien worlds**, are a popular conceit, as in Dan Simmons's **Hyperion** and Roger Zelazny's *Today We Choose Faces* (1973). Philip José Farmer's *A Private Cosmos* (1968) develops this into a **prison** without physical exits, while Schmitz's *The Lion Game* features a dispersed worldwide hotel opening on every tourist attraction.

Although individual photons have been "teleported" in the laboratory, serious matter transmission remains a very remote possibility. Larry Niven has ably explored secondary problems with conservation laws in stories like "A Kind of Murder" (1974) and the essay "The Theory and Practice of Teleportation" (1969).

Bibliography

Mervyn F. Bendle. "Teleportation, Cyborgs and the Posthuman Ideology." *Social Semiotics*, 12 (April, 2002), 45–62.

Charles Berlitz and William Moore. *The Philadelphia Experiment*. New York: Putnam, 1978.

John Gribbin. *Schrodinger's Kittens and the Search For Reality*. New York: Little, Brown, 1995.

Lawrence M. Krauss. "Beam Me Up an Einstein, Scotty." *Wired*, 3 (November, 1995), 116–130.

———. *The Physics of Star Trek*. New York: Basic Books, 1995.

Peter Nicholls, David Langford, and Brian Stableford. "Matter Transmission" and "Telekinesis and the Brute-Force Talents." Nicholls, Langford, and Stableford, *The Science in Science Fiction*. London: Michael Joseph, 1982, 135, 174–175.

Larry Niven. "Exercise in Speculation: The Theory and Practice of Teleportation." 1969. Niven, *All the Myriad Ways*. New York: Ballantine, 1971, 83–109.

Michael Okuda, Denise Okuda, and Debbie Mirek. "Transporter." Okuda, Okuda, and Mirek, *The Star Trek Encyclopedia*. New York and London: Simon & Schuster, 1994, 349–350.

—David Langford

TELEVISION AND RADIO

———————————————————■———————————————————

Overview

Consideration of new **technology** has always been central to science fiction. Before the mid-twentieth century, television and radio were depicted as wonderful new **inventions**. By the 1950s, when television began saturating world **culture** and radio had been an everyday presence for decades, writers focused, often in **satires**, on sociological aspects of broadcast **communication**.

Survey

In the early twentieth century, radio held the same mysterious, even exotic, connotations of X-rays and heavier-than-air flight—technologies in which machines seemed to produce **magic**. Before launching the first science fiction magazine, *Amazing Stories*, in 1926, Hugo Gernsback edited *Radio News*, while Howard Garis's *Tom Swift and His Wireless Message* (1911) is a representative title from the popular Tom Swift series (written under house name "Victor Appleton"). "Radio" sometimes became a universal signifier for almost any technological adventure, as in Ralph Milne Farley's *The Radio Man* (1924), *The Radio Beasts* (1925), and *The Radio Planet* (1926), novels detailing the exploits of "radio genius" Miles Standish Cabot, who, "while experimenting with the wireless transmission of matter, had accidentally projected himself through space to the planet Venus." Television, on the other hand, remained a sideshow gimmick, although the ever-innovative Tom Swift did deal with a "Photo Telephone" (1914) and "Talking Pictures" (1928), and Gernsback provided New Yorkers in the year 2660 with a "Tele-Theater" in *Ralph 124C 41+: A Romance of the Year 2660* (1925).

By the 1950s, both radio and television were familiar devices reshaping the cultural landscape. This was not lost on science fiction writers interested in social criticism. Thus, television is a matter-of-fact presence in Frederik Pohl and C.M. Kornbluth's satire of the advertising industry, ***The Space Merchants***, while the **book**-burning **dystopia** of Ray Bradbury's ***Fahrenheit 451*** is a society of media saturation and constant television watchers (a theme echoed in Theodore Sturgeon's 1956 story "And Now the News"). The potential for broadcast media to violate, or at least alter the conception of, privacy is explored in Isaac Asimov's "Dreaming Is a Private Thing" (1955), which considers the possibilities of broadcasting **dreams**. Most famously, George Orwell's ***Nineteen Eighty-Four*** presented television not as a means of placating a passive citizenry but as an active instrument of government repression. Television also figured in films like *The Twonky* (1952), about a **robot** resembling a television that takes over a man's **home** (adapted from Henry Kuttner's 1942 story about a radio), while **aliens on Earth** in the film *This Island Earth* (1955) fetishize "Interocitors," elaborate televisions with special features like deadly rays.

From the 1960s onward, science fiction writers have presented increasingly sophisticated, often pessimistic, depictions of television as a cultural force. In Robert A. Heinlein's ***Stranger in a Strange Land***, the early strategies of wise recluse Jubal Harshaw for protecting the "Man from Mars" Valentine Michael Smith depend on worldwide instantaneous television news coverage; Smith's eventual martyrdom is carried on live TV, interrupted for commercials. John Brunner's *Stand on Zanzibar* employs an experimental narrative technique that, although borrowed from John Dos Passos's 1930s USA trilogy, uses the language and images of television to present a frantic, fragmented world. Other works associated with New Wave science fiction of the late 1960s were conscious of television, including J.G. Ballard's stories "The Assassination of John Fitzgerald Kennedy Considered as a Downhill Motor Race" (1967) and "Plan for the Assassination of Jacqueline Kennedy" (1966) (collected in *Love & Napalm: Export U.S.A.* [1970]), Michael Moorcock's Jerry Cornelius novels, beginning with *The Final Programme* (1968), and Norman Spinrad's *Bug Jack Barron* (1969). Spinrad's novel in particular, featuring a television talk-show host of questionable **ethics** battling an **evil** corporate mogul, is one of the most direct, and prescient, presentations of television's ability to not just reflect the world, but alter it.

Stories like Robert Sheckley's "The Prize of Peril" (1958) and Stephen King's *The Running Man* (1982) depict men being hunted while watched by television audiences. In D.G. Compton's *The Unsleeping Eye* (1974), the **death** of a middle-aged woman is captured by a reporter with TV cameras for eyes, to entertain an audience that has largely escaped death and suffering. In Algis Budrys's *Michaelmas* (1977), the title character is a TV newscaster who collaborates with intelligent **computer** software to deal with the world's problems. As science fiction writers during this period became increasingly thoughtful in considering television, stories dealing with radio generally presented the medium as a technological means to an end, particularly sending and receiving radio signals to contact alien **intelligence**, as in James Gunn's *The Listeners* (1972), Jack McDevitt's *The Hercules Text* (1986), and Carl Sagan's *Contact* (1985).

Around this time, television began to figure in **horror** films like *Poltergeist* (1982) and *The Ring* (2002) and fantasies like Tim Powers's *Earthquake Weather* (1987), where television is bizarrely employed in **divination**. In the 1990s, **cyberpunk** godfather William Gibson considered the by-now universal presence of television. The fortunes of Berry Rydell, protagonist of *Virtual Light* (1993) and *All Tomorrow's Parties* (1999), rise and fall after his appearance on the reality TV show *Cops in Trouble*, while Colin Laney, interpreter of information patterns in *Idoru* (1996), battles a television producer who sees her network's audience as a "vicious, lazy, profoundly ignorant, perpetually hungry organism."

Discussion

The charge that "science has caught up with science fiction" usually proves false. However, considering the degree to which radio and television have permeated and transformed the world, and the extremes of both content and presentation that are commonplace in both media, one wonders whether science fiction and fantasy can offer new scenarios and ideas on this topic. It will be particularly interesting to see if science fiction can once again keep one step ahead of the present.

Bibliography

Mike Ashley. "The Amazing Story: Part 1, The Twenties." *Amazing Stories*, 66 (January, 1992), 55–59.

Isaac Asimov, Martin H. Greenberg, and Charles G. Waugh, eds. *TV 2000*. New York: Fawcett, 1982.

Thomas W. Cooper. "Fictional 1984 and Factual 1984." Robert L. Savage, ed., *The Orwellian Moment*. Fayetteville: University of Arkansas Press, 1989, 83–108.

Deborah Elkin. "Hugo Gernsback's Ideas of Science and Fiction, 1915–26." *Fantasy Commentator*, 6 (Winter, 1989/1990), 246–258.

Eun-Mee Kim. "Utopian Images of New Technology." Will Wright, and Steven Kaplan, eds., *The Image of Technology in Literature, the Media and Society*. Pueblo, CO: Society for the Interdisciplinery Study of Social Imagery, 1994, 337–343.

Chris Morgan. "Three Hundred Years Hence." Morgan, *The Shape of Futures Past*. Exeter, England: Webb & Bower, 1980, 158–179.

Jose M. Mota. "Media, Messages, and Myths." George Slusser, Colin Greenland, and Eric S. Rabkin, eds., *Storm Warnings*. Carbondale: Southern Illinois University Press, 1987, 84–93.

Gary Westfahl. "From the Back of the Head to Beyond the Moon." Westfahl, *Science Fiction, Children's Literature, and Popular Culture*. Westport, CT: Greenwood Press, 2000, 49–68.

—*F. Brett Cox*

TEMPTRESS

∎

Overview

Few hazards for literary **heroes** are as dangerous as the temptress. Follow her and you are lost; spurn her and you gain an enemy. Especially prevalent in **mythology**, fantasies, **detective** fiction, and stories of **espionage**, the temptress uses **romance** and **sexuality** to manipulate men and vows **revenge** upon those who resist her. However, while once viewed as purely **evil**, the temptress has been reconsidered by feminists in a more positive light (see **Feminism**).

Survey

Traditionally, a temptress is a woman who lures a man to do evil for her. The man may give in, or resist. If he resists, she may destroy him, or become so charmed by his strength that she reforms. Mortal or goddess, a temptress' power is almost always sexual, and she is drawn towards strength. She seeks a powerful man solely for his power, as something to use for her own purposes.

The temptress operates using sexuality and lust, but may be reformed by **love**. More than an alluring siren, she consciously manipulates the hero through sexual promise. Goal oriented, she sees men as tools. In her extreme form as femme fatale, her charms make men do things against their nature. She is not only sexy, but dangerously seductive. It is purely a one-way relationship—hers.

Some temptresses simply wish destruction upon hapless heroes. The biblical Samson is ensnared by the temptress Delilah, whose sole goal is to deprive him of his great strength. Robert E. Howard's **Conan the Conqueror** chases the seductive Frost-Giant's daughter out of lust, whereas her goal is simply that he become food for her brothers. Poison Ivy, a **Batman** villainess, can chemically seduce any male with a poisonous kiss, and uses this talent for fun and profit.

Temptresses often feel that their only value is their body; thus being denied by a man means they are nothing. A denied and defeated temptress is often shown as a pitiful figure. The Sorceress Irene in Piers Anthony's *A Spell for Chameleon* is politically motivated to seduce just about every Magician-class male in the book simply to gain the throne. Broken in the end, she is redeemed only by the wishes of the dominant male.

Temptresses will use any tool at hand, though sex appeal is most common. However, in C.S. Lewis's *The Lion, the Witch and the Wardrobe*, the evil White Witch tempts Edmund to betray his siblings with a sweet treat. Her goal is the same—usurp the male's heroic path for her own purposes. When he **escapes** her control, her anger sets up her own downfall, which is a common end for unlucky temptresses.

Other temptresses are less power-seeking and decadently use their talents to relieve their own boredom. Goddesses are prone to this: from Aphrodite in the series *Hercules: The Legendary Journeys* and both Circe and Calypso in Homer's *Odyssey* (c. 750 BCE) to the Enchantress in Marvel's Thor comics, we see goddesses of enormous might relying almost solely on their sexual attraction to manipulate mortals for selfish ends (see **Gods and Goddesses**).

Even recognizing danger, heroes are prone to fall for temptresses. "If I did less than loathe her, I should love her," states the hero of George MacDonald's *Lilith*, as he alternates between being seduced and warring with the titular character. This pattern is also common in **vampire** and **Gothic** stories, where temptation frequently crosses gender lines and is epitomized the promise of Anne Rice's vampire Lestat to "drink from me and live forever" (see *Interview with the Vampire*).

Frequently temptresses may find the tables turned, and become ensnared by love (or admiration). Edgar Rice Burroughs's Tarzan is pursued by Queen La simply because he is powerful, yet in the end, despite his polite refusal, they manage to create a bona fide relationship (see *Tarzan of the Apes*). The villaineous Lady in Glen Cook's *The Black Company* (1984) and its sequels seduces even the cynical narrator, but she also becomes a temptress who, redeemed by love, keeps her power intact. In H. Rider Haggard's *She*, She-Who-Must-Be-Obeyed is an immortal white queen of an African **city** who is desirable and deadly (see **Africa**). Yet this powerful immortal falls in love with an English explorer she believes is the **reincarnation** of her ancient lover, and in the novel's sequels seems increasingly human, and increasingly sympathetic.

Discussion

Feminists may view temptresses not as amoral **villains**, but as women justifiably employing whatever means are available to achieve their goals in brutally patriarchal societies. Thus, the famous Egyptian pharoah Cleopatra (see **Egypt**) becomes not a wanton temptress using men for her own goals but a self-confident, goal-oriented woman. Morgan le Fay, the traditionally evil femme fatale of the Arthurian cycle, is presented more as an admirable defender of a paganism threatened by **Christianity** in Marion Zimmer Bradley's *The Mists of Avalon* (see **Arthur**). And in Margaret Atwood's *The Handmaid's Tale*, any woman who can breed is presumed to be a "temptress" and treated as such, reinforcing the Cleopatra-like situation wherein a virtuous and capable woman man be falsely deemed a temptress in order to disempower her. The temptress, in such reconsiderations, becomes both the antithesis and equivalent of the **Amazon**; each is a capable women, but one uses her sexuality to achieve external power, while the other denies her sexuality to wield external power.

Bibliography

Ruth Berman. "Sirens." Malcolm South, ed., *Mythical and Fabulous Creatures*. Westport, CT: Greenwood Press, 1987, 147–153.

Maureen Duffy. *The Erotic World of Faery*. 1972. New York: Avon Books, 1980.

Karen E.C. Fuog. "Imprisoned in the Phallic Oak." *Quondam et Futuris*, 1 (Spring, 1991), 73–88.

Kathryn M. Grossman. "Woman as Temptress." *Women's Studies*, 14 (1987), 135–146.

Elizabeth Massie. "Femmes Fatales?" Bill Munster, ed., *Discovering Dean Koontz*. San Bernardino, CA: Borgo Press, 1998, 152–167.

Rick McCollum. "The Frost-Giant's Daughter." James Van Hise, ed., *The Fantastic Worlds of Robert E. Howard*. Yucca Valley: James Van Hise, 1997, 126–133.

Helmut Nickel. "The Naked and the Best." *Arthuriana*, 9 (Fall, 1999), 81–96.

Bette Roberts. "The Mother Goddess in H. Rider Haggard's *She* and Anne Rice's *The Queen of the Damned*." James C. Holte, ed., *The Fantastic Vampire*. Westport, CT: Greenwood Press, 1997, 103–110.

—*Alex (Sandy) Antunes*

TERRAFORMING

Overview

Terraforming—the process of providing a harsh alien planet with an **Earth**-like environment—is in a sense "an ancient profession," as argued in Robert Reed's story "A Place with Shade" (1995), since "Making your world more habitable began on the Earth itself, with the first dancing fire that warmed its builder's cave." Today, as people contemplate how they are unintentionally transforming Earth's climate through global warming, it does not seem unrealistic that a future **humanity**, heeding the old impulse to improve its surroundings on a larger scale, might intentionally transform other planets to inhabit them. Settlements on alien planets that do not involve terraforming are discussed under **Planetary Colonies**, while efforts to transform humans so they can survive on inhospitable worlds are discussed under **Pantropy**.

Survey

The term "terraforming" was coined by Jack Williamson in his series of stories about **antimatter**, later collected as *Seetee Ship* (1951); however, a process of terraforming was earlier described in Olaf Stapledon's *Last and First Men*, wherein humans desperate to **escape** a doomed Earth devise a way to alter **Venus**'s atmosphere and climate in order to migrate there. In the face of increasing evidence that

Venus is indeed too hot and hellish for humans to visit, the planet became a favorite target for science fiction terraforming, in works ranging from Poul Anderson's "The Big Rain" (1955) and "Sister Planet" (1959) in the 1950s to Pamela Sargent's *Venus of Dreams* (1986) and *Venus of Shadows* (1988) in the 1980s. An embryonic effort to terraform Venus is also described in Frederik Pohl's *The Gateway Trip* (1990) (see **Gateway**).

Stories about terraforming Earth's other neighboring planet, **Mars,** were at first less common, given continuing optimism that its environment might be conducive to human colonization, but Arthur C. Clarke's *The Sands of Mars* (1951) is one early novel that anticipated its barrenness and addressed the problem by having **scientists** convert one of its moons into a miniature sun, leading to warmer temperatures and more oxygen in the atmosphere. A later film, ***Total Recall***, implausibly describes the instantaneous generation of a breathable Martian atmosphere. However, a definitive vision of how Mars might actually be gradually and painstakingly made habitable is presented in Kim Stanley Robinson's Martian trilogy, beginning with **Red Mars**. Beginning with the selection of the First 100 colonists (all scientists and engineers), and continuing through to the delicate and often turbulent procedures of climatic change, Robinson's texts address all aspects of the process: scientific, economic, political, and cultural. Interestingly, one major character expresses bitter opposition to terraforming Mars, arguing for preservation of the original Martian environment, leading to an eventual compromise that leaves Martian highlands as they are while making the rest of Mars resemble Earth.

Other than Mars and Venus, the large moons of Jupiter (see **Jupiter and the Outer Planets**) have proven the most popular terraforming goal, as considered in works like Anderson's *The Snows of Ganymede* (1955) and Gregory Benford's *Jupiter Project* (1975). At the conclusion of Clarke's *2010: Odyssey Two* (see ***2001: A Space Odyssey***), unseen aliens engage in a form of terraforming, turning Jupiter into a small sun and making the Jovian moons habitable for humans. Another familiar world occasionally subjected to science fiction terraforming is, surprisingly, Earth itself, envisioned in the future as having become inhospitable and hence requiring technological intervention to be restored to its original condition; such scenarios are explored in Hal Clement's *The Nitrogen Fix* (1980) and Williamson's *Terraforming Earth* (2001).

Moving beyond the Solar System, Frank Herbert describes a massive effort to change the climate of the planet Arrakis in *Children of Dune* (1976) (see **Dune**), and an extensive terraforming project on a distant world is the focus of David Gerrold's *Moonstar Odyssey* (1977). Visions of humanity's **far future** often depict terraforming as a common profession, with practitioners traveling from world to world to complete various projects, as in Jack Chalker's *The Web of the Chozen* (1978) and Reed's "A Place with Shade." Massive terraforming projects are also depicted in novels like C.J. Cherryh's *Cyteen* (1988) and Lois McMaster Bujold's *Komarr* (1997).

Discussion

Science fiction once imagined that nearby worlds like Venus and Mars might be habitable for humans without spacesuits, generating attractive stories about humans traveling to other worlds in the manner of immigrants coming to **America**. But we now know that life on other planets of the solar system would involve a perpetual existence under protective domes or in underground chambers. Terraforming is significant in recent science fiction because it solves this problem without violating scientific laws; if humans cannot travel to planets like Edgar Rice Burroughs's Barsoom (see *A Princess of Mars*), they can now construct them. This powerful urge to live safely on distant soil may someday be responsible for the greatest engineering achievements of our species.

Bibliography

Victor R. Baker. *The Channels of Mars*. Austin: University of Texas Press, 1982.

Martyn J. Fogg. *Terraforming*. Warrendale: SAE International, 1995.

Robert H. Haynes. "Ethics and Planetary Engineering." D. Macniven, ed., *Moral Expertise*. London and New York: Routledge, 1990, 161–183.

Sylvia Kelso. "Tales of Earth." *Foundation*, No. 78 (Spring, 2000), 34–43.

James Lovelock and Michael Allaby. *The Greening of Mars*. New York: St. Martin's, 1984.

Christopher P. McKay. "On Terraforming Mars." *Extrapolation*, 23 (Winter, 1982), 309–314.

Peter Nicholls, David Langford, and Brian Stableford. "Terraforming." Nicholls, Langford, and Stableford, *The Science in Science Fiction*. 1982. New York: Alfred A. Knopf, 1983, 28–29.

J.E. Oberg. *New Earths*. New York: New American Library, 1981.

Ernest J. Yanarella. "Tera/Terror-forming and Death Denial in Kim Stanley Robinson's Martian Stories and Mars Trilogy." *Foundation*, No. 89 (Autumn, 2003), 13–26.

—Tris Kerslake

THEATRE

■

How could she have believed such an artificial life as the theatre was suitable?

—Anne McCaffrey
"Prelude to a Crystal Song" (1974)

Overview

Generally, science fiction and fantasy have not fared well on the stage, but this has not prevented writers from frequently describing plays and actors in their stories. Related to live drama are other art forms and media—**art, fashion, music, television and radio, virtual reality**—discussed in other entries.

Survey

Plays are sometimes performed within narratives: plays being staged in the **far future** of Gene Wolfe's *The Book of the New Sun* and the **post-holocaust society** of Sheri S. Tepper's *The Gate to Women's Country* are both significant accompaniments to their novels' plots. Terry Pratchett's *Wyrd Sisters* (1988) concludes with a Discworld-skewed performance of William **Shakespeare**'s *Macbeth* (c. 1606) (see *The Colour of Magic*).

Fantasy and science fiction stories may also feature traveling troupes of actors as background characters, providing young **heroes** on **quests** with colorful companions and supportive surrogate **families**. Fantasies with such groups include Peter S. Beagle's *Giant Bones* (1997), Julia Gray's *The Dark Moon* (2000), Martha Wells's *Wheel of the Infinite* (2000), and S. D. Tower's *The Assassins of Tamurin* (2002). Margaret Weis and Aron Eisenberg's novella "The Traveling Players of Gilean" (2000) features a group of immortal actors with magical powers who were later the subject of an anthology of original stories edited by Weis and Tracy Hickman, *The Players of Gilean* (2003).

In science fiction stories about **space travel**, there also appear traveling theatrical troupes, moving from planet to planet to perform wherever they can, as in Christopher Stasheff's Starship Troupers novels, *A Company of Stars* (1992) and *We Open on Venus* (1994), and an episode of *Star Trek* "The Conscience of the King" (1967), in which a company of actors including a notorious criminal performs Shakespeare's *Hamlet* (c. 1606) for the crew of the *Enterprise*. Vonda N. McIntyre's *Star Trek* novel *Enterprise: The First Adventure* (1986) reveals that James Kirk's first mission was to transport a troupe of vaudeville performers. Describing actors of a different sort, Jack Vance's *Space Opera* (1965) relates the misadventures of a spacefaring opera company.

Stories about the acting profession in the future of **Earth** are generally depressing: Wolfe's "Seven American Nights" (1978) centers on a struggling theatre company in an **America** dominated by the Arab world, and in Walter M. Miller, Jr.'s "The Darfsteller" (1954), human actors are being replaced by **robot** "doll" simulacra.

Theatres of the past or present can be effective settings for mysterious or fantastic events. Three examples are Fritz Leiber's "Four Ghosts in Hamlet" (1965), wherein a company performing *Hamlet* learns that an actual ghost is apparently playing the part of the ghost of Hamlet's father (see **Ghosts and Hauntings**); Melissa Scott and Lisa A. Barnett's *Point of Dreams* (2002), involving a theatre company in a magical Renaissance city and a murder **mystery**; and Susan Cooper's *King of Shadows* (2001), where a boy playing Puck in a London production of Shakespeare's *A Midsummer Night's Dream* (c. 1594) is transported back in time to Renaissance England, where he plays the same part at Shakespeare's Globe Theatre (see **Time Travel**).

Occasionally, science fiction and fantasy stories focus on individual actors; one example is Robert A. Heinlein's *Double Star* (1956), wherein a down-and-out actor in the future is recruited to impersonate an important Martian politician and ultimately takes his place permanently (see **Mars; Politics**). And since Leiber was the son of a stage and film actor, he brings a persuasively professional perspective to his tale of a frail future actor living in a **space habitat** who visits Earth wearing an exoskeleton, *A Specter Is Haunting Texas* (1968), Alan Brennert's *Time and Chance* (1990) involves a Broadway actor who meets, and exchanges places with, his counterpart in a **parallel world** where he chose to not pursue an acting career and instead became a salesman, with a wife and **children**, living in suburbia. In addition, many heroes and **superheroes** of science fiction and fantasy are in a sense actors, since they maintain **secret identities** or carry out missions in **disguise**, but this is rarely their profession, an exception being *Superman*'s cousin Supergirl, who in comic books once worked as an actress on a soap opera.

Finally, some **alternate histories** include famous actors, like Geoff Ryman's *Was* (1992), which refashions the life of Judy Garland, and Kim Newman's surrealistic *The Night Mayor* (1988), featuring appearances by Humphrey Bogart, James Cagney, and other film stars (see **Surrealism**). Don Sakers's anthology *Carmen Miranda's Ghost Is Haunting Space Station Three* (1990), as the title suggests, offers stories about the Brazilian singer and actress. One idea exploited for **comedy** is that of transporting actors in a science fiction television series or film into a future world where they must actually function as heroes, which is the story line of the films *The Adventures of Captain Zoom in Outer Space* (1995) and *Galaxy Quest* (1999). The idea dates back to a 1976 story, Ruth Berman's "Visit to a Weird Planet Revisited," wherein actors from the original *Star Trek* series find themselves on the bridge of the real *Enterprise*.

Discussion

Theatre and actors are ideal vehicles for exploring questions of **identity** and the difference between appearance and reality, but science fiction and fantasy texts foregrounding the profession do not always address such issues, tending more to associate acting with mere **disguise** or trickery, as conveyed by the stage magician who fools rustic fundamentalists in Tepper's *The Gate to Women's Country*. Drama is also associated with the past, the assumption being that future **technology** like virtual reality will eliminate or marginalize the archaic practice of live theatre. Still, there remains a power and dignity in stage acting that can be effectively employed even in futuristic settings, as demonstrated by recurring uses of Shakespeare in various incarnations of *Star Trek*.

Bibliography

Gerald M. Adair. "Illuminating the Ghost Light." *Journal of the Fantastic in the Arts*, 12 (2002), 364–381.

Jerrold E. Hogle. "Stoker's Counterfeit Gothic." William Hughes and Andrew Smith, eds., *Bram Stoker*. New York: St. Martin's, 1998, 205–224.

Patrick D. Murphy, ed. *Staging the Impossible*. Westport, CT: Greenwood Press, 1992, 169–181.

Steven Shaviro. "Burroughs's Theater of Illusion." Jennie Skerl and Robin Lydenberg, eds., *William S. Burroughs at the Front*. Carbondale: Southern Illinois University Press, 1991, 197–207.

Jenny B. Taylor. *In the Secret Theatre of Home*. London: Routledge, 1988.

Jennifer A. Wagner-Lawlor. "The Play of Irony." *Utopian Studies*, 13 (2002), 114–134.

Ralph A. Willingham. *Science Fiction and the Theatre*. Westport, CT: Greenwood Press, 1994.

Kazuko Yamada. "SF and Theatre." *Foundation*, No. 44 (Winter, 1988/1989), 33–41.

—Lynne Lundquist

THEFT

■

Overview

Theft—illegally taking **money, gold and silver,** or other property from another person—should be regarded as **evil** and a matter of **crime and punishment,** with perpetrators ending up in **prison.** But unlike rape or murder, theft may be viewed as a relatively unimportant offense, perhaps justified in some cases, so thieves may figure in fantasy and science fiction only as minor **villains** or even as **heroes.** Seagoing thieves, or **pirates,** are discussed elsewhere.

Survey

Theft can be justified if it is done for a good cause. Robin Hood, after all, was considered a hero because he famously took from the rich and gave to the poor, as shown in the fantastic setting of the film *Time Bandits* (1981). Following the same logic, the Society of Thieves in the future world of Charles L. Harness's *The Paradox Men* (1953) escapes readers' disapproval because they steal only to raise money to buy people out of **slavery.** In J.R.R. Tolkien's *The Hobbit,* hero Bilbo Baggins is recruited by **dwarfs** as a "burglar," but his target is a sinister **dragon.**

Fantasy heroes may dabble in theft if they are perceived as poor but worthy folk stealing from wealthy people who possess more than they need; thievery can thus be viewed as a profession, just as honorable as any other profession. A fantasy thief matching this description is *The Thief of Bagdad* (1924), featured in Douglas Fairbanks's silent film, Achmed Abdullah's novelization (1924), and four remakes; a similar film, *The Thief of Damascus* (1951), draws upon legends of Sinbad and Ali Baba and the Forty Thieves. The hero of Terry Pratchett's *Thief of Time* (2001) begins as an **apprentice** in Discworld's Thieves' Guild (see *The Colour of Magic*).

Beloved thieves include Fritz Leiber's Fafhrd and the Grey Mouser, who first appeared in "Two Sought Adventure" (1939), and Harry Harrison's starfaring *The Stainless Steel Rat* (1961); these characters carried on in numerous other stories. The young hero of the animated film *Aladdin* (1992) works as a thief before obtaining his **magic** lamp, just as Ender's friend Bean belongs to a band of pickpockets before being recruited to train as a soldier, as recounted in *Ender's Shadow* (1999) (see *Ender's Game*). Robert Lynn Asprin's anthology *Thieves' World* (1979) introduced the titular **shared world,** and various authors were soon writing **sword and sorcery** tales involving likable criminals who operate in or around the fantasy **city** of Sanctuary; along with several anthologies, Andrew J. Offutt wrote a novel featuring one of its most skillful thieves, *Shadowspawn* (1987). A science fiction story about a similarly thief-ridden environment is Jack Vance's "The King of Thieves" (1949), in which interstellar traveler Magnus Ridolph finds himself in a **planetary colony** where thievery is so common that citizens must carry around all their possessions at all times.

The scenario of sympathetic small-time thieves preying upon the rich occurs in New Wave and **cyberpunk** stories about the **near future.** Samuel R. Delany's "Time Considered as a Helix of Semi-Precious Stones" (1968) involves a member of the criminal underground who travels through the solar system carrying out his business, while William Gibson's "Burning Chrome" (1982) features shabby **computer** "cowboys" who jack into **cyberspace** and use a stolen program to loot a virtual storehouse containing a fortune.

Thieves may be recruited by government officials to perform worthwhile deeds, which is essentially what happens to Case in Gibson's *Neuromancer*. A fantasy story along these lines is Megan Whalen Turner's *The Thief* (1996), involving a king who hires a thief to retrieve a **treasure**.

Master thieves, however, are more frequently villains. Enemies in James Bond movies (see *Doctor No*; **Espionage; Technothrillers**) may plan spectacular acts of theft, like the man named *Goldfinger* (1964) who plans to steal all the gold from Fort Knox. **Superheroes** often oppose thieves: in *Batman*, the Caped Crusader tries to stop the Joker from carrying out major robberies, and in *Superman III* (1983), the Man of Steel struggles against a greedy corporate tycoon (see **Superman**).

Portentous cases of theft in science fiction and fantasy include the first film version of *Frankenstein*, which embellished Mary Shelley's story by suggesting that the accidental theft of the wrong brain for use in his experiment is what turned Frankenstein's creation into a **monster**, and *It's a Wonderful Life*, where the evil Mr. Potter finds himself fortuitously able to steal $8000 from George Bailey's bank, threatening the kindly man with disgraceful financial ruin and imprisonment. Various sorts of unusual thefts are observed: Dr. Seuss's *How the Grinch Stole Christmas* (1957) involves a monster who steals a town's **Christmas gifts** and decorations in an attempt to dampen their holiday spirit; in an episode of *The Twilight Zone*, "The Rip Van Winkle Caper" (1960), four thieves go into hibernation after stealing a large amount of gold, believing it is the perfect way to escape punishment, but when they awaken one hundred years later, they ironically discover that gold is now considered worthless; in Donald Moffitt's *The Jupiter Theft* (1977), mysterious **aliens in space** approaching **Earth** literally seize the planet Jupiter (see **Jupiter and the Outer Planets**); in Harry Harrison and Marvin Minsky's *The Turing Option* (1992), a **scientist** about to perfect an artificial intelligence (see **Computers**) has his research stolen; and in Steven Gould's *Jumper* (1992), an alienated young man becomes an effective thief by using his power of **teleportation**.

Discussion

Theft is an activity that benefits its recipients and harms its victims; how writers and readers regard a theft, then, depends upon whether they identify with the robber or the person being robbed. And, since thieves are usually poor and their targets are usually rich, a form of literature that truly sympathizes with the underdog should logically look favorably upon thieves. If this argument is accepted, then a genre's attitude toward theft might be regarded as a measurement of its social conscience.

Bibliography

Douglas Barbour. "Multiplex Misdemeanors." *Khatru*, 2 (May, 1975), 21–24, 60.

Miriam Allen DeFord, ed. *Space, Time and Crime*. New York: Paperback Library, 1964.

William W. Goodson, Jr. "The Many Adventures of Robin Hood." *Starlog*, No. 166 (May, 1991), 35–39, 76.

Lisa Hopkins. "Bilbo Baggins as a Burglar." *Inklings*, 10 (1992), 93–102.

David G. Mead. "Signs of Crime." *Extrapolation*, 28 (Summer, 1987), 140–147.

Anita Moss. "Crime and Punishment, Or Development, in Fairy Tales and Fantasy." *Mythlore*, 8 (Spring, 1981), 26–28.

Terry Pratchett and Stephen Briggs. *Discworld Thieves' Guild Yearbook and Diary 2002.* London: Gollancz, 2002.

Robert J. Sawyer and David Skene-Melvin, eds. *Crossing the Line*. East Lawrencetown, Nova Scotia: Pottersfield Press, 1998.

—*Gary Westfahl*

THRESHOLD

The fact is that thresholds exist through-out reality, and that things on their far sides are altogether different from things on their hither sides.

—Poul Anderson
"The Saturn Game" (1981)

Overview

A general trope for passage or change, thresholds are fundamental elements of **fables, fairy tales, mythology,** and **religion,** as documented by Arnold Van Gennep, Vladimir Propp, and Joseph Campbell. An umbrella term with many meanings, "threshold" can name a doorsill, suggest a psychological limit, or identify a condition called *liminality*: a state precisely on the verge of something else—spatially, temporally, or emotionally.

Survey

Three kinds of thresholds overlap: physical, **psychological,** and metaphorical. Physical thresholds include gates or portals, but similar structures also work: tunnels, holes, walls, or **mountains. Water** may be bridged or crossed by boat (like the river Styx in the underworld) though traversing **fire** can be difficult.

Psychological thresholds concern the hero's mind. **Psychology** designates perceptual lines as thresholds, so a stimulus (a sound, for example) beneath conscious perception is called subliminal. Psychological portals include **dreams** (see *Brazil*), **sleep** (Washington Irving's "Rip Van Winkle" [1819]), waking up (see *The Matrix*), psychosis (perhaps *12 Monkeys* [1995]), or states like hypnotic trance or fever's fugue (see **Hypnotism**)—or even a sharp bonk on the head (see *The Wizard of Oz*). Being poised on the threshold creates considerable **anxiety** or trauma.

Metaphorical thresholds are harder to pin down. For Norse **heroes** of Asgard, the threshold was **death,** and indeed sometimes the gate opens only one way, as a **metamorphosis** into permanent **exile.** Farah Mendlesohn argues that even when there is no literal portal, **quest** fantasy (such as J.R.R. Tolkien's *The Lord of the*

Rings) operates in a similar manner, though here through narrative strategies like point of view or diction, which can also represent this sort of phase transition.

To illustrate how types of thresholds inextricably overlap, consider doors—both physical sites and metaphorical emblems of **ritual** transformation (Van Gennep calls them "rites of preparation"). Since doors mark a physical **borderland** between familiar and alien (or in the case of religious buildings, between sacred and profane), they have a double articulation: they provide passage both *into* and *out of*, simultaneously boundaries and **escapes**. Roman mythology understood this uncanny significance: doors are secured by Janus, the god who looks both ways. At some point, all heroes must pass through a doorway and frequently must pass a threshold guardian—a human, beast (**dragon**, sphinx, snake), or deity. Sometimes ceremonies must be performed, ordeals endured, **magic** incantations recited. Everything beyond the portal is physically distinct: it may be a night world (see **Darkness**), **parallel world**, or another **time**; journeying beyond the gate requires a guide, whether it is a wise **wizard** or an ignorant **youth**.

Lewis Carroll's *Through the Looking Glass* (1871) (see *Alice's Adventures in Wonderland*) and C.S. Lewis's *The Lion, the Witch and the Wardrobe* contain famous examples of literal thresholds. Carroll's portal transits through a **mirror**, while Lewis puts his inside the wardrobe, an image repeated in *Time Bandits* (1981) and Philip Pullman's *The Golden Compass* (1995). Some portals are invisible to all but initiates, like train station platform $9^3/4$ in J.K. Rowling's Harry Potter books (see *Harry Potter and the Sorcerer's Stone*). Portals may be found by discriminating **perception**, as in Douglas Adams's *The Long, Dark Tea-Time of the Soul* (1988), where Dirk Gently finds his way to Valhalla, the hall of 540 doors.

Science fiction portals transport people through spacetime (see Dan Simmons's *Hyperion*; *Stargate*). The *Star Trek* universe provides multiple examples: in the original series ("City on the Edge of Forever" [1967]); in *Star Trek: The Next Generation* (the Iconian windows of "Contagion" [1989]); in *Star Trek: Deep Space Nine* (the wormhole); and in *Star Trek: Voyager* and *Star Trek: Enterprise* (where the *transdimensional subspace rift* is a topos).

Thresholds may require keys: devices can be magical (Roger Zelazny's trumps in *Nine Princes in Amber* [1970], Harry Potter's "Portkey"), technological (the feathers in Jeff Noon's *Vurt* [1995], which open to **virtual reality**), conceptual (the breakthrough in theoretical **physics** that permits Olympians to move **Mars** in Greg Bear's *Moving Mars* [1993]), or a combination of the three (the subtle knife in Pullman's *The Golden Compass* and its sequels). Occasionally, the portal device may be an elaborate machine, like the time-traveling police box in *Doctor Who* or quantum universe phone booth in Michael Crichton's *Timeline* (1999) (see **Time Travel**).

Discussion

Threshold liminality is more complicated, presaging a coming change (see **Progress**), posing us on the verge of revolution. Many novels are situated entirely on or against such thresholds, such as the "cultural fugue" of Samuel R. Delany's *Stars in My Pocket Like Grains of Sand* (1984) or the cultural crisis of the Festival in Charles Stross's *Singularity Sky* (2003). In some texts the line demarcating separate eras is breached (Caleb Carr's *Killing Time* [2000]), while in others the threshold passes but we cannot understand its meaning (the unification of Wintermute and Neuromancer in William Gibson's *Neuromancer*).

In science fiction, the threshold delimits or sometimes is the *novum*; in fantasy, the threshold is a transitional space distinguishing the fantasy world from the normal world against which it is juxtaposed. In science fiction, portals generally have no metaphorical resonance; in fantasy, a mere wardrobe can suggest deep psychological interiors, intimate isolation from the outside world, and so become a powerful figure of creative imagination (what Bachelard calls "intimate immensity"). Rather than minor events of the narrative, these thresholds identify moments pivotal to plot and emotional tone (**anxiety**, hope, curiosity, dread).

The crude shocks of **horror** stories notwithstanding, while most thresholds and portals are locked, some actually leak (Specters in Pullman's *The Subtle Knife* [1998], snakes in Noon's *Vurt*) and so suggest reasons to worry.

Bibliography

Gaston Bachelard. *The Poetics of Space*. 1958. Trans. Maria Jolas. Boston: Beacon, 1969.

John Hammond. "Images of the Door in *Tono-Bungay*." *The Wellsian*, No. 21 (Winter, 1998), 18–21.

Farah Mendlesohn. "Toward a Taxonomy of Fantasy." *Journal of the Fantastic in the Arts*, 13 (2002), 169–183.

Frank P. Riga. "From Time to Eternity." Cynthia Marshall, ed., *Essays on C.S. Lewis and George MacDonald*. Lewiston, NY: Edwiin Mellen, 1991, 83–100.

Philip C. Sutton, ed. *Betwixt-and-Between*. Madrid: Gateway, 2002.

Arnold Van Gennep. *The Rites of Passage*. 1908. Trans. Monika B. Vizedom and Gabrielle L. Caffee. Chicago: University of Chicago Press, 1960.

Jeffrey M. Wallman. "Flight of Passage." Gary Westfahl, ed., *Space and Beyond*. Westport, CT: Greenwood Press, 2000, 95–100.

Michael Ward. "Through the Wardrobe." *Seven: An Anglo-American Literary Review*, 15 (1998), 55–71.

—Neil Easterbrook

TIGERS

See Lions and Tigers

TIME

Time is the funniest thing, sir. It ties a man in knots.

—Clifford D. Simak
Time and Again (1952)

Overview

Science fiction is not, despite popular preconceptions, all about the future, but certainly arises from timescapes opened up by Victorian scholars like Charles Lyell and Charles Darwin. While fiction set in a future appeared late—there are few examples before the eighteenth century—by the end of the nineteenth century the idea of extrapolating social trends into a future took strong root in unlikely places. Among the explorations of post-Darwinian scientific ideas in Lewis Carroll's *Sylvie and Bruno* (1889) and its sequel (1893) are speculations about the flow of time and the effects of stopping or even reversing it.

Survey

H.G. Wells's **The Time Machine**, however, popularized a new subgenre of science fiction (see **Time Travel; Far Future**). Beginning with a discussion on the nature of time, it ends on a dying **Earth** far in the future. Such an ending opened up yet another subgenre, of eschatological fiction at the end of **history** (see **Eschatology**): William Hope Hodgson's *The House on the Borderland* (1908) took its subject on a mental voyage reminiscent of Wells's, transformed into **Gothic** modes. The same author's *The Night Land* (1912), despite its linguistic trappings of fantasy, is a more science-fictional image of beleaguered **humanity** surrounded by **monsters**. Jack Vance's *The Dying Earth* (1950), like Gene Wolfe's **The Book of the New Sun**, fuses science fiction and fantasy modes. Wolfe ingeniously expresses a sense of forgotten history by incorporating archaic words into his narrative.

Other writers construct a detailed "future history." Olaf Stapledon shows us the fate of eighteen separate species of humanity, giving a sense of scale through the use of ever-increasing time-lines (see **Last and First Men**). Robert A. Heinlein creates a more mosaic effect through stories collected in **The Past Through Tomorrow**. Heinlein is also responsible for some of the more ingenious stories about the paradoxical effects of time travel. "By His Bootstraps" (1941) exploits the "loop" effect of time travel and "'All You Zombies—'" (1959) creates a character who, through time travel, becomes his own parents.

Post-Wellsian developments in ideas about the nature of time allowed fictions which explored, as thought experiments, the idea that history could be diverted, blocked, or in some way changed. Ray Bradbury's "A Sound of Thunder" (1952) or Jack Williamson's *The Legion of Time* (1938), for example, develop these aspects of time (see **Alternate History**). *La Jetée* and its remake, *12 Monkeys* (1995), question both the idea of time travel itself, which appears a subjective experience, and the traveler's ability to change the course of events: all he has done is to replay his childhood **memories** from another viewpoint. Realms from different eras of time are accidentally or deliberately juxtaposed in Murray Leinster's "Sidewise in Time" (1934) and Fred Hoyle's *October the First Is Too Late* (1966). In the film *Groundhog Day* (1993), the **hero** is trapped in an endless loop, constantly reliving the same day. Gregory Benford explores the theoretics of temporal **communication** in *Timescape*, and Stephen Baxter's *The Time Ships* (1995), an authorized sequel to Wells's classic, places his story in the context of new theories of time.

In fantasy, time often underlies the story as nostalgia for the past, not anticipation of the future. J.R.R. Tolkien's **The Lord of the Rings** is about the *passing* of time through Age after catastrophic Age. Lord Dunsany's **The King of Elfland's Daughter** observes time as an eternal oceanic present. Time travel can appear without the mechanics of time machines (see **Timeslips**), but in both fantasy and science fiction deeper explorations of the nature of time appear. James Blish's "Common Time" (1953) shows the effect of faster-than-light travel on the subjective experience of time. His Cities in Flight sequence, beginning with *Earthman, Come Home* (1955), concludes with the end of our universe and the beginning of another. Stapledon's *Star Maker* both shows us another journey through meta-history and explores, in its last section, the idea of universes developing with different dimensional constants. One even reverses time: a concept that has fascinated a number of writers, appearing in Philip K. Dick's *Counter-Clock World* (1967), Brian W. Aldiss's *Cryptozoic* (1966), and Martin Amis's *Time's Arrow* (1991).

Discussion

It is arguable that science fiction, for which the main premise is the idea of change or difference, could not exist without a sense of collective and *secular* time. Put another way, whereas fictions focusing on changes in an individual's life in our present day, or evoking conventionally religious eschatological scenes of afterlives and judgments, are not usually science fiction, fictions exploring the potential of groups and species suggested by the gulfs of past and future usually are. The paradoxes of time—do *we* move in time, or does *it* move by us? Does it exist or is it merely an **illusion** of our limited **perception**?—are puzzles that exercise both physicists and philosophers (see **Physics; Philosophy**). Significantly, many of the thought-experiments they use to consider them, like the oft-told story of individuals estranged from their present by relativistic effects (see Joe Haldeman's **The Forever War**), are condensed science fiction stories fleshed out in science fiction texts.

Bibliography

K.V. Bailey. "Time Scales and Culture Cycles in Olaf Stapledon." *Foundation*, No. 46 (Winter, 1989), 27–39.

Russell Blackford. "Time Travel, Time Scapes, and 'Timescape.'" *New York Review of Science Fiction*, No. 144 (August, 2000), 8–15.

Boris Eizykman. "Temporality in Science Fiction Narrative." *Science-Fiction Studies*, 35 (March, 1985), 66–87.

Mark Kotani. "Time Paradox Considered as an Ideological Flux." *Science Fiction Eye*, No. 13 (Spring, 1994), 86–89.

Robert M. Philmus. "Wells and Borges and the Labyrinths of Time." *Science-Fiction Studies*, 4 (Fall, 1974), 237–248.

W.M.S. Russell. "Time Before and After *The Time Machine*." *Foundation*, No. 65 (Autumn, 1995), 24–40.

———. "Time in Folklore and Science Fiction." *Foundation*, No. 43 (Summer, 1988), 5–24.

Susan Stone-Blackburn. "Science and Humanism in Gregory Benford's *Timescape*." *Science-Fiction Studies*, 46 (November, 1988), 295–311.

Gary Westfahl, George Slusser and David Leiby, eds. *Worlds Enough and Time.* Westport, CT: Greenwood Press, 2002.

—Andy Sawyer

TIME TRAVEL

*John Albion was/is/will be living/dying/
dead; sucked into the dead/dying void.
John Albion had been/is/will be sitting in
the warmth of her home and talking of
something very small, something very
alien, something very much in his bones
which has/is/will be killed/killing him.
Conjugate the tenses of time travel.*

—Marta Randall
"Secret Rider" (1976)

Overview

People who fall asleep and wake in another time, whether it is Washington Irving's
"Rip Van Winkle" (1819) traveling forward twenty years or Mark Twain's *A Connecticut Yankee in King Arthur's Court* travelling back several centuries, have been
commonplace in fantastic literature (see **Sleep; Suspended Animation and Cryonics**).
Science fiction's great **invention** is the time machine, a device allowing travelers to
control their journeys through the fourth **dimension**. With this invention science fiction opened up vast new territory, from the Big Bang to the end of **time** and beyond,
in which stories could legitimately be set. Further, it introduced **history** as a science
that could be tested and **explored** like any other. Movements through time in fantasy are discussed as **Timeslips**.

Survey

For once one easily sees where a science fiction device has its origin: H.G. Wells's
The Time Machine. Though only vaguely described, the machine was at the core of
Wells's story, allowing him to make satirical comments about the **evolution** of Victorian society—the **class system** develops into racial differences between the Eloi
and the Morlocks (see **Satire**)—while projecting Darwinian evolution on toward the
death of **Earth** in the final haunting vision of the terminal beach (see **Eschatology**).
It is worth noting two radical developments from Wells's original story. In *The Space
Machine* (1976) Christopher Priest notes that time travel equates with **space travel**:
his time travelers end up traveling to **Mars**, and *The Time Machine* turns into
Wells's *The War of the Worlds*. In *The Time Ships* (1995), Stephen Baxter takes
Wells's Time Traveller through a series of adventures in the **near future**, **far future**,
and **alternate histories** before going to the very end of time and out again into a new
universe. Most of the writers who followed Wells, however, have preferred to create more conventional stories like Ronald Wright's *A Scientific Romance* (1997),
which resolves into a doomed **love** story set in a romantically overgrown and
depopulated future.

In one significant way, Wells himself was conventional in his invention: his traveler moved forward in time. Successors quickly realized that given a vehicle to move through time it was more interesting to travel into the past. Sometimes, as in Poul Anderson's "The Man Who Came Early" (1956), the time traveler is defeated by the guile or outright cruelty of the past. Like Twain's Connecticut Yankee, however, these were more often stories of contemporary know-how getting the better of historical ignorance, or else tales of simple historical tourism. There are, for example, numerous stories of traveling back to witness the crucifixion, notably Garry Kilworth's "Let's Go to Golgotha!" (1975) in which all the people watching Christ die are time-traveling tourists. A caustic take on the notion is provided by John Kessel in *Corrupting Dr. Nice* (1997), in which people of first-century Jerusalem are happily corrupted by twenty-first century commercialism.

The television series **Doctor Who** began as an educational program in which the kindly doctor escorted us on journeys back to significant moments in history. This idea that time travel allows us to enjoy the **romance** of the past has been a persistent characteristic of such stories. It is the basis, for instance, of the first **Back to the Future** film. Perhaps the finest example of this approach is Jack Finney's *Time and Again* (1970)—the time traveler like the author himself clearly falling in **love** with the New York of the 1880s, which he evokes with contemporary photographs and illustrations within the text. This was echoed by Peter Delacorte's *Time on my Hands* (1997), which also uses contemporary photographs to recreate Hollywood on the eve of World War II.

That Delacorte's time traveler is tempted to kill Ronald Reagan while he was still a small-time actor illustrates what would quickly become one of the most intriguing features of the time travel story, the time paradox. Traditionally described as asking what would happen if you went back in time and killed your own grandfather, most of these intellectually fascinating **puzzles** have been more subtle than that. Prime examples include Ray Bradbury's "A Sound of Thunder" (1952), in which a visitor to the age of **dinosaurs** accidentally steps on a butterfly and changes the whole of human history, and Ward Moore's *Bring the Jubilee*, in which a traveler from an alternate history in which the South won the Civil War accidentally changes the result of the Battle of Gettysburg so that history as we know it ends up happening. Time travelers intentionally or accidentally changing history are common in alternate history stories, so much so that a whole strand of stories, like Poul Anderson's Time Patrol series beginning with *Guardians of Time* (1960), John Brunner's *Times Without Number* (1969), and J.R. Dunn's *Days of Cain* (1997), feature time police whose role is to prevent changes in history. The idea of traveling in time to change history has been perhaps most successfully worked out in William Tenn's "Brooklyn Project" (1948) and R.A. Lafferty's "Thus We Frustrate Charlemagne" (1967), in which those within history cannot notice that their efforts have indeed changed the world around them.

Discussion

The time machine allows not movement in time (we already live in time, and a novelist has always been able to set a story in any future or past era), but transposition in time. It has introduced to science fiction the facility of anachronism, of looking at any one period through alien eyes. As such, it may be the most archetypal device in the genre.

Bibliography

Stephen Baxter. "Wild Extravagant Theories." *Vector*, No. 188 (August, 1996), 14–20.

Gregory Benford. "Time and *Timescape*." *Science-Fiction Studies*, 20 (July, 1993), 184–190.

Paul A. Carter. "The Paradoxes of Time Travel." Jesse G. Cunningham, ed., *Science Fiction*. San Diego, CA: Greenhaven Press, 2002, 118–130.

Bud Foote. *The Connecticut Yankee in the Twentieth Century*. Westport, CT: Greenwood Press, 1991.

Gilbert Fulmer. "Time Travel, Determinism, and Fatalism." *Philosophical Speculations in Science Fiction and Fantasy*, 1 (March, 1981), 41–47.

Paul J. Nahin. *Time Machines*. Second Edition. New York: American Institute of Physics, 1999.

Larry Niven. "The Theory and Practice of Time Travel." Niven, *All the Myriad Ways*. New York: Ballantine, 1971, 110–123.

George Slusser, Patrick Parrinder, and Danièle Chatelain, eds. *H.G. Wells's Perennial Time Machine*. Athens: University of Georgia Press, 2001.

Gary Westfahl, George Slusser, and David Leiby, eds. *Worlds Enough and Time*. Westport, CT: Greenwood Press, 2002.

—Paul Kincaid

TIMEPIECES

See Clocks and Timepieces

TIMESLIPS

Overview

A timeslip occurs when a person inadvertently, and acausally, slides from one era into another, almost always into a past era. The transition can be corporeal, but commonly only the consciousness takes the journey, either seeing past events (see **Perception**) or temporarily taking **possession** of the body of someone of that era. Generally protagonists returns to their starting points but a frequent device is that, after repeated timeslips, the "traveler" chooses to remain in the other period. Generally there is an emotional or psychological connection of some kind between the character and the earlier time—most often **love**, as when a character falls in love with someone long dead who is seen in a photograph. Unsurprisingly, timeslips are a staple of the subgenre of **romance** fiction called the Paranormal Romance, exemplified by Diana Gabaldson's *Outlander* (1991) and its sequels. Scientific **time travel** is discussed elsewhere.

Survey

There are accounts of timeslips occurring outside fiction. The best-known is probably the experience of two Englishwomen, Eleanor Jourdain and Charlotte Moberly
who, while visiting Versailles in 1901, apparently timeslipped back to 1789 and wit-
nessed scenes prior to the fall of the French monarchy; in 1911 they published an
account of their experience as the book *An Adventure*. Whether this was an actual
event, a misunderstanding, or a fabrication is irrelevant to the appeal the tale holds
for the fantasist: the possibility of spontaneously slipping into a previous time.

A fine example of the orthodox timeslip story is Daphne du Maurier's *The
House on the Strand* (1969). Through use of a **drug**, a man is mentally transported
back to fourteenth-century Cornwall, possessing the body of another man there;
repeated journeys make the fourteenth century become more real to the protagonist
than the twentieth, especially after he falls in love there. Love powers other timeslip
fantasies like David Lindsay's *The Haunted Woman* (1922), Margaret Irwin's *Still
She Wished for Company* (1924), Robert Nathan's *Portrait of Jennie* (1940) (filmed
in 1948), Jack Finney's *Time and Again* (1970), and Richard Matheson's *Bid Time
Return* (1975) (filmed in 1980 as *Somewhere in Time*). A good instance of spontaneous timeslip occurs in the film **Field of Dreams**, when Ray Kinsella goes back
some sixteen years to speak to a man who is dead by Ray's own present day;
whether the timeslip is corporeal or perceptual in nature is left moot. This illustrates
the occasional fictional explanation of ghosts as forward timeslips (see **Ghosts and
Hauntings**).

A variant of the quasi-possession theme is offered by the idea that the person
possessed in the past may be a younger version of the character himself or herself.
The protagonist of the film *The Butterfly Effect* (2004) discovers he can timeslip
back to key moments of trauma in his trauma-riddled life and change things for the
better. Among other examples of the trope are J.M. Barrie's *Dear Brutus* (1922) and
Thomas Berger's *Changing the Past* (1989). A variation of this device involves a protagonist who is blessed or cursed to live, with full **memory**, through versions of the
same time, each time attempting to sort out what went wrong with it and **escape** the
loop. A prominent example is the film *Groundhog Day* (1993), supposedly based
without credit on Richard A. Lupoff's "12:01 P.M." (1973); based directly on that
story is the more science-fictional and arguably better television film *12:01* (1993).
A more elaborate treatment of this idea is Ken Grimwood's *Replay* (1986), whose
protagonist relives his life multiple times from the age of 18 to his death at age 43.

In "He Walked Around the Horses" (1948), H. Beam Piper offers a sideways
timeslip into an **alternate history** to explain a celebrated historical mystery: the 1809
disappearance in Perleburg of the British envoy Benjamin Bathurst, who "walked
around the horses" at an inn and was never seen again. Aside from the popular
Paranormal Romance, another cross-genre mode is the timeslip **detective mystery**.
John Dickson Carr tried two of these under his own name—*The Devil in Velvet*
(1951) and *Fire, Burn!* (1957)—and one as Carter Dickson, *Fear Is the Same*
(1956), but the gimmick has been little repeated, although some writers come close
in detections involving two timelines, like Josephine Tey's *The Daughter of Time*
(1951) and Christopher Fowler's *Full Dark House* (2004). Timeslips are also common occurrences in **children**'s fantasies, two examples being Philippa Pearce's *Tom's
Midnight Garden* (1958) and Penelope Farmer's *Charlotte Sometimes* (1969).

Discussion

Timeslips, primarily a trope of fantasy, are occasionally found in science fiction, where a "scientific" explanation is implicit even if not presented. An example would be the film *Planet of the Apes*, whose protagonist does not realize that he has gone millennia into the future; knowing that he traveled in a spaceship, audiences assume that he has moved through **hyperspace** or a "space warp" of some kind, though nothing is said to explain his journey.

Related to timeslip stories are those in which a character enters an alternate reality—which may be Fairyland (see **Fairies**) but which may equally well be not—and spends a long time there, only to discover on return that little or no time has passed in the "real" world (or that the converse has happened); a typical example of this conceit occurs in C.S. Lewis's *The Lion, the Witch and the Wardrobe*.

Bibliography

John Clute. "Grail, Groundhog, Godgame." *Journal of the Fantastic in the Arts*, 10 (2000), 330–338.

Joan Forman. *Mask of Time*. London: Corgi, 1981.

Paul Horwich. *Asymmetries in Time*. Cambridge: MIT Press, 1987.

George L. Kline. "'Present', 'Past', and 'Future' as Categorical Terms, and the 'Fallacy of the Actual Future.'" *Review of Metaphysics*, 40 (December, 1986), 215–235.

Erica Obey. "Tall, Dark, and a Long Time Dead." Gary Westfahl, George Slusser, and David Leiby, eds., *Worlds Enough and Time*. Westport, CT: Greenwood Press, 2002, 157–165.

Lee Tobin-McClain. "Paranormal Romance." *Journal of the Fantastic in the Arts*, 11 (2000), 294–306.

Colin Wilson and John Grant, eds. *The Book of Time*. Newton Abbot: Westbridge, 1980.

Colin Wilson and John Grant, eds. *The Directory of Possibilities*. Exeter: Webb & Bower, 1981.

—John Grant

TORTURE

Overview

Systematic infliction of **pain** may actually be ineffective as a means of extracting truth, but fictional torture allows **heroes** to prove **courage** and endurance—or to yield with reduced **guilt and responsibility**. Its use by **villains** or oppressive **religions** and **governance systems** provides a convenient indicator of **evil**.

Survey

Dark Lords and other evil forces characteristically employ torture, from Sauron in J.R.R. Tolkien's *The Lord of the Rings* to various opponents of James Bond (see *Doctor No*). Examples appear in Geoff Ryman's *The Warrior who Carried Life* (1985) and Terry Goodkind's *Wizard's First Rule* (1994). Many fantasy heroes are motivated by **revenge** for needless torture of family and friends. A puppet villain possessed by **Satan** in C.S. Lewis's *Perelandra* (1943) (see *Out of the Silent Planet*) takes pleasure in torturing small creatures.

Crime and punishment often involves torture. Offenders in **fairy tales** are routinely consumed by **fire** or made to dance in red-hot shoes. **Sin,** according to many religions, leads to torment in **Hell,** most famously anatomized in Dante's *Inferno* (c. 1306–1321). Damned souls in James Branch Cabell's *Jurgen* demand Hell's tortures as a measure of their villainous importance. Torture was integral to the law of old **China,** as reflected in Ernest Bramah's *The Wallet of Kai Lung* (1900) and its sequels and Barry Hughart's *Bridge of Birds* (1984). In J.K. Rowling's fifth Harry Potter book, *Harry Potter and the Order of the Phoenix* (2003) (see **Harry Potter and the Sorcerer's Stone**), the minor school punishment of writing lines becomes a torture that draws **blood.**

Decadence often links torture with **sexuality,** notably in the writings of the Marquis de Sade, whose influence appears in the hideously inverted **utopia** of Octave Mirbeau's *Torture Garden* (1899). Sadistic torture forms the basis of a future society in Laurence M. Janifer's *You Sane Men* (1965).

Gene Wolfe's **The Book of the New Sun** imagines its Guild of Torturers in elaborate detail, including **rituals** and self-justifying **philosophy.** One of this Guild's many torture machines is recognizably that of Franz Kafka's "In the Penal Colony" (1919), designed to scarify the victim's flesh with an elaborately embellished description of his crime. Terry Pratchett highlights the banality of evil in *Small Gods* (1992), where Inquisition torturers drink coffee from mugs labelled "World's Greatest Daddy" (see **The Colour of Magic**).

Science fiction **technology** allows new forms of torture. Gaston Leroux's *The Phantom of the Opera* (1910) oddly anticipates **virtual reality** with its ordeal by heat and thirst in a simulated desert; the antihero of Alfred Bester's **The Stars My Destination** suffers similarly unreal agonies. Conversely, loss of **perception** in a sensory deprivation tank is the ultimate spirit-breaker in Frederik Pohl's and C.M. Kornbluth's "The Quaker Cannon" (1961).

Intense pain may be inflicted by "harmless" electrical nerve stimulation, as in Charles L. Harness's *The Paradox Men* (1953) and David Langford's *The Space Eater* (1982). Wireless versions include the "epileptigenic ray" in Robert A. Heinlein's *Sixth Column* (1949) and "neuronic whip" of Isaac Asimov's **Foundation** universe.

Easy personality transfer provides another twist in Richard Morgan's *Altered Carbon* (2002), whose tough protagonist is placed in a frail female body for savage interrogation. **Magic** torture may involve **metamorphosis** into loathsome shapes, as in Michael Moorcock's *Stormbringer* (1965), Piers Anthony's **A Spell for Chameleon,** and Harlan Ellison's "I Have No Mouth, and I Must Scream" (1967), whose **computer** torturer is effectively a cruel god.

Cordwainer Smith's "A Planet Named Shayol" (1961) depicts a functional torture world whose inmates painfully grow extra organs, harvested as spare parts (see **Medicine**). Unaugmented bodies are brutally raided for parts in the **prison** of Pohl and Jack Williamson's *The Reefs of Space* (1964) and the **clone** nurseries of Michael Marshall Smith's *Spares* (1996). Dan Simmons's **Hyperion** contains an unusual torture motive for the Shrike, a **monster** that impales victims to suffer forever on its Tree of Pain (a virtual reality construct)—eventually explained as a trap baited for the compassionate aspect of God.

Low-tech forms of torture remain effective, like the threatened drowning in a rising flood of excrement that opens Iain M. Banks's **Consider Phlebas.** Room 101 in George Orwell's **Nineteen Eighty-Four** contains "the worst thing in the world"— which, for a phobic protagonist, merely means old-fashioned rats (see **Rats and**

Mice). Here Orwell unforgettably presents torture not as a means but an end, a cruel exertion of power, which is also its own reward: "The object of torture is torture. The object of power is power."

Discussion

Torture is most chilling when practiced in the sincere belief that it benefits the victim. Deluded followers of religion traditionally maimed bodies to save souls; the torments of the Inquisition are fantastically exaggerated in Edgar Allan Poe's "The Pit and the Pendulum" (1843). Jack Vance imagines a nonreligious equivalent in *The Brains of Earth* (1966), with pain supposedly curing **possession** by aliens. Self-torment to deter possession proves ultimately futile in Pohl's *A Plague of Pythons* (1965); but torture opens the way to possession in Peter F. Hamilton's *The Reality Dysfunction* (1996). A more complex, perverse justification appears in Piers Anthony's *Chthon* (1967).

Medicine and **psychology** may also inflict "benevolent" torture, like the aversion therapy in Anthony Burgess's ***A Clockwork Orange***. C.S. Lewis's *That Hideous Strength* (1945) (see ***Out of the Silent Planet***) offers a **demon**-inspired travesty of scientific objectivity, with aspiring **scientists** stripped of emotions and empathy in the spiritually painful "Objective Room."

Bibliography

Lillian Heldreth. "The Mercy of the Torturer." Robert A. Latham and Robert A. Collins, eds., *Modes of the Fantastic*. Westport, CT: Greenwood Press, 1995, 186–194.

C.S. Lewis. *The Problem of Pain*. London: Geoffrey Bles, 1940.

John B. Reilly. "The Torture Tutorial." *Mythlore*, 21 (Winter, 1997), 39–41.

Gila Safran-Naveh. "Don't Torture Yourself, That Is My Job." Robert S. Corrington and John Deely, eds., *Semiotics*. 1993. New York: Peter Lang, 1995, 133–141.

Brian Stableford. "Introduction." Octave Mirbeau, *Torture Garden*. Cambridgeshire, UK: Dedalus, 1990, [iii–xvi].

John Swain. *A History of Torture*. New York: Award, 1969.

Ian Watson. "The Author as Torturer." *Foundation*, No. 40 (Summer, 1987), 11–15.

Edmund Wilson. "The Vogue of the Marquis de Sade" and "The Documents on the Marquis de Sade." Wilson, *The Bit Between My Teeth*. New York: Farrar, Straus & Giroux, 1965, 158–173, 174–227.

—David Langford

TOUCH

Feeling is believing.

—Edwin A. Abbott
Flatland: A Romance of Many Dimensions
(1884)

Overview

Touch—the ability to perceive the presence or physical properties of things and people through tactile contact, usually using the hand or fingers—is associated with nonverbal **communication** and is the basis of emotional bonds, courtship, and **sexuality**. Portentous, transformative, or magical touch is more prevalent in fantasy than science fiction, in exploring themes like the fear of **love**, **magic** and healing, the moral consequences of acquiring god-like abilities, the potential for **psychic powers**, and mediating desires and alliances between peoples, **cultures**, and races.

Survey

Touch, in fiction and film, is frequently presented as a measure of intimacy or catalyst for change, whether in individuals, relationships, or societies. Touching is an assumed foundation of **family** and **community**, and the lack of physical intimacy or abuse through physical contact is thought to result in antisocial behaviors or arrested emotional growth. In J.M. Barrie's *Peter and Wendy*, Wendy is shocked to find Peter Pan, the perpetual child, has never been loved, and her attempt to touch his face is rebuffed. Yet touch may also be foregrounded entirely for practical reasons, as in Edwin A. Abbott's *Flatland*, where two-dimensional beings rely on touch to determine the polygonal nature of fellow denizens (see **Dimensions**).

Monsters and **aliens on Earth** are often depicted as having supernatural or unexplained abilities associated with potent touch. The fundamental nature of touch in communication and sexuality makes it a plausible tool for control and terror, whether it is the crushing caresses of the giant **ape**, *King Kong*, the clinging parasitic aliens (see **Parasites**) in Robert A. Heinlein's *The Puppet Masters* (1951), the ominous scientific probing by extraterrestrials in Whitley Strieber's *Communion* (1987), or an alien caress that releases destructive pheromones in "Genderbender" (1994), an episode of *The X-Files*. At the other end of the spectrum are aliens with benign touch, like *E.T.: The Extra-Terrestrial*, who heals others and infuses energy into objects with his glowing finger.

Concepts of healing and therapeutic touch can be traced back to both Christian and non-Christian texts, including the New Testament stories of Jesus, who could heal the sick, raise the dead, and cast out **demons** by the laying on of hands (see **Christianity**). One common motif, especially in juvenile fantasies like Mercedes Lackey and Larry Dickson's *Owlsight* (1998) and Sara Douglass's *Beyond the Hanging Garden* (2003), depicts the **apprenticeship** of **children** or young adults gifted with healing who must learn to control magic, establish moral codes, and become responsible leaders.

For adult characters, healing touch and supernatural abilities are often attributed to **kings** and **queens**, like Aragorn in J.R.R. Tolkien's *The Lord of the Rings*. Such powers, however, may bring social costs such as disrupted lives and altered consciousness or physical capacity. Alan Bulmer, a respected physician in F. Paul Wilson's *The Touch* (1986), acquires healing touch and is subsequently hounded daily by angry mobs and a frightened medical establishment. With each healing session, he discovers he is losing his **memory** and other mental capacities. Johnny Smith of Stephen King's *The Dead Zone* (1979) regains consciousness after a six-year coma to discover that by touching others he foresees future events but at the cost of diminished physical energy and mental fatigue. His **knowledge** of specific future events presents ethical dilemmas about his potential responsibility to intervene to prevent them (see **Ethics**).

The human capacity to tolerate or control god-like power is questioned in stories about misused powers. Writers turn to the Greek myth of Midas, King of Phrygia, who was motivated by greed to wish for the ability to turn everything into gold with the stroke of his finger; after other unpleasant events, he accidentally transformed his own daughter into gold. Lynne Reid Banks's *The Adventures of King Midas* (1992) returns to the moral lesson of the traditional tale and focuses on the series of trials Midas must undergo to save his gilded daughter. Kevin Midas in Neal Shusterman's *The Eyes of Kid Midas* (1994) is a geeky high school student who finds a pair of enchanted sunglasses that seem to make all his wishes come true, but have corrupting consequences.

Touch is often a medium or a catalyst for psychic powers. Since telepathy can be defined as invasive, people illustrate their characters by carefully employing or abusing their potent touch. In *Star Trek*, Spock is a touch-telepath and a Vulcan, a race that shuns physical intimacy and rejects emotional display. However, Spock often must use his mind-meld, or psychic touch, on other alien races and humans to determine their emotional state. One popular area of *Star Trek* fan fiction, K/S Slash, explores Spock's unstated reactions to this intimate reading of human emotions and the effects on his repressed sexual desires. In *Psion* (1982), Joan D. Vinge introduces the half-alien youth, Cat, whose emotional blocks to the **horrors** of the past must be confronted before he can reach what other telepaths covet and exploit: a "joining" with others and a powerful level of collective consciousness.

Discussion

Although stories about magical and healing touch can be compelling, moral messages and plots can be clichéd and predictable (see **Clichés**). However, the theme of touch has been revitalized with relevance in Octavia E. Butler's highly acclaimed Xenogenesis series, beginning with *Dawn*, and her story "Bloodchild" (1984). Butler explores how characters strive to negotiate desires and alliances between peoples, cultures, and races for mutual **survival**. In *Dawn*, Lilith faces human cultural **taboos**, fear of miscegenation, and potential loss of her culture when she agrees to the seductive but coercive touch of the Oankali, an alien race, which saved the humans with the purpose of bonding with them genetically. Touching, whether to heal or facilitate mediated sexual pleasure with other humans or Oankali, is a central symbol in the novel for complex links between agency, choice, and consent in **survival**.

Bibliography

Dorothy Allison. "The Future Female." Henry Louis Gates Jr., ed., *Reading Black, Reading Feminist*. New York: Meridian, 1990.

Jennifer Burwell. "Speaking Parts." Burwell, *Notes on Nowhere*. Minneapolis: University of Minnesota Press, 1997, 87–130.

Naomi Jacobs. "Posthuman Bodies and Agency in Octavia Butler's Xenogenesis." Raffaella Baccolini and Tom Moylan, eds., *Dark Horizons*. New York: Routledge, 2003, 91–112.

Henry Jenkins III. *Textual Poachers*. New York: Routledge, 1992.

Carolyn Korsmeyer. "Seeing, Believing, Touching, Truth." William Irwin, ed., *The Matrix and Philosophy*. Chicago: Open Court, 2002, 41–52.

Patricia Melzer. "All That You Touch You Change." *Femspec*, 3 (2002), 31–52.

T.J. Remington. "The Other Side of Suffering." Joseph D. Olander and Martin H. Greenberg, eds., *Ursula K. Le Guin*. New York: Taplinger, 1979, 153–177.

Susan Stone-Blackburn. "Feminist Nurturers and Psychic Healers." Milton T. Wolf and Daryl F. Mallett, eds., *Imaginative Futures*. San Bernardino, CA: Jacob's Ladder Books, 1995, 167–178.

—*Nancy Johnston*

TOYS

■

Overview

Future **technology** is inevitably applied to toys and **games** in science fiction. Toys and dolls traditionally come alive in the **perception** and imagination of **children** (see **Dolls and Puppets**), an animation that can be simulated by **computer**-controlled machinery or actualized through **magic**. Adults see such attractive toys as tools for **education**.

Survey

Games of **war** with toy armies and **weaponry** almost demand the wish-fulfilment of animated soldiers, a theme found in H.G. Wells's "The Magic Shop" (1903), Philip K. Dick's "War Game" (1959), and Diana Wynne Jones's fantasy *Charmed Life* (1977). The twelve vivified toy soldiers in Pauline Clarke's *The Return of the Twelves* (1962) are those once owned by the Brontë siblings, who wrote early fantasies about them. Such military toys become serious weapons in the films *Toys* (1992) and *Small Soldiers* (1998). One of the comic-book *Superman*'s opponents, the Toyman, creates dangerous toys for criminal ends. The police girl nicknamed Toybox in Alan Moore's police-procedural superhero comic *Top 10* (launched in 1999) controls a surreal toy army (see **Surrealism**).

Animation brings drama to the supplanting of old toys by new **Christmas** gifts in Gene Wolfe's "The War Beneath the Tree" (1979) and in the film *Toy Story* (1995). The pathos of toy **astronaut** Buzz Lightyear's need to accept his essential unreality is also seen in the **robot** boy of Brian W. Aldiss's "Super-Toys Last All Summer Long" (1969) and its very different movie adaptation *A.I.: Artificial Intelligence*.

The childhood fantasy of stuffed toys as animate companions is a driving force in A.A. Milne's *Winnie-the-Pooh* (1926) and *The House at Pooh Corner* (1928), John Masefield's *The Midnight Folk* (1927), and Bill Watterson's newspaper comic strip *Calvin and Hobbes* (1985–1995). This theme is more darkly reprised in Neil Gaiman's graphic novel *The Sandman: A Game of You* (1993). Toys that come alive are among the signs of supernatural wrongness in the film *Poltergeist II: The Other Side* (1986).

More or less sinister teddy bears are recurrent figures: autonomous **robot** weapons in Dick's "Second Variety" (1953), filmed as *Screamers* (1996); the pivot of psychosis (see **Psychology**) in Frederik Pohl's "The Man Who Ate the World" (1956); a subliminal indoctrination device in Harry Harrison's "I Always Do What Teddy Says" (1965); and objects laden with supernatural malignity in John Sladek's **horror** story "Ursa Minor" (1983).

Unusually, Russell Hoban's *The Mouse and His Child* (1967) emphasizes the mechanical limitations of toyhood: its title characters are literally inseparable, a single clockwork toy that regularly and inevitably runs down. Another toy mouse comes alive in Paul Gallico's *Manxmouse* (1968). Sylvia Waugh's *The Mennyms* (1993) and its sequels portray human-sized, mysteriously animated rag dolls struggling to pass unnoticed in a British **city**.

After Santa Claus, fantasy's most famous toymaker is Pinocchio's creator Geppetto in *The Adventure of Pinocchio* (1883) by Carlo Collodi, which was adapted as the Disney animated film *Pinocchio* (1940). The eponyms of Dean R. Koontz's children's book *Oddkins* (1988) are toys that come to life when their maker dies.

Education through toys goes awry in Henry Kuttner and C.L. Moore's "Mimsy Were the Borogoves" (1943), in which **far future** playthings teach **children** about higher **dimensions**—into which they depart. Another improving future toy is the "Build-a-Man" kit of William Tenn's "Child's Play" (1947), whose use turns out to be unwise; this was adapted for the *X Minus One* radio series in 1955. With grimmer irony, Bob Shaw's "Dark Night in Toyland" (1988) gifts a terminally ill child with a similar construction kit allowing the creation of pseudo-life (see **Biology**). An entertaining magic toy in Randall Garrett's *Too Many Magicians* (1966) is designed to bring out latent magical **talent**. Defective educational toys are playfully used to simulate advanced space-drive **technology** and distract **espionage** agents in James H. Schmitz's *The Witches of Karres* (1966).

Miscellaneous toys of note include the magic ship that grows to take children on fantastic journeys in Hilda Lewis's *The Ship That Flew* (1936); the paltry fir cones that—marking the gulf between them—Lord Sepulchrave hopes will serve to amuse his son Titus in Mervyn Peake's **Titus Groan** trilogy; and exotic toys brought back from **dreams** as evidence of astral travel to **parallel worlds** in Jones's *The Lives of Christopher Chant* (1988).

Discussion

Toys are inherently subject to childish caprice, leading to tension or irony when objects are wrongly relegated to toy status. A boy's "model" spaceship in Jack McDevitt's *Infinity Beach* (2000) is the actual craft of tiny **aliens in space**; a supposed plaything in Michael Swanwick's *The Iron Dragon's Daughter* (1993) is a war machine component; a child's "bauble" holds potent magic in Lloyd Alexander's Prydain series, opening with *The Book of Three* (1964).

Such treatment of humans or **humanity** has darker resonances. Severian in Gene Wolfe's **The Book of the New Sun** suffers a prophetic-metaphoric dream of doing battle as a marionette. Victims of **miniaturization** must commit crimes in toy guise in *The Devil-Doll* (1936) and act in a toy **theatre** in Jones's *The Magicians of Caprona* (1980). The disquieting finale of **2001: A Space Odyssey** shows the coldly gazing Star Child regarding **Earth** as his toy.

Bibliography

Alida Allison. "Living the Non-Mechanical Life." *Children's Literature in Education*, 22 (September, 1991), 189–194.
Margaret Blount. *Animal Land*. New York: Morrow, 1975.
Nick Lowe. "Toys." *Interzone*, No. 72 (June, 1993), 34.
———. "Toy Story." *Interzone*, No. 108 (June, 1996), 34–35.
Frank McConnell. "From Astarte to Barbie and Beyond." George Slusser and Eric S. Rabkin, eds., *Aliens*. Carbondale: Southern Illinois University Press, 1987, 199–207.
Mark Rich. "Buck Rogers Stuff." *Science Fiction Chronicle*, 22 (July, 2001), 34–38.
John Sladek. "Ursa Minor: Afterword." Sladek, *The Lunatics of Terra*. London: Gollancz, 1984, [iii–xvi].
Mark C. Vaz. "Toy Wars." *Cinefex*, 54 (May, 1993), 54–73.

—*David Langford*

TRADE

■

Buying and selling is essentially anti-social in all its tendencies. It is an education in self-seeking at the expense of others, and no society whose citizens are trained in such a school can possibly rise above a very low grade of civilization.

—Edward Bellamy
Looking Backward, 2000–1887 (1888)

Overview

The initial currency of exchange between newly encountered **cultures** is trade. Typically, trade is the exchange of goods, though sometimes it can be information. Stories about **business** may involve **money** or **gold and silver**; certain **utopias** posit an elimination of the market economy in favor of a bartering system; trade is also characteristic of criminal or underground societies (see **Crime and Punishment**).

Survey

When alien cultures meet, trade is a rudimentary interaction. For primitive societies, like those depicted in Jean Auel's *The Clan of the Cave Bear* and its sequels and Stephen Baxter's *Evolution* (2002), barter is how a group with an excess of something obtains what it needs or otherwise does not have. For example, a seafaring folk has an excess of fish and is interested in pots made by a tribe living where clay is plentiful.

However, when a more technologically advanced culture encounters a simpler one, the culture that thinks itself superior will trade something useless, a glittering trinket, for something it values, gold or land. The classic example of this is the purchase of Manhattan from **Native Americans** by European settlers (see **Europe**) for twenty-four dollars worth of beads. Thus, trade serves as a metaphor of exploitation by invading foreigners.

Critiques of capitalist society also point to money as the root of all evil and suggests a fair bartering system of goods and services to replace it. Such commentary predates the emergence of capitalism: Plato's *The Republic* (c. 380 BC) envisions a society in which private property is abolished. Thomas More's *Utopia* (taken from the Greek word for "nowhere") elaborated on Plato's ideas that most social ills could be eliminated if the motive of private gain were abolished and all would share according to need. By the nineteenth century, in Edward Bellamy's *Looking Backward, 2000–1887,* Julian West, put to **sleep** by a hypnotist to cure insomnia (see **Hypnotism**), awakens in 2000 to a society where money is abolished and social equality attained with a system based on communal cooperation.

However, in **dystopias**, the bartering system may be just as exploitative as the purchase of Manhattan. In the last voyage of Jonathan Swift's *Gulliver's Travels*, Gulliver boasts to the Houyhnhnms about European traders who sail around the globe in search of goods: the satirical intent is to contrast how the "treasures of the world" are debased as elements of commerce.

In Cordwainer Smith's *Norstrilia*, private trading is a capital offense, though it is widely practiced by the underclass as a practical means of existence. In Adam Roberts's *Stone* (2003), there is no compelling reason to regulate the transaction of goods since **technology** has evolved to the point where their manufacture is virtually free. However, certain social customs require that services be paid for with tree leaves that are plentiful and easily plucked at will (thus demonstrating that money does grow on trees!). Though the idea of having to work to earn money with which to purchase goods and services has been eliminated, the necessity of trading one thing deemed of value for another, no matter how meaningless, remains vital to social interaction.

A harsher kind of trade takes place between the Eloi and Morlocks in H.G. Wells's *The Time Machine*. The Eloi get to live carefree lives while the Morlock do the dirty work of maintaining industrial substructures; the helpless Eloi pay in trade as a food source for the Morlocks.

The idea of trade has a less sinister, as well as symbolic, meaning in the pulp tradition where space traders serve the role of good-hearted outlaws. These characters are mavericks whose trading connections make them familiar with various alien cultures, particularly its criminal elements; they have no overt allegiance to any government, human or otherwise, but nonetheless become valuable intermediaries in times of conflict. One noteworthy trader is Poul Anderson's Nicolas van Rijn, first observed in *War of the Wing Men* (1958). Hans Solo in the *Star Wars* trilogy is a celluloid tribute to this pulp archetype, as is Quark, the Ferengi bartender of *Star Trek: Deep Space Nine*. A sort of Humphrey Bogart with big ears, Quark's dealings usually involve some sort of scam in which an even trade is defined as one that takes advantage of someone else. The Ferengi in general are depicted as ugly, greedy creatures, though ultimately comical, which risks accusations of racial stereotyping, recalling the role of Jews in William **Shakespeare**'s *The Merchant of Venice* (c. 1595) (see **Judaism**), where a debt owed is traded for a pound of flesh.

Discussion

Trade is supposed to be an equal exchange in which both parties benefit. However, in practice, it has often been the means by which one culture exploits another. It is no different in the **imaginary worlds** of fantasy and the **far futures** of science fiction, where **magic** or technology alters the human condition but does not change basic human characteristics. As for utopian visions in which societies hold goods in common and trade freely based solely on need, there is a reason why such tales are considered fantasies.

Bibliography

Merritt Abrash. "*Looking Backward.*" *Extrapolation*, 30 (Fall, 1989), 237–242.

Joan Boardman. "Ocean Trade in the Hyborian Age." L. Sprague de Camp, ed., *Blade of Conan*. New York: Ace, 1979, 45–50.

Gary Coats. "Stone Soup." Giuseppa Saccaro Del Buffa and Arthur O. Lewis, eds., *Utopia e Modernita*. Rome: Gangemi Editore, 1989, 287–310.

Jannett Highfill. "International Trade in *News From Nowhere*." *Journal of the William Morris Society*, 12 (Spring, 1997), 31–35.

Anna L. Kaplan. "*Deep Space Nine*: Ferengi Second Fiddle." *Cinefantastique*, 28 (November, 1996), 55–57.

Nancy C. Mellerski. "Structures of Exchange in Villiers de l'Isle-Adam's 'L'Intersigne.'" Olena H. Saciuk, ed., *The Shape of the Fantastic*. New York: Greenwood Press, 1990, 135–142.

Shannon Snyder and Marc Shapiro. "Another Fine Ferengi." *Starlog*, No. 190 (May, 1993), 36–39.

J.M. Walker. "Reciprocity and Exchange in Science Fiction." *Essays in Arts and Sciences*, 9 (August, 1980), 145–156.

—*David Soyka*

TRAGEDY

Overview

"Tragedy" is a term universally employed to describe any story with an unhappy ending, coloring all discussions of the genre. Still, it was defined more precisely in Aristotle's *Poetics* (c. 335–322 BCE) as the story of a person of royal **birth** and high position who demonstrates a tragic flaw—often **hubris**—that inexorably leads to an unpleasant **destiny** or **death**, evoking an audience's pity (for the afflicted person) and fear (that the same fate might afflict them). One finds tragedies of both types in science fiction and fantasy.

Survey

Ancient Greek playwrights drew upon **mythology** to write numerous plays about **heroes** who suffer tragic fates: Sophocles's *Oedipus the King* (c. 427 BCE), about the **king** who unknowingly murders his **father** and marries his **mother**, leading to blindness (see **Vision and Blindness**) and **exile**; Aeschylus's *Agamemnon* (458 BCE), about the Trojan War hero who is killed by his wife Clytemnestra upon his return **home**; Aeschylus's *Prometheus Bound* (date unknown), about the god who gave **fire** to humans against Zeus's command and is horribly punished; and Euripides's *Antigone* (c. 442 BC), about a woman executed for imprudently defying a king's order and burying her brother. Many plays of the English Renaissance were tragedies, some with fantastic elements, like Christopher Marlowe's *Doctor Faustus* (1604), about a scholar who sells his soul to **Satan**; William **Shakespeare**'s *Macbeth* (c. 1606), featuring **witches** and a ghost (see **Ghosts and Hauntings**); and Shakespeare's *Hamlet* (c. 1601), in which a king's ghost prods his son to take **revenge** on his murderer.

As argued in Joseph Campbell's *The Hero with a Thousand Faces* (1949), there is an element of tragedy in every heroic tale, as successful heroes may feel rejected and alienated when they finally return to their homelands; in J.R.R. Tolkien's **The Lord of the Rings**, for example, Frodo is unable to recapture the happiness of life in the Shire and decides to join his uncle and **elves** in a symbolic journey to the afterlife. **Messiahs** can be tragic figures, often dying unjustly with **dreams** unfulfilled; examples would include the **supermen** of Olaf Stapledon's *Odd John* (1935) and Stanley G. Weinbaum's *The New Adam* (1939).

A common motif in science fiction is the **scientist** who performs dangerous or heretical experiments and suffers as a result. Mary Shelley's *Frankenstein, or, The Modern Prometheus* is the prototypical work, announcing in its subtitle a link between its hero and Greek tragedies. Other examples include Robert Louis Stevenson's Dr. Jekyll (see **Strange Case of Dr. Jekyll and Mr. Hyde**), H.G. Wells's Dr. Moreau (see **The Island of Doctor Moreau**) and *The Invisible Man* (1897) (see **The Invisible Man**), and Edmond Hamilton's "The Man Who Evolved" (1931). As prose science fiction gradually abandoned Shelley's conceit that scientists doing research were trespassing on sacred territory and destined to fail, films clung to this attitude, sending daring scientists to tragic deaths in scores of **horror** films like *The Man Who Lived Again* (1936), *The Devil Commands* (1941), *The Fly* (1958), and *Monster on the Campus* (1958). Even more thoughtful science fiction films may harken back to the lesson of *Frankenstein*, like **Blade Runner**, which depicts the scientist who built the **androids** being killed by his own creations. However, **Forbidden Planet** better recalls classical tragedy in depicting Dr. Morbius's death as a result of his own tragic flaw—an unrestrained Id that generates a **monster**.

Other science fiction stories inviting consideration as tragedies include *King Kong*, an **ape** who dies (it is said) because of his **love** for a beautiful woman; Clifford D. Simak's "Eternity Lost" (1949), about a politician who makes an expedient decision that deprives him of immortality (see **Immortality and Longevity**; **Politics**); *The Man Who Fell to Earth*, an **alien on Earth** who fails in his **quest** to help his people and becomes a listless alcoholic; and *A.I.: Artificial Intelligence*, whose **robot** hero ultimately enjoys only one fleeting day of happiness.

Moving beyond individuals' fates, science fiction writers may envision the tragic degradation or extinction of the entire human race in the **near future** or **far future**; notable works projecting such outcomes include Shelley's **The Last Man**, Wells's **The Time Machine**, and John W. Campbell, Jr.'s sequence "Twilight" (1934) and "Night" (1935). It is not always clear that these apocalyptic events stem from some significant flaw in **humanity**'s nature and actions, as Aristotle's formula would require (see **Apocalypse**), but Mike Resnick's *Birthright: The Book of Man* (1982) is an epic recounting of humanity's future rise and fall including testimony from aliens in space specifiying that the race's demise was entirely its own fault. Kurt Vonnegut, Jr.'s *Galapagos* also unambiguously attributes humanity's devolution into unintelligent creatures to a basic defect in their design—"big brains."

Discussion

One might imagine that fantasy's characteristic devotion to heroic triumphs over evil, and science fiction's characteristic belief in **progress**, would makes these genres resistant to tragedy, as writers would prefer to be optimistic (see **Optimism and Pessimism**). Yet instances of stories that end unhappily, some of which perfectly adhere to Aristotle's pattern, can be found. Evidently, despite popular misconceptions, writers and readers of science fiction and fantasy are not unwilling to sometimes stare into dark abysses and draw unpalatable conclusions about the nature of things.

Bibliography

Alexander Argyros. "Tragedy and Chaos." Brett Cooke and Frederick Turner, eds., *Biopoetics*. Lexington, KY: ICUS, 1999, 335–346.

Roger Bozzetto. "Moreau's Tragi-Farcical Island." *Science-Fiction Studies*, 20 (March, 1993), 34–44.

J.H. Gardner. "Mary Shelley's Divine Tragedy." *Essays in Literature*, 4 (Fall, 1997), 182–197.

David Greenman. "*The Silmarillion* as Aristotelian Epic-Tragedy." *Mythlore*, 14 (Spring, 1988), 20–25, 42.

Leonard G. Heldreth. "Festering in Thebes." *Post Script*, 15 (Winter/Spring, 1998), 46–61.

P.A. McCarthy. "*Star Maker*." *Science-Fiction Studies*, 8 (November, 1981), 266–279.

Leonard Mustazza. "Fear and Pity." Tony Magistrale, ed., *The Dark Descent*. Westport, CT: Greenwood Press, 1992, 73–82.

Mary F. Pharr. "From Pathos to Tragedy." *Journal of the Fantastic in the Arts*, 2 (Spring, 1989), 37–46.

C.C. Smith. "Horror vs. Tragedy." *Extrapolation*, 26 (Spring, 1985), 66–73.

—*Gary Westfahl*

TRANSPORTATION

◼

"Transportation is Civilization," our motto runs.

—Rudyard Kipling
"With the Night Mail" (1905)

Overview

Science fiction and fantasy works regularly envision technologically advanced or magical new forms of transportation (see **Magic**), often involving movement at great **speed** and variously employed for **sea travel**, **air travel**, **space travel**, **underwater** adventure, or **underground adventure**; vehicles might be types of **automobiles** or **rockets**. Transportation may involve **time travel, teleportation**, trips to other **dimensions** and **parallel worlds**, ventures into **cyberspace** and **virtual reality**, or experiences within people's **dreams**. The purposes of transportation, perhaps assisted by **maps**, include sightseeing, **exploration**, settling new **frontiers, invasion**, and **future war**. Indeed, all human **history** might be expansively characterized as an ongoing effort to achieve more, and more advanced, forms of transportation.

Survey

Works of **prehistoric fiction** typically emphasize that humanity was originally a nomadic species, and protagonists of novels like J.H. Rosny-Aîne's *Quest for Fire* (1909) and Jean Auel's *The Clan of the Cave Bear* travel long distances on foot in search of **food and drink** and other resources. Moving into the imagined pasts of fantasy, **heroes** engaged in **quests** usually ride on **horses**, although they may fly on the backs of winged horses (see **Supernatural Creatures**) or **dragons** or ride **flying** carpets. In L. Frank Baum's *The Wonderful Wizard of Oz*, Dorothy and her friends are carried by winged monkeys (see **Apes**), and the heroes of its sequel *The Marvelous Land of Oz* (1904) assemble, and fly on the back of, a patchwork creature called a Gump. Glen Cook's Dread Empire series, beginning with *A Shadow of All Night Falling* (1979), features a magical form of teleportation.

The major science fiction writer obsessed with transportation was Jules Verne, whose heroes traveled by means of balloons (*Five Weeks in a Balloon* [1863]), steam-powered land vehicles (*The Steam House* [1880]), fabulous submarines (*Twenty Thousand Leagues under the Sea*), airships (*Robur the Conqueror* [1886]), and projectiles into space (*From the Earth to the Moon*). They were also carried *Off on a Comet* (1877) and embarked upon a *Journey to the Center of the Earth* (1863). Similar feats of fabulous transportation were less skillfully depicted in dime novels by Luis Senarens and in Tom Swift juveniles attributed to "Victor Appleton" but mostly written by Howard Garis.

While most stories of the nineteenth and early twentieth centuries involved individual heroes, later works focused more on the future of mass transportation. Hugo Gernsback's *Ralph 124C 41+: A Romance of the Year 2660* (1925) imagined that urbanites might travel on powered roller-skates, but systems of moving sidewalks became the more popular scheme, as observed in Isaac Asimov's *The Caves of Steel* (1954) (see *I, Robot*) and elsewhere, while gigantic moving roadways figured in Robert A. Heinlein's "The Roads Must Roll" (1940) (see *The Past Through Tomorrow*). Gernsback's novel also suggested constructing a large underground tube for rapid transportation from **Europe** to **America** underneath the Atlantic, while Rudyard Kipling's *With the Night Mail* (1909) envisioned a global system of air transportation.

Traveling into space usually requires spaceships, although writers also propose connecting the surface of **Earth** to an orbiting **space station** with long wires, along which vehicles would move up and down, creating a energy-efficient "space elevator." Moving beyond the solar system demands **generation starships** or methods for traveling through **hyperspace**, although Heinlein's *Tunnel in the Sky* (1955), Dan Simmons's *Hyperion*, and the film *Stargate* employ elaborate systems of teleportation to instantly move from planet to planet, and Clifford D. Simak's *Time Is the*

Simplest Thing (1961) imagines that people with **psychic powers** could mentally project themselves to distant worlds. An extravagant form of mental travel across the **stars** figures in Jayge Carr's "Webrider" (1985).

Science fiction works devise various vehicles and methods for traveling not only through space but also through time and into parallel worlds. Ironically, the most versatile vehicle of this kind—the Tardis used by *Doctor Who* and his companions—resembles an ordinary police box; a phone booth was also employed as a time machine in *Bill and Ted's Excellent Adventure* (1989).

Comic book **superheroes** sometimes employ unusual forms of personal transportation. Marvel Comics' Doctor Strange adventures as a spirit traveling through astral planes while his body remains in a motionless trance; DC Comics' Silver Age Atom shrinks himself to such tiny size that sound propels him through telephone wires from one location to another; Marvel Comics' Silver Surfer rides a surfboard through the vacuum of space; and DC Comics' Cave Carson employs a vehicle that bores through solid rock and takes him and his colleagues deep into Earth's interior.

Discussion

Forms of transportation are so ubiquitous in science fiction and fantasy that it is hard to find stories in which no transportation occurs. One of these rare works, unsurprisingly, is a **dystopia**—E.M. Forster's "The Machine Stops" (1909), which imagines a future world in which people spend their entire lives in separate underground chambers. A ubiquitous Machine delivers everything they need, and they never leave their chambers to meet others, preferring long-distance **communication**. Regarding this immobility as decadent (see **Decadence**), and transportation as invigorating, Forster achieves a happy ending by having the Machine stop working, forcing people out of their chambers to once again travel through their world. An absence of transportation, Forster concludes, makes one's life a **prison**, which people must **escape**—explaining, no doubt, why science fiction and fantasy so frequently focus on transportation.

Bibliography

Isaac Asimov. "Transportation: 21st Century." *Dodge Adventurer*, 7 (Winter, 1979), 28–30.

Arthur C. Clarke. "On the Road." Clarke, *July 20, 2019*. New York: Macmillan, 1986.

Kurt Lancaster. "Travelling Along the Lands of the Fantastic." *Foundation*, No. 67 (Summer, 1996), 28–46.

Amy Lee. "Masculinity and Fantasy (Travel) Literature." Susanne Fendler and Ulrike Horstmann, eds., *Images of Masculinity*. Lewiston: Edwin Mellen Press, 2003, 21–42.

Robert Malone with J.C. Suares. *Rocketship*. New York: Harper and Row, 1977.

Chris Morgan. "Through the Sun in an Airship." Morgan, *The Shape of Futures Past*. Exeter, England: Webb & Bower, 1980, 98–110.

Marjorie Hope Nicolson. *Voyages to the Moon*. New York: Macmillan, 1948.

Gary Westfahl and David Pringle. "Fellow Travellers." *Interzone*, No. 191 (September, 2003), 55–57.

—Gary Westfahl

TREASURE

＊

*One who cannot cast away a treasure in
need is in fetters.*

—J.R.R. Tolkien
The Two Towers (1955)

Overview

Whether the desire is as basic as feeding and clothing oneself, or as wanton as lusting for power, the need to acquire wealth is as common to humans as breathing. So it is unsurprising that **quests** for treasure and struggles over possession of treasure pervade fantasy and science fiction. Whether the treasure is **gold and silver, money,** a secret box, or even something that only alien **cultures** consider valuable, chances are that all characters will be influenced by it in one way or another.

Survey

Quests for treasure date back to Greek **mythology,** like the saga retold in the film *Jason and the Argonauts*, where the Greek **hero** leads a team of adventurers on a quest for the Golden Fleece. The fleece originally belonged to a Boeotian ram that died while saving the life of a boy named Phrixus. In memory of this good deed, the fleece of the dead ram was miraculously changed to gold and became one of the most beautiful objects on **Earth.** It was hung upon a tree in a sacred grove and was the envy of mighty **kings,** who had nothing so magnificent in their **castles.**

Humans are not the only ones interested in treasure. **Dragons,** ever an enduring presence in fantasy literature, tend to hoard stolen treasure (see **Theft**) in **caverns.** In J.R.R. Tolkien's *The Hobbit*, Bilbo Baggins travels with a band of **dwarfs** to retrieve treasure from a terrible dragon, Smaug. As is often the case with treasure, once Thorin, leader of the dwarfs, gets his hands on it, he becomes irrationally greedy and obsessed with wealth, to the extent that he would rather turn to **violence** and wage a **war** than share the treasure with those he is indebted to. But Bilbo shows vast reserves of inner strength when he attempts to thwart Thorin's greed and bring peace to the feuding dwarfs, **elves,** and humans. Like dragons, dwarfs commonly hoard treasure, as in *Snow White and the Seven Dwarfs* where every morning the dwarfs go off to the **mountains** to mine jewels and gold.

Sometimes the true value of treasure is lost on people. In J.M. Barrie's *Peter and Wendy*, **children** discover a glittering hoard of buried treasure, but instead of coveting it, they fling handfuls of diamonds, pearls, and coins at gulls, tricking the **birds** into thinking the items are food.

Robert Louis Stevenson's *Treasure Island* (1883) is one of the most frequently dramatized novels, having been variously adapted for film, television, and even a pantomime. A recent adaptation is Disney's animated movie *Treasure Planet* (2002), which retains the underlying story but shifts the action to outer space. A villainous but charming **pirate** (see **Villains**), Long John Silver, ingratiates himself with the Hawkins family after they discover a treasure **map.** The adventurers sail off (see **Sea Travel**) to find the **island,** with Jim Hawkins as cabin boy and Silver as leader. Once on the island, Silver betrays his employers despite his **friendship** with Jim (see **Betrayal**), but his plans to desert them are foiled and the treasure found.

Andre Norton's free-traders series features the travels of a crew of fortune-hunters to **alien worlds**, where they look for treasure to buy, sell, or **trade**. In *Sargasso of Space* (1955), the free-traders win exclusive rights to all tradable goods discovered on an **alien world**. The crew arrives to find the planet's surface charred but a strange pulse emanates underfoot, a secret valley of life with **monsters** lurking in rocky caves below. The traders must solve these **mysteries** so they can **escape** the planet, with or without saleable treasures. In *The Ruby in the Smoke* (1985), Philip Pullman gives readers all they could ask for in a treasure hunt novel. Sixteen-year-old Sally Lockhart gets ensnared in a deadly web of events as she encounters despicable hags and forthright heroes on her search for a mysterious ruby.

Even in modern times, the allure of ancient treasure has not lost its grip on the hearts of man, as exemplified in Douglas Preston and Lincoln Child's *Riptide* (1998). A cursed pirates' treasure valued at over two billion dollars lies deep within the treacherous **water** off the coast of Maine. All who have attempted to unearth the fortune have suffered gruesome **death**, and the latest high-tech expedition meets the same fate.

Discussion

For better or worse, love of beautiful and valuable things is a trait of **humanity**, so treasure will always be a relevant theme in science fiction and fantasy. Whether the author's purpose is to hold a **mirror** to the **evils** of greed or entertain with adventurous quests, readers can always relate to stories about treasure.

Bibliography

Christine Barkley and M.B. Ingham. "There But Not Back Again." *Riverside Quarterly*, 7 (March, 1982), 101–104.

Ruth B. Bottigheimer, ed. *Fairy Tales and Society*. Philadelphia: University of Pennsylvania Press, 1986.

Jared Curtis. "On Re-Reading *The Hobbit* Fifteen Years Later." *Children's Literature in Education*, 15 (1984), 113–120.

William H. Green. "King Thorin's Mines." *Extrapolation*, 42 (Spring, 2001), 53–64.

Bruce K. Hanson. *The Peter Pan Chronicles*. New York: Carol Publishing/Birch Lane, 1993.

Ruth Kyle. "The Wondrous Worlds of Andre Norton." *Niekas*, 40 (August, 1989), 21.

Millicent Lenz and Peter Lenz, eds. *Alternative Worlds in Fantasy Fiction*. New York: Continuum, 2001.

Brett McQuade. "Peter Pan." *Mythlore*, 20 (Winter, 1994), 5–9.

—Nick Aires

TRICKSTER

Overview

Tricksters are recurring figures in **mythology** and **religion**, who are often **gods and goddesses** who break the rules of the gods or **nature**, sometimes maliciously—for example, Loki of Norse legends—but usually with positive effects. Often, the rule-breaking takes the form of tricks. In **Native American** mythology, animals like coyotes and ravens are associated with tricksters. Tricksters are not only found in myths; they feature in any stories involving persons who deceive others, or persons who enjoy making trouble for others. A characteristic trickster is someone who is not particularly helpful, unlike **mentors**, but not particularly harmful or **evil** like **villains**. Tricksters are annoying, but never despised. A separate entry discusses **clowns and fools**.

Survey

Classic mythological tricksters sometime appear in modern texts: Loki is restored to life as a villain opposing Marvel Comics' the Mighty Thor, and in Allan Steele's *Clarke County, Space* (1990), a Native American living in a **space habitat** visits Coyote in dream **quests**. Other writers devise their own trickster gods: Rincewind, the inept **wizard** of Terry Pratchett's *The Colour of Magic*, is assisted by Lady Luck, a trickster goddess. And Piers Anthony's Xanth series, which began with *A Spell for Chameleon*, features another immortal female trickster, the Demoness Metria (see **Demons; Immortality and Longevity**). She engages in mischief because it is fun, a way to alleviate her boredom. Like many tricksters, Metria invariably gets caught, usually because of her propensity to improperly use synonyms in place of the words she means to say. One might also mention Kickaha of Philip José Farmer's World of Tiers series, beginning with *The Maker of Universes* (1965), Roger Zelazny's *Jack of Shadows* (1971), and the two-faced Chuz of Tanith Lee's Tales from the Flat Earth series, beginning with *Night's Master* (1978).

Trickster figures influenced by mythology also appear in fantasies for **children**, like Joel Chandler Harris's Brer Rabbit, whose stories were first collected in *Uncle Remus: His Songs and His Sayings* (1881), and Wile E. Coyote of the Warner Brothers cartoons, haplessly endeavoring to capture the Road Runner.

People often begin behaving like tricksters when granted the power of **invisibility**. Even Christopher Marlowe's *Doctor Faustus* (1604), when made invisible by Mephistopheles, plays a few pranks on the Pope and other characters. In the film *The Invisible Man*, unlike H.G. Wells's 1897 novel, the titular character exhibits some traits of the trickster as he enjoys bedeviling those around him. Invisible ghosts (see **Ghosts and Hauntings**), instead of being frightening, may also be tricksters. The film *Topper* features George and Marion Kirby, a fun-loving husband and wife who end an evening of jazz and champagne by smashing their car into a tree. They return as ghosts with a directive to liven up the straight-laced life of banker Cosmo Topper with various antics. Another ghost who functions as a trickster appears in the film *Beetlejuice* (1988), comically helping other ghosts get rid of the unpleasant new occupants of their **home**.

Trickster figures are also common villains who oppose comic book **superheroes**; indeed, one of the Flash's regular foes calls himself the Trickster, dressing outlandishly and employing strange devices to commit crimes. *Superman* must deal with the malicious magical pranks of the fifth-dimensional imp, Mr. Mxyzptlk, the sinister toys of the Toyman, and the bizarre gimmicks of the Prankster. However, the most famous trickster is undoubtedly the Joker, who has opposed *Batman* in the 1989 film and countless other adventures in comic books, television, and cartoons. The Joker first encounters Batman during a botched robbery (see **Theft**) at the Ace Chemical Factory. He manages to **escape** by leaping into a drainage vat of chemical waste, but later discovers that the toxins bleached his skin chalk white, dyed his hair fluorescent green, and stretched his lips into a hideous, permanent red grin. The Joker's trickster methods are simple: gain pleasure in breaking every law and moral stature known to humanity. More importantly, he derives **humor** from playing twisted **games** with Batman. Joker views every crime (see **Crime and Punishment**) as the ultimate joke—mocking Batman.

Other well known pop culture tricksters are Bart Simpson of *The Simpsons* and the advanced alien Q of the *Star Trek* universe. Q first appeared in *Star Trek: The Next Generation*, and went on to add his comedic chemistry to *Star Trek: Deep Space Nine* and *Star Trek: Voyager*. Of all the myriad beings inhabiting science-fictional worlds, none are as enigmatic as the omnipotent cosmic trickster Q, who is sometimes a playful mischief maker and sometimes a deadly threat to all humanity.

Discussion

Tricksters have been talked about in all **cultures** on **Earth** for which we have a **history**. Tricksters can be cunning or foolish or both, and they are often funny even when they are hindering a story's hero or acting as the catylyst for the storyteller's moral message (see **Fables**).

Bibliography

Tim Callahan. "Devil, Trickster and Fool." *Mythlore*, 17 (Summer, 1991), 29–34, 36.

Amanda Cockrell. "When Coyote Leaves the Res." *Journal of the Fantastic in the Arts*, 10 (Winter, 1998), 64–76.

C.S. Fredericks. "Roger Zelazny and the Trickster Myth." *Journal of American Culture*, 2 (Summer, 1979), 271–278.

Edward L. Galligan. *The Comic Vision in Literature*. Athens: University of Georgia Press, 1984.

William J. Hynes and William G. Doty, eds. *Mythical Trickster Figures*. Tuscaloosa: University of Alabama Press, 1993.

Marilyn Jurich. *Scheherazade's Sisters*. Westport, CT: Greenwood Press, 1998.

Ekkehart Malotki and Michael Lomatuway'ma. *Hopi Coyote Tales*. Lincoln: University Nebraska Press, 1984.

Jeff Rovin. "The Joker," "The Prankster," "Toyman," and "The Trickster." Rovin, *The Encyclopedia of Super Villains*. New York: Facts on File, 1987, 171–172, 270, 350, 351.

—Nick Aires

U

UFOs

—•—

Overview

In modern works on ufology one reads that the first UFO sighting was in 1947 by a U.S. pilot, who described the "flying saucers" he saw. It has also become fashionable to mention supposed UFO sightings in the Bible—especially Ezekiel 4:5-28, which describes a vision of God's fiery chariot. In *The UFO Enigma* (1977) Donald Menzel and Ernest Taves persuasively argue that this particular vision actually involves "sundogs" (parhelia), and the vast majority of UFO sightings can similarly be attributed to natural phenomena, some rare, some—like the planet **Venus**—common. However, there is no single "UFO hypothesis": ufology draws together hordes of "unorthodox theorists" and many disparate theories. To summarize, UFOs may be (a) craft from outer space (see **Space Travel**), (b) craft from other **dimensions,** (c) craft from the future (see **Time Travel**), (d) craft from inside the **hollow Earth,** or (e) natural phenomena misinterpreted by witnesses. Clearly hypothesis (e) is the least romantic option.

Survey

Perhaps the most interesting written science fiction surrounding UFOs concerns the human **psychology** underlying ufology. An example is Ian Watson's *Miracle Visitors* (1978), which explains UFO experiences as products of altered states of consciousness. Fritz Leiber's *The Wanderer* (1964) depicts UFO believers coping with the arrival in Earth's skies of a planet-sized "visitor." In his **satire** "Silly Season" (1950) C.M. Kornbluth suggests that no one would credit the arrival of a genuine flying saucer because of the tabloid media's wolf-crying. Gore Vidal's *Messiah* (1954) regards UFOs as real, but (as per Carl Jung) as portents, not spacecraft.

Relatively few written tales accepting the idea of saucers piloted by **aliens on Earth**—who may be planning **invasion** or mingling unnoticed among us—are of much interest. Though this can partly be explained by the overall paucity of written UFO-oriented science fiction, it cannot be entirely so. Exceptions include Chad Oliver's *Shadows in the Sun* (1954), depicting a Texas village populated by saucernauts; Patrick Tilley's *Fade-Out* (1975), a **technothriller** focusing on Earth's response to an alien arrival of mysterious intent; Richard Francis's idiosyncratic *Blackpool Vanishes* (1979), in which saucers are very small; and David Bischoff's series begun with *Abduction: The UFO Conspiracy* (1990), whose title is sufficient description. Stephen Coonts's *Saucer* (2002) and *Saucer: The Conquest* (2004) have a more straightforward take on things, as do Stephen King's *The Tommyknockers* (1988), filmed for television in 1993, and *Dreamcatcher* (2001), filmed in 2003. Whitley Strieber's *Majestic* (1989) is a novel designed for UFO believers and approvingly cites, as fact, the content of the spoof *An Account of a Meeting with Denizens of Another World, 1871* (1979) by David Langford "with William Robert Loosley"; Strieber's *Communion: A True Story* (1987), filmed in 1989 and detailing alien abduction, purports to be autobiographical.

More obedient to popular opinion, UFO-related screen science fiction has been prolific. The Martian spacecrafts in *The War of the Worlds* (1953) are more saucer-like than anything else (see **Mars**), as are the craft in **The Day the Earth Stood Still, The Thing (from Another World)**, **Invaders from Mars**, and other U.S. movies of the **paranoia**-fueled 1950s. *Independence Day* (1996) followed the same pattern.

The modern age of UFO movies can be said to have begun with **Close Encounters of the Third Kind**, whose plot cleverly imitates many UFO encounter stories; **communication** between humans and aliens is effected by **music**. Director Steven Spielberg returned to UFOs as a producer with **batteries not included* (1987), in which tenants of a rooming house, facing eviction, are helped by occupants of small saucers, and the more ambitious television miniseries *Taken* (2002), which follows several generations of families probing the UFO enigma. *Fire in the Sky* (1993), based on a 1975 incident in Arizona, is noteworthy in abandoning the coziness of many imitators of *Close Encounters*, focusing rather on fear of the unknown.

Television series of interest include *The Invaders* (1967–1968) and *U.F.O.* (1970–1973), in which hostile saucernauts have infiltrated human society and try to prevent this secret from being revealed—which is also the theme of John Carpenter's film *They Live* (1988). In *V* (miniseries 1983, series 1984–1985) aliens are more forthright about their intentions. Such extravaganzas contrast strongly with the series *The 4400* (launched in 2004), whose premise is that all humans abducted by UFOs throughout **history** are, without explanation, returned to Earth together, now in possession of special powers; stories follow their lives thereafter. Sober television movies include *The Flipside of Dominick Hide* (1980) and its sequel, *Another Flip for Dominick* (1982), and *Roswell* (1994)—the latter not to be confused with the adolescent series about young aliens, *Roswell* (1999–2002).

Discussion

Despite popular supposition, and a plethora of science fiction movies and television series taking alien flying saucers at face value, UFOs are rare in written science fiction, probably because most scientists regard the notion that aliens are surreptitiously visiting us as a nonstarter. In this, written science fiction goes against the grain of popular opinion: surveys show that depressingly large percentages of the U.S. population believe that UFOs are alien spaceships and their occupants abduct humans for purposes of "experimentation"; around 4 percent of the U.S. population believes *they themselves* have been abductees. For better or worse, few ideas related to science fiction have been so widely influential.

Bibliography

Joe Alves. "Designing a World for UFO's, Extraterrestrials, and Mere Mortals." *American Cinematographer*, 59 (January, 1978), 34–35, 60–62, 84–85.

Thomas M. Disch. "A Closer Look at *Close Encounters*." *Foundation*, No. 15 (January, 1979), 50–53.

George M. Eberhart. *UFOs and the Extraterrestrial Movement*. Metuchen, NJ: Scarecrow, 1986.

Charlene Engel. "Language and the Music of the Spheres." *Film/Literature Quarterly*, 24 (October, 1996), 376–384

Paris Flammonde. *Age of Flying Saucers*. New York: Hawthorn Books, 1971.

John Keel. "The Man Who Invented Flying Saucers." *Whole Earth Review*, 52 (Fall, 1986), 54–61.

Ron Magid. "Flying Saucers for **Batteries Not Included*." *American Cinematographer*, 69 (July, 1988), 66–72.

James W. Moseley and Karl T. Pflock. *Shockingly Close to the Truth*. Buffalo, NY: Prometheus, 2002.

—John Grant

UNDERGROUND ADVENTURE

Overview

Ever since the Greeks sent heroes down into Hades (see **Hell**), the world under the **Earth** has been equated with **death** and **evil**. **Caverns** were dark places where dark deeds were done. Even today we speak of a criminal "underworld" as though it were a subterranean realm distinct from, but paralleling, our own. With such a freight of symbolic meaning, science fiction and fantasy writers have tended to present the underworld in similar ways.

Survey

When H.G. Wells sent his traveler aboard **The Time Machine**, he found, in a future London, a subterranean race of Morlocks who fed off the simpler and more attractive Eloi. That the Morlocks represented the debased future of the working class while the Eloi stood for the colorless future of the upper class (see **Class System**) was made explicit in another novella Wells wrote about the same time, "A Story of the Days to Come" (1899). In this story we see the future **city** gradually being built over the workers, who become confined to a darker and ever more cramped existence underground while only the rich see the light. Obviously, "A Story of the Days to Come" marks an evolutionary stage on the way to the Eloi and Morlocks. An underground society perhaps destined to supplant our own figures in Edward Bulwer-Lytton's *The Coming Race* (1871).

This image of the underworld as dark and mean gets its clearest expression in Daniel F. Galouye's *Dark Universe* (1961), in which survivors of a **nuclear war** live like moles underground. Blind, they find their way by listening for echoes or through dim infra-red sensitivity, their retreat underground representing a cultural decay to primitivism. The underground became a familiar retreat from nuclear war in science fiction of the 1950s and 1960s, nearly always equated with cultural loss. Although rarely as dark as Galouye's novel, they are invariably oppressive. In Philip K. Dick's *The Penultimate Truth* (1964), for instance, survivors of nuclear war live a mean, restricted life in underground "Tanks" fed a diet of lies by political masters living safely and comfortably on the surface. In Harlan Ellison's "A Boy and his Dog" (1969) the underworld society first seems a sort of **utopia**, clean, bright and civilized in comparison to the dirty, dangerous existence of Albert and his **dog** on the surface. But it becomes clear that living underground involves a deliberate loss of **freedom**. This is even more explicit in Ellison's earlier "I Have No Mouth, and I Must Scream" (1967) in which nuclear survivors live a demeaned existence within the subterranean interstices of a giant, lunatic **computer** that proceeds to **torture** them for their guilt in the war.

Another variation on this theme is the underground military complex in which **scientists** find themselves constrained in works of **paranoia** like Michael Crichton's *The Andromeda Strain* (1969) and Don DeLillo's *Ratner's Star* (1976). Again, moving underground is equated with surrendering freedom and **culture**.

Of course this constricted view of the underground universe is not the only view. Ever since Jules Verne sent adventurers on *A Journey to the Center of the Earth* (1863) to discover an entire realm of **dinosaurs** and primitive people, a strand of science fiction has promoted the idea of a **hollow Earth**. Such a hollow Earth might play host to an anti-fascist **dystopia**, like Joseph O'Neill's *Land Under England* (1935), in which again we see the loss of liberty associated with being underground. Or, more playfully, it might bring together a host of science-fictional devices, as in Steven Utley and Howard Waldrop's "Black as the Pit, from Pole to Pole" (1977). Or it might be used satirically to reflect perceived losses of freedom elsewhere (see **Satire**), as in Steve Erickson's *Arc d'X* (1993).

In Lewis Carroll's *Alice's Adventures in Wonderland*, the underworld is a surreal, comic playground (see **Comedy; Surrealism**), an entire society that is a perverse variant on what we discover above ground. Subsequent writers have used this idea that one world is a distorted **mirror** for the other. In Neil Gaiman's *Neverwhere* (1996), as if continuing the theme of Wells's "A Story of the Days to Come," it is a place where the dispossessed of our world have created their own social order, a world whose pattern and meanings are imposed by the shape of the London Underground railway. The London Underground provides a similar pattern for Lisa Goldstein's *Dark Cities Underground* (1999), and in both novels it is where old gods and legends find new life, literally driven underground.

Discussion

In popular terms the "underworld" is either death or crime—in either case, a distorted mirror of the surface world we know. It is in precisely these terms that science fiction and fantasy writers use the image: a place of **darkness** away from light, of restriction on freedom—a place of the furtive, secret, and different. It is yet another way fantastic literature has found to make the familiar strange, to see our world as an alien might.

Bibliography

Peter Fitting. "Buried Treasures." *Utopian Studies*, 7 (1996), 93–112.

Thomas S. Hibbs. "Notes from Underground." William Irwin, ed., *The Matrix and Philosophy*, Chicago: Open Court, 2002, 155–165.

David Meakin. "Future Past." Edmund J. Smyth, ed., *Jules Verne: Narratives of Modernity*, Liverpool: Liverpool University Press, 2000, 94–108.

Charles Newton. "Underground Man, Go Home." *College English*, 37 (December, 1975), 337–344.

James Obertino. "Moria and Hades." *Comparative Literature Studies*, 30 (1993), 153–169.

Donald E. Palumbo. "Underground Journey." Donald E. Morse, ed., *The Fantastic in World Literature and the Arts*, Westport, CT: Greenwood Press, 1987, 211–227.

Marcelle Perks. "A Descent into the Underworld." Steve Chibnall and Julian Petley, eds., *British Horror Cinema*. London: Routledge, 2002, 145–155.

Jeff Rovin. "The Mole Man." Rovin, *The Encyclopedia of Super-Villains*. New York: Facts on File, 1987, 230–231.

—Paul Kincaid

UNDERWATER ADVENTURE

You are going to tour the land of marvels. Astonishment, amazement will become your everyday state of mind. You won't get bored with the spectacles I will provide for you. I'm going on another tour of the submarine world—for all I know, my last tour—and I'm going to review everything I've ever studied at the bottom of the seas, and you can be my fellow student.

—Jules Verne
Twenty Thousand Leagues under the Sea
(1870), translated by Walter James Miller
and Frederick Paul Walter (1993)

Overview

Undersea adventure in the technological world begins with the venerable science fiction author Jules Verne, whose *Twenty Thousand Leagues under the Sea* set the standard for submarine stories and introduced major themes the oceanic world carries with it. But in fantasy, the world beneath the ocean's surface has been the subject of tales as long as **mythology** and folklore have existed. In both genres, undersea adventure explores both the external unknown and the human unconscious mind.

Survey

In fantasy, undersea adventure is rife with **magic**. Under the ocean's surface, one may encounter not only **fish and sea creatures**, but also **mermaids**, selkies (see **Shapeshifters**), and **monsters**. The world under the ocean's surface is a natural **home** to these creatures, but humans may reach it only by using magic, unless they are unfortunate enough to sink under the waves with their homes, as occurred with **Atlantis**. In Diane Duane's *Deep Wizardry* (1985), the undersea environment is not merely the site but also the focus of a **quest**. The sea, particularly under its surface, appears more free of human influence than it actually is, so it serves as a **frontier** for young adventurers. Other underwater fantasies include Charles Kingsley's *The Water Babies*, Hugh Lofting's *Dr. Dolittle and the Secret Lake* (1948) (see *The Story of Dr. Dolittle*), and Thomas Burnett Swann's *The Dolphin and the Deep* (1968).

In science fiction, the world under the ocean serves as an alien environment near our homes. Verne's *Twenty Thousand Leagues under the Sea* is the best-known classic of undersea adventure. It features a submarine voyage with the mysterious Captain Nemo. Nemo, alienated from his society, has fled the company of other humans, except for his passengers and crew. Nemo shows passengers the wonders of sunken ships, fish, and sea creatures. His **exile** from human society has given him an **alien world** almost all to himself. Later submarine voyages were undertaken in the series *Voyage to the Bottom of the Sea* (1964–1968) and *SeaQuest DSV* (1993–1995).

The water's surface can provide a symbolic wall between characters and their everyday world. The depths of the ocean and depths of the psyche—or depths of **evil** or depravity—often coincide. In Michael Crichton's *Sphere* (1987) and its film adaptation (1998), the title object can make the characters' thoughts into reality, but the sea itself holds their fears and doubts. In *Starfish* (1999), Peter Watts addresses similar themes: the crews of deep sea stations are chosen from people with mental disorders, and the very problems that allow them to survive confinement in an unsafe atmosphere are their largest flaws and **gifts**. His characters attempt to simultaneously transcend their environmental and personal limitations.

But the world under the waves can also be a place of innocence and **nature** unspoiled by humans. In the film *The Abyss* (1989), aliens at the edge of the Cayman Trough are peace-loving and friendly, firmly opposed to **nuclear war** and willing to **flood** human **cities** to eliminate nuclear weapons. Their **wisdom** is literally deep, and their foreignness is dual in being both extraterrestrial and underwater. In *A.I.: Artificial Intelligence*, a child **robot** seeks Pinocchio's Blue Fairy to make him a real boy. At the end of the movie, after countless years have passed, advanced robots free him from his ship under the ocean's surface and provide him with a simulacrum of the human **mystery** of **love** and belonging he has been seeking for thousands upon thousands of years. However, the ocean itself does not, cannot, answer him, and the sunken **statue** of the Blue Fairy remains motionless.

The animated television series *Futurama* takes on undersea tropes with its episode "The Deep South" (2002) featuring the lost, sunken city of Atlanta, but these serve to explore themes of alienation, tolerance, and love—not to mention **humor**. The **mermaids** of *Futurama* are created by **mutations** from sunken factories of the past. Their **culture** is ultimately too different for the surface dwellers, and love does not conquer all; Fry and his friends remove their rebreathers and return to land and **space travel**.

Domed cities under the water are generally seen as much safer, as observed in works like Hal Clement's *Ocean on Top* (1973), the film *City Beneath the Sea* (1971), and Maureen McHugh's *Half the Day Is Night* (1994). While these cities are not always paragons of urban virtue, they are rarely riskier than domed cities on other planets. The dark of the **water** outside occasionally transcends its role as an exotic setting and becomes opportunity or menace, but for the most part domed cities are humanity's attempt to tame the deeps.

Discussion

While there have been some notable undersea tales, for the most part scientific speculation around the strangest creatures of the deeps has not touched print science fiction as much as it might, finding more representation in film versions. For the most part in science fiction and fantasy, the depths of the ocean are a source or representation of mystery, whether natural to the undersea environment itself, inherent to its human visitors, or visited upon it by aliens from an entirely different other world.

Bibliography

Iain Blair. "Underwater in *The Abyss*." *Starlog*, No. 146 (September, 1989), 37–40, 58.

Thomas Burgess. *Take Me under the Sea*. Salem, OR: Ocean Archives, 1995.

Ronald J. Heckelman. "The Swelling Act." George Slusser and Eric S. Rabkin, eds., *Mindscapes: The Geographies of Imagined Worlds*. Carbondale: Southern Illinois University Press, 1989.

Ben Jeapes. "Jules Verne's *Twenty Thousand Leagues under the Sea*." *Vector*, No. 184 (Summer, 1995), 10–12.

David Ketterer. "Fathoming *Twenty Thousand Leagues under the Sea*." R. A. Collins, ed., *Scope of the Fantastic*. Westport, CT: Greenwood Press, 1985, 263–275.

Joe Nazzaro. "Underwater Thoughts." *Starlog*, No. 204 (July, 1994), 54–58.

Christopher Probst. "*Voyage to the Bottom of the Sea*." *American Cinematographer*, 79 (February, 1998), 68–81.

Bill Warren. "Prepare to Submerge." *Starlog*, No. 196 (November, 1993), 44–49, 72.

—*Marissa Lingen*

UNICORNS

Overview

The unicorn is the quintessential creature of **mythology**, perhaps because people feel it *ought* to exist. Its origins are lost to **history** yet evidence of its physical existence persists in the form of travelers' tales, shadowy sightings, and alleged unicorn horns. It remains a powerful symbol of **virginity** and chastity, but in a contradictory fashion, a symbol of eroticism, **freedom**, and **escape**. The image of the unicorn has recurred in story and in art through the ages, its popularity undiminished to this day.

Survey

The earliest mention of the unicorn comes from India in the fourth century BCE, but its geographical origins are unclear. Unicorns have allegedly been sighted on all continents except Antarctica. They have been explained away as rhinoceroses, or as creatures devised to explain narwhal tusks brought **home** by sailors. Different **cultures** represent the unicorn in various ways; the Eastern unicorn was a magical being (see **Magic**), the Chinese unicorn, the k'i-lin, bringer of good fortune and sign of longevity. The Arab unicorn, the kar-kadann, was by contrast a fierce fighter. First described in the west by Ctesias, a Greek physician at the court of Darius II, the translation of the Bible known as the Septuagint included seven references to a large, fierce, horned creature, which translators called "monoceros" or unicorn, which helped to establish the creature's existence in western **culture**. It was the compilation of a bestiary in the early part of the first millennium by a writer known as Physiologus that brought the notion of an animal so fierce it could only be subdued by a virgin, and hence its association with chastity.

In heraldic terms, the combination of the lion and unicorn on the British coat of arms is an **allegory** of the joining of Scotland and England, but the fight between the lion and unicorn in Lewis Carroll's *Through the Looking-Glass* (1871) (see *Alice's Adventures in Wonderland*), allegedly representing the antagonism between William Gladstone and Benjamin Disraeli, suggests the unicorn can symbolize the "Other" in broader contexts. The unicorn's love of a battle is seen in a more sophisticated form in Roger Zelazny's "Unicorn Variations" (1981), when Martin plays Tlingel at **chess** for **knowledge** of the world's **destiny**. Tlingel is cast in the same bluff mould as Carroll's unicorn. Jewel, the unicorn in C.S. Lewis's *The Last Battle* (1956) (see *The Lion, the Witch and the Wardrobe*) is similarly loyal and straightforward, if a little bumbling.

Michael Bishop's *Unicorn Mountain* (1988) exhibits a similar rough and ready approach in portraying the association between unicorns and healing (see **Medicine**). Here, a herd of sick kar'tajans is cared for in a ranching community in Colorado, and in turn bring healing to a dysfunctional extended family, coming to terms with one member dying of AIDS. Peter S. Beagle's *The Unicorn Sonata* (1996) again touches on the idea of the unicorn as the bringer of a cure, while being in need of healing itself.

More commonly, however, the modern fictional unicorn is an ethereal, evanescent creature, shy, delicate, coaxed into the world only *in extremis*. The unicorn at the heart of Peter S. Beagle's *The Last Unicorn*, Amalthea, seeks to free her fellow unicorns, imprisoned by King Haggard in the surf at the ocean's edge. The enormity of the unicorn's task is underlined by her transformation by magician Schmendrick into a vulnerable girl. But her fragility is her strength, and through this she can restore life and meaning to the Wasteland and bring freedom for her kind. In Lord Dunsany's *The King of Elfland's Daughter* the unicorns cross from Elfland (see **Fairies**) into our world, only to be hunted down by Orion, son of King Alveric, the child intended to bring magic into the land. As such they represent lost hopes as well as creative freedom.

In *Elidor* (1965), Alan Garner explores a similar theme to that of *The Last Unicorn* but his wasteland, Elidor, is a darker, more corrupt place. Whereas Schmendrick's **quest** recognizes its self-consciously literary reference, the quest undertaken by Garner's **children** constantly confounds readers' expectations and assumptions. Their courage is exploited by Malebron, king of that place, to secure his realm while opponents exploit the girl's virginity to corner and then kill Findhorn. In his death-song Findhorn confounds his enemies and saves Elidor but the cost to the children in terms of shattered innocence is terrible. Findhorn is a muscular, corporeal unicorn and his **death** is bloody and agonizing. This resonates particularly with one of the sadder episodes in T.H. White's *The Once and Future King* (1958) when the children of Morgause decide to emulate the unicorn hunt in which their **mother** took part, only to succeed where she, not unnaturally, had failed, and then find themselves with a dead unicorn in which she has no interest. Never has the shattering of childhood innocence been more tragically portrayed.

Discussion

It is perhaps the malleability of the unicorn as a symbol, its contradictory strength and vulnerability, its presentation as a spiritual creature alongside an undeniable earthiness, which makes it so popular with modern writers and artists, who appreciate its ambiguous status.

Bibliography

Wayne G. Hammond. "Seraphim, Cherubim and Virtual Unicorns." *Mythlore*, 20 (Winter, 1995), 41–45.
Nancy Hathaway. *The Unicorn*. New York: Viking, 1980.
T.N. Roberts. "Unicorn: Creature of Love." *Mythlore*, 8 (Winter, 1982), 39–41.
Malcolm South. "Unicorn." South, ed., *Mythical and Fabulous Creatures*. Westport, CT: Greenwood Press, 1987, 5–26.
Maureen Kincaid Speller. "Unicorns, Werewolves, Ghosts, and Rhinoceroses." *Vector*, No. 204 (March/April, 1999), 10–11.
Jean Tobin. "Werewolves and Unicorns." Jan Hokenson, ed., *Forms of the Fantastic*. Westport, CT: Greenwood Press, 1986, 181–184.
Sandra Unerman. "Hunting the Unicorn." *Vector*. No. 212 (July/August, 2000), 14–16.
R.C. West "Sign of the Unicorn." T.J. Remington, ed., *Selected Proceedings of the 1978 SFRA National Conference*. Cedar Falls: University of Northern Iowa, 1979, 45–54.

—*Maureen Kincaid Speller*

UPLIFT

Not to go on all-Fours; that is the Law. Are we not Men?
Not to suck up Drink; that is the Law. Are we not Men?
Not to eat Flesh nor Fish; that is the Law. Are we not Men?

> *Not to claw Bark of Trees;* that *is the*
> *Law. Are we not Men?*
> *Not to chase other Men;* that *is the*
> *Law. Are we not Men?*

—H.G. Wells
The Island of Doctor Moreau (1896)

Overview

Popularized in science fiction by David Brin's series that includes *Startide Rising*, uplift denotes the "raising" of nonsentient or incapable species and individuals to **intelligence** (tacitly assumed to include the ability to develop and use **technology**) comparable to that of **humanity**.

Survey

The archetypal animal uplift novel is H.G. Wells's *The Island of Doctor Moreau*, presenting such enhancement as blasphemous (see **Religion**) and doomed to fail as beast-nature reasserts itself. Literary responses include Brian W. Aldiss's *Moreau's Other Island* (1980) and Kirsten Bakis's *Lives of the Monster Dogs* (1997). Large-brained sea mammals (see **Fish and Sea Creatures**) are frequently uplift candidates. Thus Larry Niven's "The Handicapped" (1967) imagines dolphins grateful for "Dolphin's Hands" as manipulative aids (see **Cyborgs**); Brin equips them with six-legged walking frames.

Uplift is entwined with the idea of animal **communication** (see **Language and Linguistics**). William C. Anderson's dolphin protagonist, *Penelope* (1963), easily masters English but speaks in supersonics, requiring conversion. Dolphins also learn speech in Robert Merle's *The Day of the Dolphin* (1967), filmed in 1973. A **role reversal** is seen in Leo Szilard's "The Voice of the Dolphins" (1961) and Douglas Adams's *The Hitchhiker's Guide to the Galaxy* sequence, in which inscrutably superior dolphins respectively save and restore the world.

Notable uplifted races include the talking **dogs** (see **Talking Animals**) of Clifford Simak's *City* and oppressed humanoid "underpeople," descended from various animals, in Cordwainer Smith's science fiction, notably *Norstrilia*. Similar animal underclasses feature in Jonathan Lethem's *Gun, With Occasional Music* (1994) and, as "moreaus," in S. Andrew Swann's *Forests of the Night* (1993).

Proto-humans are uplifted in *2001: A Space Odyssey*. In E.E. Smith's Lensman sequence (see *Triplanetary*), eugenic programs uplift both aliens and **humanity**. Poul Anderson's *Brain Wave* (1954) shows spontaneous uplift of humankind as **Earth** emerges from an intelligence-inhibiting spatial field; Vernor Vinge's *A Fire Upon the Deep* (1992) extends this concept to successive galactic zones, with limitations of brains, **computers**, and even **physics** dwindling with increasing distance from the "Unthinking Depths" of the galaxy's core. To uplift beyond the constraints of matter is, in Vinge, to Transcend; in Iain M. Banks's Culture universe (see *Consider Phlebas*) the equivalent verb is to **sublime**.

Stephen Baxter's *Time* (1999) features the **genetic engineering** of intelligent squid as space pilots; eventually, spacegoing squid survive the **apocalypse** of humanity.

The possibility of uplifted races surpassing creators—owing to greater intelligence or a different **speed** of **evolution**—figures in Theodore Sturgeon's "Microcosmic God" (1941), whose tiny, rapid-metabolism "Neoterics" evolve from protozoa to transhuman achievement, and Robert L. Forward's *Dragon's Egg* (1980), in which inhabitants of a neutron **star**, exposed to human **education** by a **exploration** team, rapidly outstrip us since they live and breed a million times faster.

Uplift of individuals tends towards **tragedy**, as in Olaf Stapledon's *Sirius* (1944), where the enhanced dog Sirius's human-scale intellect and emotions prove incompatible with life amid human prejudice. His problems are echoed in Diana Wynne Jones's fantasy *Dogsbody* (1975), in which the **star** Sirius is incarnated as a dog. The loneliness of a subnormal man uplifted beyond genius level, only to fall back again, is the theme of Daniel Keyes's ***Flowers for Algernon***. More cheerful creations are the computer-uplifted **ape** of Vinge's "Bookworm, Run!" (1966) and **drug**-enhanced **superman** rivals in Ted Chiang's "Understand" (1991).

Animals gaining speech in fantasy include the titular **cat** of Saki's "Tobermory" (1909), and many beasts are magically uplifted by Aslan the Lion after creation of C.S. Lewis's Narnia (see **Animals and Zoos; *The Lion, the Witch and the Wardrobe***). Denizens of Terry Pratchett's Discworld (see *The Colour of Magic*) are uplifted by contamination with waste **magic**, like Gaspode the Wonder Dog and a cat cooperating with rats in *The Amazing Maurice and His Educated Rodents* (2001). Rats, already intelligent and civilized in Fritz Leiber's *The Swords of Lankhmar* (1968), attain equal footing with humans via a potion that grants equivalent size. Animals metamorphosed into human form generally lack intelligence, but Philip Pullman's *I Was a Rat!* (1999) shows a bewildered character from the Cinderella **fairy tale** struggling to cope with his enduring change from rodent to small boy (see **Metamorphosis; Rats and Mice**).

Discussion

The attraction of uplift may be a yearning for companionship, especially since Earth seems alone in the universe. Brin's uplifted races owe a debt of quasi-**slavery** to less than altruistic "Patrons." To oppose uplift, intelligence itself must be distrusted. Brin's *Brightness Reef* (1995) features various species attempting to expiate crimes by devolving to pre-intelligence. This process becomes a terror weapon in Jack Chalker's *Dancers in the Afterglow* (1978). The godlike aliens of Terry Pratchett's *The Dark Side of the Sun* (1976) have regressed into animal form, allowing late evolvers to develop without being overshadowed. Kurt Vonnegut, Jr.'s **satire** *Galápagos* celebrates a **far future** where humanity has devolved toward smaller, safer brains and short lives. The alien **hive mind** of Bruce Sterling's "Swarm" (1982) rejects intelligence as **weaponry** too dangerous for routine use, while keeping this potential available to deal with intruders—like humans.

Bibliography

Gorman Beauchamp. "*The Island of Doctor Moreau* as Theological Grotesque." *Papers on Language and Literature*, 15 (1979), 408–417.

Elizabeth Man Borgese. *The Language Barrier*. New York: Holt, 1968.

Roger Bowen. "Science, Myth, and Fiction in H.G. Wells's *Island of Dr. Moreau*." *Studies in the Novel*, 8 (Fall, 1976), 318–333.

David Brin and Kevin Lenagh. *Contacting Aliens*. New York: Bantam, 2002.

Martin Gardner. "How Well Can Animals Converse?" Gardner, *Order and Surprise*. Buffalo, NY: Prometheus Books, 1983, 380–390.

———. "Two Books on Talking Apes." Gardner, *Science: Good, Bad and Bogus*. Buffalo, NY: Prometheus Books, 1981, 391–408.

David Langford. "David Brin—the Second Uplift Trilogy." Langford, *Up Through an Empty House of Stars*. Holicong, PA: Cosmos, 2003, 215–218.

Thomas A. Sebeok and Donna Jean Umika-Sebeok, eds. *Speaking of Apes*. New York: Plenum, 1980.

—David Langford

URBAN FANTASY

Overview

There are many **cities** in modern fantasy. They are essential parts of the geography of fantasyland (see **Maps**), serving as destinations, or places to avoid. But they tend to be seen from without, and are subjected to positive or negative attention from that external viewpoint. Only when a city is experienced from inside, as a way of life rather than a place to encounter during the course of a tale whose center lies elsewhere, is it possible usefully to speak of urban fantasy. Urban fantasy is a term that describes a fictional mode, not a location; stories merely about irruptions of supernatural forces within a city like Thorne Smith's *The Night Life of the Gods* (1931) or Esther M. Friesner's *New York by Knight* (1986) do not qualify. A true urban fantasy does not function as an *opposite* to other states or locations, in the way that the city can be seen, for example, to oppose the **wilderness** and physically locate itself elsewhere from the realm of **pastoral**.

Survey

All urban fantasies must of course take place in cities; but only some cities are sufficiently complex to sustain urban fantasy's modular demands, to contain whole universes of discourse within the **borderlands** that can normally be found circumambiating the central scenes. This demand for a complex, multilayered *taken-for-granted* venue may be why it is rare to find an urban fantasy set in a wholly imagined universe: the real cities of this world are not only far more complex than any fantasyland city woven out of whole cloth, but we already recognize them from previous stories. Most urban fantasies are therefore set in fantasticated versions of some real city on **Earth**; furthermore, most modern examples are set in cities that have already had stories told about them.

This is true even of forms of science fiction resembling fantasies that describe **far future** cities, such as those in Jack Vance's *The Dying Earth* (1950), J.G. Ballard's *Vermilion Sands* (1971), or M. John Harrison's Viriconium sequence beginning with *The Pastel City* (1971), as these tales almost invariably present identifiable versions of London or Paris or other European world-cities "enriched" by a vaguely Middle Eastern patina (see **Decadence; Drugs; Fin de Siècle**). China Miéville's ***Perdido Street Station***, for instance, clearly utilizes imagery characteristic of far future tales, while allowing readers to catch glimpses of a vision of London deep within.

But most urban fantasies are set in versions of a limited number of real cities: London, New York, Paris, Venice, Los Angeles, San Francisco, New Orleans, Prague, Berlin: cities already haunted, in our minds' eyes, by previous tales. Urban fantasies can be understood as fantasticated re-enactments of the drama of the city. The thinness of urban life found in Charles de Lint's Newford tales—*Dreams Underfoot: the Newford Collection* (1993) is perhaps the best introduction—may derive from the fact that the real city behind Newford, Ottawa, Ontario, the capital of Canada, is almost certainly too small and unstoried to supply the kind of multilayered background and ambience normally required. Much closer to the kind of density found in urban fantasies set in known cities are Lucius Shepard's five long tales about Trujillo, Honduras assembled in *Trujillo and Other Stories* (2004) or, even more spectacularly, Alasdair Gray's *Lanark* (1981), which is set in a darkly conceived Glasgow.

Urban fantasies are distinguished from nonfantastic stories set in world cities in their taking literally certain urban metaphors. Whereas Charles Dickens may liken London to a **theatre** in his larger novels, in *A Christmas Carol* the city literally stages the drama of Ebenezer Scrooge's sad (but salvageable) life. Whereas Upton Sinclair may liken the city to a **jungle**, in numerous modern urban fantasies—from the film ***Batman*** to William Gibson and Bruce Sterling's ***The Difference Engine***, from the stories in Harlan Ellison's ***Deathbird Stories*** to P.L. Travers's ***Mary Poppins***—we feel the city literally breathing down our necks, whether in **steampunk** terms, or more simply in the form of **magic**. Victor Hugo or Eugene Sue may envision the city as a drama in which life aboveground and life underground intersect, but in Neil Gaiman's *Neverwhere* (1996), Lisa Goldstein's *Dark Cities Underground* (1999), the film ***Brazil***, Mark Helprin's *Winter's Tale* (1983), or Michael Moorcock's *Mother London* (1988), the as-above-so-below structure of the city (see **Architecture and Interior Design**) is articulated in many ways as being *literally the case*. Thus, for example, such tales may make cities into **labyrinths** or send surface-dwellers on **underground adventures** through subways and sewer lines.

The personal dramas of the protagonists in urban fantasy tend to echo its fundamental vision of the city-world as being savagely divided but also organically one thing. In the same way that an urban-fantasy city can be seen as a riven edifice, so the lives depicted in Robert Louis Stevenson's ***Strange Case of Dr. Jekyll and Mr. Hyde*** must be seen as one life riven. **Secret identities** therefore proliferate in the form, from Dr. Jekyll and his twin to Batman and his alter ego Bruce Wayne.

Discussion

In the end, however, the masks worn in urban fantasy do tend to dissolve, catastrophically or otherwise. Given an arena so dramatic, so demanding of its inhabitants, as to require them to perform their lives properly, it is unsurprising that protagonists of urban fantasies, for good or for ill, do find themselves in the end. The urban fantasy thus serves as a theatre of discovery.

Bibliography

Walter Benjamin. *The Arcades Project*. Cambridge, MA: Harvard University Press, 1999.
John Clute. "'City' and 'Urban Fantasy.'" *Paradoxa*, 2 (1996), 19–26.
Carl Freedman. "Towards a Marxist Urban Sublime." *Extrapolation*, 44 (Winter, 2003), 395–408.
Bettina L. Knapp. *Archetype, Architecture, and the Writer*. Bloomington: Indiana University Press, 1986.
Richard Maxwell. *The Mysteries of Paris and London*. Charlottesville: University Press of Virginia, 1992.
Robert Mighall. *A Geography of Victorian Gothic Fiction*. Oxford: Oxford University Press, 1999.
Franco Moretti. *Atlas of the European Novel 1800-1900*. London: Verso, 1998.
Seymour Rudin. "Urban Gothic." *Extrapolation*, 25 (Summer, 1984), 115–126.
Kathleen L. Spencer. "Victorian Urban Gothic." George Slusser and Eric S. Rabkin, eds., *Intersections*. Carbondale: Southern Illinois University Press, 1987, 87–96.

—John Clute

UTOPIA
■

There are no easy Utopias.

—Gerald Jonas
"The Shaker Revival" (1970)

Overview

Despite similarities to visions of a lost "golden age" (see **Arcadia**), utopia attempts to achieve perfect social justice in the future. It derives from ancient Greek belief in rational **ethics**, later buttressed by Christian emphasis on a moral societal structure, especially for lower classes (see **Christianity**). Usually such posited societies involve a large degree of equality among classes and regimentation in both work and lifestyles (see **Politics**). Basic to utopian impulses is the conviction that humans can create an earthly paradise and reform themselves to live in a compliant, harmonious manner with one another. Furthermore, social harmony will lead to great gains in economic output and artistic expression (see **Art; Economics**).

Survey

The term derives from Thomas More's *Utopia*; "utopia" is neatly balanced between the Greek "eutopia" ("good place") and "outopia" ("no place"). Nevertheless, the concept of a society perfected by rational principles dates back to Plato's *The Republic* (c. 380 BCE), a seminal text for all literary utopias. Describing justice (see **Philosophy**), Socrates outlines a **city** laid out in a symmetrical fashion; the populace is governed by a small elite caste of Guardians who are carefully trained for their leadership role, who have no private property or **families**, and whose desires are entirely subjugated to the needs of the state. The entire construct is predicated on the faith that careful social planning and **education** can lead to human perfection amongst the Guardians. Their **sexuality** is controlled so as to breed a superior race. All artistic expression is censured (see **Poetry**). Plato's totalitarian state is often satirized in dystopian fiction (see **Dystopia; Satire**).

No other prominent utopian texts were composed until a spate of tracts appeared in the late Renaissance, when a sense of **progress** inspired hopes of perfection by means of human efforts. More's *Utopia* envisions a Christian communitarianism, wherein citizens of an **island** off the coast of **Latin America** share equally in its work and wealth—in marked contrast to the cruel **class system** of More's England. To prevent social tensions, equality is rigidly established and individual **freedoms** are sacrificed for conformity; Utopians need permission to go on hikes. *Utopia* is written to blur the issue of just how much of this vision More supports; the narrator's surname Hythloday, for example, derives from the Greek for "nonsense." Other utopian fictions of this era explore how science might improve humanity's lot: Tommaso Campanella's *The City of the Sun* (1602–1623) establishes a state control over sexuality more pervasive than Plato's, and Francis Bacon's *The New Atlantis* (1627) combines science and Christianity.

Since emotions are typically moderated in utopia to permit rational thought, texts rarely produce narrative interest. Some led to the creation of actual social movements, especially in the latter half of the nineteenth century, when the scientific perfection of society seemed within easy grasp. "Vera's Fourth Dream" of rural communes in Nikolai Chernyshevsky's *What Is to Be Done?* (1862) was cherished by Vladimir Lenin, founder of the Soviet Union (see **Russia**). Edward Bellamy's *Looking Backward, 2000-1887* inspired utopian clubs in the United States that hoped to achieve social reforms in the **near future** through industrial efficiency. Samuel Butler's *Erewhon* (1872) and W.H. Hudson's *A Crystal Age* (1887) were interesting though less influential.

William Morris's *News from Nowhere* (1890) answered Bellamy by calling instead for a return to harmonious **pastoral** anarchy, allowing, perhaps naively, both cooperation and freedom. H.G. Wells' *A Modern Utopia* (1905) reintroduces a ruling elite and a World State, realizing that no society can remain separate. Wells counts on modern science to free men of most labor, but worries that, as in his *The Time Machine*, this will cause **decadence**. He thus requires sexual controls and intrusive surveillance. Albeit egalitarian, most utopias remain distinctly sexist and patriarchal. Charlotte Perkins Gilman's *Herland* is the first of several feminist utopias (see **Feminism**; Ursula K. Le Guin's *The Dispossessed*, Joanna Russ's *The Female Man*, Samuel R. Delany's *Triton*, and Marge Piercy's *Woman on the Edge of Time*) positing alternatives to traditional patriarchy.

Nevertheless, during the twentieth century utopian texts were greatly outnumbered by dystopian fictions. Optimistic visions of the inevitable Communist future were written in the Soviet Union, veritably intended to be the first utopian state, but it soon became politically untenable under Stalinism to describe either that perfected future or how it would be achieved. Some readers were reminded of the U.S.S.R. by B.F. Skinner's *Walden Two* (1948), a utopia achieved through behaviorist positive reinforcement. Although Skinner's citizens do not feel constrained in their actions, his naive vision provoked a dystopic response (see Anthony Burgess's *A Clockwork Orange*).

Discussion

Utopian societies depicted in literature generally share these characteristics: economic plenitude or at least freedom from want, social conviviality, rationality, and some standardization and conformity. In several ways people live like hunter-gatherers. Many utopias envisage a return to agrarian lifestyles. Yet authors often require control by an elite (see **Governance Systems**); this undermines their denial that humans have a largely unchangeable nature resistant to social engineering. For example, utopian texts often demand disruption of the nuclear **family**, which they regard as an impediment to the creation of wider loyalty.

Bibliography

Gorman Beauchamp. "Utopia and Its Discontents." *Midwest Quarterly*, 16 (Summer, 1975), 161–174.

Marie Louise Berneri. *Journey through Utopia*. New York: Schocken, 1950.

Neta C. Crawford. "Feminist Futures." Jutta Weldes, ed., *To Seek Out New Worlds*. New York: Palgrave Macmillan, 2003, 195–220.

Robert C. Eliot. *The Shape of Utopia*. Chicago: University of Chicago Press, 1970.

Lewis Mumford. *The Story of Utopias*. New York: Viking, 1962.

Kenneth M. Roemer. *Utopian Audiences*. Amherst: University of Massachusetts Press, 2003.

Peter Ruppert. *Reader in a Strange Land*. Athens: University of Georgia Press, 1986.

George Slusser, Paul Alkon, Roger Gaillard, and Danièle Chatelain, eds. *Transformations of Utopia*. New York: AMS Press, 1999.

Richard Stites. *Revolutionary Dreams*. New York: Oxford University Press, 1989.

—Brett Cooke

VAMPIRES

This vampire which is amongst us is of himself so strong in person as twenty men; he is of cunning more than mortal, for his cunning be the growth of ages; he have still the aids of necromancy, which is, as his etymology imply, the divination by the dead, and all the dead that he can come nigh to are for him at command; he is brute, and more than brute; he is devil in callous, and the heart of him is not; he can, within limitations, appear at will when, and where, and in any of the forms that are to him; he can, within his range, direct the elements: the storm, the fog, the thunder; he can command all the meaner things: the rat, and the owl, and the bat—the moth, and the fox, and the wolf; he can grow and become small; and he can at times vanish and come unknown. How then are we to begin our strife to destroy him?

—Bram Stoker
Dracula (1897)

Overview

Vampires are a subspecies of revenants, creatures that return from the dead. Unlike revenants like mummies (see **Egypt**) or **werewolves**, vampires survive by taking **blood** from the living. Vampires have the ability to shift shape (see **Shapeshifters**) and their powers are enhanced by **darkness**. Ways of creating or destroying vampires are legion, varying according to specific narratives. Traditionally vampires were considered creatures of darkness, but some recent narratives present heroic and romantic vampires.

Survey

Folkloric vampires exist in almost all cultures. Chinese, Indian, and Pre-Colombian narratives record vampiric characters. References to vampires appear in ancient Assyrian legends, Talmudic texts, and Greek and Roman stories. Most describe night-roaming female figures that drink the blood of the living.

The first literary vampires were German, appearing in poems like Gottfried Burger's "Leonre" (1733), Heinrich Ossenfelder's "Der Vampir" (1748), and Goethe's "Bride of Corinth" (1797); these influenced English Romantic writers like John Keats, Samuel Taylor Coleridge, and Lord Byron, who employed the vampire as a tragic romantic figure. However, the major development of the vampire in fantasy came in fiction. John Polidori's *The Vampyre* (1819) created an adult, male, sexual vampire. Joseph Sheridan Le Fanu's "Carmilla" (1871) featured a lesbian vampire and influenced Bram Stoker, whose **Dracula** became the canonical vampire text, referenced by and influencing all other vampire films and fiction. *Dracula* defined the vampire as a male aristocratic predator whose hungers combined eroticism and **violence**; the novel also suggested that vampirism is both a supernatural **evil** and an infection, themes developed in later fiction. Finally, *Dracula* established the conventions that vampires **sleep** in coffins, can be destroyed by wooden stakes and decapitation, and are injured by religious objects.

In the twentieth century, the figure of the vampire became a staple of popular science fiction and fantasy. Several writers created successful series of vampire novels. The most popular is Anne Rice's Vampire Chronicles, beginning with **Interview with the Vampire**, which introduced the vampire Lestat, a self-styled "brat prince" who is central in most of Rice's dark fictions. Chelsea Quinn Yarbro's Chronicles of Saint-Germain, beginning with *The Hotel Transylvania* (1978), featured Saint-Germain, a gentlemanly, heroic vampire whose adventures span three millennia. In *The Dracula Tape* (1975) Fred Saberhagen retold *Dracula* from the vampire's point of view and followed his Dracula through a series of **horror/mystery** novels, some featuring Sherlock Holmes. Also significant are the series by Nancy Collins, beginning with *Sunglasses after Dark* (1990, which offered Sonja Blue, a young punk vampire/vampire hunter, and by P.N. Elrod, beginning with *Bloodlist* (1990). Other important vampire fictions include Stephen King's *Salem's Lot* (1975), an homage to *Dracula* set in contemporary New England; Richard Matheson's *I Am Legend* (1954), a science fiction novel that posits a world of vampires hunting one surviving human; Suzy McKee Charnas's elegant *The Vampire Tapestry* (1980), which introduced Dr. Edward Weyland, **anthropology** professor and vampire; and Whitley Strieber's haunting *The Hunger* (1981), a tale of **love** and loss set in New York.

Vampires fared well in the darkened theaters of the twentieth century, and most major vampire films were adaptations of *Dracula*. F.W. Murnau's silent film *Nosferatu* (1922), an unauthorized adaptation of Stoker's novel, depicted the vampire as a wraithlike figure of evil, in contrast to Tod Browning's **Dracula**, which established Hungarian actor Bela Lugosi as the iconic representation of Stoker's vampire. One of the numerous Dracula films that followed, Francis Ford Coppola's operatic *Bram Stoker's Dracula* (1992), dramatized the link between Transylvanian nobleman

Vlad Dracul and the fictive Dracula first suggested and popularized in Raymond McNally and Rady Florescu's *In Search of Dracula* (1972).

Among the other films that defined the twentieth-century vampire are Tony Scott's stylish, erotic adaptation of *The Hunger* (1983); Joel Shumacher's *The Lost Boys* (1987), which combines elements of vampirism with Peter Pan (see J.M. Barrie's **Peter and Wendy**), Fran Ruben Kuzui's comic *Buffy The Vampire Slayer* (1992), the first appearance of Josh Whedon's character; Neil Jordan's successful adaptation of Rice's *Interview with the Vampire* (1994); Wes Craven's interesting *A Vampire in Brooklyn* (1995), starring Eddie Murphy in a dark **comedy**; and Stephen Sommers's *Van Helsing* (2004), which reunites the famous Universal **monsters**.

Friendly vampires also appeared on television in such mainstream programs as *The Munsters* (1964–1966) and *Sesame Street* (launched in 1969). Two television series focused on more traditional vampires. *Dark Shadows* (1967–1971), a **Gothic** drama, dramatized the story of American vampire Barnabas Collins. More recently, **Buffy the Vampire Slayer** demonstrated the wide popularity of the dark narrative of vampires and their slayers.

Discussion

In the century since the publication of Stoker's *Dracula*, the figure of the vampire, in popular science fiction and fantasy, was transformed from bloodthirsty monster to a tragic, often romantic **hero**. Nevertheless, in contemporary film and fiction, the vampire remains a marginal figure, representing the strange and the other that is paradoxically part of all of us.

Bibliography

Nina Auerbach. *Our Vampires, Ourselves*. Chicago: University of Chicago Press, 1995.
Ken Gelder. *Reading the Vampire*. London and New York: Routledge. 1994.
Leonard G. Heldreth and Mary Pharr, eds. *The Blood Is the Life*. Bowling Green, OH: Bowling Green State University Popular Press, 1999.
James Craig Holte, ed. *The Fantastic Vampire*. Westport, CT: Greenwood Press, 1997.
J. Gordon Melton. *The Vampire Book*. Detroit: Visible Ink, 1994.
Carol Senf. *The Vampire in Nineteenth-Century English Literature*. Bowling Green, OH: Bowling Green State University Popular Press, 1988.
David Skal. *Hollywood Gothic*. New York: Norton, 1993.
Montague Summers. *The Vampire*. 1928. New Hyde Park, NY: University Books, 1960.
James Twitchell. *The Living Dead*. Durham, NC: Duke University Press, 1986.

—*James Craig Holte*

VENUS

Overview

Venus, second planet from the Sun, is nearly "Earth's twin" in size and approaches **Earth** more closely than any other major solar system body except the **Moon**. Its surface, however, is permanently hidden by thick clouds. Even so fundamental a parameter as its rotation period remained unknown until the 1960s. This tantalizing combination of proximity and **mystery** dominated the science fiction of "Earth's sister planet" up until the mid-1960s, when new data made scores of classic stories obsolete.

Survey

A planet permanently shrouded with clouds might imply abundant **water**, and in 1918 Nobel Prize-winning chemist Svante Arrhenius proposed that Venus was dripping wet. Based on the old Laplacian theory that the relative age of planets increased outward, it was a short step to seeing Venus as an image of a younger Earth, of (say) Carboniferous swamps, as in Edgar Rice Burroughs's *Pirates of Venus* (1934) and its sequels, and Otis Adelbert Kline's Venus series beginning with *The Planet of Peril* (1929). Stanley G. Weinbaum's "Parasite Planet" (1935) shows a fecund planet at a more cerebral level, as do Olaf Stapledon's **Last and First Men**, Malcolm Jameson's "Lilies of Life" (1945), Henry Kuttner's *Fury* (1947), and Arthur C. Clarke's "History Lesson" (1949). Even into the 1960s, Robert A. Heinlein was regularly depicting a sodden Venus ("Logic of Empire" [1941], *Space Cadet* [1948], *Between Planets* [1951], and *Podkayne of Mars* [1963]) that hardly differed from Burroughs's.

The clouds of Venus might also suggest a world entirely covered with water, as in C.S. Lewis's *Perelandra* (1942) (see **Out of the Silent Planet**). Isaac Asimov used a similar setting for his juvenile *Lucky Starr and the Oceans of Venus* (1954). An all-ocean Venus was briefly scientifically respectable in the late 1950s; unusually, Poul Anderson's disturbing "Sister Planet" (1959) uses a potentially habitable oceanic Venus as a temptation for an overcrowded Earth. The last serious "wet Venus" story is Roger Zelazny's "The Doors of His Mouth, the Lamps of His Face" (1965), describing an encounter with an enormous Venusian sea **monster**.

Even in the 1920s, though, "wet Venus" models were attacked, and as early as 1940 astrophysicist Rupert Wildt proposed high surface temperatures on Venus based on a greenhouse model that proved essentially correct. Occasionally, stories in the 1950s and 1960s portrayed Venus as a dry, hostile planet, as in two **satires**—Frederik Pohl and C.M. Kornbluth's **The Space Merchants** and Robert Sheckley's "Prospector Planet" (1959)—and in two serious stories—Dean McLaughlin's *The Fury from Earth* (1963) and Clarke's "Before Eden" (1961). Generally, such stories still fell short of describing the truly hellish conditions on Venus, as demonstrated by Clarke's rationalization of indigenous Venusian life.

After "wet Venus" was laid to rest, a few stories, mostly **survival** epics, have been set on the "new" Venus, like Larry Niven's "Becalmed in Hell" (1965). The desire to find life remains strong, however, as with the living petroleum in Brenda Pearce's "Crazy Oil" (1975) or the telepathic jewels in John Varley's "In the Bowl" (1975). In Ben Bova's *Venus* (2000), cloud-borne microbes prove a major hazard to a Venus expedition. One story in Pohl's *The Gateway Trip* (1990) (see **Gateway**) involves discovery of alien artifacts on a barren Venus. Somewhat improbably, Sarah Zettel's *The Quiet Invasion* (2000) has Venus a target of colonization by aliens fleeing an ecological catastrophe on their homeworld.

As the reality of Venus's hellish conditions settled into writers' collective consciousness, however, science fiction about Venus focused more on **terraforming**. As early as 1955, Anderson's "The Big Rain" showed colonists working to transform a hot, poisonous Venus into a new Earth. Tales like Bob Buckley's "World in the Clouds" (1980) and G. David Nordley's "The Snows of Venus" (1991) focus on the travails of terraformers, and in Pamela Sargent's *Venus of Dreams* (1986) and its sequels, terraforming Venus serves as the background of a multigenerational saga. The deadly **jungle** in Marta Randall's "Big Dome" (1985), a lost domed colony abandoned during a terraforming project, no doubt pays homage to the "traditional" science-fictional Venus. In other stories, like Nordley's "Dawn Venus" (1995), Venus is already Earth-like, further recalling early twentieth-century **romances**.

Discussion

For decades Venus was a cosmic Rorschach test, authors reading into its featureless clouds exotic but habitable settings for stories ranging from rousing adventure to pointed satire. For adventure tales or social commentary, of course, the real Venus is hardly the point. **Hard science fiction**, however, is supposed to depict possibilities consistent with current **knowledge**. An underexplored issue, then, is the degree to which such stories portrayed Venus (and **Mars**, for that matter) with roughly Earth-like environments long after such pictures had stopped being scientifically credible. Whether shirtsleeve settings reflected wishful thinking, or were merely a convenient prop for storytelling, it may be that hard science fiction has more in common with fantasy than is commonly acknowledged. In turn, the preoccupation with terraforming in later science fiction seems an attempt to recapture a lush world that never was.

Bibliography

Brian W. Aldiss and Harry Harrison, ed. *Farewell, Fantastic Venus!* London: McDonald & Co., 1968.

Robert H. Barrett. "Cloudland Revisited." *Burroughs Bulletin*, No. 51 (Summer 2002), 14–20.

M.J. Bell. "Otis Adelbert Kline's Venus Novels." *Oak Leaves*, 1 (Winter, 1972/1973), 3–6.

Andrew Darlington. "Visions of Venus." *The Zone*, No. 3 (Autumn, 1995), 30–32.

Terry Hansen. "Myth-Adventure in Leigh Brackett's 'Enchantress of Venus.'" *Extrapolation*. 23 (Spring, 1982), 77–82.

Donald M. Hassler. "Ambivalences in the Venus of Pamela Sargent." *Extrapolation*, 38 (Summer, 1997), 150–156.

Rob Marshall. "Storm World Views: Cinema SF about Venus." *The Zone*, No. 3 (Autumn, 1995), 32–33.

Sam Moskowitz. "To Mars and Venus in the Gay Nineties." *Fantastic Universe*, 12 (February, 1969), 44–56.

Eugene Warren. "Venus Redeemed." *Orcrist*, No. 6 (Winter 1971–1972), 14–16.

—*Stephen L. Gillett*

VILLAINS

Overview

Though deprecated in more upmarket work, boldly unrepentant villains and **evil-doers** frequently drive the plots of traditional **space opera** and **heroic fantasy**. Series characters like Sherlock Holmes, **superheroes**, Robert E. Howard's *Conan the Conqueror*, and *Xena: Warrior Princess* demand a steady supply of villainous opponents, a recurring arch-enemy like Holmes's Moriarty, or both.

Survey

Whether human or alien, a villain needs human-like motivations, if only the lust for power or **money**. Jekyll's dark counterpart in Robert Louis Stevenson's *Strange Case of Dr. Jekyll and Mr. Hyde* is a potent reminder that villainy begins at home. Figures of more cosmic stature, like **Satan**, Sauron in J.R.R. Tolkien's *The Lord of the Rings*, Lord Foul in Stephen R. Donaldson's *Lord Foul's Bane*, or the **mountain-**sized, sea-dwelling enemies in Gene Wolfe's *The Book of the New Sun* should not be considered mere villains—although the borderlands of villainhood are blurry. Likewise, inherently evil nonhumans like Tolkien's orcs lack the *frisson* of true villainy.

Early science fiction and the overlapping **detective** fiction genre often featured a racist (see **Race Relations**) choice of villains; the eponymous Chinese mastermind of Sax Rohmer's *The Insidious Dr. Fu-Manchu* (1913) and its sequels exemplied fear of the Oriental "Yellow Peril," already promulgated by M.P. Shiel in works like *The Yellow Danger* (1898). Though the murderous Captain Nemo of Jules Verne's *Twenty Thousand Leagues under the Sea* eventually proves (in *The Mysterious Island* [1874–1875]) to be an Indian prince, racism is not here an issue. In the James Bond film *Doctor No*, the villainous Dr. No—whose steel hands recall Rotwang in *Metropolis* and Captain Hook in J.M. Barrie's *Peter and Wendy*—fuses "Yellow Peril" **paranoia** with larger-than-life grotesquerie, exploited in later films. The gigantic, sinisterly helmeted Darth Vader of *Star Wars* continues the grotesque tradition.

Villains of stature in science fiction include the brilliant, amoral **scientist** DuQuesne of E.E. "Doc" Smith's *The Skylark of Space* (1928) and its sequels; the Mule in Isaac Asimov's *Foundation* saga; the gross Baron Harkonnen in Frank Herbert's *Dune*; the mercurial cyborg Prince Red in Samuel R. Delany's *Nova* (1968); and the unusually human **computer** HAL 9000 in *2001: A Space Odyssey*. The five Demon Princes of Jack Vance's sequence beginning with *The Star King* (1964) are characterized by different brands of **madness**, reflecting the **revenge** obsession of the hero who is their nemesis.

Madness is frequent in comic-book villains, like the **mad scientist** Luthor who forever opposes *Superman*, and the demented **trickster**, the Joker, who plagues *Batman*; Alan Moore's graphic novel *The Killing Joke* (1988) shows Batman and Joker as psychological **mirror** images driven by related obsessions.

On television, *Doctor Who* regularly confronts that chilly power-seeker, The Master, and everybody's favorite megalomaniac **cyborgs**, the Daleks. *Star Trek*'s recurring villains, the Klingons and Romulans, are less implacable and are partially rehabilitated.

Fantasy villainy has a longer pedigree. The **Arthur** legends feature the vengeful bastard son Mordred and the **witch**-girl who entraps Merlin. The **wizard** Atlantés in Ariosto's *Orlando Furioso* (1516) remains an effective figure in L. Sprague de Camp and Fletcher Pratt's comic pastiche *The Castle of Iron* (1950). Gandolf of Utterbol in William Morris's *The Well at the World's End* (1896) is a petty sadist who nevertheless inspires dread. Perhaps the best fantasy villain is the luxuriantly wicked sorcerer-**king** Gorice in E.R. Eddison's *The Worm Ouroboros*. The White Witch in C.S. Lewis's *The Lion, the Witch and the Wardrobe* is similarly obsessed with power, as is Steerpike in Mervyn Peake's *Titus Groan*—an initially sympathetic characterization, until he is devoured by his own ambition.

Classic movie images of villainous **witches** appear in *Snow White and the Seven Dwarfs* and *The Wizard of Oz*, the latter also featuring a good witch for balance (see **Yin and Yang**). Cruella de Vil of *One Hundred and One Dalmatians* (1961), based on Dodie Smith's 1956 novel, is a memorable comic monster, valuing cute **dogs** only for their fur.

Modern commercial fantasy abounds in villains, all too many of them indistinguishable. Notably, the magician Trent in Piers Anthony's *A Spell for Chameleon* is a former major villain who plausibly reforms; Terry Pratchett's Discworld novels (see *The Colour of Magic*) regularly feature quirkily obsessive or insane schemers; Lord Voldemort from *Harry Potter and the Sorcerer's Stone* has practically entered the language.

Discussion

In a natural **role reversal**, Mary Gentle and Roz Kaveney's anthology *Villains!* (1992) examines fantasy from the bad guys' side. Even orcs become viewpoint characters in Gentle's *Grunts* (1992) and Stan Nicholls's Orcs: First Blood trilogy, beginning with *Bodyguard of Lightning* (1999). Eve Forward's comic *Villains by Necessity* (1995) shows villains heroically joining to save the world from Good.

More interestingly, charismatic antiheroes like Reich in Alfred Bester's *The Demolished Man* and Alex in Anthony Burgess's *A Clockwork Orange* lure readers into semi-complicity with villainous actions. The battered mercenary protagonist of Iain M. Banks's *Consider Phlebas* is eventually shown to have chosen the wrong side. **Humanity** itself is seen as **evil** in George Orwell's *Animal Farm*, whose revolutionary leaders, pigs, become shockingly indistinguishable from the human enemy. The antihero of Oscar Wilde's *The Picture of Dorian Gray* separates himself from his own evil, but not forever; the **hero** of Ursula K. Le Guin's *A Wizard of Earthsea* must understand the enemy as his own shadow, to be embraced rather than defeated.

Bibliography

Isaac Asimov. "The Scientist as Villain." Asimov, *Asimov on Science Fiction*. Garden City, NY: Doubleday, 1981, 64–68.

Orson Scott Card. "Heroes and Villains." *SFWA Bulletin*, 14 (Spring, 1979), 21–23.

Mary Gentle and Roz Kaveney, ed. *Villains!* Harmondsworth, Middlesex, UK: Roc, 1992.

James Gunn. "Heroes, Heroines, Villains." Reginald Bretnor, ed., *The Craft of Science Fiction*. New York: Harper, 1976, 161–177.

John Mortimer, ed. *The Oxford Book of Villains*. Oxford, UK: Oxford University Press, 1991.

Mark Oehlert. "From Captain America to Wolverine." Chris H. Gray, ed., *The Cyborg Handbook*. New York: Routledge, 1995, 219–231.

Deborah W. Rogers. "Misery Loves . . . A Root of Villainy." *Mythlore*, 14 (Winter, 1987), 23–25, 40.

Jeff Rovin. *The Encyclopedia of Super Villains*. New York: Facts on File, 1987.

Gary Westfahl. "Wrangling Conversation." George Slusser and Eric S. Rabkin, eds., *Fights of Fancy*. Athens, GA: University of Georgia Press, 1993, 35–48.

—*David Langford*

VIOLENCE

■

"Violence," came the retort, "is the last refuge of the incompetent."

—Isaac Asimov
"Foundation" (1942)

Overview

Because a great deal of science fiction and fantasy is rooted in action and adventure, many of the solutions that protagonists or antagonists arrive at are violent ones. Both genres have, however, been places for thought experiments about the reasons for and purposes behind personal and collective violence.

Survey

Texts that focus on violence can be loosely organized into five categories: the first proposes that violence comes from external sources (aliens, sorcerers, gods); the second from internal, or human, causes; the third is genre-related; the fourth deals with gender; the fifth suggests alternatives to violence. In the first (external) variety, violence is embodied by **insects,** or unknown alien forces (see *The War of the Worlds; The Thing (from Another World)*; *Alien*; Orson Scott Card's *Ender's Game*) that attack **humanity** without provocation. Such texts reflect on their times and can be understood as expressions of racial intolerance, Cold War **paranoia,** or **xenophobia.** In fantasy texts, superhuman killers like **demons,** sorcerers, and **vampires** are often countered by physical strength (see Robert E. Howard's *Conan the Conqueror; Xena: Warrior Princess*), by "white magic" (see J.K. Rowling's *Harry Potter and the Sorcerer's Stone*), or spiritual authority (see C.S. Lewis's *The Lion, the Witch and the Wardrobe*). While some texts can be read as displaced cultural fear, others provide author and audience with malign forces to be hated unconditionally and wiped out without remorse.

In the second category, internal violence, are texts that identify humans as agents of our own undoing. These are often moral works, using savagery to express the authors' outrage at human behavior (see William Golding's *Lord of the Flies*; Anthony Burgess's *A Clockwork Orange*; Harlan Ellison's *Deathbird Stories*; the film *Robocop* [1987]). The violence is so extreme that the audience must consider its societal causes. Fantasy texts also engage the issue of industrial violence in conflict with personal heroism: J.R.R. Tolkien's *The Lord of the Rings* pits skill with hand-crafted **weaponry** against black **magic** and industrial forms of **war**. Critics of such texts suggest that the reason for their popularity is not their social **satire** but the pleasure audiences takes from the mayhem itself. Arguments about these texts have caused them to be moved on and off reading lists and library shelves.

The third group, genre-related violence, is bloody by tradition. Science-fictional police stories (Larry Niven's *The Long ARM of Gil Hamilton* [1976]; John Varley's *The Barbie Murders* [1980]) necessarily involve homicide, as do fantasy series that require violent conclusions to problems (*Conan the Adventurer* [1997–1998]; *Hercules: The Legendary Journeys*). The revivified noir genre (see *Blade Runner*; William Gibson's *Neuromancer*; *The Matrix*) can be characterized as both murderous and "cool." A tarnished white knight walks down Raymond Chandler's "mean streets" of urban and societal decay: social injustice drives jaded **heroes** to violent action (physically or in **cyberspace**). Although existential and spiritual questions about life anchor noir narratives, the stories are invariably ended (if not resolved) violently: the more protagonists resists violence, the more they must engage in it. Similarly, fantasy texts engage existential issues, particularly when magic causes the protagonist to reconsider the way reality is constructed, as in Roger Zelazny's Amber series beginning with *Nine Princes in Amber* (1970) and *Lord of Light*. Led by Anne Rice's *Interview with a Vampire*, vampire texts have become a venue for complex noir stories in which violence blurs the line between good and **evil**.

Both fantasy and science fiction texts in the fourth group argue that violence is the product of **gender** constructions, and the patriarchy has dedicated itself to the project of raising and rewarding violent people and technologies (see **Feminism**). Powerful criticisms can be found in Charlotte Perkins Gilman's *Herland*, Ursula K. Le Guin's *The Word for World is Forest* (1972), and Sheri S. Tepper's *The Gate to Women's Country*. These texts not only identify violence as a learned habit passed down from **father** to son, but propose ways to shift the world to more peaceful, caring kinds of living.

The final group consists of texts that offer alternatives to violence. Isaac Asimov's *Foundation* series, Iain M. Banks's Culture novels (see *Consider Phlebas*), the *Star Trek* films and television series, *Wonder Woman*, and *Superman* show humanity's better nature, finding in reason and **education** the promise of peaceful coexistence with the Other. Some fantasy texts offer utopian promises of agrarian worlds free of violent action (see **Utopia**).

Discussion

Audiences determine whether textual violence serves primarily an artistic, social, or entertainment purpose. Art need not carry a message, but excessive violence lays responsibility on the creator to examine a world made of **pain** and viciousness. Violence in **art** is something science fiction and fantasy have both furthered and questioned. Few critics have been as effective as Golding, Asimov, Tolkien, and Tepper at forcing us to reconsider what pleasure we take from violence. Is brutal entertainment always wrong? Aristotelian and Shakespearean dramas are replete with every form of ruthless blood-letting. Science fiction and fantasy have worked hard to consider not only personal and societal violence, but ways in which humanity might alter itself to be less cruel: the aliens and sorcerers that various authors have imagined are, after all, really humans in **disguise**. The violence we consume always reflects on our own values and **culture** and cannot be transferred to another: these violent texts are about us.

Bibliography

Ximena Gallardo and C. Jason Smith. *Alien Woman*. New York: Continuum, 2004.
Susan Jeffords. *The Remasculinization of America*. Bloomington: Indiana University Press, 1989.
Annette Kuhn, ed. *Alien Zone*. London: Verso, 1990.
Jerry Pournelle, ed. *Survival of Freedom*. New York: Fawcett Books, 1981.
Per Schelde. *Androids, Humanoids, and Other Science Fiction Monsters*. New York: New York University Press, 1993.
Christopher Sharrett, ed. *Crisis Cinema*. Washington, DC: Maisonneuve Press, 1993.
Richard Slotkin. *Gunfighter Nation*. New York: Simon & Schuster, 1992.
George Slusser and Eric S. Rabkin, eds. *Fights of Fancy*. Athens: University of Georgia Press, 1993.

—Tim Blackmore

VIRGINITY

Overview

Virgins—men and women who have not yet engaged in sexual relations—have inspired very different reactions in the past and in the present. Once, virginity was regarded as an admirable status conferring special dignity or even magical powers (see **Magic**); today, in a culture more inclined to celebrate and encourage **sexuality**, virginity is frequently something to be ashamed of and to ridicule.

Survey

Female virginity was significant in Greek **mythology**: three goddesses in the Olympian pantheon—Athena, goddess of **wisdom**; Artemis, goddess of the hunt; and Hestia, goddess of the hearth and **home**—were celebrated as virgins, as were the priestesses that served in temples dedicated to Greek **gods and goddesses**. The female **hero** Atalanta was also a dedicated virgin, although obliged to marry after famously losing a race by imprudently chasing after golden apples. Female virgins were sometimes sacrificed to Greek gods (see **Sacrifice**): Agamemnon sacrificed his daughter Iphigenia so Artemis would allow him to launch his expedition to Troy, as recounted in Euripides's play *Iphigenia in Aulis* (405 BCE), and Cepheus and Cassiopeia intended to sacrifice their daughter Andromeda to a sea **monster** to appease Poseidon, though she was rescued by Perseus, as described in the film *Clash of the Titans* (1980).

Virginity also became important in **Christianity**, which established as dogma both that Jesus's mother Mary was a lifelong virgin, miraculously and chastely giving birth to the Son of God, and that Jesus refrained from sexual activity. Necessarily ignored are numerous references in the Bible and elsewhere to Jesus's brothers, and there have been occasional suggestions that Jesus had married Mary Magdalene. Even in recent times, scenes in the film *The Last Temptation of Christ* (1988) suggesting that Jesus felt sexual desires inspired widespread protests and boycotts. Virgin births are rare in later fantasies, one exception being the mysterious manner in which women in Charlotte Perkins Gilman's **Herland** give birth to children without the help of men.

During the sixteenth century, Queen Elizabeth I of England widely—and inaccurately—proclaimed her virginity as one way to enhance her aura of royal authority. She was celebrated as such in Edmund Spenser's unfinished epic poem *The Faerie Queene* (1590, 1596), which was planned to conclude with the virgin Faerie Queene marrying King **Arthur**—symbolically having Elizabeth marry her nation, England. A parallel story completed within the poem was that of Britomart, a fierce virgin warrior who eventually marries the knight Artegall, representing Justice. It has remained a strong if unstated tenet of **heroic fantasy** that heroes should properly seek out virgins as lifelong mates; thus, the title of Edgar Rice Burroughs's *Thuvia, Maid of Mars* (1920) (see *A Princess of Mars*) reassures readers that the woman to be rescued and romanced by Burroughs's hero Carthoris will remain virginal until her **marriage**.

Certain traditions regarding female virgins sometimes figure in later fantasies. Alan Garner's *Elidor* (1965) embraces the ancient belief that only a virgin girl has the power to capture a **unicorn**. In certain versions of the **vampire** legend—though not the most famous vampire story, Bram Stoker's **Dracula**—vampires can only feast upon the **blood** of virgins. The notion that poltergeists (see **Ghosts and Hauntings**) are attracted by virgins underlies the film *Poltergeist* (1982), in which the chief victim is a five-year-old girl. Poul Anderson's *Operation Chaos* (1971) suggests that virgins have their own special brand of magic, to be replaced as they mature by the different magics of **mothers** and old women. The apparent virginity of the powerful women like Glinda and Ozma in L. Frank Baum's Oz books (see **The Wonderful Wizard of Oz**) is announced explicitly in Robert A. Heinlein's *The Number of the Beast* (1980), wherein Glinda bluntly informs spacefaring visitors to Oz that their women will be unable to bear **children** while they remain in Oz, a land without sexuality where no one is born and no one dies.

Contemporary fantasies typically treat virgins with little respect. In the revisionist *Andy Warhol's Dracula* (1974), a recurring joke involves Dracula's inability to locate a suitable virgin in contemporary society. And in Esther M. Friesner's Tim Desmond trilogy, beginning with *Gnome Man's Land* (1991), her young male hero is regularly embarrassed when **supernatural creatures** invading New York City make open references to his virginity. Still, at least one subgenre continues to implicitly acknowledge the power of virginity. It is often noted that in "slasher" films like *Halloween* (1978), *Friday the Thirteenth* (1980), and their innumerable sequels and imitators, the "bad" girls—those who have sex with boyfriends—tend to be attacked and slaughtered by the menace at hand, whereas the "good" girls—those who refrain from sexual activity—tend to survive, mysteriously protected from harm, it seems, by their virginity.

Discussion

While adult virginity may continue to seem less and less desirable in the future, advances in **technology** may ironically make it possible for people to enjoy the pleasures, and effects, of sexual intercourse without actually having sex. Thus, a woman might chastely enjoy sexual sensations only in scientifically induced **dreams** or **virtual reality**, or might chastely bear a child by means of a surrogate mother or cloning (see **Clones**). The end result might be people who are both virginal and sexually active, like the romantic couple of Frederik Pohl's "Day Million" (1966), who enjoy artificial sex with simulated images of each other even while they remain permanently separated, millions of miles apart. In such strange ways, forms of virginity might again become commonplace and socially acceptable.

Bibliography

Julie Brown. "Our Ladies of Perpetual Hell." *Journal of the Fantastic in the Arts*, 4 (1991), 40–52.

Maureen Duffy. "Renaissance: Sex and Violence." Duffy, *The Erotic World of Faery*. 1972. New York: Avon Books, 1980, 131–144.

Beverly Friend. "Virgin Territory." *Extrapolation*, 14 (December, 1972), 49–58.

Val Gough. "Lesbians and Virgins." David Seed, ed., *Anticipations*. Liverpool: Liverpool University Press, 1995, 195–215.

Lee B. Jennings. "Virgin, Knight, and Devil." Allienne R. Becker, ed., *Visions of the Fantastic*. Westport, CT: Greenwood Press, 1996, 51–56.

Kathleen C. Kelly. "Malory's Multiple Virgins." *Arthuriana*, 9 (Summer, 1999), 21–29.

Martin B. Shichtman. "Percival's Sister." *Arthuriana*, 9 (Summer, 1999), 11–20.

Vivian Sobchack. "The Virginity of Astronauts." George Slusser and Eric S. Rabkin, eds., *Shadows of the Magic Lamp*. Carbondale: Southern Illinois University Press, 1985, 41–57.

—Gary Westfahl

VIRTUAL REALITY

■

Overview

A virtual reality (VR) is often seen as a computer-generated artificial environment that mimics reality so accurately that it feels real to the person who enters it. While VR in this sense is a post-**cyberpunk** phenomenon, any seemingly real environment, like 3D cinema, might qualify to be so described. One could even suggest that the very experience of **reading**, becoming "lost in a book," might become like a VR experience. At the other end of this (metaphorical) spectrum lie fictions suggesting that what we consider to be "real life" is, in fact, a fake.

Survey

Aldous Huxley's **Brave New World** described the "feelies" that added another sensory perception to cinema-going. Inhabitants of Arthur C. Clarke's Diaspar, in *The City and the Stars* (1956), are entertained by adventure scenarios resembling the computer-**game** virtual worlds of later science fiction like Gwyneth Jones's *Phoenix Café* (1997). Many plots, especially those involving the "holodeck" of **Star Trek: The Next Generation**, turn on protagonists becoming trapped in a virtual world—a plot-device earlier used by Philip K. Dick's *Eye in the Sky* (1957) where a group of people are trapped inside a series of worlds generated by disturbed personalities. Dick made this theme of slipping between realities his own. In *Time Out of Joint* (1958) Ragle Gumm experiences the dissolution of his apparently real world to the extent that a soft-drink stand vanishes, leaving only a slip of paper bearing the words "SOFT–DRINK STAND."

William Gibson's description of **cyberspace** as a "consensual hallucination" in **Neuromancer** suggested that these "places" might exist as **computer** simulations, and built upon Dick's suggestion that everyday reality, for all we knew, might be the same. Computer-simulation stories also opened up scope for the exploration of human **identity**, as human personalities are downloaded into computers. Again, Dick prefigured this in *Ubik* (1969), but Frederik Pohl's *The Annals of the Heechee* (1987) presents an interesting variant, influenced by Gibsonian cyberpunk (see **Gateway**). Greg Egan, in novels like *Diaspora* (1997) or *Schild's Ladder* (2002), develops entire **communities** of such "downloads" living with autonomous Artificial Intelligence personalities.

Usually, virtual reality is seen as a science fiction trope, but that oldest of fantasy scenarios, the **dream**, might be seen as a form of VR. Many fantasies either have the vividness of lucid dream or, as in Lewis Carroll's **Alice's Adventures in Wonderland**, explicitly end with the realization that all had been a dream. William Morris's **utopia** *News From Nowhere* (1890) is explicitly a dream, but becomes more and more dream-like in its telling: "William's" attempts to not reveal his identity reflects his struggle to remain "asleep." A dream-like virtual reality (or managed lucid dream) is the location of Christopher Priest's *A Dream of Wessex* (1977); Priest explores later versions of virtual reality in *The Extremes* (1998). Both novels take place on the boundaries of these ambiguous states of consciousness. The **hero** of Stephen R. Donaldson's Thomas Covenant series (see **Lord Foul's Bane**) at first repeatedly denies the reality of his experiences. Yet many fantasy Otherworlds are reached from our world through portals or dimensional gates, sometimes suggesting an ambiguity between "base" and "virtual" worlds. Michael Ende's *The Neverending Story* (1979) considers the appeal of fantasy through a narrative where the protagonist reads his own adventures. On the other hand, Tad Williams's Otherland novels, beginning with *Otherland: City of Golden Shadow* (1996), are science fiction novels written with a "fantastic" feel, based upon the way modern computer gaming itself draws upon fantasy. The earliest cyberpunk story, Vernor Vinge's *True Names* (1981), operates like this, using motifs drawn from Tolkienian fantasy to reflect the way early software designers used terms like "daemons" and "sprites." Neal Stephenson's "metaverse", in **Snow Crash**, peopled with avatars of folk from the "real" world, also echoes the virtual worlds of gaming, as does the 2002 film *Avalon*, with its titular nod to the legends of **Arthur**.

This aspect of VR suggests the incursion of beings from the "virtual" world into ours. Rimmer, the comically obnoxious loser from the *Red Dwarf* television series, spends much of the series as a hologram, unable to interact with the physical world. Other hologram characters include the Doctor from *Star Trek: Voyager*. Such incursions can change our world. Ursula K. Le Guin's *The Lathe of Heaven* (1971), filmed in 1980, offers change through the subjective dreams of the central character, but a rogue computer program, in Mary Gentle's *Left to His Own Devices* (1994), alters the world's databases to include examples of books that never were written, and the same author's *Ash* (2000) suggests "virtual" **alternate histories**. With such possibilities, how can we point to a stable reality?

Discussion

Such fictions question our interpretations of reality—interpretations moving into confusing realms of **philosophy** and solipsism in films like *The Matrix*, where humans are kept by a vast computer in a dream-world, or *eXistenZ* (1999), which plays upon the "shared virtual reality" game players enter. They are fertile ground for the speculations of postmodernists who deny the existence of the grand unifying narratives that impose identity, or, for that matter, identity itself (see **Postmodernism**). They are also fictions where the boundaries between genre blur in a creative and interesting way, so that we can no longer be sure what *kind* of story we are in.

Bibliography

Scott Bukatman. *Terminal Identity*. Durham, NC: Duke University Press, 1993.

Mark Dery, ed. *Flame Wars*. Durham: Duke University Press, 1994.

Ross Farnell. "Posthuman Topologies." *Science-Fiction Studies*, 25 (November, 1998), 459–480.

Mike Featherstone and Roger Burrows, eds. *Cyberspace/Cyberbodies/Cyberpunk*. London: Sage Publications, 1995.

William Irwin, ed. *The Matrix and Philosophy*. Chicago: Open Court, 2002.

K. Lancaster. *Warlocks and Warpdrive*. Jefferson, NC: McFarland, 1999.

Howard Rheingold. *Virtual Reality*. New York: Simon & Schuster, 1991.

Benjamin Woolley. *Virtual Worlds*. Oxford: Blackwell, 1992.

Glenn Yeffeth, ed. *Taking the Red Pill*. Dallas, TX: BenBella Books, 2003.

—Andy Sawyer

VISION AND BLINDNESS

"Much of what you see in perceiving me—" He pointed to himself for emphasis "—is a projection from your own mind. To another percept-system I would

appear quite different. To the police, for instance. There're as many worldviews as there are sentient creatures."

—Philip K. Dick
Galactic Pot-Healer (1969)

Overview

The sense of sight has always been central to human life, so both keen vision and total blindness have great significance in fantasy and science fiction. A separate entry addresses the general topic of **perception**.

Survey

The human eye can function as a powerful icon: in the film *The Lord of the Rings: The Fellowship of the Ring* and its sequels, the embodiment of pure **evil**, Sauron, is shown only as an immense eye, looking everywhere for its **ring** of power. Large eyes are often a characteristic of **monsters**, including the one-eyed **giant** Cyclops who menaced Ulysses, in Homer's *The Odyssey* (c. 750 BCE) and various **aliens on Earth**, like the gigantic one-eyed starfish of the film *Warning from Space* (1956) and the octopus-like *The Crawling Eye* (1958) lurking on top of a **mountain**. Similarly grotesque creatures appeared so frequently on the covers of science fiction pulp magazines as to inspire the phrase "Bug-Eyed Monsters." In the future world of the film *Minority Report* (2002), retinal patterns are standards form of identification, requiring the **hero** first to obtain an illegal eye transplant to escape detection and later employ his own discarded eye as a means to break into his former headquarters. Rudyard Kipling's "At the End of the Passage" (1890) and Jules Verne's *The Kip Brothers* (1902) made use of the once-popular notion that dead people's eyes recorded the last image they had seen.

In Greek **mythology**, powerful vision was often an attribute of great heroes, like Lynceus, who could see in the dark and who joined Jason's **quest** for the Golden Fleece. Later heroes such as Edgar Rice Burroughs's *Tarzan of the Apes* and Robert E. Howard's *Conan the Conqueror* were also said to possess keen eyesight. The prototypical **superhero**, *Superman*, had several forms of amazing vision: he could see through walls with x-ray vision, long distances with telescopic vision, and tiny objects with microscopic vision. However, while *The Immoral Mr. Teas* (1958) derives pornographic pleasure from his new-found ability to see through people's clothing, a similar ability proves disastrous for *X—The Man with the X-Ray Eyes* (1963), who finally blinds himself to rid himself of that power.

The Greeks, while regarding blindness as a **curse**, also associated it with great **wisdom**. When Oedipus learns he has killed his **father** and married his **mother**, he blinds himself as fitting punishment, as depicted in Sophocles's play *Oedipus the King* (c. 427 BCE), but he returns in *Oedipus at Colonus* (c. 407 BCE) as an older, wiser man. Teiresias is blinded by the goddess Athena when he accidentally sees her bathing, but she gives him **wisdom** and the gift of prophecy (see **Divination**) (though another account has Teiresias blinded by Hera and blessed by Zeus); after Teresias's **death**, Homer's Ulysses visits the underworld to seek his counsel. The hero Perseus visits the Graeae, three wise women who only have one eye between them, and seizes their eye to force them to provide vital information—a scenario replicated in Diana Wynne Jones's *Eight Days of Luke* (1975). In Norse mythology, reflecting a similar linkage between blindness and wisdom, Odin gave up one of his eyes to obtain divine wisdom. Contemporary blind people are occasionally capable of great feats, the most conspicuous example being Marvel Comics' Daredevil, who employs his other heightened senses to function effectively as a colorful superhero despite his blindness.

An important story involving blindness is H.G. Wells's "The Country of the Blind" (1910), in which Wells contradicts the proverb by demonstrating that a man with vision, in fact, would be at a disadvantage in a society of blind people. However, in Daniel F. Galouye's *Dark Universe* (1961), a **culture** of blind people living underground after a **nuclear war** revert to barbarism, and in John Wyndham's *The Day of the Triffids*, a meteor shower that blinds almost all people on Earth leaves them at the mercy of ambulatory **plants** that begin taking over the planet, while the hero, one of the few people who can still see, resists them more effectively.

Science fiction and fantasy stories often deal with ways to improve or extend human vision. In Bob Shaw's *Night Walk* (1967), a man who is blinded and stranded on an **alien world** employs science to achieve a form of vision, while Kaw's "The Time Eliminator" (1926) is one of innumerable stories involving the invention of a remarkable device that can see anyplace in the world. Performing the same function in fantasy is the crystal ball, which can display distant places in works like J.R.R. Tolkien's *The Lord of the Rings* and the film *The Wizard of Oz*. A science-fictional equivalent is Wells's "The Crystal Egg" (1897), a glass object discovered in a shop that displays images of **Mars**. There are also magical wells that show faraway scenes, as observed in the films *Snow White and the Seven Dwarfs* and *The Lord of the Rings: The Fellowship of the Ring* (see **Magic**). Machines that show images from the past or future (see **Time Travel**) are also common in science fiction, one example occurring in John Taine's *Before the Dawn* (1934), where **scientists** observe the prehistoric adventures of a **dinosaur**.

Discussion

Today, as scientists create more and more powerful telescopes and microscopes, and soldiers wear special goggles allowing them to see in the dark by means of infra-red radiation, enhanced vision is no longer an idle dream; there are also hopes of achieving cures for blindness. Still, there remain lingering feelings that blindness may indeed represent a **gift**, especially in the case of talented musicians like Ray Charles and Stevie Wonder in real life (see **Music**) and Rhysling, "The Blind Singer of the Spaceways," in Robert A. Heinlein's "The Green Hills of Earth" (1947) (see *The Past Through Tomorrow*) in science fiction. People may always attribute a special sort of enlightenment to the blind.

Bibliography

Stephen Baxter. "The Technology of Omniscience." *Foundation*, No. 80 (Autumn, 2000), 97–107.

Alex Boulton. "The Myth of a New Found Land in H.G.Wells's 'The Country of the Blind.'" *The Wellsian*, No. 18 (Winter, 1995), 5–18.

John Christopher. "The Decline and Fall of the Bug-Eyed Monster." *The Magazine of Fantasy and Science Fiction*, 11 (October, 1956), 74–76.

Arthur B. Evans. "Optograms and Fiction." *Science-Fiction Studies*, 20 (November, 1993), 341–361.

Molly P. Hite. "Optics and Autobiography in Margaret Atwood's *Cat's Eye*." *Twentieth Century Literature*, 41 (Summer, 1995), 135–159.

James Krasner. *The Entangled Eye*. New York: Oxford University Press, 1992.

Raymond Kurzweil. "Brave New World." *Niekas*, No. 46 (February, 2001), 30–35.

Patrick Parrinder. "Wells's Cancelled Endings for 'The Country of the Blind.'" *Science-Fiction Studies*, 17 (March, 1990), 71–76.

Vernon Shetley and Alissa Ferguson. "Reflections in a Silver Eye." *Science Fiction Studies*, 28 (March, 2001), 66–76.

—*Gary Westfahl*

Voodoo

Overview

Depictions of this religious belief system, originating in West **Africa** and associated with Haiti and New Orleans, appear in all fantastic genres. Voodoo's **ritual** possessions, sacrificial offerings (see **Sacrifice**), ancestor reverence, and worship of natural forces provide rich raw material for speculative writers. Closely related traditions like Santeria and Ifa also contribute.

Survey

Pulp publications of the 1930s and 1940s represented Voodoo as essentially malign, focusing on **zombies** and **curses**: the comic book hero The Shadow fights the villainous Doctor Mocquino in Walter Gibson's *The Voodoo Master* (1936) (see **Villains**); Fredric Brown's "A Lock of Satan's Hair" (1943), the story of an attempt to kill Hitler via Voodoo, paints it as the lesser of two **evils**. The 1950s and 1960s saw little change, with Charles Beaumont's "The Jungle" (1954), the basis for a 1961 episode of *The Twilight Zone* with that name, importing the occult vengeance of an African "voodoo doctor" to the streets of New York. Voodoo was treated more sympathetically by Hugh Cave, author of genre books like *Drums of Revolt* (1957), who defended it in his travel narrative *Haiti: Highroad to Adventure* (1952).

Hollywood has often taken a dim view of Voodoo, as in *King of the Zombies* (1941), remaining largely true to sensationalistic visions of shambling corpses and devil worshipers through the 1980s. *The Believers* (1987) portrays a Caribbean "cult" engaged in child sacrifice, and *Angel Heart* (1987) offers more **clichés**. However, in David Byrne's *True Stories* (1986,) a kindly priest invokes the aid of the Voodoo pantheon's **trickster** figure, Legba, and Kasi Lemmons's *Eve's Bayou* (1997) also takes a more balanced approach. The diviner in *The Matrix* contains subtle echoes of Voodoo and Ifa goddesses Erzulie and Yemaya.

Most African-Americans writing about Voodoo present it in a neutral or even positive light. Ishmael Reed's *Mumbo Jumbo* (1972) follows a "hoodoo detective" investigating a **mysterious** psychic plague. Jewell Parker Rhodes's *Voodoo Dreams* (1993) fictionalizes the life of the legendary Marie Laveau, New Orleans' pre-eminent Voodoo priestess, also the subject of Francine Prose's novel *Marie Laveau* (1977). In Gloria Naylor's *Mama Day* (1988), a conjure woman using Voodoo-derived folk-**magic** fights for the life of her niece. Originally marketed as mainstream fiction, today these books might be categorized as **magic realism**.

1986 saw the release of William Gibson's *Count Zero* (his sequel to the **cyberpunk** novel *Neuromancer*), in which artificial intelligences take on the identities of Voodoo deities. Throughout the novel, African-derived beliefs about souls serve as analogues for cutting edge theories of consciousness. While Gibson's books excited enormous attention, Lucius Shepard's *Green Eyes* (1984) is the first novel to examine Voodoo practices in the light of scientific **knowledge**: corpses reanimated via a bacterium derived from graveyard dust show high sensitivity to magnetic fields, a sensitivity amplified by contact with veves (intricate patterns drawn during Voodoo ceremonies), which reproduce certain sequences of neuronal firing. Karen Joy Fowler's darkly humorous "Black Glass" (1991) tells how DEA agents summon the *loa*, or archetypal spirit, of their psychological forebear, the axe-wielding Carrie Nation, again with some scientific justification. Kathleen Ann Goonan's *Crescent City Rhapsody* (2000) and Richard K. Morgan's neo-cyberpunk *Broken Angels* (2004) treat Voodoo as a complex **philosophy** with unique contributions to make to modern thought.

In contrast, there remain contemporary instances of the equation of Voodoo with black magic and necromancy, as in the struggle between Anita Blake and a "Voodoo Queen" in Laurel K. Hamilton's *The Laughing Corpse* (1994), or the "Dead Man's Party" (1988) episode of *Buffy the Vampire Slayer*.

Nalo Hopkinson's *Brown Girl in the Ring* (1998) is the first work by an African-descended author published within genre boundaries that is openly influenced by Afro-Caribbean spiritual traditions. Both heroine and villain rely on supernatural assistance while warring over illegal human-organ-harvesting gangs in a gritty, **near future** Toronto. Stories by practitioners, like Constance Ash's "Flower Kiss" (1998), give an insider's perspective, and Hopkinson's 2003 anthology *Mojo: Conjure Stories* collects works on the theme by many notable authors, black and white, including Steven Barnes and Neil Gaiman. Tananarive Due's well-researched **horror** novel *The Good House* (2003) creates a terrifying atmosphere around an erring Voodoo healer without resorting to misconceptions.

Discussion

Voodoo dolls and zombies (see **Dolls and Puppets**), popular in early pulp literature and horror films, bear problematic or nonexistent relationships to the **religion** as actually practiced; authentic Voodoo **gods and goddesses**, ceremonies, and **cosmologies** provide genre writers with refreshingly different **mythologies**, dramatic milieus, and intriguing paradigms. Paralleling the improvement of **race relations**, a more objective tone has been adopted toward Voodoo, still primarily practiced by African-descended peoples. As the voices of black science fiction authors are increasingly heard, and authors of all ethnicities expand and diversify their character pools, Voodoo's thematic importance and relevance to the genre should continue to grow.

Bibliography

J. Michael Dash. *Haiti and the United States*. New York: St. Martins, 1988.

Henry Louis Gates, Jr. "On 'The Blackness of Blackness.'" Gates, *The Signifying Monkey*. New York: Oxford, 1988, 217–238.

Cosette N. Kies. "Voodoo Visions." Karen Patricia Smith, ed., *African-American Voices in Young Adult Literature*. Metuchen, NJ: Scarecrow, 1994, 337–368.

Carolyn Morrow Long. "Perceptions of New Orleans Voodoo." *Nova Religio*, 6 (December 2003), 86–101.

Sami Ludwig. "Ishmael Reed's Inductive Narratology of Detection." *African American Review*, 32 (Fall 1998), 435–444.

Steven Mizrach. "The Ghost in the Machine." *Crash Collusion*, 5 (1996), 23–27.

Rafael Sa'adah. "Eye to Eye: An Interview With Lucius Shepard." *Science Fiction Eye*, No. 2 (August 1987), 5–34.

Lindsey Tucker. "Recovering the Conjure Woman." *African American Review*, 28 (1994), 173–188.

Gwenda Young. "The Cinema of Difference." *Irish Journal of American Studies*, 7 (1988), 101–119.

—Nisi Shawl

WAR

∎

If civilization has an opposite, it is war.

—Ursula K. Le Guin
The Left Hand of Darkness (1969)

Overview

A conflict between nations involving large numbers of soldiers engaged in battle, war is regularly condemned but remains common in science fiction and fantasy, suggesting an enduring fascination with the spectacle of massive conflict and **violence**. Since other entries discuss **future war**, **invasion**, and **space war**, this entry will focus on wars in fantasies and depictions of past and present wars in science fiction and fantasy.

Survey

Since fantasies are often set in versions of **Europe**'s past, its wars unsurprisingly resemble wars in Europe's past: soldiers on foot or riding **horses** meet on battlefields brandishing **swords** and shields or shooting arrows at opponents. Most versions of the story of Camelot, for example, conclude with a battle between the forces of King **Arthur** and those of his illegitimate son, Mordred, though a different sort of bloody war concludes Mark Twain's *A Connecticut Yankee in King Arthur's Court*. The most spectacularly visualized battles of this kind were in the film *The Lord of the Rings: The Return of the King* (2003) (see *The Lord of the Rings: The Fellowship of the Ring*) with thousands of computer-generated humans and orcs (see **Goblins**) fighting with broadswords, catapults, siege engines, and immense elephant-like creatures. What can make fantasy battles unusual are the **evil** soldiers opposing virtuous **heroes**, such as the manufactured orcs of J.R.R. Tolkien's *The Lord of the Rings* and its film adaptations, the **zombie** warriors deployed in Glen Cook's Dread Empire series, beginning with *A Shadow of All Night Falling* (1979), and the walking **skeletons** of the film *Army of Darkness* (1992). Elizabeth Moon's Paksenarrion trilogy, beginning with *Sheepfarmer's Daughter* (1988), offers an unusually realistic portrayal of the travails of war in a fantasy setting. One legendary conflict, the Trojan War, has been depicted in films like *The Trojan Horse* (1962) and *Troy*

(2004); S.P. Somtow's *The Shattered Horse* (1986) is a sequel to Homer's *Iliad* (c. 750 BCE) in which Hector's son starts a second Trojan War.

When science fiction examines past wars, they usually involve either time travelers from the future observing or participating in the conflict (see **Time Travel**) or **alternate history** scenarios in which a different outcome generates an entirely different world. Sometimes, time travelers themselves accidentally or deliberately create an alternate history, as in Ward Moore's ***Bring the Jubilee***, where a time-traveling historian from a future in which the South won the Civil War alters the outcome of the Battle of Gettysburg and brings about our own world with a Northern victory. (That particular battle has so fascinated writers that an entire anthology, Brian Thomsen and Martin H. Greenberg's *Alternate Gettysburgs* (2002), was devoted to stories positing various changes in its events.) Another novel depicting a Southern victory is Harry Turtledove's *The Guns of the South* (1992). Ambrose Bierce's "An Occurrence at Owl Creek Bridge" (1891), later adapted as a 1962 short film of that name which aired in 1964 as an episode of ***The Twilight Zone***, was a different sort of Civil War story, involving a soldier who miraculously escapes being hanged and embarks on a long journey home, only to finally learn that it was all a **dream** immediately preceding his death by hanging.

While the Civil War has attracted much attention in fiction, other past wars are revisited as well. Keith Roberts's *Pavane* (1968) imagines an assassination of Queen Elizabeth I leading to a victory for the Spanish Armada and continuing Catholic domination of Europe. Diana Gabaldon's time travel **romance** *Outlander* (1991) and its sequels focus on Bonnie Prince Charlie's unsuccessful **rebellion** against the British throne, as a modern woman unsuccessfully tries to prevent him from engaging in the disastrous battle of Culloden. World War I is the subject of a 1917 play, Robert H. Davis and Perley Poore Sheehan's *Efficiency*, about a **scientist** who gruesomely figures out how to stitch together parts of soldiers' dead bodies and send the reassembled **Frankenstein monsters** back to the front. And in Robert A. Heinlein's *Time Enough for Love* (1973), Lazarus Long travels back in time to meet his mother, enlist in the American army, and fight in World War I (see ***The Past Through Tomorrow***). Turtledove's *Worldwar: In the Balance* (1994) and its sequels describe what would have happened if an alien invasion during World War II brought the Americans, Germans, and Japanese together to fight the common enemy.

Even stories in fantasy settings or the **far future** may actually be about wars in the writer's past or present. Although Tolkien downplayed the idea, many believe that images of European devastation in World War I influenced his account of the Scouring of the Shire at the end of *The Lord of the Rings*; Cleve Cartmill's "Deadline" (1944) attracted the attention of government agents because its story about the then-forbidden subject of nuclear **weaponry**, ostensibly occurring on a distant planet, involved unmistakable representatives of World War II adversaries—the American Allies (the "Seilla") and Axis powers (the "Sixa"); and the ***Star Trek*** episode "A Private Little War" (1968) is a blatant **allegory** justifying American involvement in the Vietnam War.

Discussion

By dealing so much with the imaginary and actual wars of human **history**, science fiction and fantasy implicitly agree that wars are important activities that merit one's attention and involvement, even if stories convey an antiwar message. More persuasive arguments against war, then, may be found in works that refuse to fore-ground battles and bloodshed. In Glen Cook's Garrett novels, beginning with *Sweet Silver Blues* (1987), the occasionally discussed rebellion of Glory Mooncalled is irrelevant to the daily concerns of ordinary folk in the city of TunFaire, and in Joanna Russ's "Souls" (1982), the narrator concludes by realizing what is truly important: "all the villages of Germany and England and France where the poor folk sweat from dawn to dark so that the great lords may do battle with one another." Perhaps, such works suggest, wars are not really the turning points of history, but only colorful distractions.

Bibliography

Susanne Carter. "Variations on Vietnam." *Extrapolation*, 32 (Summer, 1991), 170–184.

Christine Chism. "Middle-earth, the Middle Ages, and the Aryan Nation." Jane Chance, ed., *Tolkien the Medievalist*. New York: London, 2003, 63–92.

Janet B. Croft. "The Great War and Tolkien's Memory." *Mythlore*, 23 (Fall/Winter, 2002), 4–21.

H. Bruce Franklin. "The Vietnam War as American Science Fiction and Fantasy." *Science-Fiction Studies*, 17 (November, 1990), 341–359.

Steffen Hantke. "Disorienting Encounters." *Journal of the Fantastic in the Arts*, 12 (2001), 268–286.

Sylvia Kelso. "Connie Willis's Civil War." *Foundation*, No. 73 (Summer, 1998), 67–76.

Paul Kincaid. "The North-South Continuum." *Steam Engine Time*, No. 2 (November, 20010, 23–31.

Brian Thomsen and Martin H. Greenberg, eds. *Alternate Gettysburgs*. New York: Berkley, 2002.

Gary Westfahl. "Opposing War, Exploiting War." Westfahl, *Science Fiction, Children's Literature, and Popular Culture*. Westport, CT: Greenwood Press, 2000, 69–78.

—*Gary Westfahl*

WATER

■

Overview

As something that humans cannot live without, water plays an especially large role in secular and spiritual life, a role that carries over to works of science fiction and fantasy. Water is acknowledged as the origin of life, a crucial element in ceremonies of baptism, a substance necessary to the growth of crops that keep us alive, and a destroyer of life in **floods**. Separate entries discuss **sea travel** and **underwater adventure**.

Survey

Fantasy and science fiction often involve water because of its spiritual effects: the holy water used on a **demon** can be equated to the bucket of water thrown on the witch by Dorothy in L. Frank Baum's *The Wonderful Wizard of Oz*, and the witch melting as a deliverance for Dorothy from **evil**; in the film *Spirited Away* (2001), public baths have a cleansing effect for members of the spirit world, and a central character in the story is a river **dragon**, a figure of spiritual significance in **China**. In Robert A. Heinlein's *Stranger in a Strange Land*, the sharing of water is a key ritual of the Martian **religion**, while a new life in the water signals **rebirth** in Charles Kingsley's *The Water Babies*.

Bodies of water are also important settings in fantasy **quests**. J.R.R. Tolkien's *The Hobbit* first encounters the **magic ring** near the underground lake where Gollum dwells, and a **river** helps Bilbo and the **dwarfs** escape from captivity. *The Lord of the Rings* concludes with Bilbo, Frodo, and the **elves** embarking upon a voyage to the west that seems a symbolic **death**. Ursula K. Le Guin's Earthsea novels (see *A Wizard of Earthsea*) take place in an archipelago on a watery world, and young **wizard** Ged is safest from the Old Powers when he is out on the ocean. The sea is dangerous, but it is not malevolent, and indeed can serve as a defense and even as the last chance for Ged when he battles his shadow self.

In science fiction, water may be desperately needed for **survival** on an arid **alien world** like **Mars**. In Isaac Asimov's "The Martian Way" (1952), chunks of the icy rings of Saturn are transported to Mars to bring needed water to the colonists there. More elaborately, Kim Stanley Robinson's Mars trilogy, beginning with *Red Mars*, provides the Red Planet with water through a process of **terraforming** that, by raising its temperature and thickening its atmosphere, allows frozen underground water to come to surface in liquid form. Reflecting this transformation, the final book in the trilogy is entitled *Blue Mars* (1996), after the perceived **color** of water, signaling that the planet has become a living world of water; fittingly, the book concludes with characters enjoying a day at the Martian beach.

In Frank Herbert's *Dune*, water is necessary for survival in both physical and spiritual ways. Arrakis is a **desert** planet, the opposite of a world covered in water. Here, characters wear devices to help them reclaim the water that leaves their bodies as they breathe in order to help them live. But the **witches** of the Bene Gesserit also use the Water of Life to pass on their **knowledge**; in a sense this becomes a version of the fountain of **youth**, where the Bene Gesserit carry the accumulated **wisdom** of all their generations past. By taking the Water of Life and surviving its effects, Paul Muad'Dib takes in all of this and actually becomes the **history** that the water carries.

Stanislaw Lem's *Solaris* presents water as an emblem of both **intelligence** and **mystery**. Solaris, a sentient, water-covered planet, generates corporeal manifestations of people based on **memories** of immense personal guilt within the individuals occupying the nearby research station; here, the water acts as a device for giving **birth** to these manifestations, a sort of amniotic fluid for the darkest recesses of the guilt-ridden mind (see **Guilt and Responsibility**). At the end of the novel, all of the world's secrets remain unresolved.

As a sign of water's power, there are several **superheroes** who are closely associated with water. DC Comics' Aquaman and Marvel Comics' Sub-Mariner have both gained tremendous physical strength and psychic rapport with **fish and sea creatures** due to living in the sea; but if they are separated from water for any length of time, they become weak and may even die unless they again come into contact with the fluid they depend on. Aquaman's former wife, Mera, could command water to form into any shape she wished, thus making water her **weaponry**. Other aquatic adventurers, like DC Comics' Sea Devils, depended on their wits and advanced **technology** to triumph over menaces that threatened the peaceful world of water.

Discussion

In ancient times, water was one of the four **elements**; thus, it was a vital aspect and building block of life. Science fiction and fantasy authors have often recognized this, as well as acknowledging water's most basic roles in spirituality and in survival. As such an important aspect of life, water has served as a useful thematic device for authors in both genres. Water cleanses **humanity**, washing away both grime and **sins**, and if it is somehow dangerous to a book's characters, it is almost invariably a neutral force, without underlying maliciousness.

Bibliography

Lorenzo DiTommaso. "History and Historical Effect in Frank Herbert's *Dune*." *Science-Fiction Studies*, 19 (November, 1992), 311–325.

Neil Easterbrook. "The Sublime Simulacra." *Critique*, 36 (Spring, 1995), 177–194.

Yang Lianfen and Andrew Miller. "Water in Traditional Chinese Culture." *Journal of Popular Culture*, 27 (Fall, 1993), 51–57.

Hilary Newman. "Water in William Morris's Late Prose Romances." *Journal of the William Morris Society*, 13 (Spring, 2000), 41–47.

Phyllis J. Perry. *The World of Water*. Englewood, CO: Teacher Ideas Press, 1995.

Nicholas Ruddick. "Deep Waters." *Foundation*, No. 42 (Spring, 1988), 49–59.

George E. Slusser. "Structures of Apprehension." *Science-Fiction Studies*, 17 (March 1989), 1–37.

Sue Thomason. "Living Water." *Vector*, No. 119 (April, 1984), 33–34.

Muriel Whitaker. "Fire, Water, Rock." Kevin J. Harty, ed., *Cinema Arthuriana*. New York: Garland, 1991.

—Derryl Murphy

WEAPONRY

> *Science has toiled too long forging weapons for fools to use. It is time she held her hand.*
>
> —H.G. Wells
> *The First Men in the Moon* (1901)

Overview

Even in **magic** realms or **alien worlds**, conflicts may be settled with fisticuffs, as demonstrated with depressing regularity in the serial *Flash Gordon* (1936) and its sequels, as well as television series like *Sinbad* (1996–1998) and the original *Star*

Trek. More often than not, however, weapons will be involved in both one-on-one confrontations and massive **wars** between nations and worlds (see **War; Future War; Space War**). Separate entries address **swords** and the subgenre wherein they are often deployed, **sword and sorcery**.

Survey

While swords and knives are the most common weapons of fantasy, others are observed: Robert E. Howard's *Conan the Conqueror* often prefers to wield an axe; the elf Legolas in J.R.R. Tolkien's *The Lord of the Rings* uses a bow and arrow; and *Xena: Warrior Princess* can thwart opponents by throwing her chakram, a small disc with a cutting edge. The larger weapons employed by armies during **Europe's** Middle Ages (see **Medievalism and the Middle Ages**), like catapults and siege engines, may figure in fantasy battles like those in *The Lord of the Rings: The Return of the King* (2003) (see *The Lord of the Rings: The Fellowship of the Ring*), and the legendary Baron Munchausen famously rode on a cannonball, as depicted in the film *The Adventures of Baron Munchausen* (1989).

Today's science fiction **superheroes** may also employ ancient weapons: in addition to archers like DC Comics' Green Arrow and Marvel Comics' Hawkeye, *Batman* relies on a boomerang shaped like a bat, dubbed the Batarang, and DC Comics' Silver Age Hawkman and Hawkgirl, although they are **aliens on Earth**, use a variety of **Earth** weapons like the mace, throwing stars, the spiked glove called a cestus, nets, and the crossbow.

Guns were the weapon of choice for the pulp magazine hero the Shadow (who, unlike his radio counterpart, lacked the **psychic power** to "cloud men's minds"), and DC Comics' cowboy hero Vigilante; even Batman sometimes used a gun in early comic book adventures. Special sorts of guns include the gas gun used by DC Comics' original Sandman and the sonic gun devised by Green Lantern's villainous opponent, Sonar (see **Villains**). Elsewhere, gunfire causes *King Kong* to fall off the Empire State Building and kills the visiting alien Klaatu in *The Day the Earth Stood Still*. In the future, guns were improbably (and dangerously) used on board a spaceship returning from **Mars** to deal with a **monster** stowaway in the film *It! The Terror from Beyond Space* (1958), but guns more often figure as antiques. A character in Robert A. Heinlein's **utopia**, *Beyond This Horizon* (1949), shows off an ancient handgun he purchased, and a carefully preserved gun provides proof of **humanity**'s one-time dominance in the 2001 remake of *Planet of the Apes* (see *Planet of the Apes*).

However, the future's favorite weapons are amazing rays, beamed from either a spacecraft or hand-held projector, the notorious "ray gun." One early example of such weaponry is the heat ray used by Martian invaders in H.G. Wells's *The War of the Worlds*. By the 1930s, rays were so common in science fiction pulp magazines that when John W. Campbell, Jr. submitted the story "Space Rays" (1932), featuring one incredible ray after another, editor Hugo Gernsback presented it as a self-conscious parody of the genre's current excesses. *Star Trek* carried on these traditions with changes in nomenclature, as the "phaser" replaced the ray gun as an all-purpose weapon that could be adjusted to stun people, kill them, or disintegrate small objects; the starship *Enterprise*, which also beamed destructive rays called phasers, was additionally equipped with rays that could draw in or repel objects—"tractor beams"—and a bomb employing radiant energy, the "photon torpedo." Rays of deadly energy dominated the space battles of *Star Wars* and its sequels, though the films also introduced a novel variation of the traditional sword, the colorful "light saber," to take the place of ray guns as individual weapons.

However, there are other weapons found in the space wars of science fiction. Proclaiming that "the right to buy weapons is the right to be free," the "Weapon Shops" in the future universe of A.E. van Vogt's *The Weapon Shops of Isher* (1951) and *The Weapon Makers* (1946) sell various types of hand weapons to interested citizens as a way to prevent tyranny. Old-fashioned nuclear weapons are effective against massive dreadnoughts in the *Star Trek* episode "The Doomsday Machine" (1967) and *Star Wars*; in Heinlein's **Starship Troopers**, an elaborate suit worn in battle both provides protection and functions as a weapon in itself—which is a trope taken up and expanded upon in American cartoons and Japanese anime, as represented, for example, by Yoshiyuki Tomino's Gundam Mobile Suit series, beginning with *Awakening* (1990). Larry Niven's "The Borderland of Sol" (1975) employs a **black hole** as a weapon against spaceships; and Heinlein's *The Moon Is a Harsh Mistress* (1966) demonstrates that large rocks, hurtled toward **Earth**, would be excellent weapons. E.E. "Doc" Smith's Lensman series (see **Triplanetary**) introduces scores of increasingly powerful weapons in its ever-escalating war between the forces of good, led by the Arisians, and the **evil** alliance headed by the Eddorians. Weapons mighty enough to destroy entire planets are not uncommon in more extravagant forms of **space opera**, including the stories of Edmond Hamilton, who earned the nickname "World-Wrecker" for depicting such catastrophes.

Discussion

In Gore Vidal's television play *Visit to a Small Planet* (1955), a visitor from the future points out that war provides a tremendous impetus to technological **progress**, so it is not surprising to observe advanced future societies accompanied by advanced future weapons. For those who would prefer kinder, gentler fantasy worlds of the past, or those who dream that the future will be peaceful, the incredible numbers of weapons observed and employed in fantasy and science fiction must be depressing. Conversely, one might argue that allowing people to vicariously wield weapons in fiction and films, as well as other media like comic books, video **games**, and **computer** games, might make them less likely to use them, or encourage their use, in real life.

Bibliography

W. Haden Blackman. *Star Wars: The New Essential Guide to Weapons and Technology.* Revised Edition. New York: Del Rey Books, 2004.

L. Sprague de Camp, ed. *Blade of Conan.* New York: Ace, 1979.

Steven Eisler. *Space Wars.* New York: Crescent, 1979.

H. Bruce Franklin. *War Stars.* New York: Oxford University Press, 1988.

David Langford. *War in 2080.* New York: William Morrow, 1979.

John H. Lenihan. "Superweapons From the Past." Paul Loukides, ed., *The Material World in American Popular Film.* Bowling Green, OH: Bowling Green State University Popular Press, 1993, 164–174.

Peter Nicholls, David Langford, and Brian Stableford. "Future Weaponry." Nicholls, Langford, and Stableford, *The Science in Science Fiction*. 1982. New York: Alfred A. Knopf, 1983, 104–106.

Chris Smith. *The Lord of the Rings: Weapons and Warfare*. New York: Houghton Mifflin, 2003.

—*Gary Westfahl*

WEATHER

■

> It reminded him of other days, when weather was something to be experienced rather than to be planned. Life had lost some of its flavor, in his estimation, when the weather engineers had finally harnessed the elements.
>
> —Robert A. Heinlein
> *Methuselah's Children* (1958)

Overview

Despite Mark Twain's observation, fantasy and science fiction writers have always been very interested in doing something about the weather, regularly describing people who can achieve favorable weather conditions by means of either **magic** or advanced future **technology**. Normal seasonal changes in the weather are discussed under **Seasons**.

Survey

Like writers in other forms of literature, science fiction and fantasy writers may choose to describe particular weather conditions because they evocatively reflect the mood or situation of their characters—rain signaling sadness or misfortune, snow signally emotional sterility, and sunshine and blue skies signaling happiness. In Mary Shelley's *Frankenstein, or The Modern Prometheus* and its cinematic adaptations (see *Frankenstein*), for example, the monster was always created on an appropriately inauspicious "dreary night of November" while "the rain pattered dismally against the panes."

Weather plays a significant role in the earliest work that might be identified as fantasy, the Babylonian epic *Gilgamesh* (c. 2500 BCE) since it describes a global **flood** caused by severe rain; the account bears similarities to the story of Noah's Ark in the Bible. The ancients developed fanciful beliefs about the weather: in Greek **mythology**, lightning bolts were weapons, forged by Hephaestus and hurled by Zeus, and winds were personified as minor gods. In Norse mythology, the rainbow seen after the storm was called Bifrost and regarded as a bridge between the surface world and the **home** of the gods, guarded by the god Heimdall.

Perhaps because **children** are more influenced by weather, children's fantasies frequently involve unusual weather. In L. Frank Baum's *The Wonderful Wizard of Oz*, a tornado picks up Dorothy's house and carries it to Oz. In Dr. Seuss's *Bartholomew and the Oobleck* (1949), a **king** asks his magicians to create something new to fall from the sky, resulting in a downpour of sticky green "oobleck" causing all sorts of problems.

Since ancient times, priests and shamans have made **sacrifices** to **gods and goddesses** to improve the weather, often hoping for rain during a long drought. **Native Americans** are well known for rain dances performed for that purpose, while the titular protagonist of N. Richard Nash's play *The Rainmaker* (1955), filmed in 1956 and 1982, is a charming con man who claims that he can make it rain.

In contrast to the sporadically effective efforts of ordinary people, magical beings are sometimes genuine masters of the weather. A modern-day rain god, never realizing why he is constantly bombarded by rain, appears in Douglas Adams's *So Long, and Thanks for All the Fish* (1985) (see *The Hitchhiker's Guide to the Galaxy*), and magicians who can create a convenient storm are commonplace in fantasy. DC Comics' the Flash has as one regular **villain** the Weather Wizard, who can control the weather for his own nefarious ends, while a member of Marvel Comics' the X-Men, Storm, possesses the same power.

Regulated weather is a common feature of human **civilizations** of both the **near future** and **far future**. In Hugo Gernsback's *Ralph 124C 41+: A Romance of the Year 2660* (1925), "Weather Engineers" constantly control the weather, although a dangerous avalanche occurs when they go on strike. Theodore L. Thomas's "The Weather Man" (1962) is a classic story about the amazing technological advances, on **Earth** and in space, that allow scientists to create a desired snowstorm in a temperate zone. And there is, of course, no variation in the weather within domed cities, like the future New York of Isaac Asimov's *The Caves of Steel* (1954) (see *I, Robot*).

A favorite science fiction scenario for future **disasters** is a catastrophic change in the climate. The Earth may enter a new Ice Age, as in Anna Kavan's *Ice* (1967) and the film *The Day After Tomorrow* (2004), or the temperature may rise to either cover the Earth with **water**, as in J.G. Ballard's *The Drowned World* and the film *Waterworld* (1995), or transform the world into a global **jungle**, as in Brian W. Aldiss's *The Long Afternoon of Earth* (1962).

Some stories involve extreme weather conditions on other planets. When **Venus** was thought to be extremely wet, its constant rainstorms were depicted in Ray Bradbury's "The Long Rain" and "All Summer in a Day" (1954) as well as Poul Anderson's "The Big Rain" (1954). Hal Clement's *Mission of Gravity* (1953) opens by describing the fierce windstorms that occur at the outer extremities of the pancake-shaped world of Mesklin.

Discussion

Since the unpredictability and occasional severity of Earth's weather lead to various difficulties, fantasy writers have logically envisioned magical masters of the weather, and science fiction writers have routinely forecast future worlds of regulated weather. Still, it remains unclear whether people would really enjoy such an existence: in Robert A. Heinlein's *Methuselah's Children* (1958), the **hero** laments the carefully planned weather of his future era, longing for the old days of unpredictable conditions. Instead of changing it, in other words, some people may always prefer to simply talk about the weather.

Bibliography

Dennis Bartels. "The Road to Nowhere." *Journal of the William Morris Society*, 12 (Autumn, 1997), 39–47.

T.E. Larsen. "From Fiction to Fact." *Analog*, 114 (March, 1994), 74–79.

A. Robert Lee. "Storm, Whirlwind and Earthquake." David Seed, ed., *Imagining Apocalypse*. New York: St. Martin's, 2000, 166–180.

William Rabkin. "Tom Benedek: Retelling a Stormy Winter's Tale." *Starlog*, No. 107 (June, 1986), 48–49.

Andrew Ross. *Strange Weather*. London: Verso, 1991.

Jody D. Shannon. "A Dark and Stormy Night." *Cinefex*, 41 (February, 1990), 4–33.

Marc Shapiro. "Storm Gathering." *Starlog*, No. 219 (October, 1995), 50–53.

Michael Wilmington. "The Rain People (On the Restored Version of *Blade Runner*)." *Film Comment*, 28 (1992), 17–19.

—*Lynne Lundquist*

WEREWOLVES

—◼—

> *Even a man who is pure in heart,*
> *and says his prayers by night,*
> *may become a wolf when the wolfbane*
> *   blooms,*
> *and the autumn moon is bright.*

—Curt Siodmak
The Wolf Man (1941)

Overview

The werewolf myth in science fiction and fantasy explores or reveals people's hidden animal selves, deriving from fears that we and those we know and **love** might not be as expected, harboring beneath their civilized and loving exteriors monstrous, uncivilized bestial behaviors. Werewolves are **shapeshifters**, men and women who turn into beasts or beast-like people (see **Monsters**); usually, a mere glimpse of the full **Moon** causes the **metamorphosis**. After terrorizing local people, werewolves return to their daylight selves, though they can be killed by a silver bullet.

Survey

Over a thousand years old, the werewolf myth appears in different modes worldwide. Like **vampires**, werewolves are creatures of the night, a product of our deadliest fears of **invasion** by others: the werewolf's bite also infects, turning prey into werewolves. Unlike vampires who prefer **cities**, werewolves haunt **forests** and rural peasant territory, reflecting the fear of the dark nights that predated electricity.

Sabine Baring-Gould traces werewolves back to *Beowulf* (c. 800 CE) and Viking "berserkers," wild men with horned helmets who invaded Anglo-Saxon Britain raping, pillaging, and burning. The werewolf condition has also been related to feral upbringing and autism. The first appearance of werewolves in literature came with G.W.M. Reynolds's *Wagner, the Wehy-Wolf* (1859).

Two explanations of the fascination with werewolves and the beast within emerge from Darwinism and Freudianism. Misinterpreting Charles Darwin, nineteenth-century advocates of eugenics identified nonwhite races as inferior and less developed (see **Race Relations**), so beast men would be regarded as throwbacks to an even earlier stage of development—as in Robert Louis Stevenson's *Strange Case of Dr. Jekyll and Mr. Hyde* and H. G. Wells's *The Island of Doctor Moreau*. Thus, in Darwin-inspired werewolf tales like *The Werewolf of London* (1934), the invasion of the foreign or other is uppermost (in this case, a bite from a Tibetan beast). In contrast, Freudian-inspired tales view werewolfism as an explosion of the beast within; one example would be the film *The Wolf Man* (1941) where Larry's sexual frustration over his relationship with Jenny Williams is augmented by sexual competition with his own young **father**.

Traditional werewolf tales and films depict werewolves as figures of **horror**, and the existence of the beast in man beneath the wolf's exterior a metaphor for fear and disgust. The werewolf, though cursed, cannot be allowed to continue because he represents too great a threat to **civilization**. However, in *The Curse of the Werewolf* (1961), a more radical edge appears, associating the werewolf with poor peasantry constrained by vile economic inequalities: a beggar jailed by the violent syphilitic Marquis becomes bestial. When the Marquis attempts to rape the jailer's daughter and she bites him, she is flung into jail with the beggar who rapes and impregnates her. Upon her **escape** she lives wild in the forest and gives birth to Leon who, becoming a werewolf, must be killed by his adopted father Don Afredo.

Later films and tales employ the werewolf to call into question what we regard as normal and civilized. One key moment is in *An American Werewolf in London* (1981): young students walking alone amongst the North England moors are chased by a werewolf into an area where locals have warned they should not wander; one student is killed by the werewolf, the other bitten. The dead one returns to warn the survivor, who gradually turns into a werewolf in London with stirring, poignant moments.

Robert McCammon's *The Wolf's Hour* (1989) subverts the "beast within" motif by featuring anti-Nazi werewolf Michael Gallatin. Bitten by a werewolf as a child, he was subject to a resulting virus, releasing atavism. The novel problematically hovers between viewing werewolfism as a **curse** and as a positive force which, when managed, can expose and destroy the **evil** Nazi regime. Anne Rice's sister Alice Borchardt has written several werewolf tales set in ancient Rome, beginning with *The Silver Wolf* (1998).

Angela Carter created werewolf tales focusing on **sexuality** and power. In "Wolf-Alice" (1978) a Count's cursed legacy is lycanthropy and his werewolf self a cauldron of hidden **violence**, but he is saved from the worst of his actions by the love of another outcast, Alice. Suzy McKee Charnas's "Boobs" (1989) similarly describes a young girl who turns into a werewolf at puberty. Her protagonist is stereotyped by boys as she grows breasts, but she finds she can avoid being treated as an object and bimbo and relishes the energy and bodily control of her lithe wolf-body at the time of the full Moon; werewolf activity parallels women's **cycles**. Graduating from eating poodles, she finally takes **revenge** on her tormentor Billy Linden, who tastes quite good. This amusing, empowering tale reverses werewolf trajectories— identifying with the werewolf and realizing that the myth itself could indicate sexuality and power, and enjoying rather than suppressing and fearing the beast within humankind.

In *Wolf* (1994) Jack Nicholson is the sidelined editor who, bitten, turns into a potentially gentle, potentially violent werewolf. In revealing his wolf self, he celebrates the urge to go back to **nature**, rejecting the untruths, pretenses, and artifices of civilization. Central Park is a favorite haunt for a New York man finally recognizing his own bestial powers.

Discussion

Werewolf tales address our terrors of the defamiliarization of the everyday and familiar. Much authenticated in **history**, werewolves are night creatures who may be metaphors for foreigners, radicals, or outlaws, and they represent our fears of bodily **invasion**, the threat of racially inferior others, and our own inner **demons**.

Bibliography

Sabine Baring-Gould. *The Book of Were-Wolves*. London: Smith, Elder, 1865.
Adam Douglas. *The Beast Within*. London: Chapman, 1992.
Brian J. Frost. *The Essential Guide to Werewolf Literature*. Madison: University of Wisconsin Press, 2003.
Lillian M. Heldreth. "Tanith Lee's Werewolves Within." *Journal of the Fantastic in the Arts*, 2 (Spring, 1989), 15–24.
Richard Noll. *Vampires, Werewolves, and Demons*. New York: Brunner, 1992.
Charlotte F. Otten, ed. *A Lycanthropy Reader*. Syracuse, NY: Syracuse University Press, 1986.
Maureen K. Speller. "Unicorns, Werewolves, Ghosts, and Rhinoceroses." *Vector*, No. 204 (March/April, 1999), 10–11.
Brad Steiger. *The Werewolf Book*. Detroit: Visible Ink Press, 1999.
Marina Warner. *From the Beast to the Blonde*. London: Vintage, 1995.

—*Gina Wisker*

WESTERNS

Overview

Science fiction and fantasy stories may follow the generic conventions of the western or involve the settling of the nineteenth-century American **frontier**, often featuring cowboys as **heroes** and **Native Americans** as **villains**. Westerns often focus on the issue of **freedom**, as noble outsiders ensure the safety and freedom of the people they help at the expense of their finding personal happiness and a place to call **home**. Western heroes fight on behalf of **civilization** but ultimately cannot be a part of it; their victories ironically force themselves into obsolescence or require their moving on to another frontier realm.

Survey

Fantastic literature and the western were first linked in the nineteenth century, when dime novels about adventures in the American west sometimes featured brilliant young **scientists** who used amazing **inventions** to triumph over Native Americans and villains; examples include Edward S. Ellis's *The Steam Man of the Prairies* (1865) and Harry Enton's *Frank Reade and His Steam Horse* (1876). In the twentieth century, as pulp magazines supplanted dime novels, many writers created stories for both science fiction magazines and western magazines, and western tropes and imagery often figured in stories about **space travel**. Poul Anderson and Gordon R. Dickson's *Earthman's Burden* (1957) featured dimunitive aliens who reenact a western scenario, and Robert A. Heinlein's *Tunnel in the Sky* (1955) concludes with its hero on horseback, leading a wagon train of settlers using **teleportation** to reach and colonize a distant planet. **Planetary colonies** in their early stages may resemble towns of the American frontier, as in Heinlein's *Time Enough for Love* (1973) (see *The Past Through Tomorrow*).

Science fiction films also borrowed heavily from westerns. *Moon Zero Two* (1969), publicized as a "space western," involves a **community** of miners on the **Moon** who fight for their mining rights just as settlers fought for land and a new life on the American frontier. *Outland* (1980), based directly on the plot of the classic western *High Noon* (1952), has the marshal of a mining colony on Jupiter's moon Io (see **Jupiter and the Outer Planets**) engaged in a lonely fight against corruption and murder. *Westworld* (1973) features an amusement park offering a replication of the American west with **robot** characters. The imagery of the west plays a crucial role in *Dr. Strangelove* when an Air Force pilot sits astride the nuclear bomb being dropped on the U.S.S.R. like a cowboy riding his **horse**, signifying **America's** dichotomous nature as the world's leader in **technological** development and pre-eminent purveyor of frontier **mythology**.

On television, an episode of *Lost in Space*, "West of Mars" (1966), brings the Robinson family to a frontier planet where the villainous Dr. Smith is mistaken for a notorious gunslinger; in "Living in Harmony" (1968), an episode of *The Prisoner*, Number Six mysteriously finds himself in a western town where he must decide whether or not to use a gun; and the animated series *BraveStarr* (1987–1988) features a colorful cowboy hero on another planet. Most viewers, however, will more likely remember western elements in the *Star Trek* series. In the episode "Spectre of the Gun" (1968), aliens place Captain Kirk and his crewmates in a bizarre recreation of a ghost town and force them to re-enact the gunfight at the OK Corral, and "The Paradise Syndrome" (1968) brings Kirk to a planet inhabited by Native Americans. Later *Star Trek* series sometimes involve the American frontier; for example, in an episode of *Star Trek: Enterprise*, "North Star" (2002), the crew visits an alien recreation of the Wild West.

Present-day people may return to the actual American west by means of **time travel**. In "The 7th Is Made Up of Phantoms" (1963), an episode of *The Twilight Zone*, three soldiers travel back to the Battle of Little Big Horn, where they die along with George Custer. And in *Back to the Future: Part III* (see **Back to the Future**), Marty McFly visits America in 1885 (just as the Old West began to turn towards modern **technology** as epitomized by the coming of the railroad), takes on the local villain, and wins, allowing the town to become a safe community.

Western settings occasionally figure in works of fantasy and **horror**. Stephen King's Dark Tower series begins with *The Gunslinger* (1980), with the eponymous hero embarking on a **quest** through a surrealistic **wilderness**. In S.P. Somtow's *Moon Dance* (1990), a family of European **werewolves** immigrates to the American west. And the plots of the films *Billy the Kid vs. Dracula* (1965) and *Jesse James Meets Frankenstein's Daughter* (1966) are conveyed sufficiently by their titles.

Discussion

The western in science fiction and fantasy provides scope to explore notions of freedom, mythology, civilization, and **barbarism** in a setting that is both familiar and **culturally** important. If America's affinity with the western has grown out of a need to reaffirm cultural myths, then science fiction and fantasy stories that borrow from the western genre also conform to this sense of national dilemma. Indeed, one can argue that America's desire for **exploration** through **space travel** has replaced cowboys with **astronauts** and horses with space **rockets**, as suggested by President John Kennedy's resonant description of space as "the New Frontier." Thus, in transferring the western to stories set in the **far future**, science fiction can question the original mythology surrounding the western and suggest new possibilities for **humanity**'s first steps into a new frontier.

Bibliography

Carl Abbott. "Falling into History." *Western Historical Quarterly*, 34 (Spring, 2003), 1–24.

Robert Murray Davis. "The Frontiers of Genre." *Science-Fiction Studies*, 12 (1985), 33–41.

Jay Goulding. *Empire, Aliens, and Conquest*. Toronto, Ontario: Sisyphus Press, 1985.

Hal W. Hall. "Texas and Science Fiction." *Southwestern American Literature*, 1 (1972), 144–148.

Howard E. McCurdy. *Space and the American Imagination*. Washington D.C.: Smithsonian Institution Press, 1997.

Donald K. Meisenheimer, Jr. "Matching the Man." *Science-Fiction Studies*, 24 (November, 1997), 441–458.

David Mogen. *Wilderness Visions*. Second Edition. San Bernardino, CA: Borgo Press, 1994.

Richard Slotkin. *Gunfighter Nation*. Norton, OK: Oklahoma University Press, 1998.

Gary Westfahl, ed. *Space and Beyond*. Westport, CT: Greenwood Press, 2000.

—*Lincoln Geraghty*

WILDERNESS

■

Overview

The present entry examines depictions of fictional wildernesses and variations on more abstract idea of wilderness in fantastic fiction. Other themes relevant to the wilderness are addressed in the entries **Civilization, Frontier, Landscape,** and **Nature.**

Survey

One common conception of wilderness is that of a pristine and virginal land, untouched by human hands. Science-fictional descriptions of this kind of wilderness often deal with the initial **exploration,** or later exploitation, of uncharted territories or unknown realms, whether they are **alien worlds** or new regions of outer space. Examples of the former include Robert Zubrin's *First Landing* (2001), about the first manned mission to **Mars,** and Allen Steele's *Coyote* (2002), the story of the first interstellar colony on a planet forty-six light-years from Earth, while in David Zindell's *Neverness* (1988) and sequels, the exploration involves a vast, dangerous stellar wasteland, the Vild.

In some science fiction, entire worlds, or significant portions of them, can be considered wildernesses. Important examples include the planets Arrakis, from Frank Herbert's *Dune*; Gethen, from Ursula K. Le Guin's *The Left Hand of Darkness*; Geta, from Donald Kingsbury's *Courtship Rites* (1982); and Cadwal, from Jack Vance's *Araminta Station* (1988) and its sequels. Exploiting and "taming" an alien wilderness can present unforeseen obstacles, as happens on the worlds of Pyrrus, in Harry Harrison's *Deathworld* (1960); Athshe, in Le Guin's *The Word for World is Forest* (1972); Avalon, in *The Legacy of Heorot* (1987) and its sequels, by Larry Niven, Jerry Pournelle, and Steven Barnes; and Isis, in Robert Charles Wilson's *Bios* (1999). Closer to home, the planets of our own solar system may be wildernesses. Mars is often depicted in this manner, as in Ray Bradbury's *The Martian Chronicles*, Kim Stanley Robinson's Mars Trilogy (see **Red Mars**), and Ben Bova's *Mars* (1992) and its sequels. Parts of Earth that retain at least some of the character of wilderness are considered in Poul Anderson's "Fortune Hunter" (1972), David Brin's *Earth* (1990), and Kim Stanley Robinson's *Antarctica* (1997).

The symbolic conflict between corrupt civilization and "innocent" wilderness, especially when the latter is equated with nature, is strongest and most obvious in stories like Edgar Rice Burroughs's **Tarzan of the Apes** and the film **King Kong**, but it can also be discerned (at least implicitly) in ecological horror stories like John Brunner's *The Sheep Look Up* (1972), about humankind's transformation of Earth into a wasteland. However, the concept of wilderness cannot be limited exclusively to regions that colonizers have not yet conquered. Nor have wilderness and nature always held positive connotations: as late as the eighteenth century nature was seen as dangerous, disorganized, and chaotic. A wilderness may also be a site of desolation and destruction, a place devastated by **war**, pestilence, or advanced **technology** run amok. In such cases, wilderness is the opposite of civilization because civilization has fallen or been destroyed, and the world has been transformed into a wasteland.

Post-apocalyptic wildernesses in science fiction (see **Apocalypse; Post-Holocaust Societies**) are often the result of war, like those in Walter M. Miller, Jr.'s *A Canticle for Leibowitz* and David Brin's *The Postman* (1985).

Finally, any region characterized by lawlessness and chaos could justifiably be termed a wilderness. Examples of what might be called urban wildernesses, where order and civilization have broken down due to excessive overcrowding, are in Harry Harrison's *Make Room! Make Room!* (1966), Frank Herbert's *The Dosadi Experiment* (1978), and Barry B. Longyear's *Sea of Glass* (1987).

In fantasy, dangerous wildernesses often must be traversed by major characters, perhaps to complete a **quest**. J.R.R. Tolkien's *The Lord of the Rings* sends protagonists on such journeys, as does Terry Brooks's *The Sword of Shannara* and its sequels.

A particular characteristic of many science fiction wildernesses usually conveyed directly to readers is emotional impact. Characters pause to consider the **beauty** of a wild landscape around them, or are awe-struck by the natural wilderness through which they travel (see **Sense of Wonder**). Examples include Luna's Sea of Thirst, in Arthur C. Clarke's *A Fall of Moondust* (1961), and Martian landscapes in Robinson's *Red Mars*. In a parallel manner, a negative wilderness may arouse fear or loathing. In either case, contact with wilderness produces a strong, memorable experience.

Discussion

There are intrinsic values embedded in any understanding of the concept of wilderness, a concept that only gains meaning when placed in relation to something else, normally civilization of some kind. When wilderness is seen as a good thing, as in ecologically informed fiction, it may become equated with nature, with civilization depicted as encroaching upon it and threatening its life-affirming characteristics (see **Ecology**). When wilderness is portrayed negatively, it is a place of lawlessness, **violence**, chaos, and danger, which civilization has a duty to tame and make safe, accessible, and productive. Whether the fictional wildernesses of science fiction and fantasy are presented as sources of wonder or **horror**, they provide important contrasts and counterpoints to what civilization and its proponents offer the world, useful aids in determining just how much—and what kind of—wilderness we want in our lives.

Bibliography

William Cronon. "The Trouble with Wilderness." Cronon, ed., *Uncommon Ground*. New York: Norton, 1995, 69–90.

John Dean. "The Uses of Wilderness in American Science Fiction," *Science-Fiction Studies*, 9 (March, 1982), 68–81.

Karl S. Guthke. *The Last Frontier*. Ithaca: Cornell University Press, 1990.

David Mogen. *Wilderness Visions*. Second Edition. San Bernardino: Borgo Press, 1993.

Roderick Nash. *Wilderness and the American Mind*. Fourth Edition. New Haven: Yale University Press, 2001.

Max Oelschlaeger. *The Idea of Wilderness*. New Haven: Yale University Press, 1991.

John Pennington. "Shamanistic Mythmaking." *Journal of the Fantastic in the Arts*, 6 (1993), 34–50.

David Sandner. "Habituated to the Vast." *Extrapolation*, 41 (Fall, 2000), 282–297.

—Richard L. McKinney

WISDOM

———————————■———————————

Logic, logic, logic. Logic is the beginning of wisdom, Valeris, not the end.

—Nicholas Meyer and Denny Martin Flinn
Star Trek VI: The Undiscovered Country
(1992)

Overview

Wisdom is often regarded as the province of wise men or women whose beliefs about the proper use of **knowledge** are products of experience with life and other ways of thinking, often gained in **old age**, rather than information learned from **books**.

Survey

Wisdom is the ability to evaluate the morality or rightness of taking action. An individual may have knowledge or **technology** to accomplish goals without considering the consequences. The **mad scientists** of Mary Shelley's *Frankenstein* and H.G. Wells's *The Island of Doctor Moreau*, for example, usurp the power of **nature** by artificially creating life, with disastrous results. A century later, similar efforts through **genetic engineering** lead to **apocalypse** in Greg Bear's *Blood Music*. In fantasy, **wizards** learn the wise use of **magic** rather than the obsessive pursuit of knowledge for its own sake, as in Patricia McKillip's *The Sorceress and the Cygnet* (1991). During **education**, **apprentices** might work spells only under supervision, as in J.K. Rowling's *Harry Potter and the Sorcerer's Stone*. Sometimes, as Ged learns from his **mentor** in Ursula K. Le Guin's *The Wizard of Earthsea*, wisdom means not using power at all.

Wisdom comes not from books but from experience, which explains why wisdom is often related to old age. In science fiction and fantasy, the wise may enjoy more than a normal lifespan in which to gain wisdom; spiritual leaders in Marion Zimmer Bradley's *The Mists of Avalon* remember past lives (see **Reincarnation**), and the **elves** of J.R.R. Tolkien's *The Hobbit* and *The Lord of the Rings* are virtually immortal, as is Robert A. Heinlein's Lazarus Long, whose words of wisdom pepper the novel *Time Enough for Love* (1973) (see *The Past Through Tomorrow*; **Immortality and Longevity**). **Time travel** is another way to experience **history**, as in Wells's *The Time Machine*, while others learn by traveling in other lands, as in Thomas More's *Utopia*. That the accumulation of knowledge does not necessarily confer wisdom on **humanity** as a whole, however, is evidenced by the repeated destruction of **civilization** in Olaf Stapledon's *Last and First Men* and Walter M. Miller, Jr.'s *A Canticle for Leibowitz*. Wisdom is not always valued: in some **dystopias**, like Aldous Huxley's *Brave New World* and George Orwell's *Nineteen Eighty-Four*, slogans are perverse substitutes for the guidance of **fables** and **philosophy**.

Wisdom is usually conveyed by wise men, often **father** figures to the **hero**, like Gandalf in Tolkien's *The Hobbit*, Obi Wan Kenobi in *Star Wars*, and Morpheus in *The Matrix*. While wise men prepare the hero for **destiny**, wise women are often characterized as maternal and nurturing (see **Mothers**): **fairies** in Charles Kingsley's *The Water Babies* teach Tom proper manners, the Oracle in *The Matrix* speaks to Neo while she bakes cookies in her kitchen, and even Galadriel in *The Lord of the Rings* gives the Companions **food and drink** and clothing along with wise counsel.

Being a sage is not always a safe or comfortable job, as G'Kar discovers in the *Babylon 5* episode "The Ragged Edge" (1998). Wise men become **messiahs** to those who follow them, as Mike becomes a Christ-figure in Heinlein's *Stranger in a Strange Land*. Some wise men are depicted as **clowns and fools** and **tricksters** rather than messiahs, like Benjamin the Wandering Jew in *A Canticle for Leibowitz* or Sam in Roger Zelazny's *Lord of Light*. The figure of Monkey (see **China**) is referenced in Kim Stanley Robinson's *The Years of Rice and Salt*, while Charles de Lint's **urban fantasies** feature **Native American** tricksters as guides.

Because wisdom is rooted in **ethics**, it is often related to **religion**, as in C.S. Lewis's *Out of the Silent Planet* and *The Lion, the Witch and the Wardrobe*, as well as in David Lindsay's *A Voyage to Arcturus*. Much of the appeal of *The Matrix* lies in its allusions to Gnosticism, while works like Robinson's *The Years of Rice and Salt* and James Hilton's **Lost Horizon** evoke the **culture** of **Asia**, associating wisdom with exotic realms. Perhaps for the same reason, aliens are sources of wisdom, including the Old Ones of **Mars** in *Stranger in a Strange Land*, the Overlords of Arthur C. Clarke's **Childhood's End**, and the **aliens in space** explored in Stapledon's *Star Maker*. Occasionally, however, even **elder races** demonstrate a lack of wisdom, as do the Shadows and Vorlons of *Babylon 5*, and they are not immune to the dangers of using technology irresponsibly, as demonstrated in *Forbidden Planet*.

Discussion

Words of wisdom have been conveyed in written form since the invention of writing, and through oral traditions long before that. People have turned to fables, proverbs, and sacred texts for advice about how to act in the world and interact with others. Fantasy, with its sources in **mythology** and focus on the **quest** for **identity** and the process of coming-of-age, naturally features characters who provide guidance and advice, while arguably the central theme of science fiction has been the need to consider the consequences of **progress**, to question whether it is right to do something simply because it can be done.

Bibliography

Isaac Asimov. "Introduction." Asimov, Martin H. Greenberg, and Charles Waugh, eds., *Wizards*. New York: Signet, 1983, 7–9.

Tim Callahan. "Devil, Trickster and Fool." *Mythlore*, 17 (Summer, 1991), 29–34.

R.E. Hersh. "Lemuel Gulliver's Seven Pillars of Wisdom." R. A. Collins, ed., *Scope of the Fantastic*. Westport: Greenwood Press, 1985, 99–106.

David Langford. "Wisdom of the Ancients." *Interzone*, No. 55 (January, 1992), 43–44.

Joy Leman. "Wise Scientists and Female Androids." John Corner, ed., *Popular Television in Britain*. London: BFI Publishing, 1991, 108–124.

Janice Neuleib. "Of Other Worlds." *Extrapolation*, 19 (May, 1978), 108–111.

Roger C. Schlobin. "Survival of the Fool in Modern Heroic Fantasy." William Coyle, ed., *Aspects of Fantasy*. Westport, CT: Greenwood, 1986, 123–130.

Nancy Willard. "The Goddess in the Belfrey." Roderick McGillis, ed., *For the Childlike*. Metuchen, NJ: Scarecrow Press, 1992, 67–74.

—*Christine Mains*

WITCHES
■

Overview

Witches work **magic** for good or **evil**, often with **magical objects** or familiars like **cats**. Portrayals range from historic accounts of women making **sacrifices** to **Satan** to modern Wicca with roots in **feminism**. This encyclopedia classifies all female magic-users as "witches." For male magic-users, see **Wizards**.

Survey

When people regarded witches as real, they were universally reviled for their association with black magic and Satanism. There is nothing attractive, for example, in the portrayal of the three witches in William **Shakespeare**'s *Macbeth* (c. 1606), who drive Macbeth to murder and **tragedy**. This pattern continued well into the twentieth century: L. Frank Baum's *The Wonderful Wizard of Oz* features wicked witches in two of Oz's four realms, although he balances the picture by placing good witches in the other two. A traditionally cruel witch binds (see **Curses**) Narnia to eternal winter in C.S. Lewis's *The Lion, the Witch and the Wardrobe*.

Later portrayals grow more favorable. Fritz Leiber's *Conjure Wife* (1943) depicts housewives as witches in disguise, working benevolent magic; the novel inspired the film *Burn, Witch, Burn* (1962). The film *I Married a Witch* (1941) and the television series *Bewitched* (1964–1972) transformed witches into icons of American domesticity. Aided by a man from **Earth,** the witches of Estcarp protect their **home** in Andre Norton's *Witch World* (1963) and its sequels. Three girls with **psychic powers** alternately bedevil and assist a space traveler in James H. Schmitz's *The Witches of Karres* (1966). In David Eddings's *Pawn of Prophecy*, the witch Polgara guides Garion as he learns magic, and Romilly trains **birds** and **horses** for **war** in Marion Zimmer Bradley's *Hawkmistress* (1982). This novel provides witches with psychic powers, while continuing the fantasy motif of their connection to **nature**. Around the same time that Bradley's book was published, contemporary Wicca went public with nonfiction books like Starhawk's *The Spiral Dance* (1979), emphasizing natural **cycles**, the **gods and goddesses**, and **ethics**. These witches use their powers benevolently, often defending a special place or person, but they make fearsome enemies.

From here, interaction between fact and fiction inspires authors to more complexity. Isaac Asimov, Martin H. Greenberg, and Charles G. Waugh's anthology *Witches* (1984) includes both light and dark portrayals of witches. Patricia Kennealy-Morrison's Keltiad novels, beginning with *The Copper Crown* (1984), take witches into space (see **Space Travel**), where Aeron wields magical, military, and political power with equal skill. In Bradley's *Lythande* (1986), the titular character disguises herself as a man in order to keep her magic. This fascinating **gender** dilemma goes beyond social oppression; Lythande's order—all male, except her—draws its power from a secret, and this is hers.

Some authors choose to blur the lines of reality: in Charles de Lint's *Yarrow* (1997), Cat Midhir visits another world in her **dreams**. The juxtaposition of enchanted **forests** and city streets typifies de Lint's **urban fantasies**, which often features witches. Gael Baudino's *Strands of Starlight* (1994) presents different types of witches: the healer Miriam, the **elves** with various **talents**, and the humans who practice witchcraft as **religion**.

Witches often face significant problems involving their **families**. A witch comes into her power after unknown enemies kidnap her **children** in Holly Lisle's *Minerva Wakes* (1993). Richard Gilliam, Martin H. Greenberg, and Kathleen M. Massie-Ferch's anthology *Ancient Enchantresses* (1995) offers stories in which relatives fight together. In the television series *Buffy the Vampire Slayer*, the witch Willow gains and loses various friends and lovers. Her growing magic eventually corrupts Willow, a common pitfall suffered by many witches. In Anne Bishop's *Daughter of the Blood* (1998), Jaenelle must choose between the genetic family that rejects her and the intentional family that welcomes her, while struggling to master her powers and protect those she **loves**. These stories feature personable witches, made understandable by their family ties.

Cooperative magic is also growing in popularity. While witches in early stories tend to be solitary, like the one in Narnia, later ones display more teamwork. In Doranna Durgin's *Seer's Blood* (2000), the "Takers" (see **Parasites**) had destroyed most talented people, but one young witch helps organize a resistance. This story's charm comes from its local color, inspired by Appalachian culture, a fine tribute to the rustic **history** of witches. Folk witchcraft is also employed in Orson Scott Card's Alvin Maker series, beginning with *Seventh Son* (1987). The Fae (see **Fairies**) trace the creeping destruction of their **home** to the murder of witches, who prove to be literally *The Pillars of the World* in Bishop's novel (2001). Some witches join with the Fae to resist the Inquisitors. An antisocial girl finds unexpected friends in Ted Naifeh's *Courtney Crumrin and the Coven of Mystics* (2003), which takes an unusually faithful look at the dark side of childhood. All these stories convincingly demonstrate the drawbacks of isolationism.

Discussion

Public perception of witches has influenced literary use of this theme. As they have been transformed in the popular imagination from reviled criminals to healers, wise women, and nature worshippers, they increasingly illustrate **progress** toward religious and social tolerance. Stories question the acceptability of abusing women, outsiders, or people with unusual **talents**. Increasingly positive portrayals give more attention to the witches' own perspective.

Witches provide a crucial counterpart to wizards, over time giving female characters more power and influence. They provide subtle or spectacular magic in fantasy settings, and a hint of **mystery** in science fiction. They excite the reader's **sense of wonder** while inviting consideration of ethics in the use of magical or social power.

Bibliography

Isaac Asimov, Martin H. Greenberg, and Charles G. Waugh, eds. *Witches*. New York: Signet, 1984.

Marion Zimmer Bradley, ed. *Sword and Sorceress I*. New York: DAW, 1984.

Lester del Rey and Randall Garrett. "Witchcraft in Science Fiction." *Luna*, No. 3 (1963), 9–20.

Carrol L. Fry. "The Goddess Ascending." *Journal of Popular Culture*, 27 (Summer, 1993), 67–80.

Richard Gilliam, Martin H. Greenberg, and Kathleen M. Massie-Ferch, eds. *Ancient Enchantresses*. New York: DAW, 1995.

Katherine Kurtz. *Deryni Magic*. New York: Del Rey, 1990.

Sharon Russell. "Witch in Film." Barry K. Grant, ed., *Planks of Reason*. Metuchen: Scarecrow, 1984. 113–125.

Susan Shwartz, ed. *Hecate's Cauldron*. New York: DAW, 1982.

Starhawk. *The Spiral Dance*. San Francisco: HarperSanFrancisco, 1979.

—Elizabeth Barrette

WIZARDS

∎

Overview

Powerful and mysterious wizards are among the most popular figures in genre entertainment. A wizard is a practitioner of **magic**, especially in **fairy tales**, fantasy fiction, and fantasy role-playing **games**. The term does not commonly apply to pagans or stage magicians. Other terms often used with minimal differentiation are enchanter, magician, druid, alchemist, and sorcerer. Their tall hats, mystifying behavior, and spectacular enchantments are familiar to audiences. Wizards are often cast as **heroes**, advisors, **mentors**, or **villains**; female practitioners of magic are discussed as **witches**.

Survey

Wizards and witches are not **gods and goddesses** because there are always limits to their powers. Often this limitation is based on the nature of their magic. The magic in Ursula K. Le Guin's *A Wizard of Earthsea* is limited by the fact that all magic in Earthsea is based on true **names**, and therefore the magic a wizard can work is limited by his **knowledge** of the true names of things around him. Such clearly defined systems of magic are important elements of fantasy worlds. In J.R.R. Tolkien's *The Lord of the Rings*, though Gandalf seems at times to be an almighty wizard, he practices powerful magic sparingly because he knows it carries a dangerous price. The One Ring, the most powerful **magical object** in Middle-earth, is exceedingly **evil**, and the wizard Saruman is corrupted by the lure of its power.

Even though he plays an active role in unfolding events, Gandalf primarily functions as a wise man, a catalyst to drive other characters to action and self-realization. Without Gandalf, neither Frodo in *The Lord of the Rings* nor Bilbo in *The Hobbit* would have left the Shire, and Aragorn might never have taken his rightful place as the **king** of men. Similarly, Allanon in Terry Brooks's *The Sword of Shannara* uses druidic knowledge to guide Shea Ohmsford in his quest. Indeed, many wizards have been depicted as wise sages, particularly as advisors to their kings and queens. The most famous of which is no doubt Merlin, King **Arthur**'s trusted adviser, prophet (see **Divination**), and magician, featured in T.H. White's *The Once and Future King* (1958). In most modern popular interpretations, however, Merlin is a wizard of ultimate power, as in Marion Zimmer Bradley's *The Mists of Avalon* where he creates rain with a wave of his hand.

In some stories, wizards are effectively the lead characters, as in J.K. Rowling's *Harry Potter and the Sorcerer's Stone*, where the majority of characters are wizard students or teachers at Hogwarts School of Witchcraft and Wizardry. Harry Potter is a stereotypical **apprentice** while Albus Dumbledore, Headmaster of Hogwarts, is the stereotypical elderly, white-haired wizard with a droll sense of **humor** and twinkling eyes. Wizards who serve as heroic protagonists include Prospero in William **Shakespeare**'s *The Tempest* (c. 1611) and Vergil in Avram Davidson's *The Phoenix and the Mirror* (1969). Comic-book **superheroes** who are also wizards include Marvel Comics' Dr. Strange, DC Comics' Zatana, and Fawcett Comics' Ibis the Invincible.

Conversely, wizards can also serve as excellent, believable villains in their quests for **immortality and longevity**, absolute power, or great riches (see **Money**). Their superpowers offer a challenge to the heroes who oppose them. Tolkien's Saruman and Rowling's Voldemort are obvious examples; a comic-book equivalent is the Wizard, an implacable villain who opposed the Justice Society of America. Good and bad wizards are exploited for humor in the films *The Raven* (1963) and *Wizards* (1977).

Some people who are labeled wizards lack the requisite powers, like the ordinary man who relies on trickery to reign as L. Frank Baum's *The Wonderful Wizard of Oz*, or Rincewind in Terry Pratchett's *The Colour of Magic* and its sequels, a failed student at the Unseen University in Ankh-Morpork who spends his time running away from various people who wish to harm him. In opposition to standard wizard imagery, Schmendrick from Peter S. Beagle's *The Last Unicorn* excels at failure, not wizardry; almost all of his attempted magical feats result in **disaster**. In *A Spell for Chameleon*, Piers Anthony turns the all-powerful image around with the character Bink, whose talent is not to perform magic, but to be immune from magic. Even the Good Magician Humfrey, whose talent is information, is unable to gain knowledge about Bink.

Discussion

While wizards play different roles—from leading hero to supporting advisor to menacing villain—fantasy readers can always relate to them, relishing their abilities to manipulate their environment through use of unparalleled **wisdom** or supernatural magic. Wizards are vibrant characters that symbolize the magical allure of fantasy fiction.

Bibliography

Giselle L. Anatol, ed. *Reading Harry Potter*. Westport, CT: Praeger, 2003.

C. Stephen Byrum. "Reflections on *A Wizard of Earthsea*." *Philosophy in Context*, 11 (1981), 51–60.

Michael R. Collings. *Piers Anthony*. San Bernardino, CA: Borgo Press, 1983.
Geoff Fox. *Writers, Critics, and Children*. New York: Agathon Press, 1976.
Martin Greenburg, ed. *Wizard Fantastic*. New York: Daw, 1997.
Kerrie A. Le Lievre. "Wizards and Wainscots." *Mythlore*, 24 (Summer, 2003), 25–36.
Michael Moorcock. *Wizardry and Wild Romance*. London: Gollancz, 1987.
Deborah O'Keefe. *Readers in Wonderland*. New York: Continuum, 2003.
Michael N. Stanton. *Hobbits, Elves and Wizards*. New York: St. Martin's, 2001.

—*Nick Aires*

WORK AND LEISURE

■

Even if one has been to the moon, one has still to earn a living.

—H.G. Wells
The First Men in the Moon (1901)

Overview

To begin the process of defining science fiction's attitude toward work and leisure, one might turn to the life and works of Isaac Asimov. His move toward autobiographical reflection once he had become famous and, in particular, his hard work in editing memoirs and anthologies like *Before the Golden Age* (1974), teaches a lot about work and its reverse. He comments on stories he most enjoyed as a youth and defines a key dynamic with echoes to classical literature. The "golden age" for a science fiction fan is early adolescence when one has the leisure to read. This golden age should be followed, for Asimov, by fierce labor during the remainder of one's life, exemplified by Asimov's own labor in producing hundreds of **books**.

Survey

In Roman times, poems like Virgil's *Georgics* (37–30 BCE) celebrated industry and work with the notion that *labor*, the Latin word for work, conquers all. But georgics, also, are closely linked to **pastoral** poems in which leisure and the removal from **city** work to the peaceful country life is celebrated. Echoes of precisely that contrast resonate through science fiction and fantasy where **computers** and urbanized **technology** are often defined by opposition to more reclusive, removed, and relaxing behaviors. No narrative has seemed more pastoral in twentieth-century fantasy than J.R.R. Tolkien's **The Hobbit**, written in the midst of the turbulent decade of the thirties. Similarly, **flower** children and the protesting urban pastoralism of the 1960s greatly influenced Samuel R. Delany's epic novel of city life and escape, *Dhalgren* (1975), as well as the work of Philip K. Dick. One might even argue that **cyberpunk** itself is our most georgic expression in science fiction where hard computer work goes hand in hand with the resolve to escape and enjoy leisure.

Thus, in any well-run fantasyland, or well-run future **civilization**, there must be opportunities for both work and leisure. Fantasy heroes devoted to **quests** can enjoy the occasional raucous interlude of **carnival** or enjoy beer and companionship in **taverns and inns**. The people of Hugo Gernsback's *Ralph 124C 41+: A Romance of the Year 2660* (1925) are busier than ever, a condition ironically attributed to their labor-saving devices, but advanced technology provides them with "Vacation Cities" in the sky. If there is entirely too much leisure, as in Arthur C. Clarke's **far future** city of Diaspar in *The City and the Stars* (1956), the protagonist Alvin must rediscover the benefits of hard work by leaving the city and discovering its true **history**. The alternative policy of continuing to wallow in pleasure and relaxation will only cause **humanity** to slowly shrink into the helpless beings encountered by a distraught time traveler in John W. Campbell, Jr.'s "Twilight" (1934) (see **Time Travel**).

Several Marxian principles that ironically derive from the rigorous study by Karl Marx and Frederick Engels of the nineteenth-century work **ethic** in capitalism appear alongside classical references in some of the most political science fiction by Ursula K. Le Guin and Delany. Le Guin's *The Dispossessed* and Delany's *Triton*, in particular, are full of Marxian notions that a labor theory of value can overcome capitalist indifference to lead to more quality leisure time for all people. Similarly, the Marxian insight that modern urbanized **culture** treats everything from literature to love to **youth** itself as a commodity has had the liberating effect of inspiring polemics against commidification. Both the ghastly cityscapes and the pastoral ending to Dick's *Do Androids Dream of Electric Sheep?* illustrate this mix of the georgic and Marxian.

But information technology may represent the most vivid image in science fiction for both poles of this dialectic between work and leisure. **Robots** work very hard for humanity to provide their masters with more leisure. The inevitable tyranny, however, is often seen as dehumanizing and in need of even harder work lest the machines win. Harlan Ellison's famous short story "I Have No Mouth, and I Must Scream" (1967) screams in protest against this irony. The ultimate, ironic epitome of restful leisure, in fact, is the deep cryogenic **sleep** enjoyed by David Bowman's fellow crew members in Clarke's *2001: A Space Odyssey* (see **Suspended Animation and Cryonics**). Such forced leisure is necessary in **space travel** just as computers are necessary to keep our industrial, urbanized society working. Finally, the life work of crew members in Clarke is totally sustained by HAL 9000 the computer, and it is he who kills them.

Discussion

Thus from Virgil to Marx to cyberpunk to information technology, the message is always mixed. Work can be hard and even politically odious. Workers want to be liberated for leisure. But just as Asimov discovered for us, it is a blessing to keep working all through one's life. He said that he was happiest working on his books. And many of his books grew out of his leisurely golden age reading that he lost once he became a hard-working writer.

Bibliography

Avner Cohen. "Marx and the Abolition of Labor." *Utopian Studies*, 6 (1995), 40–50.
Fred Erisman. "Sites for Sore Souls." *Extrapolation*, 32 (Fall, 1991), 268–277.

Darren Harris-Fain. "Created in the Image of God." *Extrapolation*, 32 (Summer, 1991), 143–155.

Donald M. Hassler. "*Dhalgren, The Beggar's Opera*, and Georgic." *Extrapolation*, 30 (Winter, 1989), 332–339.

Donald M. Hassler and Clyde Wilcox, eds. *Political Science Fiction*. Columbia: University of South Carolina Press, 1997.

Louis J. Kern. "Evangelical Environmentalism and the New Commonwealth." Lisa Leibacher-Ouvrard and Nicholas D. Smith, eds., *Utopian Studies IV*. Lanham, NY: University Press of America, 1991, 42–54.

Stephen Snyder. "Family Life and Leisure Culture in *The Shining*." *Film Criticism*, 7 (Fall, 1982), 4–14.

Uri Zilbersheid. "The Idea of Abolition of Labor in Socialist Utopian Thought." *Utopian Studies*, 13 (2002), 21–42.

—*Donald M. Hassler*

WORMS

See Snakes and Worms

WRITING AND AUTHORS

Overview

Although stories about writers are common in mainstream literature, writing about writing is not an approach frequently associated with science fiction and fantasy. Nonetheless, a number of well-known science fiction and fantasy works have featured characters who are professional writers, diarists, or chroniclers. Some stories have dramatized the **business** and **economics** of authorship as well as the **anxiety** and **absurdity** of the writing life, while stories of **post-holocaust societies** often focus on diarists. And both historical and imaginary authors frequently appear in works of **metafiction and recursiveness**.

Survey

The use of letters and journals as a narrative device was commonplace in nineteenth- and early twentieth-century fiction, and many of the best-known works of science fiction and fantasy from that period present themselves as "written" records. In Mary Shelley's **Frankenstein**, Victor Frankenstein's account of his notorious career is presented as the explorer's transcriptions of Frankenstein's own words, framed by correspondence from the explorer who discovered him wandering in the Arctic. Similarly, Edgar Allan Poe's **The Narrative of Arthur Gordon Pym** claims to combine the title character's written account of his "extraordinary series of adventure" with a "few pages written by Mr. Poe." Bram's Stoker's *Dracula* is narrated as a series of diary and journal entries from several of the main characters. Such claims of verisimilitude are particularly resonant as a framework for fantastic stories.

The existence of an "actual" written record is also important in stories dealing with survivors of **apocalypse**, perhaps most famously represented by the monks who try to preserve **knowledge** after a **nuclear war** in Walter M. Miller, Jr.'s *A Canticle for Leibowitz*. In Octavia E. Butler's *Parable of the Sower* (1993) and sequel *Parable of the Talents* (1998), the **near future** collapse of American society and emergence of a new **religion** are detailed in diary entries by the religion's founder. However, the most celebrated use of diary entries as a narrative device, and one of the finest examples of attention to **language and linguistics** in science fiction, remains the record of the mentally impaired Charlie Gordon's rise to, and fall from, genius in Daniel Keyes's *Flowers for Algernon*.

In contrast to the moral authority granted to the diarist or chronicler, professional writers-as-characters are often cynical, troubled figures. Bestselling authors Chad C. Mulligan, in John Brunner's *Stand on Zanzibar*, and Jubal Harshaw, in Robert A. Heinlein's *Stranger in a Strange Land*, retreat from the chaos of early twenty-first-century society before unexpected and extraordinary events force them back into the public sphere. In Philip K. Dick's classic **alternate history** *The Man in the High Castle*, Hawthorne Abendsen, author of a **book** suggesting a different outcome to World War II, has more impact on his world than Mulligan or Harshaw have on theirs, but is targeted by assassins for his trouble. Similarly, the novelists who frequently appear as protagonists in the novels of Stephen King are usually overpowered by forces from without, as in *Misery* (1987), or within, as in *The Shining*.

This hardbitten attitude towards the profession of writing is also predominant in the subset of science fiction stories about science fiction writers, including Herovit in Barry N. Malzberg's *Herovit's World* (1973), a commercially popular but artistically undistinguished science fiction writer, and Kurt Vonnegut, Jr.'s Kilgore Trout, a recurrent character in several novels, in particular *God Bless You, Mr. Rosewater* (1965). Other notable examples of such stories are Larry Niven and Jerry Pournelle's *Inferno* (1976), in which a science fiction writer falls out a window at a science fiction convention and finds himself on a journey through Dante's **Hell**, and Norman Spinrad's *The Iron Dream* (1972), which purports to be a Hugo-winning novel by an Adolf Hitler who immigrated to **America** as a young man and became a science fiction writer.

Discussion

Even greater than the number of science fiction and fantasy stories that feature fictional writers is the number of stories in which historical literary figures appear (see **History**). Such stories have appeared periodically in science fiction, from Philip José Farmer's rendering of Mark Twain in his Riverworld series, beginning with *To Your Scattered Bodies Go* (1971), to David Barbour and Richard Raleigh's pairing of H.P. Lovecraft and Robert E. Howard in *Shadows Bend* (2000). The 1980s and 1990s in particular saw several works of short fiction featuring famous authors as characters, including Paul Di Filippo's "Walt and Emily" (1993), depicting an encounter between Walt Whitman and Emily Dickinson; Walter Jon Williams's "No

Spot of Ground" (1989), in which Edgar Allan Poe survives to become an officer in the Confederate Army; John Kessel's "The Big Dream" (1984), a striking critique of Raymond Chandler; and Jane Yolen's "Sister Emily's Lightship" (1996), in which Emily Dickinson has a close encounter, not with Whitman, but with alien visitors.

The theme of writers and writing has seldom been explored in science fiction and fantasy films. Two noteworthy exceptions are *The Trouble with Dick* (1987), a dark comedy about a science fiction writer named "Dick Kindred" (compare to real author Philip Kindred Dick), and *The Whole Wide World* (1996), a moving portrait of the final years of Robert E. Howard.

Bibliography

Edwin F. Casebeer. "The Ecological System of Stephen King's *The Dark Half.*" *Journal of the Fantastic in the Arts*, 6 (1994), 126–142.

Anthony R. Lewis. *An Annotated Bibliography of Recursive Science Fiction.* Framingham, MA: NESFA Press, 1990.

Barry N. Malzberg. *The Passage of the Light.* Ed. Mike Resnick and Lewis. Framingham, MA: NESFA Press, 1994.

———. "The Science Fiction of Science Fiction." Malzberg, *The Engines of the Night.* Garden City, NY: Doubleday, 1982, 77–84.

Peter J. Reed. "Kurt Vonnegut's Bitter Fool." Marc Leeds and Reed, eds., *Kurt Vonnegut.* Westport, CT: Greenwood Press, 2000, 67–80.

———. "Writer as Character: Kilgore Trout." Harold Bloom, ed., *Kurt Vonnegut.* Philadelphia: Chelsea House, 2000, 111–124.

Mike Resnick, ed. *Inside the Funhouse.* New York: AvoNova, 1992.

Mike Resnick and Patrick Nielsen Hayden, eds. *Alternate Skiffy.* Holicong, PA: Wildside Press, 1997.

—*F. Brett Cox*

X

XENOPHOBIA

Overview

Xenophobia, or fear of strangers, is an ancient tendency in the human species that undoubtedly once had **survival** value, enabling members of a tribe to bond together and protect themselves against menacing outsiders. However, as **humanity** expanded to populate the entire globe, and as isolated tribes gave way to large nations in constant contact, xenophobia became not a help but a hindrance to **progress**. Hostility toward other races and cultures without the element of fear is discussed under **race relations**, and specific fears about other people conspiring against someone are addressed as **paranoia**.

Survey

During the last two centuries, science fiction and fantasy have found different groups of outsiders to be afraid of. Eighteenth- and nineteenth-century Americans settling the **frontier** generally feared **Native Americans** as dangerous savages that should be exterminated—the castigated attitude of General William Henry Harrison in Orson Scott Card's **alternate history** of early **America**, the Alvin Maker series beginning with *Seventh Son* (1987). Some nineteenth-century dime novels featured heroic boy inventors deploying their amazing **inventions** against hostile Native Americans. By the dawn of the twentieth century, however, when they were confined to reservations and posed no further threat, Native Americans were regarded more benignly as quaint "noble savages," as demonstrated by the generally positive portrayal of "Indians" in J.M. Barrie's *Peter and Wendy*. The nineteenth-century British colonizers of **Africa** sometimes had reason to fear attacking African warriors, but writers generally did not view Africans as a significant menace. Instead, they regarded them with subdued respect, like H. Rider Haggard in the Allan Quatermain novels beginning with *King Solomon's Mines* (1885); or with indifference, like Edgar Rice Burroughs, whose Tarzan novels (see *Tarzan of the Apes*) generally said little about the African people; or with condescension, like Edgar Wallace's *Sanders of the River* (1911), who treats the natives like overgrown **children**.

The exotic people that both the Americans and the British feared were the Asians, particularly the Chinese and Japanese people (see **China; Japan**). M.P. Shiel's novel *The Yellow Danger* (1898) helped to promulgate the widespread variety of xenophobia referred to as the "Yellow Peril," but other works expressed fears that Asian hordes would overrun and conquer the Western world, while Kenneth Mackay's *The Yellow Wave* (1895) demonstrates that the attitude penetrated to **Australia** as well. Among the twentieth-century texts demonstrating the persistence of this theme are Sax Rohmer's novels about the Chinese **villain** Fu Manchu, beginning with *The Insidious Dr. Fu Manchu* (1913); Philip Francis Nowlan's *Armageddon 2419 A.D.* (1928), in which a twentieth-century American reawakens in the future to help America overcome Asian "Han" invaders who have taken over their country; and Robert A. Heinlein's *Sixth Column* (1949), in which a handful of **scientists** conspire to oust Asian occupiers of America. Even some fantasies set in fantasticated versions of **Europe** employ Asians as villains; for example, in Glen Cook's Dread Empire series beginning with *A Shadow of All Night Falling* (1978), the threatening Dread Empire is a thinly disguised version of ancient China.

The twentieth century also gave rise to science fiction stories about **aliens on Earth**—all too often portrayed as loathsome **monsters** fit only for extermination. H.G. Wells's *The War of the Worlds* set the pattern with its horrified description of the Martians who brought their **evil** machines to conquer the Earth. H.P. Lovecraft's monsters and **elder races** oppressing **Earth** were clear reflections of xenophobia. **Aliens in space** might be equally repugnant, one prominent example being the **insect**-like Bugs battling humanity in Heinlein's *Starship Troopers*.

However, by the middle of the twentieth century, science fiction and fantasy were shifting from expressions of xenophobia to criticisms of xenophobia, with stories about people were being unreasonably hostile to sometimes strange but basically friendly alien visitors. Films like *The Man from Planet X* (1951), **The Day the Earth Stood Still**, and *It Came from Outer Space* (1953) involved aliens initially regarded as sinister invaders who were later revealed to be benign. In James White's **Hospital Station**, staffed by and treating all sorts of different alien species, any sign of xenophobia is a cause for alarm. Specific rebuttals to *Starship Troopers* came in Joe Haldeman's **The Forever War** and Orson Scott Card's **Ender's Game**, in which insect-like aliens resembling Heinlein's Bugs turn out to be friendly but misunderstood creatures. By the time of *E.T.: The Extra-Terrestrial*, it seems that science fiction was prepared to regard even the strangest of aliens as warm and cuddly companions.

Discussion

Even as stories appear to preach against xenophobia, science fiction and fantasy may project a concealed xenophobia in depictions of unpleasant alien or monstrous foes that recall old western fears of other races. Some critics detect xenophobia toward minority groups in depictions of orcs in J.R.R. Tolkien's **The Lord of the Rings** and its film adaptation (see **The Lord of the Rings: The Fellowship of the Ring**), while critic Daniel Bernardi argues that subdued racism gradually emerged in the seemingly enlightened universe of **Star Trek** and **Star Trek: The Next Generation**. Thus, ancient fears of the other may be harder to overcome than writers of science fiction and fantasy would like to believe.

Bibliography

Henry L.P. Beckwith. "Lovecraft's Xenophobia and Providence Between the Wars." S.T. Joshi, ed., *The H. P. Lovecraft Centennial Conference Proceedings*. Warwick, RI: Necronomicon, 1991, 10.

Barry L. Bender. "Xenophobia in the Life and Work of H. P. Lovecraft." *Lovecraft Studies*, 1 (Spring, 1981), 22–38 and (Fall, 1981), 10–28.

Daniel L. Bernardi. *Star Trek and History*. New Brunswick, NJ: Rutgers University Press, 1998.

Carter F. Hanson. "1920's Yellow Peril Science Fiction." *Journal of the Fantastic in the Arts*, 6 (1995), 312–329.

John Huntington. "Impossible Love in Science Fiction." *Raritan*, 4 (Fall, 1984), 85–99.

Edward James. "Yellow, Black, Metal, and Tentacled." Philip J. Davies, ed., *Science Fiction, Social Conflict, and War*. Manchester: Manchester University Press, 1990, 26–49.

Elisabeth Anne Leonard, ed. *Into Darkness Peering*. Westport, CT: Greenwood Press, 1997.

Joseph W. Reed. "Public Enemies, Space Slime, Yellow Peril, and Crime." Reed, *American Scenarios*. Middletown, CT: Wesleyan University Press, 1989, 230–244.

—*Gary Westfahl*

YIN AND YANG

Overview

This Chinese Taoist concept of balanced opposites stands for many possible pairings, including chaos and order, **darkness** and **light**, **death** and life, left and right, female and male, and **Heaven** and **Earth** (or **Hell**). Most frequently encountered in fantasy is the moral duality of **evil** and good.

Survey

The opening trilogy of Ursula K. Le Guin's Earthsea sequence (see *A Wizard of Earthsea*) is perhaps the clearest fantasy embodiment of the Taoist principle of balance. Light and dark, or life and death, are naturally in balance with each sustaining the other. Wielding **magic** disturbs the natural order, and—paradoxically—the greatest **wizards** make least use of magic for fear of unintended consequences. When a misguided mage challenges death in *The Farthest Shore* (1972), the resulting upheaval endangers the whole world and may only be set right by a significant **sacrifice**. Likewise, Roger Zelazny's ***Lord of Light*** ultimately celebrates Death and Light as eternal complements, each as necessary as the other.

The good versus evil opposition, though endemic in commercial fantasy, is almost too trite for discussion. Often the greatest interest lies in the grey areas. Well-known examples from J.R.R. Tolkien's ***The Lord of the Rings*** (often criticized for portraying absolute blacks and whites) are the good but prideful warrior Boromir who is tempted beyond endurance by the power of the **Ring**, and the repellent, corrupted creature Gollum who retains a tiny spark of fellow feeling and eventually, accidentally, completes the **quest** when better characters fail.

In Piers Anthony's *On a Pale Horse* (1983), precise evaluation of a soul's balance of good and evil determines its destination once and for all: Heaven, Hell or Purgatory. A similar register of characters' virtuous credit or debit in Gordon R. Dickson's *The Dragon and the George* (1976) is maintained by a disembodied "Auditing Department." More in the spirit of Yin and Yang, the Swamp Thing comic's American **Gothic** storyline (scripted by Alan Moore) culminates in a vision of ultimate light and dark forces clasping hands—collected in *Swamp Thing Volume Eight* (1988). The title character of Mervyn Peake's *Mr. Pye* (1953), unable to maintain a neutral balance-point, oscillates between sprouting **angel**'s wings and **demon**'s horns.

Michael Moorcock's fantasies generally employ the more morally ambiguous axis of Law versus Chaos, whose extremes of stasis and formlessness are equally inhospitable to life. His "multiverse" features a literal Cosmic Balance which is seen righting itself when the ascendancy of Chaos is toppled in *Stormbringer* (1963), which acts as a plot device to destroy a Chaos goddess who oversteps the mark in *The Queen of the Swords* (1971), and which is left swinging freely when Law and Chaos gods alike are slaughtered in *The King of the Swords* (1971). The title character of John Brunner's *The Traveler in Black* (1971) has the task of reducing capricious chaos to the orderly, scientifically explicable universe we know.

The Recluce science fantasies of L.E. Modesitt, beginning with *The Magic of Recluce* (1991), center on a magical order/chaos balance as precise and immutable as that between positive and negative charge, or matter and **antimatter**, in **physics**. For order-magic to increase, chaos must increase elsewhere; when order-masters destroy chaos wizards (who are not all **villains**), the power of order dwindles. Similarly, David Langford's "The Arts of the Enemy" (1992) suggests that someone accumulating dark magic must create **magical objects** with healing powers as a necessary side effect.

In the role-playing **game** Dungeons & Dragons—which borrows extensively from Moorcock, Tolkien, and Jack Vance—character alignment uses independent law/chaos and good/evil axes. **Vampires** tend to be evil but, as supernatural beings constrained by strict rules, lawful; Tolkien's Tom Bombadil might be considered chaotic and good.

Imbalance between male and female principles is at the heart of many narratives addressing issues of **feminism** and **sexism**. Differently slanted popular perceptions of **witches** and wizards are examined in Terry Pratchett's *Equal Rites* (1987) (see *The Colour of Magic*). Diana Wynne Jones's fantasy *Aunt Maria* (1991) revolves around the need for male and female magic to play distinct, complementary parts. The same endangered balance is central to Robert Jordan's Wheel of Time sequence (see *The Eye of the World*).

Discussion

A simplistic opposition of absolutes—ultimate good versus ultimate evil—makes for arid storytelling. In the traditional yin-yang symbol, a wavy line of separation between the two symmetrical halves suggests mutual accommodation, or even some measure of flow or exchange across **borderlands**. Such enantiodromia, the transformation of extreme qualities into their opposites, is a driving theme of Brian W. Aldiss's *Helliconia Spring*. Another feature of the yin-yang is that each opposed region is shown as containing a tiny spot of the other. Outside physics, Manichean theology (see **Religion**) and games like **chess**, pure and balanced opposites are rare indeed.

The symbol of harmonious reconciliation does not have universal appeal. In *Aurelia* (1982), R.A. Lafferty, a Catholic, seems to value even evil above such compromise, and the book's most unpleasant and murderous faction carries bladed yo-yos decorated with yin-yang signs.

Bibliography

Richard P. Feynman. "The Great Conservation Principles." Feynman, *The Character of Physical Law*. 1965. London: Penguin, 1992, 59–83.

Robert Galbreath. "Taoist Magic in the Earthsea Trilogy." *Extrapolation*, 21 (Fall, 1980), 262–268.

Jeff Gardiner. *The Age of Chaos*. Stockport, UK: British Fantasy Society, 2002.

Martin Gardner. *The New Ambidextrous Universe*. New York: W.H. Freeman, 1990.

Gary Gygax. "Alignment." Gygax, *Advanced Dungeons & Dragons Players Handbook*. Lake Geneva, WI: TSR Games, 1978, 33–34.

Robert Jordan and Teresa Patterson. "The One Power and the True Source." Jordan and Patterson, *The World of Robert Jordan's The Wheel of Time*. London: Orbit, 1997, 17–25.

John Strysik. "Yin and Yang and Franz and Howard." *Lovecraft Studies*, 3 (Fall, 1984), 60–61.

Gary K. Wolfe. "Stasis and Chaos." *Journal of the Fantastic in the Arts*, 10 (Winter, 1998), 4–16.

J.R. Wytenbroek. "Taoism in the Fantasies of Ursula K. Le Guin." Olena H. Saciuk, ed., *The Shape of the Fantastic*. Westport, CT: Greenwood Press, 1990, 173–180.

—*David Langford*

YOUTH

———————————■———————————

I'm youth, I'm joy. I'm a little bird that has broken out of the egg.

—J.M. Barrie
Peter Pan (1904)

Overview

Fantasy has long been regarded as a form of literature most suitable for the young, who are naturally attracted to marvels and **magic** and not yet mature enough to properly focus their attention on realistic concerns. Science fiction has also aggressively promoted itself as the literature of young people, able to see beyond the limitations of the present to embrace the expansive possibilities to be created by future **technology**. For these reasons, science fiction and fantasy stories are often aimed at younger readers and feature youthful protagonists. Separate entries discuss **babies** and **children**.

Survey

A standard fantasy story concerns a young man, seemingly ordinary, who is summoned to a **quest** and eventually becomes, or is revealed to have always been, a **king** or great hero. T.H. White's *The Once and Future King* (1958) describes the youth of King **Arthur** following this pattern, and Terry Brooks's *The Sword of Shannara* features a humble lad who turns out to be the only surviving member of the family that can wield the epynomous **sword** and defeat the Warlock Lord. A science fiction variation occurs in Robert A. Heinlein's *Citizen of the Galaxy* (1957), in which a boy of the **far future** sold into **slavery** is, after adventures in space, revealed as a wealthy heir on **Earth**. In more recent fantasy and science fiction stories, of course, the heroic youth is just as likely to be a woman.

The classic fantasy of an eternal youth is J.M. Barrie's *Peter and Wendy*, though one might also mention Charles Kingsley's *The Water Babies*, featuring perpetually precocious denizens of the **water**, and Harlan Ellison's "Jeffty Is Five" (1977), the story of a boy permanently suspended at the age of five, with all associated forms of entertainment. In Oscar Wilde's *The Picture of Dorian Gray*, a man keeps himself unnaturally youthful by means of a magical picture.

Following in the footsteps of Ponce de Leon, who searched for the Fountain of Youth, writers have devised ways to allow adults to become young again. In comic-book adventures of the early 1960s, both *Superman* and *Batman* are scientifically transformed into babies; episodes of *The Twilight Zone* involve nostalgic adults returning to the past or reverting to children; and in an episode of the animated *Star Trek* series, "The Counter-Clock Incident" (1974), members of the *Enterprise* crew are turned into children. The film *Seconds* (1966) explores the **tragedy** of an older man who through a surreptitious service is given a second life as a handsome young man. Reversing the clock in another way, some stories look back at the imagined youths of familiar figures of popular culture, as in the farcical film *Young Einstein* (1988) and the earnest series *The Young Indiana Jones Chronicles* (1992–1996).

During the 1960s, a time when young people became more numerous and influential, science fiction considered the possibility of future societies that would be dominated by youth. In the film *Wild in the Streets* (1968), a teenager elected president relegates older adults to concentration camps—only in the end to be chillingly told by a twelve-year-old that he himself seems rather old. A more extreme vision was in William F. Nolan and George Clayton Johnson's *Logan's Run* (1967), wherein a future **dystopia** kills all citizens when they reach the age of twenty-one; the 1976 film adaptation more charitably allowed adults to live until the age of thirty.

A favorite conceit of science fiction is that **humanity** is a young species in the cosmos, barely beginning its **progress** toward maturity. Older **aliens in space** might look down with respect and hope for the future of the species, as in the *Star Trek* episode "Arena" (1967), or they might judge humans more harshly for their immature tendencies toward **violence**, as in the film *The Day the Earth Stood Still*. One specific plot device—a panel of advanced aliens that meets to decide whether or not to exterminate humanity—occurs in John Silbersack's *Science Fiction* (1981) and Heinlein's *Have Space Suit—Will Travel* (1958); the latter novel involves another alien in a more benign parental role called "Mother."

A related pattern involves seemingly advanced aliens who turn out to be, from the perspective of their **civilization**, only children. Two examples would be Kreton in Gore Vidal's television play *Visit to a Small Planet* (1955) and Trelane in the *Star Trek* episode "The Squire of Gothos" (1967), both beings who playfully torment and threaten humans with advanced powers before being summoned **home** by their parents.

Discussion

Today, the demographics of the audiences for science fiction and fantasy is shifting toward older readers, calling in question familiar claims that these are predominantly genres for the young. A survey of older and more recent texts might also demonstrate a shift from young, naive protagonists to more mature, even bitter **heroes**; consider, for example, the contrast between the major fantasy hero of the 1950s, Frodo Baggins of J.R.R. Tolkien's *The Lord of the Rings* and the major fantasy hero of the 1970s and 1980s, Thomas Covenant of Stephen R. Donaldson's *Lord Foul's Bane* and its sequels. Still, imaginative narratives in other media—films, television, and video games—remain popular with young people, and it may be in those forms that the spirit of youth will stay alive in science fiction and fantasy.

Bibliography

Rob Latham. *Consuming Youth*. Chicago: University of Chicago Press, 2002.

Lynne Lundquist. "Living Dolls." George Slusser, Gary Westfahl, and Eric S. Rabkin, eds., *Immortal Engines*. Athens: University of Georgia Press, 1996, 201–210.

George T. McWhorter. "Quest for the Fountain of Youth." *Burroughs Bulletin*, No. 57 (Winter, 2004), 3–5.

Kay Sambell. "Perspectives on the Meaning of Childhood in Near-Future Fantasies Produced for Young People." *Foundation*, No. 88 (Summer, 2003), 33–45.

Karen Sands and Marietta Franks. *Back in the Spaceship Again*. Westport, CT: Greenwood Press, 1999.

Gary Westfahl. "The Genre That Evolved." *Foundation*, No. 62 (Winter, 1994/1995), 70–75.

Gary Westfahl and George Slusser, eds. *Nursery Realms*. Athens: University of Georgia Press, 1999.

Jack Williamson. "Youth Against Space." Joseph D. Olander and Martin H. Greenberg, eds., *Robert A. Heinlein*. New York: Taplinger, 1978, 15–31.

Bradford Wright. *Comic Book Nation*. Baltimore: Johns Hopkins University Press, 2001.

—*Gary Westfahl*

Z

ZOMBIES

"Vampires, zombies, bogeymen, ghouls, oh my. The und—" She corrected herself. "The differently alive."

—Terry Pratchett
Feet of Clay (1996)

Overview

According to Caribbean **mythology**, zombies are the walking dead, reanimated by **voodoo** as volitionless serfs (see **Slavery**). They are stock figures of menace in **horror** and, less frequently, **heroic fantasy**. Like other **monsters**, zombies have been reinvented and rehabilitated by authors who doubt any being is inherently **evil**.

Survey

Fear of the living dead antedates voodoo; for example, the Celtic myths of the *Mabinogion* (first compiled in the fourteenth century) include the dread Crochan or cauldron, which reawakens corpses as zombie slave-warriors. Modern retellings include Lloyd Alexander's *The Black Cauldron* (1965) and Evangeline Walton's *The Children of Llyr* (1971). Hugh B. Cave evoked traditional Haiti zombies in *Legion of the Dead* (1979), *The Evil* (1981), and *Shades of Evil* (1982).

Today's images of zombies come chiefly from cinema; relevant films are numerous, the earliest of note being *White Zombie* (1932) with Bela Lugosi. *Night of the Living Dead* (1968) and its sequels *Dawn of the Dead* (1978) and *Day of the Dead* (1985) add the horror of cannibalism with flesh-eating zombie mobs. *The Evil Dead* (1982) likewise spawned sequels, *Evil Dead II* (1987) and *Army of Darkness* (1992). A **vampire**-like draining of energy leads to infectious zombieism and a zombie-populated London (see **Cities**) in *Lifeforce* (1985). There are many routine exploitation movies, like *I Was a Teenage Zombie* (1986), and even comic treatments like *Shaun of the Dead* (2004).

Indelibly impressed on popular consciousness, zombies are routine "encounter **monsters**" in fantasy role-playing **games** and book spinoffs. Fantasy treatments are more interesting. In Barbara Hambly's *The Ladies of Mandrigyn* (1984), repulsive zombie-like monsters are humans whose brains have been partially eaten by alien **parasites**. Tim Powers combines the Caribbean themes of **pirates**, zombies and voodoo in his inventive historical fantasy *On Stranger Tides* (1987). The quiet zombification of the British populace in Brian Stableford's horror-**satire** *Year Zero* (2000) passes almost unnoticed, downplayed by the government as a flu epidemic.

Piers Anthony's Xanth fantasies (see *A Spell for Chameleon*) gradually rehabilitate zombies as the series continues. From shambling though unmalign horrors who reek and drip with decay, zombies—at least the better-preserved ones—become characters with civil rights and even **love** interest. Undead rights are likewise promoted by the comically earnest zombie Reg Shoe in Terry Pratchett's Discworld (see *The Colour of Magic*), whose recruiting slogans appear inside coffin lids: "You Don't Have to Take This Lying Down."

The immortal female rivals of the film *Death Becomes Her* (1992) lead a pallid, zombie existence, killed but unable to die. A woman reanimated after embalming and burial is both pathetic and increasingly repulsive in Neil Gaiman's *American Gods* (2001); Steve Erikson's *Midnight Tides* (2004) is darkly humorous about yet another undead woman who, with a mortician's aid, makes the best of herself and enjoys restored **sexuality**.

Zombies in the real world may be simple **slave** labor subdued by **drugs**—briefly the fate of one regular character in G.B. Trudeau's *Doonesbury* comic strip. Leslie Charteris's **hero** the Saint encounters such zombies, and uncovers an attempt to exploit them in **business**, in "The Questing Tycoon" (1954). Joyce Carol Oates's serial killer in *Zombie* (1995) is motivated by the wish to create a zombie. Doris Piserchia's *I, Zombie* (1982) sees **suicides** reanimated as forced labor. Killed soldiers are recreated to fight again in William Tenn's "Down Among the Dead Men" (1954) and David Langford's *The Space Eater* (1982). Another science fiction zombie rationale appears in Robert Sheckley's *Immortality, Inc.* (1958).

Vernor Vinge's *A Deepness in the Sky* (1999) offers a modern science fiction reinvention of the theme, as deliberate infection with a psychotropic disease induces a state of "Focus"—total, autistic obsession with one's work, whether it be drudgery or advanced skills like **language and linguistics**. Greg Egan's *Distress* (1995) opens with a grisly "Frankenscience" reawakening of a corpse to brief, tormented, artificial consciousness in hopes that he will name his murderer (see **Crime and Punishment**). Lucius Shepard's *Green Eyes* (1984) blends science fiction and fantasy with a project whose experimental reanimation of the dead requires both designer bacteria (see **Genetic Engineering**) and **cemetery** earth; the revenant protagonist has a much-changed **perception** of the world and gains odd **psychic powers**.

In science fiction **humor**, the theme is represented by the rather unfunny slapstick of Harry Harrison's and Jack C. Haldeman's *Bill, the Galactic Hero on the Planet of Zombie Vampires* (1991).

Discussion

Paradoxically, the revisionist approach, allowing zombies **freedom** and **intelligence**, may intensify suffering by adding awareness of their undead condition. Fear of zombification generates horror in stories like Dennis Wheatley's *Strange Conflict* (1941) and Harrison's "At Last, the True Story of Frankenstein" (1965); the latter makes a **carnival** sideshow of the supposed **Frankenstein monster**, actually a zombie